Perspectives on Sustainable Development in Water Management:

Towards Agreement in the Fraser River Basin

Anthony H. J. Dorcey
Editor

Research Program
on
Water in Sustainable Development
Volume 1

Westwater Research Centre
Faculty of Graduate Studies
The University of British Columbia

Copyright © 1991 Westwater Research Centre,
The University of British Columbia,
Vancouver, B. C., Canada V6T 1Z2

All rights reserved.

Word processing and layout: Julian Griggs and Michael Burwash
Cover design: Ric Bains, Northburn Printers & Stationers Ltd.
Printing: Northburn Printers & Stationers Ltd.
Distributed by Westwater Research Centre

Canadian Cataloguing in Publication Data

Main entry under title:
Perspectives on sustainable development in
water management

   (Research program on water in sustainable
development ; v. 1)
   Includes bibliographical references.
   ISBN 0-920146-40-6

   1. Water resources development--British
Columbia--Fraser River Watershed. 2. Water
resources development--Environmental aspects--
British Columbia--Fraser River Watershed. 3. Water
quality management--Economic aspects -- British
Columbia--Fraser River Watershed. 4. Economic
development--Environmental aspects--British
Columbia--Fraser River Watershed.
I. Dorcey, Anthony H. J., 1944-   II.
Westwater Research Centre.   III. Series.
TC427.F7P47 1991   333.91'15'09711   C91-091281-5

Preface

In 1987 Westwater was considering the management of large river basins as the focus for its next major research program. The Fraser River Basin was being examined as an obvious and challenging case study.

In the midst of these discussions, the World Commission on Environment and Development released its report, *Our Common Future* (WCED, 1987). Shortly following this, the federal government established the National Task Force on Environment and Economy (CCREM, 1987) to suggest how Canada should respond. Together the international and Canadian reports recommended new goals and strategies for sustainable development, "development that meets the needs of the present without compromising the ability of future generations to meet their own needs" (WCED, 1987:43). The positive and widespread responses to the international and Canadian proposals encouraged Westwater to elaborate further its new research program on large river basins, and to consider how principles of sustainable development might be put into practice in water resources management.

In the autumn of 1987, the Westwater Council agreed that a new research program on water in sustainable development involving case study research in the Fraser River Basin should be designed and potential funding sources identified. A prospectus was drafted to guide a series of round table discussions during the first quarter of 1988. People from government agencies, university departments, environmental interest groups, and private sector organisations were invited to discussions that were held in Vancouver, Victoria and Ottawa. At the same time, Westwater's ideas were tested and advanced by discussions with a wider variety of people convened at meetings across Canada under diverse auspices to address the newly emerging interest in the topic of sustainable development. The feedback we received strongly endorsed the idea of a research program focussing on the implications of sustainable development principles for water management and the potential of the Fraser River Basin as a case study.

On the basis of preliminary discussions with Environment Canada and the B.C. Ministry of Environment, the Centre was encouraged to prepare an *Unsolicited Proposal* on a first phase of research for submission to the federal Department of Supply and Services in the late summer of 1988. The primary product would be a book, tentatively titled *Water in Sustainable Development: Exploring Our Common Future in the Fraser Basin*. It would utilise existing information in an illustrative analysis of science, policies and institutions for water management in the sustainable development of the Fraser River Basin. The proposal was shaped around a draft outline for the book which proposed that it be written by a research team consisting of all the faculty associated with Westwater and a number of research assistants and specialist consultants. Through the autumn, the submission was reviewed by federal and provincial government agencies and revised in the light of their comments. Final approval was received and a twenty month contract was signed in February, 1989.

Research began by drawing on the experience from discussions of sustainable development over the preceding two years and by conducting a literature review. A paper was drafted to provide a preliminary analytical framework and an initial sketch of the basic argument that might run through the book. As the analytical framework was being developed, and information available on the natural and human systems relating to water resources management in the Fraser River Basin started to be reviewed, it became increasingly evident that the comprehensiveness of sustainable development principles made it essential for the Westwater team to consult with a variety of additional experts who could advise on components of the research that went beyond its expertise. In some cases these would be people who have specific knowledge of natural and human systems in the basin. In other instances, they would be persons who have expertise with regard to policies and institutional arrangements that would be particularly relevant to sustainable development. When individuals who might be able to advise were approached, it was exciting to discover their great interest in the project and their willingness to help. Out of early discussions with these various experts came the idea of a series of background papers. This idea has ultimately resulted in the collection published in this volume and the first phase of the research has thus expanded to produce two volumes.

From the outset it was recognised that the collection in the first volume would be highly varied and would reflect the particular interests of the authors who volunteered to contribute a paper. Nevertheless it was readily agreed that it would be desirable to develop general guidelines. Potential contributors were provided with a copy of the initial analytical framework and a prospectus outlining the project, including the proposed table of contents for the original book. Each of the contributors then prepared an outline of their proposed paper which was circulated in advance of a workshop for the writers of both the background papers and the second case study volume. The highly productive exchange that ensued not only helped to develop and coordinate the paper outlines but starkly revealed the importance and challenge of dealing with different perspectives on sustainable development.

There were two general agreements with regard to all papers. Firstly, it was agreed that the authors would provide a definition of sustainable development at the beginning of their paper. Further, this would be based on the Brundtland definition as elaborated in the sketch of the analytical framework or, in cases where it differed, authors would explain how and why it had been revised. Secondly, it was agreed that each topic would be related to water resources management and wherever possible this would include examples in the Fraser River Basin.

When the first drafts of the papers were completed, they were formally reviewed by two of the other contributors of background papers, as well as by those involved in the case study volume who would have a particular interest in that topic. Several of the drafts were distributed to all authors because of their general relevance. The editor then collated the reviewers' comments and the authors revised their papers for publication in this volume.

In my editorial comments to authors, the need to address the two major issues was emphasized. The complementarity and contrast in comments from reviewers was examined and suggestions for revision were made from the editor's perspective, but the authors were left free to respond while I withheld my views for the concluding chapters and second volume. Although some of the reviewers challenged fundamental assumptions, authors were not necessarily expected to adapt significantly their conceptual and analytical frameworks. The final papers, therefore, at least partially reflect the current world views and schools of thought to which these authors subscribe. In their diversity, these papers mirror some of the challenging realities of the debate surrounding sustainable development issues in the population at large. Finally, the authors had an opportunity to critique the draft of the introduction and two concluding chapters in which comments are made on their approaches and suggestions are made as to strategies for moving towards agreement on the implications of sustainable development principles for water resources management.

This volume contributes to the second case study volume in two major ways. Firstly, it examines different perspectives on the evolving concept of sustainable development and implications for managing water resources in a large river basin. The two concluding chapters relate these perspectives to the literature and suggest how the evolving principles of water resource management are being adapted and revised in response to the emerging ideals of sustainable development. In the second volume, these management principles are used to guide both the assessment of past approaches and proposals for innovations in water management in the sustainable development of the Fraser River Basin.

Secondly, the chapters in this first volume provide specific information about selected resource systems and proposals for policy and institutional innovations. The second volume variously draws on these chapters summarizing their analyses and referring to them for more detail.

It is important to recognise that these two volumes are the products of just the first phase in a longer term, more ambitious research program—one that addresses immensely complex, wide-ranging and challenging issues. It is only right and fair to acknowledge that the authors have encountered great difficulty in dealing with both their different perspectives on the evolving concept of sustainable development and the frustrations of available data. It is crucial to appreciate the nature and implications of these two problems if future research and management initiatives in the Fraser River Basin are to be productive. For these reasons alone, the two issues are examined explicitly and strategies proposed for addressing them in each of the volumes.

Just as importantly, the two volumes should not be seen as final answers but rather as preliminary analyses, designed to stimulate vigorous discussions which need to take place on strategies for water management in the sustainable development of the Fraser River Basin. The recently announced Fraser River

Basin Action Plan in the federal government's *Green Plan* provides an unexpected and excellent opportunity to take the next steps. When Westwater began its new research program there was no sign of such an initiative on the Fraser—now, given the prospect of this major advance, the proposals at the end of the second volume are focussed on how such innovations can start to be implemented.

Anthony H. J. Dorcey,
Project Director,
February, 1991.

Acknowledgements

I am deeply grateful to the many sources of funding that have supported this first phase of Westwater's research program on *Water in Sustainable Development*. The research was made possible by funding from the Unsolicited Proposals Program of Supply and Services Canada along with support funding from Environment Canada, the British Columbia Ministry of Environment and the University of British Columbia.

Much of the initial work on this project was undertaken while I was on research leave and the recipient of a UBC Killam Faculty Research Fellowship (1988-1989).

The Social Science and Humanities Research Council provided me with a grant (410-88-0830) which supported my research leading to the development of the conceptual framework for the analysis of water resources management principles, and the resolution of conflicts in pursuing sustainable development.

Publication of this first volume—a product that was never anticipated at the outset of the research project—has been made possible by additional funding from Environment Canada, the B.C. Ministry of Environment and the University of British Columbia.

This volume brings together the work of twenty-three diverse academics, professionals and graduate students. Without their interest and willing enthusiasm, the volume would never have been conceived. I am indeed most grateful for all the time and effort that they have put into our various meetings, the initial workshop, the drafting of their papers, reviewing the first drafts of other contributors and revising their own papers in the light of comments and suggestions from reviewers. I can only hope that each of them has found the experience to be as rewarding for themselves as their contributions have been invaluable to the first phase of the research project.

In all kinds of ways the Westwater team that is conducting the research for the second volume has helped me in initiating, producing and reviewing the background papers. I greatly appreciate the continuing support and assistance that has been given to me by Ian Boeckh, Sandra Brown, Michael Burwash, Vicky Christie, Julian Griggs, Kenneth Hall, Michael Healey, Julia Gardner, Dan Moore, Harriet Rueggeberg, Thomas Northcote, John Post and Hans Schreier.

The Westwater Council members who served on the Publications Committee for this volume were Keith Henry, Les Lavkulich and Brahm Wiesman.

In conducting the reviews of draft chapters, editing the manuscripts and coordinating the word processing, production of graphics and preparation of the camera-ready copy, I have been incredibly fortunate in having the expertise, enthusiasm and continuing good humour of Julian Griggs. The only way I could ever repay him adequately would be to buy the upgraded Macintosh system that would enable him to fully exploit the potential of the graphics and layout software that are so constrained by our low end, late 1980's system. In preparing the final copy he was greatly assisted in word processing by Michael Burwash and in editing by Laurie Cooper.

Throughout the project, Jerry Pladsen has been the secretary of Westwater, supporting the research activities, trying to keep me straight and taking care of the many things I neglect. I am most grateful for all that she does.

Finally, but by no means least, I want to express my deep appreciation to Sandy D'Aquino, who, as the Scientific Authority for this project, has been both constructively critical and unrelentingly supportive at all times.

Anthony H. J. Dorcey
Project Director
February, 1991.

Table of Contents

Part III: Institutions

Part IV: Outlooks

Conclusions

List of Contributors

Peter Boothroyd
Associate Professor,
School of Community and Regional
Planning,
The University of British Columbia.

John D. Chapman
Professor Emeritus,
Department of Geography,
The University of British Columbia.

Norman G. Dale
Independent Consultant on Coastal,
Environmental and Aboriginal/Non-
Aboriginal Conflict Resolution,
Sandspit.

H. Craig Davis
Professor,
School of Community and Regional
Planning,
The University of British Columbia.

Anthony H. J. Dorcey
Assistant Director,
Westwater Research Centre, &
Associate Professor,
School of Community and Regional
Planning,
The University of British Columbia.

Dorli M. Duffy
Graduate Student,
School of Community and Regional
Planning,
The University of British Columbia.

Irving K. Fox
Professor Emeritus,
School of Community and Regional
Planning,
The University of British Columbia.

Julia E. Gardner
Assistant Professor,
Westwater Research Centre, &
School of Community and Regional
Planning,
The University of British Columbia.

Julian R. Griggs
Graduate Student,
Resource Management Science
Program,
The University of British Columbia.

Michael A. Henderson
Research Scientist,
Biological Sciences Branch,
Fisheries and Oceans Canada,
Vancouver.

Thomas A. Hutton
Assistant Manager (Policy),
Economic Development Office,
Finance Department,
City of Vancouver.

J. E. Michael Kew
Associate Professor,
Department of Anthropology and
Sociology,
The University of British Columbia.

J. P. (Hamish) Kimmins
Professor,
Department of Forest Science,
The University of British Colmbia.

Hew D. McConnell
Manager,
Sewerage and Drainage,
Greater Vancouver Regional District,
Burnaby.

Roger C. McNeill
Economist/Planner,
Inland Waters Directorate,
Environment Canada,
Vancouver.

Peter H. Pearse
Professor,
Department of Forest Resources
Management,
The University of British Columbia.

Murray T. Rankin
Professor,
Faculty of Law,
The University of Victoria.

William E. Rees
Professor,
School of Community and Regional
Planning,
The University of British Columbia.

Jean-Pierre L. Savard
Research Scientist,
Canadian Wildlife Service,
Pacific and Yukon Region,
Environment Canada,
Delta.

Anthony D. Scott
Professor Emeritus,
Department of Economics,
The University of British Columbia.

Olav Slaymaker
Professor and Head,
Department of Geography, &
Acting Director,
Sustainable Development Research
Institute,
The University of British Columbia.

Sandra E. Smith
Acting Manager,
Program Planning,
Water Management Division,
B.C. Ministry of Environment,
Victoria.

Donald M. Tate
Senior Economist,
Inland Waters Directorate,
Environment Canada,
Ottawa.

Andrew R. Thompson
Professor Emeritus,
Faculty of Law,
The University of British Columbia, &
Associate Counsel,
Ferguson Gifford,
Barristers and Solicitors,
Vancouver.

1
Water in Sustainable Development: From Ideal to Reality

Anthony H. J. Dorcey

In 1987 Westwater was considering the management of large river basins as the focus for its next major research program and the Fraser was being examined as an obvious and challenging case study (Figure 1.1). The Fraser River Basin drains a quarter of British Columbia from headwaters in the Rocky Mountains to the Pacific Ocean, supports the greatest salmon runs in the world, sustains two-thirds of the province's population and has Canada's third largest metropolis at its mouth. Yet there was no existing basinwide management system.

In the midst of these discussions the World Commission on Environment and Development released its report, *Our Common Future* (WCED, 1987). This international document together with the report of the National Task Force on Environment and Economy (CCREM, 1987), established by the federal government to determine Canada's response to it, recommended new goals and strategies for sustainable development. The positive and widespread responses to these reports prompted Westwater to further elaborate its new research program on large river basins so as to consider how principles of sustainable development might be put into practice in water resources management.

The preface describes how the first phase of this research program was designed and introduces the two volumes that are to be the major products of the program. This chapter outlines the initial analytical framework that guided the research and introduces the background papers that were contributed to the project and are published in this volume.

The Ideal of Sustainable Development

The research began by drawing on discussions of sustainable development over the preceding two years and by conducting a literature review to draft a paper that provided a preliminary analytical framework and an initial sketch of the basic

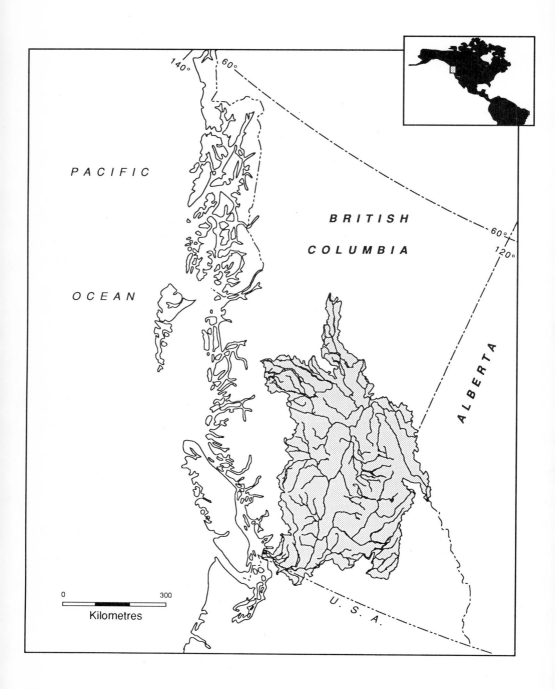

Figure 1.1: The Fraser River Basin, British Columbia.

argument that might run through the book.[1] From the outset, discussing the implications of sustainable development principles for innovation in water management presented great difficulties for those within and outside the research team. An immense diversity of opinion emerged as to the meaning of sustainable development and how it relates to the principles and practice of water management. People often found it difficult to distinguish between ideas about what *should* happen (principles) and their descriptions of what *does* happen (practice).[2]

Varied concepts of sustainable development have been in use for a long time.[3] The Greek vision of Gaia as the Goddess of Earth and Native Indian myths reflect earlier but comparable ideals of the intimate relations between humans and the planet. Millennia later, nineteenth century concepts of conservation, particularly those of the forester Pinchot, advanced the more familiar principles of sustainable utilisation of renewable resources. Progressively, the idea of constraining development so as to live off the income from the stock of natural capital has become more common. Sustained yield principles are discussed with regard to forests, fisheries, wildlife, soils, water and other renewable resources. In extending the idea to non-renewable resources, it has been suggested that they should be replaced by renewable resources wherever possible and otherwise strictly conserved. More recently, however, considerations of sustainable development have returned to re-examine the more holistic concepts and ideals of thousands of years ago, as well as the implications of potential additions to the stock of human capital.

In the last few years, the term "sustainable development" has become increasingly common as a result of its use by the World Commission on Environment and Development (WCED). This Commission, headed by Gro Harlem Brundtland, Prime Minister of Norway, was established as an independent body in 1983 by the United Nations. The mandate of the Commission was to suggest realistic policies for dealing with the increasingly serious global problems of environmental degradation and the poverty of underdevelopment. In its final report the WCED defines sustainable development as "development that meets the needs of the present without compromising the ability of future generations to meet their own needs" (WCED, 1987:43) and concludes that "[w]hat is needed now is a new era of economic growth—growth that is forceful and at the same time socially and environmentally sustainable" (WCED, 1987:xii).

In the intense debate stimulated by the reports of Brundtland and the subsequent Canadian National Task Force on Environment and Economy (CCREM, 1987), different perspectives on sustainable development have become evident.[4] They are reflected in the variations of emphasis given to economic,

---

1 A subsequent version of the initial sketch is excerpted in this and the next section.
2 The term "principle" is being used very broadly and as in the common usage of contrasting it to "practice". Principles should not be read here with the specific meaning of laws as in mathematics nor should it be assumed that there is necessarily a consensus about them. Principles are broadly conceived as ideas about "what should happen" in contrast to practice describing "what does happen". Both principles and practice may contain a variety of substantive and procedural elements.
3 For example, see discussion in Caldwell (1984) and O'Riordan (1988).
4 For discussion of sustainable development in terms of what people first think about see Barbier (1987).

environmental and social systems and associated values. Some people selectively use the Brundtland report's recommendations and variously use the idea of sustainable development to reinforce their habitual advocacy of increased economic development or greater environmental protection or accelerated removal of inequities. Thus, for example, industrial, wilderness and poverty groups respectively recast their goals of increasing GNP, expanding park areas and more decentralised decision-making in terms of sustainable development.

Other people recognize the Brundtland report's emphasis on the necessity and interdependence of each of these objectives but still attach widely varying priorities to them. First thoughts variously go to increasing economic growth or preserving the environment or reducing injustice, and only second and third thoughts turn to one of the other two major objectives. This may be the intentional result of beliefs, such as those who contend that economic growth must firstly be ensured so as to be able to afford measures that preserve the environment or reduce injustice. On the other hand it may be the unintended consequence of long held perceptions and deeply ingrained habits. Out of a concern to make clear that they believe all three objectives are important, some people have adopted tortuous qualifications, such as "environmentally sustainable socio-economic development".

Beyond these differences are those relating to the specific *meaning* of each of these objectives. For example, two people may stress the importance of the development objective but have different ideas in mind. In the case of the first, development is narrowly conceived in terms of expanding Gross National Product (GNP) as measured by the national accounts, while for the second it has a much broader meaning reflected in the use of a variety of indicators of which GNP is only one; for example, per capita GNP, under-employment, education level, poverty level etc.[5] In a similar fashion, there may well be differences in ideas about the *means used* to pursue the objectives, even though there may be no significant difference in opinion about the objectives themselves. This is well illustrated in the case of the commonly held objective of narrowly defined economic growth for which there are widely differing ideas about how it should be pursued (e.g., consider the arguments between the supply-side and demand-side economists over the last decade). Typically in any discussion about sustainable development, there is at least some degree of difference among the parties about both objectives and strategies for pursuing them when all three sets of objectives relating to environmental, economic and social systems are being considered.

Given all this, what is commonly found and novel in the recent Canadian interest in sustainable development? Among a variety of elements, the following have struck the Westwater team as significant in the ongoing debate:

(i)   *Evidence:* In recent years there has emerged increasing evidence that growth is not just affecting local environments but that it is damaging global systems in major ways (e.g., ozone depletion, climate change, acid rain, toxicant dispersion etc.). In addition, growth has not succeeded in reducing poverty in

---

5   Many authors distinguish between the two by contrasting "economic growth" and "economic" or "socio-economic development" (see e.g., discussion in Pearce, Markandya and Barbier [1989]).

the developing countries and there remains a vicious cycle between increasing poverty and environmental degradation.

(ii) *Perceptions:* There is a growing sense of unease and urgency as individuals increasingly suspect they are personally threatened (e.g., toxic materials in food and drinking water) and that the costs of remedies are much greater than avoiding the damage and risks in the first place. This is not just a personal threat, however, for there is also a widespread perception that we have reached something of a crisis point and that this is the "time to choose".

(iii) *Interdependence:* Problems and solutions are increasingly recognised as involving complex interdependencies within and between natural, economic and social systems that link the regions of the world as well as past, present and future generations. Conflicts are increasing and the need for institutional arrangements for resolving them and fostering consensus is becoming more urgent.

(iv) *Ethics:* Responses to problems are increasingly discussed as involving moral commitments and multifaceted ethics. These reflect shifting values, changing attitudes to risk and uncertainty, accepting greater responsibility towards present and future generations, and recognizing the rights of minorities and other species.

(v) *Actions:* In this context, the emphasis is shifted to anticipatory and preventive measures supported by the creation of new incentives, strategies and institutional arrangements that will support changing attitudes, perceptions, values and behaviour to be consistent with the evolving ethics of sustainable development.

Sustainable development is therefore being considered in the Westwater research program as an *evolving ethic*. It is assumed to embrace a variety of substantive and procedural elements each of which is subject to judgements about minimal conditions and relative importance. For people who are concerned about the essential interdependence of economic, environmental and social systems, as was the WCED, some variation on the following are commonly minimal elements:

- Maintaining ecological integrity and diversity;
- Meeting basic human needs;
- Keeping options open for future generations;
- Reducing injustice; and,
- Increasing self-determination.

However, the elaboration of these elements into more specific terms relevant to particular situations reveals the very different worldviews that can underlie the evolving ethic and its current indeterminacy. In British Columbia this has recently been well illustrated in the diversity of briefs submitted to the B. C. Task Force on Environment and Economy (1989).

In the Westwater research program, it is assumed that strategies for sustainable development should be based on consideration of the interdependency of economic, environmental, and social systems and should include at least the five ethical elements listed above. However, no particular set of ethics was adopted at the outset; instead, the research explores the definition and implications of adopting different ones. This approach can be contrasted with that taken in other ongoing or recent studies which adopt particular sets of ethics with varying degrees of explicitness. For example, two projects that have developed explicit but sharply contrasting statements of their particular ethical premises are the *Sustainable Society Project* at the University of Waterloo (Robinson et al., 1990) and the Fraser Institute's recent publication *Economics and the Environment: A Reconciliation* (Block, 1989). While the Fraser Institute's analyses are based on a focussed belief in the rightness and efficacy of private property rights and free market solutions, the University of Waterloo project is not so easily characterized as it is more broadly based in beliefs reflecting both the rightness and efficacy of maintaining the capacity of natural and human systems to change.

The Westwater program has adopted a strategy of exploring the implications of different beliefs. This strategy has been selected because if sustainable development principles are to be refined in the current debate and actually put into practice, it is essential

(i)   to give comparable consideration to all three systems—environmental, economic and social—and their interrelationships; and,

(ii)   to recognise the implications of different ethical and moral premises.

To ignore the first is to neglect what many people are talking about and to be silent about the second is to risk not understanding what they are questioning. From reading the literature and listening to what people are saying, there appears to be an evolving consensus that sustainable development involves at least giving much more attention to the environmental, social, and economic consequences than in the past, and that varying opinions result in critical differences about the rates and distribution of adaptation. How quickly should development adapt so as to be more sustainable? Who should incur the costs and reap the benefits of more sustainable development?

No matter what the particulars, imperatives for action based on the evolving ethic are far reaching. The Brundtland report argues that seven interrelated strategies are essential:

• Meet essential needs for jobs, food, energy, water and sanitation;
• Change the quality of growth, particularly to be less material and energy intensive;
• Conserve and enhance the resource base;
• Reorient technology and manage risk;
• Revive growth in developing countries;
• Ensure a sustainable population; and,
• Merge environment and economics in decision-making.

The Westwater studies are exploring the interrelated set of strategies required for managing water resources in the Fraser Basin under different assumptions about the evolving ethic. The analyses need to consider the extent to which the fate of water resources in the Basin is dependent on actions both in various resource sectors and outside of the basin; the focus must be on exploring the interrelated set of sustainable development strategies necessitated by these interdependencies.

The Implications for Water Management

For more than a decade, textbooks on water management have recognised, at least partially, some of the key elements of principles that are central to sustainable development. However, it is taking time for these to be translated into formal policies in Canada and practice lags even farther behind.

By the mid 1970's, experiments with elements of modern principles of water management were well advanced in Canada (Dorcey, 1987). They had been catalysed in the 1960's by growing concerns about pollution and other undesired consequences of economic development. River basin planning and impact assessment processes were coming to be seen as essential parts of management. Out of the earlier concepts of multiple purpose river basin development—using multiple means to pursue multiple objectives - came ideas of integrated resources management. The need to consider not only economic but also environmental and social consequences of water resources development was recognized in new valuation methods and procedures. Pricing of water use was believed to be the way to increase efficiency and equity. Opportunities for involving the public in impact assessment and planning were considered to be essential to the process of evaluation and a fundamental element of regional approaches to management. Such elements of principles are well reflected in the Federal Water Policy that was eventually published after much discussion in 1987 (Environment Canada, 1987).

Over the last decade, however, it has proven extremely difficult to put such principles into practice. There are two major interrelated sets of reasons for these delays. Firstly, the ambitious management experiments launched in the early 1970's were fraught with difficulties. They called for knowledge about natural and human systems that often did not exist. They also demanded unprecedented abilities to conduct interdisciplinary analyses and manage both interpersonal and inter-organizational relations. Frustrations, delays, and failure to deliver promised improvements resulted in profound disappointment among all parties. Secondly, there was not the political will and associated budgetary commitments to persevere. In the late 1970's and early 1980's, disappointment with the results of the management experiments, combined with increasingly serious problems in the Canadian economy, led to reductions in expenditure and a reversion to more partial and traditional resource management procedures, together with a search for more strategic approaches.

In the second half of the 1980's, the evolving concept of sustainable development has renewed interest in refining and advancing the earlier principles of water management. As outlined above, sustainable development is providing a new context of evidence, perceptions, interdependence, ethics and action within which to consider the principles and practice of water resources management. It remains to be seen whether this interest and newly emergent commitment from politicians can endure as other issues arise to compete on the political agenda, but many commentators believe they will prove to be more lasting than before.

The Westwater project is exploring the arguments for, and the implications of, alternative rates of change towards implementing principles of sustainable development in managing the water resources of the Fraser Basin. It is expected that a large part of what would be required by sustainable development strategies involves the implementation of well established principles, including those elements described above, and variously subsumed under labels such as "comprehensive river basin development", "integrated resources management" and "strategic watershed planning." It will, therefore, be essential to examine whether and how such principles have been applied in the Fraser Basin and to assess the reasons for their success and failure in practice. Unless the difficulties that have been encountered in the past in implementing recognised principles can be overcome, it is highly unlikely that new principles reflecting a sustainable development ethic will be successfully implemented, because they pose most of the same difficulties but in much more challenging guises.

Preliminary research suggests a number of ways in which water management in the sustainable development of river basins is becoming more challenging:

(i)   *Increased number of systems*: Water resources management in a river basin becomes progressively more complex with the growing recognition of the variety of natural (bio-physical) and human (socio-economic and political-institutional) systems and subsystems to be considered. The more developed the basin and its associated systems and the more detailed the analysis, the greater the complexity to be dealt with and the greater the interdisciplinarity required.

(ii) *Expanded spatial boundaries*: Along with recognition of the diversity of systems comes the necessity to consider much wider spatial bounds. Watersheds not only have to be examined as subsystems of river basins but the wider boundaries of associated bio-physical, socio-economic and political-institutional systems have to be recognised. These systems create important interdependencies with other river basins at the regional, continental and global level and have important interjurisdictional implications (e.g., climate change and export markets for forest and salmon products).

(iii) *Lengthened time scales*: Concern for the preservation of options for future generations draws attention to much longer time periods and a greater variety of choices. This implies examining not only the longer term consequences of proposed developments but also the possibilities for reversing the consequences of past commitments.

(iv) *Greater demands on science*: The knowledge needed to make informed decisions in water management places immense demands on science. The questions raised by the sustainable development perspective on river basin management reveal major gaps in knowledge about the behaviour of diverse natural and human systems and greatly challenge interdisciplinary science.

(v)   *Pervasive uncertainty*: Recognition that many of these gaps in knowledge cannot be eliminated in the near future and that uncertainty is to a substantial extent inherent makes it evident that management will involve extensive judgements about both facts and values that will frequently be intimately entwined.

(vi) *Heightened ethical concerns*: There is a growing appreciation of the ethical and moral judgements that can no longer be ignored in making decisions about water resources management. Explicit consideration will be required of the ethical and moral precepts that should govern both bio-physical and socio-economic analyses and the design of governance arrangements.

(vii) *Greater need for consensus*: All of these sustainable development concerns will be fertile ground for increased conflict and point to a greatly increased need for commitments to and governance arrangements for developing consensus and resolving conflicts.

Taken together, these implications of sustainable development principles suggest a major increase in the difficulty of water resources management. The Westwater research program is exploring these and other issues as they arise in the specific context of the Fraser Basin (Figure 1.2), examining how they are being dealt with presently and suggesting new initiatives that might begin to address them more effectively.

The Background Papers

A major implication of the above perspective on water in sustainable development is that the bounds of the problem and hence the breadth of the expertise required to address it are greatly expanded beyond those previously considered relevant to water resources management, even though this has traditionally been one of the most interdisciplinary fields of study. As described in the Preface, the series of background papers in the chapters that follow resulted from the Westwater team seeking advice from individuals with a wide range of expertise beyond that available in the Westwater team.

The papers were not designed to be read in any particular order but have been grouped under four headings that reflect their emphases and associated contributions to the research program.

In Part I, two papers focus on settlement and populations in the Fraser River Basin. In the first one, Michael Kew and Julian Griggs provide a perspective on the society and culture of the aboriginal peoples who have occupied and utilised the resources of the Basin for at least ten thousand years. They describe the Basin as Simon Fraser found it in 1808 when he crossed the Rocky Mountains to reach the headwaters and made his way to the mouth of the river and the Pacific Ocean. Carefully drawing on available information, and challenging common myths and misunderstandings, Kew and Griggs make the case that Native cultural and social patterns produced a system that ensured long-term sustainability. They argue that this body of knowledge and experience should inform co-management approaches today.

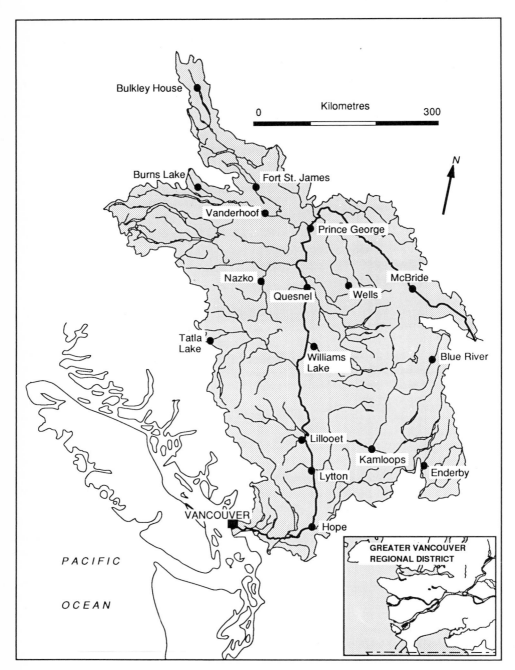

Figure 1.2: Map Showing the Mainstem and Major Tributaries of the Fraser River with Key Locations in the Basin.

In the two subsequent short centuries following Simon Fraser's arrival, the population of the Basin has increased fifty-fold, with 83% (1986) of the population concentrated in the Lower Fraser Valley. At the same time, an unimagined growth in the utilisation of the Basin's natural resources has supported the expansion of a mixed urban and rural society. In the second paper, Thomas Hutton and Craig Davis focus on the pivotal role of metropolitan Vancouver in the economy of the province and its changing links with interior and international markets. They conclude that, with careful planning that integrates economic, environmental, and social values and which anticipates threats, the prospects for Vancouver's sustainable development are broadly favourable. Hutton and Davis indicate that the stock of natural and human capital is exceptional and can be maintained and that the economy is progressing towards more advanced forms of activity with an expanding and dynamic service sector. Recent experience and the transformations now taking place suggest the Vancouver economy is becoming more resilient to the shocks and stresses of a changing world economy. Further, the developing linkages with new international markets, particularly on the Pacific Rim, are laying the foundations for exceptional long-term growth opportunities.

Part II contains a series of papers that focus on particular resources in the Basin. Olav Slaymaker points out that the erosion and sedimentation processes in the Basin are still very active 10,000 years after the retreat of the glaciers. He argues that an understanding of their spatial and temporal scales is essential to sustainable development since major forces are at work which have immense potential for surprise, benefit and damage. Sandra Smith examines the related flooding processes in the Basin and outlines the experience with floodplain management since the disastrous floods of 1894 and 1948. She draws attention to the options that are being lost as the floodplain is developed and the increasingly intensive management that is required to sustain the natural systems, the human population, and the developments at risk.

The three following papers focus on the internationally renowned aquatic wildlife resources of the Fraser Basin. The Fraser River and its many lakes and tributaries support the greatest population of salmonines in the world and fish are one of the most important indicators of the system's wellbeing. Michael Henderson focuses on the experience of managing the salmon stocks of the Fraser River Basin and describes the record of their historic depletion through overharvesting and habitat damage. He also documents the increasing successes in efforts to rebuild them to historic population levels which were at least double those in recent years. However, he suggests that achieving this goal and sustaining the stocks will be extremely difficult because of the immense challenges in managing the diverse demands in mixed stock fisheries that not only operate in the Fraser Basin but all along the B.C. coast and out into the North Pacific. In addition, rapidly expanding development throughout the Basin threatens to degrade and destroy the habitat upon which the stocks depend.

Norman Dale addresses the challenge of managing the Fraser fisheries by examining how the stakeholders interact and how they have responded to the conflicts that arise. He focusses on the importance of developing consensus and describes a number of experiments and initiatives that seek to promote cooperative management in the Basin. He argues that the integrated stock and habitat planning processes that are now being initiated in the Fraser are a major step forward. However, to meet the challenge, it will be necessary to reorient the management strategy to one that is designed to pursue collaboration and shared decision-making.

Jean-Pierre Savard documents the bird populations describing how not only large migratory and non-migratory populations are supported within the Basin, but also how major flocks are dependent on it in their migrations between habitats as widespread as Siberia and South America. He notes that the Fraser River Estuary supports the largest wintering population of waterfowl in Canada. From his analysis, Savard argues that the growing demands for non-consumptive uses of birds, together with the historic losses in habitat from floodplain and upland developments, particularly forestry, make it essential to conserve the remaining pockets of bird habitats and restore degraded areas so as to sustain the diverse populations that are one of the primary indicators of aquatic ecosystem health.

Forestry is the dominant resource based industry in the Basin and its activities are expanding. Hamish Kimmins and Dorli Duffy examine these activities and argue that management approaches must take account of local ecological conditions. More specifically, they suggest that management strategies should reflect the variation between each of the eleven biogeoclimatic zones represented in the Basin. To sustain the diversity of products and services from the forest, it is argued that it will be necessary to address issues at the global, regional and local levels, each of which focuses attention on different time scales. In particular, it is essential that management decision-making be guided by consideration of ecological rotations and an understanding of how these might change under various scenarios for climate change.

Much of the energy produced in the province comes from outside of the Basin, yet most of it is transported through, or used within the Basin. John Chapman describes the commercial energy system for the province and explores a range of future scenarios for supply and demand which he then relates to the Fraser Basin specifically. He concludes that even though the Basin has immense energy potential, it is not likely to become a major producing area in the next forty years. However, at that time he can envisage a scenario under which exploitation of the enormous hydro electricity potential of the Fraser could become an important option.

In the final paper of Part II, Hew McConnell describes water quality conditions in the Greater Vancouver area and assesses an innovative approach to planning for liquid waste management that is being employed by the Greater Vancouver Regional District as part of its program for improving water quality in the Fraser River Estuary and Burrard Inlet. He concludes that the GVRD's strategy of involving a large number of stakeholders from both inside and outside of government in a series of sub-committees, community workshops and local council meetings has been highly productive in developing a more comprehensive approach to the management of liquid wastes ultimately entering municipal sewerage systems. The substantial investment of time and money in participatory planning has been more than repaid by the understanding and commitments to action that it helped to foster.

In Part III, five authors consider the political, administrative, legal and market institutions required for water management in the sustainable development of the Basin. Irving Fox argues the case for a regionalised approach that overcomes the problems associated with single-purpose agencies that neglect interdependencies in resource uses. Such agencies are too centralised to reflect local preferences and knowledge, rely too much on bargaining between unequal parties, and are driven too strongly by narrowly conceived self-interest. Instead, he proposes a more federated system with greater utilisation of local institutions including measures to make them more representative and accountable.

Julia Gardner focuses on the role of environmental non-government organisations (ENGOs) and, in an extensive review of the literature, identifies their potential roles in sustainable development and water resources management. She argues that community based citizens' organisations have important functions to play in achieving all the key elements of sustainable development: maintaining ecological integrity and conserving the resource base, the pursuit of equity, thinking globally while acting locally, and increasing social self-determination. In relating to government, Gardner suggests that they can adopt advocacy, supplemental and transformative roles. In different situations, ENGOs might emphasize various mixes of these roles, but over time they seem to evolve towards either a focus on the need for cooperation or transformation. In the recent adoption of stewardship strategies, she sees the emergence of a role that could exploit the advantages of each, while avoiding the disadvantages and pitfalls that can undermine their success.

The system of water rights is a fundamental element of institutional arrangements for managing water resources. Anthony Scott describes the evolution of the British Columbia system in the context of regimes that have developed in other jurisdictions, and analyses how they have gradually adapted to become more sophisticated and appropriate to the demands placed upon them. Drawing on this experience, he proposes market based innovations in the B.C. water rights' system that would be appropriate to the demands of sustainable development in the Fraser Basin.

Murray Rankin questions how the law might help sustain the river by focussing on the water quality and habitat management problems that he sees as resulting in the Fraser Basin from inadequate enforcement and penalties. Drawing on evidence from other jurisdictions in B.C. and elsewhere, he argues that, given a political commitment to sustainable development, the enforcement system should be redesigned to provide for an increasing scale of automatic financial penalties while reserving prosecutions for those situations where continuing disregard or criminal intent make them essential.

In the last paper of Part III, Roger McNeill examines water supply pricing. After considering the rationale for charging for water supply as part of the institutional arrangements for sustainable development, he describes the limitations of present pricing approaches used in the Fraser Basin for domestic, municipal, agricultural and industrial supply. He concludes that there are situations in the Basin, particularly in metropolitan Vancouver and the arid areas of the interior, where the costs of metering would be more than met by the benefits of more efficient use and development of water supply systems.

The last set of papers in Part IV provide different outlooks for sustainable development in the Fraser Basin. Peter Pearse and Donald Tate review the evolution of economic thought about the role of water and other natural resources in economic development. From the viewpoint of mainstream economics today, they conclude that in real terms, prices of natural resources are not increasing. Arguing that the market has generally operated well in allocating scarce resources with the major exception of the environment, they offer recommendations for how economic instruments might be better utilised in managing future water use in the Fraser Basin.

From the increasing evidence of potentially disastrous changes in the biosphere and the perspective on ultimate limits to economic growth dictated by the laws of thermodynamics, William Rees concludes that the sustainability of development in the Fraser Basin has already been seriously compromised. He argues that rapid and fundamental changes in demands for resources and management policies must be urgently considered and that sustainable development strategies must be based on an appreciation of carrying capacities of not only the basin ecosystems but the other global ecosystems upon which the Fraser settlements are dependent.

Peter Boothroyd argues that from a global perspective the major issues in adapting to sustainable development are distributional; he doubts that economic growth as it has been conventionally understood can grow much more in real terms. In his view, it will become essential to develop institutional arrangements that can foster discussion of ethical and moral judgements and that are capable of implementing the compassionate changes that will be central to a sustainable society. He suggests the radical implications of compassion for transformation of the reigning distribution principles.

Lastly, Andrew Thompson describes the potential for a major expansion in the recognition of Native Indian rights and responsibilities in the Fraser River Basin stemming from decisions that have been made in precedent setting court cases and that are in prospect for Native claims. He argues that any outlook for the sustainable development of the Fraser Basin must anticipate that more than ninety bands will have major controlling interests in the co-management regimes that will become essential. This will also challenge Native Indian communities to reach agreement on their own visions of sustainable development.

The book concludes with two chapters by the editor which revisit the initial analytical framework for the project in light of the contributed papers and growing literatures on both sustainable development and water resources management. It is concluded that the initial framework has served well in launching the project but that it must be elaborated upon in several important regards. In particular, special attention needs to be given to the challenges of reaching agreement in sustainable development.

The first of the concluding chapters examines how different world views and disciplinary schools of thought underlie differing perspectives on sustainable development and implications for water resources management. It outlines strategies for exploiting the insights that can be obtained from the different perspectives and for moving towards agreement on the implications for water resources management of the evolving principles of sustainable development. However, it concludes by suggesting that there is a broad consensus on what should be included in the basic elements of a model of water resources management but that opinions would differ on the specifics of their implementation in any particular situation.

The final chapter examines in more detail the model of water resources management that has been evolving in the literature and relates this to the emerging principles of sustainable development. Drawing on a wide variety of literature and the background papers, the analytical framework is developed that can guide the Fraser case study in the second volume and future research. In elaborating the evolving model, account is taken of the constraints on what can be achieved in the first phase of the Fraser research which is based on only existing information. The objective is to define a model that is powerful in itself but simple enough for the first phase and capable of advancement in future research.

If your initial intent is to obtain an overview of the arguments in this volume and how they contribute to the second volume, you might like to read these last two chapters next.

Acknowledgements

Each of the participants in the project and the many groups with which earlier drafts of the initial analytical framework were discussed have influenced the content of this chapter. Christine Riek made a major contribution in undertaking the initial literature review. Many of the ideas were advanced, tested and refined while conducting research on conflict resolution in water resources management in Australia under a grant from the Social Science and Humanities Research Council (410-88-0830). This enabled me to benefit greatly from discussions with Ben Boer, Stephen Boyden, Donna Craig, Stephen Dovers, Rob Fowler, John Handmer, and Dingle Smith. Valuable comments on earlier drafts of the chapter were provided by Laurie Cooper, Sandy D'Aquino, Dorli Duffy, Irving Fox, Julian Griggs, Les Lavkulich, Bruce Mitchell, Harriet Rueggeberg, Hans Schreier and Brahm Wiesman.

References

Barbier, E. B. 1987. "The Concept of Sustainable Economic Development." *Environmental Conservation* 14(2):101-110.

Block, W. 1989. *Economics and the Environment: A Reconciliation*. Vancouver: Fraser Institute.

British Columbia Task Force on Environment and Economy, 1989. *Sustaining the Living Land*. Victoria: B. C. Ministry of Environment.

Caldwell, L. K. 1984. "Political Aspects of Ecologically Sustainable Development." *Environmental Conservation*. 11(4):299-308.

Canadian Council of Resource and Environment Ministers (CCREM). 1987. *Report of the National Task Force on Environment and Economy*. Ottawa, Ontario.

Dorcey, A. H. J. 1987. "Research for Water Resources Management: The Rise and Fall of Great Expectations." in M. C. Healey and R. R. Wallace (eds.) *Canadian Aquatic Resources*. Canadian Bulletin of Fisheries and Aquatic Sciences. 215:481-511.

Environment Canada. 1987. *Federal Water Policy*. Ottawa.

O'Riordan, T. 1988. "The Politics of Sustainability." in R. K. Turner (ed.) *Sustainable Environmental Management: Principles and Practice*. London: Belhaven Press, and Boulder, Colorado: Westview Press.

Pearce, D., A. Markandya, and E. B. Barbier. 1989. *Blueprint for a Green Economy*. London: Earthscan Publications.

Robinson, J., G. Francis, R. Legge, and S. Lerner. 1990. "Defining a Sustainable Society: Values, Principles and Definitions." Working Paper No. 1, *Sustainable Societies Project*. Department of Environment and Resource Studies, University of Waterloo.

World Commission on Environment and Development (WCED). 1987. *Our Common Future*. Oxford: Oxford University Press.

2

Native Indians of the Fraser Basin: Towards a Model of Sustainable Resource Use

J. E. Michael Kew and Julian R. Griggs

> In earlier times this Fraser River resembled an enormous dish that stored up food for all mankind...(Xa'xthelten, Peter Pierre, of Katzie).

There is both an overriding sense of loss and an edge of uncertainty in the words of Xa'xthelten. Though these words were recorded by Diamond Jenness in 1935 (1955), the underlying sentiments are apparent today in many of the public debates on ecological concerns and the sustainability of human activity in the Fraser Basin.

There is mounting concern in British Columbia that prevailing patterns of human activity and resource use are draining the region of its ecological capital. This concern has bred increasing conflict. As the cumulative impacts of development throughout the Basin are finally recognised, this concern has crystallized into forceful demands for change. While there is not widespread agreement on how best to proceed, there is an increasing and diverse political lobby calling for a re-evaluation of our style of resource use, for new approaches to development, and even for new frameworks of social organisation.

The catch-phrase for many recent initiatives has been "sustainable development", a phrase that was popularised by the World Commission on Environment and Development (WCED, chaired by Gro Harlem Brundtland). That group, in its report *Our Common Future*, defined sustainable development as

> development that meets the needs of the present without compromising the ability of future generations to meet their own needs. (WCED 1987:43).

Sustainable development, conceived in these broad terms, is an attractive idea that has been embraced by parties on all sides of the political spectrum as the key to a brighter future. Canada was one of the first nations to respond to the WCED report, establishing the National Task Force on Environment and Economy and adopting the phrase in many subsequent policy initiatives. Though the term sustainable development was given a clearer practical definition through its usage in the report of the National Task Force (CCREM, 1987), it is often used with little more than a vague notion of a new direction for development. Sustainable development is being interpreted in different circles in highly contrasting ways. While the phrase appears to state a simple directive, we find an inherent and troublesome contradiction in the term itself. 'Development' usually connotes continued economic growth and this, in all but a few cases, implies an increased demand on natural resources. Such an interpretation is consistent with the Brundtland Commission's report which called for a "new era of economic growth—growth that is forceful and at the same time socially and environmentally sustainable" (WCED, 1987:xii). We concur with many ecologically-minded critics that in a finite region, or in any relatively closed system with limited resources and limited ecological tolerance, it is inconceivable that continued development can be compatible with long-term stability (Rees, 1989).

For our purposes, therefore, we prefer a definition which avoids such ambiguity and places a stronger emphasis on social and ecological values. In this we subscribe to the suggestion of Ignacy Sachs, one of the main proponents of the concept of "eco-development", who called for

> an approach to development aimed at harmonizing social and economic objectives with ecologically sound management in a spirit of solidarity with future generations based on the principles of self-reliance, satisfaction of basic needs, a new symbiosis of... [humanity] and earth; another kind of qualitative growth. (Sachs, 1978).

In a similar vein, CUSO's (Canadian University Students Organisation) Environment and Development Education Program "Non-Government Organization Working Definition", characterizes sustainable development as an approach which

> recognizes that communities must define and develop their own solutions to environmental and development problems and that those who are closest to the environment know best how to preserve it and to protect it. In the long term, it will increase the capacity of local communities to adapt and respond to changing environmental, social and economic conditions. (CUSO, 1982).

These two hopeful proposals for planning, with their overt emphasis on decentralized decision-making and community stability, represent an approach that we believe would come closer to realizing sustainability.

In this opening chapter, we take an historical view and examine the cultures and resource-use patterns of the First Nations of the Fraser Basin. It should be stressed that we do not claim that indigenous societies meet all conditions necessary for sustainable development of all societies—it would be absurd to expect there to be a formula applicable in all socio-economic systems that would ensure continuity. But we do argue that indigenous societies of the Fraser Basin came close to sustainable use of natural resources and that there is much knowledge to be gained from revisiting the past. In keeping with the general themes of this book, we emphasize the aquatic resource base on which the First Nations depended, particularly the salmon runs of the Fraser River. We address two principal questions:

(i)   What was the First Nations' system of resource use in the Fraser Basin?
(ii) Does that system have features which may inform our approach to planning for sustainable resource use?

Native Indian people have occupied the Fraser River watershed and used its resources for at least 10,000 years (Fladmark, 1986). Their modes of resource use, population size, and scale of consumption, in short their whole cultural system, differed markedly from that of contemporary industrial society. Most striking was their stability. In contrast to industrial society's rapid rates of change, ancient Fraser cultures maintained remarkable stability of residence, cultural form, and essential features of resource use, for long periods of time (Matson, 1980; Mitchell, 1972). In measures of temporal stability, these socio-economic systems far surpass succeeding ones. More importantly, the descendants of indigenous First Nations peoples continue to live within the watershed and, to varying degrees, make use of the same renewable resources with traditionally derived cultural organization. Many of these groups are becoming increasingly powerful political actors, particularly in light of the legal momentum behind their claims to aboriginal rights (see Thompson, this volume), and in many cases the visions of development they articulate draw heavily on their cultural heritage.

The First Nations cultures of the Fraser Basin deserve consideration, therefore, for two important reasons. Firstly, they are part of the historical and present patterns of resource use, and in their early historic phases, they represent enduring and stable, that is to say, sustainable systems of resource use. They are in fact the only such systems within the Fraser Basin of which we have any empirical knowledge. Secondly, recent events such as the armed conflict at Oka, Quebec and the series of roadblocks that have followed in various parts of British Columbia have forced the issue of aboriginal rights to the top of the political agenda. With the prospect of land title settlements now a real possibility, it seems only prudent to take a closer and more critical look at the patterns of social organisation which form the basis of First Nations societies. A more refined understanding of their traditions and heritage is needed, for we believe it is these that will provide the core of the First Nations' vision of the future.

Such an historical review faces a considerable methodological challenge. Lack of indigenous written history forces us to rely on ethnographic sources of variable accuracy and reliability. Additionally, there are a number of misconceptions about indigenous peoples which must be addressed. One popular view of Native peoples sees them as warlike raiders living comfortably off the abundant and easily-had riches of the sea and forest. It views the rich and elaborate arts of coastal peoples as the result of economic surplus and leisure time provided by the natural bounty of the land. This view discounts the role which human knowledge plays in culture.

Another myth is the idea that indigenous people were nomadic wanderers hunting and gathering fortuitously with little or no attachment to place.

In this paper we challenge such myths and present a view which is more consistent with the known facts. From a review of ethnographic data, we develop an alternative model of Native Indian societies in the Fraser Basin which portrays them as stable, conserving, and inherently sustainable. This model encompasses the subtle patterns of social and political organization that provided frameworks for an enduring ecologically-oriented system. We are able to show that First Nations people developed adaptable and flexible structures of local control, and mechanisms that encouraged restraint in resource use. We argue that such societies developed, through experience, an implicit understanding of the cycles and thresholds of natural systems, and we show how conservation was a consequence of prevailing patterns of resource use. The model also underlines the strong linkage between philosophy and practice and highlights the indigenous idea of reciprocal relations between humans and the natural world, for it is these linkages and interdependences that gave the whole system its coherence and meaning. Finally, the model highlights a number of key features of sustainability, including relative closure, local control, and commitment to place.

Such a recasting of the historical record is, of course, itself just another portrayal of reality and as such is also conditioned by our perspective. In that sense, it is not different from earlier ethnographic studies now criticised for presenting First Nations cultures as lower on a scale of evolution rather than different in mode of economic organization, or fixed in form at time of contact and disappearing rather than changing and continuing.[1] We do not claim our version to be the final truth. However, we do urge attention to First Nations societies with perspectives which attend to a wider range of facts about both the past and present. We are not advocating a return to the past, nor do we think earlier societies were utopian. But we are convinced that the model developed here can have value in the context of current debate. Bound up within it, we discern features and elements that collectively formed the framework for historically real and sustainable societies. In times of mounting crisis, as we search for new approaches and new directions for the future, such models offer valuable tools for analysis and can serve to enlarge our thinking about real possibilities.

The Indigenous Societies of the Fraser Basin

There are, in the Basin, 91 separate Indian Bands as presently defined by the Indian Act (Canada, R.S.C. I-6), each with its own registered membership and elected leadership. This is a system of administration imposed by the state and developed only since the province entered confederation in 1871. These Bands are listed in Appendix 2.1, and summarized in Table 2.1, below. First Nations themselves have created larger political affiliations, many called Tribal Councils, and belong to even larger regional or national Indian associations (see Tennant, 1983). We shall refer to such changing political units at times, but in this account,

---

1   For such a critique, see Trigger (1985:114).

we shall refer mainly to language groups, a more enduring form of association. These were groups with recognized boundaries, in which people shared mutually intelligible speech and thus constituted the largest groups within which easy communication and social interaction could occur.

Within the boundaries of British Columbia there is a greater degree of indigenous cultural and linguistic diversity than in any other area of Canada. Three culture areas are recognized: Northwest Coast, Plateau, and Sub-arctic. Within these areas there were until recently as many as 30 separate languages belonging to 5 language families, and three additional language isolates, that is languages with no demonstrated affiliates. These last are Tlingit, Haida, and Kootenay (Foster, 1988; Thompson and Kinkaid, 1990).

The Fraser Basin itself was, and is still today, inhabited by indigenous people speaking six separate, mutually unintelligible languages belonging to two great language families (Figure 2.1). Within the Basin, we can also distinguish both Northwest Coast cultural forms on the lower part of the river and adjoining sea coast, and Plateau cultural forms in the middle and upper parts of the Basin.

This remarkable variety and diversity is consistent with the ten millenia time span now known to be the period of human presence in the Basin and it speaks stability of people. It also suggests that, to a great degree, and with the notable exception of occasional trade and barter or raids, each language group remained independent of neighbours and was largely self-contained and self-sufficient within its traditional territories.

In the downstream part of the system are four Salishan languages, while the two in upstream portions are Athapaskan, sometimes referred to as Dene. Although Figure 2.1 outlines their territories in relation to the watershed, it is worth noting particular features of each of these geographic distributions in turn.

Halkomelem (Salishan)

Halkomelem is the language spoken along the Fraser and its lower tributaries from Yale to the sea. It is also the language of the adjacent portion of Vancouver Island and northern Gulf Islands from Nanoose Bay to Mill Bay on Saanich Inlet. Within this region, there are different dialects of Halkomelem, and of the six languages in the Basin, the territory of these speakers extends further from the boundaries of the watershed than any other. Association of the Vancouver Island Halkomelem villages, such as Nanaimo and Cowichan, with the Fraser River was maintained, however, for these Vancouver Island people too, in the early 19th century, had summer habitat sites in the Fraser Delta and fished its waters for salmon (Duff 1952). In some degree, all Halkomelem speakers share access to the great salmon runs of the Fraser River.

Nlaka'pamux or Thompson (Salishan)

Nlaka'pamux is spoken by people whose main villages are in the Fraser Canyon, lower Thompson River and Nicola River. Their territory includes mountainous

Figure 2.1: Sketch Map Showing the Distribution and Extent of the Six Native
Indian Language Groups in the Fraser Basin.

areas in the Coast Range over to the Similkameen headwaters on the Columbia River system—an area of seasonal gathering and hunting. Their territory is mainly, but not exclusively, within the Fraser Basin watershed.

Lillooet, also Li'lwet, or Stl'atl'imx, (Salishan)

Lillooet is spoken by people who have their villages on the Fraser near the town of Lillooet, on the Bridge and Seton Rivers, and further west on the Lillooet River, from the vicinity of Mount Currie downstream to, and including part of, Harrison Lake, where their territory joins that of the Halkomelem speakers. Lillooet territory lies within the Fraser watershed and, like Nlaka'pamux territory, is a land with deep river gorges, steep hillsides, and varied biotic communities as one ascends from the river banks to alpine zones.

Shuswap (Salishan)

Shushwap is spoken by the people on both sides of the Fraser from the Lillooet territory upstream to Soda Creek Canyon, in the whole of the upper Thompson River and Shuswap Lakes watersheds and over the intervening high wooded plateau between the two great river valleys. It includes the upper part of the Quesnel River system with the lake of that name and the great sockeye-bearing Horsefly River. It lies within the boundaries of the Fraser watershed, except for a small portion of the Rocky Mountain trench extending into the upper Columbia drainage.

Chilcotin (Athapaskan)

Chilcotin is spoken by the people of the Chilcotin River system. In fact, their name means literally 'people of the Chilco River' (their name for the Chilcotin of modern maps). Except for a part of the Dean River above the high falls which were impassable to salmon, and some of the similar upper tributaries of other coastal streams, Chilcotin territory was entirely within the Fraser system.

Carrier (Athapaskan)

Carrier is spoken by the people occupying the remaining portions of the upper Fraser watershed from Alexandria upstream. There is a marked division of this group, partly in dialect but more so in social organization. The Southern or Lower Carrier, consists of people downstream from the Nechako confluence, including the other tributary basins as far as the Shuswap territory. It also includes the Algatcho who occupy part of the Blackwater and the upper Dean River, including the salmon fishing station below the aforementioned falls. All the southern Carrier except the Algatcho live within the Fraser Basin. Their kinship system is one with bilineal descent like their neighbours the Chilcotin and the Shuswap. Central Carrier, on the other hand have a system of matrilineal descent. Their territory includes a major part of the Nechako drainage and the upper Fraser itself. We will refer to both groups collectively by the term Carrier. A separate language from this, sometimes referred to as Western Carrier, is spoken by both the Natao'ten of Babine Lake, and the Wet'suwet'en of the Bulkley River system. Their territories lie predominantly within the Skeena River watershed, although the Wet'suwet'en occupy part of the upper, westernmost tributaries of the Nechako.

Ethnographic Information on Traditional Societies

In this paper, we have had to rely on existing sources of ethnographic data. Unfortunately, no single account provides an adequate overview of the data for all Fraser societies, and there are many inaccuracies and missing details. Available studies, as noted above, were shaped largely by the theoretical interests of the day. They were directed toward illustrating stages of cultural evolution or the distribution of particular culture traits, and focussed on cultures at the time of European contact. Based mainly on reconstruction from informants' memories, rather than descriptions from observation, and hampered often by language differences, they present weak accounts of the crucial processes of interaction and decision-making which governed peoples' relationships with one another and with their environment.

We have had to make the best of these problems, and have relied heavily upon four comparative studies of cultural variation which, taken together, cover the Fraser River Basin. These are Ray (1939 and 1942) and Jorgensen (1969 and 1980). Ray used published sources and the results of his own fieldwork which included interviews with a few persons from all the language groups in the Basin, except Halkomelem. Jorgensen's work was based on existing ethnographic sources. These surveys lack many details but have the virtues of being comparative studies and of being accessible. Where these reports lack specific details, additional sources were consulted.

Populations

The earliest systematic estimates of population were made by Hudson's Bay Company officers in the 1830's. These were not censuses but a combination of counts of villages known to traders, and estimates from Native informants. They are probably reasonably accurate, perhaps erring on the low side by missing some villages or seasonal encampments.

There is little doubt that the indigenous population at that time was suffering, and likely had been suffering for many decades, from the effects of diseases introduced elsewhere on the continent by European explorers and traders. Some epidemics of smallpox, for example, swept British Columbia before the first direct contacts were made with Spanish and British maritime explorers in the closing decades of the 18th century (Boyd, 1990). The effects of such contagious diseases

Table 2.1: Fraser Basin Indian Populations by Language Groups, Selected Years

Language	Number of Bands	Population*				
		1800	1835	1929**	1988	1989
Halkomelem	29	5,000	3,500	1,354	4,857	5,121
Nlaka'pamux	16	5,500	5,000	1,433	4,389	4,653
Lillooet	11	3,000	3,500	1,162	3945	4,106
Shushwap	15	5,500	5,500	2,072	5,298	5,636
Chilcotin	6	1,000	900	548	2,209	2,267
Carrier	14	4,500***	3,800***	1,477	5,021	5,301
Totals	91	24,500	22,200	8,046	25,719	27,084

Notes:
*   Populations for 1988 and 1989 are from figures compiled by B.C. Ministry of Native Affairs, and based upon DIAND (previously INAC) records. Figures for 1800 and 1835 are taken from estimates made by Duff, based on Hudson's Bay Company censuses in the 1830's which formed the basis for his more summary published population totals in Duff (1964:349).
**   Year 1929 was the year for which the lowest population total was recorded in Duff's notes and marks the nadir of First Nations populations in the Fraser Basin.
*** These Carrier totals include the Western Carrier and hence are overstatements of the Fraser Basin Carrier total.

as smallpox, measles, and whooping cough, many of which were new to the indigenous populations, were devastating. For these reasons, the earliest counts of Indian population are certainly well below peak levels.

The Hudson's Bay data were reviewed by Duff and formed the basis of published summaries (Hawthorn et al., 1958; Duff, 1964), which are described by larger linguistic units than are required for assessing sizes of Fraser Basin populations. However, his notes have been used to compile the summary presented below in Table 2.1.

Current registered Indian populations by Band are readily available and these are also provided. It should be noted that these do not include non-Status persons who are genealogically allied to band members. It may be truthfully said that counts of *registered Indians* are only a portion of the total Indian populations associated with a Band, village, or tribe. Nevertheless the records of registered Indian populations are among the most complete and useful demographic data available. Changes in these populations in the Basin, through the historic era, follow closely those for Indians in the province as a whole (Duff, 1964). The tragic decline, brought about by disease, reached its nadir for Fraser Basin peoples in the first two decades of the 20th century. Since then there have been dramatic recoveries, and populations now approximate sizes in 1800. We do not have the current rate of natural increase for B.C. registered Indians, but it will be close to that for all Canadian Indians. In 1987, this was 9.2 per thousand population (Loh, 1990), while the same index for the whole Canadian population in 1986 was 7.5 per thousand (Statistics Canada, 1990).

A recent projection of the total number of Canadian Indians forecasts an increase in the three decades following 1981 of 87 percent (Loh, 1990). A substantial portion of this would be due to additions to Indian status resulting from the 1985 change in legislation (Bill C-31) determining female Indian status upon marriage (see Jamieson, 1986). Fraser Basin registered Indian populations in 1988 totalled 25,719, and increased by more than five percent in one year to total 27,084 in 1989 (Table 2.1). This sudden high rate of increase will decline as the backlog of unjustly omitted women and offspring is added to bands of registered Indians. All evidence indicates, however, that rates of natural increase of registered Indians in the Fraser Basin will remain above those of the general population for some time.

Questions about the sizes of the Basin populations prior to 1800 and their vital characteristics, are still problematic, as there are no firm data bearing on birth or death rates. Some cultural controls, such as extended nursing of infants (reported by Ray 1942, to be two years for most of the Basin), would have moderated birth rates, as would abstinence from sexual activity which was often a feature of ritual purifications related to hunting and fishing activities. Abortion and abortifacients were also recorded as known in all Basin groups (Ray, 1942).

Duff's estimate of a 24,500 population total for 1800 applies to a time when the ravages of introduced diseases had already taken their toll. The total Basin population before then may have been twice as great and would represent the maximum size attained before contact. There are no data of which we are aware which would indicate a larger population at a far earlier time. Whether this level was as great as could be sustained upon the then existing economic base is an unanswerable question. There is no doubt, however, that the nature of food producing technology itself in 1800 was not a limitation. The Northwest Company and Hudson's Bay company posts in the Fraser area were dependent during the early days of the fur trade upon country food, mainly dried salmon produced by the First Nations (see for example, Fisher 1977). With no additional technology and little hesitation or difficulty, they also began commercial and domestic production of new plants, especially the potato (Suttles, 1951). The evidence does not suggest that the limits on aboriginal population growth are to be found either in the capacity of aboriginal technology or the resources of the region. If such controls were indeed at work, they are to be found in the more complex consequences of the whole cultural system.

Indigenous Social Organization

Despite language differences, Fraser Basin people share many features of culture. Technologies and subsistence methods were similar throughout the area, although varying in accord with major biotic region and availability of some resources. Despite some difference in rules of kinship, and in the resultant constitution of extended families, the basic units of communities were functionally similar, and political groupings were modest in size. This essential similarity of cultural form, as Jorgensen's (1980) study demonstrates, extends far beyond the boundaries of the Fraser Basin itself. In this section, we attempt to provide a summary sketch of the major features of culture throughout the Basin at the time of contact, in approximately 1800. We do not, therefore, describe the First Nations cultures of today. They continue, altered in many features but drawing from these traditional roots and maintaining distinction from the surrounding society.

Households

Among all six languages there were extended family households. Halkomelem households consisted of two or more related couples and married children. These large families were bilineally related, that is, kin were descendants through either male or female lines of ancestors identified with the household (Suttles, 1960). Households in other language groups were similar, and bilineal descent with a tendency towards patrilocal residence was the pattern among almost all the Basin groups. The *Central* Carrier, where matrilocal residence and matrilineal descent occurred, were the exception to this pattern. Despite this difference of descent, in all the groups, people lived in large kin-centred households which were primary units of domestic production and consumption.

Villages and Bands

Households formed villages throughout most of the Basin and members identified with a named village site. Among Chilcotin and Southern Carrier, the social unit to which households belonged was a geographically identified unit usually termed a band, and not a village. The two units—village and band—are similar in their functions.

In all groups, there were seasonal movements of some or all residents away from the most permanent houses or camps to temporary encampments for purposes of resource extraction and processing. Such movements were never random or permanent but purposeful, planned according to a seasonal schedule, and within the rightful territory of the band or village.

Villages or bands did not have a *formalized* political structure or local government. Leaders were recognized, but their powers derived from kinship support, as well as competence and achievement, rather than powers of office. Social order was achieved largely through internalized personal values of respect and proper ethical behaviour.

Villages or Bands functioned as self-governing bodies, however, in that members shared access to territory and acted collectively, if necessary, for defense. There were no other standing offices or regulatory military, judicial, or executive bodies. Jorgensen (1980) concludes that kin groups, and not local bands or villages, bore primary responsibility for distributing scarce food supplies and allocating access to subsistence resources. According to Ray (1939) the band organization characteristic of Carrier, Chilcotin, Lillooet, Shuswap, Thompson (Nlaka'pamux) is "...merely one unit of an expanded autonomous local group. Instead of the tiniest settlements maintaining strict independence,...a small number within a relatively small range join together in a mutually advantageous union. In this case the group is looked upon in the same light as a large village" (Ray, 1939:15).

Among the Upper Stalo Halkomelem (the uppermost division of this language on the Fraser River), Duff concluded that villages were smaller on average than among Lower Stalo, and a collective name was used for "...groups of villages which had come to be thought of as units..." (1952:86-7). Further down the river, where larger villages prevailed, the band or tribal level of identification merged with that of village. The Halkomelem villages were probably the largest among the tribes we are considering and ranged in size from about 35 to over 200 persons (Duff, 1952). Although bands and villages formed the largest political units, households and families remained primary units of economic organization.

Kinship and Marriage

Throughout the Basin, from the sea up to the Nechako confluence, marriage between first and second cousins was disallowed or disapproved, with the consequence that marriages were usually contracted between persons from different villages or local districts. Since both male and female lines are equally significant, marriages extend lineal kin ties across boundaries of villages and bands. Among the matrilineal Central Carrier, marriage was, and is, regulated by a rule of exogamy forbidding marriage between members of the same clan. This does not disallow cross-cousin marriage and some local endogamy may occur. However, clans are not localized but prevail over a wide territory and constitute kinship connections outside local communities. Thus, by different rules, bonds of kinship, cross-cut local political units.

In every part of the Basin, marriage was a formalized bond connecting different families, and these associations were marked by ritual gift exchange before marriage to confirm intentions, and in varying cycles up to several years after actual marriage. In addition, replacement of a deceased spouse by an appropriate kin was widely practiced, with the effect of maintaining established affinal bonds between families. Kinship ties thus provided enduring, close links between the seemingly separate villages and bands.

Class and Rank

In his study of Plateau culture, Ray (1939) found the Canadian portion, including the Fraser Basin tribes, to differ from the others in having social ranks or classes and slavery. In the adjoining downstream Halkomelem, within the Northwest Coast culture area, a class system with slavery existed (Suttles, 1958). Differentiation of social status according to possession of property and disposable wealth, with the accumulation of movable property and control of resources by hereditary kin groups, is thus characteristic of the whole Basin area.

While social equality was neither sought nor achieved, it is evident from descriptions that inequality, especially in terms of domestic consumption, was limited. Material signs of difference in class and rank were not great, indicating that similar levels of consumption probably prevailed in all ranks. Obligation of support among the extensive networks of lineal and affinal kin and the cycles of reciprocal gift exchange also served to reduce inequities.

Property and Economic Organization

Movable goods, tools, equipment, and foodstuffs were considered private property, shared to some degree within each household, among all the people of the Basin. Key resource extraction sites, on the other hand, were considered to be communal property, with established rules of access and use defining the rights held by members of an identified community of users.[2] While these rights were often restricted to members of an extended family, that is the family in a sense constituted the *community* of users, similar communal property rights also existed at the level of village or band. These property rights governed not only patterns of resource use, but also ceremonial artifacts, songs, dances, etc. and thus served to define the rank and authority of leaders within families and villages. Persons outside a property owning group could be granted access under certain conditions, but might equally be excluded or discouraged from entry, by physical force if necessary. Throughout the Basin, as noted, kin groups were also responsible for the distribution of foods in times of scarcity (Jorgensen, 1980).

It is illuminating to point out here an obvious but fundamental difference between First Nations, with their various levels of communal social groupings, and the units of economic organization in contemporary industrial society. The extended families, villages, and bands of First Nations consist of members recruited primarily by birth and marriage. They are kinship-based societies. Inter-group mobility is limited, and individual loyalty and obligation are locally focused. Individuals are, from birth, or marriage until death and even afterwards, associated with one place, and their close kin are also associated with the same place.

Industrial society's local residential groups—villages, towns and cities—may have members from birth but carry little kinship attachment to the community. Membership in the local community is conceived as temporary and based simply

---

2   The use of the term "communal property" follows that of Berkes (1989).

on property ownership, employment or residence. Corporate economic groups in industrial society are even less stable in membership. Corporation owners are shareholders whose connections to the group shift frequently, and typically are not resident in the local community. Corporation employees may be more fixed in residence, but their obligations to work and to residence are not necessarily connected. Citizens in industrial society are far more migratory than First Nations people.

Division of Labour and Exchange

Households were the major units of production in Native societies. Older members owned such special capital goods as canoes and nets, and acted as stewards of family owned resource sites. They also possessed specialized knowledge of calendrical cycles, animal and fish behaviour, and detailed information on the availability of resources within the village or band territory. Householders worked cooperatively, sharing tasks according to skills. Wherever available, slaves worked as bidden in these labours, living in owners' houses but discharging heavier and more burdensome labours for their sustenance.

There was no regular centralized village or band control of production or redistribution, but through the communal property systems referred to above, household and local extended family leaders do seem to have exerted control. Again, kin groups were responsible for the redistribution of some foods and goods.

Formalized gift exchange, often termed "potlatching", was an integral part of many ceremonies throughout the Basin, and served to define and maintain the prestige or social position of giver and receiver alike. Such exchanges occurred within and between local communities, and were a primary means of redistribution of surplus goods. All groups within the Basin also traded goods between communities and some standardizations of exchange values were established (see for example, Teit, 1900).

Dried and processed foods, finished goods, and raw materials, circulated between local groups within the Basin. There was also trade and exchange between these people and groups in adjoining watersheds. Well known trade routes existed between the coast and the interior, with dried salmon and oolichan oil from the coast traded inland for dried meat and hides. The Fraser and Lillooet valleys and the Nechako Basin and Upper Skeena tributaries, provided routes to and from the coast. While local groups within sub-basins could probably be self-sufficient and independent of trade when necessary, they all availed themselves of exchange when it was advantageous.

Intergroup Relations

In none of the Fraser Basin tribes were there political positions or institutions—chiefs, councils, courts, or police—responsible for deciding or punishing crimes. These were matters normally arbitrated or settled between households and kin groups without recourse to higher authority.

Warfare in the form of intergroup raiding occurred, but was of limited scale. The role of warrior was recognized, and rod and slat armour and fighting clubs were used; there were no permanent military organizations or sustained hostilities between or within the Fraser Basin tribes. Jorgensen (1980) found raiding most frequent among Halkomelem and Nlaka'pamux, and reported diverse motives for raiding: to avenge death, obtain slaves, capture women, avenge poaching, and for booty. Warfare for territorial expansion is not evident, and the endemic pattern of small scale raiding might be best understood as a means of maintaining stable jurisdiction over resources within local territories.

This generally peaceful state of affairs was described by Simon Fraser in 1808 (Lamb, 1960). Passing through what was, for him, new territory, before a state of peace could be claimed to be the result of the fur trade or colonial control, he recorded this mingling of peoples: Chilcotins present among Shuswaps; Nlaka'pamux, a Chilcotin, and possibly Shuswaps, among Lillooet; Lillooet and Nlaka'pamux together in one village; and "Swhanemugh" (most likely Shuswap) among Nlaka'pamux.

The evidence describes limited and small scale warfare, regular inter-group trade, marriage, visiting, and gift exchange. This bespeaks relatively peaceful and stable relationships between and within Nations throughout the watershed before colonial control.

Religion

Religion is a feature of First Nations culture least understood by outsiders. Yet it encompasses ideas and principles critical for understanding the First Nations world. Certainly, not all the variations of belief and ritual with which these people understood and dealt with life have been recorded in the literature. Furthermore, ethnographers have tended to approach the subject through concepts and assumptions of their discipline, so that their very words, often inadequate or inappropriate for the complex and different First Nations ideas, placed limitations on the record. Missionaries were similarly encumbered and additionally bound by an arrogance of faith in what they assumed to be a superior set of beliefs. Despite the harsh conditions and pressures of colonization, many elements of the indigenous beliefs and institutions remain extant (see for example, Kew, 1990). Imperfect and limited though the sources are, they do reveal a number of recurring themes and ceremonial cycles which appear to be fundamental. It is to these that we direct attention.

An essential idea is that humans are, in part, consubstantial with other life forms; other life forms and humans are of the same substance or essence and may transform from one appearance to the other. This is expressed clearly in mythology where animals appear alternately in human and animal form or transform appearance at will. Similarly, animals, fish, trees, and forces of nature are addressed as people on ritual occasions. A second, related idea is belief in a multiplicity of forces or powers identified mainly with life forms. These are superior in power to humans and can cause illness, death, misfortune, or the converse of these conditions. Individual humans can achieve personal helpful relationships with one or more such powers by proper training and purification. Such help was sought throughout the Basin by youths of both genders in the so-called guardian spirit quest. Successful relationships required of individuals that they observe rites of purification (bathing, fasting, separation from some human activities) and these also served to benefit, indirectly, the whole community. Private songs and dances conferred by power helpers were performed on ritual occasions as celebrations of the powers. Powers of curing and divination, often termed shamanic in anthropology, were also given to humans by these helpers.

A third idea, derivative of the first, is belief in the human-like consciousness of non-human forms. They respond like humans. For example, after spawning and dying, salmon return to the world of the salmon, where they are people. The next year, if they have been treated respectfully by people here, they return in salmon form to visit people here, bringing again the gifts which are their salmon bodies. Deer, plants, and so on are people in their own worlds. All forms are human-like in their ability to comprehend and anticipate human action and speech, and they may respond willfully to humans, providing bounty and fortune or denying success in whatever ventures are at hand.

A fourth critical point is the assumption that humans are subordinate in power. Dealings of humans with other life forms are conducted on a model of reciprocal social action in which humans are not supreme. The seeming paradox of human hunters and fishers killing the bodies of those who are superior in power and must be treated respectfully is resolved by the knowledge that the bodies are given to humans as a gift. For these reasons, there were widespread rites of supplication and purification prior to special resource gathering activities. Bathing, abstinence from food, and prayers addressed to life forms sought their favourable response to the human activity. After butchering, certain parts of some animals were specially treated, skulls for example, might be hung in trees. The first caught of one or more species of salmon, on their first arrival in the annual runs, were the subject of elaborate rites—special butchering, cooking, shared eating, and return of all bones to the water—in community ceremonies which were at once propitiatory and thanksgiving. Similar ceremonies for first fruits also exist throughout the Basin.

We suggest that these beliefs and their expressions in ritual and ceremony create a view of the world in which humans are neither independent nor dominant. They are actors and lesser participants in systems of interaction with other humans and with the features of the world and life forms they depend upon for sustenance. It is an *ethic of reciprocity* between all the personified actors in the system which governs behaviour. Conservation, in the Western sense, is a process in which humans manipulate resources in order to prevent their destruction or waste; the will of humans predominates. Among First Nations, the will of humans is but one of many, all affecting one another and responding to one another.

Traditional Food Resources

The Fraser Basin has a rich supply of diverse renewable resources including a wide range of fishes, animals, and plants for which First Nations cultures have highly developed procurement and processing techniques. Of all resources, however, it is the salmon and other anadromous fishes that are of greatest value.

Pacific salmon are born in fresh-water streams, descend to the sea, and range over a vast expanse of the ocean where they grow quickly and return to their natal streams to spawn and die. They are, in a sense, concentrators of energy, gathering the dispersed riches of their feeding grounds and concentrating them in space and time as a run of fish migrate on their final journey through the river system to their birth streams. First Nations cultures focussed around use of the salmon. Their fishing technology was efficient and productive of substantial quantities of dried fish and oil, used as staple foods through the winter season and traded widely. Despite such heavy use, there is no evidence to suggest that they pushed the productive capacity of the resource to near maximum capacity levels. Salmon stocks are resilient and capable of withstanding high levels of predation in successive cycles, as the history of the canning industry has demonstrated (see for example Foerster, 1968). Other anadromous species, such as sturgeon, steelhead, and oolichan, and freshwater fish, such as trout and suckers, were probably not exploited to maximum capacity either. Reductions of many stocks observed in this century have mainly been the result of environmental damage from agricultural and industrial development and/or grossly excessive commercial harvesting (see Northcote, 1974; Northcote and Larkin, 1988).

The relative importance of fish in the diets of Northwest Coast and Plateau peoples was well recognized and mentioned by most early observers. However, we know of no systematic studies of diet in the early historic period before imported cereals and potatoes became staples. Several authors have attempted informed guesses at the relative importance of fish, animal, and plant foods, and in general the significance of fish is upheld. Jorgensen (1980) rates fish (aquatic animals in his scheme) to have constituted at least 51% of the diet of Halkomelem, Nlaka'pamux, and Carrier, 26-50% of Lillooet and Chilcotin, and from 11-25% of Shuswap diet. Land animals and plants are about equivalent in importance among all groups in his assessment. The significance of plant foods has arguably been the most frequently underestimated. Recent research among plateau peoples has revealed an extensive knowledge of plants and their food uses, a knowledge which indicates the importance of plants to subsistence (Turner 1975; 1978; 1979; Suttles, 1962; Steedman, 1929).

Human population densities were apparently higher in the downstream areas of the Basin (Kew, n.d.) where salmon are more numerous, since all runs pass through the lower main stream. But it would be misleading to take this correlation as evidence of a simple dependence of humans on salmon. The biotic richness of the whole environment is greater in the lower altitudes and richer soils downstream, and the greater human populations are merely consistent with that greater productivity.

However, the relative importance of ocean-derived proteins, in contrast to terrestrial-derived proteins among indigenous populations, is becoming more evident from recent analyses of human skeletal remains (Chisholm, et al., 1983; Lovell et al., 1986). Marine derived proteins predominate, as one would expect, in coastal dwellers, but they are also high in pre-contact occupants in the middle Fraser as well. There is little doubt that anadromous fish, especially salmon taken in the Basin, and possibly traded from the coast, would be the main source of such protein. This evidence supports the emphasis given here to the role of fishing technologies in First Nations economies.

Technologies of Resource Use

Tools and techniques for obtaining and processing food resources are well developed and locally adapted. While availability of specific plant foods varies, equipment and techniques of plant food collection are much the same in all parts of the Basin. These techniques and a great range of plants yielding edible berries, seeds, roots, bulbs, corms, shoots, and bark are thoroughly covered in Turner's handbooks (1975; 1978; 1979).

The major hunting techniques and equipment, such as snares, deadfalls, nets, and drives into ambush vary little in fundamental features over the Basin. Similarly, means of fishing are the same throughout the Basin, and indeed over a much wider range of Western North America (see Hewes, 1947; Berringer, 1982; Ray, 1942, for major surveys).

All of the First Nations in the Basin used lines with baited hooks which were trolled, jigged, or set unattended. Harpoons and gaffs were used, usually in conditions of clear water and with torchlight at night. Weirs of brush, stones, driven pilings, or woven lattice-work, were built across streams of moderate size and current. Migrating fish, such as salmon, trout, Rocky Mountain whitefish, and suckers were taken in conjunction with weirs, by dip-nets, harpoons, double-pronged leister spears, and gaffs. A variety of lattice-work traps were often used with weirs, positioned in such a way that the fish entered them through apertures in the weir. Other lattice-work traps, some of complex design, were operated directly in streams in turbid and rapid locations, such as cataracts and under waterfalls (excellent illustrations of most of these types of fishing devices are found in Stewart, 1977).

Nets are ancient and widely distributed in North American cultures. They were used, at times, to capture both aquatic and land animals as well as fish. Halkomelem and neighbouring coastal language groups, for example, took deer, seals, and flying waterfowl with specialized nets. One of the most widespread fishing nets is the simple gill-net, made with mesh sizes designed to capture particular species. These were made and used by all the Basin people. Seines, dip-nets, and trawls, although not as common, were also widespread.

Salmon fishing technology deserves special attention. Weirs were used wherever possible to take available species of salmon bound for spawning grounds. In most of the Basin, this meant weirs on the lesser tributaries where volumes of water and current were sufficiently reduced to allow weirs to be installed. For example, in Halkomelem territory the Chilliwack river was fished by weir as well as all other smaller watercourses, probably even tiny ones supporting only brief runs of one or two species.

In smaller tributaries in all parts of the Basin, small runs of migrating fish are accessible by weir with a trap or harpoon. So, too, are large runs near spawning grounds in places like the upper Horsefly and tributaries of the Stuart system. The main Fraser itself, however, was not amenable to the use of weirs in the lower Basin. Special technologies for catching salmon in the main river were developed in the different tribal territories, each technique being adapted to the natural conditions of major sections of the Basin (see Kew, n.d. for full discussion). These are summarized in Table 2.2.

Table 2.2: Major Salmon Fishing Devices used by Indigenous Fishers in the Fraser Main Stem.

Language Groups	Nature of Stream	Salmon Fishing Device
Halkomelem	turbid, swift, partially tidal	pursing trawl-nets pulled by two canoes, fishing within communal territory
Nlaka'pamux and Lillooet	turbid, rapid, constricted, frequent canyons	large pursing dip-nets at family-owned stations
Shushwap	turbid, rapid, intermittent canyons	large dip-nets at family-owned stations
Carrier	turbid, swift, infrequent canyons	lattice-work wing weirs with traps at family-owned stations

Regulation of Access and the Question of Conservation

Regulation of access was a key component of this resource use system. Each band or village regulated access to resources, both internally and also for outsiders. Within the territories, ownership of fishing and other key resource sites rested with families, and household leaders commonly held responsibility for regulation of use. These persons were in a position to exercise considerable influence and control, especially of favourable dip-net stations or weir sites. Fish were taken not only for family sustenance, but also for gifts and for trade. Despite such requirements beyond domestic use, it seems likely that the strong ethic of reciprocity and the dictum to respect the animals who gave themselves to humans, encouraged producers to match levels of catch to technological ability and the labour supply needed to dry and preserve the harvest. Moreover, in many cases weirs were built which, though unlikely to be strong enough to dam a river indefinitely, could block completely a run in smaller streams. When sufficient fish had been caught, weirs were reportedly opened to allow passage of migrating stocks to spawn and to provide for fishers upstream who might otherwise take to raiding should their supplies fail.

It has to be conceded here that we do not have *unequivocal* evidence of deliberate restriction of harvest by First Nations peoples in the 1800's, for the purpose of conservation. It is impossible to assign an unambiguous motive for restraint. However, it is evident that their technology had the capacity, under certain conditions, to block fish migration and impede or prevent spawning and, thus, to threaten the viability of a particular run; they certainly had the means to over-fish or extinguish runs although there is no evidence that such blockages were ever created. It is reasonable to assume that adequate restraints were provided by the ethic of reciprocity which extended to both regard for the fish and for neighbouring humans as actors in a system of common relationships. This description of stream fishing by a Shuswap man provides an example:

> The people would go to the place called *See-YOO-ka,* where they would dam the creek during the night and spear sucker fish. In the morning they would break the dam. (Ike Willard, in Bouchard and Kennedy, 1979:136)

We cannot be sure that the dam was broken for the sake of "conserving" the fish, but that is beside the point when the removal of the dam is an act called for by the protocol of proper relationships with the fish who are gift-bearing visitors, and the rules of access that underpinned a system of communal property rights (see also Dale, this volume).

On a more general level, there is also evidence of deliberate manipulation of ecosystems by First Nations people to increase productivity of particular resources. Controlled burning of meadows and parklands occurred throughout western North America, in order to encourage growth of harvestable berries and to provide grazing for ungulates (Lewis, 1982; Suttles,1987). Selective harvesting of beaver and large game, such as moose and deer, by killing males and non-breeding females, is also widely reported. Such evidence belies the notion that indigenous peoples were unaware of the direct consequences of human action upon food resources. It is also clear that patterns of resource use were adaptive and flexible. The available supply, especially the salmon runs of the Fraser, fluctuated dramatically both seasonally and annually, and not in completely predictable ways. Strategies to make use of a wide range of resources were developed to match and cope with such variance. Indigenous groups moved from their villages to seasonal camps in order to harvest berries, to hunt, or to fish particular runs of salmon or other anadromous fish. The variety of known resources in a given territory provided alternate sources of food, perhaps of less than optimal abundance or ease of extraction, but enough to provide some security. Flexibility and safeguards were also built into the system through established trade and gift exchange relations with neighbouring groups (Suttles, 1987).

The religion of Native Indians is, in our view, another key factor in the stability of their culture. It was dominated by the ethic of reciprocity and their mythology carries repeated references to human manifestations of animals and fish, stressing the need to treat them with respect. This intimate linkage of humans with the powerful and humanized beings of their world encourages respect and leads to responsible and conserving action. The idea that reduced stocks of necessary resources result from improper human behaviour, including over-harvesting, encourages a long-term perspective and reinforces the imperative to use renewable resources wisely and judiciously. It does not however embody a romantic view of animals. They are necessarily killed for food.

It is clear that the renewable food resources of the Fraser Basin were not harvested at levels that threatened sustainability. We contend that the indigenous cultural systems contained mechanisms of restraint and conservation adequate for long term protection and maintenance of the resource base. The complex patterns of resource use were adaptable, were controlled locally, and were highly attuned to the cycles of supply, were regulated by the forces of social convention and political influence, and were dominated by the ethic of reciprocity. Such systems were inherently stable and sustainable.

The Effects of Contact Upon Traditional Resource Use Patterns

Traditional society was stable and adaptive, but it was far from invulnerable. Europeans proved more disruptive of the ecological system than any landslide, flood, or earthquake. The First Nations were probably capable of withstanding substantial fluctuations and change in the natural environment. Change in the human environment—in the kinds of neighbours who flooded in after 1800—was another matter.

It needs to be recognized that the First Nations system was regulated mainly by internalized values and voluntary compliance, in a relatively closed system. The ethic of reciprocity can fail, especially when other factors weaken the integrity of the prevailing cultural system. This happened in various ways with the entry of Europeans, particularly with the introduction of a market economy, different values, and new social institutions such as commercial companies, church missions, and government agencies which established ties with First Nations communities.

European agencies—state, church, and trading company—all recruited indigenous people to their service, and church and state deliberately strove to change the social and cultural fabric of First Nations life. Most destructive of all, in B.C. and the Fraser Basin, was the deliberate and unlawful denial of First Nations property rights (see Tennant, 1990, for a comprehensive review of this process). In step with this went the increasing removal of decision making about resource use from the local communities, its concentration in the provincial capital and, eventually, the far-removed boardrooms of multinational corporations.

What is remarkable about this history is that First Nations have survived. Change has occurred, but as their populations have rebounded and cultural adaptation continues anew, they will no longer be dismissed or discounted. The vigour of their voices within the Fraser watershed today is itself a resounding testimony to the vitality of their social system.

Towards a Model of Sustainable Resource Use

The picture we have drawn of the First Nations societies of the Fraser Basin is of a complex and complete socio-cultural system, capable within itself of responding and adapting to a multiplicity of variable conditions. We have tried to show how this provides a framework for sustainable resource use which would explain the apparent stability of Basin cultures over many millenia.

We have drawn out particular themes and ideas from this account and have derived a set of criteria that lead towards defining a model of sustainable resource use. Given the challenges that contemporary society now faces in the Fraser Basin, we suggest this model can inform future planning and can help to shape new styles of resource use that are more stable and which can be more enduring. The model is a tentative one, and we do not suggest that it is complete. Nor do we suggest that this approach to resource use is the *only* means of achieving sustainability but merely that it is the only one within the Fraser Basin for which we have evidence of long stability. Our intention is not to suggest that a reversal of contemporary approaches is called for, but that there is considerable wisdom in traditional systems that can and should be retrieved. We believe that the historical record can enrich the on-going debate, prompting a re-evaluation of contemporary systems of resource use and serving to enlarge thinking about possibilities.

We discern six features of the indigenous system which we offer here as *criteria* with which other systems and proposals for development may be assessed.

Commitment to Place: A sustainable resource use system must encourage commitment to place.

First nations societies are characterized by local ownership and control by persisting kin groups. This encourages commitment to place and responsibility for maintaining productive relationships to property. In contrast to the mobility of contemporary non-Indian society, indigenous peoples developed an enduring association with their homeland. This sense of attachment or identification with place generates a sense of belonging which reinforces feelings of dependence and respect. Bioregionalists (for example, Sale, 1985; Plant and Plant, 1990) have made this point forcefully, and we repeat here that people's commitment to place is likely to be a key feature of any sustainable resource use system.

Local Control: A sustainable resource use system must enable local communities to assume shared responsibility for resource stewardship and should seek to decentralise decision-making to the local level.

Throughout the Fraser Basin, the primary unit of organisation was the household or extended kinship group. These units were, by definition, small scale, personal and intimate. The cross-linkages between kin ensured continuity and a stable system of authority. Decision-making power rested not with any formal office, but on a broad base of consent maintained through elaborate protocols rooted in mutual respect. Except for the rare case of prolonged hostilities with neighbouring tribes, kinship groups were autonomous and decisions regarding resource use were made at the local level.

The sustainability of the larger system within the Fraser Basin relied on the kinship groups that assumed local responsibility for stewardship. It is our contention that for local renewable resources, similar direct participation in decision-making is a necessary condition for a sustainable resource use system. This contention is based on the recognition that individuals will contribute substantially more effort to those ventures over which they know they have some control. As Pinkerton (1989) notes, this often forms part of the rationale for developing co-operative management systems for local resources. Of course, contemporary non-Indian society lacks the kind of cohesive kinship communities that characterised First Nations societies in the Fraser Basin, but there are many promising contemporary examples where diverse and sometimes conflicting stakeholders have been brought together in a cooperative management arrangement and have developed a shared sense of responsibility much like historical systems (see Pinkerton, forthcoming 1991; and Dale, this volume). This in turn suggests that one of the challenges facing resource planners is the need to foster such cooperation and create those conditions under which smaller scale management systems can be granted the kind of authority they require to achieve sustainability.

Closure: A sustainable resource use system must demonstrate relative closure with regulated access and an identified community of users with a shared ethic of resource-use. The resulting pattern is characterised by a number of self-reliant groups which, when necessary, can act in a coordinated and responsible manner.

One of the most striking features of First Nations societies is their relative independence. Each language group was largely self-sufficient, relying on its own judicious management of the resource base within the boundaries of the traditional territories. Even on the most local scale, kinship groups relied primarily on local supplies although trade provided additional variety and sometimes support when stocks dwindled or failed. The resulting pattern can best be pictured as a series of independent units with what we might call permeable boundaries that were not entirely self-sustaining but which approached that condition.

This pattern of settlement and resource use holds a number of very general but important implications. Firstly, reliance on local stocks encourages restraint on a local scale. As anthropologists have long observed, those closest to the land and most dependent on its resources inevitably develop knowledge through familiarity and even an intimacy with the land itself that supports temperance and wise use. The very perception of vulnerability breeds humility.

Secondly, the scale of the kinship group encourages a shared sense of responsibility. Such reciprocal obligations are often encoded in the set of rules that underpin communal property systems found not only in the Fraser Basin, but also in many indigenous societies throughout the world (Berkes, 1989).

Small-scale communities in the Fraser Basin developed systems of resource use that were finely tuned to an ecological system that fluctuated seasonally and annually. Through the detailed knowledge derived from a close association of humans with their territory, the system maintained the ability to cope with dramatic changes in resource supply by shifting to an alternate food source or by rotating between local harvesting areas. The restraint from excessive harvesting, practiced on a local scale, and perceived as rewarding to resource owners, helped ensure a buffer which might be used to overcome periodic shortages, either within the local kinship group or at the scale of the level of the band or language group.

Resource use patterns in contemporary society have undoubtedly become far more complex in this century, but there is a growing recognition that conventional resource management can be substantially improved by developing cooperative systems that draw their inspiration from communal property systems of this type. This is particularly so for local renewable resources and there is a growing body of literature to support this view (see for example Berkes, 1989; Pinkerton, 1989; Griggs, 1990). The historical evidence suggests that a pattern of local groups, largely independent but capable of coordinating their efforts where and when advantageous, are more likely than other systems to achieve sustainability.

The Ethic of Reciprocity: *A sustainable system must adopt a long-term perspective on resource use and should seek to build an understanding of feedback mechanisms within the ecological system.*

The linkage between humans, animals and the spirit world which so characterised First Nations societies created a complex ethical framework which reinforced the notion of mutual dependency. Humans were not seen as dominant but played a complementary and often subordinate role in a larger ecological system. A key feature here was the concept of reciprocity and the belief that respectful human attitudes towards the resources helped to ensure the availability of future supply. Such an ethic encourages responsible use and supports an imperative of restraint.

In contemporary terms, this ethic of reciprocity embodies much of the concept of conservation and by implication, suggests the need for a long-term perspective. In light of this, we would argue that sustainability requires collective development of a more complete understanding of feedback mechanisms within the ecosystem.

This can be stated in more familiar terms. First Nations created not merely effective technologies, but an ideology of themselves and nature which informed and shaped their activities. That is to say, they were skilled in *applied* resource use within a workable *theory* of ecology. Moreover their theory was held in common, despite local differences, and before 1800 within the Fraser Basin, their theory and practice *prevailed.*

Scope and Integration: A sustainable resource use system must integrate use of different resource sectors and should seek both the adaptiveness and the resilience to cope with fluctuating levels of supply. This can best be achieved by maintaining harvest levels below maximum capacity.

The system of resource use that characterised First Nations societies shaped the relationship between humans and all of the resources in the Fraser Basin; the same underlying principles governed both the use of salmon resources in the tributaries of the Fraser itself and the game hunted on land. In this way, what we now categorize as distinct resource sectors were integrated in a comprehensive system of management and use.

Beyond this integration of specific resource use practices, the various elements that made up First Nations societies were linked at a general level. For example, the number of fishing sites was determined by the political structure of kinship groups and the authority of these groups governed the harvesting of migrating salmon, matching the catch to the level of technology available for drying and preserving the catch. While it is difficult, based on the evidence available here, to substantiate the claim that such systems were *self-regulating*, it is clear that such systems were *self-limiting*.

We suggest that this integration is critical to the sustainability of resource use in the Fraser Basin. The diversity of the resource base and the ability to shift emphasis from one resource to another in times of scarcity produced an historical system that was both flexible and adaptive. Such a system could only be enduring if the resource base was not harvested at its maximum capacity.

Summary

These five criteria contain the outline of what we believe to be a sustainable resource use system. Their value is not in defining such a system in all its dimensions, but in prompting deeper questions about existing patterns of resource use. Beyond their general value however, we believe that there is another important reason to reconsider the historical evidence and seek a more refined understanding of the resource use system of the Native Indian peoples of the Fraser Basin.

As Thompson has indicated so clearly elsewhere in this volume, the legal and political implications of aboriginal title in British Columbia are in a state of flux. Recent dramatic events have underlined that there is an acute need for settlement of outstanding Native claims. We believe that the future of development in the Fraser Basin will be overwhelmingly influenced by settlement of these claims. While few have been so bold as to predict in any detail how these events will unfold, we subscribe to the belief that the goals and aspirations of Native peoples will be heavily conditioned by their traditions and their cultural heritage. This is already evident in statements issued by many Native groups throughout the province. If this assumption is correct, there would be much value in seeking to understand the structure and dynamics of traditional systems. In a province so heavily dependent on primary resources, the issue of resource management will certainly become one of the prime foci in the debate over claims settlement.

If the future unfolds in this way, we suggest that there are two principal reasons for optimism. Firstly, we believe that our portrayal of the culture and resource use patterns of the First Nations as sustainable is close to the known facts. As the need for integration of Native political aspirations emerges, we believe that this body of experience can provide both practical and theoretical ideas and suggestions for improved management systems that are stable and that can endure.

Secondly, we believe that the criteria we have derived demonstrate that an exploration of traditional systems can provide inspiration for contemporary cooperative systems of management based on the participation of local communities. In recognising this, we suggest that contrary to much of public opinion, the needs and concerns of the majority of British Columbians are compatible with, and will be served by realisation of the goals of Native peoples. Settlement of claims deriving from Native title should then be seen not as a threat, but as an opportunity to explore new approaches to resource management that are less divisive and which result in a more conserving and ecologically-sound approach to resource use. We believe that in the Fraser Basin, we now have the opportunity not only to correct long-standing wrongs but also to choose a more enlightened way, to develop innovative systems of resource use that can be truly sustainable.

References

Berkes, F. (ed.). 1989. *Common Property Resources: Ecology and Community-Based Sustainable Development.* London: Belhaven Press.

Berringer, P. 1982. "Northwest Coast Traditional Salmon Fisheries Systems of Resource Utilization." MA thesis, Dept. of Anthropology and Sociology, University of British Columbia.

British Columbia. 1990. *The Band Data Base,* (from records of the Department of Indian and Northern Affairs, Canada). Victoria: Finance and Corporate Relations, Planning and Statistics Division, Ministry of Native Affairs, B.C.

Boyd, R. T. 1990. "Demographic History, 1774-1874." in *Handbook of North American Indians, Vol. 7, Northwest Coast.* Washington: Smithsonian Insitute.

Bouchard, R. and I. D. Kennedy, (eds.) 1979. *Shuswap Stories.* Vancouver: CommCept.

Canada, Revised Statutes, I-6, *The Indian Act.*

Canadian Council of Resource and Environment Ministers (CCREM). 1987. *Report of the National Task Force on Environment and Economy.* Ottawa: Canadian Council of Resource and Environment Ministers.

Chisholm, B. S., E. Nelson, and H. P. Schwarcz. 1983. "Marine and Terrestrial Protein in Prehistoric Diets on the British Columbia Coast." *Current Anthropology.* 24(3):396-398.

CUSO. 1982. *Sustainable Development: A CUSO Education Program.* Ottawa: Canadian University Students Organisation.

Duff, W. 1952. *The Upper Stalo Indians of the Fraser River of B.C.* Victoria: B.C. Provincial Museum.

_____ 1964. *The Indian History of British Columbia, Vol. 1: The Impact of the White Man.* Anthropology in British Columbia, Memoir No. 5. Victoria: B.C. Provincial Museum.

_____ n.d. "Notes on B.C. Indian Population". Files in Department of Anthropology and Sociology, University of British Columbia.

Fisher, R. 1977. *Contact and Conflict*. Vancouver: University of British Columbia Press.

Fladmark, K. R. 1986. *British Columbia Prehistory*. Ottawa: National Museum of Man.

Foerster, R. E. 1968. *The Sockeye Salmon*. Bulletin 162. Ottawa: Fisheries Research Board of Canada.

Foster, M. 1988. "Native People, Languages." in *Canadian Encyclopedia*. 3:1453-55, Edmonton: Hurtig.

Frideres, J. S. 1988. *Native Peoples in Canada: Contemporary Conflicts*. Scarborough: Prentice Hall.

Griggs, J. R. 1990. "Developing Cooperative Management Systems for Common Property Resources: Resolving Cross-Cultural Conflict in a West Coast Fishery." Unpublished MSc thesis, Resource Management Science Program, University of British Columbia.

Hawthorn, H. B., Belshaw, C. S., and Jamieson, S. M. 1958. *The Indians of British Columbia: A Study of Contemporary Social Adjustment*. Toronto: University of Toronto Press.

Hewes, G. W. 1947. "Aboriginal Use of Fishery Resources in Northwestern North America." PhD thesis, Dept. of Anthropology, University of California.

Jamieson, K. 1986. "Sex Discrimination and the Indian Act." in J. R. Ponting, (ed.). *Arduous Journey: Canadian Indians and Decolonization*. Toronto: McClelland and Stewart.

Jenness, D. 1955. *The Faith of a Coast Salish Indian*. Memoir No. 3, Anthropology in B.C. Victoria: B.C. Provincial Museum.

Jorgensen, J. G. 1969. *Salish Language and Culture*. Bloomington: Indiana University.

_____ 1980. *Western Indians*. San Francisco: Freeman.

Kew, M. nd. "Salmon Availability, Technology, and Cultural Adaptation On the Fraser River Watershed." in B. Hayden. (ed.). Forthcoming. Mimeo. Simon Fraser University.

_____ 1990. "Central and Southern Coast Salish Ceremonies Since 1900." in *Handbook of North American Indians, Vol. 7, Northwest Coast*. Washington: Smithsonian Insitute.

Lamb. W. K. (ed.). 1960. *The Letters and Journals of Simon Fraser, 1806-08*. Toronto: Macmillan.

Lewis, H. T. 1982. *A Time For Burning*. Occasional Publication No. 17, Boreal Institute for Northern Studies. Edmonton: University of Alberta.

Loh, Shirley. 1990. *Population Projection of Registered Indians, 1886 - 2011* Ottawa: Statistics Canada.

Lovell, N. C., B. S. Chisholm, E. Nelson and H. P. Schwarcz. 1986. "Prehistoric Salmon Consumption in Interior British Columbia." *Canadian Journal of Archaeology* 10:99-105.

Matson, R. G. 1980. "Prehistoric Subsistence Patterns in the Fraser Delta: The Evidence From the Glenrose Cannery Site." *B.C. Studies* 48:64-85.

Mitchell, D. H. 1972. "Archaeology of the Gulf of Georgia Area, a Natural Region and its Culture Types." *Syesis* 4(1):1-224.

Northcote, T. G. 1974. *Biology of the Lower Fraser River*. Technical Report No. 3. Vancouver: Westwater Research Centre, University of British Columbia.

Northcote, T. G., and P. A. Larkin. 1989. "The Fraser River: A Major Salmonine Production System." in Dodge, D. P., (ed.). *Proceedings of the International Large River Symposium (LARS)*. Ottawa: Canadian Special Publication of Fisheries and Aquatic Sciences No. 106.

Pinkerton, E. (ed.). 1989. *Co-operative Management of Local Fisheries: New Directions for Improved Management and Community Development*. Vancouver: University of British Columbia Press.

_____ 1991. "Locally-Based Water Quality Planning: Contributions to Fish Habitat Protection." *Canadian Journal of Fisheries and Aquatic Sciences* (forthcoming).

Plant, J. and Plant, C. 1990. *Turtle Talk: Voices for a Sustainable Future*. The New Catalyst Bioregional Series. Philadelphia: New Society Publishers.

Ray, V. F. 1939. *Cultural Relations in the Plateau of Western North America*. Hodge Anniversary Publication Fund, Vol. 3.

_____ 1942 "Culture Element Distributions: XXII Plateau." in *Anthropological Records*. 8(2). Berkeley: University of California Press.

Rees, W. E. 1989. "Defining 'Sustainable Development'." Centre For Human Settlement Research Bulletin. May 1989. Vancouver: University of British Columbia.

Sachs, I. 1978. "The Salient Features of Development" in G. Francis, (ed.). *Environment and Development - Phase III: Prospective and Ecodevelopment, Strategies for Action.* Ottawa: Canadian International Development Agency.

Sale, K. 1985. *Dwellers in the Land: The Bioregional Vision.* San Fransisco: Sierra Club.

Statistics Canada. 1990. *Canada Year Book, 1990.* Ottawa: Statistics Canada.

Steedman, E. V. 1929. *The Ethnobotany of the Thompson Indians of British Columbia.* Bureau of American Ethnology, 45th Annual Report. Washington: Smithsonian Institute.

Stewart, H. 1977. *Indian Fishing, Early Methods on the Northwest Coast.* Vancouver: J. J. Douglas.

Suttles, W. 1951. "The Early Diffusion of the Potato Among the Coast Salish." *Southwestern Journal of Anthropology.* 7(3):272-288.

____ 1955. "Katzie Ethnographic Notes." Anthropology in B.C., II. Victoria: B.C. Provincial Museum.

____ 1958. "Private Knowledge, Morality, and Social Classes among the Coast Salish." *American Anthropologist* 60:497-507.

____ 1960. "Affinal Ties, Subsistence, and Prestige among the Coast Salish" *American Anthropologist* 62:296-305.

____ 1962. "Variation in Habitat and Culture on the Northwest Coast." in *Akten des 34. Internationalen Amerikanistenkongresses* Vienna.

____ 1987. *Coast Salish Essays.* Vancouver: Talon Books.

Teit, J. 1900. *The Thompson Indians of British Columbia.* Publications of Jessup North Pacific Expedition. 1:163-392.

Tennant, P. 1983 "Native Indian Political Activity in British Columbia, 1969-1983" *B.C. Studies* 57:112-136.

____ 1990. *Aboriginal Peoples and Politics: The Indian Land Question in B.C., 1849-1989.* Vancouver: UBC Press.

Thompson, L. C., and M. D. Kinkaid. 1990. "Languages." in *Handbook of North American Indians, Vol. 7 Northwest Coast.* Washington: Smithsonian Institution.

Tobey, M. L. 1981. "Carrier." in *Handbook of North American Indians, Vol. 6, Subarctic.* Washington: Smithsonian Institution.

Trigger, B. G. 1985. *Natives and Newcomers: Canada's "Heroic Age" Reconsidered.* Kingston and Montreal: McGill-Queen's.

Turner, N. 1975. *Food Plants of British Columbia Indians, Part 1 - Coastal Peoples.* Handbook No. 34. Victoria: B.C. Provincial Museum.

____ 1978. *Food Plants of British Columbia Indians, Part 2 - Interior Peoples.* Handbook No. 36. Victoria: B.C. Provincial Museum.

____ 1979. *Plants in British Columbia Indian Technology.* Handbook No. 38. Victoria: B.C. Provincial Museum.

World Commission on Environment and Development. 1987. *Our Common Future.* Oxford: Oxford University Press.

Appendix 2.1

Table 2.A: Fraser Indian Bands and Populations by Language Group

Language	Watershed	Band Name	Population (1988)	(1989)
HALKOMELEM	Fraser River	Musqueam	748	775
		Tsawassen	125	135
		New Westminster	2	2
		Coquitlam	26	33
		Katzie	259	275
		Langley	98	100
		Matsqui	85	93
	Vedder/Sumas	Sumas	187	188
	Chilliwack River	Soowahlie	209	223
		Tzeachten	210	225
		Skowkale	105	116
		Yakweakwioose	30	30
	Fraser River	Lakahahmen	203	225
		Skway	86	95
		Skwah	305	318
		Squiala	85	86
		Aitchelitz	18	18
		Kwaw-kwa-a-pilt	26	28
	Harrison River	Scowlitz	179	179
		Chehalis	589	613
	Fraser River	Cheam	260	275
		Popkum	6	6
		Seabird Island	436	462
		Peters	73	86
		Ohamil	68	66
		Skawahlook	55	58
		Chawathil (Hope)	222	237
		Union Bar	63	72
		Yale	99	102
	Total	**29 Bands**	**4857**	**5121**
NLAKA'PAMUX	Fraser River	Spuzzum	100	121
		Boston Bar	160	169
		Boothroyd	201	222
		Kanaka Bar	113	125
		Siska	147	154
		Skuppah	36	47
		Lytton	1280	1330
		Nicomen	72	80
	Thompson River	Cook's Ferry	221	229
		Oregon Jack	32	36
		Ashcroft	150	155
	Nicola River	Lower Nicola	590	632

		Nooaitch	128	137
		Shackan	102	106
		Coldwater	441	464
		Upper Nicola	616	646
	Total	**16 Bands**	**4389**	**4653**
LILLOOET	Lillooet River	Douglas	158	156
		Skookumchuck	265	273
		Samahquam	181	190
		Mount Currie	1264	1318
	Anderson/Seton	Seton Lake	452	455
		Anderson Lake	162	175
	Fraser River	Lillooet	190	214
		Cayoose Creek	120	132
		Fountain	626	632
		Pavilion	302	326
		Bridge River	225	235
	Total	**11 Bands**	**3945**	**4106**
SHUSHWAP	Thompson River	Bonaparte	492	511
		Skeetchestn	312	323
		Kamloops	616	667
		Adamas Lake	475	509
		Neskainlith	400	415
		Little Shushwap	216	229
		Spallumcheen	487	508
		North Thompson	431	460
		Canim Lake	387	408
	Fraser River	Whispering Pines	67	83
		High Bar	27	34
		Canoe Creek	380	419
		Alkali Lake	467	494
		Williams Lake	331	333
		Soda Creek	210	243
	Total	**15 Bands**	**5298**	**5636**
CHILCOTIN	Chilcotin River	Toosey	168	174
		Stone	220	222
		Anaham	925	971
		Alexis Creek	486	478
		Nemaiah Valley	294	298
	Fraser River	Alexandria[1]	116	124
	Total	**6 Bands**	**2209**	**2267**
CARRIER	Fraser River	Red Bluff (Quesnel)	79	90
	Blackwater River	Nazko	217	217
		Kluskus	129	127

	Ulkatcho	478	535
Fraser River	Fort George	168	174
Nechako River	Stony Creek	582	600
	Nadleh Whuten (Fraser Lake)	253	261
	Stallaquo	255	257
	Cheslatta	168	177
	Broman Lake	125	129
	Burns Lake	47	58
Stuart River	Necoslie	986	1100
	Tl'azt'en Nations (Stuart-Trembleur)	1109	1133
	Takla Lake	425	443
Total	**14 Bands**	**5021**	**5301**

Total for All Bands in the Fraser River Basin	**91 Bands**	**25,719**	**27,084**

Source: British Columbia, Finance and Corporate Relations, Planning and Statistics Division, Ministry of Native Affairs, B.C., "The Band Data Base."

Notes:

1   Chilcotin Speakers were formerly all situated within the Chilcotin River Watershed. While Alexandria Band is now wholly Chilcotin, it was comprised of Carrier speakers in the 19th century (see Tobey, 1981).

3

Prospects for Vancouver's Sustainable Development: An Economic Perspective

Thomas A. Hutton and H. Craig Davis

As British Columbia's primary metropolis, Western Canada's largest urban area, and a leading growth centre nationally, Vancouver and its recent development have attracted considerable scholarly research. While some of this output is directed to trends and issues that are essentially in situ or localised, a growing body of research literature addresses Vancouver's growth and development within a much broader spatial setting, notably at the provincial level (e.g., Ley and Hutton, 1987; Davis and Hutton, 1989a), and, increasingly, within the dynamic Pacific Rim (Davis and Goldberg, 1988; Vertinsky and Tan, 1988; Hutton and Davis, 1989b; Edgington and Goldberg, 1989). Generally, this broader perspective is preferred, so as to capture aspects of growth and change associated with growing interdependence, economic "globalisation", and market integration, which manifestly influence the development of urban and regional, as well as national, jurisdictions.

For the most part, recent examinations of Vancouver's growth trends and development prospects have been undertaken within an exclusively economic framework. It has become apparent, however, that the future development of urban areas will be influenced not only by the familiar range of economic factors, but also a much broader (yet in many respects interrelated) spectrum of social, cultural, political and environmental variables. In particular, this broader appreciation of the factors influencing development opportunities and constraints has been generated by the burgeoning literature on sustainable development. While much of this literature addresses development sustainability from a national or international perspective, or, in other cases, focusses on sustainable development in "natural" or resource regions, the analysis and findings may be seen to have considerable significance for cities and urban regions as well.

The purpose of this paper is to examine the prospects for Vancouver's sustainable development, as part of a more extensive study of the Fraser Basin.

Although Vancouver[1] is geographically peripheral to the Fraser Basin as a whole, situated as it is on the tidal estuary of British Columbia's most important river system, it plays strategic roles in the life of the Fraser, nonetheless and numerous key relationships between the metropolis and the Basin as a whole can readily be adduced:

(i)   Vancouver is integrally part of the Fraser Basin ecological region, in terms of hydrology, climatology, geomorphology, flora and fauna.

(ii)   Dense and extensive patterns of movement (people, factor inputs, energy, and commodities of all kinds) between Vancouver and other sub-regional units of the Fraser Basin can be traced.

(iii)   Important elements of economic complementarity and interdependence between Vancouver and the rest of the Fraser Basin are in evidence, with regard to such industries as resource processing, transportation, and tourism.

(iv)   There are also aspects of core-periphery development between Vancouver and the staple-dominated economy of the Fraser Basin upriver from Hope, connoting control and dependency relationships.

(v)   The growth and development of Vancouver also has significant implications for the Fraser Basin as a whole, in terms of externalities such as pollution, energy consumption, impacts on drainage and habitat, and so on.

(vi)   Metropolitan Vancouver and other parts of the Fraser Basin are included jointly within certain regions defined for planning and administrative purposes.

(vii)   Contained by mountains to the north and the United States border to the south, expansion of the metropolitan area is proceeding up the Lower Fraser Valley.

As a consequence, there would appear to be merit in including a special examination of Vancouver within this much more spatially extensive study of the Fraser Basin as a whole.

Toward an Operational Definition of Sustainable Development

Over the past decade, academicians and public policy specialists have endeavoured to generate definitions of sustainable development, a task that "...has so far proved elusive." (Turner, 1988:5). Pezzey (1989), for example, has recently compiled a list of several dozen interpretations of sustainable development, virtually all of which differ significantly or in nuance. Much of the difficulty in achieving a consensus centres on the problem of defining "development" satisfactorily, with perspectives varying according to ideology, to the specific discipline of the various practitioners, and to changing perceptions of the issues and priorities involved (See Dorcey, this volume).

---

1   Throughout this paper references to Vancouver, unless specifically stated otherwise, are to the Vancouver Census Metropolitan Area.

Many efforts to confer meaning on the concept of sustainable development tend to emphasise interdependencies between the economy and the environment, but numerous contemporary interpretations increasingly stress the importance of social, cultural, and political considerations as well. This may lead to a more comprehensive model of sustainability in time, but the introduction of many extra variables complicates the task of establishing a consensus on sustainable development in the short term.

This heterogeneity of perspective notwithstanding, it may at least be possible to distill some essential elements of sustainable development from the burgeoning literature, as the following representative principles suggest:

(i)   Sustainable development is not directed toward "growth" per se, but rather to certain fundamental social objectives, such as increases in real income per capita, improvements in health and nutritional status, educational achievement, access to resources, and a "fairer" distribution of income (Pearce, Barbier and Markandya, 1989).

(ii) Sustainability involves using resources in a socially beneficial manner, within ecological limits: "...an economy experiencing economic growth over long periods cannot...be said to be on a *sustainable* growth path if there is evidence that the feedback from changes in environmental quality will induce non-sustainability" (Pearce et al., 1989).

(iii) Sustainable development also implies maintenance and stewardship of the capital stock: "...a society that invests in reproducible capital the competitive rents on its current extraction of exhaustible resources, will enjoy a consumption stream constant in time...this result can be interpreted as saying that an appropriately defined stock of capital...is being maintained intact, and that consumption can be interpreted as the interest on the patrimony" (Solow, 1986:141).

(iv) As a consequence of (ii) and (iii), the next (and following) generations should inherit a stock of wealth (both man-made and environmental assets) no less than the stock inherited by the previous generation (Pearce et al., 1989).

(v)   Sustainability does not, however, imply the preservation of any specific mix of assets: as development proceeds, the composition of the asset base changes; this principle acknowledges the fact that any positive rate of exploitation of non-renewable resources will eventually lead to the exhaustion of these resources (Turner, 1988:13), requiring particularly careful stewardship of these finite assets.

As these principles become increasingly accepted among practitioners, efforts can be directed toward preparing operational models of sustainable development, leading in turn to more specific policy prescriptions.

If it has been difficult to establish a consensus-based concept of sustainable development for general application, then it has been doubly so in the urban context specifically. Constraints here relate both to the problematic and exceedingly complex nature of urban development, and to the inadequacy of theories and models explaining such development. Much of the work on sustainable development has taken the form of theoretical models, or has alternatively focussed on "natural" or resource regions. This latter bias is certainly understandable, in light of the severe and evidently worsening problems of many staple-dominated regions, including resource depletion, dependency, socio-economic consequences of "boom-bust" commodity cycles, and general environmental degradation. At the same time, although these findings have significance for urban development, it is not clear that the analysis undertaken for resource regions is directly transferable to urban regions, except in very general, conceptual ways. Relative to "natural" or staple-dominated regions, urban areas

- are characterised by much more complex social, economic, and political structures, which, moreover, interact in more complex ways than those of "natural" regions;
- are influenced by a more variegated set of growth determinants than most staple regions, including both local and exogenous factors;
- in particular, are notably subject to structural change (social, economic, physical) associated with economic globalisation and market integration; staple regions are, of course, affected (sometimes profoundly) by these trends, but impacts on urban areas are more multi-dimensional in character.

As an example, most metropolitan regions are increasingly dominated by service industries, which present daunting measurement and conceptual problems, whereas the economies of staple regions are by definition characterised by natural resource endowments and associated extractive industries which are comparatively more straightforward to inventory, to assess depletion and/or renewal rates, and so on.

In light of the pace and structural nature of urban change, coupled with conceptual and measurement problems alluded to above, it is difficult, if not impossible, to reference a "satisfactory" (i.e., comprehensive and "robust") model of contemporary urban development, which in turn exacerbates the problem of adequately assessing the sustainability of urban regions. Certain of the classic models of urban growth have been seriously compromised by urban change over the past two decades, notably economic base theory (which assigns too large a role to manufacturing exports in explaining urban growth, and inappropriately assumes sector homogeneity), and also the various models positing a "closed" region concept (which fail to consider the major and evidently increasing importance of exogenous development influences associated with economic globalisation and the emergence of spatially-extensive urban systems).

More recent theoretical work is of clearly greater relevance in achieving an understanding of contemporary urban change, but again falls short of establishing a fully operational and adaptable model of urban development. Bell's (1974) thesis of a post-industrial urban society represents a benchmark contribution to our understanding of the social implications of the decline of basic production and the rise of services, but lacks an explicit spatial dimension that would assist in defining urban development trends specifically. Gottmann's work on the "metamorphosis of the modern metropolis" (1974; 1982) is of seminal importance in refining the concept of the urban service economy, but is not intended as an evaluative framework per se. Scott (1982; 1983), Stanback and Noyelle (1982), and Daniels (1985; 1986), notably, have generated persuasive models of urban service sector location and growth, but do not explicitly incorporate the range of constraints to growth and development prevalent within the burgeoning literature on sustainable development. The latter, on the other hand, is leading to a more balanced perspective on sustainable development in general terms, but tends to be weak on economic aspects, often treats "growth" (though not necessarily "development") as a given, lacks an adequate operational dimension, and is in many respects aspatial. Clearly, there is a need to synthesise the leading contributions of urban scholars with the stream of literature on sustainable development now available.

Components of Urban Sustainability

In the absence of an entirely satisfactory theory of contemporary urban development, it may at least be possible to undertake an analysis of Vancouver's "sustainability", deriving criteria from the major fields of inquiry cited above. In this context, it can be argued that the sustainability of urban areas may be assessed in terms of their interdependent capacities to

(i)   maintain and enhance their capital stock (including, notably, basic public and private sector infrastructure, transportation, tertiary educational institutions, and telecommunications; as well as social capital, and natural and environmental assets) in an era of rapidly-expanding public and corporate debt, higher real capital costs, constrained resources, accelerating urban physical decay, and environmental degradation (i.e., sustainability as the "capacity for renewal");

(ii) progress to more advanced forms of production and economic activity, in an era of urban de-industrialisation, structural change, job-shedding and displacement, and an increasingly competitive urban hierarchy at the national and international levels (i.e., sustainability as "adaptability and transformation capacity");

(iii) retain their economic vitality in an era of rapid cyclical change and frequent exogenous "shocks" (i.e., sustainability as "resilience");

(iv) create linkages to key export markets (extra-regional and international) in the context of increasing specialisation and comparative advantage in trade in all commodities (value-added production, capital, technology, and producer services) (i.e., sustainability as "market diversity").

In the absence of a fully operational model, it must of course be acknowledged that an analysis of the sustainability of an urban area can be no more than indicative. For many key questions, too, data are not readily available. Moreover, inasmuch as empirical data are, by definition, derived from past events, the predictive potential of such a framework is open to question. However, by referencing existing data sources and some recent research efforts, it may at least be possible to address, if not define, Vancouver's prospects for sustainable development in the 1990's.

Sustainability as the Capacity for Renewal

Increasingly accepted as a fundamental component of a sustainable society or region is the idea of a renewable capital stock, or stock of assets. Broadly interpreted, this capital stock is comprised of the following:

(i) *Physical assets:* public and private infrastructure, transportation infrastructure, and the like; this includes roads, schools and other public buildings, factories, commercial infrastructure, housing, and the like;

(ii) *Natural capital:* environmental assets of all kinds, including location and setting, flora and fauna, natural resources, and so on (these can be further divided into renewable and non-renewable assets);

(iii) *Social or human capital:* the embodied skills, education, culture, and entrepreneurship of the resident population.

These categories will have relevance for urban and natural regions, although of course, the proportions will vary from place to place.

The character of the capital stock represents a critical component of a society's wealth, productive capacity, and overall quality of life. An aging or otherwise inadequate capital stock will retard a society's progression to higher levels of economic activity and social well-being, while an enhanced stock of assets will, in many respects, expedite such a transformation. Moreover, since many elements of the capital stock may be subject to deterioration over time, a responsible stewardship of the asset base, combining preservation with careful levels of consumption and adequate reinvestment, is required to ensure a satisfactory capital stock for present and future generations.

The literature on sustainable development has contributed two particularly valuable principles pertaining to an appreciation of the role of capital in social development. The first such contribution insists on a higher and more explicit valuation of natural and environmental capital, when calculating (for example) costs and benefits of development options, the aggregate wealth and quality of life of a society, and so on. The second principle relates to the generational dimension: the notion that sustainable development of the resource base

> optimises the economic societal benefits available in the present, without jeopardizing the likely potential for similar benefits in the future (Goodland and Leduc, 1987:36).

Again this principle of intergenerational equity should encompass all forms of capital: natural, man-made, and human or social capital.

A Perspective on Vancouver's Capital Stock

At first glance, Vancouver would appear to enjoy almost an embarrassment of riches with respect to each category of assets or capital. These assets and advantages include the following:

- an exceptionally favourable setting, including a magnificent natural, deep-water port;
- direct access to wilderness and recreational areas that is almost unique among metropolitan regions;
- a modern stock of infrastructure, including both private and public assets, sustained by record levels of new investment in recent years, and derived both from local and more distant sources;
- an able, well-educated and culturally rich resident population, enhanced by recent large-scale inflows of particularly entrepreneurial people from elsewhere in Canada and from overseas (Davis and Hutton, 1989b).

Properly nurtured, this capital stock should provide a basis for Vancouver's prosperity and quality of life well into the 1990's and beyond.

Although in comparative terms Vancouver appears to be exceptionally well-positioned with respect to its current asset base, there are in fact some issues and concerns that will require careful management and, when appropriate, initiative. These include, notably, the following: environmental quality, municipal infrastructure and human capital.

Environmental Quality

Recent surveys have demonstrated that the quality of Vancouver's environment represents the highest value and greatest concern of the resident population. While Vancouver's overall stock of local and easily accessible natural assets is exceptionally favourable, concerns have recently been expressed about deterioration in some aspects of the natural stock, in terms of air quality (subject to growing pollution, especially from automobiles, which generate about 80 percent of atmospheric pollutants), water quality, industrial contaminants in the soil, the rapid urbanisation of the limited open space available in the region, and the impact of solid wastes. Policies and regulatory frameworks at both the local and regional levels of administration are being adjusted in order to arrest this deterioration, but there are indications that significantly higher levels of effort and expenditure will be needed to ensure that succeeding generations will enjoy similar levels of environmental quality as the present generation.[2]

A strongly positive factor is the growing realisation that the economy and environment are interdependent components of Vancouver's overall quality of life or "livability"; a vital economy can generate resources required for enhancement programmes, while high natural amenity values are seen as locational determinants for many "desirable" industries, such as higher-order services, advanced-technology production, and tourism. Part of the solution will be to explicitly "value" the natural capital when assessing trade-offs associated with development, as well as more effectively integrating economic, social and environmental policies with local and regional planning strategies. Monitoring efforts will need to be

---

2   The use of marginal cost pricing and water rights to promote economic efficiency in the use of the Fraser Basin are considered elsewhere in this volume by Pearse and Tate, McNeill, Rankin and Scott.

stepped up, including evaluation of externalities impacting not only metropolitan Vancouver, but the entire Fraser Basin.

More specific policies and overall programmes could include, for example, an overall waste management programme, including; the recycling of solid wastes and energy; a comprehensive air quality programme (Vancouver City Planning Commission, 1990); a more aggressive source control programme; an explicit strategy to integrate waterfront areas as well as streetscapes into the public amenities network; and, continuing efforts to encourage a shift to public transit from private auto commuting within metropolitan Vancouver.[3]

Municipal Infrastructure

Although Vancouver is a comparatively young metropolis, certain components of the public infrastructure are showing signs of wear and even stress. Demands for investment are generated both by the normal wear factor, as well as infrastructural requirements associated with rapid population, economic and spatial growth. Financing commitments required for adequate maintenance and enhancement appear to be well beyond the scope of local government (Technical Committee on Canada's Urban Infrastructure, 1984). It is estimated that repairs to, and replacements of, the municipal infrastructure for Canada's largest metropolitan areas will require about $15 billion over the next few years, merely to maintain (not improve) the overall quality. The lesson of the experience in the U.S. (where public investments in infrastructure have fallen from ca. 6-7 percent of GNP in the 1950's, to less than 2 percent currently) is that repeated postponement of investments leads inevitably to a serious diminution in the urban quality of life, to an erosion of productivity, and, in many cases, to urban fiscal crisis.

In the case of the City of Vancouver, the basic approach is to undertake infrastructural improvements at a pace commensurate with levels of decay. For example, for items with an approximately 100 year "life expectancy", about 1 percent of the system is replaced annually. Favourable conditions for maintaining an adequate municipal infrastructure include both a growing public appreciation of the value of Vancouver's public capital, as well as the City's AAA financial status (as evaluated by the New York bond rating agencies). At the same time, we can anticipate higher costs as the City ages, as well as a financial "squeeze" as demands for scarce public resources continue to increase.

Over time, a sustained commitment to maintaining and enhancing Vancouver's infrastructure will be required on behalf not only of local and regional government, but also senior government and the private sector. Many projects will require joint efforts, as in the case of (for example) Vancouver International Airport, which is likely to play a central role in the economy of the 1990's and beyond, as the port has historically. In this case, funding for capital improvements will be sought from both government and business, along the lines of current models of airport development in Toronto and Hong Kong. Cost-sharing for urban

---

3   While the focus here is on local efforts, it must be recognised, as Scott points out elsewhere in this volume, that the dimensions of the problem of sustaining environmental integrity are inter-regional in nature and ultimately must be considered in a global context.

infrastructure renewal will be required (for road bridges and the like), not only in Vancouver, but across Canada as a whole.

Human Capital

It is increasingly recognised that human capital is the most critical component of the post-industrial urban economy and society. Although Vancouver's population is imbued with high education and skill levels, there are concerns for future prospects in several areas. First, some analysts have pointed to British Columbia's low per capita spending on education (relative to other provinces) as a constraining factor for future socio-economic development. Secondly, the province as a whole has tended historically to rely to a degree on in-migration of skilled people. There is no guarantee that we will continue to be net beneficiaries of this trend. Finally, a recent report (The Courier, 16 May 1989) notes that since 1986, the proportion of Vancouver high school graduates proceeding to tertiary educational institutions has been declining. Again, it may be necessary to correct this trend in order to promote an adequate quality of Vancouver's human capital for an increasingly knowledge-intensive economy.

Sustainability as Transformation Propensity

While many definitions of development can be cited, there is general agreement that development must involve not only increases in wealth, but also progress toward more advanced stages and forms of economic activity, as well as improvements in socio-economic welfare. As Pearce et al. have observed, an economy

> which raises its per capita level of income over time but does so without making any transformation in its social and economic structure is unlikely to be said to be "developing" (Pearce et al., 1989:29).

To be sure, the concept of development may well include notions of "utility", political freedom and the like, but certainly the idea of economic and socio-economic transformation is quite fundamental to any assessment of the sustainability of a particular jurisdiction or society.

There are in fact several critical components of economic and socio-economic transformation relevant to a consideration of development sustainability; these include, notably:

(i) improvements in the welfare of the resident population over time, in terms of income, education, health standards, and so on;

(ii) a progressive shift to more "advanced" (i.e., more skill- and knowledge-intensive, productive, and rewarding) occupations among the resident labour force; and, fundamentally,

(iii) a broadly-experienced and continuing shift in the urban economic structure, away from basic production and the "routinised" or programmable services, toward higher-order service industries, and toward value-added and technology-intensive production.

These components are clearly linked; studies of metropolitan regions within the EEC, the U.S., Canada and other advanced societies reveal strongly positive correlations between relatively high concentrations of service industries and technology-based activities on the one hand, and favourable socio-economic indices, on the other.

This emphasis on continuing, structural economic change as a measure of a region's sustainability represents in fact something of a departure from previous planning orthodoxy, which placed a high value upon economic "stability" as a policy ideal. However desirable this notion of stability might be in theory, in practice it is now deemed to be untenable, in the face of the forces making for rapid change of both a cyclical and structural nature, including:

(i)   the impacts of economic globalisation;
(ii)   the more footloose nature of many forms of production, changes impelled by the ongoing (and now international) division of labour;
(iii) the incipient development of multinational economic and trading blocs; and,
(iv)   the liberalisation of trade across a broad spectrum of commodities, including technology, capital, and other services.

In turn, these trends and influences are manifested in a number of ways that reveal the changing nature of urban economies, for example, in terms of rapid rates of business start-ups, relocations, and closures (Birch, 1985); the continuing decentralisation of industry, especially standardised production (Scott, 1982); more generalized patterns of deconcentration, including processes both of multinucleation and dispersion (Hutton and Davis, 1985); and the functional specialisation and "internationalisation" of the Central Business District (CBD) within metropolitan regions (Conservation of Human Resources, 1977). These changes cumulatively represent a rapid and fundamental restructuring of urban economies and societies—indeed, Gottmann suggests that the term "metamorphosis" more effectively captures the nature and scale of this process than mere "change" or "evolution".

Measures of Vancouver's Transformation

In common with other advanced urban areas, Vancouver continues to experience fundamental change or "restructuring" in terms of its economic base, occupational mix, social composition, and intra-metropolitan patterns of development. Employment data categorised both by industry and occupation provide insights into the nature and pace of secular change in Vancouver's economic structure, as well as providing a basis for comparisons with other metropolitan areas in Canada and elsewhere.

Table 3.1: Labour Force Growth in Vancouver CMA, by Industry:
1961-1981, 1986, 1988

Industrial Group	1961	1971	1981	1986	1981-1986 % change	1988[1]
Agriculture	3,806	5,430	7,735	10,220	32.1	5,800
Forestry	2,518	3,355	4,175	3,890	-6.8	10,200
Fishing & Trapping	1,836	1,575	2,305	2,725	18.2	n/a
Mining	1,581	3,370	3,325	2,920	-12.2	n/a
Manufacturing	57,485	78,770	96,315	91,065	-5.5	80,700
Construction	19,897	32,034	44,575	46,155	3.5	44,300
Transportation & Communications	34,934	49,980	69,625	73,005	4.9	53,900
Trade	59,899	85,700	126,485	136,815	8.2	137,200
Finance, Ins., Real Estate	15,918	28,180	47,345	53,560	13.1	61,600
Community, Business & Personnel Services	70,380	127,775	216,715	n/a	n/a	n/a
-Services to Business	7,898	18,180	n/a	49,885	n/a	60,000
-Education & Related Services	12,113	27,530	41,015	41,940	2.3	40,800
-Health & Welfare Services	18,828	30,280	52,625	60,925	15.8	64,300
-Accommodation & Food Services	12,905	22,336	42,630	58,725	37.8	47,200
Public Administration & Defence	18,003	22,330	37,885	39,350	3.9	35,800
TOTAL: All Industries	294,759	474,560	690,955	757,520	9.6%	

Source: Census of Canada: 1961, 1971, 1981; Canada Employment & Immigration, 1988.
Notes:
1   Represents preliminary employment data (unrevised) for major industry groups within the Vancouver Census Metropolitan Area (CMA).

Underlying this multi-faceted restructuring in Vancouver is a well-established shift to service-type industries and employment, especially in the area of intermediate or "producer" services, and much slower growth or even contractions in the goods-producing industries and occupations (Tables 3.1 and 3.2). Indeed, this process has been in some ways more pronounced in Vancouver than in many other medium-size metropolitan cities within the OECD, in light of the City's relatively underdeveloped manufacturing sector (notwithstanding recent growth in Vancouver's small but significant advanced-technology production base),

Table 3.2: Employment Change in Vancouver CMA by Occupation: 1971, 1981, 1986 and 1988

Occupational Category	Employment			% Change		
	1971	1981	1986	1971-81	1981-86	1988[1]
Managerial, administrative & related	21,030	52,805	85,020	151.1	61.0	99,600
Natural sciences, engineering, math.	14,215	25,190	26,220	77.2	4.0	31,800
Social sciences & related fields	5,440	12,720	17,530	133.8	37.8	14,300
Occupations in religion	795	1,040	1,455	30.8	39.9	n/a
Teaching & related occupations	16,135	25,260	25,915	56.6	2.6	23,800
Medical & health	19,495	32,920	37,960	68.9	15.3	37,900
Artistic, literary, recreational	5,315	10,370	14,770	95.1	42.4	14,800
Clerical & related occupations	88,700	143,290	146,780	61.5	2.4	126,100
Sales occupations	55,855	75,330	81,390	34.9	8.0	87,200
Service occupations	58,715	85,355	108,120	45.4	27.1	95,200
Farming, horticultural	7,760	9,600	12,295	23.7	28.1	8,800
Fishing, hunting, trapping	1,795	1,295	2,155	-27.9	66.4	n/a
Forestry & logging occupations	2,390	2,270	2,320	-5.0	2.2	n/a
Mining & quarry (incl. oil & gas)	1,130	935	790	-17.3	-16.5	n/a
Processing occupations	18,365	21,410	19,650	16.5	-16.6	16,900
Machining & related occupations	11,794	14,090	11,640	19.5	-17.4	11,100
Product fabricating, assembling	28,935	40,785	40,690	41.0	-0.3	37,800
Construction trades	32,140	41,705	40,980	30.0	-1.7	41,200
Transport equipment operating	19,170	25,285	27,510	31.9	8.8	24,200
Material handling & related, n.e.c.	15,865	17,340	15,410	9.3	-11.5	14,100
Other crafts & equipment operating	5,730	7,730	5,925	28.0	-19.2	7,900
	430,700	646,725	724,525	50.1	12.0	

Source: Census of Canada, 1971, 1981, 1986; Canada Employment & Immigration, 1988.
Notes:
1   Represents preliminary occupational data (unrevised) for Vancouver CMA.

Table 3.3: Percentage of Labour Force Employed in Service Occupations for Selected Canadian Census Metropolitian Areas: 1986

Census Metropolitan Area	Total Employment (thousands)	Service Employment (thousands)	% Employed[1] in Services
Toronto	1,960.2	1,419.0	72.4
Montreal	1,467.3	1,073.9	73.3
Vancouver	724.5	544.6	75.2
Ottawa/Hull	454.2	372.0	81.9
Edmonton	432.1	314.2	72.7
Calgary	385.7	299.6	77.7
Winnipeg	331.5	240.0	72.4
Quebec	295.2	237.9	80.6
Hamilton	290.8	190.2	65.4
London	185.7	129.8	69.9
Halifax	160.1	125.8	78.6

Source: Census of Canada (1986).
Notes:
1   Service employment includes the following occupations: managerial, administrative and related, natural sciences, engineering and mathematics, social sciences and related fields, occupations in religion, teaching and related occupations, medical and health occupations, artistic, literary, recreational and related occupations, clerical and related occupations, sales occupations, service occupations.

the importance of its strategic trading role and export-oriented services, and its undisputed primacy within a spatially-extensive hinterland. Over three-quarters of Vancouver's employment is now in services, slightly higher than the average for Canadian metropolitan areas as a whole (Table 3.3).

Historically, Vancouver developed as the western terminus for the national rail system and Canada's principal Pacific seaport, as a processing centre for British Columbia's staple commodities, and as control centre for the province's resource economy. These roles will continue to be important, but are likely to decline in relative significance, and/or undergo substantial change, for a variety of reasons. First, processes of corporate concentration within Canada favouring Toronto, increasingly the dominant national business and financial centre, have to some extent vitiated Vancouver's role as head office centre for British Columbia's resource sector (Globe and Mail, 1989).

Secondly, and consistent with widely-experienced processes of industrial decentralisation and dispersion (Scott, 1982) much of the resource processing functions formerly carried out in metropolitan Vancouver have now migrated to ex-urban and hinterland sites.

Thirdly, while service linkages (mostly head office, producer and financial services) bind Vancouver to its hinterland, some measure of core-periphery divergence can be discerned (Ley and Hutton, 1987), characterised by increasingly different industrial structures and market orientation (Davis and Hutton, 1989a), and a general, multi-faceted "restructuring" of Vancouver's economy favouring service industries and occupations (Hutton, 1985; 1989), a theme we shall return to in the following section.

The data contained in Tables 3.1 and 3.2 demonstrate that the process of "restructuring" in Vancouver can in fact be traced back at least three decades, although the greatest momentum in terms of sectoral shifts is evident toward the latter part of this period. The producer services experienced more rapid expansion, relative to services generally and to manufacturing, during the last full census period, than during 1961-1971. During the last decade, the general pattern continues, albeit with some apparently minor modifications. In particular, growth was led by the professional and administrative occupations, in common with most Canadian cities (Table 3.4). During the period 1981-86, services continued to expand in metropolitan Vancouver, while manufacturing employment actually contracted by 5.5 per cent. These data likely reflect both the cyclical effects of the serious recession of the early 1980's, which impacted manufacturing in British

Table 3.4: Employment Growth in Managerial, Administrative and Related Occupations for Selected Canadian CMAs, 1981-86

	Employment in All Occupations			Employment in Managerial, Admin. and Related Occupations		
	1981 (thousands)	1986 (thousands)	% Change 1981-86	1981 (thousands)	1986 (thousands)	% Change 1981-86
Toronto	1,668	1,960	17.5	191	263	37.7
Montreal	1,398	1,467	4.9	146	191	24.0
Vancouver	431	647	12.0	66	85	29.0
Ottawa-Hull	380	454	19.5	47	72	52.3
Edmonton	372	432	16.2	38	47	23.7
Calgary	347	386	11.1	41	48	19.0
Winnipeg	307	332	8.0	29	35	22.7
Quebec	273	295	8.3	29	40	36.4
Hamilton	275	290	5.6	23	29	26.7
London	151	186	23.1	13	20	47.6
Halifax	142	160	12.7	14	17	27.8

Source: 1981 and 1986 Census of Canada.

Columbia especially severely, as well as longer-run trends. During the most recent period (1988-90), however, the (unpublished) data reveal exceedingly high growth rates for services (especially in terms of the producer services, which have experienced double-digit growth in each of the last two years), and also growth in manufacturing (some 4,500 in 1989), which may reflect the generally very high growth rates of the metropolitan economy, a resurgence of manufacturing, or a combination of factors.

Recent expansion of production in Vancouver reveals another facet of economic restructuring and transformation, in that this growth has been led by advanced-technology industries, while "basic" manufacturing and processing continues to decline. Provincial government data demonstrate that certain advanced-technology activities which are concentrated within the metropolitan Vancouver region, notably electronics, telecommunications, computer software, aerospace, and marine-subsea industries, have experienced double-digit growth in recent years. Further evidence of "transformation" within the Vancouver economy is the development of large (1,500 firms, concentrated within the periphery of the central area) "applied design subsector" (Design Vancouver, 1990), which in turn provides value-added to many of Vancouver's production industries, such as fashion and garment design, furniture, jewellery, industrial equipment and so on.

Vancouver's Economic Transformation as a Basis for Sustainable Growth: The Provincial Context

The preceding discussion has established that the economic structure of Vancouver has experienced a sustained process of transformation over the past two decades or more, suggesting that Vancouver is experiencing (on balance) a successful transition to more advanced forms of economic activity. Recent research has generated evidence that this structural transformation provides a favourable basis for "sustainable growth", both in absolute terms, and also when viewed in the provincial context.

Structurally, the provincial economy of B.C. is composed of three distinct regional economies:

(i) The metropolitan Vancouver economy, which is distinguished by its highly developed complex of interrelated corporate or producer services;[4]
(ii) The provincial capital region of Victoria, which is heavily oriented toward government services;
(iii) The remainder of the provincial economy, the B.C. Interior, which is largely dominated by the resource-based, extractive industries of agriculture, mining, fishing, and forestry.

Evidence for this conceptual division of the provincial economy is shown in Table 3.5. Although in terms of total employment, Vancouver is roughly the same size as Victoria and the B.C. Interior combined, the region contains over 63 percent of

---

4   Producer services are here broadly defined to include not only Finance, Insurance & Real Estate (F.I.R.E.) and Business Services, but also Transportation & Storage, Communication & Other Utilities, and Whole Trade.

the province's employment in producer services. Such services account for nearly 30 percent of the region's total employment, compared with 19 percent for the Victoria region and 18 percent for the Interior. Largely because of its specialization in the so-called "advanced" services, metropolitan Vancouver has the highest per capita income ($19,414) compared with Victoria ($18,455) and the Interior ($14,927).

The picture changes distinctly, however, with a shift of focus to public-sector or administrative services. The metropolitan Victoria region clearly stands out among the three regions, with government services accounting for nearly 18 percent of total employment in the region, approximately three times the corresponding percentages for the Vancouver and Interior regions. The Victoria region also displays the highest percentages for the Educational Services and the Health & Social Services sectors, largely because provincial administration accounts for a significant proportion of employment in these sectors. As tourism is second only to administrative services as a basic activity in metropolitan Victoria, the region also records the highest percentages in the Food & Accommodation and Retail Trade sectors.

With respect to resource-based economic activity, the Interior region dominates, with the extractive industries accounting for nearly 15 percent of total employment. This compares with 2.7 percent for the Vancouver region and 3.5 percent for metropolitan Victoria. Further analysis of the structural differences among the three regions is presented in Appendix 3.1.

In recent years, it has been thoroughly documented that service activities, as opposed to the goods-producing activities, are the prime employment generators in the developed economies throughout the world. Over the last two decades, the service sector in Canada has accounted for more than 75 percent of the growth in employment. Service activities, particularly the producer services, are expected to continue to be overwhelmingly the source of employment creation through the remainder of the century (Picot, 1986).

From their specialisation in service activities, as shown in the appendix, the Vancouver and Victoria regions would be expected to experience growth rates which exceed that of the more goods-oriented economy of the Interior. Indeed, the rates shown in Table 3.6 meet these expectations. The base year of 1984 in the Table 3.6 was chosen for two reasons. First, it is the initial year for which the 1981 boundaries of the Vancouver and Victoria CMAs were used by Statistics Canada in reporting its monthly and average annual employment estimates. (For 1983, the boundaries established in 1971 were used as the basis for employment estimation). Second, the 1984-85 period was the first in which the province had fully recovered from the general recession of the early 1980's and had begun again to register positive growth rates. From a shift-share analysis of the provincial economy (Appendix 3.2), the current divergence of regional economic growth rates in favor of the Vancouver region can be expected to continue into the foreseeable future.

Table 3.5: Labour Force Distribution: Canada, Vancouver, Victoria, B.C. Interior, 1986

Industry	Canada		Vancouver		Victoria		B.C. Interior	
	L.F.	%	L.F.	%	L.F.	%	L.F.	%
Agriculture	512,700	4.02	10,215	1.39	1,580	1.26	27,760	4.82 *
Fishing & Trapping	46,495	0.36	2,720	0.37	845	0.67	5,140	0.89 *
Forestry	112,975	0.89	3,890	0.53	1,670	1.33	35,255	6.12 *
Mining	193,340	1.52	2,925	0.40	295	0.24	16,135	2.80 *
Manufacturing	2,196,745	17.24	91,070	12.40	7,075	5.65	80,685	14.00 *
Construction	759,170	5.96	46,150	6.28 *	7,560	6.03	36,175	6.28
Trans. & Storage	565,725	4.44	45,995	6.26 *	4,355	3.47	32,155	5.58
Comm. & Other Utility	411,875	3.23	27,010	3.68 *	3,235	2.58	15,170	2.63
Wholesale Trade	584,840	4.59	41,515	5.65 *	3,365	2.69	18,550	3.22
Retail Sales	1,606,010	12.61	95,295	12.98	17,185	13.71 *	74,365	12.90
Finance, Ins. & Real Est.	690,895	5.42	53,565	7.29 *	6,300	5.03	21,840	3.79
Business Services	588,670	4.62	49,890	6.79 *	6,875	5.49	14,230	2.47
Gov. Services	969,280	7.61	39,350	5.36	22,310	17.80 *	37,165	6.45
Educational Services	838,070	6.58	41,940	5.71	8,530	6.81 *	35,075	6.09
Health & Soc. Services	1,041,450	8.17	60,925	8.30	13,515	10.78 *	40,265	6.99
Accom., Food & Bev.	806,035	6.33	58,725	8.00	10,810	8.63 *	49,120	8.52
Other Services	815,955	6.40	63,115	8.60 *	9,820	7.84	37,290	6.47
Total	12,740,230	100	734,295	100	125,325	100	576,375	100

Source: Statistics Canada 1988.
Notes:
* denotes highest percentage among the three regional economies.

Table 3.6: Regional Population and Employment Growth, 1984-89

	Population		Employment	
	1989 (thousands)	% Increase 1984-89	1989 (thousands)	% Increase 1984-89
Vancouver	1,212	14.0	773	28.6
Victoria	212	12.2	120	21.2
Interior	951	2.7	556	13.2

Source: Statistics Canada 1988; 1989a; 1989b.

Additionally, the Vancouver region has historically enjoyed unemployment rates lower than those of the other two regions. Concerns about a growing divergence between the Vancouver region and the remainder of the province, particularly as employment generators, have been expressed by Ley and Hutton (1987) and Davis and Hutton (1989a). In this context, the Vancouver-Lower Mainland Region is seen as occupying an especially favoured position relative to the hinterland regions in terms of industrial structure, urban and agglomeration economies, location, and market orientation.

Sustainability as Resilience

It can be persuasively argued that one of the most meaningful measures of long-term sustainability is that of "resilience", defined in ecological terms as the ability of an ecosystem to sustain its form, structure and vitality when exposed to exogenous pressures and shocks.

The concept of resilience has substantial relevance for assessing the sustainability of urban areas, and also has particular import for Vancouver. First, most urban areas are quintessentially "open systems", and are subject to a great range and number of external influences, including immigration, the behaviour of multinational enterprises, central government policies and regulations, and so on.

Secondly, it seems clear that the range and cumulative "weight" of exogenous influences on urban development have very significantly increased over the past decade or so. These include such trends and developments as the globalisation of markets (including financial and commodity markets), the heightened mobility of capital, the liberalisation of trade generally, advances in telecommunications, the development of incipient regional/continental trading blocs, the spatial dispersion of production, the growth in travel and tourism, and the broadly freer movement of people. Urban areas are integrally part of a more interdependent global society, and the effects will be manifested differentially but profoundly in virtually all urbanised areas.

Thirdly, the concept of resilience has special resonance for both urban and resource regions within Canada's hinterland or periphery (i.e., outside the Southern Ontario-St. Lawrence urban field). Within the Canadian hinterland, dependence on commodity production and exports has historically produced a series of "boom-bust" cycles of a classical type, documented in an extensive research literature in the tradition of Innes and more recent scholars. The impacts of boom-bust cycles are most directly experienced within the resource regions of Canada's hinterland, while urban areas within the periphery typically exhibit somewhat less sensitivity to cyclical swings as a consequence of greater industrial diversity and agglomeration and scale economies. However, while some divergence between urban and resource regions' economies is evident within Canada's periphery, the economic linkages between metropolises and their hinterlands are still extensive.

Pearce et al. (1989) distinguish between two principal classes of exogenous pressures or disturbances, *stresses* (which are defined as "regular, sometimes continuous, relatively small disturbances"), and *shocks* (defined here, correspondingly, as "irregular, infrequent, relatively large and unpredictable disturbances" [Pearce et al., 1989:41]). The boundary between these two categories of disturbance is often blurred, but examples of externally-generated "stresses" might include substantial and regular streams of in-migration to urban areas, or sustained pressures of competition from other business centres; while examples of "shocks" could include the first OPEC oil price hike in 1973, or price shocks to key commodities. Arguably, too, "shocks" could include natural catastrophes, such as earthquakes, floods and the like.

Measures of Vancouver's Resilience: The Provincial Context

Historically, metropolitan Vancouver's economy has been tightly bonded to the provincial hinterland resource economy (by virtue of head office and other service functions, resource processing and export roles, etc.), so that commodity price shocks experienced within the British Columbia periphery have been transmitted to the urban core.[5] Indeed, City of Vancouver planners have used lagged provincial GDP indicators in forecasting economic trends for the metropolitan area.

These core-periphery linkages within British Columbia notwithstanding, recent research has detected some evidence of divergence in the economic fortunes of metropolitan Vancouver and those of the remainder of the province. Prima facie evidence in support of this hypothesis includes the more rapid recovery of Vancouver from the economic downturn of 1982-85, and the much greater levels and rates of job creation in the metropolitan region in recent years, with some

---

5   For example, the severely depressed state of the provincial mining and forestry industries in the early 1980's led to a substantial downsizing of Vancouver's head offices and producer services; one prominent consulting engineering firm experiencing a contraction of employment from 1,200 to about 500 within two years.

analysts estimating that Greater Vancouver (with roughly one-half the provincial population) generated up to four-fifths of jobs in British Columbia in 1988-89 (CEIC, 1989). This trend is projected to continue; recent estimates based on data from the Central Statistical Bureau suggest that the metropolitan share of provincial employment could increase from 45.5 percent in 1986, to 55.6 percent in 2006 (GVRD, 1989).

In order to undertake some comparisons of the relative "resilience" of the metropolitan economy and that of the "Rest of the Province" (ROP), an empirical analysis was conducted of certain selected significant indicators: cyclical stability, seasonal stability, and rates of business incorporations and bankruptcies.

Cyclical Stability

To compare the recent performances of the two regional economies with respect to cyclical stability, a simple measure of economic instability was constructed for each. First, a trend equation for employment growth was estimated through regression analysis for the metropolitan Vancouver and ROP economies for the period 1975-87. Once the trend estimates of employment were constructed, the average annual percent deviation from this trend was calculated as an indicator of cyclical instability. Thus the higher the value of the indicator, the less stable is the economy. The results are shown in Table 3.7.

As demonstrated by Table 3.7, the Greater Vancouver economy exhibits a marginally lower measure of instability (2.99) compared with the index of 3.05 calculated for the ROP. It must be noted, however, that the employment figures in the table for the ROP include metropolitan Victoria, with its relatively stable public-sector employment. When Greater Victoria (the Victoria Census Metropolitan Area) is excluded from the ROP, the employment instability index for the ROP is markedly higher at 3.54.

Seasonal Stability

Similar to the measure of cyclical economic instability, a measure of seasonal instability was calculated for each of the two economies over the period 1975-1987, using monthly employment data. In this case the mean monthly percentage deviation from annual average employment was calculated for each of the thirteen years. The measure of seasonal instability was then taken to be the average of the mean monthly deviations. The results show the Greater Vancouver economy is less subject to seasonal fluctuations than is the resource-based ROP economy. Average percent monthly deviation from the annual trend for Greater Vancouver over the last thirteen years is 2.71, while that for the ROP is 3.92. As was the case with cyclical instability, when metropolitan Victoria is excluded from the ROP, the latter is shown to be more unstable; the average percentage deviation increases slightly to 4.15.

Table 3.7: Cyclical and Seasonal Fluctuations in the Vancouver and Rest of Province Economies, 1975-87

Deviations from Trend Employment Estimates, 1975-87

Year	B.C. Employ-ment	Vancouver Employ-ment	Vancouver Trend Estimate	|dev.| trend	ROP Employ-ment	ROP Trend Estimate	|dev.| trend
1975	995	538	542	0.76	457	488	6.34
1976	1,021	532	552	3.70	489	501	2.38
1977	1,050	551	563	2.09	499	514	2.90
1978	1,103	568	573	0.88	535	527	1.54
1979	1,144	591	583	1.31	553	540	2.43
1980	1,213	643	594	8.32	570	553	3.10
1981	1,270	643	604	6.47	627	566	10.81
1982	1,204	617	614	0.45	587	579	1.41
1983	1,197	604	625	3.29	593	592	0.20
1984	1,202	596	635	6.11	606	605	0.20
1985	1,228	628	645	2.65	600	618	2.88
1986	1,274	670	655	2.23	604	631	4.24
1987	1,306	670	666	0.65	636	644	1.20
Average				**2.99**			**3.05**

Source: Constructed from average annual employment figures provided by the Vancouver Office of Statistics Canada and from Statistics Canada, 1975-1987. "Employment and Earnings." Catalogue No. 72-001.

Notes: VAN Trend Eqn.: 531.85 + 10.30t; ROP Trend Eqn.: 474.76 + 12.98t

In sum, the empirical evidence shows the Greater Vancouver regional economy to be both cyclically and seasonally more stable than that of the ROP. The differences between the two economies in each case are accentuated if metropolitan Victoria is excluded from the latter.

Business Incorporations and Bankruptcies

While volatility in terms of company start-ups and closures has been termed a leading attribute of the post-industrial urban economy, comprised increasingly of small and dynamic, but undercapitalised service sector firms (Birch, 1985), comparative rates of business incorporations and bankruptcies may be useful as a rough measure of resilience.

Table 3.8: Business Incorporations, Greater Vancouver and British Columbia:
1981-88

	1981	1982	1983	1984	1985	1986	1987	1988
Greater Vancouver	13,310	7,084	8,953	9,338	10,135	11,346	12,960	12,981
British Columbia	22,368	11,432	13,787	14,052	15,581	17,067	18,691	18,703

Source: Central Statistics Bureau, B.C. Ministry of Finance and Corporate Relations.

Table 3.9: Business Bankruptcies, Greater Vancouver and British Columbia: 1981-88

	1981	1982	1983	1984	1985	1986	1987	1988
Greater Vancouver	175	366	435	512	466	524	533	479
British Columbia	505	1,025	1,246	1,474	1,334	1,456	1,251	1,165

Source: Central Statistics Bureau, B.C. Ministry of Finance and Corporate Relations.

Tables 3.8 and 3.9 show business incorporations and bankruptcies for metropolitan Vancouver and for British Columbia as a whole, for the period 1981-1988. These data yield several insights relating to the relative buoyancy of the metropolitan and hinterland economies. First, both Vancouver and the province as a whole were severely impacted by the recession of 1982-85, characterised by a steep fall in incorporations, and a dramatic increase in bankruptcies.

Secondly, the rate of recovery from the "shock" of the 1982-85 recession as measured by incorporations was much more rapid in Vancouver than in ROP. Over the last half of the decade, business incorporations levelled off to about 6,000 per annum within the ROP, while levels continued to increase in Vancouver. Overall, business incorporations in Vancouver represent about 60 percent of the provincial total. On the other hand, Vancouver bankruptcies represent only about 40 percent of the provincial total.

As in the case of data pertaining to cyclical and seasonal stability discussed above, it seems reasonable to assume that the metropolitan-hinterland disparity would be even more pronounced if Victoria was factored out of the ROP calculations.

Vancouver's Resilience in the National Context

It may be instructive to broaden the scope of our inquiry, to give some consideration to Vancouver's resilience in comparison to other metropolitan areas within Canada's urban system. Over the past twenty years, Canadian cities have experienced a succession of domestic and exogenous disturbances, both "stresses" and "shocks", and these have significantly influenced the variable economic fortunes of individual cities.

One form of "stress" to urban systems might take the form of changes or pressures within the national metropolitan hierarchy, in terms of inter-city competition for positions within this hierarchy. A dominant trend within the Canadian urban system has been the growing primacy of Toronto as the leading centre of industrial production, finance and corporate control. The most dramatic impact of this phenomenon has been the subordination of Montreal to secondary status. Rather than vying with Toronto for ascendancy within the national sphere, Montreal is now principally a regional corporate centre, with a significant international role, much like Vancouver.

Table 3.10 shows corporate relocations among major Canadian metropolitan areas, in 1980 revenues. The data reveal a very large shift to Toronto, both in the resource, manufacturing and utilities sectors, and in the services, finance and real estate sectors, the volume of the latter amounting to about double the former. Montreal is the biggest loser, with losses in the services, financial and real estate sectors being especially large, and associated in part no doubt with the economic "shock" generated by a political event, the election of the Parti Québecois in 1976. Vancouver was one of the few urban areas recording gains both in the broadly-defined goods and services sectors.

While data for the most recent period are not readily accessible, intuitively it seems reasonable to suggest that while the aggregate volume of economic activity in Vancouver continues to experience considerable growth, the city has lost ground to Toronto in terms of corporate control functions, following a trend of mergers and acquisitions, and a general concentration of head office activity in Toronto. This may, in turn, result in some loss of employment but a more significant cost will likely be diminished economic autonomy, especially in terms of head office functions related to the key resource sector industries. In the most recent period, too, there have been significant buyouts and acquisitions of Vancouver-based firms by Pacific Rim corporations, reflecting the process of globalisation and market integration alluded to above.

Another measure of Vancouver's relative resilience can be discerned with respect to comparative recovery rates from the recession of 1982-85. It was observed earlier that Vancouver experienced a more rapid recovery from this downturn than the rest of the province. However, British Columbia as a whole (including Vancouver) recovered much more slowly than the rest of Canada,

Table 3.10: Corporate Headquarters Relocations Among Major Canadian Cities, by 1980 Revenues ($ millions)

	Resource, manufacturing, utilities sector	Services, finance, real estate sectors	Net Total
Toronto	11,467	19,974	31,441
Montreal	-5,209	-15,309	-20,518
Vancouver	572	1,177	1,749
Ottawa	112	-797	-685
Edmonton	-139	410	271
Calgary	390	924	1,314
Winnipeg	234	-2,293	-2,059
Quebec City	-497	1,845	1,348
Hamilton	294	-122	172
St. Catherines-Niagara	—	-165	-165
Kitchener	—	-200	-200
London	16	62	78
Halifax	—	2,123	2,123

Source: Adapted from Semple and Green (1983).

notably central Canada, where "normal" growth rates asserted themselves fully two years in advance of those in British Columbia, underlining the peripheral status of B.C.

Interestingly, economic growth in the metropolitan Vancouver region is now comfortably exceeding that for Toronto, where a slowdown is clearly in evidence. This may reflect one or several factors in conjunction: a continuing "lag" effect, in which Vancouver has yet to enter the downturn phase Toronto has already reached; industrial mix factors; or possibly Vancouver's closer affinity to the high growth markets of the Asia-Pacific Region. This latter aspect is likely to be increasingly the key to Vancouver's future sustainability, in terms both of "transformation" and resilience, as will be addressed in the following section.

Sustainability as "Market Competition and Complementarity"

Traditionally scholars have assessed growth and development prospects of urban areas largely in terms of location, proximal resource endowments, and local-regional market characteristics. While each may still of course be significant for particular cities, the evolution of the post-industrial city within an emerging global urban network has in numerous respects undermined the criticality of these attributes. With respect to location, for example, the introduction of increasingly advanced telecommunications, and reductions in transport costs relative to overall production costs, has "loosened the glue of centrality" [in Berry's (1980) words], enabling more peripheral locations to participate more fully in economic development and trade.

Secondly, the partial "de-industrialisation" of urban areas in advanced economies, coupled with the rise of services and technology-intensive (rather than resource-intensive) production has significantly reduced the value of proximal natural resource endowments as urban growth determinants, as evidenced by the dramatic growth of resource-poor jurisdictions such as Hamburg, Milan, Osaka, Hong Kong, and Singapore.

Thirdly, metropolitan areas are becoming, to some extent at least, partially "uncoupled" from their regional markets, as more and larger secondary business and employment centres are developed in outer suburban and exurban areas, and as the central city loses much of its general, traditional central place role, in favour of more specialised business, financial, trading, and socio-political functions.

In this context, the position of metropolitan cities within more spatially-extensive urban systems becomes more important, both in understanding contemporary urban evolution, and in evaluating future development prospects. The emergence of a global urban network across which is mediated an increasing share of trade in commodities of all kinds implies inevitably aspects of hierarchy and competition as well as complementarity. Certainly, many medium-size cities play specialised regional and/or functional "niche" roles within this network but at the same time compete (unwittingly or otherwise) for shares of investment, job-generation, and markets, and it is within this broader arena that urban development will increasingly be played out.

These considerations have substantial relevance to the sustainability of Vancouver's development. Of course, Vancouver shares many of the political and socio-cultural attributes of other Canadian cities, and shares in common too a basic development configuration favouring service industries and occupations. What distinguishes Vancouver from other centres within the Canadian urban system, however, is not only its relative isolation from the mainstream business environment concentrated within central Canada, but also the leading role and impacts Pacific Basin trade, investment, immigration and institutions play in its contemporary development. Increasingly, Vancouver is becoming integrated within the network of Pacific Basin trading, commercial and financial centres, and this will over time shape Vancouver's development patterns. A brief description of some aspects of Vancouver's role as an emerging centre of the incipient Pacific Rim urban system follows.

The recent development of the Port of Vancouver and Vancouver International Airport reflects Vancouver's role as the "gateway" between Canada and the Asian Pacific. The Port of Vancouver is Canada's most important port, ranks with Los Angeles-Long Beach as the largest (by tonnage throughput) on the North

Table 3.11: Port of Vancouver in Relation to Asian Pacific Rim Ports Based On Total
Tonnage (1986 figures)

Ranking	Port	Country	Total Tonnage
1	Kobe	Japan	160,458,000*
2	Shanghai	China	133,000,000
3	Singapore	Singapore	120,716,000
4	Yokohama	Japan	110,296,000
5	Nagoya	Japan	107,743,000
6	Kitakyushu	Japan	90,075,000
7	Osaka	Japan	81,764,000
8	Keelung	Taiwan	66,200,000
9	Hong Kong	Hong Kong	62,479,000
10	Tokyo	Japan	59,546,000*
11	**Vancouver**	**Canada**	**57,593,000**
12	Kaohsiung	Taiwan	55,240,000
13	Pusan	South Korea	45,158,000
14	Inchon	South Korea	36,938,000
15	Newcastle	Australia	36,160,000
16	Sydney	Australia	35,875,000
17	Hedland	Australia	35,618,000
18	Port Kelang	Malaya	12,302,768
19	Tomakomai	Japan	10,179,246
20	Tanjung Priork	Java	9,709,446*

Notes:
*   1985 figures.

American Pacific Rim, and ranks with such major Asian ports as Hong Kong and
Kaohsiung in terms of cargo tonnage handled (Table 3.11).[6] The Port of
Vancouver has experienced very steady growth in throughput, achieving new
record levels of tonnage handled in each of the past several years, culminating in a
new historical high of 71 million tons in 1988 (Port of Vancouver, 1989). This
high volume of trade has a distinctly Pacific Rim character.

Tables 3.12 and 3.13 show the top ten destinations of exports and national
origins of imports respectively for cargo handled by the Port of Vancouver for
1988, in terms both of tonnage handled and also container tonnage. The tables

---

6   The metropolitan Vancouver port complex consists of the Port of Vancouver, the Fraser River Harbour and
the North Fraser Harbour. Tables 3.12-3.15 pertain exclusively to the Port of Vancouver, which includes the
Roberts Bank Superport in the Fraser River Estuary.

Table 3.12: Port of Vancouver Top Ten Destinations of Exports: 1988

Rank	Country*	Metric Tonnes	Rank	Country*	Container Tonnage
1	Japan (1)	25,280,508	1	Japan (1)	829,180
2	China (3)	6,205,430	2	Taiwan (2)	186,853
3	S. Korea (2)	6,129,131	3	China (5)	117,064
4	Brazil (5)	2,195,705	4	S. Korea (6)	96,059
5	U.S.A. (4)	2,154,347	5	Hong Kong (3)	90,927
6	Taiwan (6)	2,114,422	6	U.K. (4)	61,495
7	Morocco (8)	2,071,889	7	Columbia (8)	44,158
8	Australia (9)	1,524,127	8	Netherlands (9)	31,265
9	U.K. (10)	1,335,201	9	W. Germany (-)	18,856
10	U.S.S.R. (7)	1,106,073	10	Malaysia (-)	18,404

Source: Vancouver Port Corporation.
Notes:
* 1987 rankings are shown in parentheses.

Table 3.13: Port of Vancouver Top Ten Destinations of Imports: 1988

Rank	Country*	Metric Tonnes	Rank	Country*	Container Tonnage
1	U.S.A. (1)	686,494	1	Japan (1)	276,638
2	Togo (2)	654,600	2	S. Korea (3)	139,308
3	Japan (3)	407,124	3	Taiwan (2)	110,818
4	Mexico (4)	341,636	4	Hong Kong (4)	88,374
5	Morocco (-)	238,128	5	Thailand (6)	55,865
6	S. Korea (6)	167,988	6	China (5)	54,283
7	Spain (10)	146,407	7	Italy (7)	29,085
8	Australia (7)	134,853	8	France (8)	23,628
9	W. Germany (-)	119,663	9	W. Germany (10)	22,281
10	Singapore (-)	88,375	10	Singapore (-)	21,720

Source: Vancouver Port Corporation.
Notes:
* 1987 rankings are shown in parentheses.

reveal the very high volumes of export trade especially, export tonnage typically exceeding imports by a ratio of 4:1 or 5:1. Evident too is the great importance of the Pacific Rim in the Port of Vancouver's international trade, with Japan (accounting for about one-half the total volume), China, and South Korea solidly established as the top three export destinations by tonnage, and with seven of the top ten classifiable as Pacific Rim markets. With respect to container tonnage, the five largest export markets are situated within the Asian Pacific, and with Japan again dominant in the first position.

The list of nations with the largest volume of imports entering Canada through the Port of Vancouver is somewhat more geographically diversified than the top ten export destinations, with European and African countries figuring more prominently, but with Pacific Rim nations well represented with respect both to overall tonnage, and, more especially, in the area of container traffic. The top six countries of origin in the latter category for 1988 were all situated within the Asian Pacific Region (Table 3.13).

Export trade through the Port of Vancouver, while including a significant and growing volume of container trade, is largely dominated by bulk cargoes, especially resource commodities (Table 3.14). This very high level of resource exports, while contributing significantly to the development of Vancouver and British Columbia, may in the long-run be somewhat problematic, for several reasons. First, while export resource trade has been expanding in recent years, reflecting generally buoyant economic conditions, staples are after all subject to considerable volatility in demand patterns. This in turn may render more vulnerable those ports dependent to a significant degree on serving staple-dominated hinterlands for export trade, as was observed in the case of Vancouver in the early 1980's (when commodity price shocks severely impacted resource exports), and in the instance of Singapore in 1985.

Secondly, in addition to the normal fluctuations attendant upon resource export trade, there is also concern regarding the longer-term market for certain resource commodities. As is well known, there has been a secular decline in demand for certain resources among advanced economies, reflecting the shift to services and more technology-intensive forms of production, as well as the substitution of certain natural resources (Larson et al., 1987). British Columbia's important coal markets are a case in point: prospects for sustaining the very high volumes of coal exports (Table 3.14) may be threatened in the short term by downward pressures on price, in the medium-term by lower-cost competitors (notably Australia), and, perhaps more decisively in the long run, by Japan's phasing out of coal-dependent heavy industry.

Thirdly, while certainly profitable on its own terms, bulk resource exports to the Pacific Rim and elsewhere are less profitable than container trade, and, from the viewpoint of the British Columbia economy as a whole, generate less than favourable terms of trade.

British Columbia has historically been viewed as part of Canada's vast periphery, its chief economic role being the supply of resources to the more industrialized core (i.e., Central Canada) and to the U.S. Growing trade with the

Table 3.14: Port of Vancouver Export Commodities: 1988

	(in metric tonnes)
Coal & Coke	23,540,000
Grain	12,518,000
Sulphur	6,577,000
Potash	4,792,000
Lumber	2,881,000
Chemicals	1,842,000
Wood Chips	1,458,000
Woodpulp	1,194,000
Crude Oil	1,025,000
Animal Feed	1,004,000

Source: Greater Vancouver Port Corporation.

Pacific Rim nations represents a desirable element of market diversification. In light of the dominance of resource commodities within the Port of Vancouver's exports, however, there appears to be a risk of British Columbia evolving from a hinterland position within Canada, to an equally peripheral status within the economy of the Pacific Rim.

While the port has been Vancouver's most critical interface with Pacific Rim markets, Vancouver International Airport (YVR) is rapidly growing in importance. Table 3.15 shows the sustained levels of high growth in passenger throughput at Vancouver International. Much of this recent growth has been driven by Pacific Rim markets, and indeed trans-Pacific traffic is a leading element of expansion at YVR. Several measures of this Pacific Rim air traffic can be adduced. A recent study, for example, determined that the direct impact of Pacific Rim traffic at Vancouver International Airport in 1986 was valued at $243 million in annual revenues, generating some 1,070 jobs, with $30 million in wages and salaries (McNeal Associates & Consultants Limited, 1986), and this has expanded considerably over the past several years (Transport Canada, pers. comm., 1989). Given an aggressive marketing strategy, and airport capacity enhancement, both of which are in progress, it was further estimated that the direct impact of Pacific Rim traffic in terms of revenues and employment for YVR could more than double by 1998 (McNeal Associates & Consultants, 1986).

Another important measure of the growth of Pacific Rim markets to Vancouver International Airport can be derived from a profile (by country of origin) of overseas visitors to British Columbia, most of whom enter via Vancouver International. Table 3.16 provides an overseas visitors profile for British Columbia for the period 1980-1988. The data show a substantial increase

Table 3.15: Transportation - Vancouver International Airport: Passengers on Scheduled Flights

Year	Passengers
1988	9,232,932**
1987	8,023,520
1986*	8,385,356
1985	7,005,802
1984	6,895,059
1983	6,370,000
1982	5,858,000
1981	6,818,000
1980	6,777,000
1979	6,230,000
1978	5,416,000

Source: Airports Authority Group, Transport Canada.
Notes:
*   Expo 86 operated in Vancouver from May to October 1986.
**   1988 passengers consisted of 5,902,586 domestic, 1,850,986 transborder and 1,479,360 international.

Table 3.16: Visitors Profile - Origins of Overseas Visitors to British Columbia

Year	United Kingdom	Japan	West Germany	Hong Kong	Australia	Other	Totals[1]
1988	97,864	133,659	65,619	49,403	43,993	201,214	591,752
1987	81,206	104,296	57,986	37,745	38,407	173,484	493,124
1986	94,570	100,330	55,790	41,450	39,880	227,980	560,000
1985	58,270	83,290	36,140	25,170	34,350	208,780	446,000
1984	69,385	78,364	41,379	31,604	32,725	216,543	470,000
1983	77,353	67,234	41,663	29,454	26,953	202,343	445,000
1982	85,975	63,907	43,785	23,152	26,199	196,982	440,000
1981	92,966	62,820	43,774	22,410	22,897	210,133	455,000
1980	92,973	68,200	37,821	18,897	23,769	198,340	440,000

Source: B.C. Ministry of Tourism and Statistics Canada.
Notes:
1   The totals shown in this table are derived from actual counts of individuals crossing the British Columbia border from their overseas points of origin.

in overseas visitors (35 percent) over the 1980's, and with significant increases in visitations from most of those nations ranking among the top five in 1980. There is however considerable variation in growth rates, and in general Pacific Rim nations exhibit the most dramatic increases. The number of visitations to British Columbia from Australia expanded by 85 percent over the 1980's, for example, while growth in visitations was even more rapid in travellers from Japan (96 percent), and Hong Kong (161 percent). Japan is now leading in visitations to British Columbia, replacing the United Kingdom, providing another illustration of Vancouver's changing market orientation.

Airport managers have identified the Pacific Rim, and especially the Asian Pacific, as the key market for future growth. Vancouver International already handles more international and trans-Pacific air passengers than does Seattle-Tacoma International Airport, a considerably larger facility which serves a much more extensive regional market. Moreover, YVR is already serviced by many of the major Asian carriers (e.g., Japan Airlines, Cathay Pacific, Singapore Airlines, Korean Airlines, and China Air), most of which are operating at or near capacity, and are planning additional service to Vancouver. In addition to complementing British Columbia's tourist industry, these trans-Pacific air services also act as a major business development leader for Vancouver, facilitating business travel, connecting Vancouver with other centres and with the Pacific Basin's urban network, and significantly augmenting the city's Pacific Rim "Gateway" role.

Implications for Vancouver's Service Sector

Although Vancouver's export trade with Pacific Rim markets has been dominated historically by semi- and unprocessed resource commodities, an examination of the "margins of change" reveals an increasing role for services, including banking and financial, and "producer" (intermediate) services. Indeed, Vancouver's service sector represents both a potentially major source of exports to Pacific Rim markets, as well as an element of Vancouver's comparative advantage in pursuing a larger share of Pacific Rim investment, trade and commerce.

In a recent effort to identify empirically Vancouver's comparative economic advantages relative to the two major Canadian metropolitan ports of Toronto and Montreal and the primary U.S. west coast port cities (Seattle, Portland, San Francisco, Los Angeles and San Diego), Davis and Goldberg (1988) examined the industrial profiles of each region with respect to 1971-81 sector growth rates and 1981 adjusted location quotients.[7]

The location quotient analysis of each city's 48 economic sectors revealed

> Vancouver's comparative advantages to be overwhelmingly established in the service sectors. In particular, the city has developed significant advantages in transportation and communication activities, a phenomenon undoubtedly attributable in large part to the city's strategic location on the Pacific Rim. The city's advantages extend as

---

7   Location quotients are discussed in Appendix 3.1.

well into the activities of trade, finance, insurance and real estate which further enhance Vancouver's potential major role in the post-industrial economic future of the Asia Pacific Basin (Davis and Goldberg, 1988).

The comparison of sector growth rates among the ports revealed ten sectors in Vancouver that had growth rates exceeding those of the same sectors aggregated across the eight regions. Of these ten sectors,

> Services to Business Management and Banks & Other Deposit Establishments sectors stand out in that each shows a growth rate almost twice that of the corresponding aggregate. As the latter sector was estimated in the previous section to be an activity in which the Vancouver economy has already established a comparative advantage, the focus here is on the former sector, Services to Business Management. Service activities in general have indeed accounted for the major share of employment growth in the Vancouver economy over the recent past, and much of that increment results in particular from the expansion of the interwoven complex of corporate and public sector services (Davis and Goldberg, 1988).

In addition to this rapid overall growth of Vancouver's service sector, several key service industry groups exhibit significant export propensity (Davis and Goldberg 1988), a trend consistent with other advanced, "transactional" urban economies (Daniels, 1985; Beyers et al., 1986). The aforementioned study of Vancouver's producer services revealed that 11 percent of the firms sampled had conducted business in east and south-east Asia, while a somewhat larger proportion (13 percent) anticipated sales activity in Asian Pacific markets (Ley and Hutton, 1987). These service firms included engineering, architectural, management consulting, and real estate/property development companies. In terms of motivation, firms cited both a perception of significant market opportunities in Asia, as well as concerns about over-dependence on "traditional" markets within the resource hinterland in British Columbia (Ley and Hutton, 1987).

Asian-Pacific Business Presence in Vancouver

Implicit in the notion of an increasingly integrated Pacific Rim economy is the phenomenon of an expanding foreign business presence among member cities of the emerging urban network. This is seen to include, inter alia, the dispersion of production by Multi-national Enterprises (MNE's), the establishment of banking and financial subsidiaries and regional/representative corporate offices within the CBD of Pacific Rim business centres, and increasing levels of foreign investment in real estate and property development, especially (but not exclusively) in the commercial sector.

Typically this foreign business element now includes representation from increasingly far-flung jurisdictions, reflecting the effective "globalisation" of many forms of enterprise. However, there are especially large and growing concentrations of foreign firms within Pacific Basin cities. That is indigenous to the Pacific region, underlining this notion of a distinctive Pacific Rim economy within the more spatially-extensive global economy.

This phenomenon is most clearly manifested among the "first rank" Pacific Rim business centres, but a rapid expansion of foreign business activity is also evident among many of the more junior members of the Pacific Basin urban network. In the case of Vancouver, there is relatively little in the way of basic production activity directed by Pacific Rim MNE's, a notable exception being a Toyota wheel plant in suburban Richmond. There is, however, a substantial Asian Pacific business presence in Vancouver, especially in the form of banking and financial activity, various commercial enterprises, trade, and investment in real property. The level of activity in each of these areas appears to be expanding rapidly, and illustrates another dimension of Vancouver's emergence as a Pacific Rim city.

No comprehensive inventory of foreign business activity in Vancouver exists, but there is sufficient information available to trace at least the outline of Asian Pacific business presence. In general, much of this foreign business presence in Vancouver relates to the urban area's position as the Pacific gateway to the markets of western Canada or even the national market as a whole, and, in some cases, to the west coast of North America. As a result, a large proportion of the Pacific Rim business activity takes the form of banking and financial subsidiaries, regional or representative sales offices, trading companies, distribution agencies, and the like.

With respect to financial institutions, about one-half of the approximately 30 foreign banking operations in Vancouver are subsidiaries of Asian banks, the majority of the remainder being European banks. Of the Asian banks represented in Vancouver, many (e.g., Mitsubishi, Mitsui, Dai-Ichi Kangyo) are of course Japanese, reflecting the pervasive influence of Japan in the Pacific Rim capital markets generally, but the most significant Asian Pacific financial presence is the Canadian head office of the Hong Kong Bank of Canada, a subsidiary of the Hongkong and Shanghai Banking Corporation. What distinguishes the Hong Kong Bank of Canada from other Asian banks in Vancouver, in addition to the scale of its operation, and the head office function it performs for Canada, is its extensive retail banking system, resulting from the Hong Kong Bank of Canada's purchase of the Bank of British Columbia.

While the Hong Kong Bank of Canada may be seen as the flagship Hong Kong corporation in Vancouver, there is in fact a very substantial Hong Kong presence in the city and metropolitan region as a whole, reflecting the large Hong Kong-Cantonese population resident in Vancouver, and the City's attractiveness both to Hong Kong business people and emigrants. Hong Kong presence includes the regional head office of Cathay Pacific Airlines, trading, shipping and distribution companies (e.g., Dah Chong Hong and OOCL), ownership position in hotels and shopping centres, and extensive real estate property holdings. The latter include, notably, the huge 200-acre plus Pacific Place development on the north shore of

False Creek in the City's downtown owned by Concord Pacific, a subsidiary of Cheung Kong Holdings, whose majority shareholder is Li Ka-Shing. There is also an embryonic production sector controlled by Hong Kong concerns or recent immigrants from the Crown colony, specialising in garment production. This production investment is likely to expand, in light of a trend among Hong Kong industries to diversify production geographically, and in view also of the potential of serving west coast U.S. markets from Vancouver within the framework of the Canada-U.S. Free Trade Agreement.

Although the extent of overseas investment in real estate is often over-stated, there are substantial foreign holdings of property in Vancouver. There are in fact large property portfolios held by European and non-local domestic concerns, but recent attention has focussed on the purchase of real estate and buildings by Asian interests. A substantial proportion of real estate assets is held by "overseas Chinese" concerns, not just from Hong Kong, as is commonly supposed, but also from Singapore, Malayasia, Taiwan, and elsewhere. A major real estate company recently estimated that the overseas Chinese holdings might represent 7 percent of land in the downtown, including the 200-acre plus Pacific Place site (Eng, 1989).

Perhaps the most dramatic evidence of the enhanced presence of Asian-Pacific business interests can be found in the commercial sector, specifically among the cluster of a dozen or so "international class" hotels within downtown Vancouver. A decade ago, most of these were controlled by American or Toronto-based concerns; now, a large majority of these business class properties are controlled by Asian corporations. Here, there is evidence of diversification in ownership: among those firms with a controlling interest in Vancouver's hotels are corporations or individuals based in Hong Kong, Singapore, Malayasia, Macau, Japan, and the P.R.C.

Vancouver's Future as a Pacific Rim Metropolis

In conclusion, it seems apparent that Vancouver's development will increasingly be associated with its expanding roles within the Pacific Rim, and specifically its membership within the emerging Pacific Basin urban system. The precise nature of Vancouver's role is, of course, as yet undefined. In particular, it remains to be seen whether Vancouver can develop as a more fully-fledged player in the development of the Pacific Basin This implies not merely "hosting" investment from abroad, and serving as a port and distribution centre, but also a whole range of as yet underdeveloped functions. These include, notably, direct investment in Pacific Rim nations, a stronger market presence in other Pacific Basin business centres, more exports of value-added products and services, and growth in trade with a more diversified range of Pacific nations. Vancouver's past development has been hindered in part by its hinterland status within Canada, it is not to Vancouver's advantage to exchange this subordinate position merely for an equally peripheral position within the Pacific economy.

Conclusion: Toward an Assessment of Vancouver's Prospects for Sustainable Development

We have attempted in this paper to provide an analysis of Vancouver's development sustainability, with an emphasis on economic variables, but incorporating as well environmental and social factors, recognizing the critical interdependence of each. Our basic assumption is that maintaining a vital, productive, adaptable and competitive economy is fundamental to Vancouver's future as a prosperous and progressive society, but that an overall measure of quality of life and sustainability must also take proper accounting of environmental and social attributes in the interests of a balanced urban society.

Our analysis, conducted within the limited scope of this paper, cannot be considered definitive of course, but is clearly supportive of the view that Vancouver's prospects for sustainable development are broadly favourable, even very favourable, according to the measures employed. Vancouver's stock of capital assets, in terms of natural endowments, urban infrastructure (both public and private), and social or human capital, appears to be exceptional. Moreover, rates of reinvestment and renewal seem to be for the most part adequate, although there is evidence that higher levels of commitment and careful stewardship will be required over the 1990's if both productivity and livability are to be sustained.

Secondly, our examination of Vancouver's transformation propensity suggests that Vancouver's progression to more advanced forms of economic activity and employment compares favourably to other Canadian metropolitan centres, characterised by a large and dynamic service sector, which is clearly strong in the high growth producer services especially, as well as by a relatively small but dynamic advanced-technology production sector. Overall, it would appear that Vancouver is successfully undergoing the transition to a post-industrial economy and society, consistent with trends observed in advanced nations broadly.

Thirdly, Vancouver's resilience, although still subject to the vagaries of a resource-dependent hinterland economy, shows evidence of improvement according to analysis of trends over the last decade, albeit viewed from the perspective of a long boom period. Factors favouring an enhanced quality of resilience include the following: a large service sector which provides some insulation against the worst ravages of recessionary cycles; a growing metropolitan population (approaching 1.5 million) which enhances diversity and enables improvements in scale economies; and, finally, an apparently structural adjustment of export trading relations, favouring linkages with the high growth economies of the Asian Pacific and the U. S. West Coast.

This latter component of Vancouver's sustainability may in fact represent a decisive influence on Vancouver's long-term sustainability. There is a distinct opportunity to promote higher levels of integration with the most dynamic economies in the world, which should in turn generate favourable long-term growth opportunities, as well as further protection from the more extreme swings of the business cycle associated with dependence on a resource-driven economy.

This broadly-favourable prognosis should of course be tempered by an acknowledgment of potential threats and constraints. These may include, for example, the following:

- Increasing pressure on the limited land base of the metropolitan-Lower Mainland region, increasingly characterised by land use conflicts (urban/agricultural; industrial/residential; etc.). Over the short to medium term, these conflicts can be mitigated by densification and by effective planning and land use management strategies; however, constraints imposed by both natural and political boundaries, plus the social demand for livability, will inevitably place some limit on growth in the region.
- On a related issue, growing concerns about environmental quality will likely require a stronger commitment to pollution control, with respect to solid wastes, to residual industrial wastes, and, most notably, to auto-generated pollution. A deterioration of environmental quality would generate both social and economic costs, inasmuch as desirable industries are increasingly sensitive to local amenity values.
- The continuing process of corporate mergers and acquisitions associated with economic globalisation, which has already reduced Vancouver's level of commercial control and hence, could significantly undermine future decision-making autonomy, influencing in turn investment and job generation within B.C.
- The Canada-U.S. Free Trade Agreement, while seen as broadly favourable to British Columbia at present, could allow greater domination of the local market by aggressive American firms with major economies of scale and scope advantages in the long-term, unless local firms capture larger shares of the emerging continental market.
- As noted above, a failure to pursue actively opportunities in the Asian Pacific could lead to Vancouver assuming an essentially hosting or peripheral role within the Pacific Basin economy.

In addition to the above constraints and threats which have special relevance to Vancouver, there are also other, more universal concerns regarding Vancouver's long-term sustainability and socio-economic well-being. These include, for example, the potential de-skilling of significant parts of the workforce; the possibility of large-scale worker displacement as capital is increasingly substituted for labour in the historically labour-intensive service sector; increasingly serious problems associated with Canada's fiscal situation; the decline of Canada's comparative advantage in natural resources within the context of the continental and world economy; and so on.

It should be emphasised that Vancouver as a corporate entity need not react passively to this spectrum of opportunities and threats to its sustainability. Indeed, a purely laissez-faire posture is likely to generate increasing costs, in terms, of lost opportunities, foregone development potential, and increasing environmental costs. A more responsive and pro-active stance can at least help to maximize benefits, and minimize costs of change, and may well enhance prospects for long-term, sustainable development.

There are, in fact, ample precedents to draw on. Large and medium-size metropolitan areas are increasingly framing specific strategies to address the challenges associated with restructuring, market integration, and the implications of an emerging global urban network characterised both by complementarity and competition. Examples of cities undertaking such strategies within the context of different administrative structures and varying degrees of local autonomy include Hamburg, Melbourne, Singapore, and Toronto. Even in the case of Hong Kong, traditionally associated with a classic capitalistic social and economic structure, the current trend features an increasingly explicit corporate-government-community partnership in economic and socio-economic development and environmental amelioration.

Of course, strategies for sustainable development need to be specifically tailored to meet the specific values, aspirations, and objectives of individual communities. In the case of Vancouver, we are in many ways exceptionally fortunate in possessing a firm legacy of natural and man-made assets, and favourable overall prospects for development sustainability. These prospects could be effectively enhanced, in our view, by a strategy for sustainable development for Greater Vancouver which integrates economic policies and programmes with explicit social and environmental values. The basic purpose of such a strategy would be:

- To embody and convey community values and priorities, both to generate local development objectives, and also to clearly inform "external" parties (senior government, current or potential foreign investors and traders, etc.) of local preferences and opportunities;
- To enable Vancouver as a corporate entity to recognise and respond to opportunities and threats in an increasingly interdependent world society and globally integrated economic order;
- To provide a framework for action, including the more effective harnessing of collective resources;
- More specifically, to reflect Vancouver's current role and future potential as a member city of the emerging urban network of the Pacific Rim, as well as, more generally, the "global village" of communities; and,
- To operationalise the basic complementarity of economic development and environmental amenity in Vancouver, as well as to identify trade-offs where appropriate, including a more explicit accounting of economic, social, and environmental costs and benefits.

We believe, in conclusion, that it is preferable to integrate economic, social, and environmental attributes within an overall strategic approach, rather than to attempt to reconcile very contrasting and often contradictory policies for each ex post facto, which has largely been the case to date. This will require a greater degree of commitment and vision than has been demonstrated to date, within an administratively fragmented region. But is likely to be a sine qua non of achieving sustainable development in the 1990's and beyond.

References

Bell, D. 1974. *The Coming of the Post-Industrial Society.* London: Heinemann.
Berry, J. L. 1980. "Forces Reshaping the Settlement System." in H. J. Bryce. *Cities and Firms.* Kentucky: Lexington Books.
Beyers, W., M. Alvine and E. Johnson. 1985. *The Service Economy: Export of Services in the Central Puget Sound Region.* Seattle: Central Puget Sound Economic Development Department.
Birch, D. 1985. *Analysis of Entrepreneurial Potential for Vancouver.* Prepared by Cognetics Inc., Cambridge, Massachusetts for TIEM Canada.
Canada Employment and Immigration Commission. 1989. *Economic Review.* Vancouver: Regional Economic Services Branch.
Conservation of Human Resources. 1977. *The Corporate Headquarters Complex in New York City.* New York: Columbia University Press.
Courier. 16 May 1989. Vancouver.
Daniels, P. W. 1985. *Service Industries: A Geographical Appraisal.* London: Methuen.
Daniels, P. W. 1986. "The Geography of Services." *Progress in Human Geography.* 10:436-444.
Davis, H. C., and M. A. Goldberg. 1988. *Determination of the Comparative Advantages of Vancouver as an International City.* Prepared for the Asia-Pacific Initiative. Vancouver.
Davis, H. C., and T. A. Hutton. 1989a. "The Two Economies of British Columbia." *B.C. Studies.* 82:3-15.
Davis, H. C., and T. A. Hutton. 1989b. *Immigration and Ethnic Conflict in Metropolitan Vancouver: Challenge and Response.* University of British Columbia School of Community and Regional Planning, Planning Papers. Vancouver.
Design Vancouver. 1990. B.C. Design Service Sector: 1990 Survey. Prepared for the Ministry of Regional and Economic Development.
Edgington, D. W., and M. A. Goldberg. 1989. *Vancouver and the Emerging Network of Pacific Rim Global Cities.* Paper presented to the North American meeting of the Regional Science Association. Santa Barbara, California.
Eng, A. 1989. *The Influence of Hong Kong Investment in Real Estate in Vancouver.* Presentation to Pacific Rim Real Estate Investment Seminar. Vancouver.
Globe and Mail. March 1, 1989. *"Is Vancouver Trading Fur for Beads?"* Toronto.
Goodland, R., and G. Leduc. 1987. "Neoclassical Economics and Principles of Sustainable Development." *Ecological Modelling.* 38.
Gottmann, I. J. 1974. "The Dynamics of Large Cities." *Geographical Journal.* 140:254-261.
Gottmann, I. J. 1982. "The Metamorphosis of the Modern Metropolis." *Ekistics.* 49:7-11.
Greater Vancouver Regional District Bulletin. Development Services Department Monthly. 1989.
Hodes, D. A., T. Cook and W. M. Rochfort. 1989. "The Importance of Regional Economic Analysis and Regional Strategies in an Age of Industrial Restructuring." *Business Economics.* April:46-51.
Hutton, T. A. 1985. *Vancouver: Economic Structure, Growth and Change.* Prepared for the Vancouver Economic Advisory Commission. Vancouver.
Hutton, T. A. 1989. *A Profile of Vancouver's Service Sector.* Report prepared for the Tertiary Industries Workshop Group of "Metropolis '90". Plymouth, England.
Hutton, T. A., and H. C. Davis. 1985. "The Role of Office Location in Regional Tour Centre Planning and Metropolitan Multinucleation: The Case of Vancouver." *The Canadian Journal of Regional Science.* VIII(1):17-34.
Hutton, T. A., and H. C. Davis. 1989. *"Vancouver as an Emerging Centre of the Pacific Rim Urban System."* Paper presented to the Inaugural Pacific Rim Urban Development Council Conference. Los Angeles, California.

Hutton, T. A., and D. F. Ley. 1987. "Location, Linkages and Labor: The Downtown Complex of Corporate Activities in a Medium Size City, Vancouver, British Columbia." *Economic Geography.* 63(2):126-141.

Larson, E. D., M. H. Ross and R. H. Williams. "Beyond the Era of Materials." *Scientific American.* 254(6):34-41.

Ley, D. F., and T. A. Hutton. 1987. "Vancouver's Corporate Complex and Producer Services Sector: Linkages and Divergence within a Provincial Staple Economy." *Regional Studies.* 21(5):413-424.

McNeal Associates and Consultants Limited. 1986. *Pacific Rim Aviation Impact Study.* Prepared by McNeal Associates and Consultants for Transport Canada. Vancouver.

Pearce, D., A. Markandya and E. B. Barbier. 1989. *Blueprint for a Green Economy.* Earthscan Publications, for the Department of the Environment. London.

Pezzey, J. 1989. *Economic Analysis of Sustainable Growth and Sustainable Development.* The World Bank Policy Planning and Research Staff, Environment Department Working Paper No. 15.

Picot, W. G. 1986. *Canada's Industries: Growth in Jobs over Three Decades.* Ottawa: Ministry of Supply and Services. Catalogue No. 89-507E.

Port of Vancouver. 1989. *Statistical Digest.*

Scott, A. J. 1982. "Production System Dynamics and Metropolitan Development." *Annals of the Association of American Geographers.* 72:185-200.

Scott, A. J. 1983. "Location and Linkage Systems: A Survey and Reassessment." *Annals of Regional Science.* 17:1-39.

Semple, R. K., and M. Green. 1983. "Inter-Urban Corporate Headquarters Relocation in Canada." *Cahiers de Geographie du Quebec.* 27:389-406.

Solow, R. 1986. "On the Intergenerational Allocation of Natural Resources." *Scandinavian Journal of Economics.* 88.

Stanback, T. J., and T. Noyelle. 1982. *Cities in Transition.* Totawa, New Jersey: Allenheld and Osmun.

Technical Committee on Canada's Urban Infrastructure. 1984. *Canada's Urban Infrastructure: Physical Condition and Funding Adequacy.* Prepared for the Federation of Canadian Municipalities.

Turner, R. K. 1988. "Sustainability, Resource Conservation and Pollution Control: An Overview." in Turner, R. K. (ed.). *Sustainable Environmental Management: Principles and Practice.* London: Belhaven Press.

Vancouver City Planning Commission. 1990. *Clouds of Change: Vancouver and the Changing Atmosphere.* VCPC Task Force on Atmospheric Change.

Vertinsky, I., and S. J. Tan. 1987. *Strategic Management of International Financial Centres: A Tale of Two Cities.* Draft MS: Faculty of Commerce and Business Administration, University of British Columbia, Vancouver and the National University of Singapore.

Appendix 3.1: Indices of B.C. Regional Specialization

As an alternative to a comparison of the labour force profiles displayed in Table 3.5, differences in economic structures between the three B.C. regions can be delineated by means of the measures of specialization shown in Table 3.A1. The first of these two measures is the location quotient, defined here for a particular sector *i* as

$$LQ_i = \frac{R_i/R}{P_i/(P-R_i)}$$

where R_i is regional employment in sector *i*, R is total regional employment, P_i is provincial employment in sector *i*, and P is total provincial employment. The location quotient for sector *i* is thus the ratio for the proportion of regional employment in the sector to the proportion of the base economy's employment in the sector. It is designed to reveal the extent to which a region under study specialized in a particular activity in comparison with the base economy. In order to accentuate the differences between the three economies, each of the location quotients of Table 3.A1 was "adjusted" by excluding from the base or provincial economy the particular regional economy for which the quotient was constructed.

The previously discussed specialisations are clearly revealed in the Table. For the Vancouver region, the largest location quotients are in the producer service sectors of Business Services and Finance, Insurance and Real Estate. The outstanding location quotient for Victoria is, as expected, for the Government Services sector. The relative specialization of the Interior region in the resource based industries is shown by the region's exceedingly high location quotients in the Forestry and Mining sectors.

A second, complementary measure of economic specialisation is the index of concentration (Hodes et al., 1988). Location quotients by themselves can at times be misleading in that the calculations contain a number of implicit assumptions. The concentration index C_i is here defined as

$$C_i = \sum \frac{(R_i/R - N_i/N)^2}{N_i/N}$$

where N_i and N represent national labour force in sector *i* and total national labour force, respectively. In contrast with the location quotient, the concentration index does not reveal in which sectors the economy specialises. It yields instead an overall index of the degree to which the economy is concentrated or specialised with respect to a base economy. The base economy is here taken to be the B.C. provincial economy. The concentration indices are shown at the bottom of Table 3.A1. Because of the Interior's heavy concentration of labour in Forestry and Victoria's concentration of labour in Government Services, both regions show indices significantly higher than that of Vancouver.

Table 3.A1: Regional Economic Specialization in B.C., 1986

Industry	Location Quotients		
	Vancouver	Victoria	B.C. Interior
Agriculture	.33	.44	3.51
Fishing & Trapping	.43	1.12	2.15
Forestry	.10	.45	9.46
Mining	.17	.16	7.47
Manufacturing	.99	.43	1.23
Construction	1.01	.96	1.00
Trans. & Storage	1.20	.58	.95
Comm. & Other Utility	1.40	.80	.75
Wholesale Trade	1.81	.59	.62
Retail Trade	.99	1.06	.99
Finance, Ins.& Real Est.	1.82	.87	.54
Business Services	2.26	1.12	.37
Gov. Services	.63	3.05	.90
Educational Services	.92	1.16	1.04
Health & Soc. Service	1.08	1.40	.81
Accom., Food & Bev.	.94	1.05	1.05
Other Services	1.28	1.02	.76
Concentration Index:	**8.8**	**28.3**	**36.9**

Appendix 3.2: A Shift-Share Analysis of the B.C. Economy

In looking at future growth potential of the province's three regional economies, an alternative to simply observing past rates of growth is to apply shift-share analysis. While there is good reason not to rely too heavily on the results of this particular analytic approach, the technique does promote the organization of the data in such a way as to highlight the factors accounting for differences in regional growth rates and thus provides some grounds for future expectations.

To compare the three economies, the provincial economy is taken as the benchmark or base economy. In Table 3.A2, the 1981-86 labour force expansion of each of the three regional economies has been disaggregated into the three shift-share components: provincial share, industrial mix, and regional shift. The provincial share component (PS) is the amount by which total labour force in the region would have increased over the period of analysis if it had expanded at the same rate as did the provincial total labour force.The provincial share component

Table 3.A2: Regional Shift-Share Components, 1981-1986

Industry	Vancouver			Victoria			B.C. Interior		
	PS	IM	RS	PS	IM	RS	PS	IM	RS
Agriculture	8,368	1,416	431	1,254	212	114	24,209	4,097	-545
Fishing & Trapping	2,464	635	-379	686	177	-17	3,771	972	397
Forestry	4,752	136	-998	1,661	48	-38	33,267	952	1,036
Mining	3,798	-761	-112	273	-55	77	20,132	-4,033	36
Manufacturing	106,562	-16,759	1,267	9,075	-1,427	-573	96,566	-15,187	-694
Construction	49,269	-9,991	6,873	9,268	-1,879	172	54,213	-10,994	-7,044
Trans. & Storage	49,981	-1,452	-2,534	4,698	-136	-207	30,294	-880	2,741
Comm. & Other Utility	27,058	-648	592	3,032	-72	275	16,425	-389	-866
Wholesale Trade	46,676	-5,346	185	3,450	-395	310	21,509	-2,463	-495
Retail Trade	92,939	2,572	-217	16,194	448	542	72,679	2,012	-326
Finance, Ins. & Real Est.	52,279	435	851	6,884	57	-641	21,867	182	-209
Business Services	46,269	4,025	-404	5,239	456	1,180	13,805	1,201	-776
Gov. Services	41,747	-1,638	-760	23,898	-938	-650	37,215	-1,460	1,410
Educational Services	45,031	-2,330	-761	9,337	-483	-324	35,844	-1,855	1,086
Health & Soc. Service	57,572	5,528	-2,176	12,514	1,202	-201	34,569	3,320	2,376
Accom., Food & Bev.	46,649	8,273	3,803	9,300	1,649	-139	44,833	7,951	-3,664
Other Services	42,792	18,771	1,552	7,527	3,302	-1,008	26,298	11,536	-543
Total	**724,209**	**2,875**	**7,211**	**124,289**	**2,165**	**-1,129**	**587,497**	**-5,039**	**-6,083**

of the change in regional labour force between the past period *t-1* and the present period *t* is defined as

$$PS = \sum R_i{}^{t-1}(P^t/P^{t-1})$$

The industrial mix component (IM) is that portion of the change in regional labour force attributable to the difference between the region's industrial mix and that of the province.

$$IM = \sum R_i{}^{t-1}(P_i{}^t/P_i{}^{t-1} - P^t/P^{t-1})$$

The regional shift component (RS) is that portion of the change in regional labour force attributable to the difference between the region's and province's corresponding sectoral growth rates (i.e., to the region's advantage and disadvantage relative to the rest of the province).

$$RS = \sum i R_i{}^{t-1}(R_i{}^t/R_i{}^{t-1} - P_i{}^t/P_i{}^{t-1})$$

Total regional labour force at time t = PS + IM + RS.

From the results shown in Table 3.A2 it can be seen that over the intercensus period 1981-86, the Vancouver economy displays both positive industrial mix and regional shift components. The industrial mix for Victoria is also positive, but the region suffers a negative shift component. Both the mix and shift components for the Interior are negative.

The provincial share component for Vancouver reveals that the 1986 total labour force in the region would have been 724,209 had the region grown at the same rate as did the province. The actual labour force for that year exceeded this figure by 10,086, however, due to the positive mix component and, particularly, to the positive regional share component. Given the region's growth in total labour force over the late 1980's, it is reasonable to expect the magnitude of this component in the next (1986-1991) intercensus period to be even larger, with an increase in the proportional contribution to the expansion from the producer services.

Like Vancouver, Victoria's provincial share component exceeded its recorded 1986 total labour force. The region grew slightly more rapidly over the 1981-86 period than did the province. With its orientation toward the services, it too enjoyed a favourable industrial mix but, unlike Vancouver, it suffered a negative regional share component. Among the significant contributors to the unfavourable share component were Other Services, Government Services, F.I.R.E., and Manufacturing, all of which expanded at rates lower than those of the same sectors at the provincial level.

For the B.C. Interior regional economy, both the industrial mix and regional share components were negative. The unfavorable mix component is attributable in large part to the region's relative concentration of its labour force in the Manufacturing and Construction sectors. The latter sector also contributed heavily to the region's negative share component, declining by over 28.5 percent, twice that of the provincial rate of the decline over the period.

In sum, relative to the other two regions of the province Vancouver possesses both a favourable industrial mix and a set of sectoral comparative advantages that bode well for future economic performance.

4

Implications of the Processes of Erosion and Sedimentation for Sustainable Development in the Fraser River Basin

Olav Slaymaker

The implications of the concept of sustainable development as advanced in the Brundtland Report (WCED, 1987) are far-reaching. For the purpose of this discussion, the most important outcome has been a renewed emphasis on the necessity of making decisions on the basis of understanding the behaviour of both biophysical and socio-economic systems. In reviewing what is known about the biophysical processes of erosion and sedimentation in the Fraser River Basin and their socio-economic implications, one cannot but be impressed by the huge amount of information available, the disparate sources from which data can be found and the scarcity of attempts to juxtapose the data. The concept of sustainable development requires that the data be not only juxtaposed, but that they be integrated and understood together. This chapter takes a tentative step towards such a goal.

Processes of erosion and sedimentation are of fundamental importance to our understanding of large river basins. The removal of soil under the influence of gravity, running water and human agency from upstream areas of the Fraser River Basin, the storage of some of this soil en route to the sea and the net loss of soil into the Strait of Georgia constitute the core subject matter. Some aspects of the processes considered involve danger and loss of life; others add substantial costs to industry and agriculture as a result of water quality deterioration; others add benefits from accretion and nutrient enrichment and yet others have nuisance value only. From a purely economic perspective, soil erosion and sedimentation are of major concern in fisheries, forestry, agriculture and recreation (Slaymaker and Lavkulich, 1977). Forest productivity, fish habitat, road maintenance and security of recreational properties (e.g., Whistler Village development) are obvious examples of problems to which an understanding of erosion and sedimentation contributes. The dominant land use of the province, namely forestry, contributes to erosion problems through poor road construction, side casting, poor culverting, skid roads, logging across streams, large debris in streams leading to debris torrents, debris in dry ravines subject to flashfloods during rain on snow events and in many other ways (Sidle et al., 1985).

The dimensions of the problem are more than just economic. The various mechanisms responsible for removal of unconsolidated surface material differ in terms of their magnitude, rapidity, continuity over space and time and in their frequency of occurrence. Low magnitude, slow, continuously operating mechanisms (such as soil creep) present entirely different policy, management and planning questions as compared with high magnitude, rapid, discontinuous and rare mechanisms (such as the Hope Slide or volcanic eruptions at the head of Bridge River and Meager Creek, headwaters of the Lillooet River). In the context of sustainable development, all such material removal and storage mechanisms should be considered whether as aspects of hazard protection or of risk acceptance. In broaching these questions, attention is directed to the relevance of examining temporal and spatial scales of activity that are too often neglected.

The broad question that is posed is whether human intervention is necessary for, or consistent with, the sustainable development of the Fraser River Basin, as opposed to consciously allowing natural processes to take their course. There are two broad sets of principles that are commonly applied when it is thought necessary to carry out engineering works involving erosion and sedimentation (Vanoni, 1975):

(i)　In small watersheds, to use each hectare within its capacity for sustained use without deterioration of the soil resource; to develop a combination of land use practices and structural measures to control water movement; and to preserve a balance between the needs of;
　　　- each hectare,
　　　- the small watershed, and
　　　- the larger river basin to which it is tributary.

(ii)　In stream channels, to understand the fluvial morphology and present depositional environment; to maintain stream gradient; to strengthen banks to resist flowing water; to create bank roughness to reduce velocity; to divert flow from erodible banks; and to convey the water and sediment with maximum efficiency.

These are principles that guide responsible engineering practice and address the question of sustainability after the decision to intervene has been made. But what of the question whether intervention was really necessary? Decisions involving erosion and sedimentation here include consideration of intangible and ethical values that are difficult to reflect in dollar estimates of costs and benefits.

Finally, it should be pointed out that examining these issues in the Fraser Basin is particularly interesting, because it is a very active system and contains within it examples of land related natural hazards that are spectacular by comparison with river basins east of the Rocky Mountains. The reasons for exceptional activity of these biophysical processes in the Fraser Basin are at least threefold: (a) the high relief which encourages active slope and channel processes, (b) receding glaciers which are making sediment available to the river systems, and (c) the extensive distribution of unconsolidated Pleistocene sediments that cover up the bedrock of the Basin.

In order to broach the question of sustainable development specifically with respect to erosion and sedimentation, a modified definition of sustainable development is introduced into the discussion as "the maintenance, for this and succeeding generations, of an adequate quantity of land with the required qualities to support indefinitely the full range of societal demands which depend on the land resource base. These demands include the support of special esthetic values" (Manning, 1986). The management of the land resource of the Fraser River Basin requires (a) clarification of the general principles governing land response to stress, whether biophysical or socio-economic (b) identification of biophysical and socio-economic pressure points and (c) development of policy or policies at appropriate scales.

The objectives of the chapter are thus:

(i) to present a simple typology of soil removal and storage in the Fraser River Basin.

(ii) to locate the most obvious sensitive sites in the Basin.

(iii) to place the discussion of Fraser Basin sustainable development into an expanded time scale. Basin-wide policies should recognize the chain of events that is set in motion by physical disturbance of land in different parts of the Fraser River Basin.

General Principles

Questions related to material removal and storage can be examined using a sediment budget approach. A sediment budget is simply an accounting procedure that quantifies the sediment additions to, substractions from and storages in a specified control volume, in this case the Fraser River Basin. The approach is sufficiently general so as to allow the treatment of both human and biophysical effects. Dietrich and Dunne (1978), Swanson et al. (1982) and Roberts and Church (1986) provide local examples of how the effects of forestry practices superimposed on natural processes can be evaluated by means of a sediment budget approach. Over any arbitrary time period (Δt) a sediment budget can be expressed as:

$$Q_o = Q_i + \frac{\Delta s}{\Delta t} \qquad \text{where}$$

Q_o and Q_i are the sediment output and input respectively and Δs is the net change in storage. The approach has never been applied quantitatively to a basin as large

Table 4.1: Sediment Sources and Storage in the Lillooet River Basin

	Sediment Source (10³ma⁻¹)					Sediment Storage (10⁶m³)					
	Debris Flows	Landslides	Glaciers	Total	Mean	Channel	Floodplain	Fans	Fluvial Terraces	Debris Flow Terraces	Landslides
1	0	0	30-150	30-150	90	5	14	1	0	0	0
2	43-132	0-35	15-75	58-242	150	2	1	17	20	6	850
Meager	39-77	30-75	10-50	79-202	141	2	1	6	0	2	410
3	17-52	0	10-50	27-102	64	16	51	9	5	0	0
4	3-14	0	0	3-14	8	7	72	4	0	0	0
5	26-92	0	15-75	41-167	104	6	186	7	0	0	0
Green	15-60	0	20-100	35-160	98	1	7	4	0	0	30
6	0	0	0	0	0	3	57	2	0	0	0
Total	143-427	30-110	100-500	273-1037	655	42	389	50	25	8	1,290
Years of sediment yield from basin*						38**	350**	45	23	7	1,170

Source: Jordan and Slaymaker, in press.

Notes:

*   Sediment yield = 1.1 x 10⁶m³a⁻¹ at Lillooet River delta.

**   These are good estimates of residence time since all coarse sediment generated in the Basin passes through these sediment reservoirs.

as that of the Fraser. A recent study by Jordan and Slaymaker (1991) examines the Lillooet River Basin in these terms. The Basin of over 3,000 km^2 is divided into eight sectors and sediment sources and storages are evaluated for each sector (Table 4.1). For details, the original paper should be consulted and Figure 4.5 identifies locational details, but a number of points can be emphasised here. Even in this small subsystem of the Fraser Basin (1.5% of its total area), the spatial variations are huge, levels of uncertainty are high and the residence times of sediments are high. The average turnover time of the sediment reservoir in this very active and steep part of the Fraser Basin is several hundreds of years; therefore, by implication, the turnover time in the Fraser River Basin is of the order of thousands to tens of thousands of years. The time scale that needs to be seriously considered in a sediment hazard investigation is very much different than the standard engineering project time scale. The value of this approach for the present discussion is that it forces us to ask a number of questions, of which some are listed here:

(i)   Where and what are the sediment storage reservoirs that must be considered?

(ii)   In what ways are these reservoirs modified over time?

(iii)   What are the appropriate time and spatial scales at which to conduct the sediment budget?

The whole approach is, of course, analogous to that which is conventionally used in water resource management for water balance calculations, but it is intrinsically more complicated because of the longer time scales and spatial discontinuities of sediment removal.

Identification of Sediment Storage Reservoirs

First, and most extensive, is the so-called valley fill. This includes glaciolacustrine, glaciofluvial, glaciomarine, glacial and fluvial deposits, all of which are unconsolidated, and which were left behind postglacially in and close to the main trunk valleys (Figure 4.1). These materials were laid down during the last two million years and the vast majority of those exposed at the surface derive from the last period of deglaciation when the upland areas became ice free and remnants of ice blocked portions of the trunk valleys (Fulton, 1969). In post-glacial times, notably since 9,000 years B.P., the Fraser and its tributaries have incised into these sediments. Ongoing erosion of these valley fills provides an important sediment source to the Fraser River (Slaymaker and McPherson, 1977).

A second storage reservoir is that of the numerous alluvial fans distributed widely throughout the interior of the Fraser Basin and located at or close to the break of slope between mountain front and plateau or valley fill surface. Although they are too small and geographically discontinuous to be shown on a map of the Basin, they represent large volumes of stored fluvial sediment that have been largely stable over the past 9,000 years (Ryder, 1971).

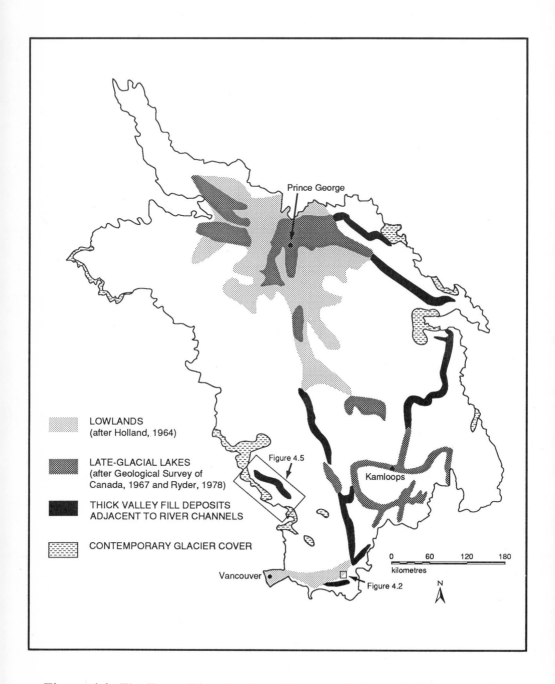

LOWLANDS
(after Holland, 1964)

LATE-GLACIAL LAKES
(after Geological Survey of
Canada, 1967 and Ryder, 1978)

THICK VALLEY FILL DEPOSITS
ADJACENT TO RIVER CHANNELS

CONTEMPORARY GLACIER COVER

Prince George

Figure 4.5

Kamloops

Vancouver

Figure 4.2

0   60   120   180
kilometres

N

Figure 4.1: The Fraser River Basin and Pressure Points with Respect to the
Sediment Problem

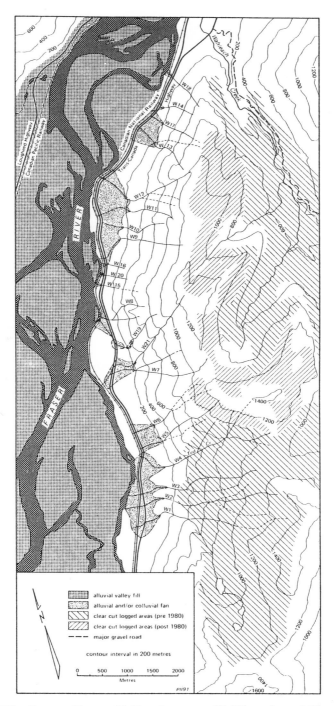

Figure 4.2: The Lower Fraser Valley between Chilliwack and Hope, Illustrating a Variety of Sediment Sources and Storage Resevoirs

A third storage reservoir is that of debris flow fans and runout zones from slides. They are also widely distributed throughout the Fraser Basin wherever a gently sloping surface abuts against a mountain front. This reservoir, by contrast with the alluvial fans, continues to accumulate and has been accumulating over the past 9,000 years (Figure 4.2).

A final storage reservoir consists of all the colluvial material that covers most of the tributary slopes of the Basin in which our mountain soils are developing. Although the depth of this material is frequently one metre or less, it represents a reservoir of the order of one hundred km^3 basin wide.

All these sediment reservoirs are geographically discrete and linkages are provided by water flows over, through or adjacent to the sediments. During low flow periods in the major rivers, sediments are moved into adjacent channels by bank undercutting and dry ravelling from steep banks, so that valley fills are the dominant source of sediments. During high flow periods, active bank erosion and river channel migration occurs and this activity also focusses on the valley fills. Periods of heavy rain or high intensity rainstorm events are necessary to activate the fans, slide material and colluvium or alternatively intensive freeze-thaw activity or even earthquake activity may be involved, such as is implicated in the Hope slide (Mathews and McTaggart, 1969).

Modification of Reservoirs Over Time

Low Magnitude, Slow, Continuously Operating Processes

Slow deformation of soil on steep hillslopes is an almost universal phenomenon in the Fraser Basin. It is evidenced by terracettes or step-like features which are most obviously expressed in the landscape in unforested areas such as the semi-arid interior around Ashcroft and Kamloops and the alpine areas above timberline. Such a process is estimated to contribute a small amount of sediment from an individual slope, but is more effective on a basin wide scale because of its ubiquity. Sedimentation in the Fraser Estuary is the storage analogue of the creep removal mechanism. Dredging costs are well known, but benefits deriving from additions of land should also be considered.

Low Magnitude, Slow, Discontinuously Operating, Frequent Processes

In certain materials, notably in silts laid down in formerly more extensive lakes and in certain glacial deposits, a phenomenon known as piping or tunnel erosion occurs. This process involves collapse and gullying leading to undermining of house foundations. In the Kamloops region, the process has been accelerated because of urbanization and intensive application of irrigation water on benchlands. The problem has become so serious that restrictions on development have had to be imposed in some areas.

Needle ice erosion is a frequent event in alpine meadows and along trails in mountainous areas. It is thought to be the major reason for degradation of intensively used fragile mountain ecosystems. The frequency of occurrence is accelerated by removal of vegetation. This may be achieved by trampling (Mt. Robson or Mt. Garibaldi Provincial Parks), by deliberate vegetation removal or by poor trail construction and/or maintenance.

Low/Intermediate Magnitude, Slow, Discontinuously Operating, Rare Processes

Earthflows are a characteristic feature of the Interior Plateau region of the Fraser Basin. In particular, the so-called Dryloch Slide (Thompson Valley), the Pavilion Earthflow (near Hat Creek) and a series of spectacular features in the middle Fraser, south of Williams Lake are textbook examples of such phenomena. Although they are large features in the landscape, their average rate of movement is not much greater than that of soil creep. In the cases of Drynoch Slide and Pavilion Earthflow, the intersection of their bases by highway construction has accelerated motion by two orders of magnitude and substantial costs in terms of road maintenance have resulted.

Large Magnitude, Rapid, Continuously Operating Processes

The removal of material by rivers in dissolved form is substantial. Although concentrations of dissolved solids may be low in the humid mountainous rim of the Basin, a large mass of dissolved material is transported and exported through the Fraser River. This may seem to be a minor problem, but it has interesting ramifications for water quality in the low flow Fraser tributaries such as the Nicola and Bonaparte, where dissolved substance concentrations are up to two orders of magnitude greater than in the mountain rim tributaries. When the transport of pollutants, resulting from intensive land use, and the cycling of nutrients and their interaction with sediments in forest ecosystems are added to the discussion, there are substantial management implications.

Large Magnitude, Rapid, Discontinuously Operating, Frequent Processes

The processes of river bank and bed erosion are responsible for the largest volumes of material moved over the greatest distances over periods of years or longer. For example, Fraser River deposits at its delta every four years the same amount of material as was brought down in the Hope Slide in January, 1965. Management costs of dredging the Fraser channel downstream from New Westminster are only a small fraction of the basin wide damage costs of normal channel deepening and widening by fluvial action upstream. Every year, the Annual Report of the B.C. Ministry of Environment reports costs incurred from river erosion on the Lillooet River, North Thompson, Shuswap, Nechako, Nicola, Coquihalla and Coquitlam rivers.

Specific costs associated with large suspended sediment loads occur in the Bridge River system. Wear and tear on the hydroelectric power generating turbines at Seton Lake, and rapid sedimentation in Downton Lake which is reducing the effective life of that reservoir, are just two examples.

Human occupance of alluvial flood plains and alluvial fans (e.g., Lillooet and Vedder Rivers), encroachments and crossings of rivers by highways, railways, pipelines and river control works (e.g., Coquihalla River), dredging, borrowing and placer mining (Coquitlam, Lower Fraser), reservoir sedimentation (Downton, Carpenter), upstream and downstream effects associated with water control (Carpenter, Downton, Nechako), and estuary sedimentation are the major types of problems resulting from bank and bed erosion.

Further issues, which are thought to affect tributary basins and not the main Fraser River, have to do with specific land use effects. Forestry, agricultural land use and mining will have distinctive impacts. Fish habitat, as influenced by fine sediment production, is of increasing concern in all areas of the Basin, but most particularly in areas immediately downstream from logging operations.

Large Magnitude, Rapid, Discontinuously Operating, Rare Processes

From a management and sustainable development perspective, these are the most difficult problems to assess. The heart of the problem is that such occurrences can be predicted only rarely.

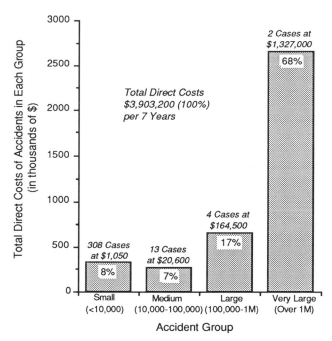

Figure 4.3: Distribution of Rockfall-Related Accident Costs, B.C. Rail System (1980-1987). (Hungr and Evans, 1989).

Debris floods and debris torrents, widely reported in B.C., have a recurrence interval of perhaps 20-100 years in debris torrent prone sites. If there are 1,000 debris torrent prone sites and a recurrence interval at each site of 100 years, there may well be 10 events somewhere in the region every year. Where they intersect transport corridors or human settlements and where they reduce forest productivity they will be costly or hazardous. The eastern end of the Fraser Valley and Coquihalla Valley have attracted most recent interest. Log jams are often associated with the initiation of debris torrents. The western rim of the Fraser Basin is most affected.

Jokulhlaups (or glacier dam bursts) are reported most frequently from the northwestern corner of B.C., but they are also important in the Coast, Cariboo and Rocky Mountains.

Rockfalls and slides (such as Hope Slide and Devastation Glacier Slide) have been responsible for rather few fatalities, but massive disruption of transportation and energy corridors (e.g., Figure 4.3). The recurrence interval of the Hope Slide is estimated at 5,000 years (on the basis of 2 post-glacial events). The probability of accidental fatality is extremely low (Table 4.2) but is rising over time (Hungr and Evans, 1989).

Seismic activity is evident from the geological column, and post-glacial faulting is not uncommon. But the Fraser River Basin seems to occupy a zone which has been less seismically active historically than would be predicted from its setting close to the edge of two continental plates. This may be a case where past frequency of occurrence is misleading. The occurrence of a mega-earthquake resulting from long term build up of stress is being seriously entertained (Rogers, 1988).

Table 4.2: Probability of Accidental Life Loss in Canada

Cause	Basis	Annual Probability per Capita	Source
Small Scale Rockfall	13 in 87 years	1×10^{-8}	Hungr and Evans 1989
Large Rockslide-Avalanche	190 in 87 years	1.4×10^{-7}	Hungr and Evans 1989
Lightning Strike	?	2.0×10^{-7}	Morgan 1986
Snow Avalanche	7/year	3.5×10^{-7}	Stethem and Schaerer 1979, 1980
Car Travel (B.C. 1984)	—	3.0×10^{-4}	Morgan 1986

Volcanism in the Fraser Basin should also be considered seriously. Quaternary volcanic activity has been substantial but the most recent activity inside the Basin was 2,500 years B.P.

Time and Spatial Scale Considerations

Time Scale

The time scale used in sediment budgeting has a major influence on the conclusions drawn. If, for example, the time scale for the adjustment of sediment reservoirs is very long, then sequences of net gain or net loss of sediment to the Fraser Basin will be impossible to detect in short-term data. Because sediments that were laid down as valley fill up to 13,000 years ago are still in storage, removal and redistribution of sediments over the Basin over shorter time scales have to be viewed as transient and not equilibrium responses to contemporary climatic, hydrologic and geomorphic conditions (Church and Slaymaker, 1989). The implication of these findings is that sediment budgeting at a basin wide scale should be integrated over the whole of the Holocene period. Alternatively, it can be argued that the impact of logging in the McGregor Basin on the Lower Fraser River Basin is, in principle, not detectable over normal planning and management time scales. McLean (1990) has argued that the appropriate time scale for studying the redistribution of gravelly bed material by the Fraser River between Hope and Mission City is 10-30 years and that shorter time periods do not permit a satifactory analysis.

Space Scale

Response times of smaller tributary drainage basins of the Fraser Basin are, of course, correspondingly shorter than those for the Basin as a whole. The problem is that exact response times are not known. What is clear is that if we wish to evaluate the impacts of land use on sediment removal, then small basins as close to the point of impact as possible must be selected. Alternatively, for the case of lowland rivers such as the Lower Fraser itself, where most sediment transfers result from ongoing bank erosion and deposition, a steady state assumption for the 190 kilometre reach from Yale to the sea over 10-100 years is probably reasonable—namely an assumption that the morphology of the Fraser River and its floodplain varies about a mean value which is unaffected by climate or land use changes. The assumption is falsifiable, probably reasonable at the scale specified but has not been demonstrated to be the case. (See below for a potential upset of this assumption.) In general, the time interval required to meet the steady state assumption will be directly proportional to the transit time.

Sensitive Sites in the Fraser River Basin

In a recent study (Kellerhals, 1985), sediment problems in B.C. were divided into two broad categories. They were (i) issues in which cumulative sediment transfer is the main concern and (ii) issues in which water quality is the primary concern. Under the first category were included floodplain occupancy, including encroachments and river training, dredging and borrowing of sand and gravel, reservoirs, upstream and downstream effects of flow regulation and estuarine problems. Under the second were forestry, agriculture and mining impacts, fisheries and general water quality. Figure 4.1 above provides an indication of the major parts of the Fraser Basin under pressure from these varied sediment problems.

Lower Fraser Valley

The Lower Fraser Valley is the focus of much activity with respect to sediment problems in the Fraser River Basin. All aspects of the sediment problem, whether cumulative sediment transfer or water quality, are of concern in this region. Dyke construction, erosion control structures and dredging and gravel mining are various responses to and aspects of the problem. Following the flood of 1948, a major programme of dyke construction was initiated (see Smith, this volume); by 1978, this was substantially completed. Dyke construction has had a major influence on the back channels in the floodplain. Filling by fine sediments and vegetative encroachment has been characteristic. Bank protection via revetments and rip rap river training structures has been another aspect of the work of the Fraser River Joint Advisory Board, on which an average of $4-12 million has been expended per year since 1978. Dredging and gravel mining has averaged about 120,000 m^3 per year since 1973 and reached 230,000 m^3 in 1982 (Kellerhals, 1985). This is potentially a problem of sustainability, in that the best estimates suggest that only 150,000 m^3 of gravel are added from upstream each year. The annual deficit of sediment can effect the equilibrium of the river in such a way that the long-term adjustment of the fluvial morphology will be disrupted. For example, a period of rapid lateral bank erosion may be initiated, posing a threat to flood plain residents in the immediate vicinity.

Problems in the Lower Fraser Valley derive from the fact that the Fraser River is flowing over its own aggradational valley fill. If the river were more deeply incised, lateral channel shift would be less probable; but because, especially from Hope to Chilliwack, it is not incised, river bank stabilization and erosion costs are high. The Chilliwack River has formed a vast post-glacial alluvial fan superimposed on the Fraser alluvial sediments and so further channel migration and bank stabilization problems arise. In addition, debris flow fans and slide run out zones, which are actively forming both on the north and south sides of the eastern Fraser Valley, cause disruption of road and rail lines (see Figure 4.2 above).

The fact of dense human occupance of the alluvial flood plains of the lower Fraser and of the alluvial fan of Vedder River, the encroachments and crossings of tributaries by highways, railways, pipelines and river control works and the dredging and borrowing in Fraser River and Coquitlam River combine to make the Lower Fraser the major sediment problem area in the Basin.

The Coquitlam, Chilliwack and Coquihalla Rivers provide the most challenging sediment related problems among Lower Fraser tributaries. The Pitt, Alouette, Stave and Lillooet have minimal impact on the Lower Fraser because of the large lakes into which they flow.

Fraser and Thompson Canyons

The Drynoch slide in the Thompson valley moves slowly but continuously towards the Trans-Canada Highway; the costs of road maintenance are substantial. The most damaging events both in terms of deaths and economic impacts are frequent, small precipitation-triggered debris flows and rock slope movements (Figure 4.4). They have formed 61% of the known damaging landslides in B.C. from 1858 to 1983 (84 such events have been documented by Evans and Clague, 1988).

Canadian National Railway's yearly budget for rockfall prevention, in British Columbia has been approximately one to two million dollars since 1971, most of which has been spent in the Fraser and Thompson Canyons. The B.C. Ministry of Transportation and Highways yearly budget for rockfall prevention such as scaling and rock cut stabilization, is 3 - 3.5 million dollars. It is not known how much of this is accounted for by the Fraser and Thompson canyons but probably at least 25%.

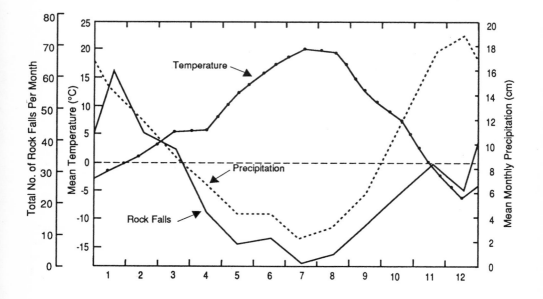

Figure 4.4: Rockfall Frequency Variations with Seasons in Fraser Canyon, B.C. (Peckover and Kerr, 1977)

A small rock fall at Hell's Gate in the Fraser Canyon during construction of the Canadian National Railway in 1914 had an effect on the Fraser River salmon fishing from which it has perhaps not yet recovered. The debris obstructed migrating salmon in their cyclic return to spawning grounds. The loss in 1978 dollars to the sockeye and pink salmon fishing amounted to $2,600 million for the period 1951-1978 (International Pacific Salmon Fish Committee, 1980; Ellis, 1989).

Sediment related problems in the canyons are quite different than those of the lower Fraser Valley. They result from the active dissection by the Fraser and Thompson Rivers of their bedrock gorges; also, the undercutting of bedrock slopes by road and rail construction has accentuated the rock fall, landslide and debris flow hazard.

Other Pressure Points

Kamloops and Thompson Valley

Urbanization in Kamloops has taken place almost exclusively on the valley fill which consists of (a) the glaciolacustrine material underlying the benchlands and (b) fluvial and fluvioglacial materials of the North Thompson, South Thompson and Thompson River floodplains. Piping occurs predominantly in the glaciolacustrine sediments. The floodplain of the Thompson River experiences similar bank erosion problems to those of the Lower Fraser.

Slides in Pleistocene sediments present a major hazard. Evans (1984) has documented five slides between 1880 and 1921 which blocked the Thompson River between Ashcroft and Spences Bridge. The river was blocked for 44 hours in October, 1880.

Pemberton - River Training and Delta Growth

In response to the biggest flood on record (October, 1940) the Prairie Farm Rehabilitation Administration carried out a massive river training project on the Lillooet River. During the 1946-1951 period, 38 km (24 mi) of dykes, 14 km (9 mi) of river cutoffs, 27 km (17 mi) of ditches and 14 km (9 mi) of service and construction roads were completed in the valley of the Lillooet River. At the same time, the high water level of Lillooet Lake was lowered by 2 1/2 m (8 ft). The net effect of the river training and the lake level lowering was an increase in the average gradient of the Lillooet River over a 50 km (32 mi) reach from 0.0008 to 0.001 (Slaymaker and Gilbert, 1972). Since 1953, the river has degraded considerably so that farmers now need to irrigate land that formerly had a high water table. At the same time, total sediment discharged into Lillooet Lake has increased, and the flood hazard appears to have increased significantly, partly as a result of the aggradation of the lower reaches of the floodplain. What was originally conceived as a flooding problem is now seen to be primarily a sediment problem. A number of problem areas tributary to the Lillooet River are Ryan Creek, Miller Creek, Soo and Rutherford Rivers (Figure 4.5).

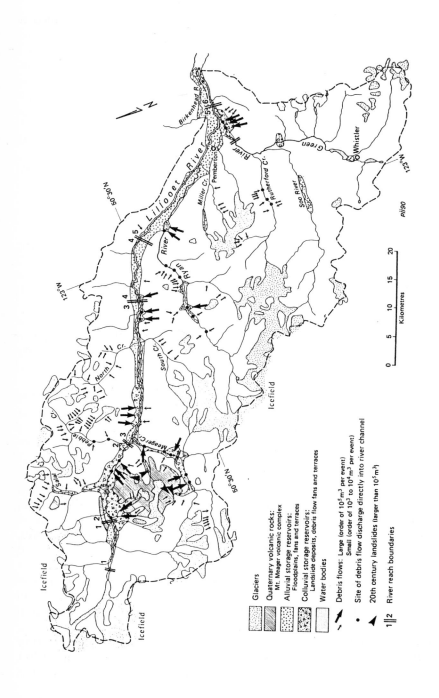

Figure 4.5: Lillooet River Watershed: Sediment Sources and Storage Resevoirs (Jordan and Slaymaker, 1991)

Middle and Upper Fraser

In the middle Fraser River valley, major inputs of sediment can be ascribed to bank erosion (Kidd, 1953). Glacial drift, extensive aggradational sand and gravel and lake silt banks border the river from Williams Lake to Lillooet, and provide a ready sediment source. There are also major earth flow problems along the west bank of the Fraser which are responsible for the dislocation of Forest Service roads and force occasional rerouting of road networks. In the Lillooet region, landslides, rockslides and washouts occur regularly around Gold Bridge and Duffey Lake.

Between Prince George and the source of the Fraser, landslides have disrupted traffic and required expensive remedial measures on a recurring basis over the past two decades. The incidence of freeze-thaw events and icings causes both road break-up and unexpected flooding.

The Mountain Rim

Volcanic activity has occurred during the Quaternary in three regions of the Fraser Basin—the Garibaldi volcanic belt, the Fraser Plateau volcanic cones and the Columbia Highlands. The greatest hazard is probably associated with the headwaters of the Bridge and Lillooet Rivers, but renewed volcanism is improbable over the short term.

Because glacier ice is widespread in the Coast Mountains, the occurrence of dramatic floods and sediment transporting events associated with the draining of glacially dammed lakes is most common on the western fringes of the Basin. However fatalities and costs have also been recorded in the Rocky Mountains during the 1980's.

Mounts Cayley and Meager are Quaternary volcanic centres with superposed glaciers. In these mountains, three major slope failures have occurred since 1930, most recently the Devastation Creek slide of 1975 which carried $26 \times 10^6 m^3$ of material. The slide generated a debris flow which killed four BC Hydro employees.

Debris flows and torrents have caused increasing concern over the past decade. There are four environmental factors which affect the occurrence of debris torrents: drainage area, channel gradient, runoff intensity and availability of debris that can be mobilized. As many as 153 potential debris torrent sites have been mapped alongside 48 km of the Trans Canada and Coquihalla Highways. Curiously enough, there is no systematic or preferred association of unstable sites with forest roads or clear cuts.

Little hard information on the implications of trampling and high density use for Fraser River Basin parks is available. It is however clear from experience, in Europe for example, that careful planning needs to take environmental degradation into account (Briand et al., 1989).

Logging roads, landings and skid trails associated with forest harvesting accentuate sediment problems. In the Lillooet River Basin between 1945 and 1969, 20,000 acres were logged. The average acreage logged per year since 1969 has been twelve times as great as in the late 1940's. Yet again there is a lamentable lack of regional information on the effects of logging on slope stability and sediment production in the Fraser Basin.

Fraser River Basin and Sustainable Development: Implications of the Physical Disturbance of Land in the Context of Climate Change

The Fraser River Basin as a Sediment Planning Unit

The Fraser River Basin is a single functioning system with respect to water resource and flood management, but only in a theoretical sense is this true for sediment management. Water released from snow melt in the Fraser headwaters may arrive at the Fraser Delta in a matter of one week; certainly, for all practical purposes, the effects of runoff generated in distant parts of the Basin are absorbed within a season. Such a view of Fraser River Basin sediment production is only approximately true over geological time scales and is quite misleading if assumed to be true over planning time scales.

It appears to be the case that much of the sediment that was exposed or produced from under the Pleistocene ice sheets 13,000 years ago is still on its way through the Fraser Basin and is hung up in a number of storage reservoirs on its way to the ocean. Because the volume of this material basin wide is so large by comparison with that which is being exposed or produced by natural processes or land use activities at the present time, the effects of contemporary activities and processes are not detectable from monitored sediment transfer information or observable channel changes. Looked at from another perspective, we can say with some confidence that the effects of logging in the McGregor Basin cannot be detected in the sediment load or channel behaviour of the lower Fraser, nor, for example, did the effects of the Hope Slide in 1965 make any direct impact on the lower Fraser.

Most erosional and sedimentation processes function discontinuously over time and space. In this respect they resemble ecosystems more closely than hydrologic and atmospheric systems which are more continuous over time and space. The more discontinuous the process, the more difficult it becomes to aggregate effects over a region or planning unit. Also, the more important become questions of surprise (Holling, 1986) and uncertainty. This argues for rather small scale planning units within the framework of a basin-wide approach.

This first group of implications suggests that the Basin must be viewed as a complex management system. Regional units and site specific planning are necessary to establish the resiliency of different regions and sub-basins to human interference. Basin-wide management is necessary for balanced and sustainable development that takes into account the variable vulnerability of land to the dynamic processes described.

The Holocene as the Relevant Time Frame

In water resources and flood management, predictions, risk analysis and scenario analysis are normally based on climatic and hydrologic record. In the Fraser Basin, such records go back to the 1890's (climate) and 1913 (runoff). But sediment problems are a function not only of climate and hydrology; they are also very sensitive to sediment availability. Given that the period of greatest sediment production and availability occurred at the close of the Pleistocene, and that this sediment is still working its way through the Basin, it is clearly necessary to extend our temporal scale of investigation to include the whole of the post-glacial period. Two interesting examples come to mind: those of the Hope Slide and the Lillooet River floodplain. In the case of the Hope Slide, the single event of 1965 provides no basis for prediction of future risk of recurrence. Examination and dating of older landslide material at the same site demonstrates that an earlier slide event had occurred during the Holocene. On the Lillooet River floodplain, evidence of sedimentation events from pre-instrumented periods is available both in the present valley fill and also in the lake bottom sediments of Lillooet Lake.

Such evidence is necessary to make assessments of the risks of inundation, sedimentation and future slide incidence, none of which can be done reliably from climatic and hydrologic records alone.

The main practical implication here is that sustainable development ideas that ignore the Holocene history of the region will surely fail with respect to the sediment problem.

Implications of Land Use and Climate Change

Road construction, logging, urbanization, mining and recreational activity in parks, all of which are intensifying land uses in the Fraser Basin, have direct and costly impacts. But none of these impacts can be detected at the Basin scale. Neither have we reliable and/or comparative data on the benefits produced by these land uses. The benefit cost calculation, which has never been made to my knowledge, must be identified as scale specific. Sustainability is a scale dependent concept; the Basin as a whole can absorb development that will destroy a small headwater tributary basin.

Similarly, it is unlikely that climate change will be recognized from basin scale erosion and sedimentation (Slaymaker, 1990). We would expect to see the effects of climate change most readily at sea level (because of sea level change), in the small fingertip tributaries of the Fraser River (because of the rapid response time of small hydrologic systems) and at timberline (because of the sensitivity of timberline to small climate changes). The Fraser Basin is so heavily buffered that the sediment carried and the erosion performed by the Lower Fraser River is unlikely to respond to climate change of the modest scale envisaged over the next 50 years.

Policy Implications

There are significant gaps in our understanding of the degree of interconnectedness of various aspects of the sediment budget in the Fraser Basin. We have identified and understand the workings of each of the diverse phenomena at the site scale. We recognise that in the mountainous and loose sediment-rich environment of the Basin, the relative importance of natural erosion and sedimentation processes is greater than that in much of the rest of Canada. We also recognise that all kinds of costs of development will be greater here. But we have considerable difficulty in tracking the source of any accelerated erosion from evidence obtained more than a few kilometres from the disturbed site, and we have similar difficulty in assessing the long term costs of development. At the scale of the Fraser Basin, there is considerable uncertainty about the functioning of the sediment system as a whole. In this respect, there is a marked contrast with the water resource system, which is modelled with a high level of accuracy. This high level of uncertainty implies a need for scoping the problem, as we have done in this chapter, and to attempt the construction of alternative kinds of sustainable futures.

A second policy implication is that an understanding of the basin-wide and long-term dynamics of the processes of erosion and sedimentation is essential for sustainable management of the Basin. An integrated land use policy with respect to erosion and sedimentation in the Basin must be sensitive to local, regional and basin-wide variations in the ability of land to absorb the impacts of human activity. The authority to recommend or to assign land for use in sustainable ways and to change land uses that are not sustainable must be vested in a Fraser River Basin management team.

A third policy implication is that regulation of sediment impacts exclusively at the basin scale makes little sense. Smaller units within the Basin need to be defined and management options at sub-regional, local or site specific scale should be considered. Because all land use change has primarily local impacts with respect to sediment transfers, all implementation of land use decisions that impact on erosion and sedimentation should be made at local and sub-regional levels. Nevertheless, this should not be interpreted as an argument against basin-wide integrated land use policy, as discussed above.

A fourth policy implication involves the heightened and more explicit ethical concern that derives from endorsing the concept of sustainable development at the full range of temporal and spatial scales. The ethical implications of accelerated erosion resulting from human intervention in the Fraser River Basin can only be defined in relation to the community for whose benefit sustainable development is being pursued. If it is the local human community, then traditional stewardship criteria will apply (Young, 1990); if the ecological community, then the Leopold land ethic is more relevant (Leopold, 1949); if the planet earth community, then Gaian criteria should be considered (Lovelock, 1988); and if the world community, some version of Brundtland's sustainability criteria would seem to be most appropriate (World Commission on Environment and Development, 1987).

The identification of explicit ethical criteria that can yield appropriate policy guidelines remains a major part of sustainable development's unfinished agenda.

References

Briand, F., M. Dubost, D. Pitt and D. Rambaud. 1989. *The Alps: A System Under Pressure*. Chambéry: International Union for Conservation of Nature and Natural Resources.

Church, M., and O. Slaymaker. 1989. "Disequilibrium of Holocene Sediment Yield in Glaciated British Columbia." *Nature*. 337:452-454.

Dietrich, W. E., and T. Dunne. 1978. "Sediment Budget for a Small Catchment in Mountainous Terrain." *Zeits. Geomorph. Supp. Band*. 29:191-206.

Ellis, D. 1989. *Environments at Risk*. New York: Springer-Verlag.

Evans, S. G. 1984. 1880 landslide dam on Thompson River, near Ashcroft. *Geological Survey of Canada Paper 84-1A*, 655-688.

Evans, S. G. and J. Clague. 1988. Catastrophic Rock Avalanches in Glacial Environments in *Proceedings, 5th International Symposium on Landslides*, Lausanne, 2:1153-1158.

Fulton, R. J. 1969. *Glacial Lake History, Southern Interior Plateau, B.C.* Geological Survey of Canada Paper 69-37.

Holling, C. S. 1986. "The Resilience of Terrestrial Ecosystems: Local Surprise and Global Change." in W. C. Clark and R. E. Munn (eds.). *Sustainable Development of the Biosphere*. New York: Cambridge University Press.

Hungr, O., and S. G. Evans. 1989. *Engineering Aspects of Rockfall Hazards in Canada*. Vancouver: Thurber Consultants.

International Pacific Salmon Fish Committee. 1980. *Hell's Gate Fisherways*. International Pacific Salmon Fish Committee.

Jordan, P. J., and O. Slaymaker. 1991. "Holocene Sediment Production in Lillooet River Basin: A Sediment Budget Approach." *Géographie Physique et Quaternaire*.

Kellerhals Engineering Services. 1985. *Sediment in the Pacific and Yukon Region: Review and Assessment*. Heriot Bay: Inland Waters Directorate Environment Canada.

Kidd, G. J. A. 1953. *Fraser River Suspended Sediment Survey: Interim Report 1947-52*. B.C. Water Resources Report 322. Victoria: Water Rights Branch.

Leopold, A. 1949. *A Sand County Almanac*. New York: Oxford University Press.

Lovelock, J. 1988. *The Ages of Gaia*. Norton. New York.

McLean, D. 1990. *The Relation Between Channel Instability and Sediment Transport on Lower Fraser River*. Unpublished Ph.D. Thesis, Vancouver: U.B.C.

Manning, E. W. 1986. *Towards Sustainable Land Use: A Strategy*. Working Paper 47, Ottawa: Environment Canada.

Mathews, W. H., and K. C. McTaggart. 1969. The Hope Landslide, B.C. Proceedings, *Geological Association of Canada*. 20:65-75.

Morgan, G. C. 1986. "Acceptability of Natural Hazards in Transportation Corridors." in *Transportation Géotechnique*. Vancouver Geotechnical Society.

Peckover, F. L., and J. W. G. Kerr. 1977. Treatment and Maintenance of Rock Slopes on Transportation Routes. *Canadian Geotechnical Journal*. 14:487-507.

Roberts, R. G., and M. Church. 1986. "The Sediment Budget in Severely Disturbed Watersheds, Queen Charlotte Ranges." *Canadian Journal of Forest Research*. 16:1092-1106.

Rogers, G. C. 1988. "An Assessment of the Megathrust Earthquake Potential of the Cascadian Subduction Zone." *Canadian Journal of Earth Science*. 25:844-852.

Ryder, J. M. 1971. "The Stratigraphy and Morphology of Paraglacial Alluvial Fans in Southcentral B.C." *Canadian Journal of Earth Science*. 8:279-298.

Sidle, R. C., A. J. Pearce and C. L. O'Loughlin. 1985. *Hillslope Stability and Land Use*. A.G.U. Water Resources Monograph Series 11, Washington.

Slaymaker, O. 1990. "Climate Change and Erosion Processes in Mountain Regions of Western Canada." *Mountain Research and Development.* 10:171-182.

Slaymaker, O., and R. E. Gilbert. 1972. "Geomorphic Process and Land Use Changes in the Coast Mountains of B.C." in Macar, P. and A. Pissart (eds.). *Processus périglaciaires étudiés sur le terrain.* 269-279.

Slaymaker, O., and L. M. Lavkulich. 1977. *A Review of Land Use-water Quality Interrelationships and a Proposed Method for their Study.* Technical Report 13. Vancouver: Westwater Research Centre, U.B.C.

Slaymaker, O., and H. J. McPherson. 1977. "An Overview of Geomorphic Processes in the Canadian Cordillera." *Zeitschrift fur Geomorphologie.* 21:169-186.

Stethem, C. J., and P. A. Schaerer. 1979-80. Avalanche Accidents in Canada 1943-78. *National Research Council of Canada, Division of Building Research* DBR Papers 834 and 926.

Swanson, F. J., R. J. Janda, T. Dunne and D. N. Swanston. 1982. Sediment Budgets and Routing in Forested Drainage Basins. *U.S. Department of Agriculture Forest Service, P.N.W. Forest and Range Experiment Station General Technical Report.* PNW-141.

Vanoni, V. A. 1975. *Sedimentation Engineering.* New York: American Society of Civil Engineering.

World Commission on Environment and Development (WCED). 1987. *Our Common Future.* Oxford: Oxford University Press.

Young, J. 1990. *Sustaining the Earth.* London: Belhaven.

5

Floodplain Management in the Fraser Basin

Sandra E. Smith

The management of floodplains is not a topic which has attracted much interest in the current worldwide debate about sustainable development stimulated by the Brundtland report (WCED, 1987). But any consideration of the implications of sustainable development principles in the Fraser Basin reveals that, at least in this situation, it is a highly relevant issue.

Put simply, activities on a floodplain cannot be sustained where serious damage from flooding can be expected and where measures to protect against flooding are not taken. While natural ecosystems associated with floodplains have adapted to periodic flooding, this has not always been the case for human activities on the floodplain. Twice in the last hundred years major flooding has occurred and caused significant damage and disruption to people and activities on the floodplain of the Fraser. Lesser but not insignificant damages have occurred in between the major floods and since, even though protection measures have been adopted to reduce the expected damages.

The principles of sustainable development elaborated by Brundtland stress the importance of maintaining the integrity of natural systems in order to keep options open for future generations. Thus, in so far as development on the floodplain involves measures that destroy the integrity of ecosystems associated with floodplains, it is contrary to this imperative. For example, salmon and waterfowl habitats may be destroyed by extensive dyking. In addition to these damages to the floodplain ecosystem, there are underlying and continuing damages from the activities that are being protected such as soil damage from agriculture and blacktopping from urbanization.

Options for floodplain management that respond to the Brundtland imperative are much greater before any development occurs than afterwards. In a watershed that has not yet been developed, consideration can be given to limiting activities in the floodplain to those that are consistent with maintaining natural systems. There are parts of the Fraser Basin where such options still exist. If, however, there is already development in place, the options are fewer and likely involve high costs of adaptation. In a situation like the Lower Fraser Valley, which is hedged in by steep mountains and where there is already major development with accelerating growth pressures, the options are much more constrained.

In either case, however, floodplain management ultimately involves ethical judgements and consideration of tradeoffs between all the costs and benefits associated with its use. From this perspective, floodplain management has to be seen in an integrated resource management context. While this has been recognized for some time, sustainable development concepts as advanced by Brundtland have introduced a new emphasis on the values to be considered.

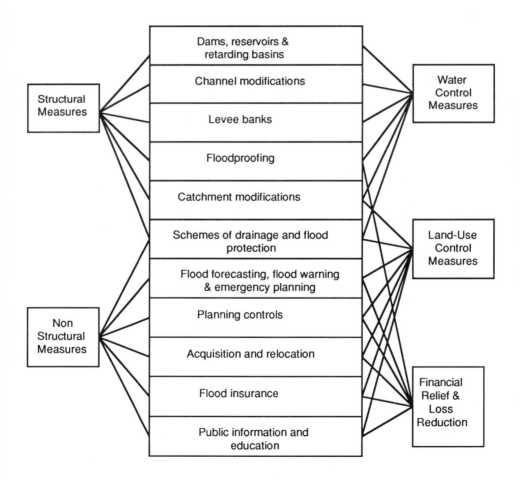

Figure 5.1: Adjustments to the Flood Hazard. (After Dingle-Smith and Penning-Rowsell, 1986:57)

Specifically, given a commitment to keep options open for future generations and maintain the integrity of natural systems, much greater attention must be given to environmental values including ethical judgments about what is considered to be good.

Accepting the Brundtland concept of sustainable development and the implications for floodplain management outlined above, this paper examines the efforts extended against the flood threat in the Fraser Basin in the past twenty-five years and indicates some of the new directions that need to be considered.

Floodplain Management

Floodplain management includes a comprehensive set of strategies which must be considered as part of the integrated management of a river basin. The concept has evolved from the seminal work of Gilbert F. White at the University of Chicago Department of Geography (White, 1964).

White determined that the significant investment in structural works such as dykes and dams for flood control was not reducing flood damage potential in the United States. Further, he explained that there is a range of other adjustments possible to achieve the same goal (Figure 5.1). The following section will describe the flood hazard and the response to this hazard which has evolved in the Fraser Basin.

The Nature of the Flood Problem in the Fraser Basin

Precipitation, temperature, topography, and land use practices are the predominant influences on the hydrology of the Fraser River system. Winter precipitation in the form of snow is acted upon by rapidly rising spring temperatures to start the first freshet in tributary streams, and then the annual spring runoff. This snowmelt runoff may occasionally be augmented by rain. Figure 5.2 shows annual maximum discharge for the Fraser River at Hope. Autumn or winter rainfall flooding occurs in some locations, but the effects are localized.

In recent years the focus of attention has moved to possible climate change associated with increasing atmospheric concentrations of CO_2. Mean sea levels of the Pacific Ocean are projected to rise from 30 cm to 1.5 metres by the middle of the next century (Environment Canada, 1989). These projections have implications for coastal erosion/sedimentation, flooding and inundation of low gradient, intertidal areas of the Fraser River Delta. Projections for other regional characteristics are less clear. However, any change may be significant both in terms of sudden localized storm events, increased snowpacks, or drought in water-short areas.

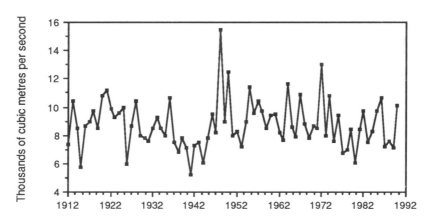

Figure 5.2: Annual Maximum Discharge: Fraser River at Hope.

Historical Evidence of Flooding

The greatest Fraser River flood in recorded history occurred in 1894, when the floodplain areas were in early stages of development (Figure 5.3). Sparse settlement prior to this period means that fewer records exist but it is known that two other major floods (1876, 1882) and seven minor floods occurred. It must be recognized, however, that much of the flooding occurred in the absence of dykes which were not constructed until after the 1894 flood.

The hazard in the Fraser Basin was again emphasized by a major flood in 1948 (Figure 5.4). The decades intervening since 1894 had seen major growth in agricultural, commercial and industrial development, and the beginning of suburban residential areas.

> At the time of the '94 flood there were few farms along the lower reaches of the Fraser. Damage, reckoned in dollars (though not in human misery), was relatively small. When, in the spring of 1948, the engineers saw the water rising fast on the Hope gauge, when they looked at the gigantic load of snow in the mountains, and learned of sudden hot weather throughout the interior, they knew they were in for trouble. ...Modern Canada had never seen a flood like this. (Hutchison, 1950)

Two thousand homes were damaged, sixteen thousand residents evacuated, and the costs of relief, rehabilitation, and repairs approached $20 million; that's $109 million in 1989 dollars! The Lower Fraser Valley received the greatest focus of attention due to the concentration of settlement in this area. However, there was also flood damage in other parts of the province, particularly Kamloops, Quesnel, and Prince George.

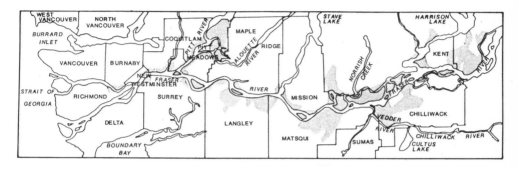

Figure 5.3: Areas Flooded in 1894.

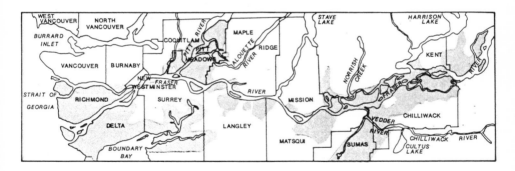

Figure 5.4: Areas Flooded in 1948.

In 1972 the Fraser and Thompson Rivers approached or exceeded 1948 levels causing substantial damage in Kamloops, Prince George, and Quesnel; the most dramatic event being the Oak Hills disaster. On June 2, 1972 a section of dyke collapsed and water inundated the Oak Hills development damaging 65 mobile homes and some 125 single family dwellings.

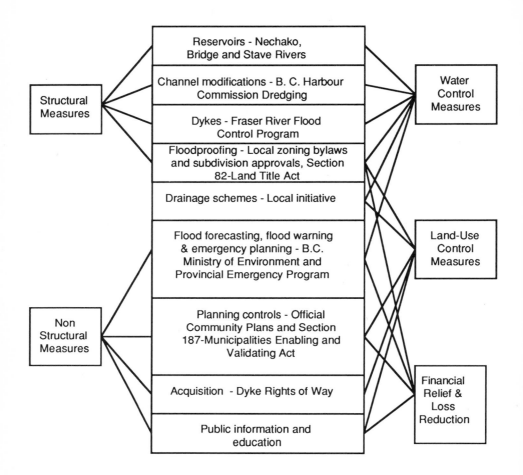

Figure 5.5: Adjustments to the Flood Hazard in the Lower Valley.

The peak in the Lower Mainland was lower than that of 1948 due mainly to lesser freshet runoff from the coastal area. In addition, the use of upstream storage reservoirs of the Nechako and Bridge Rivers and the Stave Lake Reservoir permitted a reduction of about 0.4 of a metre in peak elevation at Hope and a consequent reduction of approximately 0.3 of a metre at Mission. Without this reduction in flow, the peak elevation at Mission probably would have been about 7.5 metres, and the corresponding risk of dyke failure in the Lower Fraser Valley substantially greater.

More recently, common perception of the flood hazard has changed from "when it will happen" to "if it will happen". Complacency is only jolted by localized events such as the 1984 flooding in Pemberton which caused damages of over $8 million and damage in the Okanagan area in June 1990 which caused $18 million damage and 7 deaths.

What are we doing about the Flood Hazard?

The floodplain areas of the Fraser River drainage basin occupy only about one-half of one percent of the total basin, but they include most of the Lower Fraser Valley, parts of Prince George, Quesnel and Kamloops; and part of the Pemberton Valley on the Lillooet River. Intensification of land use and population growth in the floodplain of the Fraser River has been dramatic. For example, there was a 35% increase in population of the municipality of Richmond between 1976 and 1986. The sections that follow will describe the most important measures now taken to combat the flood hazard in the Lower Fraser Valley and in other parts of the Fraser Basin. These measures are summarized in Figure 5.5.

The Lower Fraser Valley

Dyking and Dams

The major dyke extension and improvement program for existing dykes now underway in the Lower Fraser Valley has relieved the recurrent flood threat to some extent. The Fraser River Flood Control Program was instigated following the 1948 flood by the Governments of Canada and British Columbia to repair, strengthen, construct and reconstruct dykes in the Fraser Valley. Initially, funding for the program was $18 million each from the Federal and Provincial governments, but this was increased to a total of $61 million in 1969 and $120 million in 1976. Cost sharing by local authorities (5% of bank protection, 10% of dyking, and 20% of internal drainage) was abolished in 1973, due to difficulties experienced by local authorities in funding. In 1976, due to escalating construction costs, further internal drainage works were deferred.

Today, some $134 million of the approved $161 million has been spent under the program. Figure 5.6 shows areas protected by these works. Agreements between local authorities which have benefitted from works and the Province of British Columbia stipulate that local authorities will be responsible for the operation and maintenance of the dykes and will encourage floodproofing behind dykes to reduce flood losses.

The current Lower Fraser Valley dyking program only provides flood protection to the 1894 flood level. Raising dykes above this level may be extremely costly and may generate a false sense of security where dykes are still vulnerable to a major earthquake. A recent study of the Abbotsford area (Klohn Leonoff, 1989) concluded that a 200-year earthquake occurring at any time of the year would cause sufficient damage to the dykes that rehabilitation prior to the next Fraser River freshet might not be possible. Reliance would have to be placed on evacuation procedures.

Additional flood protection could be achieved through the development of upstream storage reservoirs or diversions of major tributary rivers. The Lower McGregor diversion was found to be the only economically viable project that

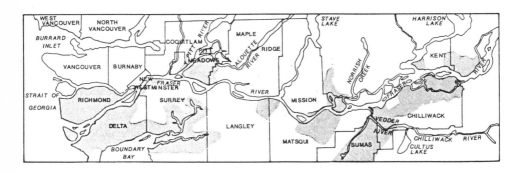

Figure 5.6: Areas Protected to 1:200 Year Flooding under Fraser River Flood Control Program.

would provide such protection by the Fraser River Upstream Storage Study (Fraser River Joint Advisory Committee, 1979). This diversion was vetoed on environmental grounds due to the risk of fish parasites migrating from the Pacific into the Arctic drainage basin.

Planning Controls

Keeping floodplain land free from urban development is the ideal solution to preventing flood damage. However, the realization of such an ideal is impossible where early settlement has already formed the nucleus for development in valley bottoms.

The need for restriction on development in the Fraser was first officially recognized in the Official Regional Plan for the Lower Mainland, enacted in 1966. This plan delineated the floodplain based on records of the extent of flooding in 1894 and 1948 (Schedule AA). The plan established a policy that floodplains were to be kept free of urban use except where committed to further development because of earlier settlement (those areas designated URBAN 1 or INDUSTRIAL 1 on the *current* schedules of the Plan). The exemptions were requested by local government in order to permit logical development of historical settlement areas protected by the dyking system. New urban growth was to be contiguous with existing development and would require floodproofing. Much of the floodplain land was designated for rural use and a 20 acre minimum parcel size established.

The introduction of the Agricultural Land Reserve in 1973 was the second major impetus to restriction of floodplain development. Lands designated under the Agricultural Land Reserve were designated as Agricultural in the update of the 1966 Official Regional Plan completed in 1980. The principle that floodplain should be kept free from urban development, where possible, was also maintained.

With the demise of the regional planning system in the early 1980's, greater reliance has been placed on local government's Official Community Plan process to keep floodplain areas free from urban development. This has met with mixed success. The controversy over development of the Boundary Bay lands in Delta and the Terra Nova lands in Richmond provide two recent examples of large tracts of floodplain land considered for development.

The total Lower Mainland population is forecast to be 1,691,500 at the end of 1990, up about 50,000 from 1989. These figures reflect the attractiveness of this area with its temperate climate for retirees, a buoyant economy, and a refuge from less stable areas of the world. Recent projections suggest that the population of the Vancouver metropolitan area will be 2,050,000 by the year 2011.[1] Pressures for development of easily accessible floodplain areas are therefore likely to be maintained.

Floodproofing-Building Standards for Flood Protection[2]

Where development of floodable land is unavoidable, protection of individual buildings can be undertaken. Provincial and municipal programs to encourage floodproofing of individual buildings, usually through the specification of standards such as setbacks from watercourses and elevation above natural ground level), have evolved over the past eighteen years. The elevation above natural ground level required to meet the strandard is based on the 200 year Designated Flood Level plus an allowance for freeboard (usually 0.6 metres). The Designated Flood Level is a flood having a magnitude with a probable frequency of occurrence of once in 200 years. Stated in another way, there is a 22% chance of this flood magnitude being equalled or exceeded in the 50 year lifetime of a typical residential structure. This level has some historic precedent (similar probability as 1894 flood magnitude) and is considered to be economically achievable in most areas.

The standards are based on general guidelines developed by the British Columbia Ministry of Environment depending on the flow record of the watercourse, and on floodplain mapping, where available.

In December 1987, the Provincial and Federal governments signed the Canada-British Columbia Flood Damage Reduction Program "Agreement Respecting Floodplain Mapping in the Province of British Columbia". This is a cost-shared agreement for 10 years with an expenditure of $5 million for the production of floodplain mapping. At the present time, mapping has been completed for the Chilliwack, Coquitlam, Coquihalla, Alouette and North Alouette Rivers. Mapping for the Fraser River floodplain is expected to take the form of publication of existing flood profile and flood schedule information.

---

1 Greater Vancouver Regional District and Central Mortgage and Housing Corporation, 1990.
2 Floodproofing means the alteration of land or structures either physically or in use to reduce or eliminate flood damage and includes the use of building setbacks from water bodies to maintain a floodway and to allow for potential erosion. Floodproofing may be achieved by all or a combination of the following: (i) building on fill, provided such fill does not interfere with flood flows of the watercourse, and is adequately protected against floodwater erosion; (ii) building raised by structural means such as foundation walls, columns, etc.; (iii) a combination of fill and structural means.

The Canada-British Columbia Agreement covering Flood Control in the Lower Fraser Valley (May 24, 1968) instituted the current major dyking program, including the following proviso;

> The Province undertakes to continue to encourage a program of land use zoning and floodproofing to diminish potential flood losses in the area covered by this Agreement.

This provision was echoed in the individual dyking agreements established with benefitting local governments. It was reinforced by the passing of provincial legislation (Section 187 of the Municipalities Enabling and Validating Act). Any plan or zoning bylaw amendments affecting the area delineated by Schedule AA of the 1966 Official Regional Plan must be approved by the Minister of Municipal Affairs who refers the issue of floodproofing requirements to the Ministry of Environment. Once a local government adopts floodproofing conditions in a base zoning bylaw, these referrals are no longer required except for Official Community Plan amendments and development variance permits.

The 1972 flooding event described earlier, and particularly the Oak Hills disaster, resulted in the passing of an amendment to the Land Title Act (Section 82) as it affects the approval of new subdivisions. The Approving Officer for all organized municipalities (Ministry of Transportation and Highways in unorganized areas) is required to submit subdivision applications on floodable land for consent of the Minister of Environment. Normally, consent is given, unless the hazard is extreme. Floodproofing conditions and "no liability" provisions are registered as a covenant against the land title of the subdivision. It is only recently that most municipalities in the Lower Mainland have complied with this legislation. The conditions are not applied in historic settlement areas which are exempted under Section 187 of the Municipalities Enabling and Validating Act. Such exemptions are significant—they account for at least one-third of the floodplain area of the Greater Vancouver Regional District.

The provisions described thus far have related primarily to newly subdivided land. An equivalent effort has been placed in encouraging local government to adopt floodproofing conditions as part of their base zoning bylaws, thereby affecting existing lots. Although 85% of local governments in the province have some form of floodproofing bylaw, there are some notable exceptions in the Lower Mainland at time of writing. Legislation supporting this program was passed in 1985 (Section 969, Municipal Act), but is being revised at present.

It was at the instigation of the Lower Mainland municipalities that a major review of floodproofing policy was undertaken in 1986. As a result of responses to a discussion paper, the Minister of Environment announced new policies in September 1987. Although existing Ministry policies were generally accepted, the Minister announced that local government could introduce some flexibility in the establishment of conditions based on the adoption of a floodplain management plan. In particular, the floodproofing required for industrial, commercial and agricultural buildings could be established by municipalities, provided certain minimum elevation standards were met.

The floodplain management plan would include a delineation of the floodplain area, background information about the flood hazard and dyke protection, floodproofing conditions, and information about compensation in the event of flooding. The plan was intended to supersede and encompass previous regulatory controls. At time of writing, legislation is being developed in support of this program.

Flood Forecasting and Flood Warning

Flood forecasting for the Fraser stem is based on snow course measurements taken at 76 stations by the Ministry of Environment and measurements taken at streamflow gauges. Once the spring runoff period commences, temperature and rainfall are carefully monitored to provide five-day warnings of flood events. Flood forecasts for rivers such as the Lillooet, Chilliwack or Coquitlam would require watershed models and input of detailed climatological data not presently available. Such models are available for the Upper Fraser and even without climatological data, now provide good forecasts up to two days before a flooding event.

Disaster Relief

The provision of disaster relief, property insurance, and emergency response are the most common means of spreading the costs associated with disaster losses. In British Columbia, it is commonly accepted that the giving of disaster relief is an appropriate responsibility of the provincial government, in association with the federal government. How this is done has varied over the years, but, in any case, it has been the responsibility of the Office of the Premier or of the Ministers of the Environment and of the Attorney General or Solicitor General in conjunction with Emergency Planning Canada.

There have been several sources and means of dealing with disaster relief. For example:

- In the 1960's, a contingency fund for flood damages was established by the provincial government, but this was soon exhausted and has not been replaced;
- Under arrangements between the senior governments, cost-sharing relating to disaster relief for any particular disaster begins when provincial expenditures exceed an amount equal to $1 per capita. When a province's expenditures exceed this level, the amount of federal financial assistance payable to a province rises progressively in stipulated amounts;
- Following recent flooding events (e.g., Pemberton, 1984) homeowners were expected to bear costs to a maximum of $10,000. In the case of Pemberton, flood damages per household frequently did not exceed this figure which prompted a review of this policy;
- The programs for disaster relief have included grants for repair of infrastructure, for structural protection such as dykes (cost-shared with local government in some cases), and agricultural subsidies;

- Court cases involving private citizens who felt that the Province or local municipalities have not adequately carried out their responsibilities in terms of flood warning, planning or compensation have been settled out of court;
- The December 1987 Federal-Provincial Floodplain Mapping Agreement designated certain floodplain areas and agreed not to fund unprotected government buildings, nor to pay compensation for buildings constructed below provincial standards, after the date of adoption of the agreement.

Today, the Ministry of the Solicitor General (Provincial Emergency Program), in consultation with Emergency Planning Canada, has certain guidelines relating to disaster relief. Approved disaster assistance payments are given as unconditional grants to individuals, businesses, and municipalities. The payments consist of a maximum of 80% of the total appraised value of uninsurable, eligible damages after exclusions, limitations, and a $1,000 deductible have been applied. There is a maximum payment of $100,000 per individual claim. Up to 100% of the appraised value of public property damage or restoration costs may be eligible for assistance. No compensation is given for the purchase of land, or the loss of use of land, in the event that reconstruction is not permitted or possible. Only those things required to replace or restore the necessities of life qualify for assistance.

The provincial government has considered the adoption of a flood insurance scheme on a number of occasions, but this has not been pursued due to lack of a willing insurer. However, there is a limited availability of flood insurance from private insurers for commercial and industrial developments.

Emergency Planning Canada and the Provincial Emergency Program of the Ministry of the Solicitor General have active programs involving local volunteers and appointed officials who coordinate and undertake emergency response.

While bearing the loss might appear to be an alternative adjustment, the common public response to natural hazards in British Columbia is seen to be similar to most developed areas of the world. The expectation is that some form of disaster relief will be forthcoming.

Public Education and Involvement

Public education regarding floodplain management has been limited up to now. The Ministry of Environment has published a guide "Floodproofing New Residential Buildings in B.C." (British Columbia Ministry of Environment, 1981) and has provided considerable service to local government officials. New programs planned include publicity programs associated with the Federal-Provincial Floodplain Mapping Agreement and floodplain management plans which are designed to provide public information.

Public involvement has been limited to public information meetings associated with dyke construction and public hearings where land use bylaws affect floodplain land.

In addition, the Provincial Emergency Program has produced leaflets giving instructions for emergency measures to be taken in the event of a flood.

Other Areas of the Fraser Basin

Floodplain management approaches in other areas of the Fraser Basin have been similar but less intensive. Examples are given for the more settled areas of the basin.

Dyking and Bank Protection

In Quesnel, some bank protection has been completed. In preparation for flooding expected in 1972, the Ministry of Transportation and Highways constructed some dyking in Kamloops. Since that time, some of the protection constructed in Kamloops has been removed, while bank protection has been placed in a few areas. In the Pemberton Valley, a program of bank protection was provided under the Canada/British Columbia Agri-Food Regional Development Subsidiary Agreement between 1979 and 1984. Following the 1984 Pemberton floods, in the order of $1.75 million was spent on dyke protection.

Planning and Floodproofing Standards

Floodplain mapping has now been completed for sections of the North Thompson, Lillooet and Nechako Rivers, as well as the Fraser and Nechako at Prince George and the Fraser and Quesnel at Quesnel. Many local governments in the Fraser Basin recognize floodplain areas in their planning process, submit subdivisions for consent to the Minister of Environment, and have adopted floodproofing standards in zoning bylaws. It should be noted, however, that the City of Kamloops, rather than enforcing protective standards, requests 'no liability' covenants against the land title of existing lots. Floodproofing is required for construction in new subdivisions. The City of Prince George has acted similarly, particularly in the industrial and commercial centre of the city.

Extent of Success

Floodplain management in the Fraser Basin has evolved considerably in the past twenty-five years. It has evolved to provide more comprehensive management. But in other ways, little has changed.

In 1965, W.R.D. Sewell cited four reasons for continued increase in flood loss potential (Sewell, 1965):

(i)   Little perception of risk by floodplain residents or makers of public policy;
(ii) Dependence on construction of flood protection works and emergency action, and flood relief and rehabilitation;
(iii) Reluctance to deal with causes of flood problems as well as their effects;
(iv) Encouragement of floodplain occupance by the construction of highways and other public works in or adjacent to floodplains.

Shanks (1972), in a study of the municipality of Richmond, found that officials were aware of the flood hazard but did not adequately perceive the function of such flood protection measures as dykes. The general public, on the other hand, were poorly informed and showed little concern for the hazard.

It would appear that little has changed regarding perception of risk by floodplain residents or makers of public policy. Without substantive evidence, it is possible only to point to continued intensification of floodplain settlement in the Lower Mainland. Slowness to adopt floodplain regulations governing land use provides another indicator.

The range of measures relating to flood protection now available to communities has been augmented. Cause rather than effect receives greater attention. Planning and regulatory controls for building on floodplains are now available for most communities in the Fraser Basin, whether floodplain mapping has been completed or not.

Flood forecasting has been improved and some attempt at public education has begun. Reliance on flood relief has been tempered by policy direction. Structural controls such as dykes and bank protection continue to have importance. Construction of dams for flood control has not been implemented. Little attempt has been made to discourage floodplain occupance by avoiding construction of highways and other public works in or adjacent to floodplains, though such options are admittedly infrequent.

Future Directions: Implications of Sustainable Development

Sustainable development principles bring new implications for advancing floodplain management. Human activities on the floodplain need protection. Therefore, planning for communities in cognisance of the flood hazard will become even more important. It will be necessary to weigh the costs of flood protection against the costs of infrastructure to accommodate a burgeoning population outside of the floodplain. Dam construction for flood control may again be considered.

Where development is directed away from lowland areas, there will be a need for detailed studies to define hazards such as alluvial fans and debris torrents affecting slopes adjacent to the valley floor. Such hazards are particularly extensive in the Dewdney-Alouette and Fraser-Cheam Regional Districts. There will be a greater need to plan for flood protection sensitive to local community needs.

Special community-based studies of the flood hazard can extend the delineation of potential flooding to flooding in the event of a dyke break. For example, in the municipality of Richmond which is surrounded by dykes, such studies have revealed the need for special emergency procedures as well as floodproofing of building sites. Consideration of building elevations used in non-floodproofed historic urban areas and improvement of these levels over the long term is suggested. The need for internal dyking was also identified and here again there is a dilemma. The effect on the agricultural community and on the natural ecosystem will have to be considered.

Flexibility of approach will be important to the success of floodplain management and sustainable development. Such an approach may be necessary for political reasons but also to adapt to new uncertainties such as climate change. Perhaps more important such an approach provides greater resilience to natural events than does a single means of control such as the construction of dams.

The Fraser River Flood Control Program ends in 1995. In the immediate future, consideration is being given to extension of the program to the City of Kamloops, but beyond 1995, the need for the program will be questioned. Since the program's inception the cost of structural works has increased considerably. Long term maintenance costs have been recognized; the knowledge of earthquake risk has increased; and the range of floodplain management measures available is better understood. The implications of climate change to areas now protected by sea dykes will also be important.

Sustainable development objectives relating to maintenance of natural ecosystems have important implications where dyke construction is considered the only viable alternative. A project completed in the municipality of Delta in 1986 at an additional cost of $2.0 million provides an excellent example of construction sensitive to the environment. Flood protection was provided while preserving the Tsawwassen salt marsh, the largest salt marsh in the Fraser River estuary. The construction included a three kilometre breakwater along the seaward edge of the saltmarsh to dissipate wave action. Several openings in the breakwater permitted normal tidal flow to inundate the marsh and improve circulation of the seawater. Flood protection was provided by minimal raising of the Tsawwassen Road and provision of upland drainage through a low profile flood box and pumping station. The project was subject to detailed environmental study throughout its design and construction. It has preserved the salt marsh wetland habitat which is a part of the Roberts Bank tidal flats ecosystem providing nutrients, fish food and refuge for fish species as well as wildlife habitat.

New evaluation techniques are required for floodplain management and this need is heightened with the recognition of sustainable development principles. Possible reduction in the costs of flood damage is frequently given as justification for floodplain management. However, a review of the literature associated with the evaluation of floodplain management finds the dominance of one theme. "Efficient use of flood-prone land must become the guiding premise, rather than an imagery limited to floods as disasters" (Changnon, 1985). Economic efficiency must become a larger part of the decision-making processes relating to floodplain management and so must ethical and equity considerations. But considerable difficulties must be faced because of pervasive misconceptions.

New forms of evaluation must address the following criticisms that are frequently voiced in some confusion about current programs:

- "An absolute reduction in the continued encroachment on flood hazard areas is not being achieved";

- "Nothing is being done to modify existing unprotected structures on floodplain lands";
- "People should just be made aware of flood hazards and then it should be up to them what they should do";

while still recognizing the realities of floodplain management in British Columbia, such as:

- The alternative to building on floodplains is often building on steep slopes;
- The reason for floodplain management is often that "there exists either some implied property right to flood alleviation or a generally altruistic desire to preserve society's members from hazards, the risk from which exceeds a certain magnitude" (Green, 1987);
- Unprotected land use in floodplain areas to the profit of a few often results in subsequent costs which must be borne by the general taxpayer.

Evaluation is needed which will take into account both who pays the costs and who reaps the benefits. Response to disaster alone whether real or scenario is insufficient.

Conclusions

It is twenty-five years since Sewell (1965) first examined the proposed integrated management approach to flooding in the Fraser Basin and found the narrow focus of considerations wanting. This paper has described the range of measures now used to combat the flood threat in the Fraser Basin. While there is still much to be done, there is now a more comprehensive approach which is essential to the sustainability of our society. At the same time, it is important to understand that measures taken in the name of floodplain management may mean the loss of valuable future options for natural systems. Careful planning, flexibility of approach, structural protection sensitive to environmental concerns and new evaluation techniques are recommended for future floodplain management.

Acknowledgements

The opinions expressed do not represent policy of the Ministry of Environment, Province of British Columbia. The author wishes to acknowledge the continuing efforts of staff of the Flood Damage Reduction Program of the Ministry of Environment in the development of the provincial program described in this paper, and particularly Neil Peters for his helpful comments on this paper. The author also wishes to thank Olav Slaymaker, Jean-Pierre Savard, Sandy D'Aquino, Kris Sharma and Tony Dorcey for their excellent suggestions during the development of the paper. Robin McNeill and Bill McInnes of the Water Management Program kindly provided graphic material.

References

Barker, M. L. 1980. *An Evaluation of Floodplain Management in the Lower Fraser Valley.* Preliminary Draft. Burnaby: Simon Fraser University, Department of Geography.

Barker, M. L. and W. B. Morgan. 1980. "Shore and Floodplain Management in British Columbia and Washington State." in Sewell W. R. D., and M. L. Barker (eds.). *Water Problems and Policies.* Victoria: University of Victoria, Department of Geography.

British Columbia. Ministry of Environment. 1981. *Floodproofing New Residential Buildings in British Columbia.* Victoria: Queen's Printer.

British Columbia. Ministry of Environment and Parks. 1987. *New Floodplain Management Policies for British Columbia Communities.* Victoria: Queen's Printer.

Burby, R. J., and S. P. French. 1985. *Floodplain Land Use Management. A National Assessment.* Boulder: Westview Press.

Canada. Emergency Planning Canada. 1988. *Annual Review 1987.* Ottawa: Minister of Supply and Services.

Canada. Environment. 1989. *Proceedings of the Impacts of Climate Variability and Change on British Columbia.* Taylor, E. M., and K. J. Johnstone. (eds.). Vancouver: Atmospheric Environment Service Pacific Region, Scientific Services Division Report PAES-89-1.

Changnon, Jr., S. A. 1985. *Journal of Water Resources Planning and Management.* 111:54-64.

Dacy, D. C., and H. Kunreuther. 1969. *The Economics of Natural Hazard: Implications for Federal Policy.* New York: The Free Press.

Dingle-Smith, D., and E. C. Penning-Rowsell. 1986. *An Evaluation of House-Raising as a Flood Mitigation Strategy for Lismore, N.S.W.* Canberra: Centre for Resource and Environmental Studies, Australian National University.

Fraser River Board. 1956. *Investigations into Measures for Flood Control in the Fraser River Basin, Interim Report.* Victoria: Fraser River Board.

_____ 1963. *Final Report on Flood Control and Hydro-Electric Power in the Fraser River Basin.* Victoria: Queen's Printer.

Fraser River Joint Advisory Committee. 1979. *Fraser River Upstream Storage Review Report.* Victoria: Queen's Printer.

Greater Vancouver Regional District Planning Committee. 1972. *Reference Book on Floodplain and Floodplain Management.* Vancouver: Greater Vancouver Regional District.

Green, W. 1987. in Handmer, J. (ed.). *Flood Hazard Management: British and International Perspectives.* Exeter: Short Run Press.

Holling, C. 1986. "The Resilience of Terrestrial Ecosystems: Local Surprise and Global Change." in Clark, W., and R. Munn. (eds.). *Sustainable Development of the Biosphere.* London: Cambridge University Press.

Hutchison, B. 1950. *The Fraser.* Toronto: Clarke Irwin.

Klohn Leonoff Ltd. 1989. *Floodplain Management Plan. Engineering Studies. District of Abbotsford.* Richmond: Klohn Leonoff.

Kreimer, A. 1989. "Disasters, Sustainability and Development: A Look to the 1990s." in Kreimer, A., and M. Zador (eds.). *Colloquium on Disasters, Sustainability and Development: A Look to the 1990's.* Washington: World Bank Environment Working Paper No. 23.

McKay, J. M. 1984. *Community Response to Flood Hazard Information.* Report for the Australia Water Resources Council. Canberra: Australia Department of Resources and Energy.

Milliman, J. W. 1984. "A Needed Economic Framework for Floodplain Management." *Water International.* 9:119-126.

Petak, W. J., and A. A. Atkisson. 1982. *Natural Hazard Risk Assessment and Public Policy.* New York: Springer-Verlag.

Rossi, P. H., J. D. Wright and E. Weber-Burdin. 1982. *Natural Hazards and Public Choice.* New York: Academic Press.

Sewell, W. R. D. 1965. *Water Management and Floods in the Fraser River Basin.* Chicago: University of Chicago, Department of Geography Research Series, No. 100.

Shanks, G. R. 1972. *The Role of Perception in Floodplain Management.* Vancouver: The University of British Columbia, Unpublished Master of Arts Thesis.

Simmons, G. E. 1980. "Approaches to Flood Control on the Fraser River." in Sewell, W. R. D., and M. Barker (eds.). *Water Problems and Policies.* Victoria: University of Victoria, Department of Geography.

White, G. F. 1964. *Choice of Adjustment to Floods*. Chicago: University of Chicago Research Paper No.93.
World Commission on Environment and Development (WCED). 1987. *Our Common Future*. Oxford: Oxford University Press.

6

Sustainable Development of the Pacific Salmon Resources in the Fraser River Basin

Michael A. Henderson

The Pacific salmon resources of the Fraser River Basin consist of six species of the genus *Oncorhynchus*; pink, chum, sockeye, coho, chinook salmon and steelhead trout. All six species share the trait of spending the initial part of their life cycle in freshwater followed by a more lengthy period of time, usually two to four years, in the marine environment before returning to freshwater to reproduce. This generalization excludes some relatively small landlocked populations of sockeye salmon referred to as kokanee. The length of the obligatory freshwater stage varies among the species and ranges from a few days to a few years following hatching.

The Pacific salmon of the Fraser River, like other renewable resources, have the ability to replace themselves. The abundance at which a species of Pacific salmon can maintain itself and the rate at which it can return to this level of abundance, if depressed, is stock specific. For the purpose of this review, a stock is defined as a group of salmon that spawn at the same location and time and hence share some genetic commonality.

The size and productivity of a salmon stock is controlled by a large array of environmental factors. For example, a stock may be large in terms of the number of fish that return to spawn. However, a heavy silt load in the gravel may result in low survival of the fertilized eggs. Consequently, this stock would have a low productivity and would be very slow to recover from the removal of a large number of fish. Conversely, a limited spawning area may keep the biomass of adults very low but excellent condition of the spawning gravel may result in high survival of the fertilized eggs. This stock would have a high productivity.

The exploitative action of fisheries also effects the abundance and productivity of a salmon stock. The removal of large numbers of fish from a stock as they approach their natal river as maturing adults may lead to a decrease in the long-term average abundance. However, up to some stock-specific level, the removal of maturing adults may actually increase the productivity of a stock.

The overall objective of this review is to provide the information on Pacific salmon required to develop a comprehensive definition of sustainable development for the water resources of the Fraser River Basin. More specifically, I provide a definition of sustainable development for Pacific salmon stocks of the Fraser River followed by a brief description of the distribution of each species within the Fraser River Basin, the management regimes associated with Fraser River salmon fisheries, and new initiatives designed to increase the abundance of Fraser River salmon. It is important to realize that the definition of sustainable development presented below is rather narrow in focus. It was developed from the perspective of the Canadian Department of Fisheries and Oceans, the agency responsible for the conservation and management of Fraser River salmon. It is the author's opinion however, that ultimately the scope of the definition will have to be greatly expanded if it is to be a meaningful construct from which to develop policy for the sustainable development of the water resources of the Fraser River Basin. The process through which an expanded definition is developed will of necessity have to involve all those who use or affect, directly or indirectly, the water resources of the Fraser River Basin (see Dale, this volume).

Sustainability of Fish Stocks and Fisheries

It is clear from the above comments that the number of fish in a stock can theoretically be sustained at any level between zero and some maximum. Within this range, and in the absence of fishing activities, the abundance attained by a stock will tend toward a particular level. The effect of fishing may be to alter the average level of abundance within this range.

The concept of sustainability in fisheries can be described from either an economic or biological perspective. For the purpose of this review, I will concentrate on the latter. A fishery is sustainable if the average annual harvest does not lead to the long-term, continuous decline in abundance of the stock that is the target of the harvest. Therefore, it is clear that a fishery can be sustained over the long-term only if there is an understanding of the relationship between the abundance of spawners or the reproductive potential of the stock, and productivity of the stock measured as the number of adults produced per spawner.

Sustainable development of the Pacific salmon resources refers to the actions taken to ensure some particular long-term average level of harvest. Over short periods of time, the stock may increase in size as the result of improved management practices. The result of such increases would be a new, higher level of long-term average harvest. The range of actions open to control long-term harvest through control of spawner abundance and stock productivity are limited. For example, we cannot easily control the number of juvenile salmon predators in the Fraser River or the amount of food in the ocean. However, we can control developments in the Fraser River Basin that may have an effect on the quality of the freshwater salmon habitat. We can also control the exploitative process of fisheries and hence the number of fish available for harvest in the future.

Description of Stocks

The Fraser River is the largest salmon production system in British Columbia and possibly the world (Northcote and Larkin, 1989). It accounts for approximately one third of the total average annual salmon catch in British Columbia. The river supports all six species of Pacific salmon although there is considerable variation in the distribution and abundance of each species within the Basin (Northcote and Larkin, 1989:192, Figure 13). The remaining discussion will not include any further reference to steelhead trout.

References are made below to spawning escapement objectives for some of the major Fraser River salmon stocks. The purpose of including the spawning escapement objectives in this review is to provide a qualitative sense of the relative size of the different stocks *within* a species and therefore of the relative importance of different areas in the Fraser River Basin to salmon production. *The spawning escapement objectives are not necessarily intended as targets in the sense that they would refer to the number of fish a manager would attempt to put on the spawning grounds nor are they necessarily indicative of the level of spawning escapement that would maximize stock size.* The same qualification applies to references to recent levels of spawning escapement. All references to spawning escapement objectives are from the Pacific Region Salmon Resource Management Plan (DFO, 1988).

Sockeye Salmon

Fraser River sockeye salmon stocks, taken as a group, form the largest run of this species in British Columbia. Historically, sockeye salmon runs to the Fraser River were much larger than at the present time. The size of runs decreased from an average of 10.5 million between 1894 and 1913 to approximately 6 million between 1964 and 1983. The largest run, which occurred in 1913, has been estimated to have exceeded 35 million fish (Ricker, 1987).

One important feature of the biology of Fraser River sockeye salmon is a four year cycle in adult abundance for some of the large upriver stocks. Prior to 1914 all major upriver sockeye salmon stocks were most abundant in the 1913 cycle year (i.e., 1905..1909..1913..). The pattern of cyclic dominance was disrupted in the early part of this century, apparently as the result of rock slides, dams and management practices. These problems have been corrected and cyclic dominance has reappeared but not on the same cycle year for all stocks.

On their return migration Fraser River sockeye salmon enter coastal waters as maturing adults anywhere from the west coast of Vancouver Island to southern southeast Alaska. The fish migrate southward either through Johnstone or Juan de Fuca straits on their way to the Strait of Georgia and the Fraser River.

Birkenhead River and Weaver Creek are the major producers of sockeye salmon in the Lower Fraser River, the area between the mouth of the Fraser River and the Fraser Canyon. These two systems have a combined spawning escapement objective of 170,000 fish. There are also five smaller stocks located in the Pitt, Harrison and Cultus river drainages.

The major Fraser River sockeye salmon stocks spawn upriver of the Fraser Canyon. Seven sockeye salmon stocks originate in the Middle Fraser, the area between the Fraser Canyon and Prince George, two of which, the Horsefly and Chilko stocks, are very large. Both of these stocks exhibit a cyclic pattern of abundance with Horsefly returns dominant in the 1989 cycle and Chilko dominant in the 1988 cycle. The spawning escapement objective for the Horsefly stock is 1,000,000, 100,000, 2,000 and 900 for the 1989, 1990, 1991 and 1992 cycles respectively. The spawning escapement objective for the Chilko stock is 150,000 each year.

The Thompson River drainage supports 15 sockeye salmon stocks. The spawning escapement objectives for these stocks are 3,140,000 and 717,000, for the 1990 and 1991 cycle years respectively and 42,000 for both the 1988 and 1989 cycle years. The extreme cyclic dominance of this stock complex is the result of a four year cycle in the Adams River stock which accounts for 75% of the total spawning escapement on the dominant cycle year (1990).

The Upper Fraser, encompassing that part of the Basin upriver of Prince George, supports 36 sockeye salmon stocks, 29 of which form the Early and Late Stuart stock complex. Both of these stock complexes exhibit cyclic patterns in abundance and are dominant in the 1989 cycle year. Spawning escapement objectives for the 1990, 1991, 1992, and 1993 cycle years are 210,000, 375,000, 90,000, and 565,000 fish respectively.

Chinook Salmon

Chinook salmon are found in the Birkenhead, Lillooet, Chilliwack, Pitt and Harrison systems in the Lower Fraser River. The Harrison stock, the largest single chinook stock in the Fraser Basin and the only major stock in the Lower Fraser River, has a spawning escapement objective of 24,000 fish. Estimates of spawning escapement of Harrison chinook have increased in recent years as the result of conservation measures.

There are nine major chinook salmon stocks in the middle Fraser with a combined spawning escapement objective of 21,000 fish. The largest of these are in the Chilko, West Road, Quesnel and Chilcotin systems. Similar to the Lower Fraser stocks, spawning escapement to some of the middle river stocks has been increasing in recent years as the result of conservation measures.

Lower Shuswap, South Thompson, Nicola, Clearwater and North Thompson rivers are the locations for the largest of 16 chinook salmon stocks in the Thompson drainage of the Fraser River Basin. These stocks have a combined spawning escapement objective of 56,000 fish. Unlike stocks in the Lower and Middle Fraser, the Thompson chinook salmon stocks have maintained a relatively constant spawning escapement in recent years.

There are 12 major chinook salmon stocks in the Upper Fraser River with a combined spawning escapement objective of 24,000 fish. The largest of these stocks originate from the Fraser mainstem, Bowron River and Slim Creek systems. Spawning escapement estimates for these stocks have increased discontinuously since the 1950's. However, at least part of this increase can be explained by an increased effort in enumerating escapement rather than an actual increase in escapement.

Pink Salmon

The Fraser River supports the largest pink salmon run in British Columbia with an average return of approximately 15 million fish over the last several cycles on odd years. Fraser River pink salmon returns in even years are very small and are not considered in this review. The current average odd year returns represent a considerable increase in the size of the run after the Hell's Gate rock slide of 1913, although it is still considerably less than the estimated run size of 48 million prior to the slide (Ricker, 1989). The Hell's Gate slide drastically reduced the size of the run by eliminating access to spawning areas above the Fraser Canyon. However, the construction of a fishway, spawning channels at Seton Creek and some reduction in exploitation rates have resulted in pink salmon re-invading the waters above the Fraser Canyon.

Pink salmon spawn in seven different systems in the Lower Fraser River including the Fraser mainstem. Total escapement has increased from an average of 1.1 million in the 1960's to 1.2 million in the 1970's to approximately 4.0 million during the first half of the 1980's. Typically the run returns in two segments. The first portion of the run, which is also the largest, spawns primarily in the Fraser mainstem while most of the second portion returns to the Harrison River.

Four pink salmon stocks from the middle portion of the Fraser Basin all spawn in Seton River. Total spawning escapement for this stock complex has increased from an average of less than 200,000 in the 1960's to over 500,000 in the 1980's. Much of this increase can be attributed to the success of Seton Creek spawning channels.

Pink salmon spawning escapement to the Thompson drainage doubled between the 1950's and 1960's to over 500,000 fish. However, it has varied erratically in recent years between 200,000 to over a million spawners. The years of poor returns were due primarily to either very low or very high water levels in the river which impeded upriver migration through the Hell's Gate area and caused an increase in pre-spawning mortality (Ricker, 1989).

Chum Salmon

Fraser River chum salmon are managed as a single stock complex and the fish spawn almost exclusively in the Lower Fraser River. The stock complex has been increasing in size in recent years following a period of low abundance. The level of spawning escapement of chum salmon to the Fraser River is currently approximately 500,000 fish. Stocks originating from the Harrison, Chilliwack and Stave river systems account for approximately 83% of the total spawning escapement.

Coho Salmon

The Fraser River is the single largest producer of coho salmon in British Columbia. Overall, there is a great deal of uncertainty associated with the status of Fraser River coho stocks due primarily to the difficulty of obtaining accurate estimates of spawning escapement. However, those estimates that are available indicate a gradual but steady decline in the abundance of Fraser River coho salmon since 1970.

The Lower Fraser River supports 110 coho salmon stocks, which, as a group, account for approximately 75% of total Fraser River coho salmon production. Major spawning stocks are located in the Chilliwack, Harrison, Upper Pitt and Salmon river systems.

Spawning coho salmon have been identified in seven streams in the Middle Fraser. The most important from the perspective of coho salmon production are the Bridge and Gate river systems.

Most coho salmon that migrate past the Fraser Canyon spawn in the Thompson River drainage. Of the 71 known spawning areas in the drainage, 12, located in the North Thompson, South Thompson and Nicola river systems, account for most of the production.

Fraser River Salmon Fisheries

On average, over the last 20 years, 66% of the total British Columbia sockeye salmon catch and 60% of the total British Columbia pink salmon catch has been of Fraser River origin. The Fraser system has also contributed approximately 16, 11 and 8% of the total annual British Columbia chinook, coho and chum catch respectively over the same period.

Commercial

Fraser River sockeye and pink salmon are primarily harvested in a series of net and troll fisheries in Johnstone and Juan de Fuca straits, the Strait of Georgia, off the west coast of Vancouver Island and in the Lower Fraser River (small numbers of Fraser River sockeye salmon are harvested in net fisheries in northern British Columbia and southern southeast Alaska). The net fisheries are mixed stock and species fisheries but their effort is directed at Fraser River pink and sockeye salmon. The timing and location of the Fraser River pink and sockeye salmon fisheries shows considerable interannual variation which also effects the incidental catch of non-Fraser River salmon. The variability in fishing patterns between years results from the combination of several factors. First, the time of return of maturing adult sockeye salmon to the Fraser River varies between stocks. Superimposed on this variability is the quadrennial pattern in abundance exhibited by some of the larger Fraser River sockeye stocks. As a result of these two features, the period of time when the fisheries are open varies considerably between years. Finally, variability in total annual fishing effort is further affected by the return of harvestable numbers of maturing pink salmon in odd years.

Fraser River chum salmon are harvested in the net fisheries of Johnstone Strait, the Strait of Georgia and the Fraser River. These fisheries occur later than the pink and sockeye salmon fisheries and are currently managed so as to increase the total spawning escapement to the Fraser River.

Fraser River chinook and coho salmon are harvested in mixed stock, mixed species troll fisheries from southern southeast Alaska to the mouth of the Fraser River. They are also harvested incidentally in south coast net fisheries.

Recreational Fisheries

Chinook and coho salmon are the primary species harvested in marine water sport fisheries in British Columbia. The sport catch of chinook and coho salmon in Georgia Strait accounts for more than 75% of the total sport catch of these two species in British Columbia. Although the Strait of Georgia sport fishery harvests chinook and coho salmon originating from throughout southern British Columbia and Washington State, Fraser River stocks make up a large portion of the total chinook catch and to a lesser extent, the total coho catch. There are also several small sport fisheries in the Lower and Middle Fraser River and in the Thompson River.

Indian Food Fisheries

Indian food fisheries were established to meet the food and ceremonial needs of Native Indian communities in the Fraser River Basin. These fisheries, of which there are many along the Fraser River, are recognized by the Canadian government as having priority, second only to the needs for stock conservation (i.e., spawning escapement). Sockeye salmon are the primary target of Indian food fisheries although chinook, chum and coho salmon are also taken in the catch.

Economic Value

The total economic value of Fraser River salmon production is a difficult figure to derive. This is due in part to the problems associated with apportioning the catch taken in marine fisheries to Fraser and non-Fraser sources. However, we are able to provide an approximation of the total value of Fraser River salmon production to the Canadian commercial fishery (i.e., this excludes the value of Fraser River salmon production to fisheries in the states of Washington and Alaska).

The landed wholesale value of the commercial salmon catch in British Columbia has ranged from $426 million to $585 million and averaged $540 million over the period 1987 to 1989 (R. Mylchreest, Canadian Department of Fisheries and Oceans, Vancouver, pers. comm.). Approximately 50% of the total annual landed wholesale value to the commercial fishery, or an average of $270 million, can be attributed to production from the Fraser River. Comparable values are not yet available for the sport and Indian food fisheries.

Salmon Habitat in the Fraser River Basin and Associated Waters

The long-term maintenance of Pacific salmon production in the Fraser River Basin depends on controlling harvest and protecting habitats that are critical to the survival and development of Pacific salmon. The Canadian Department of Fisheries and Oceans plays the lead role in regulating the catch of Fraser River salmon. This aspect of maintaining production will not be developed further in this paper. Important components of the habitat of Fraser River salmon are located in both the Basin itself and that portion of the marine environment through which the salmon move as juveniles and maturing adults. However, discussion will be restricted primarily to freshwater and estuarine habitats.

Freshwater Habitat Requirements for Fraser River Pacific Salmon

There are several freshwater habitat requirements that are common to all five species of Pacific salmon. Maturing adults that enter the river must have unobstructed access to their natal spawning grounds. Barriers that result from rock slides or velocity gradients will limit or eliminate access and hence reduce production. Once on the spawning grounds, salmon must have clean gravel through which percolates a well oxygenated supply of water for the incubation of the fertilized eggs. Anything that impedes the sub-gravel flow of water below a critical level, particularly heavy siltation of the spawning beds, will reduce egg survival. Further, the water temperature at the time of spawning and during the period of incubation must be maintained within a certain range. Excessively high temperatures will result in failure of the adults to spawn or, if spawning has taken place, it will disrupt egg development and the timing of emergence of alevins. Following hatching and emergence from the gravel, pink and chum salmon move quickly down the river and into Strait of Georgia. Most chinook, coho and sockeye salmon remain in the freshwater environment for a period ranging from a few weeks to 1-3 years following emergence. Chinook and coho salmon generally reside in streams and rivers while sockeye salmon move into lakes. During this freshwater rearing phase all three species require food, clean water, appropriate temperature regimes and refuge from predators.

Major Habitat Changes in the Fraser River Basin and Their Effects on Pacific Salmon

A vast array of changes have been made to the Fraser River Basin at various times and places over the last century. Appreciation of the effects of these changes on salmon stocks, both in the past and in the future, requires an understanding of what components of the freshwater habitat are utilized by each of the species of salmon during different times in their life history. For the purpose of this presentation, I have divided the habitat into four major types: lake, off-channel and tributary, mainstem and estuary; and life histories into three periods: migration, spawning and rearing (Table 6.1). Within each of the habitat types, I have shown the common types of changes that have occurred in the Fraser River Basin and how they effect salmon habitat (Table 6.2). A brief discussion of some of the major types of habitat alteration is provided below. This discussion draws heavily from an unpublished, internal report (1989) of the Canadian Department of Fisheries and Oceans entitled, "Status of Information on Fraser River Salmon Habitat and the Relationship Between Habitat and Production".

Table 6.1: Utilisation of General Habitat Types in the Fraser River by Coho (CO), Chum (CH), Chinook (CN), Pink (PK), and Sockeye (SK) Salmon during Different Periods of their Life Cycle

	Migration					Spawning					Rearing				
	CO	CH	CN	PK	SK	CO	CH	CN	PK	SK	CO	CH	CN	PK	SK
Lake	■		■	■				■		■			■		■
Off-Channel						■							■		■
Tributary	■	■	■	■	■	■	■	■	■	■	■			■	
Mainstem	■	■	■	■	■	■		■					■	■	
Estuary	■	■	■	■	■						■	■			■

Urbanisation of the Flood Plains

Alteration of the flood plains of the Fraser River Basin has reduced the amount of habitat available for salmon and therefore the potential rearing capacity of the Basin. Through dyking and filling, approximately 80% of the Fraser River wetlands, including intertidal and shallow sub-tidal zones, have been transformed to other uses, primarily agriculture (Environment Canada, 1986). The results of these activities have been to decrease the amount of habitat available for rearing and as a predator refuge. Further, the alteration of the flood plains has impaired the migration of smolts and fry from tributaries to the mainstem of the Fraser. A specific example of the above was the drainage of Sumas Lake between 1919 and 1923 with the resultant loss of 12,000 ha of fish habitat from the Lower Fraser River that had been used as a rearing area and predator refuge for juveniles. Also, the mortality associated with pumping to control the water level behind dykes has been estimated to be up to 20% on the Salmon River in Langley (Paish and Associates, 1981).

Armouring of river banks and channelisation are common throughout urban areas of the Fraser River Basin. These activities restrict access of salmon to both spawning and rearing habitats. Maintenance of these areas usually requires a regular regime of dredging which can result in the direct mortality of juvenile

Table 6.2: Impacts of Human Activity on Pacific Salmon Habitat in the Fraser River Basin.

Activity	Life Stage			Habitat Impacts						
	Migration	Spawning	Rearing	Flow	Temperature	Siltation	Contaminants	Food	Access	Loss
Lakes										
Landfill							■	■	■	■
Port Development								■	■	■
Municipal Effluent	■						■			
Logging		■	■		■	■	■	■		
Silviculture		■	■		■	■	■	■		
Agriculture		■	■		■	■	■	■		
Mining		■	■			■	■	■		
Dams		■	■	■	■				■	
Railway	■	■	■	■		■	■		■	■
Trans. of Dangerous Goods	■	■	■				■			
Pulp Mills			■			■	■			
Tributaries and Off-Channel Habitat										
Dyking & Channelisation	■	■	■	■	■	■		■	■	■
Landfill	■	■	■	■			■	■	■	■
Urbanisation	■	■	■	■			■	■	■	■
Municipal Effluent	■		■				■			
Logging		■	■		■	■	■	■		■
Silviculture		■	■		■	■	■	■	■	■
Agriculture		■	■	■	■	■	■	■		
Mining		■	■	■				■	■	■
Dams		■	■	■	■	■				
Road Building	■		■							
Trans. of Dangerous Goods	■		■				■			

Table 6.2: Impacts of Human Activity on Pacific Salmon Habitat in the Fraser River Basin, continued

Activity	Life Stage			Habitat Impacts						
	Migration	Spawning	Rearing	Flow	Temperature	Siltation	Contaminants	Food	Access	Loss
Mainstem Fraser and Thompson Rivers										
Dyking & Channelisation		■	■	■		■		■	■	■
Landfill			■				■			
Urbanisation	■	■	■	■	■		■	■	■	■
Dredging	■	■	■	■		■		■	■	■
Industrial Effluent	■	■	■				■			
Municipal Effluent	■	■	■				■			
Pulp Mills	■	■	■				■	■		
Wood Treatment	■	■	■				■			
Agriculture	■	■	■	■	■	■	■	■		■
Railway	■					■			■	■
Trans. of Dangerous Goods		■					■			
Estuary										
Dyking & Channelisation			■	■				■	■	■
Landfill			■	■			■			■
Port Development	■		■			■		■	■	■
Urbanisation	■		■	■	■	■	■	■	■	■
Dredging	■		■	■		■	■			■
Industrial Effluent	■		■				■			
Municipal Effluent	■		■				■			
Wood Treatment			■				■	■		
Agriculture			■		■	■	■	■		■

salmon through entrainment into the dredges and a loss of spawning habitat through gravel removal. The problems associated with armouring and channelisation are most evident in the lower portion of the Fraser River Basin. Production from approximately 20 streams that once produced coho salmon within the City of Vancouver has been lost as the result of the conversion of these systems into ditches.

Effluents

Eight major landfill sites in the Lower Fraser River are important sources of toxic materials. These sites discharge leachates comprised of organic materials, ammonia and solids totalling approximately 7.5 million litres per day into the lower river (Anon, 1978). In addition to the major sites, there are many smaller wood waste sites located adjacent to the Fraser River throughout the Basin.

The total industrial and municipal effluent discharged into the Fraser River increased from 504,000 to 1,526,000 m^3 per day between 1965 and 1985 (Servizi, 1989) and is the major source of organic and inorganic contaminants in the Basin. Some of that effluent is directed to municipal sewers and flows to sewage treatment plants prior to being discharged into the Fraser River. However, 41% of the total waste water effluent is discharged directly into the river by six pulp mills located in the headwaters of the Basin. Effluents in the Fraser River are probably responsible for contamination of some species of fish and aquatic invertebrates. Levels of organic contaminants such as PCBs (Johnston et al., 1975; Singleton, 1983) and metals have been found to be higher in fish, invertebrates and sediments in the estuarine regions of the Lower Fraser River than in the headwaters of the river. Although there has been limited sampling, adult sockeye caught upstream of Hope in 1986 and 1987 had very low levels of organic and inorganic contaminants (Canadian Department of Fisheries and Oceans, unpublished data). More recent studies have revealed the presence of dioxins and other organochlorines in juvenile chinook salmon exposed to pulp mill effluents in the upper Fraser River (Rodgers et al., 1989).

Railway and Road Construction

Railway and road construction can effect salmon habitat through sedimentation which reduces egg survival or rock slides and improper culvert installation which impedes the migration of juveniles and adults. The single largest deleterious impact on Fraser River salmon occurred as the result of rock dumping and a slide during railroad construction in the Hell's Gate area in the period between 1912 and 1915. These events, in conjunction with overfishing (Ricker, 1987; 1989) resulted in a drastic reduction in the size of the upper river runs in subsequent years. Although fishways were constructed to alleviate the blockage, passage of adults is still difficult in years of low water levels.

Dams and Irrigation

Dams block access to areas of the Basin upriver of dam sites, remove water from the system and, in the case of hydroelectric facilities, cause direct mortality to juvenile salmon as they move through the turbines. Although there are hundreds of dams in the Fraser River Basin, the ones of primary concern are those on the Nechako, Bridge-Seton, Stave, Alouette and Coquitlam rivers. There is particular concern that the global warming phenomenon, which may reduce rainfall in areas of the Basin east of the coastal mountains, will exacerbate the existing water removal problems associated with both power generation and irrigation for agricultural purposes.

Logging Activities

Logging activities have caused extensive disruption and loss of productive capacity of salmon habitat in some localized areas of the Fraser River Basin, particularly in the Weaver Creek and Nadina River watersheds. Logging operations can lead to increases in soil erosion and sedimentation, increases in water temperature (Holtby, 1988), loss of shoreline cover and increases in the use of herbicides for the control of "brush". Both the Weaver Creek and Nadina River runs of sockeye salmon have already been effected by logging activities. The Nadina sockeye run is near extinction due to siltation of historic spawning areas. There is also concern for the large Stuart Lake sockeye salmon stock complex as logging activities are being initiated in this area. A related concern is the effect of log storage on salmon habitat. Almost 1,500 ha of the Fraser River estuary foreshore is leased for log boom storage (Highman, 1983). Levy et al. (1989) showed that there can be dramatic reductions in dissolved oxygen levels at booming sites resulting in the avoidance of these areas by juvenile salmon. However, their studies did not show any direct effect of log storage on the survival of juvenile salmon.

Plans for the Future of the Pacific Salmon Resources of the Fraser River Basin

Application of the concept of sustainable development for the Pacific salmon resources of the Fraser River Basin requires an understanding of our goals for these resources and the management practices that will be implemented to attain these goals. Developing plans for the future of the Pacific salmon resources of the Fraser River Basin has received special attention in recent years for several reasons. First, Canada assumed full responsibility for the development of Fraser River salmon stocks in 1985 with the signing of the Pacific Salmon Treaty between the Governments of the United States and Canada. Prior to that time the management responsibility for sockeye and pink salmon resided with the International Pacific Salmon Fisheries Commission. Also, in recent years there has been a heightened concern among the public regarding the effect of other uses of the Fraser River Basin on the salmon resources. Finally, it has been recognized that many of the salmon stocks from the Fraser River Basin are depressed and have the potential for a much greater level of production. This is a particularly important matter as it is recognized in the Pacific Salmon Treaty that Canada should receive all the benefits from increases in production beyond base levels defined in the Treaty.

There are several plans in various stages of development that relate directly to the sustainable development of the Pacific salmon resources of the Fraser River Basin. Although the plans focus on different aspects of the resource, they all have the common overall objective of increasing the production of Pacific salmon from the Fraser River Basin. One of the plans was completed in 1986 and is known as the Canadian Department of Fisheries and Oceans Policy for the Management of Fish Habitat (PMFH). As a national policy, the PMFH has direct relevance to the Fraser River Basin. The objective of the policy is to increase the natural productive capacity of habitats for the nation's fisheries resources to benefit present and future generations of Canadians. The objective is supported by three goals. The first is to maintain the current productive capacity of fish habitats supporting Canada's fisheries resources, so that fish suitable for human consumption may be produced. This goal is being implemented using the principle of "no net loss" of productive salmon habitat as a guide. The second goal of the PMFH is to rehabilitate the productive capacity of fish habitat in selected areas where economic or social benefits can be achieved through the fisheries resource. The final goal is to create and improve fish habitat in selected areas where the production of fisheries resources can be increased for the social or economic benefit of Canadians.

The PMFH is the only plan that has been completed and received government approval to date. However, there are several other complementary initiatives that are now in progress and relate directly to the sustainable development of the Pacific salmon resources of the Fraser River Basin. As the other initiatives are in progress and are not yet government policy, it is not possible to provide all the appropriate details, particularly with regard to implementation. However, general comments can be made about the objectives.

The plans now being developed focus either on Pacific salmon habitat in the Fraser River Basin or on particular salmon species in the Basin. All these plans will contribute directly to a task force dealing with environmentally sustainable social and economic development in the Fraser River Basin.

A fish habitat management plan is being developed specifically for the Fraser River Basin. Under this plan the Basin is divided into six habitat management areas or sub-basins. For each area there will be developed a scientifically based estimate of production capacity as it relates to Pacific salmon, a description of expected salmon returns to the area, an outline of habitat and other limitations to salmon production, a list of restoration and enhancement possibilities and a description of habitat protection requirements. An overall plan will amalgamate the individual sub-basin plans.

The remaining plans for the Pacific salmon resources of the Fraser River Basin each deal with one of the five species of Pacific salmon. The Fraser River Sockeye

Salmon Management and Enhancement Plan, being prepared by the Fraser River Sockeye Salmon Task Force, has received the greatest amount of attention of any of the species specific plans to date. The objectives of the Task Force include

(i)   maximizing production from natural habitat and supplementing it with enhancement where appropriate; and,

(ii) minimizing negative effects on other species.

It is recognized, based on historical catch data, stock-recruitment (Ricker, 1975) and habitat analyses, that the Fraser River Basin has the potential to produce sockeye salmon runs that are much larger than the current levels. The upper limit to this production, based on the habitat analyses, may be on the order of 30 million fish per year, or approximately three times the current average run size. It was concluded, however, that there would be a high level of risk, both from the management and scientific perspective, in attempting to move immediately to the 30 million level. Consequently, it is likely that interim goals will be established and over the period of rebuilding the sockeye stocks to these interim levels, the possibility and practicality of producing runs of 30 million will be further evaluated. Rebuilding the Fraser River sockeye salmon stocks is predicated largely on increasing escapement to natural, but currently underutilized, spawning areas. However, the Task Force will also consider enhancement technology as a complement to natural rebuilding.

Plans relevant to Fraser River chinook, coho, pink and chum salmon, although varying in detail and approaches to implementation, all focus on increasing natural production. This will be accomplished primarily by increasing escapement to natural spawning grounds throughout the Fraser River Basin. Although, as with sockeye salmon, the emphasis will be on natural rebuilding, consideration will also be given to enhancement technology in some instances.

The Future for the Sustainable Development of the Pacific Salmon Resources of the Fraser River Basin

The concept of sustainable development presented in this paper is restricted to Pacific salmon in the Fraser River and as such is narrow in focus. Ultimately, a sustainable development plan for the Fraser River Basin will have to incorporate all major resources and stakeholders. Achieving the ultimate goal however will first require an understanding of the nature of the various resource types as well as the expectations of the stakeholders both for the present and the future. It is in this context that I discuss the future for the sustainable development of the Pacific salmon resources of the Fraser River Basin.

Any consideration for the future of sustainable development of the Pacific salmon resources of Fraser River Basin must anticipate two very important factors. First, the size of the annual salmon runs to the Fraser River can be significantly increased over the next several decades. Second, this increase in production is likely to be achieved primarily by increasing escapement to natural spawning areas. The role of enhancement in increasing fish numbers may be important in some localized areas and overall will be complementary to natural stock rebuilding.

The demands for large volumes of uncontaminated water to support the production of Pacific salmon in the Fraser River will increase as the stocks are rebuilt. This is primarily the result of the emphasis on rebuilding stocks by increasing escapement to natural spawning areas. Increases in the number of salmon returning to the Fraser River to spawn will likely require increases in water flow through certain critical areas such as Hell's Gate and possibly the construction of new fish ways to facilitate the passage of adults to the spawning areas (P. Saxvik, Canadian Department of Fisheries and Oceans, Vancouver, pers. comm.). Even at current levels of returns, water levels are insufficient in some years to permit the upriver movement of all the salmon above this area. As a result, future production is lost as some adults do not reach their spawning grounds.

Concerns for water conditions in the upper portion of the Fraser River Basin are particularly relevant for sockeye salmon. Currently, both water volume and temperature are marginal at some of the major spawning sites for sockeye salmon in this area. Further, much of the anticipated increase in sockeye salmon production described above is projected to come from the upper portion of the Fraser River Basin. The situation is complicated by other uses of the Basin which may exacerbate the problem. Logging in particular, if not performed carefully, would likely result in changes in the water flow conditions, and increases in water temperature and sedimentation (Holtby and Scrivener, 1989). Superimposed on these already difficult problems is the potential effect of global climate change on the upper portion of the Basin. In particular, the change may lead to reduced rainfall and warmer water temperatures in areas east of the coastal mountains at the same time that spawning escapement is being increased for the upper river stocks.

The production objectives for each species of Pacific salmon in the Fraser River Basin are going to be established on a sub-basin basis. In other words, the production of a species from the entire basin will be equal to the sum of the production from each of the sub-basins. Further, there are no plans to "consolidate" production for any of the five species into one or two areas within the Basin using enhancement or other technologies. As described above, the focus will be on increasing spawning escapement to natural spawning areas throughout the watershed. This approach to increasing overall production has important implications for other resource users within the Basin. In particular, all sub-basins will, to some extent, contain important salmon spawning or rearing habitat or both. As a result, close cooperation will be necessary between those who manage the fish habitat and those who use the Basin for other purposes if we are to minimize the negative effects of these other uses on Pacific salmon production.

Although the focus of this paper is on the Fraser River Basin, it is important to realize that concerns for Fraser River salmon production extend well beyond the Basin. All species of Fraser River salmon migrate as juveniles through Strait of Georgia and adjacent coastal waters on their way to the North Pacific Ocean.

Although fish from some species appear to move through the coastal waters quickly, others, particularly chinook and coho salmon, may rear in the area of the Strait of Georgia for extensive periods of time. Consequently, these fish may be more susceptible to contaminants carried into Strait of Georgia from the Fraser River. They are also more likely to be effected by annual variability in production in the Strait of Georgia which is in part, dependent on Fraser River discharge.

Another concern external to the Fraser River but potentially affecting salmon production from the Basin is the carrying capacity of the North Pacific Ocean for Pacific salmon. Theoretically, there is a limit to the number of salmon that can be reared through to the adult stage in the North Pacific Ocean. Although this number is very uncertain, we do have evidence for density-dependent growth of salmon in the North Pacific Ocean (Peterman, 1984). Further, many countries on the Pacific Rim have been dramatically increasing their juvenile salmon production in recent decades, further taxing the salmon food resources of the North Pacific Ocean. Although the ultimate carrying capacity is not known, it is important to be aware that we will be increasing the number of Fraser River salmon in the North Pacific at the same time that other countries are dramatically increasing their own production. As a result, we can not be sure that the increase in juvenile production from the Fraser River will necessarily result in the expected returns of adults.

Managing the fisheries that harvest Fraser River Pacific salmon has proven to be a demanding task. Within a species each stock has its own level of productivity which is different from other stocks of the same species. Consequently, the harvest rate that each stock can withstand, while maintaining conservation or rebuilding efforts, will vary. Current fisheries management practices attempt to "target" certain stocks at certain times so as to achieve the appropriate catch and resulting spawning escapement from all stocks within a species. However, because of the overlap in the time at which various stocks return to the river, it is rare that a fishery removes fish from only one stock. As a result, if two or more stocks with different levels of productivity are harvested at the same time, it is necessary either to catch the appropriate number of fish from the more productive stock and over-harvest the less productive stock, or to forgo some catch from the more productive stock to protect the other. The projected increases in the size of Pacific salmon runs to the Fraser River that were described above will increase the severity of the problem. This will be in part because the increase in size of some of the stocks will be much larger than for other stocks. Therefore, attempts to harvest the additional production from some of the larger stocks could have an even greater effect on some of the smaller or less productive stocks.

The problem of mixed stock fisheries within a species for Fraser River Pacific salmon may extend beyond those fisheries in the Fraser River and immediately adjacent coastal waters. For example, it is known that some Fraser River sockeye salmon are caught as maturing adults on their return migration in northern British Columbia and southern southeast Alaska. If the size of the run of sockeye salmon to the Fraser River increases as expected, they may be taken in substantial numbers in sockeye fisheries targetting on other, non-Fraser River stocks (e.g., Skeena

River sockeye salmon fisheries in northern British Columbia).

The difficulties associated with mixed stock fisheries within a species can also be extended to fisheries that while targetting on one stock, harvest more than one species. Typically, Fraser River salmon fisheries exhibit this phenomenon. For example, seine fisheries which operate in coastal waters and target on sockeye salmon often take chinook salmon as an incidental catch. If the annual sockeye salmon run to the Fraser River increases to two or three times its current level, then more fishing effort will be required to harvest the amount of sockeye that is surplus to spawning escapement requirements. However, this increase in effort will also lead to an increase in the incidental catch of chinook salmon thereby hindering efforts to rebuild Fraser River chinook stocks. Resolving the difficulties associated with mixed stock fisheries and incidental catches of other species, particularly as the Fraser River salmon stocks are rebuilding, may require alterations in the timing and location of fisheries. We may also have to consider modifications to fishing gear to make it more selective, and further research to better define the time at which different stocks pass through the fisheries.

Research Needs

Sustainable development of the Pacific salmon resources of the Fraser River Basin and the objective of increasing salmon production as described in the Policy for the Management of Fish Habitat are interdependent concepts. Both require a knowledge of the location of spawning and rearing areas within the Fraser River Basin and factors associated with the freshwater environment that limit and control salmon production. Further, it is necessary to understand better the many events occurring in the greater Fraser River estuary, including the Strait of Georgia, that effect the growth and survival of Pacific salmon. Implementing the concepts embodied in the term "sustainable development", and within the policy for the management of fish habitat require an ability to describe in quantitative terms the effects of changes to the environment of the Fraser River Basin on salmon production. The description of research needs given below reflects the view of the author and focuses primarily on examples of uncertainty in factors that limit or control Pacific salmon production in the Fraser River Basin and associated waters.

Descriptions of the spawning and juvenile rearing areas are reasonably complete for all major Fraser River salmon stocks. However, there is much less information on these characteristics for the smaller salmon stocks, particularly the small coho and chum salmon stocks. The lack of information regarding the nature and role of the smaller stocks is of increasing concern. It is now thought that a disproportionate amount of the genetic diversity of a species, and consequently the ability to survive in a changing environment, is contained within these smaller groups (Scudder, 1989). Experimental designs that can be used to quantify the effect of habitat changes on salmon production, although not commonly employed, are available (e.g., Walters et al., 1988).

Sockeye Salmon

The focus for new, major logging initiatives will be in the Upper Fraser River in the Stuart Lake area. However, very little is known about the early life history of Stuart Lake sockeye salmon. We do know that the biogeoclimatic conditions in the Stuart Lake area are very different in terms of soils, climate and hydrography from other areas of the Fraser in which sockeye have been studied. Further, there is some evidence that the productivity of Stuart Lake sockeye may be different from other sockeye stocks. Therefore, acquiring basic information on habitat, habitat-stock interactions, production capability and the impacts of logging must be considered a high priority. Some specific questions requiring answers are:

(i) Do sockeye salmon spawn primarily in areas where groundwater influences the redds, thus preventing freezing during the winter? If so, how will logging and the building of roads affect the quantity and quality of groundwater?
(ii) What is the fry production per adult in this climatic zone and how would it be affected by increases in the rate of siltation?
(iii) What effect will increasing water temperature in the spawning streams, expected as a result of the removal of the forest canopy, have on pre-spawning mortality?

Chinook Salmon

Fraser River chinook salmon are exposed to contaminants from pulp mills, particularly in the upper portion of the Fraser Basin, and to waste waters in the estuary. Although there have been a few attempts to establish the effects of contaminants and waste waters in the Fraser River on chinook (Servizi, 1989), there is little understanding of their role in controlling growth and survival. It is necessary to determine if sub-lethal effects of contaminants affect the reproductive success of adults. This is particularly important for those spring-migrating stocks which use mainstem habitats for prolonged periods on their upriver migration. There are similar concerns about the effects of contaminants and waste water on juvenile chinook salmon in the Fraser River. Juveniles spend from a few weeks to one to two years in freshwater prior to emigrating to sea. Previous studies have shown that some juvenile chinook leave their natal streams and take up residence in the mainstem of the Fraser River (Tutty and Yole, 1978) and the Fraser estuary (Levy and Northcote, 1982). Juvenile chinook can be found in the inner estuary from February through July (Birtwell et al., 1981). They have also been found downstream of pulp mill effluent diffusers at Prince George in October (Servizi, 1989), and downstream of Prince George and in the Thompson River in August (Levings et al., 1985). Overwintering populations of chinook have been detected near Prince George, Quesnel, Lytton and Agassiz and in the Thompson River (Whelen and Slaney, 1986).

The production potential of the Fraser River for chinook salmon is affected in an as yet largely undefined way by the timing and quantity of the water flow. However, as a result of dams, water diversions, land use practices and climate change the nature of the flow regime is becoming increasingly uncertain. It is necessary to quantify the relationship between production potential and the flow regime for chinook salmon, particularly at low flow levels.

Coho Salmon

Coho salmon in the tributary streams below Hope are an "urban species". Spawning and freshwater rearing habitats for coho in this area have frequently been altered over the last century. Alterations up to the 1950's were primarily the result of agricultural and flood control practices. More recent alterations in coho freshwater habitat in the lower portion of the Fraser River Basin are the result of urban expansion and include changes due to housing developments, road construction, vegetation removal, culvert installation and other land use practices. Escapement data are inadequate to assess the magnitude of the loss in productive capacity due to habitat change. A synoptic review using existing data is not practical as a result of the large number of coho streams in the Lower Fraser River Basin. A priority research strategy in this portion of the Basin would be to establish a small number of experimental watersheds where habitat could be manipulated to determine those factors limiting production.

Chum Salmon

Chum salmon fry are thought to spend several weeks rearing in the Fraser River estuary (Levy and Northcote, 1982). During this period of residence in the Lower Fraser River, chum salmon fry are dependent on the estuarine food web, feeding on insects and brackish water invertebrates. However, we do not yet understand the role of the estuarine phase with respect to the survival of chum salmon fry to the adult stage.

Pink Salmon

Significant numbers of pink salmon spawn above Hope. However, to get to spawning areas in the upper part of the Fraser and Thompson rivers adult pink salmon must negotiate velocity barriers as well as low water levels in some years. Low water levels occurred most recently in 1985 and appear to have impeded upriver migration past Hell's Gate. The role of river velocity as a factor limiting pink salmon production is also an issue when considering river narrowing associated with double tracking in the Thompson River. More information is required to determine the relationship between adult pink salmon body size, swimming energetics and energy available for reproduction.

Other Research Needs

The description of research needs described above deals with individual species and in some cases, a group of stocks within a species. However, there are other research needs that are common to all five species of Pacific salmon. An area of great interest is the effect of the Fraser River on conditions in the Strait of Georgia and in turn, the effects of these conditions on the growth and survival of juvenile Fraser River salmon is an area of great uncertainty. The Fraser River is the primary freshwater and nutrient source for the Strait contributing up to 80% of the total land runoff. Discharge from the river drives current patterns and affects nutrient distribution in the strait. It is necessary to study the linkages between the physical and chemical composition of the Fraser River and, productivity in the Strait of Georgia, growth and survival of juvenile salmon and distribution and abundance of salmon predators.

References

Anon. 1978. *Fraser River Estuary Summary Study. Proposals for the Development of an Estuary Management Plan: Summary Report of the Steering Committee.* Victoria: Government of Canada, Province of British Columbia.

Birtwell, I. K., J. C. Davis, M. Hobbs, M. D. Nassichuk, M. Waldichuk and J. A. Servizi. 1981. "Brief presented to the British Columbia Pollution Control Board Inquiry pertaining to the Annacis Island Sewage Treatment Plant and Municipal Waste Discharges into the Lower Fraser River." *Can. Ind. Rep. Fish. Aquat. Sci.* 126.

Canada. Department of Fisheries and Oceans. 1988. *Pacific Region Salmon Resource Management Plan— A Discussion Document.* Vol. 1. Inner south coast and Fraser River. Vancouver, British Columbia: Canadian Department of Fisheries and Oceans.

Environment Canada. 1986. *Fact Sheet on Wetlands in Canada: A Valuable Resource.* Ottawa: Lands Directorate, Environment Canada (Cat. No. En 73-6/86-4E).

Highman, J. 1983. *The Fraser River Log Management Review.* Prepared for the Fraser River Harbour Commission, New Westminister, B.C. May 1983.

Holtby, L. B. 1988. "Effects of Logging on Stream Temperatures in Carnation Creek, British Columbia, and Resultant Impacts on the Coho Salmon (*Oncorhynchus kisutch*)." *Can. J. Fish. Aquat. Sci.* 45:502-515.

Holtby, L. B., and J. C. Scrivener. 1989. "Observed and Simulated Effects of Climatic Variability, Clear-cut Logging and Fishing on the Numbers of Chum Salmon (*Oncorhynchus keta*) and Coho Salmon (*O. kisutch*) Returning to Carnation Creek, British Columbia." in Levings, C. D., L. B. Holtby and M. A. Henderson (eds.). Proceedings of the National Workshop on Effects of Habitat Alteration on Salmonid Stocks. *Can. Spec. Publ. Fish. Aquat. Sci.* 105.

Johnston, N. T., L. J. Albright, T. G. Northcote, P. C. Oloffs and K. Tsumura. 1975. *Chlorinated Hydrocarbon Residues in Fishes of the Lower Fraser River.* Tech. Rep. 9. Vancouver: Westwater Research Centre, University of British Columbia.

Levings, C. D., J. C. Scrivener, B. Anderson, C. Shirvell and R. Lauzier. 1985. "Results of Reconnaissance Sampling for Juvenile Salmonids in the Upper Fraser River and Selected Tributaries, August and October, 1984." *Can. Data Rep. Fish. Aquat. Sci.* 549.

Levy, D. A., and T. G. Northcote. 1982. "Juvenile Salmon Residency in the Marsh Area of the Fraser River Estuary." *Can. J. Fish. Aquat. Sci.* 39: 270-276.

Levy, D. A., T. G. Northcote, K. J. Hall and I. Yesaki. 1989. "Juvenile Salmonid Responses to Log Storage in Littoral Habitat of the Fraser River Estuary and Babine Lake." in Levings C. D., L. B. Holtby and M. A. Henderson (eds.). Proceedings of the National Workshop on the Effects of Habitat Alteration on Salmonid Stocks. *Can Spec. Publ. Fish. Aquat. Sci.* 105.

Northcote, T. G., and P. A. Larkin. 1989. "The Fraser River: A Major Salmonine Production System." in Dodge, D. P. (ed.). Proceedings of the International Large River Symposium. *Can. Spec. Publ. Fish. Aquat. Sci.* 106.

Paish and Associates. 1981. *The Implementation of a Cooperative Watershed Planning and Management Program for the Fraser River Watershed—Langley, B.C.* Vancouver: Paish and Associates. July 1981.

Peterman, R. M. 1984. "Density-Dependent Growth in Early Ocean Life of Sockeye Salmon (*Oncorhynchus nerka*)." *Can. J. Fish. Aquat. Sci.* 41:1825-1829.

Ricker, W. E. 1989. "History and Present State of the Odd-year Pink Salmon Runs of the Fraser River Region." *Can. Tech. Rep. Fish. Aquat. Sci.* 1702.

Ricker, W. E. 1987. "Effects of the Fishery and of Obstacles to Migration on the Abundance of Fraser River Sockeye Salmon (*Oncorhynchus nerka*)." *Can. Tech. Rep. Fish. Aquat. Sci.* 1522.

Ricker, W. E. 1975. "Computation and Interpretation of Biological Statistics of Fish Populations." *Fish. Res. Board Can. Bull.* 191.

Rodgers, H., C. Levings, W. L. Lockhart and R. J. Norstrom. 1989. "Observations on Overwintering Juvenile Chinook Salmon (*Oncorhynchus tschawytscha*) Exposed to Bleach Kraft Mill Effluent in the Upper Fraser River, B.C." *Chemosphere.* 19:1853-1868.

Scudder, G. G. E. 1989. "The Adaptive Significance of Marginal Populations: A General Perspective." in Levings, C. D., L. B. Holtby and M. A. Henderson (eds.). Proceedings of the National Workshop on the Effects of Habitat Alteration on Salmonid Stocks. *Can. Spec. Publ. Fish. Aquat. Sci.* 105.

Servizi, J. A. 1989. "Protecting Fraser River Salmon (*Oncorhynchus spp.*) from Wastewaters: An Assessment." in Levings, C. D., L. B. Holtby and M. A. Henderson (eds.). Proceedings of the National Workshop on the Effects of Habitat Alteration on Salmonid Stocks. *Can. Spec. Publ. Fish. Aquat. Sci.* 105.

Singleton, H. J. 1983. Trace Metals and Selected Organic Contaminants in Fraser River Fish. Tech. Rep. 1. Province of British Columbia, Ministry of the Environment.

Tutty, B. D., and F. Y. E. Yole. 1978. "Overwintering Chinook Salmon in the Upper Fraser River System." *Fish. Mar. Serv. Rep.* 1460.

Walters, C. J., J. S. Collie and T. Webb. 1988. "Experimental Designs for Estimating Transient Responses to Management Disturbances." *Can. J. Fish. Aquat. Sci.* 45:530-538.

Whelen, M. A., and T. L. Slaney. 1986. *Late Winter Sampling of Juvenile Salmonids in the Fraser River*. Report prepared by Aquatic Resources Ltd. for Department of Fisheries and Oceans, West Vancouver Laboratory.

7

The Quest for Consensus on Sustainable Development in the Use and Management of Fraser River Salmon

Norman G. Dale

Although sustainable development seems to create a new or renewed demand for technical knowledge, it is, in my view, primarily a challenge of human capacity to reach consensus. The very fact that definitions for sustainable development are so many and varied hints at this. The word *sustainable* is not problematic. Frequent reference to the need to leave future generations at least as well off as the current ones reveals a common enough understanding; but defining *development* is problematic in the extreme. The reason is that to suggest that a social system ought to develop, immediately raises the question-*towards what*? When one speaks of "development" in embryology, there is little controversy about the general direction this is to take: an egg becomes a fry becomes an adult fish. In ecology, the term "development" has also been used, with the strong suggestion that there are distinguishing characteristics of mature ecosystems (Odum, 1969). In these biophysical systems, there is a sense of directionality towards a pre-ordained final form.

But when the system to be developed is a complex human society consisting of different groups with varied and often conflicting interests then the meaning of what it is "to develop" is not at all self-evident. From the local to the global level, differences and conflicts are ubiquitous and much of the struggle arises from the all too obvious fact that people are not of one mind on what would be best for their community.

In this paper, the focus is upon the human communities who affect and are affected by the salmon stocks who spawn in the Fraser River Basin. The question is how the incredible gift of these numerous species and stocks can be used and governed so as to contribute to sustainable development.[1] This raises the further

---

1   This is not the same question as how to manage the stocks sustainably. That has been the stated intention of fisheries biologists for whom sustainable yield, preferably close to some maximum, has been an enduring if

and more profound question: what are the social, communal, economic or other purposes of governance? The answers of the key stakeholders—users, managers, and those whose actions inadvertently affect the salmon resource—would be many and conflicting.

The lack of agreement on the role and importance of salmon in the basin is seen in the contrast between fisheries biologists' and managers' views, versus those of other resource interests. The former investigate, ponder and strive for a goal of producing as much salmon as possible. Thus, for example, in recent years the federal Department of Fisheries and Oceans (DFO), has promoted a mid-range goal of doubling sockeye (*Onchorhynchus nerka*)[2] production in the Fraser Basin. Such goals are promulgated in relative isolation from others (e.g., logging interests) which could get in the way. To protect a reach of stream or a rearing lake could reduce or even preclude extractive use of timber or other resources. An implicit trade-off is involved in almost any decision to restore or protect habitat.

Stock management can also entail trade-offs. Plans to rebuild populations to maximum production levels inevitably require some curtailment of harvest rates. Commercial fishermen could readily question why they should make sacrifices to achieve the goal of maximum salmonid production. After all, fisheries biologists know and say that populations may literally be sustained within most of a wide range of equilibria (see Henderson, this volume). It is also recognized that long before today's giant fleets and habitat alteration, salmon populations underwent massive fluctuation (see Northcote and Burwash, in volume II). Thus it is difficult to defend the idea that there is some unique population that must be the goal for salmon management. Instead, the target for any given stock is open to social debate and choice.

In the absence of some coordinating measures, pursuit of individual self-interest by a large array of stakeholders with divergent values and perceptions will not lead to sustainable development; instead there will be chronic conflict and far from optimal benefits for anyone. Coordination can be achieved if one powerful stakeholder—usually government—can impose its vision on the rest. There are good reasons, however, to doubt the feasibility of this happening in the management context of the Fraser salmon. In the description of the cast of stakeholders below, the growing ability of Native and non-governmental parties to affect decision-making is highlighted. Even if particular interest groups are unable to get what they want, they frequently have the power to block others' decisions, including those of DFO.

It follows that both the means for and ends of sustainable development will have to be defined and designed multilaterally. The quest for sustainable development requires building consensual approaches.[3]

---

elusive goal (Larkin, 1977).

2   In this paper the following common names of the five species of Pacific salmon are used: coho, chum, pink, sockeye and spring. The scientific name is given at the first reference to the common name.

3   The case for consensus in the text is essentially that unilateralism is unlikely to work. There are more positive arguments for preferring consensual to coercive decision-making. These include the judgement that free and informed involvement in decisions affecting one's life is of fundamental and intrinsic value. Organizational psychology also substantiates something well recognized in everyday experience: involvement in a decision greatly enhances subsequent support for it (McGregor, 1960).

This is quite a departure from the model of authority envisioned in the *Canada Fisheries Act* where final decisions rest exclusively with the Minister of Fisheries and Oceans. However, DFO has begun to recognize the pivotal importance of consensus-building in sustainable development.

> Isolated actions by individual segments of society are no longer sufficient to address the threats to sustainable fisheries. Sustainable development can only be achieved through the coordinated efforts of all levels of government, industry and citizen groups. DFO is working to build partnerships and strengthen decision-making institutions to help promote the exchange of views and the building of a consensus for action among all key groups. (Department of Fisheries & Oceans, 1989:11).

DFO is not alone in looking for the route to consensus. In different combinations and at scales that range from local to basin-wide and beyond, governmental and non-governmental groups are increasingly involved in multilateral forums. Within these settings, stakeholders are openly seeking ways not only to share information and reach agreement but to develop a common vision of how salmon, in relation to other activities in the Fraser Basin, should be governed for sustainability. These quite preliminary experiences with consensus building are considered in the latter part of this chapter.

First, however, it is important to be clear on what is meant by consensus, since the term is often used simply as a synonym for any agreement.[4] A narrower and far more demanding definition is needed here. Consensus is taken to mean voluntary agreement by stakeholders to a set of goals and actions developed multilaterally and with which all are satisfied. Consensus is identified both with the *unanimous acceptance* of decisions and with the *process* used in reaching these decisions.

Acceptance is readily recognized by the support (or lack of opposition) of stakeholders; it does not mean that each party believes that the decision is the best one possible.

Some of the key features of the process of effective consensus-building include:

- Prior recognition that unilateralism is undesirable;
- Direct participation of all groups with a stake in the decision;
- Explicit concern for each party's viewpoints and interests;
- Commitment to inventing a decisive and binding agreement.

This understanding of consensus could make for a very demanding assessment of current decision-making regarding Fraser salmon. To do this would be premature for the new experiences in consensual approaches outlined below. But this way of thinking about consensus helps to focus our attention on the progress, problems and potential lessons encountered in those experiences.

Prior to looking at those cases, it will be helpful to review the history of

---

4   The *Webster's New World Dictionary*, for example, defines "consensus" as "(1) an opinion held by all or most (2) general agreement..."

different perspectives on salmon use and management and survey the wide array of today's cast of stakeholders.

The Succession of Dominant Perspectives in the Governance of Fraser River Salmon

Students of conflict and consensus often neglect the ways in which a bitter history has exacerbated the challenge of resolving differences (Rothman, 1989). The long history of the relationship among human groups and the Fraser salmon must be understood, if we are to comprehend the nature and degree of the current difficulties.

Humans and salmon have co-existed in the Fraser basin for at least 10,000 years. Until recently, the nature of their interaction was recorded only in the oral tradition of aboriginal people. This account has not been well preserved post-contact. Still some speculative reconstruction is possible and there is important evidence of the close relationship between aboriginal society and salmonids (Kew, 1976; see also Kew and Griggs, this volume).

Most anthropologists seem to concur that aboriginal people were strongly dependent on the salmon stocks and there is increasing evidence that a variety of cultural taboos and the explicit application of knowledge led to some admirable self-limitation among the Indian harvesters. There is little doubt that most Native groups had harvest technologies which could have exterminated local salmon populations. The existence of myths linking sparse runs to particular human misdeeds, suggests a period during which the human and salmon populations adjusted to one another.[5] There may have even been mistakes and resulting disequilibria, (at a time of unsustainable development), which destroyed salmon runs and led to the disappearance of whole villages.

Current anthropological thinking is that by the time of Indian-European contact a couple of centuries ago, a fairly stable relationship had evolved. Salmon were "managed" through the entirety of the culture—i.e., through well-recognized rights, responsibilities, taboos, and, perhaps most importantly through the application of an exquisitely detailed knowledge of the relationships within nature and between humans and nature.

During the early post-contact years, little changed in terms of the dominant way of managing and using salmon. The low population of newcomers and, as yet, the restriction of their use of salmon as food, presented no fundamental challenge to the status quo. What most characterised that period of about eighty years following contact in the late 18th century was the tremendous generosity of Native people. The newcomers were often malnourished and short of food supplies for winters in B.C. or long voyages home. Those who kept journals recorded the beneficence of aboriginal peoples, often expressed in gifts of salmon.

In the 1860's, the development of the tin canning process transformed the gift of salmon into a commodity. Concurrently, Native people were beset by an almost

---

5   Several examples of such stories from the Haida and the Kwakiutl are outlined in Bierhost (1985).

biblical sequence of plagues, real and proverbial. In the aftermath of smallpox, religious and political suppression, alcohol, and the availability of firearms, the population plummeted, taking with it the traditional systems of governance including the customary management of the salmon (see Kew and Griggs, this volume). Meanwhile, the commercial canning companies had severe impacts on the salmon populations of many major producing systems (Netboy, 1968).

In recognition of possible stock depletion, the Dominion Department of Fisheries was created and joined in what could be called the first conservation era. Especially after the turn of the century, the Department of Fisheries built its management around as firm as possible a knowledge of fisheries biology. The Department has become a world leader in fisheries management science; indeed, some of the most respected studies and theoretical developments in the field came from the salmon research undertaken by Government of Canada scientists (see Larkin, 1979).

After World War II, a challenger slowly emerged to the dominance of biologists in framing the fisheries management problem. This came from economics. The field of resource economics gained immeasurable status from the kinds of questions that dominated the minds of cold war politicians.[6] First, academic literature and later, reports undertaken on behalf of government drew stern attention to the economic wastefulness which dissipated net benefits from a fishery whether or not it was managed to maximum sustainable yield. In British Columbia, Sinclair (1960) applied Gordon's (1954) economic reasoning in citing the excessive capacity of the salmon fleet. This set the stage for major policy redirection ("limited entry") and for what was perhaps the apex of economics as the newly dominant paradigm for fisheries management—the Pearse Commission (Pearse, 1982).

The Pearse Commission was unquestionably the benchmark for DFO's and other stakeholders' discussion of the fishery throughout most of the 1980's. Thus the discipline of economics, if not fully in control of fisheries management, was powerfully affecting the fisheries management agenda. But in sparking vigorous discussion, Pearse's report had a further and little-intended consequence: during the hearing process, organized interests from all stakeholder groups came together as never before to develop positions, and unorganized interests similarly began to think more seriously about the need to represent their interests. In the aftermath of the final report, there was an even greater flurry of group activity as everyone scrambled to advocate the particular Pearse recommendations that favoured their interests or rally against those perceived as harmful. Symposia flourished. The result was a tremendous politicization of the fishery which included the emergence of numerous new voices, alongside longstanding politically-active groups like the UFAWU (United Fishermen and Allied Workers Union).[7]

---

6   One of the more influential post war resource studies was the U.S. President's Materials Policy Commission undertaken primarily in response to concerns over the security of supply of raw resource for "free world" industry. In that study, a sharp distinction was drawn between the waste of resources from physical versus economic perspectives. The point was that full physical use of a resource would rarely be economical; this set the stage for fisheries economists to challenge maximum sustainable yield as a social objective.

7   For a discussion of the politicization of groups during and after the Pearse Commission, see Marchak (1987).

Today, partly as a result of the response to Pearse and also due to the re-assertion of aboriginal rights, the major force appears to be what Amy (1983) refers to as hyper-pluralism. There are many stakeholders who have vastly improved their ability to influence decisions. This carries the potential of paralysing almost any initiative which any one player, including DFO, wishes to take. Yet the challenge of making decisions that conserve the salmon and its habitat while respecting the needs of an even broader array of interests remains. This, as I have argued earlier, underscores the importance of consensual processes. The emergence of efforts in the direction of consensus is discussed below, after a description of the array of stakeholders.

The Cast of Stakeholders

When first encountering the cast of users, managers and what might be called salmon-significant others, one can be overwhelmed with the diversity and, thereby, the difficulty of discussing, let alone coordinating, this multiplicity in an orderly, comprehensible fashion. Categories divide, blur and re-aggregate, reflecting the volatile politics, shifting alliances and the sheer complexity of the quest for consensus-based sustainable development.[8] The following distinctions or categories may be helpful in trying to sort out the cast:

(i)   Aboriginal Groups;
(ii)   DFO and Others with a Formal Mandate to Govern Salmon;
(iii)   Distinction by Fishing Motive—Food & Ceremonial vs. Recreation vs. Income;
(iv)   By Gear (Commercial Sector): Those Who Troll, Gillnet, Seine;
(v)   By Geography: In-river, Coastal, High Seas;
(vi)   Organized Labour;
(vii)   The Processors;
(viii) Those Who Affect Habitat "Incidentally";
(ix)   Environmental Organizations;
(x)   Miscellaneous Others Who Enhance, Study, Watch, Advocate and Cajole.

Aboriginal Groups

For many centuries, aboriginal people were the sole users and managers of the Fraser salmon. After more than a century of relegation to the sidelines of salmon use and management, they have returned with what is unquestionably the most important challenge to current governance.

Although many non-native stakeholders find it hard to accept what they see as racial distinctions in salmon use and management, a cursory familiarity with the Basin (and, not incidentally, with the Constitution Act, section 35[1]) reveals that

---

8   This is not to suggest that every aspect of advancing towards sustainable development would require full participation of all these groups. But consideration does have to be given to these interests in designing consensual approaches and dealing with the inevitably delicate issue of representation (see Susskind and Cruickshank (1987) for a discussion of representation issues in dispute resolution).

this dichotomy is one of increasing relevance. Within the Fraser Basin there are 91 Bands (see Kew and Griggs, this volume) as recognized by the Indian Act. There are language groups and tribal councils (often, but by no means always, based on language commonality). Moreover, salmon whose lives began in the Fraser system are extensively used by Native people far away from the Basin. Passing stocks of sockeye are extensively used by the Kwakiutl of Northern Vancouver Island, the Nuu-chah-nulth of West Vancouver Island, and many other Indians along the extensive migratory route. This includes tribes from the State of Washington.

Litigation over aboriginal fishing rights has dramatically increased in the past decade. Thompson (this volume) reviews the most important implications of leading fishing rights cases including the demise of the clear and paramount authority of the federal Minister of Fisheries. In tandem with these decisions, Native groups are organizing tribal and inter-tribal institutions to take an active role in resource management. An example is the Interior Indian Fisheries Commission, discussed below.

DFO and Others with a Formal Mandate To Govern Salmon

From a domestic point of view, mandate for the governance of Pacific salmon is quite straightforward: The Minister of Fisheries and Oceans, assisted by a department with a staff of approximately 6,000, including 1,500 in the Pacific region, is responsible for the "sea coast and inland fisheries." But this unitary authority is by no means without complication. There are several closely related anadromous salmonids which are important game fish, but whose management has been delegated to the Province of British Columbia. Instances are not rare when potential conflicts arise between the sound use of the Pacific salmon and the conservation of such species; for example steelhead (*Onchorynchus mykiss*).

The superficial simplicity of unitary federal authority over the Fraser salmon faces other caveats. Because of the international nature of the fishery for Fraser as well as other Pacific salmon, cooperative binational management involving the U.S. has long been essential. In 1985, an earlier convention was superseded by the Pacific Salmon Treaty. Although this treaty actually solidified the paramount authority of DFO over Fraser stocks, it recognized an ongoing role for both the U.S. and a permanent Pacific Salmon Commission. The Commission includes an executive of sixteen appointed commissioners and a staff of scientists, managers and technicians. The treaty also established committees responsible for annual pre-season and in-season negotiations on the fishing plan and its implementation. For the Fraser River, the most important of these is the Fraser Panel (see discussion of the annual sockeye planning cycle below for more on these entities).

There is another qualification to DFO's unitary and paramount authority and it is of rapidly growing importance. The assertion of native rights in the fishery goes well beyond demands for a larger share of harvest or special provisions for traditional harvest techniques. Indeed, the federal jurisdiction to manage is being challenged. Thompson has provided a very current overview of this issue and I need only repeat for emphasis that the Sparrow decision is but one of a number of rulings which is leading to profound changes in the distribution of management authority.

Although native people have a constitutionally-based claim to a stronger role in fisheries management, other groups have also been pressing for involvement. In the last five years, there has been wide discussion of the idea of fisheries co-management (Pinkerton, 1989). Definitions of co-management vary from an arrangement of advice-giving by users to government officials who maintain full authority, to direct participation of fishermen in decisions (see Kearney, 1989). But even the weakest version of the definition means that the flexibility of agencies like DFO in decision-making is reduced. Furthermore, co-management of any degree can entail a very significant commitment of staff time and supporting costs.

For the Fraser River specifically there is the previously mentioned Fraser Panel, created under the Canada-U.S. Pacific Salmon Treaty, and a Fraser River Advisory Committee that meets to discuss domestic pre- and in-season management issues. There are similar panels and advisory committees for other sections of the coast where the take of Fraser stocks is also a primary topic of discussion. In addition, there are several important coast-wide consultative bodies—the Pacific Area Regional Committee (PARC) which provides direct advice to the Minister on policy matters and the Commercial Fishing Industry Committee (CFIC) where attempts are made to resolve allocation issues between commercial users. DFO has established a number of local sports fishing advisory groups as well as an overall board. The B.C. Aboriginal Peoples Fisheries Commission is independent of DFO, but is generally seen as a principal mechanism for consultations with native groups.

Distinction by Fishing Motive: Food & Ceremonial vs. Recreation vs. Income

Most discussions of the fisheries sector imply a clear distinction among three broad categories of user. Some fish for food—in British Columbia only status Indians are recognized as having a special allocation for this purpose. DFO also recognizes the category of ceremonial use by native peoples. Frequent allegations are made that a significant proportion of Indian food fish are sold rather than used to feed families or villages. Native people have recently been visibly objecting to the "food fishing" category, arguing that their traditional fishery was multi-purpose including sale or trade of fish. The issue of the right to sell fish, along with the struggle for management rights, seems likely to be the next focus for aboriginal litigation.

Non-Indian fishers are generally classified as either sports or commercial. This distinction is also under fire since many of the sports-operators are involved in fishing for a living, not recreation.

Commercial sports interests have grown enormously in the recent past. Several of the entrepreneurs involved in fishing charters have many shore-based and floating lodges all along the coast. Their dependence on spring salmon (*Onchorhynchus tshawytscha*) and coho (*O. kisutch*) is high as is their commitment of time and effort to the politics of salmon management.

The "sports" category itself comprises a wide array of users with quite distinct interests and locations. There are skilled flyfishermen wading in the upper reaches of smaller tributaries, children casting buzzbombs from wharves, and solitary boatmen "mooching" lazily at the river's mouth. Fraser River and other southern spring salmon are subject to the rapidly growing pressure from large and small charter operators, in Georgia and Juan de Fuca Straits.

Sportsfishermen—recreational and commercial—are represented by numerous local and provincial organizations. The latter include the Sportsfishing Institute and the B.C. Wildlife Federation, both of which are active in lobbying to protect sports interests. There is also a Sports Fishing Advisory Board which is appointed to advise DFO.

By Gear (Commercial Sector): Those Who Troll, Gillnet, Seine

For the diverse commercial fleet, the Fraser sockeye stocks are the most important single-basin species on the entire coast. The commercial sector can be subdivided by gear type[9]: the gillnetters who set their nets to entangle fish; the seiners, operating generally from much larger vessels and whose strategy is to encircle and capture stocks with a very long purse-shaped net; and, the trollers who operate small boats with quantities of hooks slowly dragged from multiple lines strung from troll poles. Each of the gear groups is represented by at least one association; most of these organizations have become very politically active during the 1980's. For example, there are the Pacific Trollers Association, the Pacific Gillnetters Association and the Fishing Vessel Owners Association (largely representing seiners).

These in turn have given rise to a number of umbrella organizations, such as the Fishermen's Survival Coalition which was active in 1983-84 when many operators were on the verge of bankruptcy, and the Pacific Fishermen's Alliance (formerly Pacific Fishermen's Defense Alliance) which formed primarily in response to fears about the impact of aboriginal rights and claims on commercial fishing.

Political organization, lobbying and, occasionally, "protest fisheries" have enabled these interests to force their concerns onto the management agenda. Although their role in annual and longer term planning may not satisfy members, these groups are a potent influence on fisheries and related decision-making. An illustration of this influence can be seen in the recent decision of the federal government to reconsider land claims negotiations, following demands by commercial interests to be involved in that process.

By Geography: In-river, Coastal, High Seas

One of the challenges faced in defining the possibilities for sustainable development for the Fraser River concerns the efficacy of boundaries. River basin

---

9   Some vessels are equipped for use of both troll and gillnet.

planning has seemed a highly rational way of setting boundaries for resource management, but for anadromous fish, basins are too narrow. The different salmon species range widely along the northwest coast of North America and well out into the North Pacific. In addition to huge management complexities, this leads to there being several discrete fisheries with harvesters who may be only vaguely aware of others drawing on the same resource.

Thus there are important fisheries on Fraser salmon at great distances from the basin itself, including the Alaskan fishery, as well as the controversial by-catch of west coast stocks in the high seas driftnet fishery. Closer to the mouth of the Fraser are large fleets specifically targeting significantly the Fraser sockeyes and pinks (*Onchorhynchus gorbuscha*)—the Canada Department of Fisheries and Oceans (1988) distinguishes ten "major fisheries" on these species from the tip of Vancouver Island to the mouth of the Fraser.

Many of the harvesters live in the small communities of Vancouver Island and some of these communities depend heavily on the commercial fleet. This means that among the cast of stakeholders integrally affected by the Fraser sockeye are the residents of villages like Alert Bay, Ucluelet, Sointula, Bella Bella, as well as larger more diverse centres like Campbell River, home to a significant Native-owned seine fleet. Vancouver, Steveston, Victoria and Puget Sound coastal communities also house large numbers of vessels which fish significantly on Fraser stocks.

Last along the return route of the salmon are the river fishermen, primarily Native Indian, with some regional sportsfisheries. Under the Pacific Salmon Treaty, Fraser River status Indians are allotted 400,000 sockeye annually. In sheer numbers, however, the vast majority of harvested Fraser stocks are captured before the fish ever begin their voyage upriver. This geographic pattern has a powerful effect on the politics of use and management of the Fraser's rich salmon resources.

Organized Labour

The history of the organization of labour in the fishing and fish processing sectors in British Columbia is a study unto itself.[10] There are only two organizations in this category, but each has a very large membership. The United Fishermens and Allied Workers Union (UFAWU) has a membership of approximately 6,000 including both fishermen (primarily crew rather than owners) and shore workers. The UFAWU is the primary bargaining agent in labour's negotiations with the processors, but it also plays a leading role as a critic of federal fisheries policy, a participant in consultation, and, through the T. Buck Suzuki Foundation, as an environmental and peace advocacy group. The Union has been an adroit watchdog of government policy, vigorously opposing such developments as the Free Trade Agreement with the United States and the recent Vision 2000 exercise conducted by DFO. They are particularly concerned with any change that could reduce

---

10 See Marchak et al. (1987) for detailed accounts of the role and dynamics of organized labour in the Pacific sea fisheries.

employment in fishing and fish processing.

The other major fishing labour organization in B.C. is the Native Brotherhood (NBBC) which acts as a union for Native fishermen. The Native Brotherhood has other important functions which, like the UFAWU, make it a potent political force. For many years it was the only venue for the surreptitious discussion of aboriginal title and the land question and it also acts as an advocacy group on many broad matters of Native involvement in fisheries—for example, the Brotherhood recently engaged in a major policy review of licensing.

The relationship between the UFAWU and NBBC has often been a fragile one, and in recent years a lack of solidarity during major strikes and lock-outs has created overt dissent (see Marchak, 1987).

The Processors

Although there has been a trend to corporate concentration, the major fishing companies remain a diverse presence with substantial influence over the disposition of Fraser River salmon (see Pinkerton, 1987). Over the years there have been important instances of high level personnel moving back and forth between the large processors and senior ranks of the Pacific Region of DFO. At the very least this creates the appearance of what has been described elsewhere as clientele capture (Sabatier, 1975). This is but one source of what seems to be a widespread feeling among fishermen that the large fish processors exert powerful influence on fisheries managers.

The larger of the processing firms are members of the Fisheries Council of B.C., which acts as one of the leading advocacy groups on fisheries policy. More numerous smaller companies have had more difficulty in combining their voices and resources, but at least one organization, the Pacific Seafood Council, has become active as an advocate of their interests.

Those Who Affect Salmon "Incidentally"

The life cycle of the salmon exposes it to a wide variety of human impacts. As later sections will reveal, the range of people who go out to enjoy the salmon, in whatever way, is enormous. But there is also just as large a set of individuals and collectivities whose actions potentially affect salmon, but whose interests are not consciously directed towards the fish themselves.

Most of the cast in this category are important because what they do can critically impact on the salmon's environment. Henderson (in this volume) has described the diversity of actions that can harm salmon habitat. Along most of the length of the Fraser River are human communities whose domestic wastes find their way into the River. Equally, if not more broadly distributed in the Basin, are forest harvesters ranging from independent loggers to multinational corporations. Their practices can impact on the rearing and spawning habitat in a multitude of ways. The forest industry also operates processing facilities; the potential for water pollution, especially from pulp mills is of great concern to fisheries stakeholders.

Hydroelectric dams have a multitude of potential impacts on salmon habitat and also affect the flow and timing of water movement, vital parameters of the salmon life cycle. Thus B.C. Hydro, by far the largest proponent of dams in the province, is a major stakeholder in this category.

Another important group includes the users and builders of transportation corridors. These include highways, with the potential disaster of tanker trucks loaded with harmful chemicals, and the railroads whose history includes infamous accidents (most notably the Hell's Gate Slide of 1913 which severely damaged major sockeye runs). Since 1985, a major controversy in the Basin has occurred over the proposal by Canadian National to construct a second track along its route through the Thompson and Fraser valleys (see Dorcey & Rueggeberg, 1990).

These user groups include some of the largest and most powerful private companies in British Columbia. It can be argued that they have little incentive or inclination to engage in any voluntary search for a more sustainable future. Certainly, including them in future consensus-seeking approaches is a huge yet vital challenge. I will come back to this issue in the concluding section of this chapter.

Environmental Organizations

Groups whose primary focus is on environmental protection are an unquestionable force, usually poised against the stakeholders discussed in the previous category. These groups are also often vigourous critics of the performance of federal and provincial agencies whose mandate includes fish habitat protection. Examples of influential environmental organizations in the Basin include the Fraser River Coalition which has focused on water quality and habitat issues in the lower Fraser, and the Nechako Environmental Coalition which has led opposition to water diversions by Alcan.

Gardner (this volume) has discussed the variety of roles and strategies used by such organizations within the Fraser River Basin. Her analysis indicates the broad range and the rapidly increasing leverage these groups have in resource decision-making.

Miscellaneous Others Who Enhance, Study, Watch, Advocate and Cajole

Into this catch-all category fall a number of groups who have some degree of influence over, or concern with, the welfare of the Fraser salmon stocks. Compared to most of the major stakeholders described above, their influence is small. Cumulatively, however, the work these groups do and their forays into the politics of sustainable development make them far from insignificant. These include:

- A huge array of assorted organizations which undertake projects aimed at enhancing stocks and habitat. Many operate with some level of support from the Salmonid Enhancement Program; they include groups as diverse as the Alouette River Correctional Centre, the Lillooet Rod and Gun Club, and literally hundreds of elementary schools;
- Numerous research scientists for whom the salmon are intrinsically worth studying and not just because of their economic importance—UBC for example is home to a number of world-renowned salmon experts, as is the Pacific Biological Station at Nanaimo, where basic as well as applied research on Fraser salmon has long been carried out. At times these researchers become vocal critics of fisheries policy—several UBC professors have been active in the Chinook Foundation which has been very critical of recent spring salmon conservation measures;
- Increasing numbers of salmon-watchers who travel to vantage points such as on the Adams River to witness the great runs;
- Small coastal communities along the migration routes, places like the native and non-native communities of Northern Vancouver Island, who have formed a Coalition for Sustainable Fishing Communities to defend their interests in the face of shifting DFO policy; and,
- The Pacific Salmon Foundation established by the Minister of Fisheries and Oceans to raise funds and public awareness around conservation issues.

In all, I have described ten major groupings and their interests, and have noted that almost all have significant ability to influence decisions. Many of their individual actions would have to be monitored, modified, curtailed, and, most importantly, coordinated to achieve any vision of sustainable development. With such a disparate array of interest groups, a central authority can seem the only hope for concerted action. However, that alternative is unlikely to be available precisely because these interests have the power to block decisions they oppose.

In the next section of this chapter, we will see that there are already a number of "experiments" which indicate some progress in the alternative direction—consensus-building among groups that share power.

"Experiments" in Consensus-Building On Fraser Salmon Issues

With so many different parties capable of affecting the Fraser salmon, friction is inevitable. The result of destructive conflict can be seen in unresolved encroachments on habitat, excessive harvests and bitter competition among fishing groups. Each of these adversarial confrontations waste time and resources of all groups. The high costs of discord have led some stakeholders to experiment with consensual decision-making.

The sections that follow are not case studies in the sense of detailed presentations and evaluations. Rather they have been chosen first, because they are among the leading examples of fairly new consensus-building forums in the Basin and second because each sheds some light on the opportunity for, and the barriers to, consensus.[11] Five experiences are examined:

(i)   The Annual Fraser Sockeye planning cycle;
(ii)   The Interior Indian Fisheries Commission;
(iii) The Shuswap Tribal Council and its Community-Based Cooperative Fisheries Projects;
(iv)   The Fraser River Estuary Management Program;
(v)   The Fraser River Environmentally Sustainable Task Force.

The Annual Fraser Sockeye Planning Cycle

Among the five salmon species that spawn in the Fraser River Basin, sockeye have the highest value. Each year, the Department of Fisheries and Oceans orchestrates a complex and, for an outside observer, confusing set of interlocked deliberations aimed at making and implementing a plan for the Fraser River and other salmon stocks. The decision-making system—one that has evolved rapidly since the inception of the Canada-U.S. Pacific Salmon Treaty—must achieve multiple objectives, including stock conservation, and domestic and binational allocations.

The biological complexities of this problem and the resulting management challenge have been discussed elsewhere in this and the companion Westwater volume. Suffice it to say that the challenges are daunting: hundreds of stocks, some weak in numbers, some strong; a vast transnational territory within which the salmon travel; huge annual variations in numbers; a complex and interacting array of human, non-human, meteorological and hydrological forces affecting mortality and survival. Yet amidst this uncertainty and complexity, information has to be gathered and decisions on harvest rate, escapement targets, fishing openings and the like, must be made.

The system for planning mirrors the complexity of the biological and social situation. Until 1986, Fraser sockeye were managed by the International Pacific Salmon Fisheries Commission within a specific convention area. Outside this area, DFO had sole responsibility and, in the atmosphere of international conflict, had little reason to integrate its regulatory activity with the Commission. Now, the binational sharing of Fraser sockeye is calculated for the entire territory within which any fishery on these stocks takes place.

The Pacific Salmon Treaty sets forth some, though not all, of the constraints of allocation within which annual planning must operate. This includes the specific allocation of 400,000 sockeye annually to Fraser River food fisheries and target allocations for each country as a whole.[12]

The Fraser Panel was created under the treaty with responsibility for management within the old Convention area. DFO manages any domestic fishery

---

11   These case descriptions are based primarily on secondary sources and fairly brief discussions with, at most, one or two of the key actors. This is hardly the kind of basis on which one dare proffer advice for major reforms. To the extent that comments and suggestions follow from these stories, they are made entirely to provoke critical and continuing reflection, especially from those better positioned than I to see the complexities missed in my analysis.

12   See Pacific Salmon Treaty, Annex IV, Chapter 4.

on the Fraser sockeye outside this area, but these regimes are very closely coordinated in an annual planning cycle.

Let us look at how this occurs, focusing on features that contribute to consensus-building. What, then are the major steps that comprise the annual planning cycle?

(i)   The Department of Fisheries and Oceans (DFO) prepares forecasts for the principal sockeye stocks of the Fraser River. On the basis of historical data and assessment of each watershed's capacity as spawning and rearing habitat, preliminary escapement targets are set.

(ii) DFO then provides the Pacific Salmon Commission's Fraser Panel and other groups such as the Commercial Fishing Industry Committee (CFIC), with forecasts of total adult populations and goals for escapement for each stock.[13]

(iii) Concurrent discussions occur in two forums:
   -   Within Canada,[14] the Minister of Fisheries & Oceans, in consultation with several advisory bodies, determines the allocation among gear groups. This results in a specific percentage to each of four specific groups—gillnetters, seiners and two categories of trollers, those who fish in the Strait of Georgia ("the inside troll") and those fishing in other waters ("the outside troll").
   -   Within the Pacific Salmon Commission's Fraser Panel, a review is made of the forecasts and escapement goals to ensure that there are no outstanding differences of opinion on these technical issues.

(iv) Once the domestic allocations have been established, the next step is to figure out how the numerous and mixed stocks of sockeye can best be harvested— where the fish are to be taken and how long openings are to last—so as to achieve both the allocations and the escapement targets. The Pacific Salmon Commission's technical staff prepare computer simulations to yield a pre-season plan that best fits these requirements. This is subject to review by the Fraser Panel which makes recommendations to the Commissioners on changes to, and approval of, a pre-season management plan.

(v)   Once a pre-season plan has been formulated, it is taken by DFO managers to several domestic advisory bodies. There is a Fraser River Advisory Committee which includes DFO-appointed representatives from user groups operating near the Fraser mouth (southern Strait of Georgia, Juan de Fuca Strait). There is also a parallel South Coast Advisory Committee representing those who harvest Fraser sockeye in locations more distant from the river (Johnstone Strait, West Coast of Vancouver Island). These consultations focus on very detailed issues about the specific timing of

---

13   The number of stocks for which specific forecasts and targets are provided varies within the four-year cycle, because streams that have highly significant runs in one year may have negligible runs the next. In the 1988 cycle-year, for example, there were twenty stocks included in the forecasts and escapement goals (Pacific Salmon Commission, 1989).

14   In the United States the major allocative challenge has been settled by the legal decision which divided allowable catch between Treaty Indian and Non-Indian harvesters. For more on this allocation see Cohen (1986).

openings on each passing stock. It should be noted that there are major user group organizations which do not participate in either of these advisory committees. Moreover, a small but not insignificant Canadian harvest of Fraser sockeye occurs in more northerly waters (e.g., Queen Charlotte Islands and the mid-coast statistical areas).

(vi)   To this point, the sockeye have been silent in the framing of plans, but as the season approaches they too make decisions, as it were, which have immense effects on the pre-season management plans. The most important of these is the diversion rate, the relative proportions of stocks that return to the Fraser via the West versus the East side of Vancouver Island. This, as well as the timing and the actual versus predicted size of each run, makes all the difference in the world to the applicability of the pre-season plan. Frequently predictions are far from accurate and this triggers numerous meetings of the Fraser Panel and domestic advisory committees, aimed at improvising changes to the pre-season plan, so that escapement and allocation objectives can be attained. This flurry of meetings is part of what is called in-season management.

(vii) In-season management includes several steps (naturally, these are going on at different phases for each of the separate stocks):
- Test fisheries are made to gauge run size;
- Openings occur and, from the fishing success, data is compiled to revise estimates of run size;
- Scheduled and non-scheduled (i.e., emergency) meetings and teleconferences are held to adjust fishing openings and allocations (i.e., actual numbers per gear group, not percentages);
- New schedules for fishing are promulgated in accordance with revised fishing plans.

(viii) At the end of the fishing season, the Fraser Panel and other advisory committees will have final meetings, at which some preliminary summary of the season will be proffered by DFO. However, it is rarely until the various committees and panels reassemble for the subsequent year pre-season planning that a clearer picture of what happened is available.

This is a very simplified and sanitized version of the actual process, for there are further biological complexities which impact powerfully on pre-season and in-season management. Moreover, the above account says nothing of the sources of confusion and tension that strongly influence the mood and process of consultative meetings. Space does not permit a fuller analysis of even one working year in this annual planning cycle. Here we can only give some flavour for the enormity of the challenge by noting some of the biological and political complications.

As an example of some of the biological surprises that can occur, we can look at highlights of the 1988 season, for which a formal summary has been prepared by the Pacific Salmon Commission (1989). These include:

• The run of Chilko Lake sockeye which had been a prime pre-season conservation concern came in at only 50% of that predicted;

- Early summer stocks held at the Fraser River mouth for much longer than expected, leading to uncertainty about whether specific stock escapement targets were likely to be met;
- Mounting concerns over spring salmon during the season led to curtailment of certain Johnstone Strait net-fisheries with the result that some anticipated harvest of major passing Fraser sockeye stocks were foregone; this was made worse, from the netfishermen's point of view by some miscalculations in the timing of migrations through the area;
- The Weaver Creek sockeye stock came back at twice its pre-season forecast strength, but this brought its own problems. The danger was that weaker stocks, mixed with Weaver Creek sockeye, could be exploited too heavily if the harvest rate appropriate to the unexpectedly strong stock was maintained.

Such biological "surprises" are not at all uncommon; indeed, they are quintessential features of the resource regime. But there are equally severe difficulties on the social and political side of the management equation and these can exacerbate the effects of biological uncertainties.

There has been continuous and extreme difficulty in reaching agreement on domestic shares of sockeye for each gear group. The Commercial Fishing Industry Committee (CFIC) is supposed to seek consensus on an allocation plan which goes to the Minister of Fisheries and Oceans for approval. However inter-group hostilities plague CFIC; consensus on allocations is rarely reached. The Minister is then forced to make the final determination on shares. In response, one or more parties almost inevitably cries unfair treatment.

A particularly sore and chronic problem lies with the share afforded to trollers. This group's targeting on Fraser sockeye developed rapidly during the years preceding the completion of the Pacific Salmon Treaty. Troller groups were encouraged to expand their sockeye harvest to exert pressure on the U.S. in treaty negotiations (see Urquhart, 1989). After the treaty was signed, the Government of Canada no longer needed this effort. Trollers felt, however, that they had earned a substantial allocation in perpetuity. Net-fishermen in the CFIC argue their case, instead, on the basis of a longer period for historical averages and see the trollers as usurping traditional shares.

Clearly lacking in these discussions are efforts to transcend the year-by-year struggle by developing *durable and objective criteria*. Also, because the responsibility for the decision lies not with CFIC but with the Minister, there is a strong incentive to use one's persuasive force with him and not with one's fellow members. "End-runs" around the bargaining table are frequent.

These debates are neither settled within nor restricted to CFIC but spill over into other advisory forums. There, frustration often runs high as DFO staff strive to keep discussions to the specific details of scheduling particular openings. Spokespeople for gear groups who are displeased with Ministerial allocations feel that they are being asked to merely "rubber stamp" decisions prejudicial to their interests.

Another unresolved problem of this highly charged political process of annual planning lies in the vague nature of the responsibilities of gear group representatives. The selection of such representatives is quite informal, frequently having no basis in any selection process by the constituency. Furthermore, no resources are provided nor procedures specified whereby the member of a given panel or domestic advisory committee reports back to the constituency. Thus, for many fishermen, information is restricted to marine radio announcements with minimal, if any, justification provided for decisions that have profound impacts on their livelihood. This can only exacerbate mistrust and indignation at what can seem capricious changes in plans that were poorly received, even in their initial formulation.

My intention here is not to cast too harsh a light on the existing consultative process. Indeed, it is truly remarkable in light of the complexity within this system—both human and salmonid—that allocation and escapement targets are often closely approximated—and without bloodshed! In the 1988 season, used as an example above, Canadian domestic allocations were off by only a very little— trollers got more (11.1% rather than targeted 8.8%), gillnetters less (36% rather than 38.4%) while seiners were almost dead on (53.0% rather than 52.8%).

But the fact of CFIC failing once again to negotiate an allocation, the exasperation of many advisers with unexpected and poorly explained changes in fishing openings, and the sense among some user groups of being intentionally cut out of the fishery, suggests that there is much room for improvement. From my own direct experience with the South Coast Advisory Committee, and from discussions with CFIC members, what is most striking is the contrast between the relative sophistication of the natural science versus naivete regarding group dynamics (VanGundy, 1984) principled negotiations (Fisher & Ury, 1984) and simply the art of making meetings work (Doyle & Straus, 1976). These practical areas of knowledge are highly accessible and very familiar to a large community of scholars and practitioners who work with human organizations. But there seems to be almost no attention paid to them by those who convene the plethora of consultative forums on fisheries.

Consensus-building in stock management requires very substantial changes in the skills and attitudes of all participants, but especially in DFO which assumes responsibility for the design and operation of consultative mechanisms.[15]

The Interior Indian Fisheries Commission

In 1986, as tension grew between Natives and non-Natives over fishing issues, interest arose in a new and vague concept called co-management. This was variously seen along a spectrum from truely joint-control between Indians and DFO, to merely technical co-operation in local enhancement projects. In response, many non-native fishermen and their representative organizations formed the

---

15 Lest the reader feel that my assessment is too harsh, the following quote is from a discussion document released last year by DFO: "Consultative Process...It is a fractured decision-making process, not structured to resolve in-fighting and internal conflict. It is short term...There is no single focus for the three sectors, with multiple advisory groups crossing sectors, with multiple and often overlapping players...Generally, decision-making is insular, not open to general public scrutiny or community involvement" (Canada, 1989:10).

Pacific Fishermens Defense Alliance (PFDA). The primary thrust was opposition to any degree of devolution of authority to Native groups. In the hortatory materials PFDA circulated, the clinching argument posed against Native authority was the statistic that in the Fraser system alone there were 92 bands, [16](c.f,. Kew and Griggs)—how, PFDA asked rhetorically, could a resource management system with so many managers ever work?

PFDA's arguments ignore the fact that many of the First Nations of the Fraser and also the Columbia watersheds had already recognized the critical task of coordinating their fishing interests. This was one of the motivations for forming the Interior Indian Fisheries Commission (IIFC). The Department of Fisheries and Oceans was initially enthusiastic about the fledgling IIFC because it provided a coordinating mechanism for dealing with Indian food fish allocation for the Fraser River.[17] Since then, as the IIFC took on a more assertive role on the issue of aboriginal fishing rights, some conflict has arisen. More recently, DFO, the IIFC and the provincial government have been exploring ways of developing a cooperative framework.

The evolving model of the IIFC is worth examining as one way of coordinating groups that are numerous and which have roughly equivalent power. And if the current trend continues for more and more groups to demand a voice in the fate of the Fraser salmon, we will need models for the sharing of authority among parties who are treated as equals—something that Canadian fisheries institutions have not previously had much experience with.

IIFC is one of several inter-tribal Native fishing organizations formed in the mid 1980's. The rationale was inspired by two Aboriginal organizations in the U.S. Pacific Northwest. The Northwest Indian Fisheries Commission and the Columbia River Inter-tribal Fisheries Commission were established after judicial decisions in 1973-74 affirmed substantial Indian treaty rights for fisheries (see Cohen, 1986).

The IIFC struggled through several years of staff and organizational development with an enormous diversity of language, custom and interests among its membership. In 1989, the member First Nations signed a formal treaty codifying objectives, principles and procedures.

There are several noteworthy features in this agreement. First, although the treaty is based on mutual recognition of sovereignty, all members have formally agreed that there is a greater, shared inter-tribal interest—salmon conservation. The treaty envisions the formulation of fishing laws by each autonomous tribe, including, significantly, laws which have previously been traditional and

---

16   The figure of 92 bands was used by Pacific Fishermen's Defence Alliance (n.d.). It is slightly higher than the more recent figure used by Kew and Griggs (this volume). Such discrepancies are not unusual since amalgamations and administrative divisions of Bands do occur.

17   Under the 1985 Pacific Salmon Treaty, there was an immediate need for Canada to get very specific about its domestic allocation requirements for Fraser River sockeye. As a result, an allocation of 400,000 pieces was made for Fraser River Indian food fish; this remains one of the few allocations of its kind on the coast. With this blanket allocation came an immediate need to manage the harvest with great accuracy and among a very scattered set of Indian fishers. It was therefore in DFO's interests to encourage the IIFC and, in its first year, the new Comission was quite reliant on DFO not only for funds but also for administrative assistance. This has changed dramatically since 1987-88, as the IIFC members have become both better organized and more focused on the goal of restoring traditional management authority. Nonetheless, IIFC still receives much of its support funding from the federal government.

unwritten. Yet, such laws are subordinate to the broader agreement. One of the stated objectives is to "adopt the principle that Inter-Tribal rights supersede (sic) individual tribal rights if the two are in conflict in order to ensure the survival of the salmon."[18] Observance of the principles of the treaty is to be monitored by the IIFC staff and detailed procedures have been created to address non-compliance.

A second key aspect is the central role afforded to what is called the "Common Inter-Tribal Fisheries Policy." The policy was not articulated in the treaty but rather anticipated by it. As a result of this treaty, technical analyses and negotiations are proceeding to develop a working policy. This policy will detail salmon management, harvest, protection and enhancement throughout the Fraser (and Columbia) watersheds.

The treaty also specifies the means for achieving consensus and for resolving any outstanding inter-tribal disputes over fishing policy. These and the underlying philosophy of the treaty, contrast sharply with the dominant federal management regime. The latter is strongly based on the idea of a single paramount authority, the Minister of Fisheries and Oceans; at this person's discretion, other stakeholders will be consulted but final decisions rest solely with the Minister.

The IIFC in contrast is based on the idea of equals voluntarily submitting to a broader interest, one defined and legitimized by consensus rather than coercion. If political and judicial developments continue to strengthen recognized aboriginal rights in the fishery, the model of a consensus-oriented and multi-group salmon management system may become inevitable. The governments of British Columbia, Canada and the IIFC are presently exploring possible agreements that could lead to such arrangements without the need for judicial imposition.[19]

The Shuswap Tribal Council and Community-Based Cooperative Fisheries Projects[20]

The Shuswap Tribal Council (STC) represents nine bands in the lake district of the Thompson River (the largest tributary of the Fraser Basin). Like most Native groups in the Basin, the Shuswap have always depended on annual salmon runs for sustenance and trade. Since the late nineteenth century Indians of the area have largely been left out of fisheries management, and have been basically bystanders as resource decisions, harvesting and other activities affecting the environment in distant places, weakened the salmon runs to the Shuswap home waters.

In the last decade, this has changed. Bands have participated in management projects in several different ways and with varying success. The Shuswap were also members of the now defunct Central Indian Tribal Council (CITC) whose

---

18 Interior Indian Fisheries Commission. "Intertribal Fishing Treaty Between Indian Nations: A Treaty of Mutual Purpose and Support," (27 July 1989), Article 1(g).

19 At the time of writing (late 1990) a framework agreement is in preparation involving the IIFC's ten member tribal councils, the federal Department of Indian and Northern Affairs as well as DFO, and the B.C. Ministries of Environment and Agriculture and Fisheries. The purpose is to provide a framework within which to rebuild stocks and develop a *fair* approach to sharing the resource.

20 This case is based on records of interviews with Mr. Dave Moore, Director of the Shuswap Tribal Council's Fisheries Program, Mr. Wilf Kip and Mr. Dubs Pulley. The interviews were conducted by Dr.Julia Gardner of the UBC Westwater Research Centre, August 1989.

Fisheries Committee initiated a number of enhancement projects focusing on the training of band members. While skills were acquired, the absence of a recognized aboriginal role in on-going fisheries management meant that financial support was derived almost exclusively through government-initiated "make-work" programmes.

After the CITC folded in the early 1980's, enormous changes began to unfold in the context within which aboriginal fisheries management could occur. The recent history of the struggle for such a role has been taken up in this volume by Thompson and is covered in several papers in Pinkerton's (1989) collection. Suffice it to say that the Canada Department of Fisheries and Oceans has had to take the demand for co-management opportunities far more seriously in recent years. This has been difficult in the absence of any consensus among stakeholders on what co-management means.

Within this changing context, the STC has nurtured a community-based planning effort involving other local stakeholders. Indeed, it seems that the creative efforts of STC and its member bands have helped demonstrate to DFO and others the possible shape that co-management can take.

The initial work of STC was intentionally kept as small-scale as possible. As is often the case, a fresh start requires dissatisfaction if not despair with the status quo. The Shuswap Lakes region has relied economically on the tourist attraction of good sportsfishing; in Spence's Bridge, for example, an almost year-round sportsfishery had developed based on a spring and summer trout season, a fall chinook salmon fishery and, in winter, steelhead.

In response to declining populations in the late 1970's, DFO drastically curtailed sports openings, particularly in the case of the fall chinook. Local businesses, dependent on the influx of tourist dollars, suffered. This included members of the Skeetchestn (Deadman's Creek) Band, one of the Shuswap Bands. Band members had done well in sales of vegetable produce to visitors; as the sportsfishery was cut, so too were their incomes from this source.

With this negative lesson firmly in mind, the STC was supportive of the efforts made by Dave Moore, a former Provincial Fish & Wildlife biologist, who came to them with a proposal for fisheries enhancement. The core idea was to attract local groups—Native and sports—into a hands-on project for stream and stock rehabilitation for Deadman's Creek.

On behalf of STC, Moore and a co-worker initiated a series of meetings with several local sportsfishing interest groups. A project was launched which focused on habitat restoration and on training Skeetchestn Band members. This went beyond the level of basic techniques, and on to the development of an understanding of the rationale for habitat assessment, counting, tagging, brush removal, etc. The initial project entailed a cooperative assessment of the habitat involving the Kamloops Flyfishing Association, the Kamloops Fish & Game Club and Kamloops Steelhead Society. Inevitably, contact between sports interests and Indians has led to changes in attitudes. This was essential because of longstanding conflict between sportsfishers and Band members over the Native harvest of the steelhead. This is a prize species to the sports sector.

As the project unfolded, DFO and the B.C. Fish & Wildlife Branch became increasingly interested. According to Moore, financial support is no problem any more; indeed there is concern that the STC Fisheries Program should not expand too rapidly with the accompanying risk of exceeding its ability to manage quality projects. As the project has developed, there has been an emphasis on the issue of capacity-building: the scope of educational programmes has expanded to include training in communication, so that tribal members can become effective emissaries in the whole community on behalf of cross-cultural cooperation in fisheries projects.

To date, the Fisheries Program has very consciously avoided the most politically divisive issues. Instead, it has concentrated on small projects where the probability is high for "win-win" outcomes. The STC has capitalized on resulting good will in creating a "community working group" within the Shuswap Tribal Council's territory. This brings a multiplicity of stakeholders to regular, informal get-togethers. The plan is to evolve a permanent forum within which new projects can be formulated and any problems quickly resolved.

As yet, there is no indication of how this emerging local network will handle any dramatic changes that may result from legal decisions similar to the Sparrow case. For example, will STC get involved directly in the issue of aboriginal sales of food fish allocations? And if so, how well will the "community working group" hold up as a forum for education and conflict resolution? The Fisheries Program's avoidance of politically controversial matters means that there have been no demanding "tests" of cooperative spirit and mechanisms. It is reasonable to surmise, however, that the existing network of working and personal relationships will increase the ability of those involved to find constructive solutions when, inevitably, they face more troublesome issues.

The Fraser River Estuary Management Program (FREMP)

FREMP has been described as Canada's most successful coastal management program (Dorcey, 1990) and also as a "working model of an environment-economy partnership" as espoused by The World Commission on Environment and Development (McPhee, 1989). While concerned with a good deal more than the salmon, FREMP comprises analytical and regulatory efforts to protect fish as well as wildlife habitat through an explicit process of multi-agency, multi-government planning. Thus it represents a clear attempt to forge consensus on issues central to both salmon management and sustainable development. Brief historical background may be useful though the reader should consult other sources for detail (Dorcey, 1990; Kennett and McPhee, 1988).

FREMP began in the late 1970's, an era of ambitious comprehensive planning schemes. Coastal zone management had joined river basin planning as a major preoccupation of both government, and also non-government organizations who advocated a break from narrow, compartmentalized resource management. The two literally met in the Fraser estuary. The deterioration of water quality and the increasing incidence of multiple use conflict (Dorcey, 1976), fixed public attention on this the most heavily populated and industrialized estuarine region along Canada's west coast.

In 1977, the Fraser River Estuary Study began under a federal-provincial agreement. The initial purpose was to prepare a comprehensive plan for a 1,000 metre strip along the shores from the River's mouth up to head of tide near the Pitt River. During the first eighteen month phase, background physical and land use studies as well as concepts for a future management entity were assessed. This work was completed by a Federal-Provincial Steering Committee that provided an early opportunity for partial multi-agency consensus building (see Dorcey, 1990).

In Phase II, which lasted for three years, the Steering Committee was enlarged and became the Fraser River Estuary Planning Committee. Its 1982 Final Report outlined the options for managing the estuary in terms of institutional structures, coordinating mechanisms and planning tools. After a lengthy review period, an agreement was signed for the establishment of the Fraser River Estuary Management Program, including a program office in New Westminster.

From its earliest days as the Fraser River Estuary Study, the paramount challenge facing this program has been precisely the one that is the focus of this paper—the existence of a multiplicity of government agencies, not to mention users and public interest groups, each of whom has some kind of stake in resource decision-making. This is reflected in FREMP's Management Committee with its five agency executive[21] and twenty-seven members at large including other federal and provincial agencies, regional and municipal governments and several Indian Bands.

Protection and enhancement of fish stocks and habitat were among the leading public concerns motivating the creation of FREMP and with DFO as one of the signatories to the formative agreement, these rank high in the program activities. The most explicit opportunity for dealing with salmon protection arises in the work on habitat. It is to be emphasized that salmon stock management, still seen as almost solely under DFO's authority, is not directly within the purview of FREMP. Single agencies continue to look after their own mandate whether that be DFO's for fish stocks or the Harbour Commissions' for port management: FREMP plays a role only where the regulated activities begin to affect one another.

The question here is to what extent does FREMP provide an opportunity for these and other stakeholders to reach better and more consensual decisions apropos the Fraser River salmon?

There are several mechanisms used for this in FREMP:

- The Coordinated Project Review Process—essentially a multi-agency sharing of information and an orderly circulation of detailed applications for making joint decisions on projects within FREMP's boundaries;
- An evolving system of Area Designations whereby optimal use(s) of each coastal sub-area is negotiated by member agencies on the basis of full sharing

---

21   The five agencies who were co-signatories of the FREMP Agreement include: B.C. Ministry of the Environment, Environment Canada, Fisheries & Oceans Canada, the North Fraser Harbour Commission and the Fraser River Harbour Commission.

of resource use information;
- Activity Work Groups which meet to consider both specific current issues and to develop profiles of their focal activity (e.g., Port & Industrial Development Work Group, Log Management Work Group);
- Development of detailed environmental management plans for major subsystems of the estuary (e.g., North Fraser Harbour Environmental Management Plan).

More detailed reviews of these elements have been presented elsewhere (Dorcey, 1990; McPhee, 1989; Kennett & McPhee, 1988). Here, we can look only at the aspects of these activities that are most relevant to salmonid protection and management.

DFO's Habitat Division is a leading player in all of the above mechanisms. The force it brings to any decision-making in the estuary arises from the Fisheries Act and, with greater specificity, from the recent strengthened habitat policy. This authority would give DFO tremendous influence over what goes on in the estuary, even in the absence of FREMP or anything like it. What then is gained in subjecting this mandate to the multi-agency forums and procedures that constitute FREMP?

DFO's participation in FREMP provides exactly the opportunity for shared understandings and consensus-building which, as I have suggested above, is vital to the quest for sustainable development. Outside of a setting like FREMP, DFO's defense of fish habitat is likely to be confrontational (i.e., the regulator pitted directly against the developer) and narrow in purpose. Moreover, without the kind of guidance furnished through area designations, each case would be regulated with little regard for how the habitat at a specific location relates to the larger ecosystem.

We can better understand the ways in which FREMP complements DFO's salmon habitat mandate by looking at the recent development of the North Fraser Harbour Environmental Management Plan. This plan, co-signed by the Chairman of the North Fraser Harbour Commission and the Minister of Fisheries & Oceans, details a new relationship between the agency with development responsibilities for the North Fraser and the most powerful and omnipresent regulatory agency, DFO.

Some of the key features reflecting a new kind of developer/regulator relationship are:

- Agreement to determine the broad acceptability of future activities on the basis of a continually refined habitat inventory and classification;
- Incorporation of a single agency's policy (i.e., DFO's "no net loss" habitat policy) in a bilateral inter-agency agreement;
- Creation of a "habitat compensation bank" within the agreement area, administered by the Harbour Commission to provide compensatory habitat where development leads to unavoidable habitat loss; and,
- Commitment to a multi-faceted "cooperative management program" aimed at strengthening the working relationship between the Commission and DFO.

From one perspective DFO is voluntarily fettering its legitimate pursuit of its mandate with a formal and explicit recognition of the Harbour Commission's legitimate interests in the Fraser estuary. Yet this is done in a planning or anticipatory mode, not as an ad hoc reaction in the midst of political controversy. This bears comparison to other interactions in the Fraser Basin, where DFO has been accused of having compromised its responsibilities in the heat of battle.[22]

FREMP, then, provides one model of how consensus and a more cooperative spirit can be approached in the context of sustainable development. The Program is not without critics, especially environmental groups who argue that it lacks the necessary (satisfactory) dedication to preservation and environmental quality enhancement (Dorcey, 1990). Moreover, FREMP does not foster direct involvement in decision-making by public interest groups and is therefore criticized for being too insular; public participation has been multi-faceted but not at all empowering.

FREMP has moved recently to enhance the role of local governments, particularly in its efforts to facilitate the negotiation of "statements of intent", whereby municipalities would be centrally involved in the system of area designation. Several non-government organizations are also involved in the Activity Work Groups.

The experiment remains preliminary and the concrete achievements for protecting salmon habitat are as yet difficult to identify clearly. What is most encouraging perhaps is that some advancement has been made in this the most complex, multi-interest zone of the Fraser Basin. Perhaps this augurs well for extending the underlying concept up the river where the cast is smaller and the conflicts have not advanced quite so far.[23]

The Fraser River Environmentally Sustainable Development Task Force

The Department of Fisheries and Oceans may well have the strongest mandate for environmental protection of any agency, federal or provincial. In the mid-1970's, regulations pursuant to the Fisheries Act bolstered the authority for protecting fish habitat; more recently the intent and methods of DFO were laid out in an aggressive new habitat policy. Within some understandings of sustainable development this would signal a great forward step. But as I have suggested several times above, singlemindedness—a disregard for the socio-economic trade-offs of protecting a single resource or activity—hardly qualifies as "sustainable development." To qualify, fish habitat protection has to be integrated within a broader set of social objectives.

---

22 In the case of Alcan's proposed Kemano Completion Project, the proponent of a major water diversion from the Nechako (a Fraser tributary) to the Kemano River took DFO to court. Its arguments were that early contracts gave Alcan rights to such water for hydroelectric development. In the long shadow of the court, negotiations took place whereby DFO sanctioned the project. Local environmental groups and some DFO staff felt that this agreement impinged on DFO's legislated mandate to protect fish habitat.

23 Some of the tools and philosophy of FREMP were discussed as possible models for application to transportation issues in the lengthy corridor from Agassiz on the lower Fraser up to and along the Thompson River as far as Valemount. (See Dorcey & Rueggeberg, 1990).

Towards this end and in recognition of its own internal schism between habitat protection and salmon stock management, DFO has recently established a Task Force devoted to exploring sustainable development concepts in relation to the Fraser River Basin. To what extent is this entity addressing the need for consensus-building which, according to the focus of the present paper, is a pivotal requirement of sustainable development?

First, a brief overview of the Fraser River Environmentally Sustainable Development Task Force is needed.[24] The Task Force was established in 1989 as a way of focusing DFO's hitherto fragmented efforts at habitat and stock management planning for the Basin. Like many other Canadian resource agencies, DFO has responded to the report and recommendations of the Brundtland Commission. Among the Commission's major thrusts was the idea of more holistic integration of single-purpose resource management. The fact that within DFO itself habitat and stock management had been poorly integrated, had been a subject of concern for several years (see Paish & Associates, 1985). DFO's habitat protection had been criticised as too reactive, another theme of the Brundtland Commission's criticism of existing resource administration. Sustainable development provided a new and politically well-liked rubric under which to do some long-awaited integration and reformulation of DFO's primary responsibilities. The Fraser River is the natural choice for this somewhat experimental approach in light of its dominant position among B.C.'s salmon-producing rivers.

The goal of the Task Force is to produce a sustainable development plan for the entire Basin. This is envisioned as involving several additive steps:

(i)   Preparation of detailed habitat and stock management plans for sixteen sub-basins that comprise the whole watershed;
(ii) Integration of these into a plan for sustainable development of fisheries resources for the whole system;
(iii) In conjunction with managers and users of other resources of the Basin, negotiation of a cross sector sustainable development plan.

Since the Task Force has only two years to conduct its work, the emphasis is primarily on the first of these steps with the intention of at least setting the stage for more holistic planning. The focus of discussion in this paper is restricted to early experience with one key component: the preparation of detailed habitat management plans. As will be seen, even the early stages of this aspect of the Task Force's work well illustrate the challenges of consensus-building as a prerequisite for sustainable development planning.

It must be noted, however, that this preliminary component of sustainable development planning has barely begun and so it is too early to hold the experience up to close scrutiny. Yet what is intriguing is that the planning for the first three sub-basins provides, unintentionally it would seem, three distinct

---

24 This overview and the ensuing discussion of the habitat management planning is based on a workshop held in May, 1990 among task force members and the Westwater Research Centre at UBC and discussions between myself and several of the task force members.

models. And first impressions are that, with some initial reluctance, the Task Force is learning about the exigencies and even the advantages of multilateral planning.

Each habitat management plan is based on a detailed account of the current status of salmon stocks, and spawning and rearing habitat. Consultants lead in assembling and organizing the relevant data. The first planning area was the Stuart-Takla sub-basin in the Upper Fraser. In fact, the consultant's work commenced before the formal establishment of the Fraser River Environmentally Sustainable Development Task Force. The study was completed to the stage of a full draft before any discussions occurred with stakeholders (e.g., the Carrier-Sekani Indians) or other resource users and managers. This has led to a minimal commitment by these stakeholders to the objectives of the plan and, perhaps, some apprehension among them.

In the Shuswap sub-basin, the second selected for detailed planning, the Task Force took a much more proactive approach to the involvement of other interests. In cooperation with DFO, the consultant visited major stakeholders of the basin to explain the purpose and procedures of the habitat management planning process. The Shuswap Nation Tribal Council, whose activities are described above, was approached about its participation.[25] Similarly, discussions have been held at an early stage with most forest companies. The intention is for the consultant to provide detailed information to all stakeholders including local governments of the many small towns in this basin. Interest generated by this early involvement is expected to lead to a sense of shared purpose in finalizing and implementing a sustainable development plan.

In the third case of sub-basin planning, now just underway, events have taken a different course. Well before the Task Force had intended to begin planning in the Cariboo sub-basin, local public awareness of the need for balanced watershed planning had risen. This appears to have come about largely through the office of the local Member of Parliament, Dave Worthy. Concern arose both from stakeholders interested in protecting salmonid resources and from loggers who feared that DFO habitat planning would unduly constrain their activity.

Worthy and his staff pressed DFO to come to a series of public meetings in the Cariboo Chilcotin area. These have been aimed at laying the groundwork for a process of multiple resource planning. The Task Force staff had seen multiple sector discussions and negotiations as a later phase of plan preparation. Nevertheless, the Task Force has expedited the process of habitat management planning for this sub-basin. A consultant was being selected as this paper was in preparation. Meanwhile, another firm had been hired especially to convene continuing meetings within the study area.

It is far too early to comment on the relative merits of these very different approaches to habitat management planning. Yet a reasonable surmise is that if the Cariboo sub-basin process produces a plan, it will be perceived as much more a

---

25 Quite different accounts were given to me by DFO versus Shuswap staff on the amount of successful consultation. The former felt that a positive start had been made while the latter were more inclined to see the interaction as meagre and not especially relevant to their ongoing interests. This divergence of views underscores the gap between what DFO can or will provide and the rising expectations of other stakeholders.

local product than something imposed by bureaucrats from outside. The role of the Task Force in supporting the compilation of the best possible information on the state of the watershed will be no less than in the Stuart-Takla, yet local commitment seems sure to be much higher.

My discussions with Task Force members suggest that despite the sense of losing some control over the timing and momentum of planning, they see clear advantages. They recognize that in both the Cariboo and the Shuswap sub-basins, much-needed public support is being generated by public involvement at an earlier stage. In a time of fiscal restraint and programme cutbacks, this support and, in the case of the Cariboo, the potential backing of a local politician, is no small benefit.

If there is one overall lesson from these "experiments in consensus-building", it is that the need for more and better collective planning is broadly recognized. How else does one explain the frequency with which these and many other attempts are made to bring people and groups together, whether this be in formal inter-organizational structures, one-day seminars or through the plethora of various referral processes. We seem to keep urging each other towards more and more consultation despite the risks, costs and time requirements.

In the conclusions, I will make some more specific observations on the nature of the challenge of consensus-building for sustainable development. These will centre on the lessons of these "experiments".

Conclusions

This chapter has focused on the social diversity of those with a stake in the use and management of Fraser River salmon. We have seen how the resulting diversity of interests and values evolved and we have been through the diverse array of harvesters, managers and significant others. This underscores the daunting challenge of building a consensus on what we as a society want to do with the extraordinary gift of Fraser salmon.

In the immediately preceding section, highlights were presented of five quite recent experiences, all of which are more or less directed at achieving consensus. This quest for consensus, I have argued, is a prerequisite to deciding what the state of "sustainable development" is to be.

A way of understanding the meaning of consensus was presented in the first part of this chapter. The key features ascribed to consensual decision-making included commitment to multilateral rather than unilateral approaches, direct participation of key stakeholders, explicit concern for each group's views and interests, and the desire to reach decisions that all stakeholders abide by.

The experiences we have described vary in the degree to which these features are evident, yet all cases reveal some movement away from unilateralism and single-purpose orientations. While DFO sticks to the official line of sole ministerial responsibility and continues vigorously to promote such single purposes as doubling Fraser sockeye production, it has also ventured into a wide range of consultative experiences. CFIC has been asked (albeit unproductively) to come up with an allocation formula for Fraser sockeye; a framework agreement is in the works with IIFC for stock sharing and rebuilding; some assistance is now provided for others like the Shuswap to foster local coalitions; the North Fraser Harbour Commission is consulted on fish habitat matters under an umbrella agreement; and sustainable management plans have been opened to local involvement at earlier stages of planning in the upper Fraser.

Aboriginal groups whose power is growing rapidly are also discovering—or rediscovering—cooperative mechanisms through basin-wide forums like the IIFC and through step-by-step building of relationships at the local level.

In many though not all cases, the forest industry, municipalities and others whose actions affect habitat in the basin, have become more and more interested in participating in multilateral forums. Thus, for example, such stakeholders have been increasingly involved in both FREMP and the Fraser River Sustainable Development Task Force. We saw how pressure from these interests has led to the Task Force's reshaping of its procedures and priorities in sub-basin planning for the Cariboo.

Consensus is not at hand but one cannot fail to be impressed by the emergence of forums in which former adversaries are at least talking face-to-face. Incomplete and preliminary as the experiences are, they offer some hope in the face of the challenge created by a competitive history and the awesome melange of distinct interests.

To move closer to consensus on sustainable development in the context of Fraser salmon will require stakeholders to build on these preliminary experiences. A more exacting analysis than that presented here would be required as a basis for social learning. Still, several points can be made, drawing on the experiences outlined here and some general perspectives on the nature of consensual processes.

We need to reflect more critically and fundamentally on the goals of salmon stock and habitat management in order to better understand each stakeholder's interests.

An essential step towards consensus is to understand what motivates each major group. Fisher and Ury (1984) have described how all too often, people bargain over staunchly held positions. At the same time, they work on the basis of simplistic assumptions about what the other side seeks or values. Some of the more important consultative forums are plagued by this kind of thinking that leads only to "win-lose" confrontation.

Narrow ways of thinking and talking about interests are endemic. Native leaders have not come out with understandable visions of how they would like the fishery to be, if aboriginal title was resolved. This leaves predictions of disaster open to the most vivid imaginations (e.g., Pacific Fishermen's Defense Alliance, n.d.). DFO likewise, has for several years, advanced a one-dimensional image of the goals of fisheries management; for example, Fraser sockeye are to be doubled. But to what purpose? Just because the river could produce more fish? How, precisely, is the welfare of putative beneficiaries to be enhanced? And what about interests that could be harmed in trying to achieve such a goal? These are the kinds of questions that need to be addressed constructively, not rhetorically, in forums of multilateral consensus-seeking.

To really honour the insights and recommendations of the Brundtland Commission, those involved in sustainable development planning in the Basin must re-examine the issue of goals. They need to ponder the objectives articulated in *Our Common Future* (WCED, 1987) and ask how well they are dealt with in current fisheries resources planning in the Fraser Basin. This might be a sobering experience for those who believe that their institutions or programmes have already achieved sustainability.[26]

We need to take people and their behaviour as seriously as we take the dynamics of the salmon. Technical and scientific capacity far outstrip our present sophistication in dealing with the group and organizational-process side of the salmon management equation.

There is reason to believe that the Pacific salmon are the most thoroughly studied resource species anywhere in the world (Hilborn & Peterman, 1977). Yet most DFO and other stakeholders seem fixated on the idea that the most important area for improvement in salmon management lies in even more fisheries science. This emphasis exists in spite of continual and dramatic evidence that human behaviour rather than ecological dynamics underlies much of the chronic conflict.

Unquestionably, there are very important outstanding scientific questions and issues. But we know much less—or use much less of what we know—on how the humans involved in salmon governance think and act. This is not due to a lack of potential sources of information and understanding. There is a vast popular and academic literature on how groups work. Yet the simplest ideas—for example, building commitment to the process by joint-design of agenda—seem to elude those who convene many of the more important advisory meetings.

Beyond a sorely needed understanding of "meeting dynamics" is a broader and profound gap in appreciation of the organizational and inter-organizational dynamics of the major stakeholder groups. Since the mid-1960's, there has been growing awareness that organizations vary enormously in their capacity to deal with turbulent settings. Inter-organizational processes have also been the focus of action research (Williams, 1982; Trist, 1983). The implication of this work has been that organizations and societies must become active learning systems (including, most importantly, learning about the forces and features that limit their effectiveness). There is little evidence that the numerous stakeholders in the Fraser

26 DFO, when discussing the imperatives of the Brundtland Commission, frequently asserts that it has always been managing for sustainability. The long-time preoccupation with the concept of maximum sustainable yield (Larkin, 1977), is equated with the Commission's much broader and more profound concerns for global ecological welfare. FREMP similarly evaluates itself as an exemplar of sustainable development, while continuing to largely exclude public interest groups from its deliberations. Native leaders likewise speak as if their history of longterm sustainability is a genetic endowment, thus ignoring the enormous gap that can open between those traditional achievements and the desperate search for funds to correct serious social problems which many aboriginal groups feel forced to undertake (see Cassidy and Dale, 1988).

salmon domain are making an effort to understand their own and other organizations' dynamics. This leads to frustrating repetitions of old and less effective strategies in dealing with other groups.

Progress in consensus-building can occur simultaneously on various scales. Let us be open to multiple paths to sustainable development and not get hung up on debating the relative merits of centralized versus decentralized approaches.

One of the many precepts of the Brundtland Commission report was that greater reliance should be placed on grass-roots and locally-directed planning. This raises a question in a large river basin like the Fraser of the scale of decision-making, or just how local we need to get. The question is far from theoretical; the general advance of aboriginal rights through court decisions and the resulting political organization of some who fear this development, has led to a renewed debate over unilateral versus multilateral decision-making. This is closely related to the issue of whether local communities should play a lead or merely ancillary role in decision-making.

But when one looks at the various "experiments" in consensus-building within the Basin, scale is not necessarily the issue. Some decisions such as the management of the harvest of major sockeye stocks cannot be decentralized to the local level without also decentralizing the fishery itself (i.e., terminal fishing). Somehow, collaborative problem-solving must remain broad in geographic scope. In other cases, such as habitat enhancement (including habitat planning), local education and participation is critical and can practically occur only through small scale forums (e.g., the experience of Skeetchestn Band and Kamloops sports groups on Deadman's Creek). For the Fraser River estuary, multilateral planning will of necessity encompass a wide area and many users and resource managers; yet the format and the coordinating mechanisms may be adaptable up-river to less complex inter-organizational challenges (Dorcey and Rueggeberg, 1990).

The important point is that achieving a consensual framework for sustainable development should not be posed as an "either/or" selection between locally-led or centrally-organized initiatives. The recent interest by DFO in sustainable development planning for the entire basin is commendable, but so too is the work undertaken by the Shuswap on smaller sub-basins such as Deadman's Creek. DFO can, as needed, use its strong mandate to bring potentially harmful activities into line; the Shuswap, so far, have taken more the approach of gentle persuasion. Neither excludes the other; to the contrary, with a little better coordination, the efforts could be complementary.

The sharing of power (and its obverse, vulnerability) is absolutely essential and should not be seen as a zero-sum affair.

The final and perhaps most important point concerns attitudes towards power and its allocation. Not many years ago, consensus-based fisheries management in

Canada would have been seen as a legal impossibility, a violation of the sacrosanct principle of exclusive ministerial authority. Now there are forces of change, most notably the pursuit of aboriginal fisheries and fish management rights. As well, the system created under the Pacific Salmon Treaty provides a clear counter-example to the precept that there must be only one authoritative fisheries decision maker.

If further evidence is needed, there is the experience in the U.S. Pacific Northwest of evolving co-management mechanisms between state fisheries officials and inter-tribal Indian fishing organizations (Dale, 1989). The U.S. story provides additional lessons on the slow pace but essentiality of changing attitudes towards the sharing of power. Until state fisheries managers fully accepted permanent Indian participation as equals in fisheries planning, litigation and confrontation were incessant. Later, the benefits of multilateralism became apparent.[27]

Cultivating new attitudes is one of the Brundtland Commission's leading themes but it is usually seen primarily in terms of changing our outlook towards nature. The argument here has been that it is at least as crucial to confront our present assumptions about the distribution of authority. This questioning is inherent in the Brundtland Commission's perspective.[28]

The quest for sustainable development in the context discussed here, will be an exciting, often frustrating and always intimidating experience, both for those who have had the power and for those who have lived in its shadow. But, as stated, the energy and commitment to consensus-building is clearly in evidence within the vast array of people and groups whose future is tied to this gift of Fraser River salmon.

References

Amy, D. J. 1983. "Environmental Mediation: An Alternative Approach to Policy Atalemates." *Journal of Policy Sciences.* 14:345-365.
Bierhost, J. 1985. *The Mythology of North America.* New York: Morrow.
Canada. Dept. of Fisheries & Oceans. 1988. *Pacific Region Salmon Stock Management Plan. Volume I. Inner South Coast and Fraser River.* Vancouver: DFO
Canada. Dept. of Fisheries & Oceans. 1989. "Pacific Region Strategic Outlook. Vision 2000. A Vision of Pacific Fisheries at the Beginning of the 21st Century." Discussion Draft.
Cassidy, F., and N. Dale. 1988. *After Native Claims?* Lantzville: Oolichan Books.
Clement, W. 1987. *The Struggle to Organize.* (xx-incomplete citation).
Cohen, F. 1986. *Treaties on Trial: The Continuing Controversy over Northwest Indian Fishing Rights.* Seattle: University of Washington Press.
Dale, N. 1989. "Getting to Co-Management: Social Learning in the Redesign of Fisheries Management."

---

27 A positive assessment of the new multi-party approach to fisheries management was given by Gaffney (1986), who had actively opposed Indian fish management rights in the early post-Boldt years. For more on this, see Dale (1989).

28 This is most visible in the Commission's discussion of the role for non-government organizations. In a speech Brundtland made subsequent to publication of the Commission's final report, she stated: "The Commission found that a major prerequisite to sustainable development is a political system that secures effective citizen participation in decision-making. ...A major theme of Our Common Future is that a new multilateralism will be crucial for progress. (citied in Starke, 1990:64)."

in Pinkerton, E. (ed.). *Co-operative Management of Local Fisheries.* Vancouver: UBC Press.

Dorcey, A. H. J. (ed.). 1976. *The Uncertain Future of the Lower Fraser.* Vancouver: Westwater Research Centre.

Dorcey, A. H. J., and H. I. Rueggeberg. 1990. "Developing a Coordinated Environmental Review Process for the Fraser-Thompson Corridor." Report on a Workshop. Discussion paper for the Fraser-Thompson Corridor Transportation Environmental Steering Committee.

Dorcey, A. H. J. 1990. "Sustainable Development of the Fraser River Estuary: Success Amidst Failure." Paper prepared for Coastal Resource Management Group, Environment Directorate, OECD, Paris.

Doyle, M., and D. Straus. 1976. *How to Make Meetings Work.* New York: Playboy Press.

Fisher, R., and W. Ury. 1984. *Getting to Yes.* Toronto: Penguin.

Gaffney, F. 1986. "Beyond Boldt: When Ten Years of Law Suits Failed to Add Another Steelhead." *Trout.* (Winter 1986): 51-53.

Gordon, H. S. 1954. "The Economic Theory of a Common-Property Resource: The Fishery." *Journal of Political Economy* 62:124-142.

Hilborn, R., and R. M. Peterman. 1977. "Changing Management Objectives." in Ellis, D. V. (ed.). *Pacific Salmon Management for People.* Victoria: University of Victoria. Dept. of Geography.

Kearney, J. 1989. "Co-management or Co-optation?: The Ambiguities of Lobster Fisheries Management in Southwest Nova Scotia." in Pinkerton, E. (ed.). *Co-operative Management of Local Fisheries.* Vancouver: UBC Press.

Kennett, K., and M. McPhee. 1988. *The Fraser River Estuary: An Overview of Changing Conditions.* New Westminster: Fraser River Estuary Management Program.

Kew, M. 1976. "Salmon Abundance, Technology and Human Populations on the Fraser River Watershed." Unpublished ms. Dept. of Anthropology & Sociology, U.B.C.

Larkin, P. A. 1977. "An Epitaph for the Concept of Maximum Sustainable Yield. " *Trans. Amer. Fish. Soc.* 106(1):1-11.

Larkin, P. A. 1979. "Maybe You Can't Get There From Here: A Foreshortened History of Research in Relation to Management of Pacific Salmon." *J. Fish. Res. Bd. Can.* 36:98-106.

Marchak, P. 1987. "Organization of Divided Fishers." in Marchak, P., N. Guppy and J. McMullan (eds.). *Uncommon Property.* Toronto: Methuen.

Marchak, P., N. Guppy and J. McMullan (eds.). 1987. *Uncommon Property.* Toronto: Methuen.

McGregor, D. 1960. *The Human Side of Enterprise.* New York: McGraw-Hill.

McPhee, M. 1989. "Implementing Area Designations in the Fraser Estuary." in *Coastal Zone 89* V:4206-4212.

Netboy, A. 1968. *The Atlantic Salmon: A vanishing species?* Boston: Houghton Mifflin.

Netboy, A. 1980 *The Columbia River Salmon and Steelhead Trout, their Fight for Survival.* Seattle: University of Washington Press.

Odum, E. P. 1969. "The Strategy of Ecosystem Development." *Science.* 164:262-270.

Pacific Fishermen's Defense Alliance. no date. "Canada's fisheries...in crisis." Brochure from Box 1264, Station A, Surrey, B.C.

Pacific Salmon Commission. 1989. *Report of the Fraser River Panel to the Pacific Salmon Commission on the 1988 Fraser River Sockeye Salmon Fishing Season.* Vancouver: Pacific Salmon Commission.

Paish, H. & Associates. 1985. *Salmon Resource Stock Rebuilding: A Habitat Overview.* Report prepared for DFO, Pacific Region.

Pearse, P. H. 1982. *Turning the Tide: A New Policy for Canada's Pacific Fisheries.* Commission on Pacific Fisheries Policy, Final Report. Ottawa: Minister of Supply & Services.

Pinkerton, E. 1987. "Competition Among B.C. Fish-Processing Firms." in P. Marchak, N. Guppy and J. McMullan (eds.). *Uncommon Property.* Toronto: Methuen.

Pinkerton, E. (ed.). 1989. *Co-operative Management of Local Fisheries.* Vancouver: UBC Press.

Rothman, J. 1989. "Developing Pre-Negotiation Theory and Practice." Policy Studies No. 29, Leonard Davis Institute, Hebrew University, Jerusalem.

Sabatier, P. 1975. "Social Movements and Regulatory Agencies: Toward a More Adequate View of Client Capture." *Policy Sciences.* 6:301-342.

Sinclair, S. 1960. *License Limitation - British Columbia: A Method of Economic Fisheries Management.* Report to Canada Dept. of Fisheries.

Starke, L. 1990. *Signs of Hope: Working Towards Our Common Future.* Oxford: Oxford University Press.

Susskind, L., and J. Cruickshank. 1987. *Breaking the Impasse.* New York: Basic Books.

Trist, E. L. 1983. "Referent Organizations and the Development of Inter-Organizational Domains."

Human Relations. 36:269-284.

Urquhart, I. T. 1989. *International Relations, National Regulations: The Politics of Salmon Fishing in the Pacific Northwest.* Unpublished manuscript.

VanGundy, A. B. 1984. *Managing Group Creativity.* New York: Amacom.

Williams, T. A. 1982. *Learning to Manage Our Future: The Participative Redesign of Societies in Turbulent Transition.* New York: Wiley.

8

Birds of the Fraser Basin in Sustainable Development

Jean-Pierre L. Savard

The Fraser River Basin is renowned for the diversity and abundance of its birds. It encompasses 11 biogeoclimatic zones (B.C. Ministry of Forests, 1988), each characterised by particular climatic and vegetative component habitats and each supporting a distinct avifauna. However, agricultural, industrial and residential development affects the birds by modifying or destroying these habitats through physical alteration, pollution and disturbance. The challenge of sustainable development is to minimize these impacts.

Sustainable development is defined here as a positive socio-economic change that does not undermine the ecological and social systems upon which communities and society are dependent (Rees, 1989). It implies the preservation of options for future generations. Central to this definition of sustainable development is the belief that the integrity of the natural ecosystem must be maintained and, where necessary, restored. This is further elaborated to encompass the imperative that species diversity should be maintained. In the case of birds, this means that we should maintain the integrity of the habitats required to insure their diversity. Determining how large the population should be depends on the values associated with them; the size of population that is necessary to insure viability sets a minimum which only becomes the bottom line in situations where other resource development benefits make it unavoidably necessary to accept reductions in their numbers.

The objectives of this paper are

(i)   to highlight the principle components and associated habitats of the avifauna of the Fraser Basin;
(ii) to provide examples of the sustainable use of the bird resource within the Basin;

(iii) to review the impact of past development and major threats facing birds in the Basin; and,

(iv) to identify research on birds that is needed to guide sustainable development of the Basin.

Habitat Diversity

The Fraser Basin includes 11 of the 14 biogeoclimatic zones of British Columbia which makes it one of the most diversified river basins in Canada. The zones represented include the Coastal Western Hemlock, Interior Cedar Hemlock, Interior Douglas Fir, Ponderosa Pine, Bunchgrass, Mountain Spruce, Engelmann Spruce-Subalpine Fir, Mountain Hemlock, Sub-boreal Spruce, Sub-boreal Pine Spruce, and Alpine Tundra (B.C. Ministry of Forests, 1988). Some zones cover an extensive portion of the Basin, while others only a small section (Table 8.1). Each biogeoclimatic zone can be further subdivided into several different habitat types based on other characteristics such as vegetation age, type, location and degree of wetness.

Thousands of lakes and ponds of various size are found within the Fraser Basin. They range from fresh to highly alkaline (Topping and Scudder, 1977) and support a variety of aquatic vegetation and marshes. The estuary of the Fraser is the largest in British Columbia, supporting a diversity of large marshes of high biological productivity (Butler and Campbell, 1987; Yamanaka, 1975).

Table 8.1: Area Covered by the Different Biogeoclimatic Zones in the Fraser River Basin

Biogeoclimatic Zone	Area Within the Fraser Basin (ha)
Coastal Western Hemlock	839,798
Interior Cedar Hemlock	2,125,799
Interior Douglas Fir	3,292,015
Ponderosa Pine	220,943
Bunchgrass	327,811
Mountain Spruce	647,954
Engelmann Spruce—Sub-Alpine Fir	5,003,156
Mountain Hemlock	456,006
Sub-Boreal Spruce	6,874,301
Sub-Boreal Pine Spruce	2,359,961
Alpine Tundra	1,079,198

Birds of the Fraser Basin

Waterfowl

The most visible avian resource associated with the Fraser is waterfowl with twenty-one species of waterfowl breeding within the Basin. In fact the most productive waterfowl breeding areas of British Columbia are located within the Fraser Basin (McKelvey and Munro, 1983; Boyd et al., 1989; Savard, 1990). The waterfowl community of central British Columbia is also one of the most, if not the most, diversified in Canada in terms of species numbers (Boyd and Savard, 1987; Savard, 1990).

What sets the waterfowl community of the Fraser Basin aside from that of other areas in Canada is the predominance of cavity-nesting species (Savard, 1990). The relative abundance and diversity of breeding waterfowl are particularly high near Williams Lake (Table 8.2). Those species breed on lakes and ponds within the Basin and reach their highest densities on alkaline ponds (Boyd et al., 1989; Savard, 1990). The centre of distribution of Barrow's Goldeneye *(Bucephala islandica)*, a species for which over 60% of the world's population both breeds and winters in British Columbia (Savard, 1987), and the highest densities of Barrow's Goldeneye and Bufflehead *(B. albeola)* in North America are both found within the boundaries of the Fraser River Basin (Munro, 1942; Erskine, 1972; Savard, 1987).

Two species, the Common Merganser *(Mergus merganser)* and the Harlequin Duck *(Histrionicus histrionicus)* are closely associated with the Fraser River and its tributaries. The Common Merganser is a common breeder on the River, but little is known of the breeding distribution of the Harlequin Duck within the Fraser Basin (Brèault and Savard, 1991). Harlequin Ducks prefer mountainous streams and frequent tributaries of the Fraser River. The Common Goldeneye *(Bucephala clangula)* is a common breeder in the upper part of the Basin within the Sub-boreal Spruce biogeoclimatic zone, whereas the Barrow's Goldeneye is most abundant in the Interior Douglas Fir zone. Barrow's Goldeneye tend to avoid lakes with fishes and prefer highly productive alkaline ponds (Savard, 1984).

The interior portion of the Fraser Basin is not only a breeding area for waterfowl but also an important migratory corridor for several species (Savard, 1980; Butler and Savard, 1985), an important moulting site (Munro, 1941; 1949), and an important fall staging area for waterfowl (Munro, 1941; Ducks Unlimited, unpublished data). Important moulting species within the Fraser Basin include Lesser Scaup *(Aythya affinis)*, American Widgeon *(Anas americana)*, Mallard *(A. platyrhyncos)*, Green-winged Teal *(A. crecca)* and Blue-winged Teal *(A. discors)* (Savard, 1990).

The most productive area of the Fraser Basin is the estuary with its associated tidal marshes. These marshes provide wintering habitat for thousands of waterfowl, especially dabbling ducks (Table 8.3). Mallard, American Wigeon, Northern Pintail *(Anas acuta)* and Green-winged Teal are the most abundant dabbling ducks wintering in the delta. The waterfowl associated with the Fraser

Table 8.2: Average Abundance (n=7 years, 1980-1986) of Breeding Adult Males for Waterfowl near Riske Creek, British Columbia in a 10km² area

Species	Average	%
Mallard	93 ± 15	5
Gadwall	19 ± 1	1
American Widgeon	122 ± 11	7
Northern Pintail	38 ± 3	2
Green-Winged Teal	66 ± 3	4
Blue-Winged Teal	363 ± 69	19
Cinnamon Teal	26 ± 6	1
Northern Shoveler	71 ± 10	4
Redhead	41 ± 4	2
Ring-Necked Duck	60 ± 7	3
Canvasback	28 ± 3	1
Scaup	276 ± 22	15
Barrow's Goldeneye	371 ± 19	20
Bufflehead	171 ± 4	9
Ruddy Duck	127 ± 10	7
Total	1872	

Source: Savard (1990).

delta has been the subject of several studies (Taylor, 1970; Vermeer and Levings, 1977; Blood, 1978; Savard, 1985; McKelvey et al,. 1985; Butler and Campbell, 1987). Dabbling ducks outnumber diving ducks by a factor of four during winter in the intertidal marshes, foraging extensively in the agricultural fields adjacent to the estuary. In early March, there is an influx of diving ducks and an exodus of dabbling ducks possibly indicating departure for breeding areas. Aerial surveys conducted in the mid-1960's (Taylor, 1970) and in the early 1980's (McKelvey et al., 1985) indicate the seasonal and overall abundance of dabbling ducks on the Fraser delta and highlight the importance of the delta for wintering waterfowl (Table 8.4). The delta also supports some moulting seaducks during the summer, but the largest number of moulters is found in the adjacent Boundary Bay (Savard, 1988b).

Table 8.3: Ground Counts of the Number of Waterfowl Wintering in the Intertidal Marshes of the Fraser Delta in 1977

	December 20-21	February 8-9	Feb. 28-March 1
Mallard	361	53	237
Northern Pintail	196	9	1,099
Green-Winged Teal	1,297	793	682
American Widgeon	1,690	240	856
Dabbling Duck sp.	8,707	7,022	1,232
Canvasback	115	56	346
Scaup	1,182	663	2,559
Common Goldeneye	19	41	37
Barrow's Goldeneye	9	8	31
Bufflehead	109	17	182
Oldsquaw	87	22	105
White-Winged Scoter	44	38	116
Surf Scoter	249	314	435
Black Scoter	121	201	174
Scoter sp.	22	22	90
Ruddy Duck	795	756	1,300
Red-Breasted Merganser	16	4	25
Duck sp.	307	35	17
Total Dabbling Ducks	12,251	8,117	4,106
Total Diving Ducks	3,075	2,177	5,417
Total Ducks	15,326	10,294	9,523

Source: Savard (1985).

Table 8.4: Seasonal Abundance of Waterfowl within the Fraser Delta

Month	Taylor (1970)[*] April 1966 - January 1970	McKelvey et al. (1985)[**] 1982 - 1984
September	28,981[***]	4,694 ± 1477
October	39,304	34,869 ± 0
November	60,763	28,682 ± 4357
December	41,640	37,345 ± 6613
January	29,644	20,890 ± 6516
February	10,228	10,060 ± 3195
March	16,765	3,377 ± 630
April	20,877	2,748 ± 1074
May	—	37
June	—	490
July	—	979
August	—	157

Notes:
[*]   Includes diving and dabbling ducks.
[**]   Includes only dabbling ducks.
[***]   Number of birds estimated from aerial surveys.

Geese and Swans

The Canada Goose *(Branta canadensis)* is the only goose to breed within the Fraser Basin. It breeds throughout the whole Fraser Basin but in low densities. In recent years, populations in the Fraser delta have increased due to introductions that began in the early 1970's and a moratorium on hunting that ended in 1978 (Leach, 1982b). Today, there are approximately 9,000 Canada Geese in the lower Fraser valley (McKelvey, Can. Wildl. Serv., pers. comm.).

The spring and fall migrations of geese are spectacular in the interior, especially near Vanderhoof on the Nechako River. Both Snow Geese *(Anser caerulescens)* and Canada Geese stage there during migration. Few geese winter in the interior within the Fraser Basin; most migrate south. However, the Fraser estuary supports large populations of wintering Snow and Canada Geese (Taylor, 1970; Jeffrey and Kaiser, 1979; McKelvey et al., 1985; Savard, 1985; Butler and Campbell, 1987). Migrant White-fronted Geese *(Anser albifrons)* also occur regularly but in very small numbers.

Snow Geese arrive in the Fraser delta from their breeding area on Wrangel Island in the Soviet Union in early October and remain in the delta until late December when most depart for the Skagit estuary. They return to the Fraser delta in late February to accumulate the necessary energy prior to their departure for Wrangel Island in late March. Snow Geese feed on rhizomes of Scirpus found in the intertidal brackish marshes (Burton, 1977). In recent years, geese have increased their use of agricultural fields (Hatfield, 1991). This coincided with an increase in population size. In the late 1970's, the Snow Goose population of the Skagit and Fraser numbered between 12,000 and 24,000 birds (Jeffrey and Kaiser, 1979), while it now numbers around 50,000 (S. Boyd, Can. Wildl. Serv., pers. comm.).

Numbers of Tundra Swans *(Cygnus columbianus)* and Trumpeter Swans *(C. buccinator)* wintering in the Fraser valley have increased from a few individuals in the 1970's to approximately 150 birds in 1984, and to 500 in 1989 (McKelvey, 1986; 1989). This parallels an increase in the overall wintering population of Trumpeter Swans in British Columbia (McKelvey et al., 1989). Swans in the tidal marshes are mostly Trumpeters (70%) whereas those frequenting the upper Fraser valley are mostly Tundra (75%) (McKelvey, 1989).

Trumpeter Swans traditionally winter in small numbers on some open rivers of the Fraser Basin. In 1980, 93 swans wintered near François Lake, 46 on the Nautley River and 33 on the Stuart River (McKelvey and Noble, 1980). Approximately 50 Trumpeter Swans also winter on the Crooked River near a hot spring north of Prince George.

Loons and Grebes

One species of loon and five species of grebes breed within the Fraser Basin. The Common Loon *(Gavia immer)* frequents lakes with fishes and is widely distributed throughout the Basin. In British Columbia, the Pied-billed Grebe *(Podilymbus podiceps)*, Horned Grebe *(Podiceps auritus)*, Red-necked Grebe *(P. grisegena)* and Eared Grebe *(P. nigricollis)* reach their highest breeding densities within the Fraser Basin, frequenting small ponds and lakes. Over 40% of the known breeding sites of Eared Grebe in British Columbia are located within the Fraser Basin (Brèault et al., 1988) especially in the interior Douglas Fir biogeoclimatic zones. The abundance of the Western Grebe *(Aechmophorus occidentalis)* has decreased within the Fraser Basin from four active colonies in the mid-1960's, to only one now located on Shuswap Lake (Forbes, 1984; Campbell et al., 1990). Causes of the decline have been attributed to industrial development and human disturbance (Campbell et al., 1990). Four species of loons and six species of grebes winter in the Fraser estuary (Blood, 1978; Savard, 1985), the Common Loon and Western Grebe being the most abundant.

Raptors and Owls

Nearly all species of raptors and owls breeding in British Columbia can be found within the Fraser Basin. Two species have been classified as threatened—the Flammulated Owl *(Otus flammeolus)* and the Barn Owl *(Tyto alba)*—and one as endangered in Canada—the Spotted Owl *(Strix occidentalis)* (World Wildlife Fund, 1988; COSEWIC, 1990). Barn Owls breed and winter in the Fraser delta (Campbell and Campbell, 1984) and Spotted Owls are found in old growth coastal forests surrounding the delta (Campbell and Campbell, 1986). Both species are at the northern limit of their range. Flammulated Owls are associated with old growth in the interior Douglas Fir biogeoclimatic zone (Howie, 1988).

Other species breed in various habitats of the Fraser Basin, but in low densities. Two species are closely associated with water: the Bald Eagle *(Haliaeetus leucoephalus)* and Osprey *(Pandion haliaetus)*. Bald Eagles concentrate in late fall and early winter along salmon-bearing streams to prey on dying salmon. Bald Eagles breed in sparse numbers throughout the whole Fraser Basin. Ospreys breed throughout the Basin and sometimes in relatively high densities as on Shuswap Lake.

The highest concentration of raptors in the Fraser Basin is found in winter within the Fraser delta (Blood, 1978; Grass and Grass, 1978; Butler and Campbell, 1987). Rough-legged Hawks *(Buteo lagopus)* arrive in the delta in November from their northern breeding area and stay until April (Grass and Grass, 1978). Other raptors, whose numbers increase in winter within the delta include the Peregrine Falcon *(Falco peregrinus)*, Merlin *(Falco columbarius)* Northern Harrier *(Circus cyaneus)*, Red-tailed Hawk *(Buteo jamaicensis)*, Snowy Owl *(Nyctea scandiaca)* and Short-eared Owl *(Asia flammeus)* (Table 8.5). Most of the hawks and owls feed on small rodents which are found mostly in old field habitat and in pasture fields.

Shorebirds, Herons and Gulls

Twenty-nine species of shorebirds have been recorded in the Fraser delta (Butler and Campbell, 1987). Four species dominate in numbers: the Western Sandpiper *(Calidris mauri)*, Least Sandpiper *(C. minutilla)*, Dunlin *(C. alpina)* and Black-bellied Plover *(Pluvialis squatarola)*. Butler and Campbell (1987) estimated that in 1977, 500,000 Western Sandpipers used the delta (Boundary Bay included) in the spring, and 1.2 million in the fall. Only two species of shorebirds winter in significant numbers within the delta: the Dunlin, numbering between 30,000-40,000 during this period (McEwan and Farr, 1986), but up to 109,000 during fall migration (Fry, 1980); and the Black-bellied Plover, with a wintering population fluctuating between 1,000-2,000 birds (Butler and Cannings, 1990).

Over 30 colonies of Great Blue Herons *(Ardea herodias)* are found within the Fraser Basin, most of them near the Fraser delta (Forbes et al., 1985). Herons are closely associated with the Fraser River and feed mainly on fish captured in the river and its associated marshes (Krebs 1974; Butler, 1989). The three colonies associated with the Fraser foreshore hold approximately 400 nests (Forbes et al.,

Table 8.5: Seasonal Abundance of Raptors in the Fraser Valley[1]

	Month							
Species	Oct	Nov.	Dec.	Jan.	Feb.	Mar.	Apr.	May
Accipiters	0	5	11	4	9	5	5	3
Marsh Hawk	35	67	88	85	54	62	52	18
Rough-Legged Hawk	3	10	38	29	26	35	29	2
Red-Tailed Hawk	14	40	57	66	32	33	28	21
Bald Eagle	0	1	3	15	29	33	9	5
Falcons	3	8	9	10	7	2	5	3
Short-Eared Owl	0	6	7	12	17	3	4	2
Snowy Owl	0	0	0	3	8	3	0	0
Total	55	137	213	224	182	176	132	54

Notes:
1   Grass and Grass (1978), number of individuals seen in the sampled areas.

1985). Herons also winter in large numbers within the Fraser Valley especially near the estuary (Blood, 1978; Butler and Cannings, 1990).

Seven species of gulls frequent the Fraser Basin (Butler and Campbell, 1987), but only two breed there: the Glaucous-winged Gull *(Larus glaucescens)*, which breeds in the Fraser Estuary, and the Bonaparte's Gull *(Larus philadelphia)* which breeds inland. Most species frequent the Fraser estuary in fall and winter, when they feed in the fields, refuse dumps and intertidal areas.

The Greater Sandhill Crane *(Grus canadensis)* breeds within the Fraser Basin, but in low numbers. There is a small relict population within the Pitt valley near Vancouver, but the majority breeds within the Interior Douglas Fir biogeoclimatic zone (Campbell et al., 1990). The Lesser Sandhill Crane, which breeds in the Yukon, Alaska and the Northwest Territories, migrates and stages in large numbers through the Fraser Basin in the central interior.

Passerines and Other Families

Over 80 species of passerines have been recorded in the Fraser delta (Butler and Campbell, 1987) and over 150 within the Fraser Basin. The species most closely tied with the Fraser River and its tributaries are those associated with riparian habitats, habitats that are usually highly productive and support a great diversity of birds (Oakley et al., 1985; Thomas et al., 1979; Faber et al., 1989). The type and extent of riparian zones vary considerably throughout the Fraser Basin, but these zones are usually more productive than adjacent habitat. Species using riparian habitats within the Fraser Basin include: American Dipper *(Cinclus mexicanus)*, Spotted Sandpiper *(Actitis macularia)*, Belted Kingfisher *(Ceryle alcyon)*, Alder Flycatcher *(Empidonax alnorum)*, Willow Flycatcher *(E. traillii)*, Yellow Warbler *(Dendroica petechia)*, Common Yellowthroat *(Geothlypis trichas)*, Northern Waterthrush *(Seiurus noveboracensis)*. Riparian habitats are especially important in coniferous forests where they often provide a deciduous component to the forest, attracting distinct species of birds. In heavily logged areas riparian habitats often provide the only remaining nesting areas for cavity-nesting species. Cottonwood trees associated with riparian areas are extensively used by cavity-nesting species.

Forest ecosystems are very diversified in the Fraser Basin and harbour a great diversity of passerine birds. Cavity nesting birds constitute an important component of the avifauna of the Fraser Basin as more cavity nesting birds breed within the Fraser Basin, especially in the Interior Douglas Fir biogeoclimatic zone than anywhere else in Canada. Twelve species of woodpeckers breed within the Fraser Basin and provide cavities for more than 22 species of secondary cavity nesters.

Grasslands of the Fraser Basin are breeding grounds for the Long-billed Curlew *(Numenius americanus)*, Horned Lark *(Eremophila alpestris)*, Western Meadowlark *(Sturnella neglecta)*, Vesper Sparrow *(Pooecetes gramineus)* and Savannah Sparrow *(Passerculus sandwichensis)*.

International Importance of the Birds of the Fraser Basin

Over 80% of the birds breeding and/or wintering within the Fraser Basin are migratory. Band recoveries indicate that some of the Mallards, Northern Pintails, American Wigeons and Green-winged Teals that winter in the Fraser delta come from the Yukon, Alaska and Alberta (McKelvey and Smith, 1990). Among the breeding American Wigeons banded in the Fraser Basin near Williams Lake, only 14% were recovered from the Fraser delta compared to 28% from Washington, 28% from Oregon and 23% from California. Most band returns of Green-winged Teals, Northern Shovelers *(Anas clypeata)* and Northern Pintails breeding in central British Columbia are from California (McKelvey and Smith, 1990).

Most Lesser Scaups *(Aythya affinis)* and Buffleheads breeding in the Fraser Basin winter in California. Wintering populations of these species in the Fraser delta originate from Alaska and the Yukon. Blue-winged Teal breeding in the Fraser Basin winter in Central and South America (McKelvey and Smith, 1990). Most species of waterfowl breeding within the Fraser Basin are harvested locally in early fall. However, as most do not winter in British Columbia, late fall and early winter harvests occur in the United States. Conversely, most of the birds harvested in the Fraser Basin in winter come from Alaska, the Yukon and Alberta.

The Snow Geese wintering and migrating through the Fraser delta breed in the Soviet Union and winter partially in the United States. In fact, the Fraser and Skagit estuary form a wintering unit for the Snow Geese which travel frequently between the two estuaries.

Over 60% of the passerines breeding within the Fraser Basin winter either in the southern United States, Central America and/or South America (Diamond, 1986). Some species spend more time in their wintering areas than here. Most species of warblers and vireos winter in the tropics. Some other common species of the Fraser Basin wintering in tropical areas include the Eastern Kingbird *(Tyrannus tyrnnus)*, Western Wood Pewee *(Contopus sordidulus)*, Black-headed Grosbeak *(Pheucticus melanocephalus)*, Western Tanager *(Piranga ludoviciana)*, and Swainson's Thrush *(Catharus ustulatus)*.

Because a great portion of the avifauna of the Fraser Basin is migratory, their population could be affected by conditions outside the Fraser Basin. For example, the increase in the Snow Goose population wintering in the Fraser delta is mostly due to several years of good reproductive success on Wrangel Island, Soviet Union. Several of our passerine populations wintering in the tropics could be affected by deforestation in their wintering areas. There is mounting evidence suggesting a negative impact (Robbins et al., 1986; Collins and Wendt, 1989; Terborgh, 1989). There is even stronger evidence of a decline of species wintering in the southern United States, an area heavily impacted by agricultural, industrial and urban development (Erskine et al., 1990). The problems of determining whether declines are due to changes in the breeding or wintering areas or both is difficult and requires a good understanding of the ecology of each species.

Sustainable Use of the Bird Resources

Utilization of the bird resources by humans can be broadly classified as consumptive and non-consumptive.

Consumptive Use

Consumptive use includes scientific collecting, capture for aviculture purposes, some scientific research and hunting. Geese, waterfowl and upland gamebird hunting are practised in a sustainable fashion; their harvest is being closely monitored so that it does not negatively affect their populations. In the winter of 1982-83, 465 hunters hunted Snow Geese in the Fraser delta, spending a total of 3,035 hunter-days and killing an estimated 1,590 Snow Geese. Figures for 1983-84 were 448 hunters, 2,580 hunter-days and 668 Snow Geese killed (Boyd, pers. comm.).

Waterfowl hunting within the Fraser Basin constitutes an important economic activity. Jacquemot et al. (1986) estimated that in 1981 waterfowl hunters of British Columbia spent an average of $160.72 for a total of $6.4 million and that upland gamebird hunters spent an average of $143.20 each for a total of $12.2 million. A large proportion of these activities occurred within the Fraser Basin.

The number of waterfowl hunters in British Columbia has been decreasing steadily since 1981 when 29,000 hunting permits were sold, compared with only 13,000 sold in 1989. This decline is attributed to a combination of changes in the age structure of the population, a greater degree of urbanization of the population, reduced hunting opportunities in some areas, and increased costs of hunting (Boyd and Cooch, 1986). This reduction in hunters translated into a significant reduction in duck harvest from 188,000 in 1981 to 101,000 in 1989.

Several mechanisms are in place to ensure that hunting activities do not significantly impact the resource and that populations are maintained. The National Harvest Survey (Cooch et al., 1978; Dickson, 1987, 1989) monitors waterfowl kills in British Columbia. Special surveys and questionnaires are in place to monitor the harvest of Snow and Canada geese within the Fraser valley. Breeding waterfowl populations in the most productive areas of British Columbia are now being monitored and the wintering Snow and Canada geese of the delta are surveyed every year. Hunting regulations are adjusted according to these data to ensure sustainable use of the resource. Federal and provincial enforcement officers ensure that hunters comply with regulations. Hunter compliance with regulations is high.

Scientific use of birds has increased in recent years mostly because of their usefulness in assessing contamination levels in various habitats. Most pesticides, especially organochlorines, some herbicides, heavy metals and toxic by-products like dioxins concentrate through the food web and are most easily detected in organisms at the top of food chains (Peakall, 1972). Within the Fraser Basin, waterfowl have been used to assess contamination levels in recent years (Vermeer and Levings, 1977) particularly Great Blue Herons, which have been used to monitor dioxin levels (Elliott et al., 1988, 1989). Birds are often used as indicators of ecosystem integrity, because of their high visibility and their sensitivity to change in habitat structure.

Non-Consumptive Use

Non-consumptive uses of the bird resources are increasing in British Columbia and have surpassed consumptive use (Jacquemot et al., 1986; Filion et al., 1989). Jacquemot et al. (1986) estimated that in 1981, each British Columbian spent an average of $151.86 on non-consumptive use of wildlife; a total of $68.9 million for the province. In 1981, non-consumptive activities provided about 55% of the total net value of wildlife related activities to residents of British Columbia whereas hunting of waterfowl and gamebirds provided only 32% (Jacquemot et al., 1986).

Because of the diversity of habitats found within the Fraser Basin, viewing opportunities for wildlife are numerous. Each spring, spectacular migrations can be observed. Waterfowl concentrate in early spring on ponds and lakes of the Interior Douglas Fir biogeoclimatic zone, waiting for more northerly ponds to open. Large numbers of arctic breeding Sandhill Cranes fly over the Fraser River near Riske Creek en route to their breeding areas. The most impressive spectacles are found in the Fraser delta during winter. Each year, Snow Geese attract thousands of visitors to the Reifel Refuge, and the Alaksen National Wildlife Area. A yearly festival has been established to celebrate the arrival of the geese. Snow geese provide for both consumptive and non-consumptive use with no significant conflicts between the two usages. This is a good example of sustainable use of a resource, in that the use by one group does not preclude utilization by another group. A provincial program is now in place to identify and develop wildlife viewing areas (Maurer, 1989; Mol, 1991).

Birds and the Sustainable Development of Other Resources

The concept of sustainable development implies that the exploitation of a given resource does not jeopardize the utilization of other resources in a permanent way, reducing options available in the future.

Only one species of bird occurring within the Fraser Basin has been classified as endangered in Canada: the Spotted Owl (World Wildlife Fund, 1988; COSEWIC, 1990). The Spotted Owl has been the subject of several studies in the United States (Forsman et al., 1984; Campbell et al., 1984; Gutierrey and Carey, 1985) but, besides preliminary inventories, nothing is known of its ecology within the Fraser Basin (Campbell and Campbell, 1986).

The Spotted Owl has been identified as an old growth dependent species (Gutierrey and Carey 1985; Campbell and Campbell, 1986) and is found mainly within the Coastal Western Hemlock biogeoclimatic zone. Important areas within the Fraser Basin where this species has been recorded include Mount Lehman, Chilliwack, Vedder Crossing, Hope, Lillooet River watershed, and Spuzzum (Howie, 1980a; Campbell and Campbell, 1986). Intensive logging, and urban and industrial development within the Spotted Owl's range have undoubtedly negatively affected the species. Besides habitat destruction, logging has fragmented the remaining forest, favouring the establishment of the Barred Owl (*Strix varia*), a superior competitor (Hamer et al., 1989). The Burrowing Owl *(Athene cunicularia)* once nested within the Fraser Basin, but is now very rare and may no longer breed in the area (Wedgwood, 1978; Howie, 1980b).

Seven species have been classified as rare nationally, and thus of concern. They are the Barn Owl which is common within the Fraser delta, the Caspian Tern *(Sterna caspia)* of which a few birds nest in the estuary (Campbell et al., 1990), the Cooper's Hawk *(Accipiter cooperii)*, the Flammulated Owl, the Great Grey Owl *(Strix nebulosa)* which breeds within the Fraser Basin, the Peregrine Falcon which winters within the delta, and the Trumpeter Swan whose numbers have been increasing and which feeds mostly within the intertidal marshes of the estuary and the aquatic marshes along the river.

Although not considered rare in Canada, the American White Pelican *(Pelecanus erythrorhynchos)* is considered endangered in British Columbia as there is only one colony, located on Stump Lake (Dunbar et al., 1980). The Western Grebe is also represented in British Columbia by only a few small colonies and their numbers have been decreasing. The disappearance of these two species from the Fraser Basin would be a great loss in terms of reduced biodiversity within the Basin and loss of two spectacular species. Special care should be taken to ensure the survival of these two small populations and possibly their expansion.

Because birds require specific habitats to breed and healthy ecosystems to survive, several economic developments affect them. Wetland alienation has been extensive in the Fraser Estuary due to agricultural, industrial and urban activities (Leach, 1982a; 1982b; Butler and Campbell, 1987) (Table 8.6). Seasonal wet meadows, bogs, and tree and shrub communities have been replaced by cultivated fields and urban or industrial complexes. There has been relatively little wetland loss in the interior portion of the Fraser Basin (McKenzie, 1983; 1985), but the quality of several wetlands has been reduced because of overgrazing. Other habitat types have been greatly modified by some form of resource development (Pojar, 1980). Below I will address some of the major types of activities that negatively affect birds within the Fraser Basin.

Table 8.6: Habitat Composition (%)[1] of the Fraser River Delta (681.5 km[2]) in 1880 (prior to European Settlement) and in 1985

Habitat	1880	1985
River	10	10
Sand and Mud Flats	38	38
Seasonal Wet Meadows	22	~ 0
Bog	13	1
Trees and Shrubs	16	5
Cultivated Field	0	19
Suburban and Industrial	0	28

Source: Adapted from Butler and Campbell (1987).
Notes:
1   Two habitats are not represented here: Tidal and brackish marshes and salt marshes. The values presented in Butler and Campbell (1987) for these habitats are inaccurate and should not be used.

Forest Exploitation

Logging is one of the main industrial activities of the Fraser Basin affecting birds. For some species the impact is positive, but for most it is negative (Bunnell and Eastman, 1976). Species adapted to early succession habitats benefit from clearcutting. These include MacGillivray's Warbler *(Oporornis tolmiei)*, Song Sparrow *(Melospiza melodia)*, Rufous-sided Towhee *(Pipilo erythrophthalmus)*, White-crowned Sparrow *(Zonotrichia leucophrys)*, Dark-eyed Junco *(Junco hyemalis)* and Fox Sparrow *(Passerella iliaca)* (Gebauer, 1989; Seip and Savard 1990).

The effect of forestry practices is most severe for species associated with mature and old growth forest at some stage of their life history. Within the Fraser Basin, species associated with mature and old growth forests include the Spotted Owl, Northern Goshawk *(Accipiter gentilis)*, Pileated Woodpecker *(Dryocopus pileatus)*, Hairy Woodpecker *(Picoides villosus)*, Flammulated Owl, Brown Creeper *(Certhia americana)*, Varied Thrush *(Ixoreus naevius)* and Marbled Murrelet *(Brachyramphus marmoratus)*. Research is needed to determine the extent to which these species depend on mature and old growth forest for their long term survival.

Studies in the United States and Europe have shown that current forestry practices (clearcutting, homogeneous plantations, short rotation periods) have the greatest impact on cavity nesting species (Balda, 1975; Kessler, 1979; Nilsson, 1979; Mannan, 1982; Helle, 1985). Cavity nesters need trees or snags infected with heart rot fungi in order to excavate their breeding and roosting cavities (McClelland and Frissell, 1975; Miller and Miller, 1980). Secondary cavity nesters, which depend upon cavities excavated by the primary cavity nesters for breeding, are equally affected.

Clearcutting, thinning and selective logging practices often eliminate snags and large trees, greatly reducing nest site availability and foraging substrates for cavity nesting species. Studies have shown that the density and diversity of breeding and wintering birds in clearcuts can be increased by the retention of snags (Dickson et al., 1983; Marcot, 1983; Scott and Oldemeyer, 1983; Zarnowitz and Manuwal, 1985). Studies have also shown that densities and diversities of breeding cavity nesters in the forest increased with snag densities (Haapanen, 1965; Balda, 1975; Mannan et al., 1980; Brush, 1981; Raphael and White, 1984; Scott and Oldemeyer, 1983). Mature and old growth forests also provide the best wintering habitat for most resident species (Manuwal and Huff, 1987).

Barrow's Goldeneye, which breed in tree cavities, are adversely affected by the harvest of large trees, as only these provide cavities large enough. Only Pileated Woodpecker cavities are large enough to accommodate Barrow's Goldeneye. In several areas within the Fraser Basin, there is a shortage of suitable nesting cavities for goldeneyes (Peterson and Gauthier, 1985; Gauthier and Smith, 1987; Savard, 1988a). The maintenance of viable populations of woodpeckers in harvested areas is not only important from a biotic diversity point of view but also from an economic point of view. Studies have shown that birds can reduce the frequency of insect outbreaks (Otvos, 1965; McCambridge and Knight, 1972; Massey and Wygant, 1973)—especially important within the Fraser Basin where forests are subjected to frequent outbreaks of Mountain Pine Beetles.

Our current methods of exploiting forests are not compatible with the concept of sustainable development, as they often pose a threat to other existing resources. Several techniques have been developed to minimize the impact of logging on wildlife (Thomas, 1979; Hoover and Wills, 1984; Brown, 1985) but they are not used within the Fraser Basin. Harris (1984) proposes various ways of exploiting forests while maintaining biotic diversity on a regional scale. The key to proper forest exploitation is the retention of all habitat components within a management unit. Complete logging of watersheds is not compatible with maintaining biotic diversity and future options. Significant portions of watershed should be left intact or in long rotation cutting in order to maintain the presence of the species associated with mature and old growth forests. This would also facilitate the recolonization of the growing forest by these species. Riparian zones should be preserved as they serve as corridors for moving between forest patches and also often support the greatest number of species.

An increasingly important issue affecting forest birds is the fragmentation of mature and old growth forests. Large species such as raptors, owls, and Pileated Woodpeckers require large tracts of forest. Studies in eastern North America have shown that the reproductive success of forest interior species is reduced in small patches of forest because of increased predation rates and an increase in Brown-headed Cowbird *(Molothrus ater)* parasitism (Robbins, 1979; Whitcomb et al., 1981; Janzen, 1983). Similar studies are needed in western North America.

Forest diversity is also an increasingly important concept in terms of maintaining biodiversity and as a safeguard against the effect of climate warming. Large planted monocultures reduce forest diversity, affect the diversity of the avifauna, and increase the susceptibility of the forest to fires and disease. The loss of the deciduous component in these forests further contributes to reduce biodiversity as several species of birds are associated with deciduous vegetation.

A more holistic approach to forestry is needed within the Fraser Basin to achieve sustainable development of the resource. The maintenance of biotic diversity, an increasingly important issue, depends on more global planning of forest exploitation.

Agriculture and Ranching

Agricultural activities, like logging, modify habitats and thus directly affect bird use of these habitats. Agricultural activities are dominant within the lower portion of the Fraser Basin. Two species have already been extirpated from the Fraser delta mostly as a result of these activities: the Horned Lark and the Western Bluebird *(Sialia mexicana)* (Butler and Campbell, 1987). Wintering waterfowl of the delta, however, have adapted and use remnant and forage crops as food sources in winter (Hatfield, 1990; Hirst and Easthope, 1981). The draining of Sumas Lake in 1923 was probably the single most important modification of the natural habitat, displacing thousands of migrant waterfowl and creating Sumas prairies (Leach, 1982b).

Hawks and owls wintering in the delta rely mainly on small rodents which tend to be less abundant in intensively farmed areas and could be affected by intensified levels of agricultural activities. Several species breed in hedgerows found around the fields. The absence of hedgerows in intensively farmed areas greatly reduces the biotic diversity of the agricultural environment.

Ranching is the main agricultural activity in the mid section of the Fraser Basin. Grazing occurs mainly on the grasslands bordering the Fraser River in the Bunchgrass and Interior Douglas-fir biogeoclimatic zones. Grazing is not without its effects on bird populations (Graul, 1980; Kantrud, 1981). Intense grazing changes the structure of grasslands, affecting the density and height of vegetation. This in turn favours some species but not others (Ryder, 1980). Long-billed Curlews for example tend to benefit from moderate grazing as they prefer short grass prairies. However, intense grazing removes the cover necessary for the protection of their young and makes them more vulnerable to predation (Bicak et al., 1982).

Intense grazing also affects waterfowl nesting success. Species such as the Mallard, American Wigeon, Blue-winged Teal and Lesser Scaup nest in upland areas and require high grasses to conceal their nests. In intensively grazed areas, the nest and even the female becomes more vulnerable to predation.

Grazing has also an impact on the very important riparian vegetation. Because of their high productivity, riparian areas usually suffer higher amounts of grazing than adjacent areas. Trampling by cattle often destroys the sensitive riparian and aquatic vegetation. Transformation of natural grasslands into agricultural areas is another increasing threat to the avifauna of these habitats. Irrigation of the dry grasslands of the Fraser Basin modifies these grasslands, while directly using the water resources of the Fraser River and its tributaries. When water is taken from ponds, these can become unsuitable as breeding sites for waterfowl. Forest ecosystems are slowly replaced by agricultural land in the valleys of the Fraser Basin mostly for forage crop production. This is especially acute from Williams Lake to Prince George and through the Nechako and Bulkley valleys (Pojar, 1980).

Finally, pollution is an indirect but very significant effect of agricultural activities on the environment. The use of fertilizers, herbicides and pesticides increases every year, reducing insect populations and polluting waterways over large areas. These impacts can have long term effects, affecting the sustainable use of other resources (i.e., fisheries, tourism and even agriculture). Several cases of bird mortality related to use of pesticides in the Fraser Delta have been documented (Table 8.7).

Mining

The direct effect of mining on the habitat is more localized than that of forestry or agriculture. However, it is usually associated with a complete destruction of habitat, as in the case of open pit mining and placer mining. Mining is quite important within the Fraser Basin and efforts should be made to minimize its effect on the environment.

Placer mining destroys riparian habitats and thus has a significant affect on bird communities at least at a local level. It also increases the sediment load in the

Table 8.7: Examples of Bird Mortality Related to Agricultural Activities in the Fraser Delta Area

Date	Victim	Pesticide	Crop
December 16th, 1973	60 Ducks	Carbofuran	Turnip
November 25th, 1974	60 Ducks	Carbofuran	Potatoes
November 1975	110 Ducks	Carbofuran	?
January 1975	20 Ducks	Carbofuran	?
December 3rd, 1979	70 Mallards and Pintails	Dasamit (fensulfathion)	Cabbage and Cauliflower
July 26th, 1982	12 Canada Geese	Dasamit (fensulfathion)	Cauliflower
September 17th, 1986	500-1000 Savannah and Lincoln Sparrows	Carbofuran	Turnips and Radishes
July 1987	Several Rock Doves and Passerines	Dasamit (fensulfathion)	Radishes

Source: Can. Wild. Serv. unpublished data.

water, reducing productivity and impairing feeding of aquatic birds such as diving ducks, Belted Kingfishers and American Dipper. The stripping of bogs for peat in the lower Fraser Basin has affected several species of birds. The Sandhill Crane which once nested in the Fraser delta in significant numbers is now very rare (Butler and Campbell, 1987) and may no longer breed in the area.

Urbanization

Urbanization has significant effects on bird populations as it usually destroys the natural landscape, fragmenting it into isolated parcels. Its effect is especially great on riparian habitats. Dyking in the lower Fraser Basin has destroyed large amounts of riparian vegetation communities and their associated avifauna. Most bottomland forests and forested wetlands of the Fraser delta have been destroyed by urbanization (Pojar, 1980).

Besides direct destruction of habitat, urbanization affects the environment by increasing air pollution levels, contaminating waterways and increasing levels of disturbance in remaining habitats. For example, the colony of Western Grebes on Williams Lake that had been active for at least 30 years was likely abandoned due to an increased level of human disturbance on the lake (Campbell et al., 1990). The reproductive success of Great Blue Heron colonies in the Fraser delta is sometimes affected by human disturbance. Rapid urbanization of farmlands in the Fraser Delta could have a major effect on wintering populations of raptors and waterfowl, notwithstanding the removal of prime agricultural land.

Within the Fraser Basin, greater attention should be paid to minimizing urbanization impacts on the environment. Both the environment and the urbanites would benefit from increased biotic diversity within and adjacent to urbanized areas. Also, the potential for recreation and tourism development centred on bird watching is important. Wildlife abundance and diversity can be increased in urban settings with proper management (Weber, 1972; Savard, 1978; Lancaster and Rees, 1979).

Within the last few decades some birds have adapted to urban environments and are beginning to create problems. Gulls have benefitted from urbanization by using dumps as sources of food. This easy access to food increases the survival rate of young birds and contributes to an increase in the population. Gulls have also started to nest on man-made structures, creating health and safety problems (Eddy, 1980; Vermeer et al., 1989). Within the Fraser delta Canada Geese nest very successfully in urban areas and concentrate in parks and other green areas every fall to avoid hunting pressure. They have been so successful that they now have to be controlled to limit the damage they cause on the few open spaces of the city.

Industrial Pollution

The impact of industrial pollution is becoming more and more obvious and serious (Waldichuk, 1983). Acid rain and the toxic pollution of aquatic environments are common occurrences today affecting us all. The resources of the Fraser Basin are affected by these. Pulp mills in the interior pollute the Fraser River. As of November 1989, seafood related fisheries (crabs, mussels, clams, crustaceans) have been closed in several areas of the Strait of Georgia because of dioxins originating mainly from pulp mill effluent. Levels of dioxin in Great Blue Herons feeding in the Fraser estuary are high and have been increasing since 1983 (Elliott et al., 1988; 1989). Levels of furan in Great Blue Herons are highest in the herons frequenting the Fraser Estuary.

Mining and industrial effluent discharges contribute significant amounts of heavy metals into the environment. These concentrate in food chains, affecting wildlife and even people. The persistence of these contaminants in the environment and their obvious direct and indirect effects on some resources should be a great source of concern not only for the wildlife of the Fraser Basin, but also for its human population. Oil pollution is frequent in the lower portion of the Fraser Basin and directly affects birds through plumage soiling leading to death, and through habitat destruction and/or food reduction. The effect of oil pollution on birds is well known (Hooper et al., 1987; Rodway et al., 1989). A major spill within the Fraser Estuary would have a considerable impact on birds, especially in winter. Another large scale factor likely to affect the avifauna of the Fraser Basin is climate change. The effect of climate change on birds is difficult to predict but could be drastic as many birds are closely tied to their habitat and several species are specialized. Undoubtedly, climate change will be positive for some species and negative for others. With the warming of temperatures, southern vegetation will move north bringing associated fauna. The location, quality and quantity of staging and migrating areas could be affected and thus disrupt staging and migration patterns. Also, sea level rise will affect the Fraser estuary vegetation and animal communities.

Research Needs

Lack of knowledge on the distribution, behaviour and ecology of several species of birds within the Fraser River Basin impairs our ability to manage on a sustainable basis. Research needs are especially great in the context of forest exploitation, where there is an absence of information on the effects of various harvest techniques on bird populations. Efforts are also needed to develop modifications to harvest techniques to reduce their impacts on bird populations.

A greater understanding of the ecological requirements of the birds wintering and staging in the Fraser River delta is urgently needed in view of the great developmental pressures and flood control measures in the delta. Such information is crucial to the guiding of development so that it does not unnecessarily jeopardize the survival of the wintering and staging populations of the birds of the delta.

Harlequin Ducks, now endangered in eastern Canada (COSEWIC, 1990), breed along streams and are very susceptible to disturbance (Brèault and Savard, 1991). Their distribution and abundance within the Fraser River Basin is unknown. This greatly impairs our ability to protect their habitat.

Waterfowl staging and moulting areas are poorly known within the Fraser Basin and need to be located so that the most important are adequately protected.

Birds are used to monitor toxic pollution, but little is known of the effect of that pollution on the survival of affected birds. More research is needed in this sector. Also, the effects of various developments and flood control measures on bird populations are poorly understood, and a greater understanding is needed. Little is known of the structure and dynamics of riparian avian communities along the Fraser River and its tributaries. Such information is needed to ensure the maintenance and enhancement of biotic diversity throughout the Fraser Basin.

Conclusions and Recommendations

The avifauna of the Fraser Basin is very diverse, perhaps the most diversified of any river basin in Canada. It has great tourism potential which is now beginning to be exploited (e.g., Snow Goose festival in Delta). Residents of British Columbia spend more on wildlife related activities than residents of other provinces (Jacquemot et al., 1986). As most of the birds frequenting the Fraser Basin are migratory, we have a national and international responsibility to maintain viable populations. Hunting is an important economic activity which has to be managed on a sustainable basis. Birds of the Fraser Basin are hunted locally but also in other countries. We harvest birds from the Soviet Union, the United States, Central and South America. Therefore, populations have to be managed internationally.

Management plans have been prepared for waterfowl and geese (Anonymous, 1986; 1989a) and are being gradually implemented. Two recent initiatives that will benefit waterfowl of the Fraser Basin include the Arctic Goose Joint Venture (Anonymous, 1989b) and the Pacific Coast Joint Venture which are in their initial phases (Anonymous, 1990).

Because of the lack of long term data, it is difficult to compare the actual populations of birds utilizing the Fraser Basin with those of the past. Leach (1982b) provides an historic perspective of the use of the Fraser Estuary by birds and suggests a general decline in the number of waterfowl and geese using the estuary today. Butler and Campbell (1987) review changes in the population of birds of the Fraser estuary over the last few decades.

Five species of birds have already been extirpated from the Fraser delta, mostly as a consequence of development: the Yellow-billed Cuckoo *(Coccyzus americanus)*, Purple Martin *(Progne subis)*, Western Bluebird, Horned Lark and Burrowing Owl (Munro and Cowan, 1947; Weber, 1980; Butler and Campbell, 1987). The only breeding colony of Yellow-headed Blackbirds *(Xanthocephalus xanthocephalus)* in the estuary is now threatened by the expansion of the Vancouver Airport. The Sandhill Crane is close to being extirpated from the lower mainland as only a few birds occur in the area now (Robinson, 1980). Brant numbers wintering within the delta have decreased but the causes of the decline are unclear (Butler and Campbell, 1987).

Four species have increased within the estuary, the Snow Goose, Canada Goose, Trumpeter Swan and Glaucous-winged Gull; the latter as a result of reduced persecution and increased feeding opportunities provided by human refuse.

Economic developments in the Fraser Basin have significant impacts on bird populations. Several ecosystems of the Fraser Basin are threatened by development and, of course, their avifauna is threatened also (Pojar, 1980). Greater attention should be paid to the avian resource in industrial development. Current developments are often not carried out on a sustainable basis and, as a result, impact too greatly on other resources. A significant proportion of impacts could be reduced without any significant economic impact. The key is more holistic and global planning of resources and a commitment by managers to work towards no net loss of important habitats. This requires greater communication between agencies and a greater appreciation of short and long term consequences of development. Environmental reviews of development projects would permit a better appreciation by development agencies of the ramifications of their projects on the environment, and hopefully identify ways of minimizing, if not eliminating, some of the negative effects.

Because of their position at, or near, the top of the food chain, their conspicuousness and their wide distribution, birds constitute excellent indicators of the health of ecosystems. They can provide early warnings of imbalances within ecological systems. Monitoring of harvested species permits the adjustment of harvest levels on a yearly basis. Breeding bird surveys (Collins and Wendt, 1989), and Christmas bird counts provide reliable indices of the abundance and distribution of several species of non-game birds and have already indicated a continent-wide decline in several species (Collins and Wendt, 1989; Robbins et al., 1986; Erskine, 1978; Butcher et al., 1990). Birds have been and are currently used as an early indicator of toxic pollution. Because several toxic substances accumulate within the food chain, they become easier to detect in birds. Within the Fraser Basin, Great Blue Herons and several species of waterfowl are regularly monitored to track the level of several toxic substances in the environment (Elliott et al., 1988; 1989).

The avifauna of the Fraser Basin is a major component of the biotic diversity of British Columbia. The maintenance of regional biotic diversity represents a challenge that should be taken up by all resource development agencies from the forest industry to industrial and residential development. It is the moral duty and the civic, national and international responsibility of the agencies exploiting British Columbia's resources to ensure that their activities are carried out in a sustainable fashion and that they do not significantly and irreversibly affect other resources.

References

Anonymous. 1986. *North American Waterfowl Management Plan.* Ottawa, Ontario: U.S. Department of the Interior, Fish and Wildlife Service and Can. Wildl. Serv.

Anonymous. 1989a. *Cooperative Management Plan for British Columbia.* Can. Wildl. Serv., B.C. Ministry of Environment and Ducks Unlimited.

Anonymous. 1989b. *Arctic Goose Joint Venture.* Edmonton, Alberta: Can. Wildl. Serv., Western and Northern Region.

Anonymous. 1990. Pacific Coast Joint Venture. *Pacific Coast Habitat: A Prospectus.* Delta, British Columbia: Can. Widl. Serv. and Portland, Oregon: U.S. Fish and Wildlife Service.

Balda, R. P. 1975. *The Relationship of Secondary Cavity-nesters to Snag Densities in Western Coniferous Forests.* Albuquerque, N.M.: U.S. For. Serv. Wildl. Habitat Tech. Bull. 2.

B.C. Ministry of Forests. 1988. *Biogeoclimatic Zones of British Columbia.* Map-BC553. Victoria: British Columbia Ministry of Forests.

Bicak, T. K., R. L. Redmond and D. A. Jenni. 1982. "Effect of Grazing on Long-billed Curlew (Numenius americanus) Breeding Behaviour and Ecology in Southwest Idaho." in Peek, J. M. and P. D. Dalke (eds.). *Wildlife Livestock Relationships Symposium: Proceedings 10.* Moscow, Idaho, Univ. Idaho, Forest, Wildl. and Range Exp. Sta.

Blood, D. A. 1978. *Migratory Bird Use of South Arm of Fraser River, December 1976 through November 1977.* Regional Report. Delta, British Columbia: Can. Wildl. Serv.

Boyd, H., and F. G. Cooch. 1986. *Recent Changes in Sales of Migratory Game Bird Hunting Permits and Prospects for the Near Future.* Progress Notes No. 162. Ottawa: Canadian Wildlife Service.

Boyd, W. S., and J-P. L. Savard. 1987. *Abiotic and Biotic Characteristics of Wetlands at Riske Creek, British Columbia - A Data Report.* Techn. Rep. Ser. No.16. Delta, British Columbia: Canadian Wildlife Service, Pacific & Yukon Region.

Boyd, W. S., J-P. L. Savard and G. E. J. Smith. 1989. *Relationships Between Aquatic Birds and Wetland Characteristics in the Aspen Parkland, Central British Columbia.* Tech. Rep. Series No.70. Delta, British Columbia: Canadian Wildlife Service, Pacific and Yukon Region.

Brèault, A. M., K. M. Cheng and J-P. L. Savard. 1988. *Distribution and Abundance of Eared Grebes (Podiceps nigricollis) in British Columbia.* Tech. Rep. Ser. No. 51. Can. Wildl. Serv., Pacific and Yukon Region, B.C.

Brèault, A. M., and J-P. L. Savard. 1991. *Status Report on the Distribution and Ecology of Harlequin Ducks in British Columbia.* Tech. Rep. Ser. No. (In press). Can. Wildl. Serv. Pacific and Yukon Region, B.C.

Brown, R. E. 1985. *Management of Wildlife and Fish Habitats in Forests of Western Oregon and Washington.* U.S.D.A., Forest Serv. Pacific Northwest Region and U.S.D.I., Bureau of Land Management.

Brush, T. 1981. *Response of Secondary Cavity Nesting Birds to Manipulation of Nest Site Availability.* M.S. Thesis, Arizona: State Univ. Tempe.

Bunnell, F. L., and D. S. Eastman 1976. *Effects of Forest Management Practices on Wildlife in the Forests of British Columbia.* IV F.R.O. World Congress, Proceedings XVI group 6, Norway.

Burton, B. A. 1977. *Some Aspects of the Ecology of Lesser Snow Geese Wintering on the Fraser River Estuary.* MSc. Thesis, Vancouver: Univ. British Columbia.

Butcher, G. S., M. R. Fuller, L. S. McAllister and P. H. Geissler 1990. "An Evaluation of the Christmas Bird Count for Monitoring Population Trends of Selected Species." *Wildl. Soc. Bull.* 18:129-134.

Butler, R. W. 1989. "Breeding Ecology and Population Trends of the Great Blue Heron (Ardea herodias fannini) in the Strait of Georgia." in Vermeer, K., and R. W. Butler (eds.). *The Ecology and Status of Marine and Shoreline Birds in the Strait of Georgia, British Columbia,* Ottawa: Spec. Publ. Can. Wildl. Serv.

Butler, R. W., and J-P. L. Savard. 1985. *Monitoring of the Spring Migration of Waterbirds Throughout British Columbia: A Pilot Study.* Regional Report. Delta, British Columbia: Canadian Wildlife Service. Pacific and Yukon Region.

Butler, R. W., and R. W. Campbell. 1987. *The Birds of the Fraser River Delta: Populations, Ecology and International Significance.* Occasional paper No.65. Ottawa: Can. Wildl. Serv.

Butler, R. W., and R. J. Cannings. 1990 *Distribution of Birds in the Intertidal Portion of the Fraser River Delta, British Columbia.* Tech. Rep. No.93 Delta, B.C.: Can. Wildl. Serv., Pacific and Yukon Region.

Campbell, E. C., and R. W. Campbell. 1984. *Status Report on the Barn Owl (Tyto alba).* Ottawa, Ontario: Committee on the Status of Endangered Wildlife in Canada.

Campbell, E. C., and R. W. Campbell. 1986. *Status Report on the Spotted Owl in Canada (Strix occidentalis caurina).* Ottawa: Committee on the Status of Endangered Wildlife in Canada.

Campbell, R. W., E. D. Forsman and B. M. Van Der Raay. 1984. *An Annotated Bibliography of Literature on the Spotted Owl.* Land Management Report No. 24. Victoria, British Columbia: Ministry of Forests.

Campbell, R. W., N. K. Dawe, I. McTaggart-Cowan, J. M. Cooper, G. W. Kaiser and M. C. E. McNall. 1990. *The Birds of British Columbia.* Royal B.C. Museum and Canadian Wildlife Service.

Collins, B. T., and J. S. Wendt. 1989. *The Breeding Bird Survey in Canada 1966-1983. Analysis of Trends in Breeding Bird Populations.* Can. Wildl. Serv. Tech. Rep. No. 75.

Cooch, F. G., J. S. Wendt, G. E. J. Smith and G. Butler. 1978. "The Canadian Migratory Game Bird Hunting Permit and Associated Surveys." in Boyd, H., and G. H. Finney (eds.). *Migratory game bird hunting in Canada.* Can. Wildl. Serv. Rep. Ser. No. 43.

COSEWIC: Committee on the Status of Endangered Wildlife in Canada. 1990. *List of Species with Designated Status - April 1990.* Ottawa, Ontario.

Diamond, A. W. 1986. *An Evaluation of the Vulnerability of Canadian Migratory Birds to Changes in Neotropical Forest Habitats.* Regional Report. Ottawa, Ontario: Can. Wildl. Serv.

Dickson, K. 1987. *Migratory Birds Killed in Canada during the 1986 Season.* Progress Notes No. 171. Ottawa, Canada: Can. Wildl. Serv.

Dickson, K. 1989. *Migratory Game Birds Killed in Canada during the 1987 Hunting Season.* Progress Notes No. 179. Ottawa, Ontario: Can. Wildl. Serv.

Dickson, J. G., R. N. Conner and J. H. Williamson. 1983. "Snag Retention Increases Bird Use of a Clearcut." *J. Wildl. Manag.* 47:799-804.

Dunbar, D., L. Koza and F. L. Bunnell 1980. "White Pelicans in British Columbia." in *Threatened and Endangered Species and Habitats in British Columbia and the Yukon*. Victoria: B.C. Ministry of Environment.

Eddy, G. 1982. "Glaucous-winged Gulls Nesting on Buildings in Seattle, Washington." *Murrelet*. 63:27-29.

Elliott, J. E., R. W. Butler, R. J. Norstrom and P. E. Whitehead. 1989. "Environmental Contaminants and Reproductive Success of Great Blue Herons *(Ardea herodias)* in British Columbia." *Environmental Pollution*. 59:91-114.

Elliott, J. E., R. W. Butler, R. J. Norstrom and P. E. Whitehead. 1988. *Levels of Polychlorinated Dibenzodioxins and Polychlorinated Dibenzofurans in Eggs of Great Blue Herons (Ardea herodias) in British Columbia, 1983-87: Possible Impacts on Reproductive Success*. Progress Notes No. 176. Ottawa, Canada: Can. Wildl. Serv.

Erskine, A. J. 1972. *Buffleheads*. Monogr. Ser. No. 4. Ottawa, Canada: Can. Wildl. Serv.

Erskine, A. J. 1978. *The First Ten Years of the Co-operative Breeding Bird Survey in Canada*. Rep. Ser. 42., Can. Wildl. Serv.

Erskine, A. J., B. T. Collins and J. W. Chardine. 1990. *The Cooperative Breeding Bird Survey in Canada, 1988*. Progress Notes No. 188. Ottawa: Can. Wildl. Serv.

Faber, P. M., E. Keller, A. Sands and B. M. Massey. 1989. *The Ecology of Riparian Habitats of the Southern California Coastal Region. A community profile*. Biol. Rep. 85 (7.27), U.S. Fish and Wildl. Serv.

Filion, F. L., E. DuWars, A. Jacquemot, P. Bouchard, P. Boxall, P. A. Gray and R. Reid. 1989. *The Importance of Wildlife to Canadians in 1987: Highlights of a National Survey*. Ottawa, Canada: Environment Canada, Can. Wildl. Serv.

Forbes, L. S. 1984. *The Nesting Ecology of the Western Grebe in British Columbia*. Regional Report, Delta, British Columbia: Can. Wildl. Serv., Pacific and Yukon Region.

Forbes, L. S., K. Simpson, J. P. Kelsall and D. R. Flook. 1985. *Great Blue Heron Colonies in British Columbia*. Regional Report. Delta, British Columbia: Can. Wildl. Serv. Pacific and Yukon Region.

Forsman, E. D., E. C. Meslow and H. W. Wight. 1984. *Distribution and biology of the Spotted Owl in Oregon*. Wildl. Monog. No.87.

Fry, K. 1980. *Aspects of the Wintering Ecology of the Dunlin (Calidris alpina) on the Fraser River Delta*. Regional Report. Delta, British Columbia: Can. Wildl. Serv., Pacific and Yukon Region.

Gauthier, G., and J. N. M. Smith. 1987. "Territorial Behaviour, Nest-site Availability, and Breeding Density in Buffleheads." *J. Anim. Ecol.* 56:171-184.

Gebauer, M. B. 1989. *Relations Between Shrub Cover and Bird or Small Mammal Abundance or Diversity on Forest Plantation in Central British Columbia*. MSc Thesis. Vancouver: Univ. British Columbia.

Grass, J., and A. Grass. 1978. "Vancouver Natural History Society Raptor Census Results 1976-1977." *Discovery*. 7:1-5.

Graul, W. D. 1980. "Grassland Management Practices and Bird Communities." in *Management of Western Forests and Grasslands for Non-game Birds*. Gen. Tech. Rep. INT-86. Ogden, Utah: U.S. Forest Ser.

Gutierrey, R. J., and A. B. Carey. 1985. *Ecology and Management of the Spotted Owl in the Pacific Northwest*. Gen. Techn. Rep. PNW-185. Portland, Oregon: U.S.D.A., Forest Service, Pac. Northw. For. and Range Exp. Station.

Haapanen, A. 1965. "Bird Fauna of the Finnish Forests in Relation to Forest Succession." *Ann. Zool. Fennica* 2:153-196.

Hamer, T. E., S. G. Seim and K. R. Dixon. 1989. *Northern Spotted Owl and Northern Barred Owl Habitat Use and Home Range Size in Washington*. Preliminary Report Washington Department of Wildlife and Wildlife Management - Non Game.

Harris, L. D. 1984. *The Fragmented Forest: Island Biogeography Theory and the Preservation of Biotic Diversity*. Chicago and London: Univ. Chicago Press.

Hatfield, J. P. 1991. *Use of Alaksen Wildlife Area by Waterfowl, 1973-1987*. Techn. Rep. Ser. No. 113. Pacific and Yukon Region, British Columbia: Can. Wildl. Serv.

Helle, P. 1985. "Effect of Forest Regeneration on the Structure of Bird Communities in Northern Finland." *Holarctic Ecology*. 8:120-132.

Hirst, S. M., and C. A. Easthope. 1981. "Use of Agricultural Lands by Waterfowl in Southwestern British Columbia." *J. Wildl. Manage*. 45:454-462.

Hooper, T. D., K. Vermeer and I. Szabo. *Oil Pollution of Birds an Annotated Bibliography*. Tech. Rep. Series No. 34. Can. Wildl. Ser. Pacific and Yukon Region.

Hoover, R. L., and D. L. Wills. 1984. *Managing Forested Lands for Wildlife*. Colorado Division of Wildlife in cooperation with U.S.D.A. Forest Service, Rocky Mountain Region, Denver, Colorado.

Howie, R. R. 1980a. "The Spotted Owl in British Columbia." in Stace-Smith, R., L. Johns and P. Joslin. *Threatened and endangered species and habitats in British Columbia and the Yukon*. Victoria, B.C.: B.C. Ministry Environ. Fish and Wildl Branch.

Howie, R. R. 1980b. "The Burrowing Owl in British Columbia." in Stace-Smith, R., L. Johns and P. Joslin. *Threatened and endangered species and habitats in British Columbia and the Yukon*. Victoria, B.C.: B.C. Ministry Environ. Fish and Wildl Branch.

Howie, R. R. 1988. *Status report on the Flammulated Owl (Otus flammeolus)*. Committee on the Status of Endangered Wildlife in Canada, Ottawa, Ontario.

Jacquemot, A., R. Reid and R. L. Filion. 1986. *The Importance of Wildlife to Canadians. The Recreational Economic Significance of Wildlife*. Ottawa, Canada: Environment Canada, Can. Wildl. Serv.

Janzen, D. H. 1983. "No Park is an Island: Increase in Interference from Outside as Park Size Decreases." *Oikos* 41:402-410.

Jeffrey, R., G. W. Kaiser. 1979. "The Snow Goose Flock of the Fraser and Skagit Deltas." in Jarvis, R. L., and J. C. Bartonek (eds.). *Management and Biology of Pacific Flyway Geese*. Symp. Northwest Sect. Wildl. Soc. Corvallis, Oregon: Oregon State Univ. Book Stores.

Kantrud, H. A. 1981. "Grazing Intensity Effects on the Breeding Avifauna of North Dakota Grasslands." *Can. Field Nat.* 95:404-417.

Kessler, W. B. 1979. *Bird Population Responses to Clearcutting in the Tongass National Forest, Southeast Alaska*. Report 71. Ketchikan, Alaska 99901: U.S. Dept. Agriculture, Forest Service, Tongass National Forest.

Krebs, J. R. 1974. "Colonial Nesting and Social Feeding as Strategies for Exploiting Food Resources in the Great Blue Heron." *Behav.* 51:99-134.

Lancaster, R. K., and W. E. Rees. 1979. "Bird Communities and the Structure of Urban Habitats." *Can. J. Zool.* 57:2358-2368.

Leach, B. 1982a. "Waterfowl Habitats of the Lower Fraser Valley Wetlands." in Day, J. C., and R. Stace-Smith (eds.). *British Columbia Land for Wildlife Past, Present and Future*. Victoria, B.C.: B.C. Ministry of Environment, Fish and Wildlife Branch.

Leach, B. 1982b. *Waterfowl on a Pacific Estuary*. British Columbia Provincial Museum. Spec. Publ. No. 5.

McCambridge, W. F., and F. B. Knight. 1972. "Factors Affecting Spruce Beetles During a Small Outbreak." *Ecology.* 53:830-839.

McClelland, B. R., and S. S. Frissell. 1975. "Identifying Forest Snags Useful for Hole Nesting Birds." *J. For.* 73:414-417.

McEwan, E. W., and A. Farr. 1986. *Foraging Tactics of Dunlin (Calidris alpina)*. Regional Report. Delta, B.C. : Can. Wildl. Serv.

McKelvey, R. W., and W. Munro. 1983. *Cooperative Waterfowl Management Plan for British Columbia*. Regional Report, Delta, B.C.: Can. Wildl. Serv. Pacific and Yukon Region, and Victoria, B.C.: B.C. Fish and Wildl. Branch.

McKelvey, R. W., D. W. Smith, G. E. J. Smith and R. A. Keller. 1985. *The Interaction of Birds and Air Traffic at Boundary Bay Airport*. Unpubl. Rep. Delta, B.C.: Can. Wildl. Serv.

McKelvey, R. 1986. *The Status of Trumpeter Swans in British Columbia and Yukon, Summer 1985*. Tech. Rep. Ser. No.8. Delta, B.C.: Canadian Wildlife Service, Pacific & Yukon Region.

McKelvey, R. W. 1989. *The Status of Trumpeter Swans in Southwestern British Columbia in 1989*. Proc. of the 12th Trumpeter Swan Society Conference (In press).

McKelvey, R. W., R. G. Davies and K. Morrison. 1989. *The Status of Trumpeter Swans Wintering on Vancouver Island, British Columbia in 1989*. Unpubl. Report. Delta, British Columbia: Can. Wildl. Serv., Pacific and Yukon Region.

McKelvey, R. W., and M. D. Noble. 1980. *Swans Wintering in the Cariboo-Chilcotin Areas of British Columbia*. Unpubl. Report Can. Wildl. Serv. Pacific and Yukon Region, Delta, B.C.

McKelvey, R. W., and G. E. J. Smith. 1990. *The Distribution of Waterfowl Banded or Returned in British Columbia, 1951-1985*. Tech. Rep. Ser. No. 79. Delta, B.C.: Can. Wildl. Serv., Pacific and Yukon Region.

McKenzie, E. 1983. *Preliminary Assessment of Wetland Alienation in the Cariboo-Chilcotin Area, B.C.* Regional Report. Delta, B.C.: Can. Wildl. Serv., Pacific and Yukon Region.

McKenzie, E. 1985. *Preliminary Assessment of Wetland Alienation in the South Thompson-Okanagan and Peace River-Fort St. John Areas of B.C.* Regional Report. Delta, B.C.: Can. Wildl. Serv., Pacific and Yukon Region.

Mannan, R. W. 1982. *Bird Populations and Vegetation Characteristics in Managed and Old-growth Forests, Northeastern Oregon.* Ph.D. Thesis, Oregon State Univ.

Mannan, R. W., E. C. Meslow and H. M. Wight. 1980. "Use of Snags by Birds in Douglas-fir Forests, Western Oregon." *J. Wildl. Manage.* 44:787-797.

Manuwal, D. A., and M. H. Huff. 1987. "Spring and Winter Bird Populations in a Douglas-fir Forest Sere." *J. Wildl. Manage.* 51:586-595.

Marcot, B. G. 1983. "Snag Use by Birds in Douglas-fir Clearcuts." in Davis, J. W., G. A. Goodwin and R. A. Ockenfels (eds.). *Snag Habitat Management.* June 7-9, 1983. Northern Arizona Univ.

Massey, C. L., and N. D. Wygant. 1973. "Woodpeckers: Most Important Predators of the Spruce Beetle." *Colo. Field Ornithol.* 16:4-8.

Maurer, A. L. 1989. *Boundary Bay Wildlife Viewing Development Plan.* Victoria: B.C. Ministry of Environment, Wildl. Branch.

Miller, E., and Miller, D.R. 1980. "Snag Use by Birds." in DeGraaf, R. M. (ed.). *Proceedings of the Workshop on Management of Western Forests and Grasslands for Nongame Birds.* UT. Gen. Tech. Rep. INT-86, Ogden U.S.D.A. Forest Serv., Intermountain Forest and Range Experiment Station.

Mol, A. L. 1991. *Watching Wildlife in Southwestern British Columbia* (in press).

Munro, J. A. 1941. "Studies of Waterfowl in British Columbia: Greater Scaup Duck, Lesser Scaup Duck." *Can. J. Res.* 19:113-138.

Munro, J. A. 1942. "Studies of Waterfowl in British Columbia: Bufflehead." *Can J. Res.* 200:133-160.

Munro, J. A. 1949. "Studies of Waterfowl in British Columbia: Baldpate." *Can. J. Res.* 27:289-307.

Munro, J. A., and I. McT. Cowan 1947. *A Review of the Bird Fauna of British Columbia.* Spec. Publ. No. 2, Victoria: B.C. Prov. Mus.

Nilsson, S. G. 1979. "Effect of Forest Management on the Breeding Bird Community in Southern Sweden." *Biol. Conserv.* 16:135-143.

Oakley, A. L., J. A. Collins, L. B. Everson, D. A. Heller, J. C. Howerton and R. E. Vincent. 1985. "Riparian Zones and Freshwater Wetlands." in Brown, E. R. (ed.). *Management of Wildlife and Fish Habitats in Forests of Western Oregon and Washington.*

Otvos, I. S. 1965. "Studies on Avian Predators of Dendroctomus brevicomis Le Conte *(Coleoptera: Scolytidae)* with Special Reference to Picidae." *Con. Entomol.* 97:1184-1199.

Peakall, D. B. 1972. "Polychlorinated Biphenyls: Occurrence and Biological Effects." *Res. Reviews.* 44:1-21.

Peterson, B., and G. Gauthier. 1985. "Nest Site Use by Cavity Nesting Birds of the Caribou Parkland, British Columbia." *Wilson Bull.* 97:319-331.

Pojar, J. 1980. "Threatened Forest Ecosystems of British Columbia." in R. Stace-Smith, L. Johns and P. Joslin. *Threatened and Endangered Species and Habitats in British Columbia and the Yukon.* Victoria, B.C.: B.C. Ministry Environ. Fish and Wildl Branch.

Raphael, M. G., and M. White. 1984. "Use of Snags by Cavity Nesting Birds in the Sierra Nevada." *Wildl. Monogr.* 86.

Rees, W. E. 1989. *Planning for Sustainable Development: A Resource Book.* Vancouver: University of British Columbia Centre for Human Settlements.

Robbins, C. S. 1979. "Effect of Forest Fragmentation on Bird Populations." in DeGraaf, R. M. and K.E. Evans, *Management of North Central and Northeastern Forests of Nongame Birds.* U.S.D.A. Forest Service General Technical Report NC-51.

Robbins, C. S., D. Bystrak and P. H. Geissler. 1986. *The Breeding Bird Survey: Its First Fifteen Years, 1965-1979.* U.S. Dept. Inter. Fish & Wildl. Ser. Resour. Publ. 157.

Robinson, W. 1980. "The Greater Sandhill Crane." in Stace-Smith, R., L. Johns and P. Joslin. *Threatened and Endangered Species and Habitats in British Columbia and the Yukon.* Victoria, B.C.: B.C. Ministry Environ. Fish and Wildl. Branch.

Rodway, M. S., M. J. F. Lemon, J-P. L. Savard and R. McKelvey. 1989. *Nestucca Oil Spill: Impact Assessment on Avian Populations and Habitat.* Tech. Rep. Ser. No. 68. Can. Wildl. Serv. Pacific and Yukon Region.

Ryder, R. A. 1980. "Effects of Grazing on Bird Habitats." in *Management of Western Forests and Grasslands for Non-game Birds.* Gen. Tech. Rep. INT-86, Ogden, Utah: U.S. Forest Serv.

Savard, J-P. L. 1978. *Birds in Metropolitan Toronto: Distribution, Relationships with Habitat Features, and Nesting Sites.* M.Sc. thesis. Toronto, Ontario: Univ. of Toronto.

Savard, J-P. L. 1980. *Some Observations on Spring Migration of Waterfowl in Central British Columbia.* Regional Report, Delta, British Columbia: Can. Wildl. Serv., Pacific and Yukon Region.

Savard, J-P. L. 1984. "Territorial Behaviour of Common Goldeneye, Barrow's Goldeneye and Bufflehead in Areas of Sympatry." *Ornis Scand.* 15:211-216.

Savard, J-P. L. 1985. *Fall and Winter Inventories of Ducks on the Fraser River Delta and Boundary Bay, 1977-1978.* Regional Report, Delta, B.C.: Can. Wildl. Serv., Pacific and Yukon Region.

Savard, J-P. L. 1987. *Status Report on Barrow's Goldeneye.* Techn. Rep. Ser. No. 23. Canadian Wildlife Service, Pacific and Yukon Region, Delta, British Columbia.

Savard, J-P. L. 1988a. "Use of Nest Boxes by Barrow's Goldeneyes: Nesting Success and Effect on the Breeding Population." *Wildl. Soc. Bull.* 16:125-132.

Savard, J-P. L. 1988b. *A Summary of Current Knowledge on the Distribution and Abundance of Moulting Seaducks in the Coastal Waters of British Columbia.* Tech. Rep. Ser. No. 45. Can. Wildl. Serv. Pacific and Yukon Region, B.C.

Savard, J-P. L. 1990. *Waterfowl in the Aspen Parkland of Central British Columbia.* Techn. Rep. Ser. No. (in press). Delta, B.C.: Can. Wildl. Serv., Pacific and Yukon Region.

Scott, V. W., and J. L. Oldemeyer. 1983. "Cavity Nesting Bird Requirements and Responses to Snag Cutting in Ponderosa Pine." in Davis, J. W., G. A. Goodwin and K. R. A. Ockenfels (eds.). *Snag Habitat Management.* June 7-9, 1983, Northern Arizona Univ.

Seip, D. R., and J-P. L. Savard. 1990. *Maintaining Wildlife Diversity in Managed Coastal Forests.* Unpubl. Report. Can. Wildl. Serv. and B.C. Forest Service.

Taylor, E. W. 1970. *A Review of the Wildlife and Recreation Potential of Boundary Bay, British Columbia.* Regional Report, Can. Wildl. Serv. Pacific and Yukon Region, British Columbia.

Terborgh, J. 1989. *Where Have All the Birds Gone?* Princeton Univ. Press.

Thomas, J. W. 1979. *Wildlife Habitats in Managed Forests: The Blue Mountains of Oregon and Washington.* Agri. Hanb. 553. Washington, D.C. U.S.D.A., Forest Serv.

Thomas, J. W., C. Maser and J. E. Rodick. 1979. "Riparian Zones." in Thomas, J. W. (ed.). *Wildlife Habitats in Managed Forests the Blue Mountains of Oregon and Washington.* U.S.D.A., Forest Service, Agriculture Handbook No.553.

Topping, M. S., and G. G. E. Scudder. 1977. Some Physical and Chemical Features of Saline Lakes in Central British Columbia. *Syesis.* 10:145-166.

Vermeer, K., and C. D. Levings. 1977. "Populations, Biomass and Food Habits of Ducks on the Fraser Delta Intertidal Area, British Columbia." *Wildfowl.* 28:49-60.

Vermeer, K., D. Power and G. E. J. Smith. 1989. "Habitat Selection and Nesting Biology of Roof-nesting Glaucous-winged Gulls." *Colonial Waterbirds.* 11(2):189-201.

Waldichuk, M. 1983. "Pollution in the Strait of Georgia: A Review." *Can. J. Fish and Aquat. Sci.* 40:1142-1167.

Weber, W. C. 1972. *Birds in Cities: A Study of Populations, Foraging Ecology, and Nest-sites of Urban Birds.* M.Sc. thesis. Vancouver: Univ. of British Columbia.

Weber, W. C. 1980. "A Proposed List of Rare and Endangered Bird Species for British Columbia." in Stace-Smith, R., L. Johns and P. Joslin. *Threatened and Endangered Species and Habitats in British Columbia and the Yukon.* Victoria, B.C.: B.C. Ministry Environ. Fish and Wildl Branch.

Wedgwood, J. A. 1978. *The Status of the Burrowing Owl in Canada.* Ottawa: Committee on the Status of Endangered Wildlife in Canada.

Whitcomb, R. F., C. S. Robbins, J. F. Lynch, B. L. Whitcomb, M. K. Klimbiewiez and D. Bystrak. 1981. "Effects of Forest Fragmentation on Avifauna of the Eastern Deciduous Forest. in *Forest Island Dynamics in Man-dominated Landscapes* (ed.). by R. L. Burgess and D.M. Sharpe. 125-206. New York, Spring.

World Wildlife Fund. 1988. *Endangered Species in Canada 1988.* Can. Nat. Sportsmen's Shows and World Wildlife Fund.

Yamanaka, K. 1975. *Primary Productivity of the Fraser River Delta Foreshore: Yield Estimates of Emergent Vegetation.* M.Sc. Thesis. Vancouver: Univ. British Columbia.

Zarnowitz, J. E., and D. A. Manuwal. 1985. "The Effects of Forest Management on Cavity-nesting Birds in Northwestern Washington." *J. Wildl. Manage.* 49:255-263.

9

Sustainable Forestry in the Fraser River Basin

J. P. (Hamish) Kimmins and Dorli M. Duffy

Located on the west coast of the continent, British Columbia enjoys a prevailing westerly flow of moist Pacific air, which, in combination with a series of mountain ranges that parallel the coast, ensures that much of the province receives abundant precipitation. This combination of landform and location results in a disproportionate amount of the total national precipitation falling in B.C. The abundant precipitation ensures that 46% of the B.C. landscape is covered with forest and much of the major river flow originates from precipitation falling on forested lands. There is thus an intimate connection between the quality, quantity, and timing (the regimen) of streamflow and the manner in which the forests of B.C. are managed or impacted by natural disturbance.

Much of the Fraser Basin is forested, and forestry-related activities (mostly timber production and harvesting) provide a very substantial contribution to the total employment and gross domestic product of this part of the province. Most of the communities within the Basin are dependent wholly or in large part on the forest industry, which is largely timber-management-based. As a result of this dependence, employment, job security, and the economic and social fabric of these communities are largely a function of the well-being and health of the forest-related activities in this region.

Clearly, forestry is a very important land use and economic activity in the Fraser Basin, and the quality and sustainability[1] of forest management has important implications for water, fish, wildlife, range, tourism, recreation, future supplies of timber and community stability in the area. Failure to practise sustainable silviculture, or environmental changes that result in significant alterations in forest cover, would have significant implications for the sustainable development of the Basin. Forestry thus plays a pivotal role in determining the future development in the Fraser Basin in general, and of its water resources in particular.

---

1   The definition of sustainability as used in this paper is provided in a later section.

There are several reasons to think that forestry in B.C. will change significantly over the next fifty years. Public attitudes towards the environment are undergoing rapid change, and there is a growing demand for an increase in reserves of wilderness, "old growth", and parks. Public concern over the aesthetics of forestry, and public perceptions about impacts of timber harvesting on the integrity of both local ecosystems and entire landscapes, may lead to significant changes in both silviculture and timber harvesting systems in some areas. Public concern may prevent the use of some traditional timber management practices altogether, irrespective of the technical or environmental merits thereof. These concerns have entered the political process and will probably result in policy changes that will alter how the forested landscapes of the Basin are managed. Sometimes these changes will be positive, but because some of the changes may not be adequately based on scientific evidence, this will not always be so. The nature and extent of these policy changes will influence the contribution of the forestry sector to the economic activity of the Basin.

In this chapter, we examine the biophysical variability of the Fraser Basin landscape and how this variability is represented in the biogeoclimatic classification of the Basin. We then discuss the concept of sustainability in forestry from a biophysical perspective and the need to examine this topic at different temporal and spatial scales. This is followed by a presentation of the concept of "ecological rotation" and a discussion of the extent to which current and probable future rotations are equal to, or shorter than, ecological rotations. The next section examines the need to develop and use ecologically-sound yield prediction and planning tools that are sensitive to the question of sustainability. We make the point that many of the forest planning tools currently in use are insensitive to questions of climate change and soil degradation. Only when these and other related issues are considered in management planning can we reach meaningful conclusions about the long-term biophysical sustainability of the forestry sector.

The final section addresses possible future changes in the management of forests in the Fraser Basin. Inter-relationships between forest and water resources are both intimate and extremely complex. Our premise, therefore, is that biophysical sustainability in the forestry sector is a prerequisite for sustainability of aquatic resources in the Fraser Basin. However, to achieve sustainability in the forestry sector as a whole, social and institutional goals must be met, in addition to sustaining the productivity of our forests. Although the major emphasis in this paper is on biophysical considerations, there is a brief discussion of some social and institutional considerations that are important to the sustainability of the forestry sector.

The Biophysical Variability of the Fraser Basin

An accurate evaluation of the forestry sector in an area as geographically-extensive and ecologically-diverse as the Fraser Basin must be stratified on the basis of the major biological, geological and climatic (i.e., biogeoclimatic) units of the area. Very few useful broad generalizations can be made outside of such a stratification, and all statements and analyses of the biophysical sustainability of forestry must be related to relatively homogeneous biogeoclimatic units of the landscape. This section of the chapter will describe the variability of the Basin in terms of B.C.'s biogeoclimatic system of land classification. The system was pioneered by Professor Vladimir J. Krajina (Emeritus Professor of Botany, U.B.C.) and his students (Krajina, 1969), and elaborated by the Research Branch, B.C. Ministry of Forests (Klinka et al., 1990).

British Columbia's location on the west coast of North America between latitudes 49°N (Vancouver Island extends to just south of 48° 30'N) and 60°N results in prevailing winds which move moist Pacific air inland from the west and southwest. As it crosses the province, this humid air mass encounters a series of mountain ranges extending roughly NW-SE. These ranges cause the air to rise and cool, leading to precipitation on the windward slopes, followed by a warming and drying as the air sinks and warms on the lee slopes. The result is a west-east sequence of repeated wet and dry belts from the coast to the Alberta border. This sequence is particularly well developed in the southern third of the province, where there is a series of tall mountain ranges. Further north, the lower temperatures, shorter growing season, and somewhat less dramatic inland topography result in the climatic patterns being more closely tied to elevation than to the longitudinal sequence of major topographic features.

The combination of air mass movement, topography, distance from the coast and latitude result in a diverse mosaic of climates in the province. Of the five major types of climate to be found in the world, only Tropical climates are not represented in the province, and it could be argued that the similarity of the climate on the southern tip of Vancouver Island to a Mediterranean-type gives us a minor representation of sub-tropical.

Because climate is such an important determinant of vegetation, the mosaic of climates is accurately reflected in the overall characteristics of a broad mosaic of vegetation. The climate-specific components of this mosaic are referred to as biogeoclimatic zones and subzones. The effect of climate is modified by local variations in soil moisture and nutrient regimes caused by local topography. Aspect can also contribute to the mosaic by altering moisture and temperature regimes. This is especially true in temperature-limited (both low elevation hot zones and high elevation cold zones) and moisture-limited biogeoclimatic zones (Table 9.1).

Within a biogeoclimatic zone (a broad climatic unit defined by the dominant species in mature ["climax"] stands on average or "zonal" sites), one can identify variations in climate that are not great enough to cause a change in the dominant climax species, but are sufficient to cause a change in the accompanying tree and minor plant species, and subtle changes in soils. For example, in the Interior Douglas fir zone there is a dry subzone characterized by ponderosa pine (*Pinus ponderosa* Dougl.) as a so-called pioneer tree species, whereas in the wet subzone the pioneer role is played by lodgepole pine (*Pinus contorta* Dougl.). In both

Table 9.1: Some Climatic Features of the Biogeoclimatic Zones Represented in the Fraser Basin

Zone	Selected Climate Characteristics				
	Monthly temp. range	days >5C	days <0C	May - Sept. ppt (mm)	Oct. - April ppt (mm)
Alpine Tundra	-11.1 - 9.5	427	1763	287	469
Engleman Spruce-Subalpine Fir	-10.9 - 13.3	629 - 801	879 - 1189	205 - 425	271 - 1597
Montane Spruce	-12.5 - 17.4	891 - 1310	847 - 890	158 - 252	223 - 469
Sub-boreal Spruce	-14.6 - 16.9	884 - 1510	792 - 1369	189 - 353	250 - 1383
Sub-boreal Pine-Spruce	-13.8 - 14.3	697 - 1044	1140 - 1405	243 - 300	218 - 222
Interior Cedar-Hemlock	-10.7 - 20.8	1267 - 2140	238 - 820	200 - 439	294 - 1098
Interior Douglas-Fir	-13.1 - 21.3	903 - 2366	235 - 1260	107 - 291	149 - 1022
Ponderosa Pine	-8.6 - 21.6	1505 - 2442	258 - 861	86 - 270	170 - 334
Bunchgrass	-10.8 - 22.4	1771 - 2516	230 - 878	98 - 175	108 - 208
Mountain Hemlock	-2.3 - 13.2	919 - 933	307 - 352	694 - 707	1857 - 2260
Coastal Western Hemlock	-6.6 - 18.7	1059 - 2205	5 - 493	159 - 1162	695 - 3225

subzones, Douglas-fir (*Pseudotsuga menziesii* (Mirb.) Franco) is the characteristic climax dominant. The dry subzone typically has "eutric brunisol" soils (a higher pH, more nutrient rich type of brunisol), while the wet subzone is characterized by "dystric brunisols" (a lower pH, less nutrient rich type of brunisol). The dry subzone is characterized by a shrub-rich understory, whereas the wet subzone tends to have more herbs, especially pine grass (*Calamogrostis rubescens* Buckl.). On the coast, the wet subzone of the Coastal Western Hemlock zone has Pacific silver fir (*Abies amabilis* (Dougl. Forbes) and deer fern (*Blechnum spicant* (L.) Roth) as characteristic secondary species, and "ferro-humic" podzol soils, while these are replaced by Douglas-fir, swordfern (*Polystichum munitum* (Kaulf.) Presl.), and "humo-ferric" podzols, respectively, in the dry subzone. In both subzones, western hemlock (*Tsuga heterophylla* (Raf.) Sarg.) is the characteristic climax dominant.

Within a biogeoclimatic subzone, there are local topographic sequences which create gradients of soil moisture and soil nutrients: landscape sequences from moist and fertile valley bottom and lower slope sites, through mid-slopes to dry and often nutrient-poor ridge top sites. These sequences occur where the difference in elevation between valley bottom and ridge top is not sufficient to cause a significant change in climate. The forest ecosystems found along these gradients tend to exhibit a series of fairly discrete, mutually-exclusive plant communities that vary in structure, species composition, and productivity (Figure 9.1). These discrete communities are typically associated with characteristic conditions of the forest floor (the surface organic accumulation, also called the "humus type") and mineral soil. The combined biotic community/soil units are referred to as ecosystem-types (or site-types). All ecosystem-types that have the potential to develop a similar climax plant community are grouped together, irrespective of soil type, into "ecosystem-associations" (or "site-associations").

Each ecosystem-association, or sometimes each ecosystem-type, will have a unique response to a given forest management treatment, a unique pattern of recovery from natural or management-induced disturbance, and a unique productivity potential. It is accepted in forestry in B.C., and it is written into the Forest Act, that all stand-level silvicultural and management decisions, prescriptions, and actions must be at least biogeoclimatic-subzone and ecosystem-association specific. This ecological basis for the management of forest resources has only been introduced in the past ten years and is still being implemented for the first time in many areas. However, it is expected that the legal requirement that forestry must be practised on the basis of such a biogeoclimatic stratification will contribute to a steady improvement in the quality and success of the silvicultural aspects of forest management over the coming decades.

Sustainable Forestry in the Fraser Basin

Before discussing the sustainability of the forestry sector in B.C. in general, and in the Fraser Basin in particular, we offer the following definition of sustainable development of forests. Our definition is complex, reflecting several aspects of biophysical sustainability in forestry.

We believe that the sustainable development of forests is a set of silvicultural and other management actions that result in the maintenance or enhancement of the existing biotic diversity[2], and a sustained or enhanced regional supply of a variety of material products and other values from the forest, notably, industrial wood biomass; employment in the forest sector; fish and wildlife habitat and populations; a "natural" regimen (seasonal flow patterns) of clean, cool water; a visually attractive landscape; a variety of recreational opportunities; and, where appropriate, range and other miscellaneous values (e.g., honey and other minor forest products).

---

2   Note that there is a wide diversity of meanings of the phrase "biotic diversity". There is genetic, species, life form, and community structure diversity. There is local (alpha) and landscape (beta) diversity, regional and continental (ecoclinal or geographic) diversity, and functional diversity. Finally, there is temporal diversity; several of the above types of diversity vary over time.

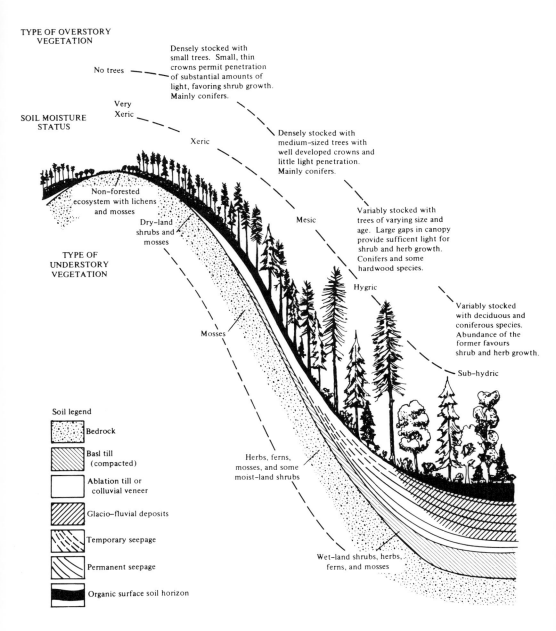

Figure 9.1: The Effect of Local Topography on Gradients of Soil Moisture and Nutrients, and the Resulting Variation in Structure, Composition and Productivity of Forest Vegetation. (The details of this local site variation vary from zone to zone. The figure shows the general pattern that is found in many forested zones.)

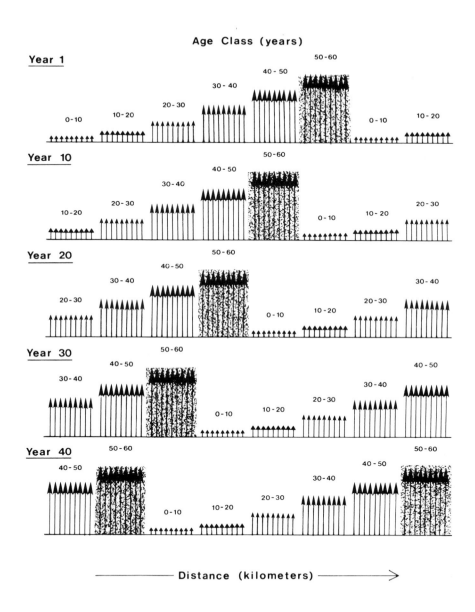

Figure 9.2: Diagrammatic Representation of the Age Class Structure of a Managed Forest.

This definition refers to sustainability at a regional level rather than at the individual stand level. This is necessary because most forests in the Fraser Basin are and probably will continue to be managed using and even-aged silvicultural system.[3] Resource values provided at any one point on the landscape will vary considerably over the tree crop cycle if even-aged management is practised, even if the overall long-term average condition of that point in the landscape is sustained. Sustainable, even-aged forest management will result in a mosaic of stands at different stages of the cycle which will, in aggregate, provide a sustained regional supply of forest products and values (Figure 9.2). This diagram shows how there is a continuous supply of areas for harvesting (the shaded stand age) across the area occupied by a single complete set of stand age classes, but that the geographical location of that timber harvesting will vary with time. Similarly, other values that are associated with particular stand ages will be supplied continuouly from the region occupied by this set of forest age classes, but the geographical location of those values will change over time. The sustainability of forest resources must be considered at the global level and the stand level as well as the regional level. The following discussion examines biophysical sustainability at all three levels: global, regional, and local.

Sustainability at the Global Level

The soils and vegetation of a region reflect a variety of regional environmental conditions and factors. If there are substantial changes in any of these, one or more of the components or characteristics of the ecosystem may be expected to change. There is a significant risk that climate, of all these factors, may be changing because of global events.

At the global level, we are facing a serious threat of climatic change (Bolin et al., 1986; Shands and Hoffman, 1987; Harrington, 1987; Schneider, 1989). Climates are always changing, of course, daily, seasonally, from year to year, and from decade to decade. On a much longer time scale (from tens of thousands to hundreds of thousands of years), ice ages have come and gone, and on even longer time scales (hundreds of millions of years), continents have changed their latitudes. Normally we do not consider climatic change on such time scales when we talk about sustainability. However, most atmospheric scientists now agree that the unprecedented rates of change over the past century in atmospheric concentrations of so-called greenhouse gases will result in higher average global temperatures by the middle or latter part of the next century than at any time in the last million years. The increase in greenhouse gases is the result of a complex mixture of land use changes, technology changes, and a rapid acceleration in the quantity of fossil fuels being used around the world.

There is evidence that on a geological time scale we are at or near the end of the current warm "interglacial" period. For the past million or so years, such warm periods of about 12,000 years duration have interrupted the periodic

---

3   In the hotter, drier biogeoclimatic zones or sites in the Fraser Basin, non-clearcutting timber harvesting systems should be, and are, used. Such zones and sites are relatively small portions of the Basin. These harvesting systems may result in even-aged or uneven-aged stands.

advance of continental ice sheets, the whole cycle occurring over about 120,000 years. The present interglacial has prevailed for about the past 10,000 to 13,000 years. Interglacials are followed by a long period of slow cooling that leads, over tens of thousands of years, into a new "ice-age". Uninterrupted by human activity, it is predicted that 5,000 years from now the climate would have cooled significantly, with the maximum development of "ice-age" conditions being achieved sometime between 23,000 and 60,000 years from now (the glacial period is not uniformly cold, there being warmer periods, but not warm enough or long enough to be called an interglacial).

Such natural long-term climatic fluctuations have been accompanied by slow latitudinal and elevational migrations of the world's major vegetation types. These migrations are reflected in the pollen record of lake sediments, which suggests that species migrations northwards and up mountains are still occurring in some areas in the wake of the last glacial period, or at least following the "little ice age" of the 1400-1800 A.D. period. However, the industrial revolution, the population explosion, and now the transportation revolution have caused the addition of so much "greenhouse" gas to the atmosphere since 1800 that the average global temperature is expected to warm up over the next 50-100 years by almost as many degrees as normally separates the peak of an interglacial from the peak of an ice age. A temperature change of this magnitude in the past has required a period of 10,000-20,000 years. The consequences of a climatic change of this magnitude and rate for the precipitation, snowfall, snowpack accumulation, streamflow, vegetation, and soils of the Fraser Basin are unknown and can only be guessed at.

Statisticians still insist that, given the past variability of climate, we cannot yet say with statistical confidence that the global climate has started to undergo change attributable to greenhouse gases. However, we can be fairly certain of one thing. Although it is true that there is still great uncertainty about the effects of climate warming on clouds and ocean currents, and the degree to which such effects could act as a negative feedback mechanism that would reduce climate warming, the action of the basic physical mechanisms by which an increasing proportion of incoming solar energy will be trapped within the atmosphere is being intensified. In the face of this evidence, it would be foolish to consider the sustainability of the forests of the Fraser Basin without considering the possible consequences of plausible climate change scenarios. These include either a warmer and drier climate, or a warmer and wetter climate.

If the climate of the Fraser Basin were to get warmer and drier, much of the current area of forest at lower elevations would give way to savanna and open grassland. Snowpacks in the mountains would decline, glaciers would retreat, the lowest elevation of significant snowpack would rise, and climatic belts would move north. Through management, crop tree species could be moved latitudinally and elevationally to follow the climate, but it is not known how soils, non-crop vegetation, animals, and microbes would change, and whether the non-crop organisms could migrate fast enough to prevent a major disruption of ecosystem processes.

If, on the other hand, the climate became warmer and wetter, snowpacks would increase at the highest elevations and some glaciers would advance, but the lowest elevation of snowpack would be raised. Some present-day grasslands might be invaded by forest. Many species would have to change their geographical range.

Because of the inability of the current global circulation models to predict the details of future local and regional climate change, we cannot yet say how climate change will impact the Fraser Basin. We cannot choose which of the above two scenarios, or some other scenario, will develop. However, there seems to be widespread agreement that significant climate change of some sort will occur, and that this will produce sufficient ecosystem change to affect terrestrial resources and their management. Recent warm spells in the middle of winter have resulted in extensive budkill in many tree species at all elevations in the Fraser Basin. Few of these bud-damaged trees will experience any measurable loss of growth, but many have already developed double or multiple stems which may greatly reduce their value for lumber when they are old enough for harvest. The occurrence of such "atypical" winter weather is one of the predictions of the climate change theory, and some believe that this widespread forest damage is a prelude to what will happen if major climate change occurs.

The water resources of the Fraser Basin would be substantially effected by climate change if spatial and temporal patterns of precipitation and snow pack accumulation and melt are altered. The overall impact of climate change on the hydrology of the Fraser Basin would be virtually independent of activities in the forest sector.

Sustainability at the Regional Level

In the absence of climate change, the flow of logs to mills and the level and geographic distribution of employment over the next century would be primarily a function of the age class structure, size class structure, and tree species composition of the existing forest. This is so because these variables determine the area and species composition of forest that is available for timber harvesting each year. The geographical distribution of these forest attributes in a region is also important. However, while primarily a function of the age class structure and location of timber resources, the continued flow of products through mills and sustained employment in local communities is also dependent on how the forests are managed.

A timber-production forest managed under an even-aged silvicultural system would in theory have approximately equal areas of all the different age classes of forest of the desired species of trees on each of the different ecosystem types in the forest (Figure 9.2). These stands would be distributed spatially in a way that ensures continuing even supplies of forest products to particular mills without excessive haulage distances, and sustained employment in local communities without excessive travel distances to work. The distribution would also ensure a sustained supply of other forest values (e.g., wildlife, water).

Imagine a large area of mature (ready for harvest) or old-growth (ecologically mature) forest that has never been managed or harvested. If this area is dedicated to timber production but is harvested at a rate that is faster than the rate of reforestation and regrowth on the harvested areas, there will come a time when most mature, harvestable forest has been logged, but the trees in the second-growth forest are not yet large enough for harvest. This results in a decrease in the supply of harvestable forest until the young forest reaches an average tree size at which it is harvestable. Natural large-scale disturbances like large fires, insect outbreaks, and diseases which kill substantial areas of mature forest that were being relied upon for timber harvesting at some time in the future can also result in the depletion of the mature forest before the second growth forest is ready for harvest. Fire, insect outbreaks or diseases in particular age classes of the second growth forests can similarly cause problems in log supply at some time in the future.

Sustained yield forestry has been the espoused cornerstone of B.C.'s forest policy since the 1950's. One of the main reasons for this focus has been the argument that a regulated flow of timber will stabilize a community or region.

However, if the sustainable rate of cutting is calculated over too large a region, and if the calculated cut is not distributed into several local "cutting cycles" (a cutting cycle is a complete set of stand age classes), local areas may experience "boom-and-bust" logging cycles (Figure 9.3). This may occur even though over the entire region the cut may be occurring at a sustainable rate. Social and economic sustainability at a smaller scale (a small local community) may be imperilled by forest management which ensures a sustained flow of logs at a larger geographical scale (a large timber supply area).

Community or regional stability is not ensured solely by a regulated flow of wood to mills. Rather, regional economic stability can only be achieved if annual harvest flows are equal, if market product prices are stable and if relative costs of production are constant.

Wildlife may experience a similar problem. Many species are specialized in their habitat requirements, and as habitat conditions change over time as a clearcut harvested area develops back to mature forest, there is a corresponding succession of both plant and animal species occupying the area. Where the scale of the mosaic of forest patches of various ages in a region is small enough, animals are able to move from patch to patch as conditions in any one patch change, thereby maintaining themselves in the appropriate habitat conditions. Where the patches are too large (e.g., a large valley continuously clearcut over a few years), some species of animal may not be able to move to an appropriate new area as habitat conditions change or as weather conditions require a change in habitat (e.g., a move to "winter range" during heavy winter snow). This can result in large variations in their abundance in the area over time and suggests the need for small, geographically dispersed clearcuts (i.e., many cutting cycles). However, this may not be desirable everywhere and for all species.

A. One cutting cycle

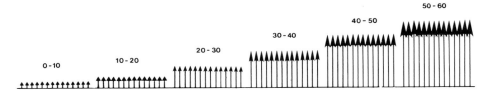

B. Two cutting cycles

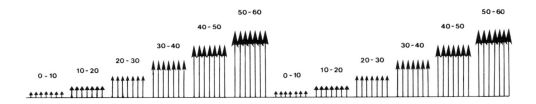

C. Three cutting cycles

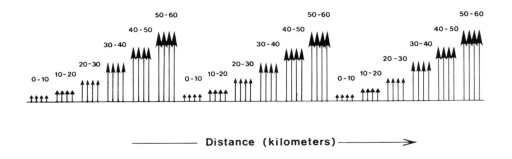

Figure 9.3: Distribution of the Annual Harvest of a Forest from a Single "Cutting Cycle" or from Several. (Clearly, if the total annual harvest is taken from several cutting cycles, there will be a more continuous provision of a variety of forest resource values from any one sub-unit of the forest than if the forest has a single cutting cycle.)

Recently, concern has been increasing over the effects of regional harvesting patterns on some aspects of biotic diversity. It is suggested that the few species in B.C. that are known to depend exclusively on mature second growth or old growth for habitat may not be able to survive in the small patches (20-40 ha on the coast and 5-20 ha in some parts of the interior) that would result from having the annual cut distributed over many cutting cycles. This "fragmentation" of the forest increases the area of "forest edge", which is good for many species of wildlife that use clearcuts, but can have a negative effect on species that have an absolute requirement for mature or old growth forest. Maintenance of maximum regional wildlife diversity will require a compromise between these two rather mutually-exclusive management approaches and will probably require a diversity of sizes of harvested areas.

The discussion in this section has emphasized even-aged stand management that involves clearcut harvesting or some closely related system which results in all the trees in the stand being roughly the same size and age. There is growing public pressure to switch to uneven-aged management with some type of selection harvesting, or to a non-clearcut method of even-age management (e.g., shelterwood). Uneven-aged management would result in all sizes and ages of trees being represented in each stand. Experience in British Columbia, Scandinavia, and elsewhere has shown that uneven-aged management is often the best system for very hot, dry forests, and in some snow-dominated subalpine forests. However, in most cool, humid forests, and most forests with very cold winters, clearcutting, albeit with small openings, has been found to be environmentally sound and silviculturally effective, whereas uneven-aged selection-harvesting of such forests can result in a reduction in their productivity and yield of timber products.

There is certainly a need to replace clearcutting with alternative even-aged silvicultural systems and to increase the use of uneven-aged management in some parts of B.C. However, regional sustainability of timber products will be achieved best if harvesting and management systems are chosen on a site-specific basis that reflects the ecological characteristics of the ecosystem and the ecological requirements of desired tree species. Because the majority of forests in the Fraser Basin are environmentally suited to even-age clearcut harvesting, this harvesting technique will almost certainly continue to be used, subject to wildlife, range, watershed, soil, aesthetics, and recreational concerns.

Forest management activities will have little effect on overall regional hydrology within the Fraser Basin because timber management regulations generally restrict the proportion of regional watersheds (e.g., 4th or 5th order watersheds) that are in a recently harvested condition. Where this proportion is less than about 25%, there will generally be little measurable effect on streamflow at the outflow of the watershed (Bosch and Hewlett, 1982). Salvage logging of extensive areas of insect or fire-killed forests will probably result in measureable hydrological effects in the affected watersheds because of alterations in snow pack accumulation and snow melt. Where such effects occur, they would be expected to persist until the area was reforested.

Sustainability at the Local Level

Global and regional sustainability questions have great potential significance for the Fraser Basin, but so does the sustainability of structure, species composition, and site productivity at the individual stand level. These factors would be affected by global climate change if it occurs, but, in turn, they determine the response of the stand to climate change. Sustainability of timber production at the stand level ultimately determines sustainability of timber flows at the regional level because it affects the volume of timber that will be available for harvest as each stand reaches the age at which it is ready for harvest.

The maintenance of productivity of individual stands has several determinants. Pre-eminent amongst these is soil conditions. Loss of soil organic matter, loss of nutrients, excessive drying or waterlogging, and loss of soil physical structure (due to compaction during harvesting, or intense slashburning) all lead to significant declines in tree growth in all but the most unusual circumstances. Loss of "forest microclimate" caused by clearcutting in hot, dry, or very windy climates can also be important. It may lead to delayed regeneration, lengthened rotations, and a loss of average annual timber production, even if a site's growth potential as determined by soil resources (nutrients, moisture) is unaltered. Competition for light, moisture and nutrients by non-crop species during the early years of a plantation or a naturally regenerated site can similarly delay the formation of a closed forest and therefore reduce timber yields over a given rotation, even though potential site productivity (determined by the climate and soil) remains unchanged. Diseases and insects can similarly reduce the yield of timber products.

As in agriculture, repeated cropping by monocultures of susceptible tree species can sometimes lead to extensive timber volume losses by death or decay due to the build up of populations of pathogens. In other cases, repeated populations of a single tree species is the way nature does things and artificially-established single species forests have proven to be both stable and productive. There is nothing inherently "wrong", "unnatural", or "unstable" about monocultures, as long as they are created and managed in an ecologically sensitive manner. However, in many cases, using natural patterns of forest development following natural disturbance as a guide to stand management will help avoid costly mistakes. Where multi-species forests are harvested, it is generally desirable that we establish a new tree crop of similar species composition. In most of our forests, processes of natural regeneration ensure that we finish up with mixed species stands, even where we plant only one tree species, but sometimes it is necessary to plant appropriate mixtures of species. Useful generalizations about these issues are difficult to find. Individual site evaluations at the ecosystem type or ecosystem association level are necessary.

"Good silviculture" should result in at least sustained, and generally enhanced, site productivity of timber resources in comparison with an unmanaged forest. In most cases, this requires that the natural adaptations of individual tree species are respected, and that the natural successional sequences of plant communities are mimicked to a considerable extent in our stand management. Failure to practice "ecologically-sympathetic" silviculture may not cause problems in the first or even the second rotation, but cumulative changes in soils and abiotic conditions can result in negative impacts on ecosystem function and/or biotic diversity in succeeding rotations, and a subsequent loss in the sustainability of yield.

Local wildlife and water resources are normally subject to much greater changes as a result of timber management than wildlife and water resources considered at the regional or the entire Fraser Basin level. Forest stand management results in significant changes over time in wildlife habitat at the local site level. Habitat changes caused by timber harvesting will result in an increase in the abundance of some animal species and a decrease in the abundance of others, but these changes are ephemeral. Over time, the processes of ecological succession return harvested areas to a forested condition and there is a consequent change in wildlife habitat values and the relative abundance of different species.

Timber harvesting can have a very significant impact on the quantity, quality and regimen of first order streams, because most or all of a first order watershed will be contained within a harvested area, and first order streams generally lack well developed vegetation. These effects will be greater where clearcut harvesting is used than in the case of partial cutting (e.g., shelterwood, patch or selective harvesting). Clearcuts of the size common in much of the Fraser Basin will generally have much less effect on second order streams, and relatively little effect on most third order streams. Salvage-logging of first and insect-killed timber may cause measurable effects in these higher order streams.

The sustainability of visual, recreation and range resources has not been discussed in this chapter. Neither has the maintenance of the traditional values of B.C.'s Native people that are based on forested ecosystems. They are beyond the scope of this paper, but must be considered in a more broadly-based evaluation of the sustainability of forest-based activities in the Fraser Basin.

The Concept of "Ecological Rotations"

Whether or not the various values of the forest resource are being sustained under current forest management practices cannot be judged solely on the basis of short-term evaluations of a site following forest harvesting. Recently harvested forests are frequently ugly, there is often some degree of soil disturbance and/or damage, some aspects of wildlife carrying capacity may have been impaired, and there may have been some negative impacts on water quality and fish habitat. Over the short-term, which can vary from as little as one year to as many as 20 years, the "quality" of a particular site may have been reduced in terms of one or more resource values (although it may have been increased in terms of some others). However, in common with all living systems, ecosystems have the ability to recover. Were this not so, life on earth would long since have collapsed and gone extinct because ecosystems always have, and always will be, disturbed periodically. Their rate of recovery from disturbance will vary according to the particular ecosystem condition by which recovery is judged, the degree to which this ecosystem condition has been altered by disturbance, the climate, and the resilience of the site.[4]

Even severely disturbed ecosystems can recover many of their pre-disturbance conditions and values within decades if they have a mild climate and a moist, fertile soil. Conversely, relatively lightly disturbed ecosystems may take many decades or even many centuries to recover if the climate is severe and/or the soil is infertile and subject to significant growing season drought, or has some other physical condition that impedes plant growth. Evaluations of the sustainability of ecosystem conditions at the local level thus require the definition of:

(i)   the intensity of ecosystem disturbance;
(ii)   the spatial extent of the disturbance;
(iii) the anticipated frequency of the disturbance; and,
(iv)   the resilience of the ecosystem.

Whether or not a particular management practice or natural disturbance event threatens the sustainability of the resource has more to do with whether the mechanisms of ecosystem recovery have been impaired than with the short-term visual alteration of the ecosystem. For example, a relatively severe ecosystem disturbance will not threaten long-term sustainability of the ecosystem if the plan is to repeat this disturbance only once every 100 years, and the ecosystem has the ability to recover the lost values within 50 years.

The lack of any simple criteria by which to evaluate sustainability at the local site level suggests the need for the concept of "ecological rotations"—the time taken for a specific ecosystem parameter to recover to its pre-disturbance condition following a particular type, intensity, and extent of disturbance (Figure 9.4).

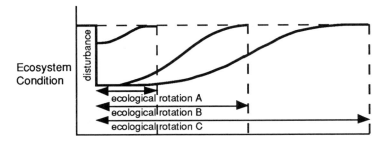

Figure 9.4: Diagrammatic Representation of the Concept of "Ecological Rotation". (Different ecosystems, or different ecosystem parameters, recover from a given disturbance at different rates. Each will have its own "rotation of recovery" or ecological rotation.)

---

4   Resilience is the ability to "bounce back" or recover from disturbance, also called the "elastic stability" of the ecosystem, or simply its elasticity. Resilience of an ecosystem within any particular climatic region is largely determined by soil and biological resources.

If the combination of the intensity and extent of harvest-related disturbance and the natural or management-assisted rate of recovery of a particular ecosystem results in an ecological rotation that is longer than the planned tree crop rotation, long-term "decline" in ecosystem condition can be expected. If management considerations suggest a frequency of harvest on a particular site that is greater than that suggested by the ecological rotation for that site with a particular type of harvesting system, then the intensity of harvest disturbance must be reduced to ensure long-term sustainability. Similarly, if technical considerations result in a degree of ecological disturbance to the site being greater than that which the ecosystem can sustain for a given frequency of harvest, the rotation will have to be lengthened. Obviously, there will be greater latitude of management on a resilient site than on a site that recovers slowly (Figure 9.5).

Estimation of Ecological Rotations

As a theoretical concept, "ecological rotation" may be quite useful. The problem is, how does one estimate ecological rotations? The best way, of course, would be to have rotation-length experience of ecosystem recovery from various different types and intensities of disturbance. Lacking such experience, one can use ecologically-based ecosystem management simulation models such as FORCYTE (Kimmins, 1988; 1990). FORCYTE-11 is a model that permits the examination of short (10-20 years), medium (one rotation) and long-term (multi-rotation) consequences of a wide variety of types and intensities of management-induced or natural (e.g., fire, insects) disturbances to a forest ecosystem. The model predicts the effects on production, yield, soil fertility, sustainability of production and yield, stand-level economics, and energy-use efficiency. A more advanced model called FORECAST (Kimmins and Scoullar, in preparation) provides the opportunity to predict the consequences of an even wider range of management impacts than is possible with FORCYTE-11, and the impacts of climate change can be examined. Appropriately calibrated, models of this type provide one way of estimating the various possible combinations of disturbance and rotation length for a particular ecosystem that will result in long-term sustainable ecosystem condition and productivity.

Are Presently-used Rotations Greater or Less than Ecological Rotations?

Because of the lack of rotation-length experience, and because of the failure to use ecosystem-based forest yield predictors, there has been no systematic, quantitative evaluation of the relationship between current rotations and ecological rotations in the Fraser Basin, or anywhere else in British Columbia (FORCYTE is being used for this purpose in Oregon). However, qualitative assessments of the impact of harvesting on soils have suggested that substantial physical damage has been done to the forest soils of British Columbia in the past, that this damage is continuing to occur, and that substantial growth and economic losses have resulted (Utzig and Walmsley, 1988). Loss of soil organic matter and nutrients caused by soil erosion

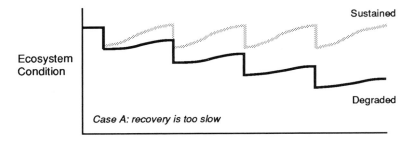

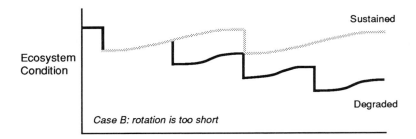

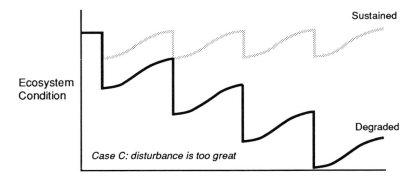

Figure 9.5: Diagrammatic Representation of the Effects of
Variations in the Intensity of Disturbance, Frequency
of Disturbance, and Ecosystem Resilience on the
Long-term Sustainability of Ecosystem Condition

and compaction, by slashburning, or by whole-tree harvesting (also called full-tree harvesting) can result in reductions in long-term site productivity unless rotations are used that are long enough to permit ecosystem recovery, or unless management actions (fertilization or use of nutritional nurse crops) compensate for the nutritional losses.

In addition to soil damage, clearcutting in the drier biogeoclimatic zones has led to the loss of forest microclimate, frequently delaying reforestation. In cold, high elevation forests with short growing seasons, slashburning following clearcutting causes the loss of advanced regeneration, and this can also delay reforestation. Failure to control non-crop vegetation in successfully established plantations and/or failure of natural or artificial regeneration has led to prolonged regeneration delays in weed-prone areas. However, in some cases the elimination of non-crop vegetation can reduce the rate at which the ecosystem recovers from harvest disturbance, and the elimination of nitrogen-fixing species may have negative implications for long-term site productivity.

Research and qualitative field experience have led to the conclusion that, for some forest ecosystems in B.C., it will require longer than the planned rotation to recover from the impacts of harvesting to some desired, sustainable condition under current management regimes (see papers in Gessel et al., 1990; Lousier and Still, 1988). In short, the planned rotations for these types of forest are shorter than the ecological rotation for the planned intensity of disturbance and anticipated management inputs. If this is true, it implies that some of the forestry being practiced in the Fraser Basin may not result in sustained tree growth and sustainable yields.

There is an urgent need to reduce the extent of harvest-induced physical soil damage and soil nutrient depletion, and to improve our understanding of the implications of such soil changes for long-term site productivity. The role of soil organic matter and the forest floor in sustaining site production must be given much greater consideration, and soil organic matter and site nutrient management must become a routine component of forest management. Similarly, in low elevation dry forests and high elevation cold forests, it should be mandatory to employ harvesting methods that facilitate regeneration. In many cases it will be much easier to practise "environmentally friendly" forestry in subsequent rotations than it is in the first managed rotation. The period of transition from old-growth unmanaged forests to managed second growth forests poses a variety of problems that are not found in managed forests. The solutions to these problems can result in undesirable environmental impacts of variable duration.

Ecologically-Sound Yield Prediction and Planning Tools in Forestry

The forests of the Fraser Basin are variable in climate, soils, topography, age since last major disturbance, species composition, and plant community structure. The single most important factor in achieving sustained use of these forests is the explicit recognition of this physical, chemical and biological variability in an ecological site classification system. This fundamental requirement for sustainable forestry is satisfied in the Fraser Basin by the biogeoclimatic classification of the Ministry of Forests, and the requirement of the Forest Act that there be a pre-harvest, ecologically-based description of the site and an associated prescription of the silvicultural and harvest system that is to be used.

A second requirement of sustainable forestry is the ability to predict, on a site-by-site basis, the sustainability of timber yields and other resource values that will result from different silvicultural and management strategies. Lacking empirical experience over rotation or multi-rotation time scales, the ability to make such predictions requires the use of ecologically-based ecosystem management simulation models. Qualitative predictions can certainly be made based solely on the biogeoclimatic classification in combination with our scientific understanding of how ecosystems function and our short-term experience. However, it is difficult to synthesize our knowledge of the myriad of factors that determine long-term site productivity without the use of an appropriate ecosystem-level model, and predictions based on short-term experience are often very different from predictions based on long-term experience. Consequently, prediction of ecological rotations and evaluation of the sustainability of yield under a variety of possible stand management strategies requires the use of such models in conjunction with ecological site classification.

Possible Future Changes in the Management of Forests in the Fraser Basin

Forestry has developed at various times in history and in various places around the world, but always in response to the need to sustain certain forest conditions, supplies of material goods, and/or non-consumptive forest uses. In most cases, forestry has evolved through a predictable series of stages (Kimmins, 1987). It may be relevant, therefore, to examine this characteristic pattern of historical development for clues concerning the future of forestry in the Fraser Basin.

Early societies used forests as they needed them or cleared them for agriculture with no thought for future supplies of forest products. This resulted in local shortages of timber for fuel, building or other uses, which led to the unregulated exploitation of more remote forests. As these lands in turn became denuded, attempts were often made to colonize the forests of other countries, either economically (by trade) or militarily. Acquisition of timber for strategic purposes played an important role in the building of empires during periods when political and economic strength depended on the power of a wooden navy and the extent of a wooden merchant fleet.

This sequence of exploitation and colonization only postponed the day when countries had to initiate some form of regulation to ensure continued supplies of forest resources from their own territories. Thus, the human endeavor of forestry developed.

Early attempts at forestry were generally not very successful. Lacking an explicit recognition of the spatially variable and temporally-changing character of forest ecosystems (although such knowledge existed in the writings of botanists in Greece at least as early as 300 B.C.), the centralized, legalistic, administrative approach that characterizes early attempts at forestry rarely succeeded in its objective. The failure of the administrative approach to ensure sustained future supplies of forest resources has generally led to the adoption of a more ecologically-sensitive approach to silviculture, and this ecologically-based silvicultural phase of forestry is sooner or later accompanied by an increasing sensitivity to the broader social values of the forest and the needs of local communities. The origins of modern forestry can be traced back to central Europe where the need for a biological/ecological approach was recognized at least half a millennium ago. However, the formalization of earlier European attempts to conserve and sustain forest resources by means of ecologically-based silvicultural and management systems is more recent, dating back less than three centuries.

This same sequence of development has occurred in B.C. forestry, but over a much shorter time scale. Initial unregulated exploitation at low elevations on the southern coast in the 19th century and first decade of this century created local shortages. This lead to the logging of higher elevations and more remote areas, and to the institution of forest regulations in the first half of this century. The coast wood supply was fully committed under sustained yield management by the end of the second World War, and this led to the "colonization" of the interior forests in the 1940 to 1960 period.

The approach to forestry on B.C.'s publicly owned forest land was largely administrative in character until the past two decades. Increasing difficulty with forest regeneration, increasing evidence of site damage from inappropriate harvesting, slashburning, and regeneration practices, and increasing recognition that regeneration failures and excessive rates of forest harvesting were going to lead to future reductions in yield lead, in the 1975 to 1985 period, to the adoption of a more ecologically-based approach to silviculture. However, before the "ecological/silvicultural" phase of forestry became fully implemented in the province, and before sufficient time had passed for its effects on the quality of forest management to become apparent, rapidly changing public attitudes towards forestry and the environment have begun to push B.C. forestry into the next phase—social forestry.

B.C. forestry to date has thus developed in much the same way as forestry elsewhere in the world. So what can the experience in countries with a longer history of forests teach us? Looking at Europe and Scandinavia one sees a much greater control of forested landscapes by local communities, greater importance placed on the recreation and protection roles of forests, and a greater constraint on what foresters and loggers are permitted to do. Comparisons between forestry in Europe and British Columbia are difficult, of course, because of differences in population density, in the economic importance of timber production in the economy, in forest ownership, and several other important factors. However, the trend towards forest management that is sensitive to a wide variety of social issues, as well as being sensitive to the specific ecological characteristics of the local forest site is one which will probably characterize forestry in British Columbia over the next few decades.

If this prediction is correct, we can expect to see much greater care taken in the future over the aesthetic impacts of forestry in the Fraser Basin because of the importance of recreation and the high visibility of forest harvesting practices in the mountainous terrain of the area. Forest harvesting will probably be constrained to ensure that log supplies to particular mills and employment in local communities are sustained to ensure community stability. The latter will also require changes in access to forest resources to allow the development of small-scale, locally-based operations, and greater diversification of products ("value-added" products) in addition to the staple products currently produced for the export market.

Clearcutting of even-aged forests will undoubtedly continue to be the dominant silvicultural system in B.C., but other forms of silviculture, including shelterwood and some type of selection, will probably see increased use in those forests where they are ecologically and silviculturally appropriate, and where public concern over aesthetics requires some form of continuous forest cover. Finally, public concern about smoke from slashburning, the use of herbicides, and soil damage caused by conventional harvesting practices will almost certainly result in changes in these practices, whether or not they actually threaten the biophysical sustainability of forest resources. All these changes will have implications for the nature of forestry in, and the contribution of forestry to, the economic and social development of the Fraser Basin.

Social and Institutional Aspects of Sustainability in the Fraser Basin

We recognize that biophysical sustainability is a necessary, but not sufficient, condition for the overall sustainability of the forests and forest sector in the Fraser River Basin. Additional factors, such as area-based rather than volume-based forest management, secure long-term tenure systems, and policy and economic incentive structures that encourage stewardship and sustainable practices are equally important. Further research is necessary to determine changes in policy and management that are needed to ensure that the social and institutional goals of sustainability are met.

Using the types of analysis suggested in this paper, biophysically sustainable forest management practices and silviculture regimes could be assessed. Similar analyses must be conducted to determine the social goals associated with the forests of the Fraser River Basin. These will likely include assessments of community stability, recreation, aesthetics, wilderness and non-timber values. Without a clear understanding of these societal goals, the aforementioned forest management practices may be biophysically sustainable, and environmentally appropriate, yet socially inappropriate. This point was alluded to earlier with reference to the implication of a move from an "ecological/silvicultural" phase of forestry to social forestry.

Institutional arrangements associated with the forests of the Fraser River Basin must also be investigated. Unless the decision-making structures and planning processes are sensitive to the changing nature of societal goals, it is unlikely that they will be achieved. Current conflicts associated with increasing demands for citizen participation, increased access to resources for smaller-scale and community-based operations, and the Native land question illustrate challenges to the existing institutional arrangements. The question then follows: how should the forest resources of the Fraser River Basin be administered? What structural and institutional changes are necessary to achieve these socio-economic and biophysical goals? A thorough examination of the structure of the industry, of governments, of relationships between forest stakeholders, and of government policies is necessary if these questions are to be pursued.

Conclusions

Forestry is the major land use in the Fraser Basin. The sustainability of communities, the economy, the wildlife, range and recreation resources, and the water resources of the Basin are all intimately related to how the forests are managed. Faced with changing public attitudes about the environment, the probability of climate change, and increasing demands for both timber and non-timber values from the forest, there will inevitably be a change in both the forests of the Basin and how they are managed.

Whether or not desired forest values are sustained will depend on the magnitude of climate change, on whether or not forest crop rotations approximate ecological rotations (i.e., whether or not long-term site quality is sustained), and on how harvesting is distributed spatially and temporally in the landscape. An appropriate pattern of forest plant communities of different ages and species is required to maintain regional biological diversity, and appropriate silvicultural strategies are required to sustain the long-term diversity of individual stands at desired levels.

There is little doubt that some of the harvesting and site preparation practices that have been used in the Fraser Basin do not constitute sustainable forestry and have had a negative impact on the forestry sector and on the water resource, at least in low order watersheds. However, there appears to be little basis on which to suggest that forestry in the Basin is not sustainable. There is every reason to anticipate that the rate of forest growth and yield of timber products can be significantly increased in the future by the application of ecologically-sound management practices. This can occur even if some additional areas of forests are reserved for non-timber uses, and if additional constraints are placed on silviculture (e.g., the banning of slashburning or herbicides) in order to ensure an adequate supply of non-timber resources and protection of the water resource in low order watersheds. However, in many cases slashburning and herbicides are appropriate managements tools, and may be much less environmentally damaging than alternatives.

Forestry in the Fraser Basin can be sustainable in the broadest sense of this term and can increase its contributions to the economy and social fabric of the area. It can achieve this without negative impacts on the water resources of the Basin, but some changes from current practices may be necessary if this is to be achieved.

This chapter advances the premise that sustainability in the forestry sector, in which biophysical, social and institutional goals are met, is a prerequisite for the sustainability of aquatic resources in the Fraser Basin. This chapter has focussed on the implications of biophysical sustainability of forestry in the Basin. In doing so, a framework for analysis has been developed which is readily applicable to the sustainability question from social and institutional perspectives. Through the application of this approach to these questions, management and policy implications at the local, regional and global level would be revealed, thereby assisting efforts to achieve sustainability in our forests.

References

Bolin, B., B. R. Doos, J. Jager and R. A. Warrick. 1986. *The Greenhouse Effect, Climate Change, and Ecosystems.* SCOPE Report 29. New York: Wiley.

Bosch, J. M., and J. A. Hewlett. 1982. "A Review of Catchment Experiments to Determine the Effect of Vegetation Changes on Water Yield and Evapotranspiration." *J. Hydrology.* 55: 3-23.

Gessel, S. P., D. S. Lacate, G. F. Weetman and R. F. Powers. 1990. *Sustained Productivity of Forest Soils. Proceedings of the 7th North American Forest Soils Conference.* Vancouver: University of British Columbia, Faculty of Forestry Publication.

Harrington, J. B. 1987. "Climate Change: A Review of Causes." *Can. J. For. Res.* 17:1313-1339.

Kimmins, J. P. 1987. "Development of Forestry and Forest Ecology." Chapter 2. in *Forest Ecology.* New York: MacMillan.

Kimmins, J. P. 1988. "Community Organization: Methods of Study and Prediction of the Production and Yield of Forest Ecosystems." *Can. J. Bot.* 66:2654-2672.

Kimmins, J. P. 1990. "Modelling the Sustainability of Forest Production and Yield for a Changing and Uncertain Future." *For. Chronicle.* 66:271-280.

Klinka, K., M. C. Feller, R. N. Green, D. V. Meindinger, J. Pojar and J. Worrall. 1990 "Ecological Principles: Applications." in Lavender, D. P., R. Parish, C. M. Johnson et al. *Regenerating British Columbia's Forests.* Vancouver: U.B.C. Press.

Krajina, V. J. 1969. "Ecology of Forest Trees in British Columbia." *Ecol. West. N. Amer.* 2(1):1-147.

Lousier, J. D., and G. W. Still. 1986. *Degradation of Forested Land: "Forest & Soils at Risk".* Proceedings of the 10th B.C. Soil Science Workshop. Land Management Report #56. Victoria: British Columbia Ministry of Forests.

Schneider, S. H. 1989. *Global Warming. Are We Entering the Greenhouse Century?* San Francisco: Sierra Club.

Shands, W. E., and J. S. Hoffman (eds.). 1987. *The Greenhouse Effect, Climate Change, and US Forests.* Washington: The Conservation Foundation.

Utzig, G. F., and M. E. Walmsley. 1988. *Evaluation of Soil Degradation as a Factor Affecting Forest Productivity in British Columbia: A Problem Analysis.* Phase 1. FRDA Report 015. Ottawa: Canada Forestry Service.

10

The Evolution of British Columbia's Energy System and Implications for the Fraser Basin

John D. Chapman

The purpose of this chapter is to review the state of knowledge about the future development of the British Columbian commercial energy system and consider its implications for sustainable development in the province as a whole and the Fraser River Basin in particular. The introduction deals briefly with the author's perception of the terms "natural resource" and "sustainable development", the components of commercial energy systems in general and the current state of the provincial system. The body of the chapter is divided into four sections. The first deals with the general topic of energy futures in order to set the context for the second and third sections on projections of future requirements and plans and proposals for future supply in B.C. The fourth section considers the implications of future energy developments for the province as a whole and the Fraser Basin within it. The treatment in the first three sections is general and summative and, in the fourth section on implications, it is speculative.

Concepts and Energy Systems

Natural Resources and Sustainable Development

Natural resources may be defined as "those aspects of the biophysical environment which humans value and from which they benefit". Four streams of benefits may be identified providing, respectively, materials and energy, space for built facilities, opportunities for experiences and the operation of life support, biophysical processes and functions. Inclusion of these four benefit streams expands the concept of "natural resource" beyond the conventional focus on the provision of materials and energy and the associated concern for adequacy of future supplies. In particular, this definition recognizes biophysical processes and functions ("nature's services" as Westmann [1977] calls them) as an integral part of the meaning of 'natural resource'. This, in turn, leads to an holistic approach to resource issues (rather than the single benefit stream focus of the past) and opens the way for more ecologically sound practices as well as providing a framework for internalizing environmental and experiential values in an economic sense.

In this context, the concept of "sustainable development" may be interpreted to mean the human use of the biophysical environment in ways which maintain an optimal balance between the four benefit streams potentially embodied in any natural resource. It should be noted that this working definition excludes explicit concern for social systems and implementation processes required to bring about change (Rees, 1989).

Energy Systems and The Environment

The mobilization and use of inanimate energy involves four major stages, plus the provision of transportation and storage facilities and the production and disposal of residuals (Figure 10.1). Each of the stages and activities identified in Figure 10.1 has implications for environmental functions and processes and, to a greater or lesser extent, competes with the other benefit streams.

Conversely, the state of the environment influences both the supply of and demand for energy. The character of the past and present biophysical environment largely determines the existence and quality of primary energy sources. Thus, geological and geophysical conditions determine whether fossil fuels are present, the hydrologic regime and landforms whether a hydro-electric potential exists and the climate-soil characteristics underlie the basic productivity of biomass. From an operational point of view, all stages of energy chains may be affected by unfamiliar or extreme environmental conditions requiring the development of new technologies or procedures in order to avoid service delays or interruptions of supply.

The environmental conditions also affect the potential demand for energy. The seasonal temperature regime determines the general level of the potential demand for heating and cooling built space, while short term temperature extremes may lead to dramatic peaks of demand. Such abrupt temperature changes can place a heavy strain on energy distribution systems and require production systems to include expensive peak load and storage capacity.

Secular changes of climate will clearly influence the potential supply of energy from such sources as rivers, wind, and solar radiation as well as the demand for energy for heating and cooling and for such tasks as pumping water (e.g., maintaining drainage in the Lower Fraser Valley or providing irrigation in the south central interior Fraser Basin).

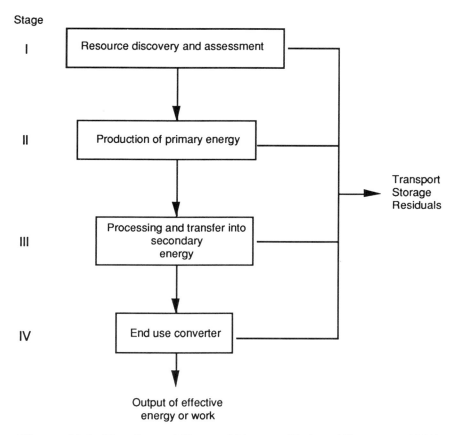

Stage

I   Resource discovery and assessment

II   Production of primary energy

III   Processing and transfer into secondary energy

IV   End use converter

Transport
Storage
Residuals

Output of effective
energy or work

Figure 10.1: The General Form of Energy Chains. (Chapman, 1989).

The B.C. Energy System

The general characteristics of the B.C. energy system in 1988 are depicted in Figure 10.2 and Table 10.1.

Almost three-quarters of the primary energy produced are fossil fuels, dominated by coal, with the remainder divided equally between hydro-electricity and wood waste.[1] Almost two-thirds of the primary energy consumed are also fossil fuels (mainly hydrocarbons and very little coal) and the remainder wood wastes (a distinguishing feature of B.C.'s energy consumption mix) and hydro-

---

1   Wood waste includes "hog-fuel" (the residual from the initial processing of logs) and "black liquor" (a residual from bleaching wood chips in the pulping process). Collectively these potential energy sources are often referred to as renewable resources. However, supply depends first on the availability of timber which will decrease as the "fall-down" effect develops and second, upon the level of activity in and technology used by the wood processing industry. The latter are subject to market variables and the rate of technological innovation. Consequently, to use the term renewable in the same sense as say, the potential energy of a river, seems inappropriate.

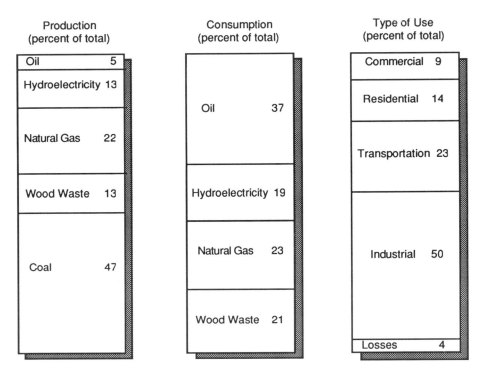

Figure 10.2: Primary Energy Production and Consumption, 1988. (After British Columbia Ministry of Energy, Mines and Petroleum Resources)

Table 10.1: B.C. Primary Energy Balance, 1988 (in Petajoules)

Commodity	Production	Consumption	Export	Import	Balance
Coal	688	8	680	0	+680
Natural Gas	343	226	117	0	+117
Wood Waste	201	201	0	0	0
Hydroelectric	247	222	33	8	+25
Oil	82	438	3	359	-356
Total	1,561	1,095	833	367	+456

electricity. The end-use of primary energy is dominated by the industrial and transportation sectors.

From the point of view of total energy balance, B.C. has a large surplus of production over consumption as the result of the magnitude of the export-based coal and natural gas production. For oil, however, the province is in a strongly deficit position, relying on Alberta for over 80% of its supply.

The Fraser River Basin

The Fraser River Basin may be conveniently divided into the large, thinly populated interior portion and the small densely populated coastal portion or the Lower Fraser Valley downstream of Hope. For the purpose of this paper the Lower Fraser Valley refers to the area, including all of Greater Vancouver, conventionally included in the term even though it extends beyond the watershed boundary of the Fraser River Basin proper.

From an energy point of view, the interior Basin contains some primary energy sources and production, but most of the current energy-related activities are the result of the bulk transfer of energy from outside the Basin to coastal B.C., the USA and offshore. The major energy consumers in the interior Basin are the forest product and mineral industries, followed by the transportation, residential and commercial sectors of the growing urban settlements. The distribution of refined petroleum products, gas and electricity also gives rise to local and sub-regional transportation and storage facilities.

The coastal portion of the Basin has several small hydro-electric plants but no other primary energy production. There is a potential for natural gas but to date exploratory drilling has not led to any reported discoveries. The Lower Fraser Valley is, however, the major energy consuming centre of the province, the centre of oil refining (four plants) and the focal point for the energy transportation facilities which pass through the interior portion of the Basin.

Energy Futures

Statements about energy futures are in the form of conditional probabilities. They state what could happen if specified conditions are met, not what will happen. At best, they project the appropriate direction and order of magnitude of change.

Scale

Projections about the future state of commercial energy systems are made at a range of temporal, spatial and phenomenal scales.

Temporal

Projections may be applied to time periods as short as days or weeks and as long as half a century. Within this range a distinction may be made between short, medium and long-term projections representing up to 5, 25 and 50 years respectively.

Short-term projections, used for operational and tactical purposes, have the highest probability of being correct. Despite the predictive expectations associated with short-term projections, unforeseeable events such as political and labour disruptions, abrupt price changes, or extreme weather conditions may render them unreliable. Medium-term projections of conditions up to 25 years in the future deal with a time-frame long enough for existing strategies to be implemented and new ones formulated. Thus, although rooted in the technologies, supply patterns and use habits of the date of formulation, significant changes can arise from decisions taken early in the projection period. Uncertainty about what decisions will be taken, as well as the relatively long period during which unexpected events may occur, reduces the predictive capacity of projections over this time scale. Long-term projections of conditions up to 50 years have the least predictive capacity because, on the one hand, the long lead time is sufficient for order-of-magnitude alterations in the state of the system and, on the other, for unimagined circumstances to develop.

Currently in B.C., the Ministry of Energy, Mines and Petroleum Resources (MEMPR) publishes a 20 year, comprehensive energy forecast at two year intervals which is updated in intervening years for the next 5 year period. B.C. Hydro (BCH) publishes a 20 year electric load forecast which is updated annually. Private sector corporations (e.g., Westcoast Transmission, Transmountain Pipeline) also prepare forecasts to guide their operations but these are rarely made available beyond the firm.

Spatial

The spatial coverage of projections may range over widely different sized areas, but those that are published are usually at the regional, provincial or national scale. In Canada, the Department of Energy, Mines and Resources and the National Energy Board produce comprehensive energy projections for the country broken down by province for some components.

In B.C., the MEMPR projections cover the province but, for some components, Vancouver Island and the Mainland are dealt with separately. There are no published data available for the Fraser River Basin or its subdivisions. Most of the published BCH electric load projections extend over the BCH Integrated System (BCH, 1989a) but for internal use they are reduced first to the four operational divisions and then to the distribution sub-station level and individual large electricity users (mostly industrial plants).

Phenomenal

Energy system futures may consist of one or more of the following components:

(i) By sector—dealing with the energy requirements and supply sources of each consuming sector and sub-sector (e.g., transportation, aviation);

(ii)   By total energy—dealing with the demand for and supply of total energy (e.g., total energy requirements of B.C. in 1990 in Petajoules); and,

(iii) By energy source—dealing with the demand for and supply of individual energy sources and forms (e.g., coal or electricity).

The MEMPR projections deal with all three of the above with the emphasis upon requirements rather than supply and excluding contracted exports in the former. BCH's projections are limited to electricity which is dealt with in total and by sector and includes firm power exports already contracted.

Methodology

This is not the place to attempt a review of the complexities of the various methodologies available for use in the preparation of energy futures. The two major demand forecasting agencies in B.C. both publish details of the methodology they use (MEMPR, 1983; BCH, 1989a), and it is noteworthy that BCH has replaced the unsophisticated approach used up to the time of the Peace River, Site C hearings by much more elaborate procedures accompanied by uncertainty analyses of the output. Despite these changes, the models currently used for demand projections by both agencies require further development or replacement in order to include the effects of demand side management (DSM).

Future Energy Requirements

In the most general terms the projection of energy demand involves:

(i)   Description of the magnitude and structure of current demand;
(ii)   Identification of the variables which affect the current scene;
(iii) Calibration of the influence of each variable upon demand;
(iv)   Estimation of the future magnitude of selected variables; and,
(v)   Projection of the effect that each of these variables will have.

Variables

The consumption of energy derives from the goods and services which its use provides. Thus the amount and composition of energy consumed is a function of the general demand for these goods and services which, in turn, is subject to the influence of many variables, some major and fundamental and others of importance over a restricted range of space and time (Table 10.2).

Economic Activity

The general level of economic activity is the major variable determining the total amount of inanimate energy consumed. During periods of rising production, trade and consumption of goods and services, the overall demand for energy also rises.

Table 10.2: Variables Influencing the Consumption of Energy

First Order	Second Order	Third Order
Level of Economic Activity	Structure of Economy	Technology and Equipment Stock
General Price Level of Energy	Difference in Price between Energy Sources	Regional Variations in Price
Population-Numbers	Income and Settlement Patterns	Cultural Characteristics and Lifestyles
Environment-Temperature Regime	Environmental Regulations	Spatial Extent

Within this major variable, the structure of the economy and the technology and equipment stock are important sub-variables. In the first instance, economies with large manufacturing sectors (particularly primary processing such as B.C.) are likely to use more energy per unit of GNP or GPP than those in which the tertiary or quaternary sectors are dominant. Secondly, the thermodynamic efficiency with which work is carried out in an economy (and thus the amount of energy required for a specific task) is determined by the technology used, the character of the equipment stock, and the manner in which it is operated.

Estimates of future GNP/GPP values are made either on the basis of projections of population, labour force and productivity or by extrapolation of historical trends adjusted to take account of consistency requirements and judgements about the influence of changing circumstances. Among the latter are maintenance of environmental quality, political instability, capital availability and, emphasizing the interdependency between demand and supply, the price and availability of energy. British Columbia's GPP is projected to increase at an annual average rate of 3.0% until 1998 and 2.8% until 2008.

The relation between energy demand and GNP/GPP is commonly expressed by two measures: the amount of energy used to produce one unit of GNP (the energy/GNP ratio or energy intensity) and the percentage change in energy used in relation to the percentage change in GNP (the energy/GNP elasticity). Both of these aggregate measures represent the outcome of the interplay of a number of variables including the structure of the economy, prevailing technologies and stocks of equipment, and, once again, the price and availability of energy. British Columbia's energy intensity has been slowly declining since 1982 and is expected to continue to do so.

Price

A second major factor determining the consumption of energy is its real price in comparison with other factors of production. If the real price of inanimate energy declines relative to labour or capital, there will be a tendency to substitute it (with a time-lag) for the other inputs in the production of intermediate goods and services.

In the consideration of the effect of price upon energy futures, it is useful to distinguish between the conditions which cause prices to change and the effects of those changes upon future energy demand and supply. In practice this is much easier said than done because of the considerable degree of interdependency between the two.

Price changes may be initiated from the supply or the demand side. From the former, price increases may result from increased scarcity, production moving to higher recovery-cost reserves (e.g., to frontier or deep off-shore oil reserves), from governments increasing the administered element of energy prices (e.g., Canada and B.C. continuously), and from major interruptions of supply such as that caused by the Iran-Iraq war. Supply side influences may also serve to decrease the price if production exceeds market requirements (e.g., oil in 1986). From the demand side, upward pressure on prices occurs during periods of high economic activity and associated energy requirements or, in the shorter term, the occurrence of extreme temperature conditions in the heavily populated areas of the developed world. Low levels of economic activity and attendant diminished energy requirements serve to depress prices.

However induced, upward price changes tend to diminish demand and vice versa. The sensitivity of demand to price changes varies between energy sources, forms and uses—and changes occur only after a time-lag, the length of which also varies. The study of energy-price elasticities receives considerable attention from economists but the results, while confirming the direction of change expected from first principles, unfortunately appear to have limited generality and applicability to prediction. Nevertheless the prediction of energy prices is probably a greater problem than dealing with the relationship between price and demand.

Population

Demographic considerations play a basic role in assessing the medium and long-term outlook for energy demand in two ways. First, every additional person generates a small increase in the demand for goods and services and, thus, the energy required to produce them. Second, the magnitude of a population, in conjunction with its age structure, determines the size of the work force and, thus, the potential output of goods and services. The size of the energy requirement associated with each net addition to population is determined by a number of variables including income, settlement pattern, housing preferences and lifestyle. B.C.'s population is projected to increase at an annual average rate of 1.4% until 2008.

Environmental Considerations

The state of the environment influences the demand for energy primarily via the temperature regime and its effects upon the amount of energy required for heating and cooling. BCH, and presumably the private sector hydrocarbon companies, use degree day data as one of the variables in forecasting but it must be noted that this relates primarily to the demand in the residential and, to some extent, the commercial sectors only.

In this context it may be useful to consider to what extent climatic change may be included as an operational variable in projecting energy requirements. Referring to the five steps involved in projecting energy demand identified at the beginning of this section, step one is reasonably well quantified (though perhaps not at an adequate scale), air temperature is clearly identified as a variable in step two and, in step three, the energy suppliers have calibrated its influence on the demand for their product. Step four however, cannot be quantified in an operational way at this time. First, it has to be determined whether climatic change is occurring in B.C. and its regions or whether current trends are within the range of variability of, say, the last 30 or even 60 years (Pacific Northwest Laboratory, 1990). If it is determined that the magnitude or rate of change is unprecedented, then it is necessary to quantify future values before step five can be taken. At this time, the only practical approach appears to be to assume, say, three possible temperature scenarios over the next 30 years and, using the values assumed in the scenarios, arrive at a first approximation of the influence of each upon energy requirements (Taylor and Johnstone, 1989; World Meteorolgical Organization, 1990).

Although the temperature regime is the most widely recognized and used environmental variable influencing energy requirements, the recognition of broader environmental considerations have more pervasive and, ultimately, more important effects. The amount and type of energy consumed and the residuals which result have major environmental implications and B.C. society is increasingly (though far too slowly for many) moving toward energy consumption patterns which minimize environmental impact. The regulatory and fiscal mechanisms which bring about these changes have more influence on the type of energy used and the performance of conversion technology than they do upon the total amount of energy consumed. However, to the extent that such changes result in a higher real price for energy, total consumption will at least be constrained if not reduced. It is worth noting that changes toward the use of energy sources with more benign environmental consequences at the end use stage may only shift the undesirable impact, not remove it. For example, substituting electric motors for internal combustion engines in vehicles will improve air quality in urban areas but decrease it elsewhere if the greatly expanded electricity requirements are supplied from new coal burning plants.

Exports

The existence, magnitude and term of firm export contracts is a variable influencing the demands upon the energy resources of a given area. Thus the amounts of coal and gas covered by existing export contracts constitute a part of B.C.'s energy requirements for the term of the contracts and, in projecting the total future requirements, account must be taken of what export commitment will be entered into and for how long.

B.C. Ministry of Energy, Mines and Petroleum Resources Projection

The most recent MEMPR energy projection was published in December, 1987 (MEMPR, 1987), and, because of the changed value of a number of the key variables since its preparation (e.g., population, economic activity and electricity prices), there is little value in reviewing its contents here. Unfortunately, the 1990 projections are still not available at the time of writing (August, 1990).

B.C. Hydro Projection

B.C. Hydro's latest published Electric Load Forecast 1988/89 - 2008/09 is based upon data assembled in 1989 (BCH, 1989a). The output is summarized in Table 10.3 and Figure 10.3. The forecast refers to the total B.C. Hydro system which

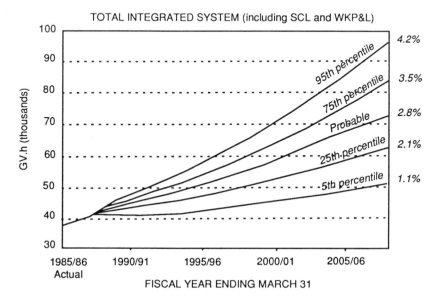

Figure 10.3: B.C Hydro: Gross Electric Load Requirements Forecast, 1988/89 - 2008/09.

Table 10.3: B.C. Hydro Probable Gross Load Requirements (GW.h) by Major Sectors: A Summary (including SCL and WKP&L)

Fiscal Year	Residential	Commercial	Industrial	Other	Total Sales	Losses/ Accruals	TOTAL GROSS REQT'S	Less Non-Integr.	Integrated System TOTAL GROSS REQT'S	Peak
Actual 1987/88	9,902	9,060	16,427	679	36,068	4,725	40,793	167	40,626	7,060
Forecast 1998/99	12,576	13,355	21,562	1,455	48,948	6,350	55,290	230	55,060	9,670
Avg. Ann. % incr. 11 years: 87/88–98/99	2.2 %	3.6 %	2.5 %	7.2 %	2.8 %	2.7 %	2.8 %	3.0 %	2.8 %	2.9 %
Forecast 2008/09	15,024	19,165	27,865	2,039	64,093	8,320	72,410	320	72,090	12,650
Avg. Ann. % incr. 10 years: 98/99–08/09	1.8 %	3.7 %	2.6 %	3.4 %	2.7 %	2.7 %	2.7 %	3.4 %	2.7 %	2.7 %
Avg. Ann. % incr. 21 years: 87/88–08/09	2.0 %	3.6 %	2.5 %	5.4 %	2.8 %	2.7 %	2.8 %	3.1 %	2.8 %	2.8 %

supplies slightly more than 75% of B.C.'s total electric requirements and includes firm commitments to West Kootenay Power and Light (WKP&L) and Seattle City Light (SCL), the latter under the terms of Skagit Valley Agreement. The forecast does not include provision for additional exports, the effects of the recently announced price increase nor the Power and Resource Smart programs (see section on future supply below). It is interesting to compare previous forecasts with one another and with the actual (Figure 10.4).

Future Energy Supply

In the past, the conventional approach to future energy supply has been to assess the provincial resource base and develop individual resource opportunities in anticipation of increased demand. This supply-side approach has characterized the development of the B.C. electricity and hydro-carbon industry. Today, however, it is increasingly recognized that the least cost (in all respects) approach is to increase the efficiency of use and thus decrease the physical capacity that must be developed. This demand side management (DSM) approach is particularly suited to the supply of electricity, though in, the broad sense, applicable to other energy sources.

Supply Side Management

Two options are available in supply side management: (i) develop the energy potential of the area concerned; and/or, (ii) import from beyond its boundaries. Development of domestic resources has the advantages of relatively high degree of control and security, probably (but not necessarily) lower cost and some spin-off benefits to the domestic economy. On the other hand, the depletion of non-renewable resources is hastened and environmental disturbance and foregone opportunities are borne by the source area.

Potential Physical Resources

For the next 20 years, B.C. has sufficient coal, natural gas, hydroelectric and wood-waste resources to meet its own projected requirements plus expanded exports. Provincial oil reserves, however, are expected to be largely depleted. The potential of alternative energy sources (wind, solar, geothermal and municipal solid waste), with the exception of solar in the south-central interior and solid waste in Vancouver and Victoria, is likely to be of only local importance and contribute little to the total supply.

If the time scale is extended to 40 years hence, B.C. will still have large reserves of coal but gas reserves are likely to be significantly depleted, oil reserves gone and, quite possibly, all major hydro potential utilized except for the Fraser River main stem. The major supply problems will be centred on petroleum

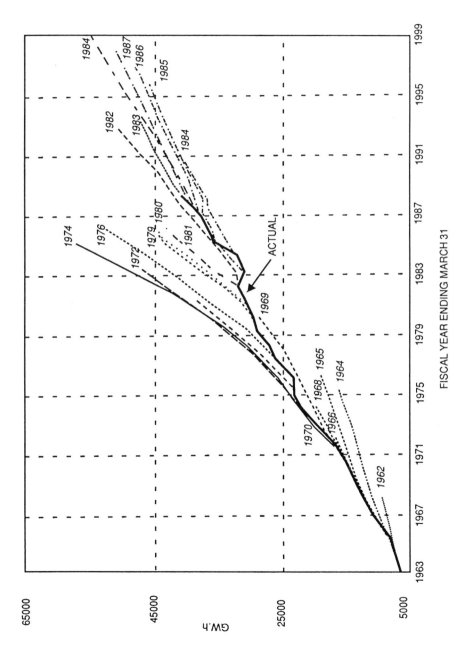

Figure 10.4: B.C. Hydro: Gross Electrical Requirements - Comparison of Actual with Forecast Made in 1962 through 1988.

products. By then it is probable that Alberta's conventional crude oil reserves will be gone and the oil industry will be based upon heavy oil and the bitumen of oil sands.

Imports

At present, B.C. imports over 80% of the crude oil and petroleum products consumed in the province. Most of this comes from Alberta with some heavy fuel oil from the U.S.A., a flow which will cease when the Vancouver Island gas pipeline is operational. In the next 20 years, B.C.'s petroleum requirements will increasingly be imported from Alberta and, as the result of location economics, one or more of the refineries in Vancouver will be closed. Over the longer term, supplies of conventional crude from Alberta may not be sustainable and offshore supply, with all its implications, may become necessary. Domestic natural gas supplies appear sufficient over a 20-25 year period after which imports from the northern frontier gas fields will probably still be available.

Small amounts of electricity are imported now on a short term, operational basis. There are significant cost advantages to expanding the import of electricity in order to defer the building of domestic capacity and B.C. Hydro's resource plan includes provision for agreements with Trans-Alta and Bonneville Power to this end (BCH, 1989b).

Demand Side Management

Explicit demand side management is now an integral part of BCH's resource plan (see next section). The B.C. government, in addition to being party to BCH's plans, is phasing out the Industrial Electricity Rate Discount Act and the Critical Industries Act both of which encouraged the use of electricity by providing for lower rates. It is also requiring B.C. Hydro to increase its return to general revenues, thus raising the price and encouraging its more efficient use. Because of its jurisdictional powers, government influence is greatest over the electricity industry but there is evidence of a demand-side approach (but more with respect to the mix of energy sources used than total consumption) in its support for the use of compressed natural gas or propane as a fuel for vehicles. This program is actively being pursued by B.C. Gas.

B.C. Hydro's Twenty Year Resource Plan

In April 1989, B.C. Hydro published a plan to meet the projected electricity requirements for the period 1989-2027 (BCH, 1989b). The plan is divided into two stages, 1989-2000 and 2000-2027. The first stage consists of a mixture of demand side management (the Power Smart Program), increased efficiency of production and transmission (the Resource Smart Program), co-ordination and purchase agreements with Trans Alta, Alcan, Bonneville and private producers in B.C. yet to be identified, the repatriation of downstream benefits arising from the

Columbia River Treaty and new construction (Figures 10.5-7). For the second stage, 2000-2027, three scenarios are presented emphasizing hydro, thermal and intensified demand side management plus alternative sources respectively (Table 10.4). BCH initiated public debate upon these proposals in the spring of 1989 at the 2nd Electric Power Forum (BCH, 1990) and has continued it with an information campaign and a third Electric Power Forum held in Prince George in May, 1990.

Table 10.4: B.C. Hydro Scenarios for Meeting System Electricity Requirements, 2000-2001

PROJECT		GWh	ESTIMATED COST	
		per year	Capital (1988) 10^6	Energy c/KWh
Hydro Scenario				
Columbia	Downstream Benefits	480-4,600	30	<1.0
	Construction on Tributaries	1,900	1,296	2.3-4.4
Coast Mountains	Homathko	3,500	1,844	5.4
	Elaho	1,560	?	?
Fraser River	McGregor	1,720	?	?
Northern Rivers	Stikine-Iskut	15,570	6,439	5.0
	Liard	18,380	7,044	5.4
Small Hydro	Dispersed Throughout B.C	possible 5800	?	?
Thermal Scenario				
Coal	Hat Creek[1]	13,000	3,020	4.0
	East Kootenay	3,940	?	>4.5
Wood Waste	Quesnel, Prince George	600	?	3.0-4.0
Municipal Solid Waste	Vancouver, Victoria	380	?	6.0
Intensified DSM and Alternative Source Scenario				
Marginal Pricing		6,000-11,000	?	?
Off-Electric for Cooking, Hotwater, Heating		up to 3,000	?	?
High Efficiency Building Design and Convertors		4,000	?	?
Solar/Wind		230	?	?

Source: Compiled from B.C. Hydro, 1989b.
Notes:
1 Three project arrangements have been studied of different capacity. This figure refers to the largest.

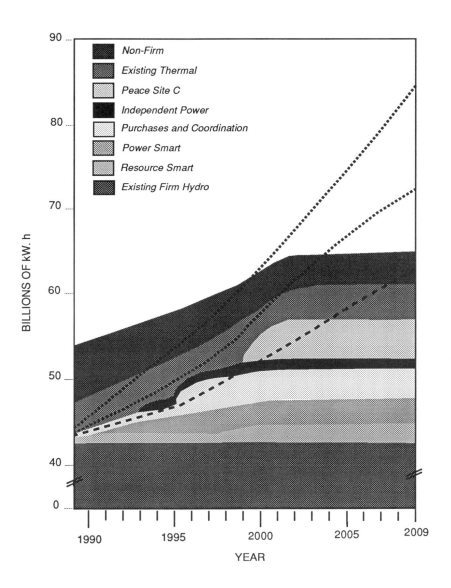

Figure 10.5: B.C. Hydro: Recommended Electricity Supply Plan, 1989 - 2000

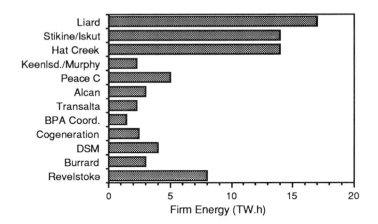

Figure 10.6: Comparison of Magnitude of Energy Supply Proposals.

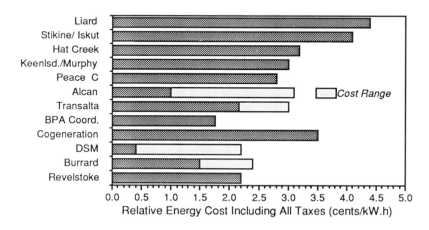

Figure 10.7: Comparison of Energy Costs of Projects in B.C. Hydro Recommendation. (After EMR, 1989:21)

Implications for British Columbia and the Fraser River Basin

The implications of future energy developments upon British Columbia and the Fraser River Basin will be determined by:

(i)   The growth of energy demand (intra and extra-provincial);
(ii) The mix of energy sources selected to meet the projected demand;
(iii) The location of the resources selected for development;
(iv) The sensitivity to other economic and experiential opportunities and to the biophysical environment with which the facilities are designed, constructed and operated.

This speculative section adopts a long term time scale of 40 years, until the year 2030. During the previous 40 years, since 1950, nuclear electricity has developed from a single demonstration plant to supplying almost 20% of global capacity, natural gas has emerged as a major fuel, electricity can now be economically transmitted over 1500 km rather than 200 km and, in North America, the use of coal is essentially confined to the thermal electric and iron and steel industries. In 1950, B.C. consumed approximately 200 PJ of energy; in 1990, 1095 PJ; coal was the dominant fuel, whereas today there is virtually no coal used; and in 1950, the majority of the crude oil and petroleum products was imported from the USA. In comparison with these dramatic changes in the past 40 years, those suggested below for the same period in the future are conservative to say the least.

British Columbia

Energy Requirements

Over the 40 year period to 2030, it is inescapable that the total amount of energy required will be very much larger than now, probably in excess of two-fold. However, the rate of increase would be constrained if economic activity and population growth were to decline and real energy prices substantially increase. Of these only the latter is likely. More realistically, and less dramatically, the rate will be constrained in comparison with recent years to the extent that the structure of the provincial economy changes (with energy intensive resource processing industries assuming a relatively smaller role) and demand side management is more actively pursued not only with respect to electricity but, and in many ways more necessarily, to petroleum products as well. Attractive as demand side management is, there are limits to the rate at which it can be introduced to British Columbian society (e.g., direct public demand side management of petroleum products or natural gas would require a significant shift in majority public values before becoming politically viable). BCH's current Power Smart program is based upon user education coupled with financial inducements. An intensified program, such as that in place in the U.S. Pacific Northwest, would involve stringent energy efficiency regulations for new buildings and energy using equipment (changes in the B.C. building code are currently under consideration), and specification of the type of energy that may be used for given tasks. Most effective of all would be real price increases, administratively or market driven. Judging by the press reaction to recent proposals by both B.C. Hydro and the provincial government to increase electricity prices, it will take some time before public values change sufficiently to make such actions an acceptable part of demand side management (Vancouver Sun, December 18, 1989).

The growth of demands upon provincial energy sources could also be constrained by the limitation or cessation of exports. The conventional argument in support of exports is that they create income for the public and private sector which, in the case of coal, would not occur at all without exports. However, there remains considerable doubt whether there has been a net economic benefit to either sector as a consequence of the development of the northeast coalfields. For natural gas, there is a substantial and rapidly growing market in the province but without the opportunity to augment this market with exports, it is argued, the private sector would not mount the exploration effort necessary to maintain the discovery of reserves. In the case of electricity, the export option is the most discretionary as the resources will eventually be developed anyway and there is no 'discovery rate' to be influenced by exporting. However, the timing of the building of new capacity and the speed with which that capacity can be fully used, and thus operate under the most favourable economic conditions, will be influenced by serving export markets so that the opportunity for real economic net benefits is potentially high.

In assessing the desirability of exports, a much broader view might be taken. It could be argued that B.C. should expand its production and export of those energy sources which, when used, are the most benign so far as the effects upon the global environment are concerned and cease the export of those that contribute to global degradation. Such a view would lead to the closure of the provincial coal industry, more rapid growth of natural gas exports (and its attendant long-run depletion of reserves) and the more rapid development of hydro potential and the export of electricity to California. In this way British Columbians would contribute to global sustainable development at the expense of sustainable development at home. The dilemma such a situation poses underlines the relevance of spatial scale in the debate on sustainable development.

Energy Supply

Turning to energy supply, the question is what options will be exercised to meet provincial energy requirements by 2030? One option is to focus on the development of domestic resources, the most abundant of which is coal. However, with the exception of use by the electricity supply industry (see below) it is difficult to imagine the circumstances which would lead British Columbia to return to coal as a major energy source. The prospect of an offshore-funded integrated iron and steel industry in B.C., although under consideration, surely cannot be taken seriously. Consequently, it is likely that coal mining and transportation will only expand to the extent that export markets exist and British Columbians choose to compete for them. Natural gas, on the other hand, is in all respects the most attractive fuel with the least damaging environmental implications. Demand will increase rapidly in both domestic and U.S. markets particularly as it becomes a substitute for gasoline. In the context of sustainable development, natural gas has one major disadvantage: it is a non-renewable resource. To be sure, in the short to medium term expanded production would sustain an active exploration program and thus maintain reserves, but over the longer term such production would only hasten the depletion of the resource.

There seems little doubt that the most important energy supply issue facing the province by 2030 will be the supply of petroleum products. It is highly probable that by then there will have been large real price increases which will significantly influence their use and accelerate the development of alternatives such as compressed natural gas, propane and the electric vehicle. Nevertheless, there will probably still be a substantial demand by the transportation sector. Will there still be a competitively priced supply available from the heavy oil and bitumen in Alberta and Saskatchewan, or will there have been large-scale discoveries in the northern frontier areas by then? If yes, the existing pipeline system (perhaps enlarged) will probably be adequate to serve provincial needs, though transporting only petroleum products (not crude) because the coastal refineries will be closed. Such a scenario would meet some of the requirements of sustainable development at the provincial scale because the quality of the atmosphere in the Lower Fraser Valley would be improved by the closure of the refineries. However, there would be significant environmental degradation in Alberta and Saskatchewan.

Another scenario would include the waterborne import of either crude or petroleum products from offshore or, if further large scale discoveries were made in Alaska, by a combination of tanker/pipeline (the West Coast Oil Port Inquiry revisited). As unwelcome as this option appears today, it would be prudent for British Columbians to start considering now under what conditions it could become marginally acceptable if it became necessary. It should be remembered that many areas of the world currently depend on import supply systems on a scale far larger than would be required for B.C. in 2030, and that such a system has been in operation in the U.S. Puget Sound area for many years. In either of these scenarios offshore hydro-carbon exploration (and production if the opportunity presents itself) will occur off the B.C. coast during the period.

Electricity: The Three Scenarios

Electricity, which currently supplies 20% of British Columbia's total energy requirements, is the only form of energy for which there is a carefully considered and formally presented choice of options extending forward almost to 2030 (Table 10.4).

The hydro-electric option meets some of the requirements of a sustainable development strategy. First, it is based upon a renewable primary resource, stream flow. Over the 40 year period, climatic change might result in a reduction of flow beyond the variability already experienced; on the other hand, it might increase it. Second, all stages of the production chain are free of chemical residuals and, third, some multiple use of the completed projects is possible. However, there is considerable biophysical impact as the result of replacing a natural river regime with one managed primarily for power and, upstream of the dam, replacing a riverine environment by a lacustrine one.

The hydro option includes small as well as large projects. Harnessing the potential energy of a large number of small streams means dispersing small production structures and an associated web of low capacity transmission lines through landscapes which otherwise would be unaffected by energy developments. Regulating the environmental disturbance, monitoring the safety of the installations and adapting to a lower level of reliability of supply make this component of the hydro option problematic. Nevertheless, B.C. Hydro is currently preparing development guidelines and by 2030 there will probably be some small hydro, but its total contribution is likely to be of local consequence only.

The thermal-electric scenario proposes that a large component of future electricity supply be based upon coal, municipal solid waste and waste from the wood processing industries. Forty years hence there will still be large supplies of the first two but wood-waste supplies will probably be reduced. Five of the six projects listed in Table 10.4 under this scenario are based on residual fuels which, when burned, produce gaseous (CO_2, SO_2), particulate and solid residuals, and all require water both for process steam and cooling so that the natural hydrological regime will to some extent be disrupted. It is notable that neither natural gas nor nuclear fuels are mentioned in this scenario. However, in the case of the former, gas would be used to fuel the Burrard plant for as long as it remains economically serviceable and several of the private proposals currently being considered by BCH are gas-fired. The use of gas by these projects, at 35% conversion efficiency, is incompatible with sustainable development in the medium to long term. Despite the potential advantages that nuclear fuelled plants have from a sustainable development stand point, B.C. society appears not willing to even consider it for use in the next 40 years. Maybe that will and should change.

The third electricity scenario is based upon a pro-active, intensified demand side management (DSM) strategy with some only tentatively specified input from the energy potential of wind and solar radiation. Intensified DSM would involve large real price increases, prohibition of some end uses and demanding regulations to maximize efficiency of use. Perhaps B.C. society will be ready to accept such measures by 2030; in 1990 the majority would regard them as draconian. The potential role of wind, solar and geothermal in B.C., even assuming greatly improved conversion technology, will be small because of the very limited 'resource' base and, in the case of wind and solar, because of their inherent irregularity of availability (diurnal, seasonal).

It seems that, for electricity supply, the principles of sustainable development can most nearly be met by adopting a mixture of the three scenarios plus some features of the short term (1990-2000) recommended plan. Specifically, these principles will be met to the extent that DSM is practiced, interconnection agreements are made with utilities in neighbouring jurisdictions and downstream benefits are repatriated. As production facilities have to be developed, large scale hydro would be preferred over coal-fired plants. Furthermore, it would be prudent for British Columbians to review the prospect of nuclear plants for there may come a time when nuclear conversion and residual treatment technology improves sufficiently for them to accept the remaining risks and thus avoid or delay the development of northern rivers.

Finally, if any new plant development is to be acceptable within a sustainable development framework, it will be mandatory for the practices of the past to be greatly modified. In the first place, it is necessary that, notwithstanding the uncertainties involved, a longer view be taken by all concerned. In this context, B.C. Hydro's 20-25 year proposals are commendable. Secondly, developer and regulator must commit themselves jointly to the principles of minimizing environmental disruption, practicing adaptive management, providing for multiple use operation and accepting the cost of realistic relocation compensation. Thirdly, society has to be willing to pay a considerably higher price for electricity.

The Fraser River Basin

This section refocusses the spatial scale from that of the province to the Fraser River Basin. As noted the Fraser Basin may conveniently be divided into a large, biophysically diverse and relatively sparsely populated interior basin, and a small, relatively biophysically homogeneous, densely populated coastal basin or Lower Fraser Valley. With some exceptions noted below, the Basin is not now and will not become by 2030 a major energy producing area. Rather, it's role as a conduit for (interior basin) and terminus of (Lower Fraser Valley) major transportation systems for oil, gas, coal and electricity will expand over the next 40 years.

Interior Basin

The potential energy sources of the interior basin include coal in the Bowron Valley and lignite in the Hat Creek Valley, large scale hydro on the Nechako, McGregor and Fraser (at Moran) Rivers, wood waste at the major wood processing centres of Prince George, Quesnel, Kamloops and other centres, small scale hydro in the Upper Fraser-North Thompson and Lillooet River sub-basins and solar radiation in the south central area. To date hydro-carbon potential is not thought to be significant.

Of these potential sources, the most likely to receive serious attention for development by 2030 are the Nechako River (currently underway), the McGregor River, the Hat Creek lignite deposit, wood waste supplies (currently underway at Williams Lake) and some small hydro. The expansion of the Nechako River power system is taking place in the framework of the Nechako Fisheries Conservation Program between the federal and provincial government agencies and the developer, Alcan Ltd. This agreement in many ways appears as an encouraging model for co-operative, adaptive management serving the principles of sustainable development.

There are two options for the development of the McGregor River. One requires the diversion of waters from Peace River system into the McGregor and the other does not. The former, while more energy efficient, raises the spectre of the introduction of organisms from the Peace into the Fraser River with its attendant risks for the Fraser salmon stock. The second option appears to more nearly fit into a sustainable development framework though, to date, minimal environmental assessment has been carried out.

The Hat Creek proposal has already received a good deal of study and public review (BCH, 1981). Of all of the potential developments in the Basin it appears to be the least compatible with the concept of sustainable development. It is based upon a non-renewable (though large) resource and involves considerable environmental disturbance (surface, air, water) at site and more distantly. The preliminary design and environmental assessment considered in some detail the matter of gaseous and particulate emissions into the atmosphere. It did not, however, include consideration of the CO_2 component of the gaseous emissions nor the dispersal of residuals beyond the Hat Creek basin under varying meteorological conditions. In the large potential project category it is noteworthy that the largest hydro potential site in B.C., the Moran gorge on the mainstem of the Fraser, is not mentioned in BCH's hydro scenario. Nevertheless, the potential is there, and, despite the currently unthinkable implications for the salmon runs, it was seriously considered in the 1950's and may be again.

The use of wood waste from sawmills and pulp mills as fuel for the cogeneration of process steam and steam for power generation is an appealing option on several counts. First it can be less expensive than other production choices; second, it makes use of residuals in a manner which results in greatly reduced particulate emissions (but increased CO_2) in contrast with current beehive burning and third, although somewhat incorrectly, it is perceived to be a renewable resource. As a consequence short to medium term expansion of wood waste projects might be expected after which the levelling-off or even curtailment of supplies associated with changes in the annual allowable cut of timber will put a ceiling on the development (Jaccard, et al., 1989).

Small hydro opportunities are not widespread in the interior basin and, even if a significant portion of the potential were developed, its contribution to other than local requirements would be small and, as a consequence of the spatial dispersal of small structures and power lines, the total environmental disturbance could be quite considerable.

If energy production facilities are not going to be a major part of the 40 year future of the interior basin, transportation facilities will certainly be expanded. Short term additions to the electric transmission system are shown on Figure 10.8. The expected increase in sales of natural gas (some taking place already) will require expansion of transportation capacity first by increasing the capacity of existing facilities and then by building additional lines. How disruptive the construction and operation of these facilities will be depends upon the care with which they are carried out. In the past with a few exceptions, the construction phase of pipelines and electric transmission lines has been conducted with minimal and short lived disruption. Once in place, however, the transportation corridors are considered by some to constitute 'visual blight' and there are implications for wild life (some positive, some negative), surface erosion, localized electric fields and the creation of access to former wilderness areas.

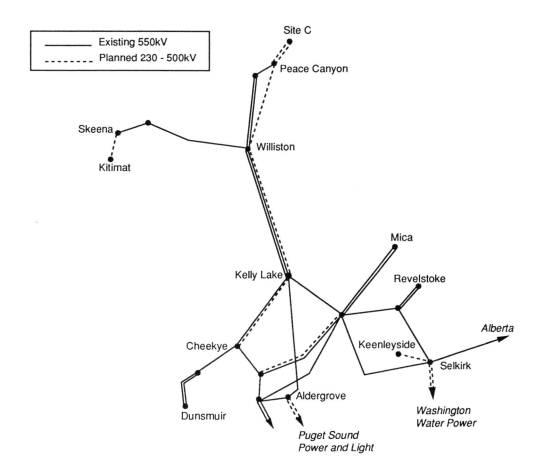

Figure 10.8: B.C. Hydro: Integrated System Major Transmission Additions to Year 2000

Coastal Basin - Lower Fraser Valley

Currently the Lower Fraser Valley has several energy producing and processing facilities including relatively small scale hydro plants (Wahleach, Alouette, Stave Falls), one large gas burning thermal electric plant (Burrard), a small gas-turbine electric plant (Port Mann), and four oil refineries fed by pipeline. It is plausible to speculate that 40 years hence the hydro plants will have been up-graded and still in operation and there will be at least one gas burning thermal electric plant to meet peak load requirements. Two possibilities exist for the oil refineries: they may be all closed and the Lower Fraser Valley will be supplied with petroleum products by pipeline from Alberta or one or two may continue to exist (but probably in a different location) relying on offshore crude. It is also possible that there will be small scale natural gas production in the area.

Forty years from now, the Lower Fraser Valley will probably consume an even greater proportion of the total provincial consumption than now and air quality controls will have been considerably strengthened. From the point of view of end use emissions, the most benign energy forms are electricity and natural gas. BCH's newly introduced Power Smart program is in some instances encouraging a shift from electricity to natural gas (e.g., domestic water heating). In the short to medium term such a shift appears laudable but in the long term it steers consumption toward a non-renewable energy source and one which results in some emissions when burned.

This last example illustrates once again that an acceptable strategy for one area or one time period may be less acceptable for other areas or times. Achievement of sustainable development objectives requires strategies that are dynamic and flexible and continuously aware of the complexities of spatial, temporal and phenomenal linkages.

Conclusions

The first draft of this paper was reviewed by several interested readers. The issues raised by the reviewers have been addressed in part by making changes in the body of the paper but mainly in this concluding section.

Definition of Sustainable Development

The necessary specific working definitions of concepts used in a paper should reflect conventional definitions where they exist or indicate how they differ and what are the implications of the differences. This paper uses the following statement as the conventional definition of sustainable development:

> Sustainable development is positive socioeconomic change that does not undermine the ecological and social systems upon which its communities and society are dependent. Its successful implementation requires integrated policy, planning and social learning processes; its political viability depends on the full support of the people it affects

through their governments, their social institutions and their private activities (Rees, 1989:3).

The working definition given on page one of the paper is narrower than the one above in that it does not explicitly incorporate social systems nor the implementation processes required to bring about change. The definition used for the paper was narrowed because:

- the breadth and complexity of the conventional definition is so great that a careful, considered paper based upon it would have had to be at least twice as long; and,
- the focus on the biophysical component permitted the linking together of two other widely used concepts (resource and environment) in a manner which is considered helpful to the general sustainable development debate.

Significant commentary on the social aspects of B.C.'s energy system is better undertaken by those with a more appropriate disciplinary background than the author (e.g., sociology, political science) provided it is set within the reality of an essentially urbanized society whose energy requirements are highly concentrated and specialized. Furthermore, to deal in an objective and thorough way with the processes by which order of magnitude changes in the structure of B.C.'s energy system can be brought about also requires an appropriate disciplinary context. In this paper, passing reference is made to some of the processes of change but a more penetrating analysis is beyond the present scope.

Climate Change

One reviewer was particularly concerned about the implications for energy production and use in B.C. of the adoption of a program to reduce "warming emissions". Perhaps the first question that should be asked is whether B.C. should adopt a program that specifically targets the emission of "greenhouse" gases expressly for the purpose of reducing global warming? Readers are referred to the three very recent and authoritative reports included in the list of references (B.C.-MEMPR, 1990; PNL, 1990; WMO, 1990, a, b, c) on the basis of which they may come to their own conclusions for appropriate answers. The author of this paper accepts the high degree of uncertainty that continues to exist and would not, at this time, advocate the initiation of programs targeted on the reduction of the emission of "greenhouse gases" for the prime purpose of influencing climate change. Similarly, undertaking programs to influence the role of vegetative cover as a carbon dioxide sink is probably premature considering the views expressed in documents by MEMPR (1990:20-22, 37-46) and PNL (1990:3.2.).

Notwithstanding the above, it is prudent to adopt strategies which will accomplish other objectives of sustainable development as well as contribute to the reduced emission of greenhouse gases. The most obvious directions are to improve the inventory and process information about climate change, increase the efficiency of production and use of all forms of energy, change behaviour patterns, develop and install more effective scrubbing technology, and switch to energy sources which produce less environmentally deteriorating waste products.

In this context, it is instructive to review the CO_2 emission scene in B.C. recently documented in MEMPR, 1990. The major CO_2 emissions in 1988 came from the combustion of petroleum products (16,200 kt p.a.), pulp liquor (14,700 kt p.a.), hog fuel (14,600 kt p.a.), and natural gas (12,000 kt p.a.). The major producers of the CO_2 were the pulp and paper industry (20,800 kt p.a.), prescribed slash burning (13,300 kt p.a.) and road transportation (11,200 kt p.a.). By 2005, the pulp and paper industry contribution is expected to increase to 22,600, road transport to 15,500 and prescribed slash burning to decrease to 9300 kt p.a. Clearly, increasing the efficiency of use of fuels will diminish the rate of increase of emission of CO_2, as would the greater use of public transportation systems, the wider use and improvement in the operation of emission control systems and a move away from the high CO_2 producing fuels.

The latter strategy provides some interesting dilemmas. For example, the use of biomass as an alternative fuel has been widely advocated on the grounds that it represents a shift to what is perceived to be a renewable energy source. Within this view, the use of process wastes from the sawmilling and pulp and paper industry is seen to have the additional advantage of disposing of wastes in a less harmful way than beehive burners, landfill or dumping into the nearest water body. But the burning of these fuels is now shown to be the major source of CO_2 emissions in the province and the Fraser River Basin.

Leaving aside the question of how to dispose of these wastes if they are not burned, what fuel could the pulp and paper industry use in their place? Natural gas would be an obvious choice but it is a non-renewable (non-sustainable) resource, more plentiful in B.C. and Canada generally than conventional oil, but non-renewable nevertheless. The heat required could be supplied by electricity thereby doubling (or more) the already large electricity requirements of pulp and paper manufacturing and thus further increasing the need to expand the electricity supply industry. The latter would have to be either hydro or nuclear based if it were not to emit more CO_2 than the biomass it replaced. And so on.

Alternative Sources

Several reviewers were disappointed with the treatment of such energy sources as solar radiation, wind, geothermal heat, municipal waste and small hydro and the opportunities for "decentralization" of production that harnessing these sources could provide. The potential of "alternative" sources must be considered in the following context:

- The magnitude of B.C.'s current (1988) and future total energy requirements—1095 PJ and over 2000 PJ respectively (Table 10.1);
- Most energy users require a high level of availability and reliability of supply.
- Energy consumption is highly concentrated:

- spatially - over 80% of energy consumption in B.C. takes place in less than 5% of the area of the province;
- sectorally - almost 75% of energy is consumed by 2 sectors (Figure 10.2);
- end use - over 80% is fuel to provide heat (Figure 10.2).

Solar radiation and wind are, by contrast to the above, areally dispersed, intermittently and unpredictably available and only locally available in significant amounts. Similarly, geothermal sources are limited to only a few sites in B.C., are not as renewable as usually thought (in that the supply of the energy carrier, water, may become restricted) and often have undesirable wastes. It was as a result of taking these considerations into account, that it was concluded that these alternatives would have only limited potential.

Other Comments

Two reviewers considered the discussion of energy exports to be inadequate. It is suggested by one that B.C. should use the lower CO_2 emission which results from burning natural gas "...as a bargaining chip in negotiating with the U.S. on policies designed to reduce global warming". Although the author is not aware of any such negotiations being underway or planned, it is agreed that this attribute of natural gas is a further reason for demanding a high price and adopting a careful marketing strategy for this relatively benign fuel.

Other matters mentioned by reviewers included the scope of alternatives considered by forecasting agencies, quantitative data on the energy system of the Fraser River Basin, the use of GNP/GPP as a measure of economic activity and demand side management. In very brief terms, the following observations are made in respect of these comments:

- The methodology, variables and scope of the forecasts are elaborated in depth in the cited references (MEMPR, 1983; BCH, 1989a);
- Regional energy data are not publicly available for the Fraser River Basin;
- As a measure of economic activity GNP/GPP are the best summative indices available but as is generally recognized, they do not include allowances for resource depletion or environmental degradation;
- Demand side management is explicitly considered and the reader is referred to the major publication outlining the BCH program (BCH, 1989a; 1990).

References

B.C. Hydro (BCH). 1981. *Hat Creek Project: Environmental Impact Statement.* Vancouver: BCHPA.

_____ 1989a. *Electric Load Forecast, 1988/89-2008/9.* Vancouver: Forecasting Department, Corporate Affairs.

_____ 1989b. *Twenty-Year Resource Plan: For the Period 1989-2008, Resource Plan: For the Period 1989-2008.* Vancouver: Forecasting Department, Corporate Affairs.

_____ 1990. *Second Annual Electric Energy Forum.* Vancouver: Communications Planning.

B.C. Ministry of Energy, Mines and Petroleum Resources (MEMPR). 1983. *B.C. Energy Demand Forecasting and Planning Model.* Staff Paper.

_____ 1984. *B.C. Energy Supply and Requirements Forecast, 1982-2000.* Victoria: Forecasts and Special Projects Branch, Energy Resources Division.

_____ 1986. *B.C. Energy Supply and Requirements Forecast, 1984-2005.* Victoria: Forecasts and Special Projects Branch, Energy Resources Division.

_____ 1987. *B.C. Energy Supply and Requirements Forecast. Update 1987-1992.* Victoria: Forecasts and Special Projects Branch, Energy Resources Division.

_____ 1990. *Carbon Dioxide Inventory for British Columbia.* Prepared for MEMPR by B.H. Levelton and Associates et. al.

B.C. Ministry of Finance and Corporate Relations (MFCR). 1989. *B.C. Economic and Statistical Review.* Victoria: Communications Branch.

Canada, Department of Energy, Mines and Resources (EMR). 1989. *Demand Side Management in Canada.* Ottawa: Programs Section.

Chapman, J. D. 1989. *Geography and Energy: Commercial Energy Systems and National Policies.* London: Longman.

Jaccard, M., et. al. 1989. *Electricity from Wood Waste: Integrating Energy and Environmental Analysis in British Columbia.* Burnaby: Natural Resources Management Program, Simon Fraser University.

Pacific Northwest Laboratory (PNL). 1990. *Global Warming: A Northwest Perspective.* Proceedings of Symposium, February 9, 1989. Olympia, Washington. Richmond, Washington: PNL 99352.

Rees, W. E. 1989. *Defining "Sustainable Development".* CHS Research Bulletin. Vancouver: UBC Centre for Human Settlements, University of British Columbia.

Taylor, E., and Johnstone, K. (eds.). 1989. *Proceedings of the Symposium on the Impacts of Climate Variability and Change on British Columbia, December 14, 1988, Vancouver,* Scientific Services Division Report. PAES-89-1. Vancouver: Atmospheric Environment Service, Environment Canada.

Vancouver Sun. December 18, 1989. *Editorial.*

Westman, W. E. 1977. "How Much are Nature's Services Worth?" *Science* 197:960-64.

World Meteorological Organization (WMO). United Nations Environment Programme (UNEP). Intergovernmental Panel on Climate Change (IPCC). 1990:

_____ 1990a. *Policymakers Summary of the Potential Impacts of Climate Change.* Report from Working Group II. Mimeo.

_____ 1990b. *Policymakers Summary of the Formulation of Response Strategies.* Report from Working Group III. Mimeo.

_____ 1990c. *Overview and Conclusions. Climate Change: A Key Global Issue.* Draft mimeo.

11

Planning for Metropolitan Liquid Waste Management in the GVRD: An Innovative Approach Towards Sustainable Development

Hew D. McConnell

This chapter describes the Greater Vancouver Regional District's (GVRD) Liquid Waste Management Plan and the process used to develop it. This innovative approach demonstrates how government agencies can involve a range of stakeholders in the planning of environmentally-sensitive projects and programs, and can achieve substantial and timely success in their design and implementation. It is argued here that such processes are models for future planning in the Fraser River Basin, leading towards sustainable development.

The GVRD's Liquid Waste Management Plan

The GVRD's Liquid Waste Management Plan (LWMP) is the latest step in updating the master sewerage and drainage plan for the Greater Vancouver area in Canada. The purpose of the LWMP is twofold; first, to determine how well existing sewerage facilities can handle existing and future sanitary flows; second, to find the most environmentally acceptable and cost-effective ways to dispose of Greater Vancouver's liquid wastes. The LWMP will recommend sewerage and drainage practices (facilities and operations) to protect the receiving environment for other uses such as bathing and aquatic life and habitat.

The GVRD's approach to the LWMP is innovative in two very significant ways. First, the District set out to involve the key stakeholders, both inside and outside of government, in the LWMP from the outset. While requiring a significant commitment of time and resources, the process was effective and produced a timely result that was well received. Second, the LWMP involves a holistic approach to waste management by coordinating, in a single project, decisions on the sewage treatment options, combined sewer overflow and urban runoff management, and industrial waste control. Stage 1 of the LWMP process

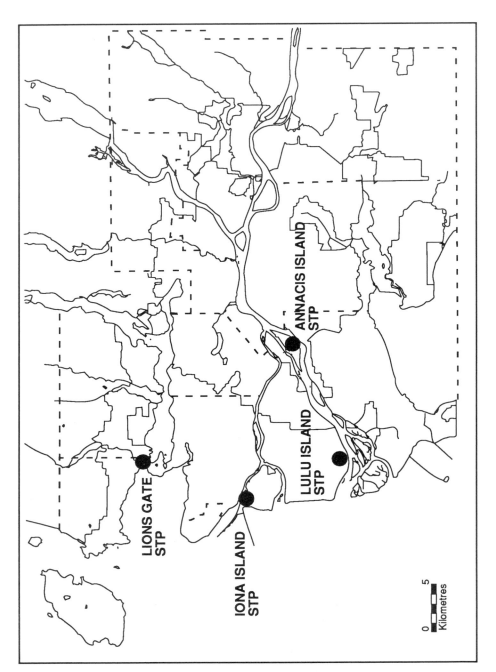

Figure 11.1: The Greater Vancouver Regional District Sewerage Service Area

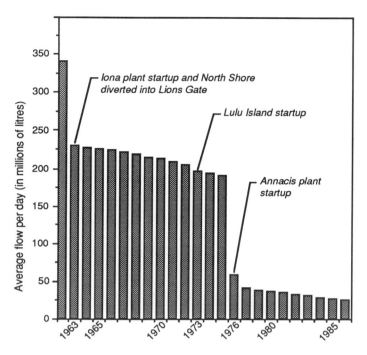

Figure 11.2: Estimated Volume of Untreated Sewage

has provided a model for all future GVRD waste management planning. Furthermore, the LWMP principles can also be applied to liquid waste planning in other areas of the Basin.

The Greater Vancouver Regional District is a federation of 18 municipalities with a combined total population of about 1.5 million (1990); and with a sewerage service area of over 280,000 hectares (see Figure 11.1). Figure 11.2 shows how the volume of untreated sewage discharged from Greater Vancouver has declined over the years. Until the early 1960's, all sewage and drainage flowed directly, to local waterbodies, without treatment. Sewage treatment was first introduced to the region in 1961 and, since then, the District has progressively intercepted more sewage for treatment. From 1976 onward, virtually all sanitary sewage has been treated. A small amount, however, still overflows when heavy rain overloads existing combined sewers in Vancouver, New Westminster and parts of Burnaby. Since 1913, the District has spent about $1 billion building sewerage and drainage facilities within the region.

Municipal sewers collect sewage from private properties and deliver it to regional interceptor and treatment facilities. The District now operates four primary sewage treatment plants, two of which discharge to the Fraser River, one to Burrard Inlet, and one directly to Georgia Strait through a long deep sea outfall. Municipal storm sewers collect storm drainage from private properties and roadways, and discharge it untreated to local waterbodies. Vancouver, New

Westminster, and some parts of Burnaby are serviced by combined sewers which collect sanitary sewage and rainfall runoff in the same pipe. Because the pipes cannot handle peak rainfall, overflows of mixed sewage and runoff occur to local waterbodies. The number of overflows varies from site to site, but estimates indicate over one hundred each year to Burrard Inlet and to the Fraser River North Arm and Main Stem.

In the 1980's, the public became much more concerned about the environment and believed that wastes should be managed better. To address these concerns, the District completed Stage 1 of its LWMP in 1989. Now that virtually all sanitary sewage is collected and receives primary treatment, the emphasis of the LWMP is on a broader range of environmental issues including higher levels of sewage treatment, controls on industrial discharges, and controls on combined sewer overflows and rainfall runoff.

Stage 1 of the LWMP collected existing information, examined existing conditions, developed waste management alternatives in conceptual form and presented a set of realistic waste management options. Stage 2, to be completed in 1992, will examine selected options in more detail and will include recommendations for capital works.

The sections which follow outline the LWMP process in more detail. In particular, they describe the steps taken to involve the public and other key stakeholders in the project. The paper concludes with an outline of lessons learned and future challenges in liquid waste planning for Greater Vancouver.

LWMP Development: A Co-operative Approach

Because the Liquid Waste Management Plan (LWMP) considers a broad variety of issues and interests, the District involved federal, provincial, and municipal agencies, industry, and public groups directly in the process. Many of the participants were also involved in the Fraser River Estuary Management Program (FREMP).

Figure 11.3 shows key features of the co-operative process, namely:

(i)   A multi-agency Steering Committee to advise the District on the scope and general direction of the LWMP;

(ii) Four multi-agency Technical Committees to advise the District on specific technical issues:
- The Water Use and Water Quality Committee looked at existing receiving water conditions, and evaluated their impact on existing and future water uses;
- The Treatment Upgrading and Sludge Disposal Committee developed options and costs for sewage treatment upgrading and sludge disposal, and assessed their applicability to the District's plants;
- The Combined Sewer Overflow and Urban Runoff Committee developed a clear understanding of pollution arising from combined sewer overflows and urban runoff, and evaluated alternatives for reducing contaminant discharges to local receiving waters;

- The Source Control Committee made recommendations on the need for and scope of programs to control industrial waste discharges to sewers at their source.

All of the technical material produced in the LWMP was subject to extensive peer review. For example, the District distributed almost five hundred copies of the "Draft" Stage 1 Plan to individuals and agencies for input and comment. Furthermore, as outlined below, the District took significant steps to involve the public and public interest groups in the process.

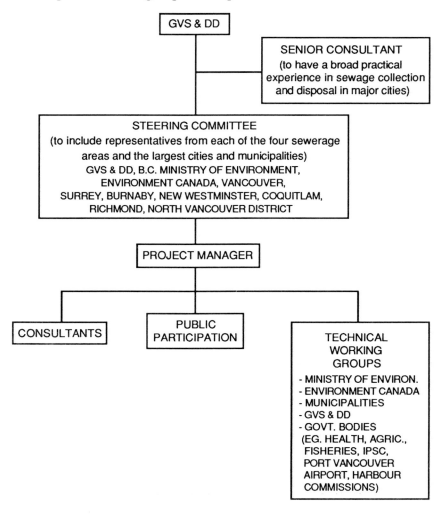

Figure 11.3: Liquid Waste Management Plan for GVRD (Sewage)

It took four years to complete the LWMP Stage 1, and while requiring a significant commitment of resources, built greater awareness about liquid waste planning issues, and contributed significantly to achieving broader acceptance of the Stage 1 Plan.

Stage 1 Liquid Waste Management Plan Findings

Figure 11.4 shows the major waterbodies in Greater Vancouver, and Table 11.1 provides an overview of their environmental quality. Based on limited data, it appears that 14 out of 21 major waterbodies in the region can be rated either "fair" or "poor". This means that water quality is periodically below standards required to support designated uses such as bathing, crop irrigation, and fish. All parts of the Fraser River within the region are rated "fair", with the North Arm of the Fraser River being in the poorest condition.

In all cases, the chemicals of greatest concern in Lower Mainland waterbodies are those which do not break down naturally in the environment, but which persist and accumulate. Examples of these are chlorophenols from wood preserving operations, and lead from car exhausts.

The Fraser River already has a significant load of contaminants when it enters the region. For example, estimates show that wastewater sources in the region contribute less than 10% of the total amount of metals in the Fraser at its mouth (see Figure 11.5). Some of the upstream contaminants are natural, and some come from wastewater discharges in areas outside Greater Vancouver. The District expects the provincial government to evaluate the environmental significance of these upstream sources in more detail and to implement improvement programs.

Within the region, a wide variety of sources contribute contaminants to local receiving waters. Sources which fall within the District's and its member municipalities' jurisdiction are sewage treatment plant (STP) effluents, combined sewer overflows (CSO), and urban stormwater runoff (UR) discharges. Other sources include industrial operations which discharge directly to receiving waters under Permit from the Province, rainfall runoff from agricultural land, sewage discharges from boats, leachates from woodwaste and landfill sites, and spills from ship repair and ship loading facilities.

Sewage treatment plant effluents, combined sewer overflows, and urban stormwater runoff all discharge significant quantities of contaminants to local receiving waters. However, very little data exists on the impact they are having on the environment and on what benefits, if any, improvements in effluent quality would have. There is also insufficient data to determine if the impact of sewage treatment plant effluents is higher than that from combined sewer overflows or urban runoff. Therefore, a co-ordinated, comprehensive environmental monitoring program is required to determine the need for, and scope of, improvements to wastewater facilities, and to form a basis for waste management decision making.

Figure 11.4: Waterbodies Within the Greater Vancouver Sewerage & Drainage District

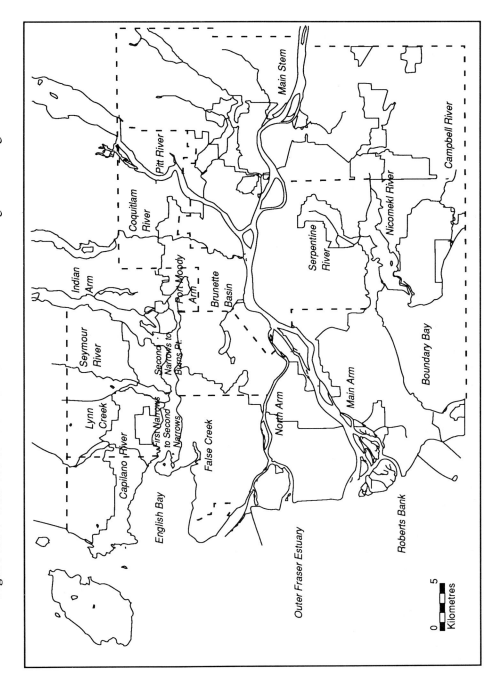

Table 11.1: Overview of the Environmental Quality of Greater Vancouver's
Receiving Waters

	Rating	Apparent Environmental Condition
Fraser River System:		
Fraser River		
Main Stem	Fair	Occasional high concentrations of fecal coliforms and heavy metals.
Main Arm	Fair	Occasional high concentrations of fecal coliforms and heavy metals.
Lower Main Arm	Fair	Occasional high concentrations of fecal coliforms and occasional depleted oxygen levels in sloughs.
Upper North Arm	Fair	Presence of chlorophenols and elevated concentrations of metals in water and sediments.
Lower North Arm	Fair	Chlorophenol concentrations occasionally exceed sub-lethal effect levels, heavy metal contamination in local areas.
Pitt River	Good	Based on pre-1980 data.
Coquitlam River	Good	Based on conditions upstream of gravel operation; water quality decreases downstream of gravel operation due to impact of suspended solids.
Brunette Drainage Basin		
Still Creek	Poor	Frequent exceedances of Criteria for fecal coliform, copper, lead and cadmium.
Burnaby Lake	Fair	Occasional exceedance of various Criteria.
Deer Lake	Fair	Occasional exceedance of Criteria for fecal coliforms, copper and lead.
Brunette River	Fair	Occasional exceedance of Criteria for fecal coliforms, copper and lead.
Roberts Bank	Good	Based on limited data. High biological productivity. Routine operations at coal terminal are not expected to impact water quality.
Sturgeon Bank	Fair	Approximately 10% of the Bank was degraded due to dissolved oxygen depletion resulting from the original Iona Island STP discharge; the discharge has been relocated to deep water in Georgia Strait. Remainder of Bank appears good based on limited data.
Georgia Strait	Good	Based on 1979 monitoring data and pre-operational monitoring for the Iona Island deep-sea outfall.

Boundary Bay System:

Boundary Bay	Fair	Based on 1979 data. Levels of fecal coliforms remain above limits for shellfish harvesting. Pre-1979 data indicate exceedances of Criteria and Objectives for dissolved oxygen and copper.
Serpentine River	Poor	Periodic low dissolved oxygen levels resulting in fish kills; fecal contamination; dissolved cadmium and copper levels frequently do not meet Criteria.
Nicomekl River	Poor	Low dissolved oxygen; elevated fecal coliform counts; ammonia, orthophosphate and copper levels in water regularly exceed Criteria.
Little Campbell River	Poor	Low dissolved oxygen resulted in fish kills as recently as 1985. Elevated fecal coliform counts; concentrations of orthophosphate and copper exceed Criteria.

Burrard Inlet System:

Port Moody Arm	Fair	Limited database. Evidence of localized sediment contamination which exceeds Ocean Dumping Control Act limits.
Second Narrows to Burns Point	Unknown	Database is very limited. Some localized contamination of sediments is evident.
Vancouver Harbour (First Narrows to Second Narrows)	Poor	Sediments from localized areas shown to be highly toxic during sediment bioassays. Metal and PCB concentrations judged to be very high in sediments from localized areas. Organotins measured in sediments and water in localized areas are of concern.
Indian Arm	Good	With exception of periodic fecal coliform contamination at Deep Cove.
Seymour River	Good	Based on limited data. Contamination sources minimal other than urban runoff to lower sections of the river.
Lynn Creek	Unknown	Elevated levels of metals and nutrients due to landfill leachates reported prior to 1985. No recent monitoring data available to evaluate remedial measures.
Capilano River	Good	Based on pre-1979 data.
Outer Burrard Inlet (e.g., English Bay)	Fair	Fecal coliforms occasionally exceed bathing standards in some areas. Subject to combined sewer overflows and occasional oil spills.
False Creek	Poor	Sediment quality exceeds Ocean Dumping Control Act limits. Poor water exchange in Eastern Basin results in continued poor water quality with respect to fecal coliforms and dissolved oxygen.
Queen Charlotte Channel (In Howe Sound)	Fair	Based on 1985-86 closures of bathing beaches. 1978-79 monitoring data suggest large scale releases of mercury and copper.

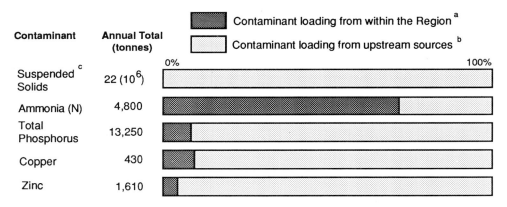

a Annual contaminant loadings from STP's, UR, CSO, and NPS.

b Annual contaminant loadings at Pattullo Bridge.

c Insignificant SS loadings from the Region.

Figure 11.5: Annual Contaminant Loading to the Fraser River System

One of the most effective ways of improving wastewater quality is to prevent contaminants being discharged to sewer at their source; this is called "source control". The District has adopted a new Regional Source Control Bylaw which will ensure consistent controls on industrial discharges to sewers region-wide. However, this program can only be partly successful in reducing contaminants in sewage. Figure 11.6 shows that as much as 60% of some toxic contaminants in sewage originate from private homes and small businesses. Home-owners flush things like old oil, drug prescriptions, and pesticides down the drain. Improved public information programs are required to raise awareness of this issue.

Secondary sewage treatment could take the flow from existing primary plants and provide further contaminant reductions. However, secondary treatment does not remove 100% of the contaminants in waste water, and many nutrients and metals would remain in the discharge to local waters. Also, the higher the level of sewage treatment, the more sludge is generated for disposal. Contaminants become concentrated in the sludge and can restrict options for sludge disposal. Upgrading to secondary treatment at all four District plants, would cost an estimated $500 million, and would add annual operating costs of over $25 million.

A common measure for controlling combined sewer overflows is sewer separation. Sewer separation involves constructing an extra pipe so that sanitary and storm flows are collected in separate pipes. All sanitary sewage is treated and all rainfall runoff discharges untreated to receiving waters. However, research has now shown that separate stormwater runoff, itself, is contaminated, and that sewer separation may not achieve the desired environmental benefits. In fact, sewer separation may make matters worse in some areas.

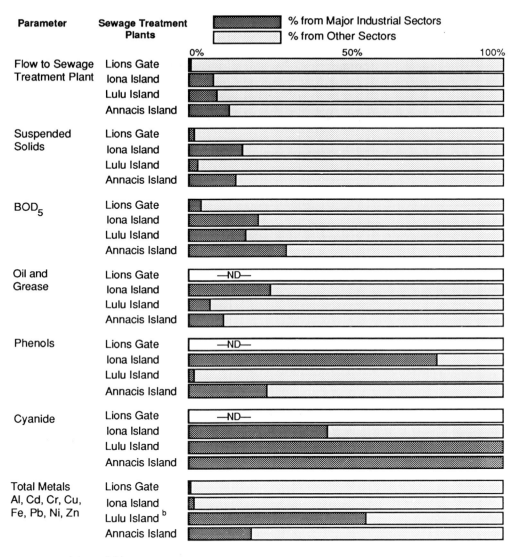

Figure 11.6: Estimated Flow and Contaminant Contributions to GVS & DD Sewage Treatment Plants from Major Discharge Sectors[a]

Another CSO control alternative being used by many North American cities is storage. Storage tanks collect and retain a portion of combined sewer flows until the storm has passed; the stored wastewater is then returned gradually to the combined sewers and to the sewage treatment plant. Storage tanks can be located above or below ground and can be integrated into neighbourhoods to minimize the impact on local amenities. In fact, the tops of underground storage tanks can be used for parking or tennis courts and can increase the amenity of an area.

The cost to reduce combined sewer overflow volumes by 50%, and some contaminants by 75% using storage in Vancouver, New Westminster, and Burnaby, would be almost $500 million. The cost could be higher or lower depending on the level of CSO reduction required. The cost for sewer separation could be higher or lower than storage depending on how quickly the separation proceeds. Existing sewer separation programs in Vancouver, and New Westminster will take about 70 years to complete.

There are a wide variety of options for controlling urban rainfall runoff. Some are more practical than others. An example of a practical option, already in widespread use in Surrey, is the "wet pond". The solid particles in runoff settle out in these ponds, and relatively clear flow passes through to the receiving waters. Sediments and accumulated contaminants can be cleaned out from the ponds periodically as required. However, again, contaminants can be concentrated in sediments which can restrict options for sediment disposal. Regionwide urban runoff controls could cost about $500 million, depending on the level of control required.

To date, the major expense for the Region's wastewater facilities has been borne by the local taxpayer. If this process continues, costs for the regionwide upgrading programs described above could add about $200 - $300 per year to the taxes for each household. Present costs for sewerage and drainage vary from municipality to municipality, but are generally in the order of $100 per year per household. Therefore, priorities must be set to ensure the most benefit is realized for the additional money spent.

Public Information

Over a three month period from October to December 1988, the District presented the findings and issues from its "Draft" Stage 1 Liquid Waste Management Plan (LWMP) to municipal councils, federal and provincial politicians, and the public. This program cost $75,000, and provided opportunities for individuals and groups to have input before the Regional Board received the final Stage 1 Plan for approval.

District staff attended 17 council meetings and held 5 public meetings throughout the Region. To ensure individuals and groups were notified of the public meetings, the District:

(i)   sent over 200 letters from the Chairman of the GVRD Board to federal, provincial and municipal politicians of the Greater Vancouver area;

(ii) sent over 350 letters to non-governmental organizations (such as environmental interest groups);

(iii) contacted by telephone over 100 local neighbourhood groups throughout the region;

(iv) distributed 7,000 flyers announcing the public meetings to elementary and secondary schools, public libraries, public interest groups, and homeowner/ratepayer groups in all municipalities;

(v) made telephone contacts with the university community;

(vi) ran 14 paid advertisements in local community newspapers.

Over 300 participants attended the public meetings and provided the District with valuable insight into the public's perception of liquid waste planning. At each meeting, a lively two to two and half hour question and answer period followed the District's presentation. Even a power blackout at the Coquitlam meeting did not stop the question and answer period, a tribute to the participants' enthusiastic response to the process.

Over 6,000 copies of the LWMP brochure titled "Be Part of the Solution" were distributed to the public libraries in all member municipalities of GVRD, to agencies involved in the Liquid Waste Management Plan, and to people at the public meetings.

Considering the municipal and federal elections were underway during the District's program, media attention was significant. Local community newspapers and major daily newspapers ran in-depth articles on the Plan, and television stations produced several interviews with detailed footage on LWMP issues. As well, local radio news, current affairs, and hot-line programs discussed the issues.

The LWMP Public Information Program enhanced the public's understanding of liquid waste issues and promoted greater communication among participants in the program. Participants became more knowledgeable about the environmental, economic, and social costs and benefits of proposed actions; in return, their suggestions and recommendations helped the District to understand local attitudes and values, and assisted in identifying sensitive issues and concerns in the communities. The program showed that a genuine public interest clearly exists on environmental issues.

Public Response

About 100 questions and concerns were expressed on liquid waste management issues at the public meetings. They fell into major categories as follows:

Source Control

Individuals supported more aggressive source control of waste discharges to District sewers. Many individuals believed that the District needs stricter penalties for industries which fail to comply with the GVRD source control requirements. There was concern that, in many cases, the fines are less than the cost of good waste management practices. As well, individuals expressed the need for a mechanism to control the production of products which contain hazardous chemicals in addition to a mechanism for disposing or recycling. There was general consensus on the need for facilities to handle industrial waste residues, as well as for more public education on the environmental impact of hazardous chemicals.

Sewage Treatment

Individuals were generally concerned about the impact of sewage treatment plant discharges on the environment, and asked the District to consider state of the art sludge disposal methods. Individuals also expressed their desire to make sewage treatment plants comply with existing Provincial Permits.

Waste Management Planning

There was consensus that careful liquid waste planning is needed in the GVRD. However, some individuals expressed concern about continuing studies indefinitely without clear action to resolve problems. Some individuals wanted immediate action in areas where wastewater is clearly impacting the environment. Some people questioned the cost of deferring projects; some suggested that the cost to rehabilitate the environment in the future would be greater than the cost of upgrading now.

Funding

The majority of questions focussed on the funding issue. Many individuals expressed concern about the large costs of upgrading wastewater facilities. Some individuals advocated cost sharing between municipalities and the provincial and federal governments. However, some believed that all government funds ultimately come from local taxpayers and so local taxpayers should bear the burden. Individuals noted that Halifax and Montreal had received commitments of federal funding for upgrading their sewerage facilities and that local politicians should show more initiative in demanding federal funding.

Household Hazardous Wastes

Many individuals expressed concern about how to dispose of household hazardous wastes. In particular, there was consensus that practical collection and disposal methods need to be implemented in the Region. As well, individuals expressed a desire for regulatory agencies to do more to inform homeowners about hazardous wastes and their proper disposal methods.

Combined Sewer Overflows and Urban Runoff

Many participants were unfamiliar with these two sources of contamination and questioned their significance. All participants were surprised by the high frequency of CSO's as well as by the significant quantity of contaminants originating in rainfall runoff.

Water Quality

Participants expressed concern that the 70-year capital sewer reconstruction and "separation" programs in Vancouver would take too long to achieve water quality improvements.

Public Information Programs

At each public meeting, there was acknowledgment and support for the District's open and public process for preparing the LWMP. Individuals encouraged the District to continue with an open public program as the liquid waste planning process continues. People were clearly interested in liquid waste planning issues and the broader questions of waste management in today's society.

Future Challenges in Liquid Waste Planning

Many challenges lie ahead for Greater Vancouver's liquid waste planning process. Some of the major ones are outlined below.

(i)   There is a need to satisfy the public desire for action to improve liquid waste management practices. At the same time, there is a need to take sufficient time to plan major upgrading programs to ensure that money is well spent, and that real progress will be achieved.

(ii)   Elected officials must balance the high public demands for environmental protection, against the ability of governments and the people to pay.

(iii)   Liquid waste management programs must keep ahead of the increased pressure on the natural environment which will be created by substantial population growth.

(iv)   Ways must be found to make environmental legislation and enforcement more pro-active rather than reactive.

(v)   Liquid waste management programs should include measures to reduce public "demand" for sewerage service, for example, reductions in sewage flow through water conservation.

(vi)   The ability to measure contaminants has outstripped the ability to understand the meaning of the measured data. Steps must be taken to understand better the impact of contaminants on water, sediment, and biota, to assist in answering the question of "how clean is clean".

(vii)   Steps must be taken to co-ordinate better the existing regulatory and bureaucratic structure between agencies for environmental management.

(viii) Creative financing options will be required to meet the high costs of upgrading liquid waste management programs.

(ix) Pro-active public information and involvement programs are required to make the public aware of liquid waste management issues. In particular, environmental education should be integrated into the school curriculum.

Reflections on the Liquid Waste Planning Process

The Greater Vancouver Liquid Waste Management Plan is innovative in that it integrates decisions on sewage treatment operations, combined sewer overflow and urban runoff management, and industrial waste control in a single project. From the outset, all sectors of the community recognized the LWMP as an ambitious project.

The Technical Committee and public information programs were keys to involving the many agencies, industries, public groups, and the general public in the liquid waste planning project. The major challenge for GVRD staff was to keep the programs well focussed and to achieve timely progress. The major benefits were that most of the individuals involved in the process achieved a "sense of ownership" of the Plan, and the general public gained heightened awareness of liquid waste planning issues.

All participants in the LWMP process clearly appreciated the District's openness and honesty. As a result, many individuals came to recognize the complexity of liquid waste planning issues, and to appreciate that, while criticism is easy, finding practical solutions is much tougher.

As a result of the Stage 1 LWMP, the District has already completed or is well underway with the following projects:

(i)   Effluent dechlorination was implemented at the Lions Gate Sewage Treatment Plant for the 1990 bathing season at a cost of $250,000. Dechlorination reduces the toxicity of chlorinated effluent being discharged to Burrard Inlet;

(ii) Construction is proceeding with sludge handling facilities at the Lions Gate Sewage Treatment Plant at an estimated cost of almost $5 million. Sludge discharges to Burrard Inlet will cease when these facilities are completed towards the end of 1991;

(iii) The District is working jointly with the UBC Forestry Department on a three year research program to evaluate the potential for disposing of sewage treatment plant sludge beneficially on forest lands. The District has already committed over half a million dollars to this program, now in its second year;

(iv) The District is proceeding jointly with the City of Vancouver on design studies estimated at $1.5 million, to select the most effective measures for reducing contaminant discharges from combined sewer overflows to Burrard Inlet and False Creek. The District is also proceeding jointly with the City of New Westminster and Burnaby on a similar study, estimated at $720,000, to select measures for controlling combined sewer overflows to the Fraser River at New Westminster. Both studies are scheduled for completion by the end of 1991;

(v) The District has adopted a Regional Source Control Bylaw and is now making arrangements for its implementation;

(vi) The District has completed, at a cost of $85,000, a comprehensive Action Plan for improving environmental conditions in Burrard Inlet. The Federal and Provincial Governments, the GVRD, and the Vancouver Port Corporation have established a joint process for implementing the recommended actions;

(vii) The District is proceeding with work to implement secondary treatment at its Lulu and Annacis Island Plants which discharge to the Fraser River. Scheduled for completion in 1994 and 1996, respectively, the projects are expected to cost a combined total of over $300 million;

(viii) The District will submit a Stage 2 of its Liquid Waste Management Plan to the Provincial Minister of Environment in 1992.

Conclusions: The Liquid Waste Management Plan and Sustainable Development

The Stage 1 LWMP process provides a model which can be applied to waste management planning in many areas. Its ongoing success demonstrates that such an integrated approach, involving key stakeholders in the development of the plan, can be effective in achieving timely progress on waste management issues and can contribute to sustainable development in the Fraser Basin and beyond.

12

Institutional Design for the Management of the Natural Resources of the Fraser River Basin

Irving K. Fox

This chapter is divided into three parts. The first part suggests a set of basic considerations to be taken into account in the design of institutional arrangements for management of the natural resources of a river basin in British Columbia. The second part employs these basic considerations in developing an outline of an institutional arrangement for managing the natural resources of the Fraser River Basin. The concluding part highlights and emphasizes the critical issues that need to be addressed in order to strengthen institutional arrangements for management of the natural resources of the Fraser River Basin on a sustainable basis.

Basic Considerations

Sustainability of Biological Resources

An initial consideration is acceptance of the view that biological resources must be so managed that their long term sustainability is not compromised. Furthermore, it is assumed that to assure the realization of this objective, genetic and species diversity must be maintained. All resource development activities must accord with this constraint.

Since the dawn of the industrial era, there has been a growing acceptance by our culture of the view that maintaining the sustainability of natural resources could be a secondary concern because science and technology will assure the production of goods and services to meet human requirements through the manipulation of natural systems. It is increasingly evident that natural biological systems are so complex that society runs great risk by relying on technological advance to compensate for man-made changes in these systems. The conservative policy, therefore, is to maintain sustainability (including the diversity) of biological resources (see Rees, this volume).

This is a complex matter and a thorough justification of the foregoing conclusion would require many pages. A highly respected study by Barnett and Morse published in 1963 has been interpreted to support the view that resource shortages do not constitute a serious problem in the modern world. This study demonstrated that in the U.S. between 1870 and 1957 the costs of natural resource products (with the exception of forest products) declined instead of increased as would be the case if there were a growing scarcity of such products. It is noteworthy that the costs of forest products rose. Also, the authors suggested that "[p]opulation growth constitutes a special problem" (1963:12) and that the threat to the quality of life by population and industrial growth could become very serious. Thus, even this study did not provide convincing evidence that advances in science and technology will assure adequate supplies of natural resource products for a growing population and economy.

I find convincing the views expressed by such writers as Mumford (1970), and Ornstein and Ehrlich (1989) that confidence in science to solve our natural resource and human welfare problems in a world of continuing population and industrial growth is misplaced. This concern arises, in part, because of the effect of industrial growth as well as population growth on the quality of life and social stability, and in part because of the great difficulty of fathoming the complexity of the natural world and assuring the sustainable use of resources over the indefinite future. Therefore, the wise course with regard to the use of natural resources is to avoid development that undermines the sustainability of natural systems. Species and genetic diversity should be preserved, because scientists cannot predict the long-term consequences of the increasing rate of extinction that is now occurring and the consequent loss of the diversity in biological systems that have evolved over millions of years.

In considering how "sustainable development" should be defined, it is concluded that development is appropriate if it is compatible with the long term sustainable use of the biological resources affected and, within this constraint, the development has been decided upon through democratic processes that faithfully reflect a balancing of public preferences and priorities.

Democratic Decision-Making Processes

An underlying premise of this paper is that decisions on the use and management of natural resources should reflect the preferences of members of society affected by a decision. For public preferences to be reflected in decisions in a reasonably accurate fashion, the value frameworks of those affected must determine the decision. An ideal situation exists when all costs and all benefits associated with a decision are borne by those who make the decision, as in the case of the purchase and sale in a fully competitive market of a commodity which involves no external effects. In this kind of situation, self-interest motivations produce a socially optimal result—the classic example of the operation of the "invisible hand". However, because of

(i)   the external effects of some resource uses;
(ii) the economies of scale associated with the production of some resource commodities which result in natural monopolies;
(iii) the indivisibilities of some resource products (e.g., a scenic vista); and,
(iv) the impact of some resource developments and uses upon quality of life and the welfare of future generations,

a market frequently does not allocate resources in accord with the preferences of the individuals affected. Therefore, for many categories of private commercial activities, collective decision-making processes are required to provide a framework for private decision-making that will reflect a democratic balancing of public preferences about how resources should be used. For still other resource based economic activities, either governmental organizations, government supervised private organizations or some type of collective may be required to conduct the activities. *Since a very large proportion of resource use and management activities require some degree of collective decision-making, the development of procedures, processes, and entities through which these decisions are made constitutes the major challenge in the management and use of natural resources.*

It may be argued that through the application of advanced techniques of economic analysis, values incapable of measurement through use of market prices can in fact be determined through technical economic analysis (for example Bowes and Krutilla, 1989; Krutilla and Fisher, 1973). These ingenious techniques can be of great value when applied by a neutral professional economist. However, they are still unsatisfactory in three respects. First, they do not identify the relevant alternatives which merit consideration. Such identification is determined by the value framework of the individual making the evaluation. One of the major criticisms repeatedly made of resource planning organizations is that they have not evaluated the relevant alternatives (Crenson, 1971). Second, the application of economic analyses can still be biased by the value framework of the analyst. This conclusion has been well documented (see Fox and Picken, 1960). Third, some of the issues are not capable of any type of economic analysis. Instead they are concerned about what is right for the society in terms of such matters as the quality of life in a community, the proper distribution of effects, and the welfare of future generations.

In brief, it is proposed that the following conditions must exist in each significant decision-making situation for decisions to accord with public preferences and priorities:

(i)   The alternatives perceived to be relevant by those holding differing value frameworks must be identified;
(ii) Each alternative identified must be evaluated in terms of bio-physical, economic, and social consequences, and the uncertainties that exist;
(iii) Those having differing value frameworks must have the opportunity to negotiate and reach consensus on what constitutes an appropriate decision;

(iv) For all significant decisions, a body elected by majority vote of the public should make the final decision in light of the results of the negotiations among those representing the range of value frameworks.

Dunn (1971) makes an important distinction between growth and development. He states that "[g]rowth implies that an activity system is increasing the scale of its social structure and the quantitative level of its activities". On the other hand, "[d]evelopment implies that an activity system is transformed in its mode of behaviour" (1971:8-9). He characterizes development as "an open process of creative learning". It is evident that in order to adapt to the requirements of sustainable use of resources, there must be a great deal of creative learning. Therefore, it behooves us to develop processes of social decision-making which are in fact creative learning processes. The interactive processes of negotiation in which individuals must contend with others having differing perspectives and holding different values can appropriately be regarded as processes of creative learning.

Natural Resource Interrelationships

Another consideration bearing upon the design of resource management and use institutions is the nature and extent of natural resource interrelationships. Water use in the upper part of a river system affects flow regimes in the lower part of the system. Emissions to the atmosphere may have continent-wide effects. Of major importance is recognition of the fact that the components of the ecological system are intricately interrelated. It is essential that resource management institutions be capable of taking into account these interrelationships in order to maintain sustainability and make best use of resources.

Human Behaviour and Decision-Making.

A widely held perception of human behaviour as it relates to decision-making is that an individual considers the choices available, weighs the consequences of each alternative, and selects the alternative that best serves his or her self-interest—a "rational" process in the terminology of economists. It is now recognized that this model is an over-simplification of human behaviour which has features other than self-interest motivations that are important for institutional design. (There is an enormous literature on human decision-making behaviour; for example, see Janis and Mann, 1977). For the purposes of this paper, the following features are important.

(i)   Self-interest is an important human motivation but it must be taken into account within a broader picture of human behaviour;

(ii) Individuals often do not become well informed about the consequences of alternative courses of action. *Cognitive dissonance* may cause an individual to ignore information that conflicts with preconceived notions or what he/she

would prefer to believe. The burden of becoming well informed may cause a person to make decisions without considering all relevant information;
(iii) Tightly knit organizations or groups may evolve an internal discipline which has been referred to as the "group think" phenomenon—a situation which causes an individual to exclude from consideration information which conflicts with the position prevalent in the group (Janis and Mann, 1977);
(iv) As a result of common educational and work experiences, members of a profession tend to develop a uniform way of processing (or rejecting) information;
(v) And, of major importance, it is now well recognized that the self-interest motivation of individuals is tempered, and at times replaced by what is considered to be socially desirable—i.e., moral considerations. The importance of these motivations of individual behaviour in institutional design is emphasized in a growing body of literature (see Mansbridge, 1990; Etzioni, 1989; Solomon, 1990; Daly and Cobb, 1989).

These behavioural considerations are important for the design of institutional arrangements for resource management and use in several respects:

- Self-interest motivations provide a sound basis for the design of processes in which market forces take into account all costs and all benefits involved in a market transaction. In many cases (such as where there are external effects like those of air and water pollution), the imposition of constraints on the way the market functions are required in order to assure that values not capable of valid measurement through market forces are in fact weighed through collective action.
- Processes to foster the consideration of all relevant information bearing on a resource use decision should be built into the institutional design. This can be done by requiring the interaction of individuals with differing value frameworks, who thus have different perceptions of what constitutes relevant information, in arriving at collective decisions.
- Explicit provision should be made to build on the natural moral motivations of people to arrive at the collective decisions required to manage and use resources in accord with the overall public interest. This point merits further elaboration.

Since, as previously noted, a large proportion of the decisions relating to the management of natural resources cannot be made through the unrestrained operation of market forces, collective decisions are required in order to take into account the welfare of the affected population. Thus, the common good rather than the self interest of individuals must dictate what is done. The "invisible hand" operating through the forces of a competitive market cannot serve the common good unless it functions within a framework prescribed by society to serve the public as a whole.

Within a community there is a natural emotion of human beings to do what is right in terms of the welfare of others (Solomon, 1990). These moral motivations have their greatest influence in small communities because the effects of actions upon others in the community are much more evident than when one lives in a larger, more impersonal society. Therefore, the decentralization of public and private decision-making to social environments in which the welfare of the community is strongly felt will tend to be more conducive to the effective implementation of practices that serve the common good than through centralized decision-making. This does not imply that the common good will always be served nor does it imply that the good of the nation or the province will be properly weighed. As noted below, a system of inter-governmental checks is therefore required to assure the integrity of the system.

Collective decisions involve negotiations among the members of the collective group. It may be argued that the negotiators will be motivated by self-interest in the conduct of their negotiations.[1] Certainly some negotiators will be motivated by self interest to some degree, but it is now well established that perceptions of what is best for the community will motivate participants to a substantial extent. For example, advocacy groups concerned about global warming, the preservation of biological diversity, or the effects of water pollution are generally motivated by a concern about what is right from a social point of view rather than what will best serve their self-interest.

The moral dimension of resource management and use decisions implies that local ownership and control of private resource development and use organizations is preferable to absentee ownership. Since decisions by private organizations which are based outside of the region are remote from the social concerns of the community, their decisions are not subject to the same degree to the moral motivations that influence the decisions of locally based organizations. Morevover, large corporate enterprises have the capability to exercise a degree of political influence that is incompatible with democratic decision-making. That influence will be used to serve the corporate interest as opposed to the common good to a greater extent than if it were a regionally-based organization.

Balancing the Preferences and Countervailing Influences

Of major importance in the design of institutional arrangements for the management of natural resources in a region of British Columbia is the premise that management and use decisions should reflect an appropriate balancing of the preferences of the people of Canada. Implicit in this premise is a requirement that certain authorities and responsibilities for management of natural resources be assigned to regional jurisdictions, to the provincial government, and to the federal government.

In view of the fact that with few exceptions the people of a region are most directly affected by the way the resources of the region are managed and used, and since members of the regional public are in a better position to be informed

---

1   "Public choice theory" seeks to demonstrate that government decision-making is a product of self-interest motivations (see for example Russell, 1979; Breton, 1974). Recent literature opposes this theory (see for example Mansbridge, 1990).

about the resources, their potentials, and the consequences of alternative management and use decisions, it is concluded that planning and implementation of the management and use of regional resources should be the primary responsibility of regional jurisdictions. Furthermore, there is substantial support for the view that smaller units of government are more conducive to democratic processes than larger units and, therefore, reflect public preferences more accurately.[2] However, control over the exercise of these responsibilities should not be unrestrained. In order to insure that the provincial and federal interests are not compromised, the Provincial jurisdictions should have authority and responsibility to restrain regional actions, when there are significant consequences for people outside of the region in the province. Similarly, the federal government should have such authority and responsibility when there are significant consequences from regional or provincial actions for people outside of the Province. This formulation departs from the present institutional structure by envisioning a major role for regional jurisdictions.

It should also be kept in mind that in any jurisdiction, political forces may operate contrary to the public interest, no matter how well they are designed. A charismatic politician or an economically powerful organization may have an inordinate influence on governmental decisions. A sharing of responsibilities for resource management will create countervailing influences that will help to limit the opportunities for using natural resources in a manner contrary to the overall public interest. The provincial levels must contend with a well informed local jurisdiction which will be able to reveal weaknesses in actions the province proposes. The regional jurisdiction should be subject to the coordination of its programs with those of other jurisdictions and to an audit of regional programs to assure conformance with sustainability standards. The federal government must carry out its responsibilities in light of well informed agencies at both the provincial and regional levels (for a rigorous and detailed analytical rationale for a "compound" system of government, see Ostrom, 1987).

Determining Public Preferences: The Problem

The foregoing considerations lead to the need to examine the practical problems of designing arrangements at each level of government which will reflect reasonably well public preferences within the jurisdiction served. As previously noted, for this to be achieved, the options that merit consideration with regard to a potential resource decision must be identified and the consequences of each option determined. If this is not done, the concerned members of the public are in no position to decide which alternative accords with their preferences. Furthermore, without the identification of the options and a reliable assessment of

---

2   It is of interest that de Tocqueville, in his famous treatise , *Democracy in America,* (first published in 1835) extolled the virtues of the decentralized governments he found in the United States at that time. See, for example, his Chapter V on townships and municipalities. In their study of *Size and Democracy,* Dahl and Tufte (1973) conclude that "....very small units seem to us necessary to provide a place where ordinary people can acquire the sense and the reality of moral responsibility and political effectiveness in a universe where remote galaxies of leaders spin on courses mysterious and unfathomable to the ordinary citizen."

their consequences, there is no basis for responsible and effective negotiation among those holding different preferences—an essential requirement for democratic collective decision-making. There are several obstacles to the realization of these conditions, namely:

(i)   Under the current governmental system, minority preferences tend to receive limited consideration because legislative representatives are elected by majority vote in each district. Thus, the options preferred by the minority often are not clearly defined and assessed by governmental organizations responsive to a majority view, and the minorities often lack the expert assistance required to define the alternatives in an explicit fashion;

(ii) Natural resource issues are technically, economically, and socially complex so that it is difficult for the interested citizen and groups to marshall the expertise required to identify the choices that merit consideration and their biological, social, and economic consequences;

(iii) Because of this technical complexity of resource management issues, governmental decisions tend to be highly influenced by professional experts and the bureaucracy in which they function. There is a well entrenched presumption that once policies are established by elected representatives, program design and implementation is simply a technical task. However, early in this century Robert Michels, in recognizing the need for a bureaucracy, saw a dilemma for democratic governments, stating that "democratic social action is possible only through bureaucratic organization, and bureaucratic organization is destructive of democratic values" (as quoted by Crozier, 1964:176). Studies have established that each profession tends to develop its own set of values and operates within a social discipline stemming from the organization within which it functions. Thus, professional and bureaucratic values influence the range of options considered and the design of programs implemented (see for example, Janis and Mann, 1977). This results in decisions that do not reflect public preferences, as would be arrived at through negotiation among different interests in light of responsibly conceived and carefully evaluated options. Some means must be found to deal with this problem, if Michels' dilemma is to be avoided.

With regard to elected officials, an alternative to the existing system of election is to adopt a system of proportional representation, as is employed in some European countries. Even if this were done—and it does not appear to be a practical alternative in Canada—the other two problems would remain. It is evident that if the public is unwilling to turn over decision-making completely to the majority and the professional experts, members of the public, or representatives of a full range of interests found in the body politic must devote a great deal of time to understanding resource management issues, the options that merit consideration in individual cases, and the consequences of each option. This will entail the unprecedented involvement of members of the public in policy development, progam planning, and the monitoring of policy and program implementation. It will also require negotiations by representatives of the public with one another in an effort to reach consensus on resource policies and programs. All interests will need to have access to the technical resources required to conceptualize and evaluate alternatives that accord with their preferences.

Determining Public Preferences: The Process

In the preceding section, it was concluded that if public preferences are to be properly weighed, members of the public holding differing value frameworks must be involved in the decision-making process. They must participate in the identification of alternatives that merit consideration, they must become well informed of the biophysical, social, and economic consequences of each alternative, and they must negotiate with others holding differing views in an effort to reach a public consensus.

The activities of government are manifold and it cannot be expected that for each governmental activity all members of the public will be capable of identifying alternative courses of action that merit consideration and evaluate the consequences of each alternative. The time available to an individual is simply not sufficient for such a task. Sociologists have found that, faced with this problem, individuals follow the lead of a collective or reference group with members whose values they share (Etzioni, 1988). Furthermore, even if a large number of people could become well informed on a given issue, it would be impracticable to conduct negotiations effectively through a large group. These considerations suggest that individuals accepted by others as representing a given value framework should be designated to participate in the decision-making process.

To be well informed on resource management and use matters requires that an individual become familiar with a substantial amount of technical analyses, usually produced by professionally trained experts. Therefore, an individual who represents a given value framework in the decision process must have access to technical evaluations of the biophysical, social, and economic consequences of alternative decisions.

With the foregoing considerations in mind, institutional arrangements for arriving at collective decisions at each level of government must provide

(i)   for a suitable way of selecting the representatives of differing value frameworks who are to participate directly in the identification of alternatives and the negotiation of consensus agreements; and,
(ii) an appropriate means of supplying such representatives with the technical analyses they require.

Finally, it must be recognized that the process envisioned should be subject to a periodic check by all interested members of the public. For example, when a resource management and use plan is being devised, the public should have the opportunity to react (preferably in a public meeting), first when the alternatives have been identified, and second, when the alternatives have been evaluated but final conclusions have not been reached.

Native Claims

A final consideration relates to the issue of Native claims. A large proportion of the Canadian population recognizes that Native people have been deprived of resources which are rightfully theirs, and believes that land claims should be settled to redress this injustice. Such settlements appear likely to return very substantial resources in British Columbia to Native control (see Thompson, this volume). When such settlements are made, it would be only reasonable for the Native people to have the same control over the returned resources as is exercised by a private property owner. This should mean that these resources should be used and managed on a sustainable basis. Since there may be differences over how sustainability is defined, provision should be made for joint agreement by the Native people and the provincial government on the definition of sustainable use. The definition would apply not only to Native-owned resources but also to other privately owned resources and crown-owned resources. Since understanding of the requirements that must be met to assure sustainability will evolve over time as scientific knowledge advances, it will be necessary to make provision for updating the definitions from time to time. Also a Native-provincial monitoring system for the management and use practices being applied to all resources, regardless of ownership, would be required.

Pending the settlement of land claims, Native involvement in regional resource management activities is essential to assure that native perceptions of what constitutes appropriate management and use practices are taken into account in the design of resource management and use plans.

An Institutional Structure

This description of an institutional structure for the management and use of the natural resources of the Fraser River Basin is no more than a very broad outline. A detailed description would require book-length treatment. Therefore, this section identifies only the main features of a proposed institutional structure which stem from the basic considerations specified in the preceding section of this paper. The description does not cover the role of the federal government, which can be important with regard to fisheries, and some other matters of national significance, such as resource use practices related to global warming.

Provincial Responsibilities and Structure

The provincial government is the primary source of authority over management and use of the resources of the province. Therefore, provincial legislation must establish the role and responsibilities of subordinate jurisdictions, such as regional districts, as well as decide upon what activities will be undertaken by the provincial government itself and what policies it will pursue. This section outlines the main features of the proposed provincial level framework, including policies and responsibilities.

Defining and Enforcing Standards of Sustainable Resource Use

There has been a great deal of discussion of the meaning of "sustainable development" since this term was coined. However, little progress has been made in defining how the concept should be applied in the day-to-day management of resources. As previously stated, my position is that resource use should be constrained by a requirement that such use not limit the ecological sustainability of the resource base. Developments undertaken within this constraint are acceptable if they reflect public preferences and priorities. In accord with these concepts, definition of the requirements which must be met to assure the sustainability of agricultural resources, forestland resources, wildland resources, water resources, and atmospheric resources are essential if the concept of sustainable use is to be implemented.

An important responsibility of the provincial government should be to develop these definitions in terms of acceptable practices (standards) for the use and management of each category of resources so that they can be applied by those engaged in these activities. Representatives of the Native people should participate in the development of these standards. Also, it will no doubt be necessary to update these standards periodically in order to take into account scientific advancements in understanding what sustainable use entails. Furthermore, it is suggested that the regional districts be responsible for enforcing adherence to the standards and that the provincial government make a periodic audit of the application of the standard practices. The provincial government should have responsibility to act on appeals of actions by the regional districts in the implementation of the standards. These processes are essential if British Columbia is to give more than lip service to the concept of sustainable resource use.

It will not be easy to arrive at acceptable standards for sustainable resource use because it is evident that scientific knowledge is not adequate to indicate with certainty what practices are fully compatible with sustainable use. Therefore, it will be necessary to negotiate a definition in light of scientifically established knowledge, the uncertainties that exist, and the practices available to minimize uncertainties.

Tenure Arrangements for Resource Use

A wide range of tenure rights to resource use exist under provincial law. These include private property rights in land, rights to divert and utilize specified quantities of water, rights to cut timber on crown land, and rights to guide hunters and recreationists on certain areas of crown land. It is not practicable to examine the many aspects of these rights in this paper, even if I were qualified to do so (see Scott, this volume). It is recognized that the purpose of such tenure arrangements is to provide the prospective resource user with sufficient security to justify the investment required, or to provide the security essential to the welfare of an individual. It is suggested that such tenure arrangements should adhere to the following principles:

(i)   Resource use by all tenure holders should be subject to the constraint of sustainable use;

(ii) The tenure holder should be responsible for any costs or adverse impacts on others resulting from using resources available under the tenure right;

(iii) Tenures for use of crown-owned resources should be for a period no longer than necessary to amortize the investment required to use the resource efficiently or to meet the objective of individual security. During that period, the tenure should be subject to sale by the tenure holder to another qualified party;

(iv) Where multiple products can be derived from crown-owned resources and the tenure does not apply to all of the potential uses, a multiple use plan for the area for the period covered by the tenure agreement should be developed by the regional jurisdiction at the time the tenure is granted, and the tenure holder should be required to conduct activities in a fashion compatible with this plan;

(v) Tenure arrangements should not be permitted to create monopoly or oligopoly conditions over resource supplies in a region;

(vi) The province should receive payments for the resource products derived from crown resources by tenure holders that are equivalent to those that would be derived under competitive market conditions. (A paper by Scott [1976] provides an innovative way of applying this principle to timber production);

(vii) The majority of the investors in an organization awarded a tenure, and the majority of the investors of an organization producing the primary products from the tenured area, should preferably be residents of the regional jurisdiction in which the tenure is located. As a minimum, they should be residents of British Columbia.

Provincial Involvement in Resource Use Planning

There are a number of responsibilities related to planning the management and use of resources that should be discharged by the provincial level of government, including the following:

(i)   The establishment of a uniform system of resource data collection to be employed by the regional jurisdictions;

(ii) Identification of opportunities for resource development and use that transcend regional boundaries and, in cooperation with the affected regional jurisdictions, the preparation of coordinated plans and implementing arrangements for taking advantage of such opportunities;

(iii) Identification of the trans-regional consequences of proposed regional programs for resource use and development, and regulation of regional actions to prevent adverse effects of a regional program on other regions or to capitalize on potentials for maximization of benefits to the province as a whole through resource use and development.

Provision of Professional Assistance

Each regional district probably would not be able to afford employment of a full range of specialized professionals on every aspect of resource management. Thus, it is suggested that the provincial government should employ such a range of specialists and make them available to assist regional districts when their assistance is needed.

Report on the State of Provincial Resources

In the section below on the reponsibilities of regional districts, it is proposed that each district prepare an annual report on the state of the region's resources. This report would cover the supply of the various resources, including the quality of the supplies, an assessment of the outlook for maintaining the current level of use of the supply in the future, and any significant changes in the supply outlook since the previous report. The provincial jurisdiction would consolidate the information in the regional reports into a report covering the province as a whole.

Undertaking Scientific Research on Natural Resources

The field of natural resources is fraught with many uncertainties and will continue to be for the indefinite future. The provincial government should, therefore, support a strong research program. A significant part of this research should be undertaken within the natural resources agency because without the opportunity to engage in research, it will be difficult for the natural resources agency to maintain a staff of well qualified scientists to advise on government programs and assist regional jurisdictions. At the same time, half or more of the research can appropriately be undertaken through grants for support of research by universities and research organizations.

Provincial Organization Structure

No effort will be made to suggest a detailed design for the provincial organization structure required for the management of natural resources. Several features are regarded to be of fundamental importance for the effective discharge of provincial responsibilities.

It is assumed that it will continue to be necessary to have separate ministries to deal with minerals and agriculture. Minerals are not renewable resources and involve policy and program issues that are quite different from those encountered in the management of renewable resources. Agriculture is concerned with resources largely in private ownership and government's primary role is to provide services and an economic environment that fosters a healthy agricultural industry. In contrast, for water, crown lands including forestlands, wildlife, fisheries, and the atmosphere, the provincial government has custodial responsibilities. Furthermore, these resources are highly interrelated and must be managed on an integrated basis. It is proposed, therefore, that provincial responsibilities for these resources be assigned to a single ministry, a ministry of renewable resources. It is proposed that the ministry of renewable resources would participate with the ministry of agriculture in the development of sustainable use standards, and the ministry of renewable resources would audit and enforce compliance with established standards. Similarly the ministry of renewable resources would participate with the ministry of mines in establishment of sustainable use standards applicable to mineral development activities and the ministry of renewable resources would audit and enforce compliance with established standards.[3]

The aim of the ministry of renewable resources should be to assure that provincial renewable resources are managed and used on a sustainable, integrated basis so as to assure maximum benefits to the people of the province. Accordingly, instead of having major subdivisions of the ministry deal with individual resources (e.g., water, forests, wildlife, etc.), major subdivisions would have responsibilities relating to resource managment in defined geographic areas and these areas would, for the most part, be defined along river basin boundaries. (See Aberley, 1985, for the rationale of employing "bio-regional " subdivisions). One such geographic area might well be the Fraser River Basin. Each such unit within the ministry would be staffed with professional specialists in different fields, such as hydrology, timber production, wildlife biology, outdoor recreation, etc. With reference to the regional jurisdictions in its area, the geographic area management unit would be responsible for auditing adherence to adopted sustainable use practices, the review and critiquing of regional plans, the coordination of interregional resource management activities, producing a periodic assessment of the resource base in the geographic area, and assisting the regions in securing expert assistance when needed. In addition to these subdivisions by geographic area, the ministry would no doubt require a research division composed of professionals in the various scientific fields, a unit that would work on a continual updating of the definitions of sustainable resource use practices, and a statistical division that would process and make available data on the resources of the province.

Associated with the minister's office, there should be what will be referred to as the *Citizens Resource Management Council.* This body, which should consist of no more than ten or twelve members, would make an annual review of the policies and programs of the ministry in light of the annual report on the status of the natural resource base of the province, a review of the coordination activities of the ministry, and any special analyses it found necessary to have made of such matters as tenure arrangements, resource use fees, and the sustainable use standards being applied by the ministry.

A major responsibility of the Council would be to participate in the development of sustainable resource use standards. The professional staff of the

---

3   It is a well known feature of bureaucratic behaviour for an agency to become an advocate of the interests which it serves. To assure effective enforcement of sustainable use standards, this responsibility for minerals should not be assigned to the ministry of mines and similarly the responsibility for agriculture should not be assigned to the ministry of agriculture.

resource ministries should make the analyses required to arrive at suitable standards. As previously noted, a great many uncertainties exist. Council members should consider these uncertainties and seek to reach a consensus on how these should be dealt with in arriving at acceptable standards. Final decisions should be a ministerial responsibility.

Considerable thought should be given to the design of the Council arrangement. It would be important that political considerations of the party in power not determine membership on the Council.[4] It would also be important that the individuals selected reflect the range of perceptions with regard to resource management found in the public at large. Finally, it would be desirable that members serve for a limited term, such as three years, and not be eligible for reappointment. This is necessary to avoid having members of the Council develop relationships with the bureaucracy of the ministry which would colour their judgements on the issues they should address. One possibility, with regard to selection of Council members, would be to assign this responsibility to a committee composed of the presidents (or vice presidents) of the provincial universities. Nominations could be made by members of the public for consideration by the committee. It would be essential that members be paid and that the amount of payment be determined by the amount of time devoted to the work of the Council.

Should the ministry undertake to coordinate a planning activity involving two or three regional districts, the planning should be undertaken by the *Resource Management and Use Councils* (for a full description of these bodies, see below) of the affected regional districts and the staff of the ministry should have a coordinating role. The process should be similar to the one outlined below for the regional districts. If basin-wide planning should be required for proper management of some responsibilities (as will likely be the case), a separate planning Council should be organized to conduct this activity and the processes followed would be similar to the one outlined for regional districts. It is suggested that each district Council designate one or two of its members to serve on the basin-wide Council. Ministry personnel together with staff seconded from individual districts would serve as the staff of the basin-wide planning Council.

Regional Jurisdictions: Role and Responsibilities

It is proposed that the primary responsibility for planning and implementing governmental resource management and use programs and policies be assigned to regional jurisdictions, in accord with the standards for sustainable use prescribed by the provincial government, provincial policies governing tenure, and the coordination of external effects by the provincial level, as described in the preceding section. The regional jurisdictions might have responsibilities for activities other than resource management as well. As a minimum, it would appear logical that they absorb the responsibilities of the current regional

---

4   Final decisions are, of course, of a political nature. Therefore, the political level must make final decisions on matters considered by the Council.

districts. The sections which follow relate only to the discharge of resource management responsibilities.

The Nature of the Regional Jurisdiction

The basic purpose of the regional jurisdiction would be to manage the resources of the district for which it is responsible on a sustainable basis in accord with the public preferences of the residents of the region. The regional district would be governed by an elected regional board of no more than ten members. The boundaries of the district would follow drainage basin lines within a major river basin.

Regional District Responsibilities

The regional district would have three major responsibilities. One responsibility would involve integrated management of crown resources on a sustainable use basis, including air, land, water, fisheries, forests, wildlands, and wildife. With regard to air and water, this includes regulation of emissions to the atmosphere and discharges to waterways in the interest of protecting public health, as well as in maintaining resource use sustainability. Its second responsibility would be to regulate the use of privately owned agricultural lands, forestlands, and wildlands, in the interest of assuring the long term sustainability of these resources. Finally, it would be responsible for making an annual assessment of the status of the resource base in the district in terms of its sustainability over the long term.

There appears to be some confusion over what is meant by integrated resource management. In this paper it is assumed that the aim of integrated resource management is to realize maximum benefits from an interrelated set of resources, within the constraint of sustainable use. This entails first a determination of what practices (plan) will maximize benefits from each potential use when considered without regard for the impact of each use on other uses. Then the relationships among the separate plans are identified and a determination made of how the various single use plans must be changed to maximize benefits from the interrelated set of resources as a whole. This task is complicated by the fact that there are often major uncertainties about the effects of a given use and the inability to measure benefits and costs from each use in the same quantitative terms.

Public Involvement In the Planning and Management Process

As indicated in an earlier section of this paper, in most cases of government decision-making on resource management and use matters, economic analysis by itself cannot be expected to produce results that reflect a balancing of public preferences. It was concluded that a group of representatives of the range of interests found in the public at large should be responsible for the initial formulation of alternative resource management and use plans. These alternatives would then be subject to review and criticism by those interested members of the public before final recommendations are made to a body elected by majority vote.

With this general structure and process in mind, the planning and monitoring of the management activities of each regional district would be the responsibility of what will be referred to as the *Resource Management and Use Council*. It would be organized and function as follows:

(i)   Members of the Council would represent the range of values of the residents of the regional district. It would consist of no more than ten members, with members serving a term of no more than three years, and the terms of approximately a third of the members expiring each year;

(ii)   Members would be selected by a magistrate of a court in accord with the instruction to select a body of residents who will capably represent the range of values found in the district. Where Native people are residents of the district, at least two Native people should serve as Council members. Any resident of the district would be able to nominate individuals for consideration by the magistrate;

(iii) A body of qualified professionals would serve as the staff of the Council in order to provide the Council with the technical support it requires;

(iv)   When a planning activity is to be undertaken, the first task of the Council would be to work out with the staff an understanding of the information it will require for the planning. With this information in hand, the following process would be followed:

-    The Council, with the assistance of the staff, outlines a plan for each use of the resources involved (timber production, recreation, wildlife, fisheries, irrigation etc.) which will optimize returns from that use, *if effects on other uses are not taken into account;*

-    Employing these single use plans as a foundation, the Council and staff then formulate and evaluate in rough form a set of alternative integrated resource management plans believed to merit consideration. The differences in the alternative integrated plans will be the result of different weights being given to values associated with each resource use or a different approach being taken to the uncertainties about the consequences of the various potential uses;

-    A public meeting is held to review the draft alternative integrated plans and the information on which they have been based. The aim of this meeting would be to determine whether the alternative plans reflect the views of the public about the alternatives that merit consideration. This might result in additions to or subtractions from the list of draft alternative plans presented;

-    The Council, with the assistance of the staff, will then prepare a detailed evaluation of each alternative integrated plan in terms of its biophysical, economic and social effects, if it were implemented;

- A second public meeting is then held to secure public reactions to the alternatives, in light of the evaluation of each alternative;
- Following the public meeting, the Council members, taking into account the evaluations of each alternative and the reactions received at the public meeting, endeavour to reach agreement on a single plan to recommend to the regional board. If agreement cannot be reached on a single plan, two or more plans will be submitted to the regional board together with a statement of the views of each Council member for supporting or opposing each alternative plan;
- The Board reviews the recommendations and views of Council members and decides upon the plan to be implemented;
- At periodic intervals, while the plan is being implemented, the staff of the Council monitors adherence to the adopted plan. In case of departures from the adopted plan, the Council will assess their implications and report its assessment to the regional board and the public;
- If during the time the plan is being implemented, those involved in its implementation conclude that changes in the plan are called for, the conditions giving rise to this conclusion will be reported to the Council, which will assess the proposal and submit its recommendations to the regional board for decision.

Council members would be paid for their services in accord with the amount of time devoted to Council matters.

Regulation of the Management and Use of Privately Owned Resources to Assure Sustainable Use

It is assumed, as previously proposed, that the provincial government, will develop detailed specifications of what constitutes sustainable use of all resources, and the penalties to be applied if a property owner fails to adhere to these standards. All private owners of resources will be informed of these standards. At periodic intervals, staff members of the regional district will audit resource use practices of private owners. If violations are found, penalties provided for in provincial legislation will be applied and the violations and penalties imposed will be reported to the public.

Annual Report on the State of the Natural Resources of the Regional District

Each regional district would be expected to produce annually a report on the state of natural resources of the district, covering both privately owned and crown resources. Like the capital of a business firm, the resources of the district constitute the capital on which the long term welfare of the public depends. A business firm requires a periodic accounting of the state of its assets. It is equally important that the public know the state of its vital capital, its natural resources. What is the current supply of various kinds of resources, what changes have occurred in the supply and quality over the preceding year, and what is the supply outlook for the indefinite future if current practices are continued? At the outset, there will undoubtedly be major deficiencies in knowledge about the state of the natural resource base of the region. As time goes on, the extent of these deficiencies should be reduced. The first time the annual report is prepared, it will, no doubt, be a substantial task, but subsequently it will largely be a task of updating information from the previous year.

Determining the Boundaries of Regional Governments

In developing a regional structure for resource management, an important task is to determine what constitutes an appropriate geographic area and population size for each region. It is suggested that this task should be guided to the extent practicable by the following criteria:

(i) *The region should embrace an area that has relatively uniform biophysical characterisitics. Ideally its boundaries should coincide with those of a drainage basin (i.e., a river basin or tributary watersheds).*
There are several reasons for this criterion. Relative uniformity of biophysical conditions limits the complexity of plannning and management of resources and thus facilitates public understanding of the problems and issues that must be addressed. Since stream flows produce biophysical interrelationships, jurisdictional boundaries that accord with watershed lines simplify the task of taking these relationships into account.

(ii) *The area should not be so large that residents have difficulty in familiarizing themselves with the area, its resources, and its economic activities.*
If the residents of a region are familiar with its resources and its economic activities, they develop a "feel" for the area and can react much more intelligently to proposals for the use of its resources. For some thinly populated parts of the Fraser River Basin, it may be difficult to delineate a region that meets this criterion and which has sufficient resources and people to warrant designation as a separate regional jurisdiction.

(iii) *The location of population centres and transportation routes should permit easy communication among residents of the region, an elected governing board, and the resource management staff.*
For the jurisdiction to function most effectively, those concerned with and interested in resource management should not find it difficult to meet with one another. Lack of ability to communicate easily can lead to misunderstandings and unnecessary conflicts.

(iv) *Ideally the population of the region should be of relatively modest size so that those directly concerned with resource management in the region—the regional board members, the planning council members, the regional resource management staff, interest group leaders, and individual concerned citizens—can get to know one another.*

It is unlikely that this criterion can be met in the Greater Vancouver metropolitan area but it should be possible to adhere to it in the rest of the Fraser River Basin.

Observance of the foregoing criteria should foster public consensus and the development of a feeling of common purpose within the region. This in turn should lead to strong support for the proper husbandry of the resources of the region, their sustainable use, and realization of the potential benefits of these resources by the people of the region.

An Illustrative Sketch of Regional Boundaries

The accompanying map illustrates how the foregoing criteria might be applied in establishing the boundaries of regions in the Fraser River Basin. There are eight regions with approximate populations as follows:

(i)   The Upper Fraser East, approximate population 80,000.

(ii)   The Nechako-Stuart, approximate population 22,000.

(iii)   Upper Middle Fraser, approximate population 60,000.

(iv)   Lower Middle Fraser, approximate population 22,000.

(v)   North and South Thompson, approximate population 105,000.

(vi)   Lower Fraser Valley, approximate population 200,000.

(vii)   Greater Vancouver Metropolitan Area, approximate population 1,000,000 plus.

(viii) Lillooet, Squamish, and Coastal Drainages, approximate population 13,000.

It will be noted that the Squamish and Coastal Drainages lie outside the Fraser River Basin. However, the Lillooet drainage biophysically is much more similar to the Squamish and Coastal Drainages than to the drainages to the east of the Lillooet drainage. The Lillooet drainage is so thinly populated that it would not warrant designation as a separate region.

The foregoing sketch has been based on a relatively superficial examination of relevant data. Much more detailed study of data on resources including biophysical characteristics, economic activities, the relationship of processing

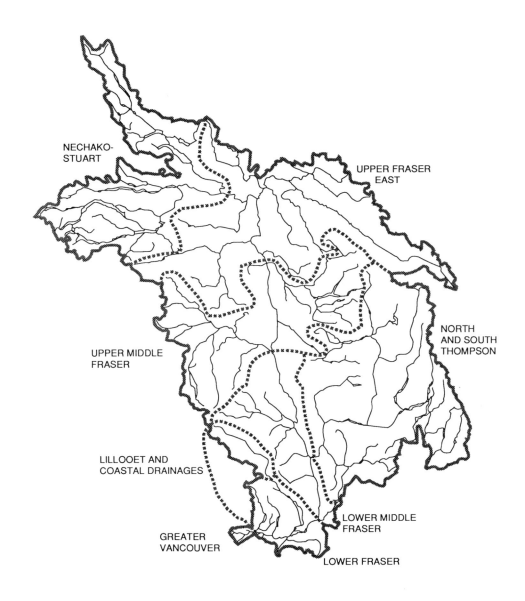

Figure 12.1: The Fraser River Basin: An Illustrative Sketch showing
Proposed Regional Boundaries and the Principal Drainage
Network

activities to sources of supply and communication routes would be required to provide a solid basis for recommending regional boundaries. One problem that needs to be examined carefully is how to locate regional boundaries in relation to some of the major population centres. For example, in the the foregoing sketch, Prince George lies near the western boundary of the Upper Fraser East region. However, it draws upon resource supplies from several of the adjoining regions. Kamloops is in a similar situation. Further study may indicate that this is not a serious problem, because economic considerations result in a flow of raw materials over substantial distances to processing facilities.

Conclusion

There are several perceptions of the current resource management and use problem in British Columbia which underlie the proposals made in this paper. Of major importance is the lack of any explicit institutional provision to assure the management and use of resources on a sustainable basis. Secondly, the current institutional structure fails to bring public preferences to bear effectively on decisions about how resources are to be managed and utilized. Finally, the current structure tends to mute rather than foster the application of the natural moral sentiments of people with regard to decisions about resource use.

Three suggestions are made, aimed at assuring the sustainable use of resources. These are: (i) the preparation by the provincial government of a set of specific resource practices—a set of standards—that must be applied to assure sustainable use of resources; (ii) provision for the audit of practices being applied and the imposition of penalties for the violation of standards; and, (iii) an annual report on the state of the resources within each region as well as an overall Provincial report.

An interrelated set of measures are suggested to assure that resource management and use decisions faithfully reflect public preferences and priorities. These include the following:

(i)   It is proposed that decision-making be decentralized to the fullest extent possible. It is recognized that this can be most effectively achieved through a fully competitive market, where all costs and all benefits are taken into account by the participants in a transaction. However, for a number of reasons specified, collective action is required for many resource use decisions, as well as to establish the rules governing operation of the market, where necessary to assure protection of the overall public interest. In addition, it is proposed that primary responsibility for public planning and implementing resource management and use programs be assigned to regional districts of modest size, operating under the direction of a regionally elected board. This brings the decision-making closer to the public most directly affected, and simplifies the task of decision-makers in becoming informed about the consequences of alternative decisions and in understanding public preferences. For the private sector, it is proposed that majority owners of an organization holding a tenure right to crown resources preferably be residents of the region, and as a minimum be residents of the Province. This will eliminate the enormous unwarranted political influence of multinational corporations on government decisions. Of major importance, decentralization of responsibilities to regional districts will enhance the role of moral motivations in resource management and use decisions.

(ii) Recognizing that regional resource decisions can have system effects that may extend well beyond the region, it is proposed that both the provincial and federal governments have an important role in resource management. Since all governmental institutions can fail at times to reflect faithfully the public interest, it is proposed that the three levels of government be so designed as to have a countervailing influence upon one another.

(iii) Finally, it is proposed that explicit provision be made for representatives of the range of values found in the region and in the province to be involved in resource management and use planning. These representatives, at the regional level, would be responsible for the identification and evaluation of alternative integrated resource management and use plans, and endeavour to negotiate a consensus on the plans to be recommended for adoption by the regional board. This system assures that representatives of each value framework will be well informed of the consequences of alternative plans and the rationale underlying the preferences of others, thus providing an environment conducive to effective negotiation. The interaction of individuals having differing perceptions and values should provide for a dynamic planning body that should lead to what Dunn (1971) characterizes as "creative learning".

It has been concluded that the current design of institutional arrangements for resource management and use have failed to give sufficient weight to the moral considerations that guide individual actions. The importance of these considerations was well recognized by one of the intellectual founders of modern capitalism, but has been neglected because of a preoccupation with the importance of self-interest as a motivating force in society. In 1759 Adam Smith, the author of the *Wealth of Nations,* made the following statement:

> But upon the tolerable observance of these duties [justice, truth, chastity, fidelity] depends the very existence of human society, which would crumble into nothing if mankind were not generally impressed with a reverence of these important rules of conduct. (Smith, 1759:231-232)

It is evident from this statement that one of the architects of capitalism assumed that participants in the market would be constrained by moral considerations. A decentralized structure of governmental and private institutions to regions of modest size would be conducive to the operation of these constraints, which tend to be lacking in the impersonal environment of highly centralized organizations.

References

Aberley, D. 1985. *Bioregionalism: A Territorial Approach to Governance and Development of Northwest British Columbia.* Unpublished MA thesis. School of Community and Regional Planning, University of British Columbia.

Barnett, H. J., and C. Morse. 1963. *Scarcity and Growth: The Economics of Natural Resource Availability.* Baltimore: Johns Hopkins University Press.

Bowes, M. D., and J. V. Krutilla. 1989. *Multiple-Use Management: The Economics of Public Forestlands.* Washington, D.C.: Resources for the Future.

Breton, A.. 1974. *The Economic Theory of Representative Government.* Chicago: Aldine Publishing Company.

Crenson, M. A. 1971. *The Un-Politics of Air Pollution,* Baltimore: Johns Hopkins University Press.

Crozier, M.. 1964. *The Bureaucratic Phenomeno.* Chicago: The University of Chicago Press.

Dahl, R. A., and E. R. Tufte. 1973. *Size and Democracy.* Stanford: Stanford University Press.

Daly, H. E., and J. B. Cobb, Jr. 1989. *For the Common Good.* Boston: Beacon Press.

Dunn, E. S., Jr. 1971. *Economic and Social Development.* Baltimore: John Hopkins University Press.

Etzioni, A.. 1988. *The Moral Dimension: Toward a New Economics.* New York: The Free Press.

Fox, I. K., and I. Picken. 1960. *The Upstream-Downstream Flood Control Controversy in Arkansas-Red-White Basins Survey.* University of Alabama Press.

Janis, I. L., and L. Mann. 1977. *Decision Making: A Psychological Analysis of Conflict, Choice, and Commitment.* New York: The Free Press.

Krutilla, J. V., and A. C. Fisher. 1973. *Economics of Natural Environments.* Washington, D.C.: Resources for the Future.

Mansbridge, J. J. 1990. *Beyond Self-Interest.* Chicago: The University of Chicago Press.

Mumford, L. 1970. *The Myth of the Machine: The Pentagon of Power.* New York: Harcourt Brace Jovanovich.

Ornstein, R., and P. Ehrlich. 1989. *New World, New Mind.* New York: Doubleday

Ostrom, V. 1987. *The Political Theory of a Compound Republic.* Lincoln: University of Nebraska Press.

Russell, C. S., (ed.). 1979. *Collective Decision Making: Applications from Public Choice Theory.* Baltimore: Johns Hopkins University Press.

Scott, A. 1976. "The Cost of Compulsory Log Trading." in W. McKillop and W. J. Mead (eds.) *Timber Policy Issues in British Columbia.* Vancouver: University of British Columbia Press.

Smith, A. 1966. *The Theory of Moral Sentiments.* New York: Augustus M. Kelley.

Solomon, R. C. 1990. *A Passion for Justice.* Reading: Addison-Wesley.

de Tocqueville, A. 1961. *Democracy in America.* New York: Random House.

13

Environmental Non-Government Organisations and the Management of the Aquatic Environment for Sustainable Development

Julia E. Gardner

Resource development is increasingly required to be sustainable and ecologically sensitive, as governments become more aware of connections between environment and development and of growing concern for the maintenance of ecological integrity (WCED, 1987). But unilateral measures by government to meet this priority are out of the question for several reasons. Economic restraint means that institutional resources for the governance of resource use are at a premium. A changing political culture in Canada, and especially in British Columbia, calls for closer public accountability on the part of government, and more citizen involvement in the regulation of human affairs (Resnick, 1986; Ruff, 1986). And elected governments do not seem to be able to keep pace with emerging societal values which emphasize closer human links with nature and a deeper appreciation of our natural heritage. In combination, these trends point to the timeliness of a stronger role for citizens and their organizations in environmental management.

Internationally, approaches to environmental management which are decentralized and cognizant of the potential for citizen initiative, going beyond the traditional role of government-initiated public participation programs, are increasingly promoted. Citizens' organizations are perceived to have an essential role in the re-establishment of modes of human-environment interaction that allow for development with environmental conservation, and conservation with equity—central themes of sustainable development.

The objective of this chapter is to review a number of literatures in order to generate an analytical framework that will be applied to a case study in the Fraser Basin in Westwater's second volume, *Water in Sustainable Development: Exploring Our Common Future in the Fraser River Basin*. That case study explores the roles of community-based, environmental non-government organizations (ENGOs) in protecting the aquatic environment of the Fraser River Basin, with special attention to the ways in which these organizations interact with government. A second objective of this literature review is to promote an enhanced appreciation of the role of citizens' organizations in sustainable development.

The literatures examined are predominantly those of sustainable development and environmental politics or environmentalism. Some resource economics and policy theory is also drawn upon. The first part of this chapter focuses on the roles of citizens' organizations in sustainable development. The second part examines the roles of ENGOs in relation to government and politics. The analytical framework for the case study in the second volume is derived directly from this discussion.

Sustainable Development and Citizens' Organizations

The following discussion addresses the functions that citizens' organizations play in sustainable development at the most general level and then focuses on the role of environmental groups in the sustainable development of water resources. First, some clarification of terms is in order. The term "citizens' organizations" is the most all-encompassing label for the subject of discussion. Used interchangably with this term here is that of "interest group," assuming that the groups included are public, or community-based, rather than private (i.e., industry or profession-based). Most of the discussion focuses more specifically on "environmental interest groups" or ENGOs. A working definition of ENGO specific to this analysis is presented later. The collective activity and social and political relationships of these environmental interest groups over time is referred to as the "environmental movement".

The Roles of Citizens' Organizations in Sustainable Development

Citizens' organizations have important functions to play in achieving virtually all the key elements of sustainable development, namely, maintaining ecological integrity and conserving the resource base, the pursuit of equity, thinking globally while acting locally, and increasing social self-determination. The relationships between citizens' organizations and each of these themes are delineated here.

The Pursuit and Maintenance of Ecological Integrity

Environmental interest group work has been centrally important in the pursuit and maintenance of ecological integrity and diversity. The longest-standing branch of the environmental movement in North America is that of wilderness advocacy—a continuing central thrust of the movement in B.C. Currently, Earthlife Foundation and the B.C. Chapter of the Canadian Parks and Wilderness Society are designing a cooperative strategy for the conservation of biological diversity through a system of protected areas in the province. Coterminous with wilderness advocacy are interest group efforts toward conserving and enhancing the resource base, the objectives of which include keeping options open for future generations. In this province, attention has been paid most publicly to the forest sector, with strident calls for the preservation of old growth forests and improvements in logging techniques to make them more ecosystem-friendly. A coalition of social movements organized the second "Tin Wis" conference, held in Port Alberni in 1990, on themes of environmental and community sustainability in a forestry-based economy.

Fisheries, too, have been the target of conservation campaigns. The most visible version is the anti-pollution lobby of groups such as Greenpeace and the West Coast Environmental Law Association, an example being Greenpeace's posting of unofficial health warnings regarding fish caught in Burrard Inlet. In addition to such high-profile campaigns are countless smaller volunteer projects for the stewardship of fish habitats and the rearing of salmon for the enhancement of depleted stocks, facilitated in part by the Department of Fisheries and Oceans' Salmonid Enhancement Program. Further observations on the role of citizens' organizations in the conservation of aquatic resources are made later in the chapter.

The Pursuit of Equity

The role of interest groups in the maintenance of ecological integrity and resource conservation is straightforward when considered in the narrow terms of concern for the natural environment. When an equally crucial sustainable development principle—the pursuit of equity—is brought into consideration, ideological and strategic complexities begin to cloud the picture. Some of these complexities are explored here.

Achieving conservation *with* equity is increasingly recognized to be the central challenge to sustainable development (Jacobs and Munro, 1987). The logic, based in the experience of global development, is that "[p]ure conservation—in its isolation from economic reality—is doomed to fail in all but the most privileged circumstances" (Sandbrook, 1986:299). The dominant explanation for this interdependency is that underprivileged people whose basic needs are not met are driven to seek to meet these needs through behaviour that can lead to drastic environmental impacts—like desertification through the gathering of firewood. A more subtle connection, perhaps more relevant to the developed world, is that "efforts to protect the environment must fail as human society loses its capacity for equity,...and as people become increasingly harsh and insensitive in dealing with each other and, as a result, with the natural world around them" (Booth, 1988:307). Likewise, equity cannot be achieved if a deteriorating environment provides the excuse for the abuse of human rights, or if the negative impacts on quality of life of environmental degradation are inequitably distributed (see Boothroyd, this volume).

Observers of the environmental movement have closely watched the conservation-equity relationship outside the context of sustainable development as well. Prominent among these in the North American literature are Alan

Schnaiberg and Denton Morrison. Schnaiberg states that "[f]rom a sociological perspective, it is never sufficient to point to *the* environment as having been protected. The question must always be asked, for whom and from whom has it been protected? Environmental quality and social welfare issues are not socially or politically separable" (1980:5). Morrison concurs that the ideology of the equity movement and related social movements are the "social and political climate in which the environmental movement has evolved" (1986:206).

The discussion of equity in relation to ENGO activity has largely revolved around two issues. The first is the question of the membership of the groups, with the frequent accusation being that it is predominantly middle class—an elite sector of society. The second issue is the question of who benefits from ENGO activity, where the criticism is that the working class suffers fewer of the benefits and more of the costs, by way of lost wages, for instance. Milbrath (1984) has taken some of the impact out of such assertions with his findings based on empirical studies that, regardless of the membership of the environmental movement, the values and priorities that the movement expresses are held across the social strata. At the very least, the broadest ends of the environmental movement, such as clean air and water, have to be seen as serving the public good as opposed to the interests of a narrow segment of the population. In further support of the argument against an elitist environmentalism, Morrison (1986) points out that the alternative technology movement (developed by Schumacher and Lovins) had a progressive impact on the environmental movement, by providing environmentally sound, decentralized, higher employment-based technologies rather than simply raising the costs of energy. Unfortunately, the conservative administrations of the 1980's largely stifled the influence of "soft technology paths" (although we are now seeing a revival of mainstream support for them, as western governments are reminded of the tenuousness of their access to Middle-Eastern oil). Morrison goes on to argue that social movements for equity "have shifted environmentalism to the left, and, even more than that, environmentalism has moved the new left toward environmental consciousness" (1986:212-3). In B.C., examples of this merging are the Tin Wis coalition, mentioned above, with its labour, native and environmentalist membership; the "One Conference" held in October 1990, calling together the full range of social and environmental interest groups in the province; and the Green Caucus of the New Democratic Party which emphasizes the common ground between environmental and NDP interests. Discussions of the green movement in European politics (e.g., Eckersley, 1988) carry further the theme of environmentalism's connection to the political left (or lack of such).

An additional trend counteracting the elitist tendencies of today's environmentalism is the increasingly "grass-roots," or community-based, nature of the movement. Grass-roots groups are more involved in local issues with inequitable impacts (e.g., in the area of waste disposal which often disproportionately affects the poor), and are better able to support local management arrangements which can work for conservation in the community's self-interest. Globally, the grass-roots movement can be described as people operating in their own community at the local level, "looking for small improving steps on a pathway to a more equitable future which is nature-conscious and sustainable" (Sandbrook, 1986:291). But optimism for the potential of the grass-roots movement (more fully explored later in this discussion) has to be tempered by awareness of countervailing circumstances.

The growth of corporatism in the environmental movement in North America towards the increased professionalization and bureaucratization of ENGOs is one trend which could counterbalance the spreading equity effect of the grass roots. And powers in government and industry whose interests are vested in the status quo present a formidable barrier to change. Morrison poses the difficult question of "whether and how environmental reform can be organized so as to be an integral, functioning part of a political-economy with an overriding goal of equity/redistribution" (1986:216). At the coarsest level of analysis, we can envisage reforms that restructure government and society or reforms that modify our existing system of governance and social organization. The choice depends largely on what perspective is taken on the sources of inequity at the broadest scale, particularly with regard to the concentration of wealth in the hands of the economic interests with the best access to government decision-making power. Varying perspectives represented in the current literature are summarized here.

Gadgil (1987) has suggested that the World Conservation Strategy has not been well-implemented because those who control most of the world's resources do not perceive a commonality of long-term interests, so that disparities within societies and between nations increase, and an elite acquires more of a hold over resources. Durning, writing for Worldwatch Institute's *State of the World Report* for 1989, likewise points out that a world economy of concentrated power and entrenched vested interests in a few countries limits the potential of the grass roots to work towards sustainability (1989).

Similar trends in the concentration of power and access to natural resources have been demonstrated within North America. Canada's frontier economy historically led government to enter into arrangements with companies that would agree to make the necessary investments in physical plant to enable the exploitation of a primary resource, in return for guaranteed access to that resource (Marchak, 1983; Pross, 1986). During the Roosevelt years in the U.S., this economic efficiency priority competed with two other themes of conservation associated with the Progressive era, namely, equity and aesthetics. The objective of the equity proponents was to keep natural resources in public control so the benefits of resource development would be distributed fairly, fostering grass-roots democracy (Koppes, 1988). But efficiency conservation devoid of equity concerns proved more appealing to those who would further capitalist expansion and to efficiency-oriented bureaucracies, so the equity branch of the early conservation movement was eventually overshadowed by the other two themes. A strong argument can be made that the concentration of capital and power, whether for economic efficiency or other causes, continues to challenge the best efforts of social movements both for equity and conservation.

Today, different branches of the environmental movement can be distinguished on the basis of whether they identify power centres—"the iron triangle"(Rees,

1985), "monopoly capital"(Schnaiberg, 1980; Morrison, 1986), or the "sub-government" (Pross, 1986)—as targets for change, or ignore such structural circumstances. Morrison suggests that environmentalists on the whole adopt the latter attitude.

> From an old left perspective environmentalism puts some technological reforms on the means by which profits are produced, and makes proper public statements about equity (and makes a few changes in environmental programmes in that direction), but in theory this does not threaten monopoly capital, since environmental costs can ultimately be passed down the line (1986:121).

Science, rather than equity (or aesthetics) is now the driving force for mainstream environmentalism.

Nevertheless, observers of various political persuasions are calling for structural reform in the name of conservation with equity. Durning maintains that "[d]eep reforms in broader institutions are the key to unleashing a wider grass-roots mobilization, because no popular effort exists in an institutional vacuum... Whether intentionally or not, these institutions create many of the opportunities and incentives for organized action; they also create many of the obstacles" (1989:168). Gadgil recommends the "restoration of control over resources to small, largely homogeneous local communities" (1987:93). And Schnaiberg suggests that for a joint conservation and equity movement to succeed, "it must focus social movement efforts on the state in order to control these inherent limits in oligopolistic market systems...At this point in movement history, the most crucial need is to establish firmly the dual ecological-equity goals..." (1980:393).

Those who take the perspective that structural change is too onerous, or is not necessary—holding that elitism is *not* built into our system of governance—seek other pathways towards sustainable development. And even those working for fundamental change often support more moderate approaches as necessary measures for buying time, pending systemic transformation. The demands of the less radical branch of the environmental movement for greater government accountability and more open decision-making receive broadly-based support. The World Commission on Environment and Development, for example, points out that,

> In many countries, governments need to recognize and extend NGOs' right to know and have access to information on the environment and natural resources; their right to be consulted and to participate in decision-making on activities likely to have a significant effect on their environment; and their right to legal remedies and redress when their health or environment has been or may be seriously affected (1987:328).

Reciprocating this accountability, interest groups can be pivotal in building the constituency of political support required for a government attempting reforms for sustainable development—witness Environment Minister Bouchard's quick turn to the public with his "Green Plan" when he did not attain support for this environmental agenda from the federal Cabinet. Furthermore, still without necessarily dismantling the capitalist system condemned by more radical factions, interest groups can counterbalance its failings by articulating environmental considerations which are not revealed through market forces, in essence "acting as a substitute (for the price mechanism) in indicating the proper path toward sustainable development" (Salim, 1987:338).

Thinking Globally While Acting Locally

Regardless of their role in, or attitudes towards, structural change, citizens' associations, amongst all forms of social organization, currently have the best capability for thinking globally while acting locally—a central theme in the quest for sustainable development.

Turning our attention back to the potential of the grass roots, Durning believes that "grass-roots action for sustainability is a formidable force...setting its sights on everything from local waste recycling to international trade and debt issues" (1989:158) The capabilities of citizens' organizations in facilitating progress towards sustainable development are now widely recognized. The World Commission on Environment and Development (1987) identifies the following roles of NGOs: planning, monitoring, evaluating, and carrying out projects; the creation and maintenance of public awareness and political pressures that stimulate governments to act; identifying risks, assessing environmental impacts and designing and implementing measures to deal with them. Durning sees in these organizations "the capacities to tap local knowledge and resources, to respond to problems rapidly and creatively, and to maintain the institutional flexibility necessary in changing circumstances. In addition, although few groups use the words sustainable development, their agendas in many cases embody its ideal" (1989:155). Finally, Canadian journalist and commentator on sustainable development, Michael Keating, holds that environmental groups "have been the source and the repository of many of the best ideas about sustainability for decades" (1989:287).

The most local level from which action can originate is, of course, the level of the individual. Support is extensive for the view that change, indeed, *has* to originate from this level. U.S. observers put this message forward most strongly:

> Only the individualist can succeed,...for true success comes only from within...[I]ndividuals working together, or even alone, at the grassroots of America, *have* worked miracles (Frome, 1988:254);

> I can't imagine how else [the land ethic] will come about, the actualizing of this cosmic idea, other than in small but vivid increments of individual choice and collective action (Little, 1988:277).

In Canada, the National Round Table on Environment and Economy has demonstrated support for this theme in its exploration, with Environment Canada, of a "participaction" program to encourage individual action for environmental protection. Likewise, Canada's *Green Plan* (1990) devotes a section to the promotion of "environmental citizenship."

Increasing Social Self-Determination

Though perhaps over-stated at times, the potential of the grass roots is real. A new, de facto, global coalition has formed which is "largely concerned with putting sustainable development into practice of the community level (sic)...[h]undreds of thousands of small but contributory activities are being carried out at the very point where the environmental problems are most evident" (Sandbrook, 1986:300). Well before the publication of the Brundtland report, Hodge and Hodge pointed out that environmental interest groups "can provide a valuable bridge in local problem solving between the assessment of local needs and the assessment of the technical and global issues which nowadays characterize so many problems confronting local decision makers" (1979:36). And the individual involvement that is characteristic of grass-roots activity also contributes to the sustainable development priority of increasing social self-determination. Commenting on the challenge of global sustainability, Emil Salim suggests that the growth of non-governmental organizations, or "self-reliant institutions," should be encouraged, as the "[p]romotion of these institutions is based on the recognition that sustainable development requires changes in people's outlook and perception of development; changes which can be achieved most effectively through people's direct involvement in the process" (1987:338).

Yet we must not be carried away by the growing enthusiasm for the grass-roots remedy. Durning appropriately cautions that "[l]ocal groups eventually collide with forces they cannot control...Thus, perhaps the greatest irony of community action for sustainability is that communities cannot do it alone. Small may be beautiful, but it can also be insignificant" (1989:168). The solution, Durning suggests, is to forge an alliance between institutions and community groups. This is a difficult prescription because the institutions involved are often powerful and rigid, but it is important, for, "[t]o succeed, sustainable development will have to come from both the bottom and the top" (1989:155). An investigation below of the forms of interaction between interest groups and government agencies elucidates some of the issues and the potential of this complex challenge to achieving sustainability.

Citizens' Organizations, Sustainable Development and Water

The potential of grass-roots efforts to promote the sustainable development of aquatic environments in North America has been well-demonstrated through the activities of citizens' organizations across the continent for the conservation and restoration of coastal and riverine ecosystems. Examples of the attention being paid to these activities include Lerner's (1986) study of volunteer stewardship in the Great Lakes area and several U.S. government and volunteer programs for coastal ecosystem conservation (e.g., Dreyfoos, 1987; Taylor, 1987; Puget Sound Water Quality Authority, 1990). Byrne and Horn, speaking at the 1989 Conference of the Canadian Water Resources Association, summarized the growing citizen interest in river systems.

> With rivers dominating so much of the regional landscape, it is not surprising that concern over their quality and manipulation has served as a focus around which public interest could coalesce. Over the course of this century, water issues have brought together wilderness preservationists, landowners, native groups, fish and wildlife supporters and recreationists. These groups, which initially waged their own individual river battles, came together during the 1960's and 1970's and collectively ushered in a new era of publicly supported water conservation efforts...Public support for clean water and free-flowing rivers is now a potent political force (1989:3).

These authors echo the views of those above on the capability of grass-roots organizations to act locally while thinking globally: "In North America, public perception and understanding of these [global] issues are transforming complacency into concern and action at the community level. This trend to local action is an appropriate expression of a citizen's individual contribution to the global commons" (Byrne and Horn, 1989:4). Like the World Commission on Environment and Development, Byrne and Horn urge governments to encourage and support the role of citizen participation.

In Canada, reports from the *Inquiry on Federal Water Policy* (Pearse et al., 1985), and the Science Council's report *Water 2020: Sustainable Use for Water in the 21st Century* (1988), similarly emphasize the importance of nongovernment organizations. The Science Council recognizes that environmental groups are enthusiastic, knowledgeable, and "ahead of the game" in their interests and activities. Accordingly, it recommends that "[t]he fuller involvement of these groups in shaping the research and political agenda is necessary if Canada is to develop strategies to overcome current and future environmental problems and muster the political will for their implementation" and that "a whole series of issues concerning water use, water science and a range of international, national, and regional water programs...require sustained and informed public participation and response" (1988:29). Pearse (1985) also emphasized the importance of public involvement in improving decision-making for water resources. His Commission saw citizens' organizations as providing channels of communication with large numbers of interested Canadians.

As well, commentary in the Pearse report reinforces the broader, societal rationales for increasing citizen involvement made at the opening of this chapter:

In recent years, governments have increasingly sought the views of special interest groups and the public at large before making decisions, especially when they involve natural resources and environmental matters. This reflects, among other things, a growing anxiety about the way we have traditionally used our natural resources, deep concerns about the environment's widespread degradation, citizens' feeling alienated from their governments, and frustration with the ability of traditional political structures to register public opinion about particular issues and decisions (Pearse 1985:174-5).

The important role of environmental interest groups in aquatic resource management has also been recognized in B.C., and in the Fraser Basin in particular. Consultants commissioned by federal and provincial environment agencies to undertake a *State of the Environment Report for the Lower Fraser Basin* (Quadra Planning Consultants Ltd. and Regional Consulting Ltd., 1990) emphasized the role of "public interest organizations," or "environmental conservation organizations," in promoting public awareness of and interest in environmental management. These consultants also observe that in the Lower Fraser Basin,

in the past twenty years, public interest groups have been active in promoting environmental protection and conservation. …Other non-government organizations are directly involved in preserving, acquiring and rehabilitating natural wetlands. Ducks Unlimited, the Nature Trust of B.C. and the Pacific Estuary Conservation Foundation have assisted in acquiring wildlife habitat at various locations. Many local fish and wildlife clubs, along with the B.C. Wildlife Federation, work closely with government programs such as the Federal Salmonid Enhancement Program. School groups are also active… (Quadra Planning Consultants Ltd. and Regional Consulting Ltd., March 1990:114-115).

These are the kinds of activities that will be elaborated upon in the case study in Volume 2.

Environmental Non-Government Organisations (ENGOs) and their Roles

The analysis of this chapter is primarily concerned with the role of ENGOs as proponents of conservation and the relation of this role to governance and social change for sustainable development. This section introduces ENGOs in more detail and establishes a system for classifying the roles of interest groups in relation to government, to support the focus on the interaction between ENGOs and government agencies involved in environmental management in the case study.

ENGOs

For the purposes of this analysis, an ENGO is a citizens' interest group whose activities include efforts for environmental conservation. "Conservation" activities are those that strive to protect or promote the natural integrity ("health") of ecosystems or components of ecosystems through the rehabilitation of degraded ecosystems or the prevention of negative impacts on ecosystems (or components thereof). The membership of the group is voluntary; the group does not aim to be profit-making; it is autonomous (free to make its own decisions); it provides mainly services as opposed to material benefits; it seeks changes on behalf of its members, wider society, and/or the environment. Groups are included here whose activities may not be *primarily* directed at conservation, but do include conservation activities as described above (such as fish and game clubs).

There are virtually as many ways of categorizing environmental interest groups as there are commentators on the environmental movement. Classifications are primarily based on the *roles* played by groups and the *phases* of evolution of ENGOs. *Phases* can describe shifts in environmentalism in broad historical terms, such as the above description of the early conservation movement in North America, where equity priorities were replaced by efficiency priorities over time. Phases can also be applied in an ahistorical sense, describing the stages that individual ENGOs are expected to evolve through, for example, from a single issue-orientation to a multiple issue-orientation. This second perspective is taken at the end of the next sub-section, where the relationships between interest group roles are discussed.

Various *role* classifications differently emphasize ENGO relationships to politics, government and the public, or the practical functions performed by groups. Thus ENGO roles can be described in a supposedly value-neutral way, especially when addressing the empirical effectiveness of groups; or in an ideological way, emphasizing the roles of ENGOs in their political-economic context—as generally demonstrated in the discussion of equity implications above. Naturally, roles and phases overlap, with one being described in terms of the other in many classification systems.

Other bases for categorizing ENGOs secondary to, and partially encompassed by, the above, include the *scale* of activity of the ENGO (e.g., local or national— see Petulla, 1987:110), its *strategies or tactics* (e.g,. lobbying or direct action) and its *organization* (e.g., centralized or decentralized, membership-oriented or otherwise). In her 1972 thesis, Draper nicely summarized the traditional approaches to ENGO classification, and O'Riordan (1981) provides another survey of schemes for describing ENGOs. Canadian academics who have recently analysed patterns in the environmental movement include Paehlke (1985 and 1989) and Toner (McIlroy, 1990). Pross (1986) and Kernaghan and Siegel (1987) discuss the roles of interest groups in Canadian politics more generally.

A selection of taxonomies of ENGOs from the literature is described below. In this overview schema related to governance and social change are emphasized, in concert with observations on the role of interest groups in sustainable development from the discussion above. That discussion pointed to varying levels of emphasis in the environmental movement on structural reform for the achievement of sustainable development principles (namely, ecological integrity, equity and social self-determination), and to the importance of institutional contexts to the success of grass-roots conservation efforts. The classification schema reviewed here encompass these themes and support the construction of an analytical framework specific to the present focus on government-interest group interaction.

Classifications that address the relationship between ENGOs and government tend to emphasize either (i) levels of cooperation (or conflict) in that relationship; or, (ii) the attitudes of the ENGOs towards partisan politics; or, (iii) the degree to which ENGOs appear to take issue with (or accept) the dominant political and economic system. Ideological questions related to mechanisms for social change towards the principles of sustainable development inevitably enter into such schema.

Allan Schnaiberg is one of the most frequently-cited commentators on the forms of the environmental movement in the U.S. (especially *From Surplus to Scarcity*, 1980). He identifies an increasing politicization of the movement, and a concomitant refinement of goals and means, away from the virtually apolitical version of the early 1900's. He also establishes four profiles of environmental organizations and participants based on perceptions of social and economic reality that emerge from historical *phases* of the movement. His "cosmetologists" and "meliorists" are described as having limited perspectives on ecological and socioeconomic dimensions, emphasizing consumption issues and voluntary consumer action, and being subject to manipulation by producer groups. His "reformists" and "radicals," on the other hand, "see the broader ecological needs as dictating broader reorganization of production and consumption" (1980:375). The reformists, in the 1960's, provided the impetus for a shift towards the use of legislation and litigation in environmental protest. The radicals, most recently emerged, focus on appropriate technology and confront the forces of social inequality.

Schnaiberg's assessment of the state of the movement in 1980 as one characterized by "intensive and extensive negotiation rather than marches and protests" (1980:377) is still applicable a decade later. He cautions of this mode that,

> [n]egotiation, of course, entails the clear and present danger of cooptation by antienvironmental opponents, whether in the state or in capitalist sectors. To some extent, this has occurred in the incremental decision-making logic tacitly agreed to by environmental reformists...Yet the continuing presence of radicals, including radicalized reformists and meliorists with a passion for single issues, helps offset some of this tendency toward absorption (1980:378).

Overall, Schnaiberg joins company with those who call for systemic reform, as reflected in his belief that "[p]erception of [environmental] threats must be more closely integrated into programs of reform and challenge to existing production patterns and existing controllers of surplus allocation" (1980:374).

In a publication of the same year as Schnaiberg's well-known work, Watts and Wandesforde-Smith trace three stages in the evolution of environmental political initiatives which parallel Schnaiberg's categories. At the first level, equivalent to Schnaiberg's meliorists, is local level action by ad hoc groupings of individuals, in which the "cognition by those involved of the environmental problem is consensual and naive,"omitting broader scale considerations (1980:350), and "[t]he search is for a simple solution...in which the adjustment people have to make is at the individual level" (1980:351). Watts and Wandesforde-Smith believe that groups are ineffective in bringing about change at this level, and to be successful (i.e., to overcome institutional obstacles) they must mobilize at a higher level. Then they become reformists, "interested in policy formulation and in changing the policy process to make it more open, more accessible, more transparent, and, from their own point of view, more legitimate" (1980:351). Frustration on the part of groups that are ineffective in finding influence at the first two levels leads them to the third, in which they "call for a transformation of the system, calling into question the legitimacy of its policy processes and the economic, scientific, and technological rationality of the industrial society that sustains it" (1980:352).

Stepping back to the chronological approach to categorizing styles of environmentalism, observations from several authors (Borrelli, 1988; Buttel, 1986; Paehlke, 1985; Slocombe, 1984; Weinberg, 1989 and others) can be selectively combined into the following overlapping phases:

(i) The early conservation movement that emerged under Roosevelt and continues in the form of the more conservative national wilderness organizations;

(ii) Growing mass awareness of environmental problems and some grass-roots organizing from 1960 (the publication of Rachel Carson's *Silent Spring*) to 1972 (c.f. Schnaiberg's meliorists and cosmetologists);

(iii) The stage from Earth Day, 1970, to the mid-1980's, with a mixture of special interest organizing, some liaison with the appropriate technology movement of the late 1970's and early 1980's, and increasing litigation and "rearguard politics" based on efforts to see implemented new environmental legislation (c.f. Schnaiberg's reformists);

(iv) From the mid-1980's to the present, with extensive grass-roots mobilization for environmental advocacy and stewardship, increasing polarization between the most politicized ENGOs (Schnaiberg's radicals) and members of a neoconservative backlash; and the contrasting emergence of a so-called "third wave environmentalism," involving increased cooperation between professionally organized, non-local ENGOs and government and industry (c.f. Schnaiberg's reformists).

One final approach to categorizing ENGO styles in relation to government derives from the literature on public participation rather than environmentalism. This literature looks at forms of interest group involvement from a less ideological perspective, yet its descriptors nicely mirror the themes discussed above. Sadler (1980) summarizes three styles of public participation in environmental management that have emerged in North America over time:

(i)   *Pre-1960's;* participation by invitation, meaning closed consultation of selected interest groups at the central level;
(ii) *1960's;* participation by intervention, stemming from a more diverse range of pressure groups demanding citizen involvement through protest; and
(iii) *1970's;* participation by integration—the move by governments to integrate opportunities for public review of environmental policies and resource projects into the decision-making process.

Sadler's three categories closely correspond to Susskind and Elliott's (1983) description of the forms of community involvement in urban planning in Europe:

(i)   "Paternalism" (Sadler's participation by invitation);
(ii) "Conflict" (intervention); and,
(iii) "Coproduction" (integration).

Interest Group Roles in Relation to Government

Here, a three-part approach to describing ENGO roles that will frame the Fraser River Basin study is presented. The three categories are derived from the approaches summarized above and the sustainable development themes discussed earlier; they are set forth in a language that refers to the roles played by ENGOs in relation to government and associated strategies rather than to phases of activism or ideological types. The categories of roles are advocacy, supplemental and transformative. There is overlap among the three groups, especially in the area of the strategies they employ.

Advocacy

This category encompasses the broad range of activities undertaken by ENGOs to strengthen and expand the accountability of government and industry without restructuring economic or governance systems. The motivation to undertake such activities stems from dissatifaction with government performance. ENGOs in this category act as "watchdogs" to make government meet its commitments and fulfil its responsibilities in their area of concern for the environment, by demanding that government agencies adhere to their stated environmental policies, follow through on programs that help maintain ecological integrity, and enforce existing environmental regulations. They also attempt to expand the government's consideration of environmental issues by forcing it to incorporate ecological principles in planning processes, pass new environmental legislation and regulations, and inject new concerns about environmental issues into the decision-making arena. Halle and Furtado highlight this "prodding" role in a discussion of the furtherance of national conservation strategies:

> Government bureaucracies generally favour compromise and stability which makes them disinclined to radical change. Therefore, they should be effectively counterbalanced by strong participation from non-governmental organizations whose role often includes that of a "watch-dog" or lobby. (1987:283-4)

ENGO participants in advocacy activities, as defined here, are the reformists. They demand better access to environmental decision-making and to the information base related to those decisions. While they may ask for changes to make government more accountable through enhanced public input, they would leave political processes essentially unaltered. They want to "make government do a better job" but they are content with the general structure of our liberal democratic system, and their moderate approaches to reform essentially legitimate that system. Yet the importance of this moderate approach should not be underestimated in the context of our current political culture. Observers like Keating (1987) see ENGOs as providing "articulate voices of comment and criticism" essential to democratic processes. The goal of accountability held by these ENGOs is also considered to be of central importance by other social movements (Andrews, 1980). In discussing the state of "public interest liberalism," McCann (1986) asserts that the "new activists" across the sectors are distinguished by their attempt to make institutions that are public in *function* more public in *form*, (i.e., open, accountable, and representative).

The activities of the advocates revolve around communication processes. Advocates take the opinions of ENGO memberships, and by extension, sectors of the broader public, to government agencies or politicians via a range of communication avenues. These avenues include letter writing, meetings, use of the media, participation in consultative processes, and protest activities. The content of their message to government derives from their surveillance of government programmatic and planning activities, and the priorities amalgamated from their membership and their observations of environmental issues. Ongoing interaction of ENGOs with a number of government agencies lends the ENGOs an enhanced capability to see, and communicate back to agencies, a broader picture of environmental problems, because of the array of information and depth of perception these groups acquire through their work (Hodge and Hodge, 1979). This educational effect spreads to the public as groups seek to increase their lobbying power by mobilizing public support for their cause.

The style of the communication process can range from confrontational to cooperative, even though some commentators associate advocacy with a predominantly confrontational style (e.g., Maw, 1987). At the confrontational extreme lie the direct action or civil disobedience strategies (discussed in more detail below). This is involvement through intervention and conflict, as opposed to invitation or integration. At the cooperative extreme is the "third wave environmentalism" mentioned above, characterized by increasing centralization and close links with industry (Commoner, 1988; Devall, 1980). At this end of the spectrum, ENGOs run the risk of co-optation by non-environmental interests, and where input from ENGOs is invited by government, paternalistic, if not cooptive, relationships may emerge. Nevertheless, many ENGOs believe non-confrontational stances to be more effective in the long term because better access to decision-makers can be maintained, as the following excerpt from a fundraising letter indicates:

> CPAWS [Canadian Parks and Wilderness Society] policy has always been to work *with* government and industry in a spirit of cooperation. We believe this is the best way to get results. ... we are with the decision makers, directly influencing the future of Canada's ecosystems (CPAWS, 1990).

Sometimes more adversarial stances are taken if alternative strategies have failed, if avenues for cooperation are seen to be missing or inadequate, or if government performance is otherwise seen to warrant a more activist response. For example, the letter cited above goes on to state that "[w]e use confrontation only as a last resort".

Levels of politicization also vary, but partisan politics, like confrontational tactics, are usually avoided in an attempt to ensure continued support from citizens of various political inclinations (Lowe and Goyder, 1983). Doherty of the Sierra Club of Western Canada believes the non-partisan stance of most ENGOs is counter-productive: "Since public-interest lobbying eventually depends on the ability to influence voting, this reluctance has diminished the political clout of environmental organizations" (1984). Milbrath describes the tendency of ENGOs to become politicized (although not necessarily in a partisan sense) despite inclinations to the contrary.

> Even though environmentalists have become very disenchanted with the unresponsiveness of government, their sense of urgency compels them to try to influence government because they perceive it to be a major lever for forestalling catastrophe and fostering social change. Like it or not, then, environmentalists who want to turn a society around must get involved in politics.(1984:81)

Advocacy work depends on organization and on resources. Gaining access to the corridors of decision-making power may require a sophisticated organizational structure including offices and full or part-time employees (Lowe and Goyder, 1983; Pross, 1986). Meaningful and effective input into decision-making calls for a solid information base, expert advice and money for travel and other expenses (Sandbach, 1980). Sometimes these resources can be accessed through membership in an umbrella organization, such as the Federation of B.C. Naturalists; sometimes lack of access to them precludes the participation of less-advantaged interests. Certainly, with respect to resources, ENGOs are at a disadvantage in relation to lobbyists with constituencies based in economic interests—namely business, industry and professional or labour organizations (Devall, 1980; Lee, 1987; Pross, 1986; Sabatier and Pelkey, 1987). (Although U.S. environmental lobbyists are now contributing funds to Congressional candidates in the same order of magnitude as other lobby groups [Globe and Mail, 1991]). Ease of access varies also in relation to the scale of activity and the level of government addressed: grass-roots efforts may stand a greater chance of influencing regional or local bureaucracies than central government in Victoria, but the impact of that influence may be correspondingly small. Large-scale organizations, which increasingly rely on professionals, risk bureaucratic structures that are more like those of the establishment they are lobbying, making the advancement of more radical causes difficult and increasing the potential for cooptation (Friedmann, 1987; Lowe and Goyder, 1983; M'Gonigle, 1986; O'Riordan, 1981). However, the failure of the large groups to advance certain causes cannot be solely attributed to this creeping bureaucratization—major victories are simply hard to come by in the face of the entrenched economic interests described above (Wilson, 1988).

Supplemental

The supplemental role refers to the work undertaken by ENGOs to supplement government functions for environmental conservation. The focus here is not political but practical—a "do it yourself" approach that includes servicing the needs of ENGO members as well as efforts to protect the environment. The motivation to work towards these ends arises from a desire to be involved in environmental management in a "hands on" way, or from a recognition that government either cannot, or will not, undertake the measures that are necessary to maintain ecological integrity. Most of the activities encompassed by this category are addressed by an emerging field of investigation known as "voluntary environmental stewardship" (Lerner, 1986). If the advocacy activities are the highest profile, stereotypical roles played by ENGOs, the supplemental activities are the "dark horse" of today's environmental movement. Berger (1987) concludes from his review of efforts by American citizens to restore damaged environments that such efforts go beyond conservation and traditional environmentalism. Many participants, indeed, would not even consider themselves as ardent environmentalists; rather they are citizens "who feel a proprietary concern for the river or resource in jeopardy" (Dreyfoos, 1987:1803).

Supplemental work may be undertaken in cooperation with government agencies, often through programs designed for that purpose such as the Salmonid Enhancement Program; or independently of government, at the sole initiative of the ENGO and its non-government affiliates. If responsibilities and duties are being performed that would normally be held by government, or that supplement the regular management activities of government, the ENGOs involved are virtually "agents" of government. Activities typical of the agent role are ecosystem monitoring, inventories, education, facility construction, research, and surveillance work. The agent role falls into Susskind and Elliott's coproduction category, and into Sadler's integration, depending on how the latter is interpreted. The World Commission on Environment and Development supports this role in its statement that "NGOs and private and community groups can often provide an efficient and effective alternative to public agencies in the delivery of programmes and projects. Moreover, they can sometimes reach target groups that public agencies cannot" (1987:238).

If the supplemental activities undertaken are beyond the normal scope of government responsibilities then a "modelling" function may be performed, in which creative experiments or innovative initiatives may be undertaken by the ENGOs (Langton, 1982). The modelling role may surpass not only the mandate but the capabilities of government agencies. Work with intermediate technology, such as horse logging or organic farming, demonstrates the modelling function. Habitat enhancement or restoration and environmental education activities can fall into either category.

There is clearly potential for significant contributions to the maintenance of ecological integrity from these stewardship activities, and they can be a positive force for social self-determination as well. The actions of stewardship groups are pivotal in building local constituencies of support for environmental protection and they often underpin the success of ENGOs with broader mandates (Lerner, 1986). However, the supplemental role is not without its hazards. When cooperation with government agencies is close, the ENGOs risk the loss of autonomy as a result of entering into contractual or less formal agreements. Langton questions "[w]hether or not voluntary associations can retain their distinctive qualities that recommend them as an alternative to government service bureaucracies," and he goes on to caution that

> one of the major problems of voluntary associations is the threat of seduction and cooptation by the governmental sector. This threat is implicit in the acceptance of the supplemental service function in three respects. First, increased financial dependence on government can temper the prophetic passion of a voluntary organization for fear of biting the hand that feeds them. Second, the style and objectives of an organization can be modified excessively to serve the government's agenda. Third, the growing presence of voluntary association leaders in the governmental sector may subtly influence leaders of voluntary associations to be more cooperative with governmental agencies than they might otherwise be because of the lure of potential governmental service. (1982:9)

As well, both parties to such agreements risk losses if one party should renege on its promised contribution—a high level of trust and commitment is required. At a more general level, government could conceivably take advantage of the opportunity to "off-load" its stewardship responsibilities onto the shoulders of volunteers. On the other hand, the ENGOs involved might come to expect, in return for their extra efforts, a special voice in decision-making or preemptive rights of access to areas in which their efforts have been invested, to the detriment of the wider community interest, and with a potential loss of public accountability. Finally, when groups are trying to work more independently of government, they may encounter legal or bureaucratic barriers to their initiatives that can at times be insurmountable.

Transformative

The transformative role encompasses ENGO activities that strive to transform government and society. Schnaiberg's radicals, who are not satisfied with the existing system of governance and seek fundamental restructuring, fall into this category. Cotgrove similarly categorizes as radicals those environmentalists who "use the environment as a lever to try to bring about the kind of changes they want" (1982:34). He elaborates by describing these environmentalists as finding themselves at the periphery of institutions and processes of industrialist society, holding a distinctive ideology or social paradigm, and driven to protest their alienation through "outsider politics." These latter are actions taken beyond legal bounds—civil disobedience or more violent protests—aiming at fundamental social change. Road blockages in the name of native land claims are a topical example in B.C., albeit in a different context. Watts and Wandesforde-Smith (1980) identify as an alternative action towards transformation of the system the establishment of new political parties such as the Green Party.

The non-confrontational "modelling" functions described above can also be directed towards societal transformation. By innovative example, these activities can set the stage for forms of environmental management that place the principles of sustainable development on a higher plane than do current, mainstream systems. Deep ecologists, in particular, do not seek confrontation in their questioning of the dominant social paradigm as they "prefer to act as exemplary models and to teach through acting" (Devall, 1980:229). Commentary from Friedmann supports this emphasis on individual action: "One might further argue that a political practice aimed at social transformation can be effective only when it is based on the extra-political actions of ordinary people gathered in their own communities" (1987:297). Similarly, M'Gonigle eloquently makes the case for decentralization towards community control on the grounds that "the actual experience of balanced community provides the best guide to [fundamental] change" (1986:294), and that "[e]mpowerment at the periphery will force the center to adapt" (1986:310).

One hope is that transformation may find its humble beginnings in the "hands on" experience of stewardship projects, through which communities enhance their awareness of and sensitivity towards ecosystem needs and their sense of responsibility for the quality of the environment. These forces might lead in turn to the emergence of an environmental ethic with a potentially transformative influence. The experience of working in community-based organizations can also promote social change by enhancing community cohesion and self-determination. Social learning can take place which leads to demands for institutional restructuring, including the devolution of power and the decentralization of management responsibility. This kind of change—through "social mobilization" (Friedmann, 1987) at the grass roots level—may have had effectiveness to some extent immune from the hazards of cooptation and elitism more prevalent at the national level.

Relationships Between Roles and the Evolution of Roles

Not only are the above types of roles overlapping and interconnected, but any particular group's goals and strategies evolve over time, often in relation to government actions or reactions. As pointed out above, the supplemental role can lead to a transformative role through the effects that stewardship activities can have on a community. Involvement in stewardship activities can also act as a force for the politicization of communities resulting in a transition to the advocacy role (Lerner, 1986). For example, an ENGO that invests effort into the rehabilitation of a stream and then sees that stream insufficiently protected by government agencies may turn to lobbying tactics; in essence, it becomes politicized. Reformists may become radicals if they consistently encounter blockages to their reform objectives and lose faith in the system of governance at which their efforts have been targeted. They may also shift from a cooperative stance to a confrontational one if they find cooperative channels are inadequately responsive, or if they consider the risks of cooptation too high. Alteratively, a group may use different approaches concurrently, as they lend themselves appropriately to different types of problems (Wilson, 1988).

Other observers maintain that strategies employed in a particular role can work against the achievement of ends associated with other roles. For instance, opinions differ as to the wisdom of the "third wave" tactics which emphasize the negotiation processes that Schnaiberg flagged as posing some risks. While observers like Slocombe (1984) see the "emerging environmentalist professionalism" as the way of the future, those of a more radical bent like Weinberg (1989) and Commoner (1988) see the abandonment of the adversarial approach as holding dangers such as compromise solutions to environmental problems favoring industry, counteraction of grass-roots efforts, and reinforcement of "the highly centralized techno-bureaucratic political structures of the late twentieth century" (Weinberg, 1989:9). Paul George of the Western Canada Wilderness Committee graphically described the compromise implicated in environmentalist participation on a government-appointed advisory committee for the review of logging in the Carmanah Valley as "like sitting on the team planning to build the ovens at Auschwitz" (Bell, 1991).

More simply, efforts towards social transformation may be neglected because of the level of commitment taken to maintain a vigilant stand on reforms achieved to date, and to respond to invitations for participation from government. Mitchell elaborates such a dilemma:

> The legislative response to the nation's environmental problems
> has been sufficiently extensive that most environmentalists will
> be too busy defending the existing laws and calling for new ones
> to push for a radically decentralized society in any serious way
> in the years to come. (1980:356)

Sandbach is also pessimistic, observing that environmentalist campaigns focussed on particular issues have not been "sufficiently broadly based to have seriously threatened the power that major corporations are able to wield, nor their sources of profit which are often the root cause of environmental problems" (1980:135). Reed and Amos (1988), in turn, argue that the biggest failing of the U.S. environmental movement has been its inability to respond to issues at the local and regional levels because of its "misdirected" focus on Washington and national wilderness reserves.

Yet, as mentioned earlier, the potential power of advocacy efforts beyond their immediate meliorist image should not be underestimated. Like the stewardship activities of the supplemental role, advocacy work can have a transformational influence. Nerfin draws attention to this potential from a global perspective:

> The principle of accountability and its enforcement emerges perhaps as the central theme in the efforts to re-assert people's autonomous power vis-a-vis the Prince and the Merchant. ...As an instrument of democracy (that is, strictly speaking, people's power), accountability may progressively circumscribe the power of those who hold it. The act of making Prince and Merchant accountable may instil a new sense of self-confidence among the people. (1987:177)

Schumacher makes virtually the same point in his classic book, *Good Work* (1979) as he suggests that the roles that people have taken on in non-government organizations challenged them "to think and act in larger arenas, accepting responsibility for more people and/or dealing with more complicated issues and information and wider horizons. Their performance created in their eyes and in others a vastly increased sense of the scope of their own capacities and of 'common people' in general" (1979:160).

On a less positive note, the current trend in B.C. towards civil disobedience strategies is drawing unprecedented levels of attention to the environmental movement in this province (e.g., Mitchell, 1989; Rose, 1991). Direct action is often a result of high levels of frustration over a perceived lack of access to decision-making through more moderate approaches. It is a form of protest that can be directed at particular issues, in the realm of advocacy, or at more fundamental social change, in the transformative category. Milbrath observes that "[e]nvironmentalists probably will continue to use direct action to influence policy as long as they believe that they are unable to affect change through normal political channels" (1984:90). Cotgrove ascribes the growth of direct action to "a deep-seated loss of confidence in political institutions" (1982:97) and cites Habermas as also having identified "a widening of the gap between citizen and government, and...an emerging crisis of legitimacy in politics" (1982:98).

Members of the political or corporate mainstream, in contrast, are less likely to explain the movement towards more extreme strategies in terms of structural flaws in society. For example, an article in the *Report on Business Magazine* describes the attitude of Canadian ENGOs which are unwilling to enter into cooperative arrangements with business as behind-the-times, petty, malevolent, zealous and irrational: "For a descent into true environmental madness, it's necessary to take a trip to Canada's West Coast" (Mitchell, 1989:77). Likewise, a wildlife manager in B.C. recognizes that the most vocal environmental group representatives in B.C. get identified by decision-making authorities as trouble-makers, radicals and extremists, and he recommends to them, "If you want a fair hearing, and want to convince the businessmen, the miners, the foresters and the subdividers, learn to talk like one!" (Walker, 1988:113). Thankfully, not all decision-makers are so accusatory. A corporate president speaking before the annual conference of the Foundation for Public Affairs in Washington, D.C. shared the following insightful remarks, worthy of quotation at length:

> First we must dispel the myths about the activist movements by some careful definition of the activist community. For the most part, activist movements are peoples movements, initially amorphous but soon coalesced and then organized around a commonalty of interests and concerns. An articulate spokesman for a single issue of emerging concern can soon become the lynch pin of a movement. Critics of conscience are quickly attracted to those who are willing to devote all their energies to righting a wrong. Underestimating the ethical seriousness of these critics is a serious mistake. And issue managers who dismiss or attempt to discredit activism as creeping socialism are doing business a terrible disservice. Activism has moved as far beyond Saul Alinsky as industry has beyond the industrial revolution. Activists are not overzealous adolescents having a go at the adults. They are for the most part serious-minded people who believe that they are working for a cleaner, safer, healthier, saner world (Pagan, 1989:178).

Conclusion

A hypothesis can be drawn from the above analysis that the life-cycle of an ENGO follows one of two paths. The first is that described earlier from Watts and Wandesforde-Smith (1980), in which local-level action by ad hoc groupings of individuals is followed by higher-level mobilization towards changing the policy process, which in turn evolves into a questioning of the legitimacy of the system and a call for its transformation. The alternative life-cycle is similar in its first two stages, but culminates in "third wave" cooperation rather than increased radicalism. In the latter scenario, the tendency towards conservatism may be counterbalanced by groups in earlier phases of the cycle or by ones that follow the first sequence described, although this effect is debatable.

In either case, ENGOs with highly different role-orientations will co-exist at any time, and there is no consensus amongst analysts on the compatibility of strategies associated with those roles. Moderates advocating more accountability from the governance system tend to be more accepting of the full range of strategies than are radicals seeking systemic transformation. Rather than ascribe this apparent open-mindedness to greater maturity or generosity of spirit, deeper practical and ideological explanations can be identified. First, the moderates almost by definition have more faith in the functioning of a pluralistic, liberal democracy, and so assume that the system provides fair access to all interests, including the radicals (should they choose to partake). Second, radical environmentalist activities rarely detract from the effectiveness of more moderate advocacy work except to the extent that the whole movement may be seen to be "tainted" by the high-profile actions of the extremists. The threat of radical action is even seen as an advantage by many moderates, in that it serves as a forcefull back-up to failed cooperative efforts—as a "best alternative to a negotiated agreement." From the perspective of the radicals, on the other hand, the system is not seen to be equitably accessible to all interests and indeed it is so inadequate as to deserve boycotting. Cooperation from moderates, in the eyes of the radicals, absorbs precious ENGO resources, derails critical protest activities and further legitimizes the rules designed by the elite to serve their own interests.

Nevertheless, each role does possess its own good intentions, integrity, and potential to promote fundamental social change towards the principles of sustainable development. Furthermore, most observers of the current state of the environmental movement, whether reformists or radicals, agree that the naively apolitical days of earlier phases are past, and that ENGOs are increasingly obliged to enter the political forum (Paehlke, 1985). At the same time, the trend towards direct action, and the new development of ENGO surveillance by security forces (Berlet, 1990), reflect a widening gap between ENGOs and government that is cause for concern. To Milbrath, the question of trust is central: "A profound question for governance in all societies is the extent to which groups trust each other to make wise policy choices" (1984:92). Recent Canadian poll results support his empirical findings on this topic in the U.S.: the general public's trust in the viewpoints of environmentalists has grown as its confidence in government has diminished.

Proponents of the cooperative approach like Colin Isaacs, a Canadian activist who left Pollution Probe over this issue, hope to restore trust through more intense, supportive interaction between ENGOs and the establishment (Morris, 1990). Proponents of direct action, like the U.S.-based Earth First!, hope to see the system succumb to their demands for fundamental restructuring, replaced by a decentralized form of governance more worthy of a cooperative relationship. While the hard choice between these two options threatens to split the environmental movement, a third path is emerging. Contemporary with the increasing politicization of the movement is the development of a new form of apolitical environmental activity, described under the supplementary category above—volunteer environmental stewardship. The stewardship role holds the promise of support for the grass roots, self-determining approach prescribed by the principles of sustainable development. It offers a set of strategies that does not necessarily expend energy in a negative way confronting the system; nor does it always endorse the system. Stewardship strategies instead demonstrate constructive ways of moving towards an environmentally and socially sustainable future.

The Hodges (1979) summarize the qualities that community-based ENGOs have to offer as innovation, energy and commitment, capability, and information and knowledge. They suggest that ENGOs can apply these attributes to both local environmental problems and to "the functional problems of environmental management which have much broader orientations than the locality." Furthermore, these authors believe that community ENGOs

> can provide a valuable bridge in local problem solving between the assessment of local needs and the assessment of the technical and global issues which nowadays characterize so many problems confronting local decision makers. It could probably best be achieved by a cooptative mode of participation rather than a conflict mode. But whether decision makers will offer citizens a partnership in community problem solving and gain the assets that community groups possess is still, as distressing as it seems, a crucial and unsolved question. (1979:36)

A decade later, the question rests unanswered, and myriad institutional blockages to the creative work of community-based ENGOs remain. Many diverse voices are now calling for the replacement of those impediments with positive incentives:

- The World Commission on Environment and Development (1987:328) calls for "substantially increased financial support [for community-based NGO's] to expand their special roles and functions on behalf of the world community and in support of national NGOs. In the Commission's view, the increased support that will allow these organizations to expand their services represents an indispensable and cost-effective investment."
- Shirley Taylor, of the U.S. Sierra Club declares that "smart and responsible" coastal managers "might do well to extend their friendship and cooperation to the interested public waiting at their door, eager to be admitted to help reach common goals. They will cooperate when possible, confront only when necessary. They can take the lead to propose policies that managers might wish for but dare not do...Coastal managers will not be weakened if they open that door—but only strengthened" (1987:2196).
- Stuart Langton maintains that the capacity of the voluntary sector needs to be strengthened through "enormous support efforts" if interest groups are to play their roles, for example through reforms in government tax and regulatory policies and greater commitment from the corporate sector, equitably at both centralized and grass roots levels (1982:16).
- Canada's *Green Plan* (1990) apparently supports the above philosophy in its promise of increased core funding to smaller ENGOs. The sincerity of this gesture can only be proven with time. Indeed, as the supplementary role expands, largely in the form of voluntary environmental stewardship, its

performance must be carefully monitored for pitfalls like cooptation, off-loading of government responsibility, and others listed above.

The monitoring of the supplementary role and its interplay with the more traditional, activist roles of ENGOs is the challenge for the observers of the environmental movement whose works are reviewed in this chapter and their successors. The Fraser Basin case study in Volume 2 contributes to this cause by seeking preliminary empirical evidence of the phenomenon discussed in this chapter, focussing on the interactive processes described above under the advocacy, supplemental and transformative role categories.

Acknowledgements

The author would like to thank the Social Science and Humanities Research Council of Canada for the financial assistance which supported the production of this paper.

References

Berger, J. J. 1987. *Restoring the Earth: How Americans are Working to Renew our Damaged Environment*. New York: Doubleday.

Andrews, R. N. L. 1980. "Class Politics or Democratic Reform: Environmentalism and American Political Institutions." *Natural Resources Journal*. 20:231-241.

Bell, S. 1991. "Eight Named to Committee to Review Valley Logging." *The Vancouver Sun*. 12th January 1991.

Berlet, C. 1990. "Taking off the Gloves." *Greenpeace*. Sept/Oct:18-22.

Booth, R. S. 1988. "Forging a Viable Future." in Borrelli, P. (ed.). *Crossroads: Environmental Priorities for the Future*. Washington: Island Press.

Borrelli, P. 1988. "Environmentalism at a Crossroads." in Borrelli, P. (ed.). *Crossroads: Environmental Priorities for the Future*. Washington: Island Press.

Buttel, F. H. 1986. "Discussion: Economic Stagnation, Scarcity, and Changing Commitments to Distributional Policies in Environmental-Resource Issues." in Schnaiberg, A., N. Watts and K. Zimmermann (eds.). *Distributional Conflicts in Environmental-Resource Policy*. England: Gower.

Byrne, J. M., and T. F. Horn. 1989. "Citizen Participation in River Conservation and Water Quality Protection: A Regional Approach." Submitted to the Conference of the Canadian Water Resources Association, 20 June 1989.

Canada. Environment Canada. 1990. *Canada's Green Plan*. Ottawa: Ministry of Supply and Services.

Canadian Parks and Wilderness Society. 1990. Fundraising letter to membership. 9th April 1991.

Commoner, B. 1988. "The Environment" in Borrelli, P. (ed.). *Crossroads: Environmental Priorities for the Future*. Washington: Island Press.

Commoner, B. 1990. "Environmental Democracy is the Planet's Best Hope." *Utne Reader*. July/August:61-63.

Cotgrove, S. 1982. *Catastrophe or Cornucopia: The Environment, Politics and the Future*. Chichester: John Wiley and Sons.

Devall, B. 1980. "The Deep Ecology Movement." *Natural Resources Journal*. 20:299-322.

Doherty, M. 1984. *Environmental Non-Governmental Organizations in Canada and the U.S.A.* Sierra Club of Western Canada. mimeo. 1st November 1984.

Draper, D. 1972. *Eco-Activism: Issues and Strategies of Environmental Interest Groups in British Columbia.* Unpublished M.A.thesis, Department of Geography, University of Victoria.

Dreyfoos, W. W. 1987. "Estuarine Protection through Public Participation." in Magoon, O. T. et al. (eds.). *Coastal Zone '87: Proceedings of the Fifth Symposium on Coastal and Ocean Management. Volume 2.* New York: American Society of Civil Engineers.

Durning, A. B. 1989. "Mobilizing at the Grassroots." in Brown, L. R. et al. *State of the World 1989.* New York and London: W.W. Norton and Co.

Eckersley. 1988. "Green Politics: A Practice in Search of a Theory?" *Alternatives* 15(4):52-61.

Friedmann, J. 1987. *Planning in the Public Domain: From Knowledge to Action.* New Jersey: Princeton University Press.

Frome, M. 1988. "Heal the Earth, Heal the Soul." in Borrelli, P. (ed.). *Crossroads: Environmental Priorities for the Future.* Washington: Island Press.

Gadgil, M. 1987. "Culture, Perceptions and Attitudes to the Environment." in Jacobs, P. and D. A. Munro (eds.). *Conservation with Equity: Strategies for Sustainable Development.* Gland and Cambridge: IUCN.

Globe and Mail. 1991. "Wallets Mobilized in U.S. Forest Battle." 12th January 1991.

Halle, M., and J. I. Furtado. 1987. "The Role of National Conservation Strategies in Attaining Objectives of the World Conservation Strategy." in Jacobs, P. and D.A. Munro (eds.). *Conservation with Equity: Strategies for Sustainable Development.* Cambridge: Cambridge University Press.

Hodge, G., and P. Hodge. 1979. "Public Participation in Environmental Planning in Eastern Ontario." *Plan Canada.* 9(1):30-37.

Jacobs, P., and D. A. Munro. 1987. *Conservation with Equity: Strategies for Sustainable Development.* Cambridge: Cambridge University Press.

Keating, M. 1989. "Marking Changes for the Better: Monitoring Advances in Sustainable Development." in *Environment and Economy, Partners for the Future: A Conference on Sustainable Development: The Proceedings.* Winnipeg.

Kernaghan, K., and D. Siegel. 1987. "Public Administration in Canada." in *Pressure Groups, Political Parties and the Bureaucracy.* Toronto: Methuen.

Koppes, C. R. 1988. "Efficiency, Equity, Aesthetics: Shifting Themes in American Conservation." in Worster, D. (ed.). *The Ends of the Earth.* New York: Cambridge University Press.

Langton, S. 1982. "The New Voluntarism." in J. D. Harman (ed.). *Voluntarism in the Eighties: Fundamental Issues in Voluntary Action.* Washington: University Press of America.

Lee, P. G. 1987. "Dealing with the Civil Service on Environmental Issues." in Public Advisory Committees to the Environment Council of Alberta. *Need-to-know: Effective Communication for Environmental Groups. Proceeding of the 1987 Annual Joint Meeting of the Public Advisory Committees to the Environment Council of Alberta.* Edmonton: Environment Council of Alberta.

Little, C. E. 1988. "In a Landscape of Hope." in Borrelli, P. (ed.). *Crossroads: Environmental Priorities for the Future.* Washington: Island Press.

Lerner, S. C. 1986. "Environmental Constituency-Building: Local Initiatives and Volunteer Stewardship." *Alternatives.* 13(3):55-60.

Lowe, P., and J. Goyder. 1983. *Environmental Groups in Politics.* London: George Allen and Unwin.

Marchak, P. 1983. *Green Gold: The Forest Industry in British Columbia.* Vancouver: The University of British Columbia Press.

Maw, R. 1987. "Cooperative Activities." in Scace, R. C. and J. G. Nelson (eds.). *Heritage for Tomorrow: Canadian Assembly on National Parks and Protected Areas.* Ottawa: Minister of Supply and Services.

McCann, M. W. 1986. *Taking Reform Seriously: Perspectives on Public Interest Liberalism.* Ithaca and London: Cornell University Press.

M'Gonigle, R. M. 1986. "The Tribune and the Tribe: Toward a Natural Law of the Market/Legal State." *Ecology Law Quarterly.* 13:233-310.

McIlroy, A. 1990. "Environmentalists: Who's Who in the Green Movement and should they be Doing Business with Business?" *The Ottawa Citizen.* 18th October 1990.

Milbrath, L. W. 1984. *Environmentalists: Vanguard for a New Society.* Albany: State University of New York.

Mitchell, J. 1989. "No Deals." *Report on Business Magazine.* October 1989.

Mitchell, R. C. 1980. "How 'Soft,' 'Deep,' or 'Left?' Present Constituencies in the Environmental Movement for Certain World Views." *Natural Resources Journal.* 20:345-358.

Morris, J. 1990. "Environmental Groups Urged to Take Less Radical Approach." *The Ottawa Citizen*. 8th June 1990.

Morrison, D. E. 1986. "How and Why Environmental Consciousness has Trickled Down." in Schnaiberg, A., N Watts and K. Zimmermann (eds) *Distributional Conflicts in Environmental-resource Policy*. England: Gower.

Nerfin, M. 1987. "Neither Prince nor Merchant: Citizen—An Introduction to the Third System." *Development Dialogue*. 1987(1):170-195.

O'Riordan, T. 1981. (2nd edition) *Environmentalism*. London: Pion.

Paehlke, R. C. 1985. "Environmentalism: 'Motherhood', Revolution, or Just Plain Politics." *Alternatives*. 13(1):29-33.

Paehlke, R C. 1989. *Environmentalism and the Future of Progressive Politics*. New Haven and London: Yale University Press.

Pagan, R. D. Jr. 1989. "Framing the Public Agenda: The Age of New Activism." *Vital Speeches of the Day*. LV(6):177-180. Delivered before the Annual Conference of the Foundation for Public Affairs, Washington, D.C., 29th September 1988.

Pearse, P. H., F. Bertrand and J. W. MacLaren. 1985. *Currents of Change: Final Report Inquiry on Federal Water Policy*. Ottawa: Environment Canada.

Petulla, J. M. 1987. *Environmental Protection in the United States: Industry, Agencies, Environmentalists*. San Francisco: San Francisco Study Centre.

Pross, A. P. 1986. *Group Politics and Public Policy*. Toronto: Oxford University Press.

Puget Sound Water Quality Authority. 1990. *Public Involvement and Education Model Projects Fund: 47 Success Stories from Puget Sound*, Seattle: Puget Sound Water Quality Authority.

Quadra Planning Consultants Ltd. and Regional Consulting Ltd. 1990. *State of the Environment Report for the Lower Fraser Basin*. Report prepared for Environment Canada and B.C. Ministry of Environment. March 1990 draft.

Reed, N. P., and A. S. Eno. 1988. "Looking Backwards." in Borrelli, P. (ed.). *Crossroads: Environmental Priorities for the Future*. Washington: Island Press.

Rees, J. 1985. *Natural Resources: Allocation, Economics and Policy*. London and New York: Methuen.

Resnick, P. 1986. "Democratization and Socialism." in Magnusson, W., R. B. F. Walker, C. Doyle and J. DeMarco (eds.). *After Bennett*. Vancouver: New Star Books Ltd.

Rose, A. 1991. "Log Jam, Woolly Ethics of Disobedience." *The Toronto Globe and Mail*. 5th January 1991.

Ruff, N. 1986 "Towards Interactive Government." in Magnusson, W., R.B.F. Walker, C. Doyle and J. DeMarco (eds.). *After Bennett*. Vancouver: New Star Books Ltd.

Sabatier, P. A., and N. Pelkey. 1987. "Incorporating Multiple Actors and Guidance Instruments into Models of Regulatory Policymaking: An Advocacy Coalition Framework." *Administration and Society*. 19(2):236-263.

Sadler, B. 1980. "Towards New Strategies of Public Involvement in Environmental Management." in Sadler, B. (ed.). *Public Participation in Environmental Decision Making: Strategies for Change*. Edmonton: Environment Council of Alberta.

Salim, E. 1987. "Indonesia's National Conservation Strategy." in Jacobs, P. and D. A. Munro (eds.). *Conservation with Equity: Strategies for Sustainable Development*. Cambridge: Cambridge University Press.

Sandbach, F. 1980. *Environment, Ideology and Policy*. Oxford: Basil Blackwell.

Sandbrook, J. R. 1986. "Towards a Global Environmental Strategy." in Park, C. C. (ed.). *Environmental policies: An International Review*.

Science Council of Canada. 1988. *Water 2020: Sustainable Use for Water in the 21st Century*. Science Council of Canada Report 40. Ottawa: Science Council of Canada.

Schnaiberg, A. 1980. *The Environment: From Surplus to Scarcity*. New York: Oxford University Press.

Schumacher, E. F. 1979. *Good Work*. New York: Harper and Row.

Slocombe, D. S. 1984. "Environmentalism: A Modern Synthesis." *The Environmentalist*. 4(4):281-5.

Susskind, L., and M. Elliott. 1983. "Paternalism, Conflict, and Co-production: Learning from Citizen Action and Citizen Participation in Western Europe." in L. Susskind and M. Elliott (eds.). *Paternalism, Conflict, and Coproduction: Learning from Citizen Action and Citizen Participation in Western Europe*. New York and London: Plenum Press.

Taylor, S. 1987. "Overlooked Tools that Build Coastal Constituencies." in Magoon, O. T. et al. (eds.). *Coastal Zone '87: Proceedings of the Fifth Symposium on Coastal and Ocean Management*. Volume 2. New York: American Society of Civil Engineers.

Walker, J. H. C. 1988. "The Role of the Public in Wildlife Decision-Making." in Fox, R. J. (ed.). *The Wildlife of Northern British Columbia - Past, Present and Future*. Smithers: The Spatsizi Association for Biological Research.

Watts, N., and G. Wandesforde-Smith. 1980. "Postmaterial Values and Environmental Policy Change." *Policy Studies Journal*. 9(3):346-358.

Weinberg, B. 1989. "'Third Wave' Environmentalism... Imagine there's no Exxon..." *The New Catalyst*. Winter 1989/90(16):8-9.

Wilson, C. 1988. "A View from the Trenches." in Borrelli, P. (ed.). *Crossroads: Environmental Priorities for the Future*. Washington: Island Press.

World Commission on Environment and Development (WCED). 1987. *Our Common Future*. Oxford, New York: Oxford University Press.

14

British Columbia's Water Rights: Their Impact on the Sustainable Development of the Fraser Basin

Anthony D. Scott

This chapter deals with one of the institutions that must be involved in the development of the Fraser Basin: the water rights held by those who divert and consume its flows. It shows that, although widely regarded as an administrative device, the present system of rights is an adaptation of systems that have a long history. One of my purposes is simply to present aspects of the twists and turns of this history and to attempt some explanations of how and why systems have from time to time been altered. A second is to use this background to assess the present Fraser Basin system and suggest how it may be changed to become suitable for sustainable development.

Water Licences and Sustainable Development

Sustainable Development

Dorcey, in the opening chapter of this volume, refers to sustainable development as an evolving world view. Within this he distinguishes five goals or "elements":

- Maintaining ecological integrity and diversity;
- Meeting basic human needs;
- Keeping options open for future generations;
- Reducing injustice;
- Increasing self-determination.

What is new about this list, as opposed to those of the older conservation movement or the later environmental ethic is the first element. For conservation-minded economists and all those taking a discounted-benefit-cost view of social decisions, there is nothing new about concern for the welfare and freedom of future generations. That concern has been, by itself, enough to motivate a whole campaign, but its goals and difficulties are already well known and analysed. Reducing injustice and meeting basic needs, especially the injustice of hunger and poverty in the developing world are also familiar concerns. The strength of the Brundtland report is that it keeps the developing world as a constraint in its discussion of our options for dealing with the ecological and physical challenges of global survival. No policy that neglects the welfare of the developing world is ethically acceptable; in any case no such option is available.

Thus, sustainable development has a moral imperative that is also a necessary condition for the achievement of any other goal. Unless we meet the needs of the developing world our own descendants will not long have opportunities to enjoy the resources of the Fraser Basin or the luxury of debating how they should be preserved and exploited.

Certain considerations help to shape an ethic for the care and use of our resources over the next twenty years. First, they must be used: we owe it to the developing world to play our role as a source of basic necessities, so that the pressure on tropical lands, oceans, streams, forests and minerals can be eased. That is, we must continue to produce wood products, foods, energy, fish and metals. Second, we must make sure that aid and trade open our purses and our markets, and in all ways make the developing world benefit from our production and resources. The components of this second step, however, are less under our local control as a matter of resource policy. Third, we must increase the efficiency of our production: the more we produce from a given resource pressure, the less we need to expand that pressure to other resources. As well, this means the more we can share with the world.

Fourth, with respect to Fraser Basin water resources, we need to adopt water-use methods that maintain the ecological integrity and diversity of the tributary creeks, lakes and rivers, and of the interdependent communities, forests and lands, while at the same time making possible human use of the "resources". All human purposes, commercial and otherwise (including simple preservation or non-use as one human purpose), deserve equal consideration in deciding on uses. To dedicate a stream to one use only is probably to misuse it; on the other hand it, is probably beneficial to dedicate some streams to particular purposes and preserve them from many of the other purposes and uses.

Fifth, consideration of the four points mentioned above indicates that there are a range of alternative sustainable development strategies for B.C. One strategy is to conserve our resources and to adopt policies for sustainable development within B.C. At the opposite extreme to this is a second strategy; to develop our resources intensely so as to maximise their near-future yield. Which one to choose depends on how we wish to divide the burden of sustainable development between ourselves and the developing world. Following the "develop" strategy, we can intensify those water uses that increase the income that is enjoyed or accrues to today's generation of B.C. people: uses in agriculture, industry, power, mining, forestry, fish migration, tourism, hunting and fishing. In general, every increase in these activities increases our material and financial self-sufficiency. Carried to the limit, we could for a while become independent of the resources of other regions. The implications of such a choice can be appreciated by considering reductions in this developmental, resource-using, strategy. Every reduction would mean an increase in our dependence on the resources of other regions and countries. Carried to its limit, this reduction would bring us to a negligible productive use of our resources, restoring the rivers completely to their natural flow in quality and quantity. Then, unless we could will our life styles to become proportionately austere and frugal, we would depend completely on production taking place elsewhere, remaining economically dependent but minimising the pressure on and the delay in restoring our own resources, as though we lived in a combined national park and wilderness area.

If our reduction of land and water uses were carried to this extreme, we would have opted out of that part of the international streams of aid, assistance, trade and migration and forced the rest of the world to use its resources to provide for us. On the other hand, if we intensified our land and water uses, we would reduce our dependence on the world, increase their dependence on us, and enable them to "conserve" their resources.

Obviously, we will not choose either of these drastic extremes, but something between them. We will trade off development against local sustainability, until we arrive at a strategy that makes some contribution to global sustainability but which also satisfies the feeling that environmentalist action must begin at home. The point is that the trade-off here is not zero-sum. While we can start by envisaging a simple choice between damaging an acre-foot of land-and-water here or in the tropics, the *impacts* and *products* of these alternatives are not the same. We must go on to observe the differences. It seems that *global* damage done by an increment of tropical forest destruction is now greater there than the damage done by an equal increment of forest destruction in B.C. Furthermore, it seems the *global* gain in product (food, timber, fish, metals, electricity, etc.) from that increment is greater in B.C. than in the tropics. (Our labour productivities, capital productivities and land yields are higher). To the extent these perceptions about damage and productivity are correct, we should help the tropical countries to stop being the world's specialists in sustaining ecological impact by sustaining more of it in B.C. At least we should not hesitate to suffer more. (And, to the extent the perceptions are not correct, we should encourage the world's economies to press even more on the developing world's resources and should reduce our non-sustainable use of our own.)

Here is a dilemma, only partly ethical and mostly informational and economic. Our global ecosystem and production information are not so far collected in a fashion to help us to compare the global impacts of an extra ton of paper or aluminum produced in B.C., with that of a ton processed in the developing world. Nor is it always correct that labour and capital are always more productive when used in producing ordinary goods and services here. The ethical problem is whether we are willing to increase the development, or the conservation of our resources according to what inquiries would show.

My tentative opinion is that neither those who are concerned about our common future nor those who are most indifferent to it are thinking in these terms. Neither side is considering what role we can play most advantageously; neither has adequate information and neither is empowered to make this overwhelming choice. Neither sees that her/his self interest depends on this comparison. Reports (such as *Sustaining the Living Land* [Strangway, 1989] for B.C.) suggest that many thoughtful Canadians intend to press for the preservation of *our* resources regardless of facts about the choice above. However, to the extent that aspects of the choice are reflected in world market values of food, fibre, timber, etc., Canadian producers are being induced to develop our resources extensively and intensively, also regardless of facts about the trade-offs. For example, both sides are content that paper and lumber production should migrate from B.C. to the tropics; one side is relieved to see the end of pressure on our forests, while the other anticipates enjoying greater returns from tropical than from temperate logging.

Water Licencing as an "Institution"

We may expect that information about this trade-off between development and protection will become available only slowly. Not enough will be known in the near future to justify either a current policy of increasing exploitation of the Fraser River Basin's resources even at irreversible environmental cost, or a policy of going backward from the present general level of development, even at great export and income cost. It would be wrong to re-develop our institutions in a way that would bias our future in either direction, yet we must keep them flexible enough to adapt smoothly to whatever needs, information, opportunities and attitudes emerge. What we need to know now is how our institutions work and how they can be changed as needed.

In this essay, the institution is the system of water rights that underlies individual water use—and non-use—in the Fraser Basin. We will see that such institutions, even when they are based on a statute, cannot easily be changed by simply planning to amend that statute. Such institutions are properly slow to change, because they are relied on by all to provide a certain context for day-to-day activity and future planning, private and public. They are respected because they are relatively more stable than the decisions and transactions conducted in their shelter. Water rights have never been exclusively an instrument of government policy. Indeed, government has often simply enforced the water usages that individuals have invented and instituted. Thus the question arises about the institution that will guide and constrain our water choices over the next twenty years. What can we say about who will protect, and allocate, and how, and for what reward, our stream levels and flows?

For any purpose, the variety of organizational systems that are both available and suitable is very large. Some are better than others, less clumsy and costly, fairer, or less biased in their outcomes. In theory a resource user's basic functions can be performed within almost any institutional set-up that will:

- Obtain information;
- Make policies and decision(s);
- Share the yield, enjoyment or ownership; and,
- Monitor and enforce decisions and feed back experience as new information.

However, institutions also are specialised in the costs, ease and fairness with which they allow these functions to be performed. History suggests that a blend of institutions gradually tends to replace a monolithic introduction. For example, even the working of the old feudal system of land use was tempered by such exceptions as free cities, church land uses, royal forests and both chartered and privately-conveyed lands, fishing rights, water power privileges, mineral rights, port rights and so forth.

Similarly, on the scale of water resources alone, *pure* versions of the various types of water regimes, such as government regulation, custom, riparian rights, appropriative rights, and their Mediterranean and Islamic equivalents, have never existed. Water resources are probably too complicated and heterogenous for reliance on any single system. The numbers of users and uses are too numerous for either government regulation to make decisions about each one or for rival systems to make one rule for all. A mixed system has always emerged, and there is always good reason for reconsidering the mixture.

In the early days a system was selected for its apparent distributive connotations. A riparian system favoured old-established land owners; an appropriative system favoured first-comers and their descendants; a religious system favoured the faithful; an Islamic system favoured migratory uses; a public system favoured the voting majority: these and other distributional generalizations are said to have been sufficient explanations of changing mixtures of systems.

Today, however, it is recognised that a water system has no unique distribution of wealth to go with it. For example, a governmentally-regulated system can favour any set of users and, as well, either produce revenues or absorb government expenditure. The same is true of a modified riparian rights system, an appropriative system, a "taxed" system and an appropriative-rights system. Thus, in analysing systems and choosing among them, we may, to a first approximation, neglect their fairness, justice and rent-producing or absorbing aspects. For example, an appropriative-rights system can be almost literally a sinkhole for government money or a lucrative mine of public or private revenue; both these outcomes can be found in the U.S. mountain states today.

What we must do is investigate how a system affects the *uses* that are made of surface water and ground water (see below) and with what ease or cost it allows the chosen combinations to be made or changed. The system of private water rights, including water licences, has "characteristics" that do this. By itself or in combination, the right allows a number of users to choose among a number of uses. In most variants, it allows market mechanisms to play a major role in answering the five great questions of water use: what? where? how? when? and for whom?

The main part of this chapter is about these characteristics. Before that I discuss the history that led us to our present licencing. Apart from serving my own historical interests, I find it important to do this so that I can allow the reader to hear about our experiences with earlier systems, descendants of which are still around. Each system's characteristics are constantly being modified and each is to be seen as in competition with others. A vast literature includes many comparisons of the systems' merits. New choices of system are being suggested all the time. For example, in the 1960's, Ontario went over to a permit system; in the 1970's, Saskatchewan put all water rights under a Crown corporation. In the 1990's, water users everywhere are getting accustomed to suggestions about how water *as a commodity* should be priced, protected and provided. How our own system here in B.C. emerged is outlined below.

I have a special reason for doing this historical analysis. In spite of the background of choice and controversy regarding water systems, I am skeptical of the implicit belief that a society such as ours is free just to adopt whatever system it fancies. Like all institutions, the water systems that are actually in use change very slowly. Courts may re-interpret private rights, and governments may pass new Water Acts, but the exercise of accepted rights may stay stubbornly on a course that is determined as much by custom, belief, technology and preferences as by formal law. Knowing this, judges and politicians are reluctant to tinker with a working water-rights system. Consequently, when new needs or uses emerge, as is happening today in terms of water quality, actual water practices do not instantly conform. It follows that it is not enough to read histories that chronicle changes in laws and court rulings; we must also know which were effective and which merely tentative, or symbolic.

For example, before the story narrated in the next part began, England and New England had been through several versions of the common law of rights to divert rivers. "Riparian rights" as they were called, were an integral part of ownership of land on the bank of a river. For the most part, this "riparian" law was agreed to be less a branch of the old law of prosperity than an implicit body of court decisions about nuisance, loss or injury suffered by parties whose opportunities to use flowing water had been harmed. Their damage suits had gradually accumulated into the outline of a system of rights to divert.

Most suits involved water power, as used for cloth mills, sawmills, flour mills and for mines and smelters. Until about 1800, whichever user had first been harnessing the fall of a stream was likely to be confirmed in his right to divert. This era is sometimes referred to as the period of "prior-use rights". After 1800, however, this clear doctrine was obscured by the large number of law suits arising from the key role of water power in the Industrial Revolution in textiles. In these cases, the courts seemed to try one doctrine after another. First, they formally disavowed their prior-use doctrine and proclaimed that *every* riverside proprietor had a right to that river's "natural flow". This really settled nothing, so the courts next took to deciding between conflicting water power uses on the basis of "reasonableness". Since this was essentially a system of leaving every decision to a judge's discretion, it worked after a fashion and the "reasonable-use" principle was retained for many kinds of water-right questions.

Just how this version of riparian law compared with the new system that followed *after* it, is discussed at some length below. However, the point I wish to make is that this legal ferment about court principles and procedures in water-use disputes is a misleading guide to the history of water rights. While the courts, and the legislatures, were fine-tuning the notion of reasonable use (in, say, the 1840's), water was still allocated and transferred by rights under the pre-1800 prior-use system. Agriculture and industry (and navigation, too) were based on the idea that the prior user had rights to divert that were virtually unassailable. These recognised priorities very often hardened in a defined period of time into real property rights, by the workings of the process known as "prescription". Even when they did not harden in this way, they were not only held, but transferred by contract or agreement or by sale or lease of riparian rights to divert. Thus riparian property owners could benefit from their riverside locations, while the water itself was "promoted" to ever better-paying uses.

The trade in these rights, referred to by the generic name of "privileges", was apparently immune not only to changes in common-law procedure and principles, but also to the politicking and law making that ushered in the age of canals and city water and sewer systems. The prior user never lost out. Although there were of course many exceptions and many "hard cases", the systems of negotiable prior use rights flourished as long users demanded it.

The lesson: neither judges nor legislatures can easily change a working system of water rights. It was and is much easier to recognise, confirm and build on these rights than transform them. Short of revolution, no court or legislature will participate in a wide-spread cancellation of custom and privilege, especially one that the holders believe themselves to have paid for.

However, notwithstanding this observation, water systems have changed. To see the great change of 1849, read on.

The Western States Replace Riparian Law

History

The Western appropriative-rights laws represented a self-help approach to law-making. They were born in California and the mountain territories purchased from Mexico in 1848. Although pioneers were flowing to the mineral and ranch lands, the regions lacked courts and law-making assemblies.

As a result, in the subsequent California gold rush, miners grouped in their camps agreed and apparently enforced a new water law incident to their new mining-claim law.[1] Both laws were later enforced by the new state. Somewhat

---

1   That mining property law was generally established by force among the miners themselves in their camps is widely agreed. But detailed evidence on the origins of water law is surprisingly conjectural. For example, Umbeck is able to say no more than: "I suspect that in the early 1850's water rights were rationed like land rights—by force." The general thrust of Anderson and Hill (1975) is that early farmers and raisers of cattle, already investing in storage and control works, borrowed the water property system from the mining regions. The chief contemporary source is J. H. Shinn (1884). In one of his few references to water or to ditch-building, Shinn writes of the large Columbia camp in 1850-52 that its mining laws included "...full regulations to prevent persons from diverting water flowing naturally through gold-bearing ravines, from its course, without the consent of all parties interested..."(Paul, 1965:245). Strictly speaking, this was not an appropriative, but a

similar initiatives were taken by mining, ranching or irrigation groups in other American states and the new water law was carried by miners, irrigators and administrators to still other states and other countries.

In its first years the system's important characteristic was "first in time, senior in right". In other words, the scale of seniority (precedence) remained, even after the right had been re-assigned to late comers. That the use must be beneficial (i.e., active and not potential nor wasteful) was the only other condition. The right became a "vested property interest," the characteristics of which are examined below.

Why the Change in System?

Why did the miners and settlers not use the riparian water law which was in use in the eastern states? It is often said that they believed it was suitable only for "humid" regions, not for the "arid" west! Actually, it was not that they objected to riparian law, but that they simply improvised a water system that would blend with mining practices. In any event, it is unlikely that they knew much about water law.

What the miners and settlers devised was a system that turned out to hearken back to the seniority principle of the prior-use water rights of pre-1800. As contractual rights and "privileges" these were still in effect in New England. Rejecting these, the miners now invented a system that both rehabilitated the old individual, quantity-specific rights and divorced them from riparian, or indeed any form of land-ownership.

Later in the century, the eastern and western systems were to converge. The riparian rights system was modified in the courts and by statutes to permit, or even to force, diversion to properties away from the stream. The new western system was modified by a variety of acts and decisions to accept some riparian owners' claims to water and to attach water to irrigated lands, Indian lands, federal forests, navigation requirements, and so on. This recent convergence is startling to anyone who has been exposed to the vehement statements of the 19th century champions of the two contending systems. It tends to discredit the oft-repeated idea that a common law system was infeasible for an arid region.

The Six Characteristics of a Property Right

A right has six characteristics, the amounts of which are continuously variable.[2] If one regards a water right as a type of interest in real property, then the result,

---

riparian, rule. Lawyers recounting the history of the appropriative doctrine refer most frequently to Shinn, (1884; which deals, however, mostly with minerals, not waters), George Thomas (1920) on Utah irrigation, Wiel (1911), and Wells Hutchins (1928) on the effects of Spanish law in the form of the *Acequia*.

2   See Alan Randall (1975) and Furubotn and Pejovich (1974) who, in contrast to the present discussion, describe the characteristics of rights in an *ideal* system of interests such that participants in a competitive market could together arrive at an efficient, flexible and progressive economy. For example, their lists require that the system of individual rights have zero spillover effects. My criticism is that their requirements are not available for describing the structure of an imperfect or "attenuated" system. They amount to an all-or-nothing requirement. They are therefore of no use for a policy of incrementally making a system of property rights

indeed one meaning, of a change in a property system is that a typical user obtains a different amount of each *characteristic*. These are duration, flexibility, exclusivity, quality of title, transferability and divisibility. The contrast between the riparian and appropriative systems that follows neatly illustrates the dimensions of these characteristics.

Duration

Under the old riparian system, prior-use rights and prescriptive rights had durations as long as the riparian's interest in the adjoining land. In the age of reasonable-use, these durations had become more uncertain because, as time passed, the chances that an old use would be less reasonable than a newer increased. The new appropriative right, in the typical western state, was permanent, and its holder could also transfer it out for a limited period. (See the paragraphs on transferability below).

Flexibility Among Uses

In the 18th Century the rights of riparians had only limited flexibility. For example, prior-use and prescriptive rights were in early times limited to a precise original dam or diversion, later to a precise amount of water. A transitional era, when judges required all riparians not to interfere with a concept known as "natural flow", also had rigid requirements. In the later reasonable-use period, permitted uses became flexible, only needing to be more reasonable than another party's use. Reasonability was almost capriciously vulnerable to re-examination in changed circumstances. In matters of quantity consumed or quality discharged, what was reasonable only a few years ago might become unreasonable with a changed technology or use, and vice versa.

Rights under the appropriative system represented, in a large part, a reaction against this unpredictable flexibility of the common law system. Water held in most states' appropriative rights systems could be flexibly re-allocated between uses by the original holder or his assign. However there were limits to the right of the individual irrigation farmer to change uses, places or owners. This will be discussed further under "transferability."

Exclusivity

One should not expect any water rights system to give great exclusivity to individual streamflow users, so overwhelming is the interdependence upstream and downstream. Furthermore, so-called instream uses, such as navigation, fisheries habitat, and ecosystem protection, are not easily separated "uses". In other systems, an individual's property right cannot usually be defined to be "specific" to a single use or purpose, or made free from the "externalities" or "spillovers" of other

---

somewhat less "attenuated." In such non-idealised situations, the theory of the second best applies. Numbers are needed. *Natura non facit saltum.*

users. Since 1800, it has become increasingly difficult to design a right in which the enjoyment of any given degree of water *quality* has freedom from externality, or is exclusive, though *quantity* may be guaranteed to a favoured few.

Under prior-use and prescriptive rights, although a typical or usual amount and quality was appurtenant to each riparian property, the rights had been basically neither quantitative nor qualitative. (In low-flow periods, the system apparently forced users to a sharing procedure, driving riparian users to invest in storage reservoirs, or move closer to the source.) In the reasonable-use era, although more attention was given to defining numerically-stated levels and flows, the courts actually attempted to reduce the exclusivity enjoyed by the typical user, leaving it to statute law to grant water rights to waterworks and the like. The problem of defining water quality was scarcely touched by this formulation of the property-rights system.

Under the new appropriative rights system, the goal of quantity exclusivity was regained. The amount belonged to the *user*, not to the use nor to the riparian land. Had natural flows been steady, holders would have enjoyed dependable quantities and confidence to invest in irrigation or mining capital. Actually, during seasonal low flows, the strict order of seniority was followed to ration out the available flow; the senior appropriator took *all* his, and so on till the available flow was exhausted. Thus only seniors', not juniors', rights were dependable.

The attempted exclusivity of an appropriative interest did not apply to water quality. The holder was forced to share the waste-disposal features of the stream, accepting whatever amount of waste or pollution came along. Another priority governed water quality, reflecting the number of waste emitters located upstream. When water quality did become a goal, the new rules, and rights were made quite independant of both the polluters' and the victims' water rights.

Quality of Title

Under the old common law, the riparian land proprietor had a good title to use naturally flowing water, but a non-riparian could not acquire title. A record of prior use strengthened a title. Title did not require uninterrupted use. A riparian could "sit on his right" for years, then interfere with or divert the flow. Western miners and settlers are said to have known about and rejected this dog-in-the-manger aspect of common-law rights.[3]

Under the appropriative system, the title of those who first claimed the water was the best, if the appropriator had maintained continuous "beneficial use." However, even beneficial users could have a poor title: (i) The quantity was often wrongly specified. Later, title questions required water surveys, title search, and "adjudications" of whole rivers; (ii) When common-law water rights re-appeared in half the western states, old appropriators lost water to new unanticipated

---

3   In 1989, in Boulder, Colorado, David Getches in conversation suggested to me that the appropriative system was not a "necessity" for western settlement, saying "only in N. California or Colorado on public lands was prior appropriation a necessity since there was no land ownership, property rights security was needed." (See Irwin v Philips). But with freehold land, riparian doctrine could be used successfully. In Coffin v Left Hand Ditch 6 Colo. 443 (1882) lawyers polarised the issue and defeated riparianism in Colorado.

riparian claims; (iii) Reserved or treaty rights of present or future Native Indians, foreigners and other states reduced flows apportionable to individuals; (iv) Available flows were cut to provide for such "in-stream uses" as fisheries, navigation, wilderness, waste disposal and ecosystem integrity.

Transferability and Divisibility

Early riparian rights were a "stick in the bundle of rights of a riparian landowner"[4] so that the real right could be transferred to a non-riparian with and only with a transfer of riparian land. With the coming of the reasonable-use rule, the limitations on transferability continued. But they were eroded in some places by statutes and in others by the manipulation of the reasonableness definitions to permit transport of the legal right and/or the water to remote destinations, sometimes outside the watershed.

Appropriative rights, in principle, were quite different. Acquired independently of land ownership, they were also independently transferable in two senses. First, water might be carried to and used on suitable land away from the stream. Second, water rights could be *divided* with the land where used, or parts might be assigned to "anyone."

However, in the new age of appropriative rights, much water was not easily transferable. In the new appropriative-rights states, much water was tied to lands within one irrigation district.[5] For financial and political reasons, districts did not want to lose irrigation-farming members. Another reason is that irrigation water used upstream will flow back into the river, making a larger amount available below than if all the water were transferred to another district. Though net, or option-rights, schemes have been devised, they may be costly to introduce and operate.[6] Consequently, legal and political instruments have been mobilised to prevent such transfers.

Two Tests

The characteristics of a system's individual rights can be inspected only when they grapple with a problem.

One test is the allocation of water during seasonal and irregular *low-flow periods*. Under the old riparian law all diverted water had to be returned. So in droughts, downstream users got their water, though timing and quality might

---

4   See Gould (1989:457) for a recent discussion of transferability. There is much evidence however that in New England extensive trading of mill privileges took place amongst mill owners. Hunter writes that "water privileges had early been recognised as a form of real property, subject to sale, rental and lease, by fractional shares or as a whole, often offering attractive opportunities for speculative investment."(1979:224). Bagnall (1873) details many examples of sales of privileges and leasing of them in the period between 1696-1717. There is even evidence of joint ownership agreements where water rights were divided into rights to use a mill so many hours/days per month, and that "these rights were widely sold, and further split by inheritance into fractions sometimes as small as minutes." (Gibb, 1950:118).

5   Many economists have joined legal writers in discussing particular interferences with complete transferability under appropriative statutes. In particular they have suggested ways of organizing net transfers that harm third parties. See Gould (1989) for many citations. Burness, Cummings, Gaffney, Gardner, Gisser, Howe, Milliman, Quirk and Smith, with numerous co-authors, are important names.

6   See Vernon Smith (1985), Gisser and Johnson (1983), and also a new study by Miller (1987).

suffer. Bargains could be struck so that the system led to agreed releases and sharing. Accordingly, under the later riparian system it was sometimes said that proprietors had "equal rights" (at least until laws began to allow diversions out of the watershed). Under mid-twentieth century versions of these systems, judicial procedures allocate scarce water supplies. These are combined in many states with superimposed water permit laws enacted in the 1960's; the riparian law is amended to require permittees' "equal" dividing of low flows, under officials' supervision.

Under the appropriative system, the response to low-flow periods worked quite differently.[7] In principle, the senior user got water but juniors did not. In practice, Utah and perhaps other states tended to share water shortages proportionately (Maas and Anderson, 1978).[8] Furthermore, the system's formal transferability of individual rights eased this drastic result by permitting trades from seniors to juniors. The outcome would be something like the sharing under the riparian system or the appropriative system without transfers. How much water was actually traded needs more research; the transactions costs would be low within water-using communities but high between them. Costly permanent transfers were simpler. Lack of funds, and no transferability, left juniors with unpredictable and wildly fluctuating residual flows.

A second test is allocating streamflow between public (or instream) uses and private uses. Public uses include navigation, fisheries, waste disposal, wildlife habitat, recreation and general support of river ecosystems.

The combining of intense private and public uses is an old problem for legal systems. It is difficult to imagine how conflicting users would, by contracting, allocate the streamflow themselves. Consequently the common law settled the matter by assigning complete priority to public users (navigation) on the relatively short tidal streams, and to riparians and private users (domestic and waterpower) inland and upstream (LaForest, 1973).[9]

Most conflicts seem to have arisen from riparians' dams and other obstructions to boats rather than from their reductions of water levels. This is probably because riparians, being compelled to leave something like a natural flow for their downstream neighbours, incidentally also left a depth adequate for navigation. As for enforcement, private individuals could bring an action against riparians provided they could show *special* damage. This private right was stiffened by a right of the Crown to bring an action to protect the general right of navigation.[10]

---

7   To compare riparian and appropriative systems one should stick with one use, although many writers perhaps unknowingly are comparing waterpower and irrigation. What is said here would apply for irrigation under *both* systems.

8   According to Hirshleifer, DeHaven and Milliman (1960), Colorado, Idaho and Nebraska have dry-season systems which give absolute preferences to domestic and farm uses; however low-preference users must be compensated.

9   On any tidal or navigable stream, the public right of navigation is a paramount right; whenever it conflicts with the rights of the owner of the bed or of a riparian owner, it will prevail. A leading case is A.G. v. Johnson (1819) 2 wils ch. 87. See Anger and Hornsberger (1959) for the tendency in North America to substitute navigability for tidal action in identifying which category a stream falls into. For example in Quebec and British Columbia there is a public right of navigation on any *de facto* navigable river.

10 See section on "Navigation" (Halsbury [4th Edition], 1973:643).

Under the appropriative system, the U.S. federal government also has power to keep navigable streams clear.[11]

There is now considerable debate as to how amounts needed for eco-systems are to be guaranteed. One straight forward proposal is to buy sufficient high priority water rights. Of the Western states, however, only Arizona and Utah allow a private party to hold a water right simply to maintain flows for recreation, wildlife or aesthetic purposes. In Colorado, appropriation by public bodies is allowed (Colby, 1988).[12]

Another proposal is for the state to reserve the minimum flow, as with navigability. This does not appear to have been done, as most states require only that impacts on instream users must be considered when approving new appropriations (Colby, 1988). Phasing-in environmental protection in this way, however, has the major disadvantage that holders of existing rights will be reluctant to make transfers, as the quantity of water available to them might be restricted to take account of new environmental concerns. It is difficult to see how these reservations or prohibitions would be allotted among water users. Canada has some experience with fisheries as an instream purpose, discussed below.

Summary of Characteristics

To senior users, the new appropriative system gave more duration, exclusivity, transferability, and quality of title, than they would have had under the 1850 version of the riparian system. Divisibility and flexibility, probably, were unchanged.

In other words, with the appropriative system, each right had come closer to being a property interest, having some of all six characteristics. Even junior users, whose rights gave them clear title to widely-varying and unpredictable levels and flows, had a mature property-like interest in which all the characteristics were represented. In my belief, westerners' demand for this improved right is a better explanation for their states' abandoning the old riparian system, and constructing their own than is the anecdotal historical theory, with its reliance on inherent differences between "humid-land" and "arid-land" rights. For example, I believe that the property right system inherent in the new western system would travel well to the streams of New and Old England.[13]

---

11 This power has been used in the past to pre-empt a state reclamation project; see First Iowa Hydro Electric Corp. v. Federal Power Commission 318 U.S. 152 (1946).

12 These have typically been junior rights however, and could not guarantee minimum flows.

13 Indeed it has shown this by its transference to the humid parts of Washington state and to several mid-west states such as Michigan. Adapted to government control, it is widely used in Canada and Australia, including their humid regions, as is apparent from the state of Victoria's new Water Bill in which the Crown re-affirms its primary right to the use, flow and control of all water, and sets up a system of licences and priorities. See further Clark and Renard (1970), and Dragun (1989). On the other hand even the western states have been slow to apply the system to ground water, for which it needs considerable adaptation, and probably, government participation.

Transactions Costs

The characteristics of an individual right cannot be enjoyed without transactions costs. These are first payable for the *initial* increase of a characteristic in a typical interest in water. Examples are the legal costs of getting an interest re-examined and eventually changed, and the lobbying or rent-seeking costs of getting politicians and officials to change legisled water law. When a characteristic has been changed, the associated *day-to-day* transactions costs also change, such as those spent on information, bargaining and enforcing.[14]

Under the riparian systems of England and the eastern states, transactions costs were unexceptional. The initial costs of changing water rights' characteristics were evidently divided between *litigative* and *legislative* actions. The day-to-day costs of trading and enforcing the changed rights seem to have been incurred as legal expenses. No studies of the actual amounts have been made; one has the impression that despite a reputation as a litigious society, even New England waterpower users managed their transactions and disputes outside the courts.

For the western appropriative rights system, the initiating transactions costs were large, as would be expected for a new body of property law. In the first months, force was required to initiate the system and to keep it going. Later, start-up costs stretched over 50 years. First, the new system had to be tried in the courts and enacted in the legislature. Then its champions had to confront the counter-attacks of riparians in court, and also to attempt compromise legislation. Even today, new aspects of inter-basin and inter-state water transport, Indian water reservations, and groundwater control are testing and re-shaping individual water rights. It should not be assumed that the system was *given* once and for all. Large court and lobbying expenses are purposively incurred to change it or to protect it.

As for day-to-day transactions costs, the cost of enforcement or a particular transaction depends on the state. States differ in the extent to which they rely on the law courts rather than on administrators. Decisions in the former have been said to be made on "legalistic" criteria, while decisions in administrative tribunals are described as being in the "public interest". Why or how their initial transactions propelled the states in these divergent directions has not been studied, though it is noteworthy that they also seem now to differ in the extent to which they depend on surface streams rather than ground water. In any case, in a state of the first type, Colorado, owners employ water rights lawyers to act for them in minor disputes and, in whole-river "adjudications", partisan witnesses provide much of the data. In New Mexico, the individual's transactions costs are lower, as more information-collecting responsibilities and also decision-making authority are assumed by a state agency. Shared systems for registration, stream-measurement, engineering reports, watermasters and wardens can appear in either system, but private legal expenses predominate in Colorado, public agency costs in New Mexico.[15] In a tentative conclusion, Howe et al. suggest that

---

14   Howe et al. (1990) distinguish 6 elements in transactions costs of sales or transfers. They include, unusually, externality costs borne by third parties.

15   Howe et al. (1990) and Colby et al. (1989). Those who are opposed to market transfers might complain that there is some bias in the Howe et al. studies in that it is taken for granted that ceteris paribus the best system is

> Colorado's water court setting appears to create a litigious environment in which the parties feel the need for independent technical studies. In New Mexico where the state engineer's office first evaluates a proposed transfer and makes recommendations, there appears to be a presumption that the parties will accept those recommendations without the need for opposition, independent studies and [or] extensive legal representation. Evidence of these effects of the institutional setting have been found [by Colby et al]. The data indicate that the occurrence of protests is much higher in Colorado than in New Mexico [probably resulting in higher day-to-day transactions costs for a standard 50 acre-foot water transfer.][16] (1990:20)

It is encouraging that such studies are being made, yet they do not cast much light. We do not yet know which type of appropriative system transfers water ownership at the least private and public expense. Furthermore, we are as far as ever from comparing the transactions costs under the riparian system with those under any appropriative system. Although transactions costs are only one aspect of a water rights system, the necessary rigorous examination of them has been neglected.

The B.C. System

History: The Origins of the B.C. System in a Nutshell

British Columbia was established as a separate colony in 1858, mainly to provide law and order for the Fraser River gold fields (Nugent, 1944).

It was unclear whether the colony would follow Vancouver Island and enforce riparian law. The first "Colonial Proclamation dealing with Water Rights", published on February 14, 1859, was ambiguous in this respect, as it linked water rights to land leases, mining claims and sales, while leaving open the use of water from off site sources for mining and agricultural development.[17]

In the "Rules and Regulations for the Working of Gold Mines", published seven months later, it was clear that dissectors did not need to own riparian, or indeed any land, as the regulations established that ditch or water privileges could be applied for which did not have to be used on riparian land.[18] This meant that water supply need not be appurtenant to a mine or any piece of land. The

---

that with the lowest transactions costs for transfers. Getches suggested to me that in Colorado, where water-rights ownership is concentrated, legislators act as though their role is to protect property holders, resist change, public-interest bills. Is this chicken or egg?

16   Their data include private transactions costs but not public outlays.

17   "Unless otherwise specially notified at time of sale, all such sales of Crown Land shall be subject to such public rights of way, and of leading or using water for animals, and for mining and engineering purposes, as may at the time of sale be specified by the Chief Commissioner of Lands and Works." *Colony of B.C. Proclamation* Feb. 14,1859:56.

18   They were to pay a rent for the privilege, the amount derived from their water rental revenue. See *Colony of B.C. Rules and Regulations for the Working of Gold Mines.* September 7, 1859, and *Proclamations and Ordinances, 1858-65,* Provincial Library Rs. NW 346B 862 1858-68 Provincial Archives.

regulations also provided for priority of access based on priority of appropriation.[19]

Subsequent proclamations and legislation added very few other principles. The first explicit reference to water rights for those *bona fide* cultivating lands was made in 1865 (Wilson, 1989). Thus a new appropriative-rights system was in the making, the first in the British colonies, where the common law of England had otherwise been taken for granted.

The water systems continued to be an element of land and mining law till 1897. Then, with its first real Water Act, the Water Clauses Consolidation Act, the B.C. government at last set out to create a system of individual water rights. The features that emerged or were consolidated are described below.

First, the basic principle was that all water uses came under provincial control. The 1892 assumption, that private water rights ran with Crown-granted riparian lands, was progressively abandoned. At the same time, the presumption strengthened that all water uses, whether or not on granted land, belonged to (was vested in) the province. In 1897, all crown-granted riparian common-law water rights were effectively transferred to the Crown.[20] The provincial Crown now held both these and the water rights incidental to its ownership of unalienated public lands.[21]

These provisions should have made the new water policy universal, but federal-provincial friction over water rights in the "railway belt" (along the lower Fraser and the south Thompson Rivers) soon showed that a mere provincial declaration could not loosen the hold of underlying riparian rights. A belt of crown lands had been conveyed to Ottawa in 1880 prior to the 1892 declaration to help finance a transcontinental railway. Near Lillooet, Ottawa granted timber berths in this belt to loggers. When, in 1906, B.C. granted a conflicting licence for a hydro project, Ottawa went to court to protect the loggers' riparian water uses. Eventually, in 1911, the Privy Council found that the loggers did have riparian rights. The implication was that B.C.'s powers to grant licences did not run where lands had been transferred to Ottawa and which Ottawa had conveyed to the licencees of its public lands.

This Burrard Power case illustrates that, whatever the legal foundation of American appropriative rights, the basis for the B.C. water-rights system was the province's own remaining riparian proprietorship.[22] To this was added its legislative powers to recapture riparian rights already in existence, and its legislative powers to create a licencing system to allow users to occupy the Crown's own water rights. B.C. could convert its extensive riparian rights into licences, but it could not convert or abolish Ottawa's proprietary riparian rights.

---

19 Loc. cit.
20 This was confirmed by the Privy Council in Cook v. Vancouver Corporation (1914) A.C. 1077. In 1985, MacMillan Bloedel v B.C. (1985) 69 BCLR 76 confirmed that B.C. was a royalty-charging owner, not simply a tax collector.
21 As did all Crown Colonies in trust for the Imperial Government. By the time B.C. became an organized colony in 1865, it had already been settled that the revenues from the sale of such lands should go to the local assemblies and not the government in London. Indeed it was taken for granted in correspondence between Sir Edward Lytton, the Colonial Secretary, and Douglas, that the disposal of Crown lands should be a means of the colony obtaining funds. Correspondence in Howay and Schofield (1914). See also LaForest (1969).
22 See Burrard Power v. The King (1911) A.C. 87. Parts of the informative judgement are reprinted in Cail (1974).

The B.C. system was, to that extent, not universal. Furthermore, as the licencee of the crown, a riparian, the B.C. user's title was less proprietorial than in most American water states.[23]

Second, water was licenced to whoever applied first. This feature, rank precedence or seniority, which gave the "appropriative" system its name, was derived from the system chosen in California miners' camps and Utah settlements. Governor Douglas accepted the seniority custom of the camps (or miners' boards, as the initial orders called them).[24]

Third, provisions were included to insure that scarce water rights were not held unless the water was being fully (or "beneficially") used. As early as 1865 it was demanded that the licencee be a *bona fide* farmer or miner. Later, the legislation was amended to provide administrative methods of approving, and of cancelling, unused rights. These methods were supplemented in 1914 by a ranking of types of uses, from most to least preferred. At one time, it was apparently thought that such a ranking could be used by the Comptroller to allocate licenced water from a lower to a higher use. However, the Act was not drafted so as to make this possible. The chief functions of the ranking of uses have been in the interpretation of existing licences, which have given seniorities and specified uses. For example, if two date seniorities happen to be the same, the use ranking will come into play. Or, if land is subdivided, the licenced water is also subdivided, but only if the new water uses have (at least) the same preference ranking as the purposes under the old licence.[25] Thus the named purpose or use and the ranking of uses can sometimes be influential in dispute settlement. However, my general belief is that purpose ranking is not an essential element in the Water Act.[26]

Fourth, after some initial wavering, the law made licences appurtenant to land although later it appeared to follow the spirit of American appropriative law in not requiring appurtenancy at all, especially if the users were ditch companies. B.C.'s slap dash 19th century methods of recording rights did not always include appurtenancy information, or even the holder's address. By 1897, however, the problems of enforcing beneficial use and seniority principles probably induced the government to tie, definitely, a water right to one location. By that time too it had become well established in the United States that an appropriative right must be attached to a site.

---

23 Probably an important function of the B.C. (1897) declaration had been to force riparians to obtain regular water licences. Commenting on a similar declaration in Utah, the Utah court suggested another consequence: the government, in claiming waters on behalf of the people, thereby assumes a duty to alienate it in the best interests of the people (not just fairly or according in order of seniority). More broadly, such American declarations assert powers to regulate and administer, not to withhold or supply water.

24 Not only did Douglas undertake extensive visits to the goldfields to gain as much firsthand information as possible, but in writing to the Colonial Secretary, Sir Edward Lytton, he expressed his approval of "the ingenious contrivances for distributing water; wherever the natural supply was not convenient, small streams had been diverted...even from a distance of 3 miles...owners of the ditches charging a certain sum per inch for water supplied." Sage (1937:229). See also Howay and Schofield (1914), Maclean (1955), Cail (1974) and Ormsby (1971). See Wells Hutchins (1957) for an account of the gradual conversion of riparian rights into appropriative rights in all but name.

25 See Appeal 85/11 and Water Act 20 (2)a.

26 Backman (1982) says that in Utah similar categories "have almost never been used" for application. Zimmerman (1969, at footnote 35) comes to a similar conclusion about the non-use of the equivalent preference rankings in the prairie legislation, and William McLeod (1977) agrees. Percy (1988) however suggests that the preference ranking might be considered in applications to transfer a water right.

Fifth, as a corollary, B.C. laws made water rights transferable. As in the U.S., a licenced amount appurtenant to a site is transferred with the site keeping its seniority intact. The use might be changed. The Act and regulations on transfers to new sites, or to uses that require different amounts or have different return flows are not precise. Transferability is discussed below (Percy, 1988).[27]

Sixth, the provincial government sometimes by-passed the licencing procedure. Since 1914, however, even a politically-promoted water project must be validated by the issue of a right by the Comptroller.[28] In the early 1900's the cabinet began to issue "reservations", reducing or ending the Comptroller's power to grant other licences on certain unlicenced streams. Sixty of these are still outstanding.[29]

Seventh, licences were quantitative in principle. The 1859 Rules and Regulations had set out that flows must be measured (in miners' inches). But in fact most 19th century licences and records were not quantity-specific. The "record" was mostly just a receipt for a fee. Not until 1909 did a Board set out to review and classify the many informal, under-recorded licences.

Eighth, a right could be issued whether or not there was enough streamflow to satisfy it. There was no limit to the quantity of a stream's flow that might be recorded. Cail (1974) wrote that many streams had been recorded ten times beyond their available supply. Not till 1916 could the Board reconcile railway-belt riparian rights with B.C.'s records and link each new "licence" to its site. Even today, governments' reservations are vague in amount.

Today, much stream flow information is slowly accumulated in government licence folders. For example, data acquired each time a licence is transferred, disputed or divided is saved and compared with adjoining files. The province does meter a few streams regularly, and has made special studies of others. Data from the many federal hydrographic stations are always available, although these have not been located in order to serve the licencing system.

A surprising amount of administrative information is still deduced by simply inspecting a licencee's diversion system. For example, the mere completion of the water diversion system signals that an applicant's intentions to make beneficial use are credible. Further the dimensions of the system signify the maximum flow actually to be diverted; the "water duty" expected; and the likely amount of return flow, waste or excess water.

Added together, however, these makeshift estimates cannot present a complete picture. They do not match the comprehensive "adjudications" conducted in most American states. It is fortunate that the flexible seniority system accustoms licencees to uncertain and unpredictable privileges.

---

27 See Percy (1988:27), including references to Campbell, Pearse and Scott (1972), and to inquiries by Christine Riek.

28 As early as 1873, the government gave Victoria the right to expropriate water in any river system within 20 miles of the city (MacLean 1955). Other early exceptions, for similar purposes, are referred to in the preamble of the Water Privileges Act, 1892.

29 See Water Act 1897, Section 44. See Zimmerman (1969, at footnote 52) for similar powers to reserve unappropriated water in Saskatchewan and Manitoba. These reservations are discretionary, unlike American water "reserves" which usually provide for federal government spheres of influence over state water systems, for parks, military bases, Indian lands, and national forests. They often appear to be the riparian rights of federal lands. For a recent reference see Colby, Saliba and Bush (1987).

Ninth, the law implied that in low-flow periods the senior right was to get the available flow, the system of preferred uses not applying. Today, neither act nor regulations make explicit provision for low flow periods. Probably the seniority principle still applies. Casual economics would predict that excluded juniors would be induced to rent some of senior licencees' water.[30] There *is* evidence that juniors have been impelled to join seniors in building storage works; their reward being a larger diversion or withdrawal from storage.[31] Originally, I was told that government engineers apply moral suasion to induce more equal sharing of low flows, but this has not been confirmed by my inquiries.[32]

Tenth, since the ordinance of 1857, the legislation has accumulated provisions to set up, assist and regulate "ditches" and more complex collective water systems. The interim and final approval procedures for applications for rights were linked to the beginning and completion of diversion works. Public and private water-district communities were first mentioned in the Act of 1914, providing wide powers of self-government, pricing, taxing, and expropriation. Improvement districts were created in 1920. Similar provision for large-scale public irrigation became prominent features of all provincial (and American) water acts at the turn of the century (Wilson, 1989).

Eleventh, the Water Act itself has been kept compact. Legislation to do with floods, energy, the governance of water districts, and the environment have been detached into separate Acts, thus also being removed from the mandatory procedures of the Water Rights branch.[33] At the same time, B.C. and federal legislation have steadily considered and refined the division of powers concerning rivers. Canada's powers are very extensive, being mostly concerned with what I earlier refered to as "public" or instream uses: fisheries, navigation and with waters flowing or serving lands belonging to the government of Canada, or flowing across provincial boundaries. The full extent of many of these powers has yet to be tested. For example, in 1990, the courts are considering Canada's powers to veto projects if they failed to meet Ottawa's regulatory requirements. These requirements included an obligation to undergo an environmental impact hearing and assessment even in cases where the projects were supported by actions or financing under federal powers.

30　In fact, from an examination of the Appeals Reports, it appears that juniors bring a complaint to the Comptroller that their right to water is being infringed. See appeal 87/04, where a user was not receiving sufficent water for his needs, during low flow months, yet brought a complaint that the intake tank shared with a senior user should be modified to give him more water, even though he was already getting all he was entitled to under his licence.

31　See for example Appeal 84/03 where this was the case.

32　Certainly moral suasion is applied in other areas. See Appeal 82/27-28 where the Comptroller is reported as having tried to effect an agreement between users regarding flooding, rather than using the strict terms of the Water Act.

33　See for example Flood Relief Act RSC 1979 c.138 concerning the building of dykes and other works to prevent flooding, and compensation following floods, the Pollution Control Act RSBC 1979 c.332 which prohibits discharge of waste without a permit, and the Health Act RSBC 1979 c.161, which deals with guidelines for prevention of contamination of groundwater, the Environmental Appeal Board and the Waste Management Act SBC 1982 c.41. All of these acts deal with different aspects of water.

Characteristics: The B.C. Water Licence as a Property Right

In the sections above I have used the framework of six "characteristics" to analyse the property right aspects of water rights at various times. Here I do the same for B.C.'s water rights system.

Duration

The B.C. water right is issued for a period that is at the pleasure of the Comptroller. Licences are usually perpetual but can be granted for limited periods. Today very temporary diversions need approval but no licence. Licences are renewable, and various initial and annual fees are charged, depending on use and quantity.

The granting of licenses to whoever was first in line created an incentive to become prematurely committed to a water diversion. Economists, especially Mason Gaffney (1969), have criticized this for its wasteful advancement of investment and settlement. Other critics have echoed Henry George's criticism of the unearned gains to speculators who could afford to buy early and sell later at higher water values. Still others feared that too-early alienation of water could obstruct later, better, projects from going ahead. Whatever the justness of these general criticisms, the damage is already done and bygones are bygones. Most original appropriators have made their gains and disappeared, their modern assignees having paid a market price for their seniority (Gaffney, 1969; Trelease, 1954; Hirschleifer et al., 1960).

A few speculative owners do hold on. It appears B.C. does not disturb users who make less than beneficial use until another licencee, or applicant, complains. The stir probably induces the owner to make at least more visible show of beneficial use. This may end the matter unless large land values are at stake. In that case, a cancellation procedure, provided for in the Act, will be instituted. Cancellation, which seems to deprive the owner of his property, is reluctantly attempted by the government, and then only if its success seems assured.[34]

Thus the system tries to strike a balance between a wasteful non-use of a water right and a wasteful show of beneficial use. This balancing effort may actually be infeasible. Beneficial use is so vague a concept and its enforcement is so uncertain that some potential investors, interested in holding a water right for a later project, may decide to skip the whole opportunity.

It would probably be better to consider replacing discretionary cancellation with a higher carrying-cost of an unused water right. Most fees are too low to induce relinquishment of the licence. True, the fees (royalties) for such high-value

---

34 The cancellation procedure replicates a common "forfeiture for non-use" procedure in American states (Colby, 1988). No evidence is available to suggest either how frequently any jurisdiction including B.C. has initiated cancellation procedures or how successful they have been. However licences which are granted conditional on beneficial use are often not made final for lack of beneficial use. There is evidence that partial cancellation takes place, as in Appeal 89/07 although in that case the Comptroller expressly stated that "cancellation was not to be undertaken lightly". In Colorado and Utah, an owner loses the right to recapture and re-use his own waste water unless mitigating circumstances are pleaded. However, the owner is believed to transfer it rather than lose it "....the market mechanism may be relied upon to place the water..in its most valuable use." (Backman, 1982:37).

uses as hydro power are now very high,[35] but unused hydro sites can be informally and cheaply held by charge-free reservations. The fees for domestic, farm and irrigation uses are similarly negligible, and encourage licencees to hold on to their seniority for future gains. Higher fixed fees, or periodic bidding, would quickly shorten the duration of some licences, as well as clarifying just how scarce water really is.[36]

Thus, the near-permanence of B.C. licences is not an indication that some users are going short. In fact, many use water without a licence. The real questions are whether either fully-used or speculative licences are easily transferred or acquired for more urgent or valuable uses.[37]

Flexibility

Individual users are given flexibility by the transferability of the licenced flow between uses and even between properties "within the amount granted."

The flexibility of the system as a whole is much greater than is apparent from examining the characteristics of a single licence, stemming from very wide governmental discretion to bend or by-pass the individual applicant/user procedures. At the field level, there is discretion exercisable by the engineer/manager in granting licences, permitting transfers, and inserting, remembering and enforcing conditions. In Victoria, the water Comptroller has similar, though more visible, powers. At the political level, the power of the government to make reservations (without hearings or appeals) forestalling individual applications, and indeed to change the Water Act, adds a flexibility unknown in American appropriative-rights systems.

From the point of view of achieving water-user goals, the present flexibility is a mixed blessing. It does free water use to keep up with changing goals and technologies.[38] At the same time, it leaves the river-use open to being used as a political pork barrel. The resulting added uncertainty must deter some fixed investment and prevent a commitment to environmental improvement by users or administrators.

Exclusivity

As noted earlier, a property interest can gain exclusivity by increasing the control of one user both over the physical extent of the resource and over the number of uses (competing or complementary). Gaining exclusivity of the second type is considered below under the heading of divisibility. Here I consider the first type.

---

35 Royalties increased from $16 million in 1980 to $178 million in 1982 leading McMillan Bloedel to bring an action against the provincial government to try to have them declared void. See footnote 20, above.
36 For information on fees, see Campbell, Pearse and Scott (1972) and Water Act 1979 RSBC c.429, and the Regulations O.C. 889 May 12, 1988 Part III Schedule A., containing exact fee scales. McNeill (this volume) also contains more complete information.
37 I have been told of some grumbling that recent 15-year licences for bulk water exports have been too short to amortize the exporters' start-up costs.
38 See comment by Zimmerman (1969, at footnote 53) emphasizing the "desirability" of the wide political discretion governing water rights in all Western provinces.

The question is whether, in instituting its licence system, British Columbia has done all possible to permit the holder to manage the designated diversion, as its sole owner, without interference or spillover. Here we must recognize that the characteristics of exclusivity, duration and divisibility are interdependent. Long-run exclusivity enhances the value of the duration and divisibility characteristics. On the other hand, exclusivity tends to be eroded by the flexibility characteristic (Hannah, 1987).

Has the B.C. water right excessive or insufficient exclusivity? It gives senior water users *short-run* exclusivity. Juniors get a nominal exclusivity but no water. Their exclusivity has permitted seniors to contract to trade amounts of water to juniors; but more research is needed to learn how much short-run trading or sharing actually takes place. The right has about the same *long-run* exclusivity as all U.S. western appropriative-rights systems, and also the same vulnerability to new politically-made reservations, flexibility, and changes in policy toward property.

Quality of Title

Willingness to respond significantly to incentives to invest, arrange multiple uses, or improve water quality all increase with the quality and *security* of a title. It is difficult to devise credible rights to anything as fleeting and versatile as running water, especially when it is fully subject to political attack and politicians' discretion. On paper, the B.C. system does not give the holder a title as secure as in some American states having an appropriative-rights system,[39] but its long standing as an administrative system should reassure the risk-averse water user about conflict with other rights holders.

The security of today's licence may have some technical weaknesses. From the time of application there are delays, providing opportunities for legalistic competitors to prevent or forestall applicants' success. Even after success, the lack of authoritative flow data, and the lack of a published water-right registry, can make somewhat uncertain the robustness of a holder's interest in a stream as against present users and unknown future applicants.[40]

A second category of weakness lies in the uncertainty of B.C.'s own title to certain lands, and the uncertainty of how it will resolve such issues. For example, Pasco v. C.N.R. (1985) 69 BCLR 76 now before the courts, may show that Indians, or the federal government in trust for them, still own riparian rights arising from the creation of reserves.[41] The licencee's uncertainty arises because it is all too likely that the B.C. government will meet its obligations in such cases[42] by simply subtracting the quantity from existing licencees. Its alternative, to buy

---

39 Indeed, Backman (1982) uses the security and full-use characteristics of water in Utah as a model for a better interest in land.
40 See Environmental Appeal Board, hearings 88/12, where a licencee lost a licence to a water source on her property because it was unlicensable groundwater. The Board was critical of the ambiguity in the Water Act.
41 See Thompson (this volume), suggesting this assumption.
42 For meeting Indian claims, and also fishery enhancement needs, or large-scale water-export or power-export projects.

the quantities required from the licencees, would in my opinion be out of character for B.C. governments.[43]

Transferability

Designed as an administrative instrument rather than as a title to private property right, the B.C. licencee gets a C+ for transferability. The system does allow the holder to transfer the right, with the land, to another person, keeping the same seniority or precedence (Water Act, section 13). It also permits a licence holder to change to a new purpose (even one less preferred in the official scale) with the same stream seniority or precedence so long as the amount taken is within the former licenced amount. However, this permission has been discretionary. It does not normally allow a holder to transfer a right, with its seniority, to a new intake or new appurtenant site. In this respect, it probably lacks the smoothness of changed-site or changed-intake transfers in most American states, although comparison is not easy.[44] The administrative problem, of course, is to reconcile the wholesale displacement of water flows and stocks with the continuing expectations of settled downstream senior, and even junior, diverters.

An obvious way to effect this, especially among non-permanent transferees, is to pool or bank water in an elevated lake or other storage where it can be drawn upon as demanded. Where this is physically possible, its implementation runs into obvious problems with return flows and also into less obvious problems of pooling seniorities. For example, if amounts from licencees with different seniorities are pooled, what is the seniority of the combined right? What seniority has a participant who wishes to withdraw from an operating bank? The owner of an old senior water right who later constructs a storage dam will keep senior rights to the normal flow but acquire junior rights to diversions from his own storage. Here the seniority requirement raises the amounts of water to which one or more juniors have exclusive rights. They become free riders on his storage. It is of course possible that the parties can agree to share the cost of the dam. The worry is that the free riding will deter the senior from an investment that would otherwise be undertaken.[45]

It is extremely difficult to learn how much water is successfully transferred between licencees by informal agreement or even by default. I believe that the number of permanent transfers between B.C. licencees is very small, compared, say, with the 50 or more said to take place in Washington every year.[46]

---

43 This strong statement is expected to attract debate. Contrary recent evidence is found in the B.C. government's attempts to protect mining permits and forest licencees threatened by park developments, and in its gestures toward compensating the losing licencees. Evidence for the proposition is found in its readiness to set aside protection for owners depending on the agricultural land reserve, the Islands Trust, and other zoning arrangements, its delay in acting on a royal commission report on an expropriation policy, and its requirements that land developers provide public access to water resources. Of course, some of these policies were popular and defensible. The point is that they have weakened property owners' quality of title obtained from the B.C. government, all being initiated without compensation to losers.

44 Most states require state agency approval; B.C. would probably require a new application with the accompanying loss of seniority. (Johnson & DuMars, 1989).

45 These questions were provoked by reading Appeal 84/03 concerning, in part, a case where an agreement among licencees to build and pay for a dam was, in the 1920's, made a specification of a water licence.

46 Reported in Johnson and DuMars, (1989:373-4)

Divisibility

For a property interest to enable the user to make good use of water, it must have not only exclusivity of both types but also divisibility.[47] With more of both characteristics, the holder is less restricted in combining alternative and overlapping uses of a stream.

For example, consider divisibility in an interest in land. A farmer's ownership not only permits changing combinations of crops, grass and trees, but also amounts of space for public and private watershed protection, wildlife, recreation, garden, workshop, house, stable and so on. The exclusivity of his ownership determines how many uses he controls, while its divisibility determines how many he can sever as distinct services, enterprises or ownerships.

Private water right characteristics in the B.C. system, and under the appropriative system everywhere, do not contain divisibility (or exclusivity) adequate to permit a holder to provide or hive off a wide range of uses. Licences convey rights to divert, store and use, and to build suitable dams and intakes. Purposes not provided for are mostly of a public, not private, benefit. They involve maintaining lake and stream depth, flow, and quality by holding water upstream in soil, vegetation, marshes, ponds, and lakes. There is little active demand for licences to include these functions because private sale of these benefits is not remunerative. The benefits are, loosely, public goods.

One example is in-stream flow. In many B.C. streams flows in various seasons must have depth and velocity suitable for salmon migration. This is arranged by a regulation outside the licensing system. Licencees get no recompense for water reserved (Hannah, 1987).

It is instructive to consider how the holder of a more divisible licence could respond to demands for in-stream flows. One method would be to licence all water in a stream to one *public* "holder". The holder, a district trust or crown corporation, would provide levels or flows for in-stream uses. If the trust's licence had divisibility, it could also sell the usual off-stream diversions and other privileges to other users, getting the best monthly combinations of, say, fisheries habitat and mineral concentrating. An alternative method would be to licence a whole stream to one *private* user such as a mine, with powers to divide and sell water flows among uses including in-stream deepening for a fisheries habitat. The advantage of either method would be more precision in the division of a stream's flows between public and private purposes, instead of today's over—or under—provision. Each public or private authority would have wide discretion to judge how to allocate the stream. Possibly their provision of instream flows would be

---

47   In another work, I distinguish between several kinds of divisibility. Here I refer to the power of one owner to make multiple uses of his licenced water. Other kinds of divisibility are equally important: divisibility of the income or "equity" among joint or common owners and divisibility of the resource into several properties. The B.C. land and water systems put little difficulty in the way of changing single to joint ownership of land and the water appurtenant to it. See Water Act s.16 and s.17. The B.C. water system could require re-application of a holder attempting to divide one water right into several of smaller amounts or with different purposes. The Comptroller would certainly not allow one holder to issue new rights, these would not be enforced or valid against third parties. However he might agree to sub-leasing of some kind; the question would probably turn on the total amount to be used and on the appurtenancy of each sub-divided part.

guided by a price offered by the federal or provincial fisheries or the provincial wildlife agencies. I would favour experimenting with this approach. However, on many streams this attempt at pricing competing uses would be faced by the difficulties of few bidders, non-competitive behaviour, and very high transactions costs.[48]

Examining the B.C. System

Legal and Commercial Aspects

Our examination of the characteristics of the B.C. water licence system has shown many of its strengths and weaknesses. These have been interesting in their own right. When we try to add them up, what do we get?

From the legal point of view, a "licence" is all that it is. Our courts do not accord it the status its American appropriative progenitor enjoys—a distinct property interest giving its owner the triple powers of water management, water alienation or sale, and water rent or revenue. Our courts see the province as the continuing owner of three powers over British Columbia's waters. It has clutched to its bosom what in the American jurisdictions has become the subject of its private right, licencing out on a conditional and non-permanent basis only a few of its retained rights and obligations. Our courts rarely see our water licences, for their issuance, transfer and cancellation can all be dealt with without further litigation, legislation, or market activity. Although, as water rights become a little scarcer, disputes are not unknown, nearly all of them are handled locally by regional officers. A fraction are important enough to be the subject of a hearing, and/or to gain the special attention of officials in the central bureau of the Branch in Victoria. Beyond this lie appeals to a panel under the Environment Act—of which there have been forty over the past seven years. Where complainants feel that they have been dealt with unfairly, there lies a reference to the Ombudsman: there are a few of these every year. Appeals to the courts are not unknown, as the footnotes have shown, but they have less to do with whether the Act has been administered correctly than whether the scope of the Act has been properly interpreted by its administrators or by tax collectors and others. For example, the recent MacMillan case[49] dealing with revenues from hydro power sites, ruled on whether the user fee should be regarded as a kind of tax or as a kind of royalty. None of these review or appeal procedures makes much of a contribution to the amplifications or development of the water licence as a real property right in the eyes of the law. If anything, it has become more confined than ever to its role as an instrument of the administration of a static piece of legislation.

Seen through the eyes of a business economist, however, the B.C. water licence appears to have rather more of what it takes to be analysed as a property right. It has significant proportions along all six dimensions. Thus, when it is examined as

---

48 Today's system of protecting fish habitat already has high administrative and compliance costs, some of which would be avoided by licencing in-stream uses.

49 See footnote 20, above. See also Appeals 84/03 and 87/19 concerning the entanglement of three 1925 water licences which went to the B.C. Supreme Court.

an element governing diversions and storage, it is obviously the key institutional building block, conveying to its holder secure amounts of duration, exclusivity, transferability and flexibility in a title to specific amounts of stream flow and storage. Most users, by taking direct market action and following fairly open administrative processes, can acquire the management, disposal and income of all the water they desire for several of water's final purposes.

So long as B.C. users are mostly concerned about making streamflow available for some manufacturing industries, for irrigation, and for hydroelectric facilities, it seems to have what welfare economic theorists demand.

But, to farm, industry, and power users it also has many of the defects of any administrative licence. The combined effect of emphases on seniority, beneficial use and, to a lesser extent, the ranking of uses, leads to a kind of hoarding of old licences. So-called users evidently feel it is better to hang on to their rights to the detriment of the entire structure of business and farm water uses.

Scarcity and Low-flow

Still concentrating on farm and other "economic" uses, we may follow the general criticisms just levelled by examining how B.C.'s system responds to two perennial problems of any system: coping with low cyclical and seasonal flows, and integrating the licencees' appropriation of surface waters with ground water supplies.

Earlier I touched on the low-flow characteristics of the riparian and (the U.S.) appropriative systems, and also I have noticed how B.C. users tend to hoard rather than rent, sell or abandon rights. The result is that many licencees continue to run unmeasured amounts through old, leaky, polluting and inefficient channels and processes rather than give up some or all of their entitlement. Unenforced conditions, obscure registries, and overly-generous provision for unlicenced uses work the same way. Whatever the Branch's own priorities, the government's goals for the water system are very limited: tough scrutiny of revenue-yielding licencees and easy accommodation of all others.

A probable result of this is a distortion in the attitudes to water among different kinds of users. Water-power licencees, forced to pay *heavily* for every cubic metre, have learned to economise on their demands even more than would be dictated by the construction costs of dams and power houses. This influence has doubtless increased the caution with which B.C. Hydro, for example, now proposes new projects. Irrigation and small-industry consumers, on the other hand, sometimes act as though there is already increasing water scarcity. With negligible carrying costs but high expected future acquisition costs, bloated individual licences account for more than the normal stream flow of many creeks. Relations between neighbours are not the easy give and take of fellow-participants in a commodity market but the acrimonious parsimony of participants in a zero-sum game.[50] No "surplus" water is admitted to exist; any large new use is said to be impossible to accomodate on most interior watersheds.

Thus, even humid B.C. is locked into an absurdly tight water situation. The licences are avidly retained rather than being transferred with mutual gain to new uses and even to new locations. Low licence fees and charges encourage this tightness, as do the precious prerogative of seniority and use preference. If greater transferability is to be achieved, under present rules and traditions, it will be by the exercise of administrative or political discretion, not market incentives. Such discretion, creating reserves and allowing for large-scale uses, has created uncertainty about the long-run quality of a licencee's title. Under the B.C. system, we saw, creeks and lakes with great seasonal differences in levels and flows are usually over-recorded in the dry season. Senior diverters get all or most of their water, while juniors get little or none. As a result, juniors must adapt by adopting a land use that requires almost no irrigation, or by spending on storage dams and other works.

In the long run, one would expect to find that the markets in land and water had led to a final equilibrium in which water and capital were re-allocated across the landscape to minimize the cost of their joint outputs. The trading of land and water in B.C., however, does not seem to tend to this best-use equilibrium. Instead, I have heard, the holders of senior rights continue to make water-intensive use of their land while juniors have recourse to capital, or to land-intensive techniques. Why? Differences in land quality and location can account for some of this contrast. But most must be due to the high transactions costs of transferring water from one user to another. The system prevents water from being as transferable as land, capital, labour or management. Thus, the inelastic supply of existing water rights unduly dominates decisions about location, product, technique and timing.

Groundwater

The B.C. water right is usually regarded as dealing with surface water alone. Although the Water Act contains a provision allowing groundwater to be licenced in the same regulatory manner as surface water, it has not yet been brought into force. The current policy is that ground water is "not licensable". Thus, the system does not take into account that licensable water may flow from springs that are affected by wells or pumping "upstream"; nor that licensed water may after use become ground water on which users downstream depend. The probable reasons for excluding groundwater are that the information necessary for the independent applications of concepts like seniority is totally lacking, that serious disputes about well-water are infrequent, and that the Branch is not in any case staffed adequately to investigate groundwater matters.[51] The Branch already spends a good deal of its time on domestic and small farm water licences. As the government evidently

---

50　The Environmental Appeals Hearings are characterized by the Board's criticism of the "personal animosity" between participants which prevents harmonious solutions of the problems.
51　See Appeal 86/29 where the Board noted that "the law cannot be strictly enforced as the Water Management Branch doesn't have the resources to provide supervision."

believes that the most valuable uses of water are large-scale, it is not surpising that the difficulties implicit in groundwater conservation and allocation have been avoided.

Among the difficulties is that of scale of management. Observe the difference between surface and underground water management. Centuries of experience have shown that many surface-water conflicts can be resolved among two, or several users. The most costly assumption is that every one of the users in a valley or river-basin must be contacted and their use contractually co-ordinated. This is undoubtedly an over-estimate, for not every use sensibly affects every other. In any case, the total numbers on some streams are small. Once B.C.'s licencing regime was in place, it was applicable *mutatis mutandis* to users on streams running in all major basins. This would not be true of an attempt to adapt it for groundwater management. The mountainous terrain means that throughout the province there are very many distinct water tables, strata and aquifers. Most users do not know which other users affect them. Thus such concepts as seniority, return flow, and preferred uses are extremely difficult to apply. The work of Helen Ingram and others on Arizona's groundwater law-making suggests the magnitude of that state's information problem; yet Arizona's users are more concentrated than those in British Columbia, and its groundwater problems are "simplified" by the existence of several huge acquifers (Ingram and Weschler, 1982). It is far from obvious, for example, who would be the winners or losers if British Columbia should attempt to apply the principles of its current Water Act to users who augment the licencing system by using wells or bores.[52]

Instream and Public Uses

So far, I have examined the B.C. system by looking at how it can handle farm, industry and other "economic" uses that can be licenced to use water. But how does it provide for those uses that depend on the natural flow? As we have already seen, the jargon of water law refers to the provision of a natural flow as the allotment of water for public or *in-stream uses* to maintain ecosystems, especially the migration and spawning of salmon.

In British Columbia, the main use is not consumptive irrigation but power production; this is in some locations diversionary and wholly consumptive. But on many streams its effect is to change the timing of the flow as dams are filled and discharged. Thus, whatever its regulatory philosophy in the matter, the B.C. system could not rely on issuing diversion licences to protect salmon. Probably for this reason it uses the second of the two systems—stated formal and improvised informal reserves from the licenced flows.

We must distinguish between the rights and duties existing among the water users, and those rights among the users and the general public. So far as the

---

52 See the recent reports on the campaign by the government of Victoria, Australia, to create one simple Water Act that will comprehend surface waters not running in watercourses, river waters and groundwater. In my opinion the resulting Act, if it works, will be largely an exercise that nominally lumps all kinds of water together, then distinguishes them again by giving discretion to several kinds of local and regional council with managerial and licencing powers.

former are concerned, we may focus on the right of a downstream water user to be free of waste disposal or pollution of an upstream party. Under common law, he could bring a private suit for damages or an injunction against a user who reduced the quality of the natural flow,[53] subject to being able to identify the user that caused the pollution, and to the source not being entitled by prior use, prescriptive rights, easement or personal agreement to use the stream for waste disposal.

The appropriative system works much the same way. One cannot have a senior right to water quality, but must depend on common law rights.[54] This was demonstrated in B.C. in 1988-89, when the courts examined the Water Act's implications for a person whose domestic water supply was contaminated by roadwork uphill from his house. Successive judgements showed that he had a right to sue in nuisance,[55] as he would have had under riparian law.[56]

More important is waste emission by a water licencee that affects the general public. The common law is ineffective on this and B.C. like most other jurisdictions depends on special clean-water laws (Laurer, 1970; McLaren, 1983; Lucas, 1969). These work by banning emissions, unless a permit is obtained. Water pollution is governed by a provincial permit statute. Waste disposal is forbidden without a permit. The procedure for granting a permit provides an opportunity for specifying conditions referred to often as guidelines. These typically set maximum effluent concentrations and call for mandatory equipment and industrial practices. The permit system is augmented by other provincial pollution policies and by the federal Fisheries Act, which forbids the dumping of deleterious substances into streams.

The general picture is that, while the various anti-pollution policies and instruments have each been designed in knowledge of the others, all seem to have been designed in almost total disregard of the water licence system. One would think that it would be advantageous for the system of pollution control to be able to control a waste-emitter's water supply, since water is used to transport and dilute the wastes. But this has not been attempted. The Branch personnel administer the Water Act to deliver water to licencees; other people worry about pollution. There is even unity of system here in that waste be found under the system of riparian rights to "natural flows".

---

53 For a discussion, see Lucas (1969). In the reasonable-use version of common law, pollution is unreasonable *per se*. In older versions, a complainant would also have to show actual damage from the pollution.

54 See Wright v. Best, S.C. Cal. (1942) Sac. 5393, 121 Pacific Reporter 2d Series 702. In this case an obligation or agreement by an injured party not to sue is regarded as an easement, the "privileged" property being the dominant tenant.

55 Steadman v. Erickson 35 B.C.L.R. (2d) 129. The plaintiff had no licence, but this is legal in B.C. for a domestic user, so long as there is no conflict with a licenced user. The case was first tried in Chambers in 1987, 43 D.L.R. (4th), and an informative judgement handed down.

56 See also Zimmerman (1969, at footnote 11). Wright v. Best shows that some American states have evolved rules entitling senior appropriators to emit "reasonable" amounts of pollution at the expense of juniors. This is a common-law approach.

Comparison with Prairie Provinces

So far, the comparison in my discussion of the Water Act has been limited to the United States. In this brief section, I will make reference to the legislation in Alberta, Saskatchewan and Manitoba.

The general principles are the same. All had adopted, by 1894, the appropriative models then current in the United States, after brief experience with the common law system (Percy, 1988). The reasons were not the same however. In the humid Fraser Basin the miners, largely American, had wished to complement an appropriative mining law with an appropriative water law. Later, in the prairie territories, the railways, land promoters and governments sought to encourage settlement by providing for irrigation using the ready-made water laws recommended by American experts familiar with the laws of Utah and Colorado. Probably familiarity was the chief reason for the adoptions (Gossage, 1985). The Fraser mining boom and the prairie irrigation boom both soon passed, leaving their hastily-adopted water systems to be modified later, to serve power production in British Columbia and to dry-farm water systems on the prairies.

Differences have emerged. One frequently mentioned is that prairie ordinary or domestic users are entitled, automatically, to water as though they were holding proprietorial rights under the riparian system. In B.C., this is not so; domestic users must acquire a licence to protect their supplies.[57]

Otherwise, all provincial laws have seniority provisions, priority uses, provision for political and judicial override of the Comptroller or Board, and extremely wide administrative discretion. All have proved inadequate for direct application to major changes in water use such as north-south diversions, very large power projects, flood prevention,[58] environmental impact, water exports, or inter-provincial transfer. Thus, they all should be regarded as instruments for allotting routine water uses, rather than providing for large changes in water policy, revenue policy, in-stream policy, or, today, provision for "global change."

All this is illustrated by the provision in the Alberta Act allowing the Minister to waive licencing procedures "if he considers it expedient and fit and proper to do so."[59] It is also illustrated by the tendency of the three prairie provinces and the N.W.T. and the Yukon to allow water for general agricultural purposes without recourse to the Act and to allow the small scale use of groundwater without a licence.[60]

These features, common to all provincial systems, are also illustrated by Saskatchewan's impetuous 1984 abandoning of its water law. A new water Corporation was evidently intended to integrate various Crown water bodies, including those having functions connected with the delivery of water from the Diefenbaker Dam. As with the system of water permits in Ontario, the system of

---

57 For other comparisons, see especially a long discussion in Percy (1988) and also W.H. Ellis (1984).
58 For example, the administrators of the Act did not approve a cut-off in a river meander to relieve flood pressure. R v. Placer Development Ltd. (1983) NWTR 329. (Supreme Court).
59 See Friends of Oldman River Society v. Alberta (1987) 56 Alta L.R.(2d) 368.
60 In the prairie provinces, there is some variation in application of licence systems to groundwater, some requiring licences for all domestic users as in Alberta, some only requiring licences in problem areas. See Nicolls (1982).

individual water rights appears to have had low priority in the excitement of creating the new agency. It seems that the idea was to place both investment in water supply and the allocation of water under a single non-political control. Thus, discretionary decisions and non-market decisions were as likely here as in the other western and northern jurisdictions, but were to be exercised centrally and not by river-basin councils or Ministers. Seen from the outside, however, the locus of control over water projects seems still to be at cabinet level. As with the other provinces, the corporation still has no special capacity to provide for public, reserved, or Indian uses.

As for individual water rights, they are the stepchild of the whole setup. One author has said of the rights system *plus ca change plus c'est la meme chose* (Percy, 1988). He adds, however, that since its construction activities give the Corporation a direct interest in securing water rights, its routine water rights decisions may become suspect, as being made by a person that is both a regulator and an applicant. One result has been an increasing number of appeals to the administrative tribunal, perhaps reflecting some dissatisfaction with the performance of the licence-granting role.[61]

Transaction Costs

In an earlier section, I observed that any increase in the amount of a characteristic built into a water right system is probably associated with an increase in transactions costs. Indeed, it may be the cause of the increase.[62] These may be payable up front, for the *initial* obtaining of the characteristic, or on a *day-to-day* basis for the continuing costs of managing and disposing of water.

As for the *initial* transactions costs of getting the characteristics of rights in the B.C. system revised, every decade or so, one wants to know about spending on lobbying, rent-seeking, litigation and their variants. No research has been done. For example, the most serious decision about the system may have been taken in the first months of the gold rush. The first proclamation clearly suggests that Douglas had envisaged riparian law such as in the colony of Vancouver Island and in Upper Canada. The initial transactions costs of changing this system must have been incurred in the mining camps, where the rights were debated and the new water and mining-claim systems tried out. The organization and extent of lobbying are unknown. B.C. probably got a free ride from earlier American water law debates.

Other large-scale revisions were apparently touched off by the government's desire to promote irrigation districts and electric power generation, and to shore up its ownership during the railway belt disputes. History tells us little, so far, about the campaign that produced these revisions.[63]

---

61 See the discussion in Percy (1988:36-48). Percy uses as one criterion of potential performance the procedures for cancelling licenses in the western provinces. Presumably the increased number of appeals also reflects growing water shortage. Since there is no plan to charge for water, some users have no recourse but to take it from each other.

62 For example, more transferability will naturally entail more total transactions costs. But if unit transactions costs declined, the decline could be the cause, or the effect, of the increase in transferability.

63 But see Wilson (1989), concerning campaigns for change in the Okanagan Valley.

We turn now from up-front lobbying costs to day-to-day transactions costs. My treatment must be somewhat inductive, because so far as I know no examination of B.C. transactions costs can match that by Colby, Howe and their associates, referred to above and below.

In the present context, the word "transactions" minimises the costly activities referred to. As already explained, they include the costs of owners or decision-makers—managers—in making and following through on transactions involving resource use. Information, bargaining, pleading, enforcement and monitoring are important costly categories. However, these magnitudes are fairly uninformative unless we also include the transactions costs of the alternatives to appropriative water rights. To the extent that alternatives involve internalisation of management into a single firm, cooperative trust, transactions costs fall as they are replaced by *internal* organization costs of the entity. In a sense, the comparison of a corporation's internal costs with its external contracting costs, originated by Coase in 1937, is applicable. Indeed it *has* been applied in studies of enforcement on village commons versus exclusion on individual farms. Thus, if B.C.'s individual water rights were replaced by more planned day to day water allocations, we would have to add to the reduced costs of getting along with neighbours, the increased cost of internal information gathering and processing by a government or water district.

What follows does not make this full comparison. We should know, but do not, the costs of the public administration that complement the private activities analysed. It would be good if the Branch attempted to assign its budgets functionally, so that researchers *could* appraise how much are both the public and private components that make it work. The rights are treated as though they form the basis of a rather imperfect market, at which users and owners may, at some cost, make transfers over time and space.

Transaction Costs of Searching for a Trading Partner

On streams where some flows are still unlicenced, finding a partner is not urgent. Sellers may seek buyers, but buyers have the option of applying for a new licence. In areas where water is fully licenced, a user must seek a seller. In some places, where water may be transferred long distances, the search may be costly. But as the B.C. law now prevents all but short-distance transfers, potential buyers or sellers probably already know each other. Thus, finding a partner may be costly chiefly where the buyer is a newcomer, the seller an absentee, or the transfer is to be made over a long distance.

In some transfers today a lawyer or intermediary may be used as a finder. Their fee is probably a small percent of the value of traded water.[64] If transfers are to be made over longer distances, future search costs may be very high.

---

64   Brajer (1984) and co-authors say that in New Mexico it is the same as real-estate brokers' fees: 6 percent.

Preliminary Information Costs

The potential buyer must be able to describe precisely the flow he seeks, and the points of diversion and use. Because downstream users who may get involved are also affected, he also needs data on amounts and timing of return flows. In the case of a new application, the engineer will need data on proposed diversion and storage works, and their times of construction. In the case of a proposed trade, especially a contracted trade, the potential buyer will ask for information about the quality of title and seniority of the physically defined and timed diversions and return flows. These may come down to describing the flow and checking the licence register. The first is likely to be the more expensive; on some streams flow and depth records are sketchy. Checking the legal ownership of active licences is easier. If an application proposes the cancellation of an allegedly inactive licence, much more information must be acquired, by the engineer and the applicant.

I have so far obtained no suggestions about the dollar costs involved in any of these. Most informants have emphasized that the process is slow, so that the main cost may well be that of the time of the waiting buyers and sellers.

Costs of Making Transfer

Consider two types of transfer—temporary and informal, or official. If the transfer is informal, unrecorded, and/or for a very short period, the costs may run from that of a mere handshake, up to that of instructing professionals to draw up a complex agreement. Even if an informal agreement is enforceable between the parties as a contract, it is not necessarily accepted as affecting the licence(s) by the Water Branch. Recognition of this may lead to exercising costly skill and care in conveyancing.

If the application or transfer is official, it requires approval; the applicant and others must deal with the engineer. Whatever water information, mapping and measurement, surveying, adjudication, exists may well be re-checked and extended by government. The fees for such new information, as well as for the ensuing decision-making and registration, are small (the balance is borne by government, as with land-registrations). When applications and transfers are large, the parties may choose to be represented by professionals—lawyers or brokers. While their fees can be considerable, the heaviest costs to the parties will be that of the time required plus that of waiting.

Cost of Protest, Appeal, Litigation

Informal deals and agreements will run into situations requiring renewals, liquidations, disputes and disagreements, as over the years the parties and their water uses change. Most agreements never come to litigation, but are negotiated and settled by parties concerned.

Water applications and rulings officially made by the engineer's office are frequently challenged, often after some years. Many rural neighbours seem to prefer not to resolve their water disputes or those with the engineer, by discussion.

The Appeal Board continually criticizes this lack of co-operation.[65] Perhaps the questions are too technical for participants to have confidence in their own negotiating ability. In any case, the Act prevents disputed awards going to litigation, review and appeal procedures having always been kept within the government.[66]

Monitoring and Enforcement Costs

Reading the judgements of the Environmental Appeal Board, I agree with informants who have told me that compliance with many licences, awards and transfers is not good. Yet, without protests from injured neighbours, there is no government enforcement. Those who feel they are wrongly losing water can complain, and they also have limited rights of self-help, falling short of violence. There are almost no water bailiffs in B.C., and resources to enable monitoring are not given to the Water Management Branch (except within organized irrigation and drainage districts), so there is little keeping track of the timing and amount of actual individual diversions.

When a crisis does arise, as when large interests are in conflict, the Water Act is probably adaptable enough for the Comptroller to issue conditional licences, observe their working, and reconsider the conditions. This was shown by the deferred decision-making in connection with the licence for the B.C. Hydro Revelstoke Dam, for which hearings were held in 1976. In the hearings, the environmental impact of the dam and construction on the local communities and the quality of their water supplies, fisheries, wildlife and recreation was raised in objection. The Comptroller responded by granting Hydro a *conditional* licence, calling for the installation of several monitoring committees and officers, and to arrange communication so that during construction Hydro could "mitigate" undesirable impacts as they became perceptible to the monitors and the public. In their study of this monitoring, Bankes and Thompson (1980) applaud this creative extension of the Comptroller's powers to issue a conditional licence. But they criticise its organization, under which the monitors found they had inadequate access to Hydro engineers or to the Comptroller. Consequently, their monitoring might as well have been secret, for all the influence it had on mitigation.

This experience with monitoring needs careful study. It showed recognition that when a water licence has numerous unknown effects, postponed monitoring can be a method of reducing the delays arising from inadequate initial information, and the various kinds of transaction costs discussed above. But it also showed that just spending on monitoring is not enough; the licencing procedure must be interactive with both public participation at later hearings and professional

---

65 See Appeal 84/03 concerning a sharing agreement since 1925, to build a dam and share the stored water, which led to disagreement when the dam had to be reconstructed. See also 85/11, where land was sold, but the water right appurtenant retained by agreement, and 85/3 concerning an arrangement among neighbours for the supply of domestic water, which the supplier wished to end.

66 For the years 1982-1989 there were 40 appeals concerning water to the Environmental Appeals Board (set up by the Environment Management Act 1981). Most appeals were against the issuance of a water licence by other stream users who objected that there wouldn't be sufficient water to satisfy all licences.

"monitory" if the cost of the monitoring is to be justified. When it is used effectively, it may be very expensive.

This general lesson is confirmed by remarks contained in recent judgements of the Environmental Appeal Board. It is clear that wherever fine-print specifications of water licences for relatively small amounts are not monitored early and frequently the appeal proceedings often require considerable manpower to clarify what went wrong and what is now possible and just. Indeed, it appears to an outsider that much of the information collating capability of the Branch has been allocated to clearing up misunderstandings in old licences, rather than providing swift information for granting and recalling new licences and new uses. This suggests the reflection that if the province is to retain its waters, rather than disposing of them outright, it is in for subsequent monitoring costs just as surely as when it retains its forests and parklands (Scott, 1958).

Some Summary Comments on the B.C. Water Act

"Guiding the Design of Dynamic Institutional Arrangements"

One theme of this chapter has been that the system of water rights in B.C. is an *institution*. That means that relative to our numerous private and public decisions about day-to-day water use, decisions about the system of rights itself are taken very seldom. They may be taken either by the courts or by government, but they are only a tiny fraction of each year's stream of government orders and statutes and of judicial orders and decisions. We saw that in the 19th century whole decades passed between revisions of the precursors of the Water Act, and even in this century the Act has been amended infrequently. This does not mean it was in disuse, only that each time it was amended its structure was considered deliberately enough that it provided a predictable framework giving certainty to individual water users. Under its regime, users could look forward to allocating water among themselves, among uses, and through a period of time. Users could also count on having enough of the six characteristics to justify their investments in water diversion and storage works, and in productive capital generally.

Government, too, has found it adequate as a framework for its water policies. This is suggested by examination of its own water-using projects, some of them of very large scale. Few of these have done violence to the province's system of water rights; most of them have been fitted into the overall system with water-rights of their own. In short government too has regarded it as a permanent institution.

A second theme is that the system of water rights, although sometimes referred to as an administrative system, can profitably be regarded as a system of individual interests in water use—property rights. The best reason is that they work like property rights: licencees have obtained a combination of the characteristics permitting them to act as though they held individual interests in water, and so to act, observably, like property-owners. A second reason is that they are copies of actual property rights; the individual licence is a little-altered version of the appropriative right to be found in south-western states where courts treat it as a free-standing real interest.

A third theme is that the water right is slow to respond to attempts to redesign it. Like any property institution, it is valued by many simply because it is relatively tinker-proof. Neither does it evolve, like the old common law riparian rights. The reason seems to be that the legislation has taken it out of the courts, from which many revisions used to arise. It is exposed to almost no judicial or general oversight, not even from an ombudsman or administrative tribunal. There is, of course, a sort of case law internal to the department and its own appeal board, but these sources have little scope for encouraging evolutionary development.

Thus the government is the only source of change in the characteristics of the institution of the B.C. water rights. Within government, some expectation of change is to be found in the divisions among branches and bureaus in the water business. They can be regarded as alternative sources of new characteristics, in a sort of suspended or potential competition relationship. We need not name departments, but it is obvious that in addition to the Water Management Branch itself, influence and power can be expected from additional governmental segments concerned with hydro electricity, health, waste disposal, water quality, wildlife habitat, commercial fisheries, sport fisheries, tourism, Native rights, recreation, mining, logging, agriculture, navigation, and ferries, bridges and highways.

Most of these have had little success in re-directing the evolution of water rights. True, some have wielded local political power, notably departments connected with hydro power and irrigation. And a few have even displayed strength in the courts, relying on constitutional law to outgun the B.C. system in the names of fisheries, railways, navigation and transboundary river management. Apart from these exceptions, however, the system is borne along by its own strength. This has guaranteed the characteristics of its licences. The system is supported by users now holding licences, all of whom have a vested interest in the continuance, not only of the Water Act, but also of the independence and strength of the Branch that tends it. Neither elected governments nor opposition politicians have any intention of offending or frightening these holder-voters. Governments have had their way with water policy either by working within it (as with using water for irrigation and hydro power goals), or by avoiding it (as with those B.C. governments who, by putting reserves on certain water bodies, have quietly removed them from the domain of the system.)

Hence, to return to the heading of this section, the idea of guiding the dynamic development of the water right system is an ambitious one. It has developed in the past in response to the dynamics derived from new technologies, products and populations. But some of the channels for these dynamic forces have been removed. A water-right revolt is unlikely. The courts have little jurisdiction. Only the legislature now can re-allot water, and we should concentrate on the statutory path to change. Here are suggestions to the B.C. government concerning the characteristics of individual rights and their administrative context.

A word about the timing of developmental changes in water law. It follows from what I have said about the glacial pace of revision of individual rights, that the agenda must be carefully worked out. Very small changes, such as those that are constantly at work perfecting tax legislation, should be avoided. The government should move only when it is prepared to carry through a well-understood change. Attention must be paid to those who might lose from the reform. Such substantial changes as will be essential should be introduced after groundwork among users has been done. Political opposition arising only because users have been surprised is always to be avoided; here the danger is even more severe because opposition and debate can undermine the whole licencing system as a right, weaken holders' reliance on the quality of their titles, and induce water uses that are compatible only with a perceived short and risky time horizon.

In brief, if change is essential, start early and work slowly. Furthermore, minimise unpredictable effects by making the changes incremental to the system, rather than replacing its main characteristics and features.

Areas for Possible Improvement

The purpose of this short section is to point to areas for reconsideration of the system for possible substantial, but nevertheless incremental change.

Decentralization

One of these is decentralization. Obviously in a province as large as British Columbia, there are always opportunities to decentralise, with both administration and records being localised in important sub-jurisdictions of the province. The material presented here suggests two avenues for further exploration.

One of these is decentralization not only of administrative but also of political and adjudicative functions. The water-rights system is so simple, and so widely used internationally, that there are no insuperable obstacles to placing it under district, or regional boards. Irving Fox's chapter in this volume shows much of how such a decentralization would look. The objective would be to bring the motivation and the expertise of local residents to bear on multiple-resource ecosystems.

Another avenue is decentralization of the water-allocation right down to the level of the individual user. For example, where water diversion for irrigation is the only use, the holders along a stream or in a sub-basin can either pool their interests to form a cooperative district water management, or make pair-wise agreements cooperating in water use. Either of these can be for long-run storage projects or short-run diversions and water loans.

Flexibility

A characteristic of the present water right system that needs thought is the capacity it gives individual users to respond to changed circumstances. The common sense response by any government to a new challenge is to modernise itself and adapt its laws. With a water property institution, however, the urge to modernise and reform must be done very carefully, for fear (to mix a metaphor) of throwing out the baby with the bathwater—the working part of the system with less efficient elements. For example, history has shown it is difficult to give a water right both exclusive use of a flow and flexibility in how that is to be used. (To define the user's exclusivity, it has historically been necessary to tie it to a specific place, time, use or user, thus reducing the flexibility of use.) The present B.C. licencee has little legal flexibility, apart from what the extensive discretion and good feelings of the administration can give.

Revenue, Rent, and Price

The present B.C. individual water right system produces very little revenue. The benefit of the stream of rents from present and future water users accrues to the first licencee, both in his use and in the price he extracts when he sells it to the next right holder. The time has come to decide whether this original transfer of wealth from the Crown to the individual should continue. (In the case of rights to hydro-electric power sites, large lump sums, more or less than the rent, to an unknown extent have already been captured from a small group of water-using entities and they from their customers.).

The issue of revenue is complementary to the issue of water pricing. Economists can provide many reasons for adopting a procedure that will lead to the equating of the value of a unit of flowing water to its marginal productivity and to its opportunity value in alternative uses. These procedures do not require a market price, but having a competitive market certainly helps, particularly in reducing the transactions costs of information. For example, where the best alternative uses of streamflows would be on neighbouring lands, the process of allocating the flow requires only that each rancher, in a profit-increasing frame of mind, decide for himself how much to take or release each period at the going price. If the institutional set up is that use of the flow belongs to the government, paying yields public revenue. If it is that it belongs to private licencees, paying the price increases their sales revenues. Even if it is found that water pricing yields little public revenue, it may well be that water pricing would add efficiency to the whole system. In any case, whether to have water pricing is a question independent of whether to give more property characteristics to water licencees. Pricing and revenue arise from transferability, a characteristic that can be made a feature of either private or public ownership of water rights.[67]

---

67   See the extended discussion by Pearse and Tate (this volume). Note that water pricing is not simply an internal question for urban water supply systems. Scott, Renzetti and others working on the "water export" question have noted that economic decision-making on any proposed large scale diversion, transfer or export becomes extremely difficult in the absence of prices to serve as indicators of loss or gain. For example, if emotional objectors could learn what a cubic foot per second would have to be worth to deny any export, their energy would be diverted into thinking productively about how and how much they value water. By the same token, several of the most feared water-export projects would be shown to be so uneconomic and privately unprofitable as to cause them to disappear altogether from discussions.

Integration with Provincial Policies for Participating in Global Sustainable Development Goals

This area brings us back to the place of water rights in a program of sustainable development. In the discussion above, I stated that efficient *global* sustainable development could well require that B.C. use its natural resources *more* intensively, even dangerously. Recognising the possibility that we ought to play such an extreme role indicates that we must at least keep our options open. We must rely on systems of rights, administration, and dispute settlement that enable us to allocate our water resources to adapt to global demands.

This is not an abstract goal. Water resource law and rights have in the past and will in the future become specialised to meet whatever demand emerges. For example, if our role (or the effects of global warming) call for more water diversion, local storage and irrigation uses, we may want to encourage the continuance of the present system of individual water rights in the directions it is already following. However, if energy problems dictate more specialisation in large-scale hydroelectric developments, individual rights may be less effective than special-purpose legislative charters. Again, if the provision of locales for fisheries, recreation and wild-life habitat is to be our appointed function, a local-government control of the form outlined by Irving Fox may be the best system. In all of these, property-like water rights play some role. But in the first they are the main instrument by which individual and/or market behaviour guide water uses, while in the other examples they are merely instruments facilitating the working of basically non-market administrations. In this and the next section, I survey some aspects of two options. In this one, I assume that the decision will be made to keep B.C.'s system of private water rights in the framework of a strong government regulatory authority.

Under this assumption, the future problems of the water rights branch can be seen as falling under two very general headings—accomodating new uses and reducing the costs of carrying out the present functions. I assume that global pressures and local growth both will make these two problems more intense.

Basin Administration

Following this route, the province will wish to retain all that is good in the present system. From an administrative point of view, we are fortunate that we have a well-tried water system within which experienced officials and staff sympathetically run and guide water allocation. There is a minimum of fuss. Considering the vast area under administration, information requirements have been economically reduced to a minimum. Furthermore, administration and transactions costs have been kept down by frugally and somewhat informally devolving record-keeping, monitoring and decision-making to regional offices.

It seems likely that a policy inspired by sustainable development to maintain ecological integrity, avoid making many irreversible decisions and (as an end in itself) increase self or local determination, will be forced to further decentralize the present set-up. One can foresee efforts to increase ecological integrity by joining decisions about water uses to planning the uses of other resources in the same regional ecosystem. Irving Fox's and Tony Dorcey's chapters (this volume) on this approach cover the ground well. This means that there must be regional desks, bureaus, or governing councils. Fox and Dorcey both suggest that if these joint regional bodies were representative and responsible, they would be a good thing, even if they could make little ultimate improvement in joint resource allocation and planning.

We may predict that under this regime, water licences would be issued or approved by the local body. Dispute settlement, maintaining flexibility among uses, revenue collection and pricing would be among their functions and concerns. What can be said about their probable evaluations of the system of water rights?

First, at the very least, it would continue as a convenient and well-understood administrative and information device, allowing some use of water preservation and allocation by expropriation or purchase of private water rights in conflict with regional plans.

Second, it could form a new base for local revenue, just as land registration now provides a base for municipal tax rolls. It is true that records that form a tax roll are likely to become unreliable. Old-timers will remember when strictly local valuations were scandalously out of date and suspiciously discriminating among tax payers. Partly for this reason, B.C. has added an assessment authority to its local-government fiscal institutions; would this idea be needed for appraising the values of water rights too? At this stage, we can only give the opinion that running water has a value in B.C., that the rent is not being collected by the present administration, and that some regional bodies might find it a good source of finance for their activities. Furthermore, economists would suggest that revenue-maximisation, a proxy for rent maximisation, adds to the general-equilibrium efficiency of resource allocation.

Third, the process of selling, auctioning or granting water licences can provide an interactive information system. Deliberative councils are unwilling to collect information and study it unless some decision requires it. As they process water-licence applications, and price the rights, they will provoke local reactions that will produce more public and private information. These reactions will lead to revisions of the attitudes of pressure groups and the plans of private users, and second and third rounds of fine-tuning of land and water uses. Among the reactions will be a tendency to build up knowledge on a geographical or river-valley basis.

This broadening of the licencing decisions would lead to more thorough "beforehand" investigations and choice. At the present time, the small amount of information available to the officers of the water rights system results in what are essentially tentative water rights, only confirmed and perfected "afterhand" or *ex post facto* when errors are corrected, expensively and distractingly.

This brings us to dispute-settlement procedures. I have presented some evidence on how this works by summarising recent tribunal decisions. The contributions by Tony Dorcey to this volume, and his writing elsewhere indicates the value of avoiding arbitrary and confrontational dispute resolution. He explains how structured negotiation can produce ordered and better-informed resolutions and decisions. The mechanism implies a certain degree of delegated decision-making, for the value of the individual negotiator's information will increase if it is felt that it will to win a favourable outcome, and will decline if it is only regarded as a form of lobbying or public relations.

What is the bearing of the system of individual rights on negotiated dispute settlement? It can be helpful, especially in getting discussions going and thus reducing transactions costs. Indeed, it appears that if the parties to a dispute are all stakeholders, owning or claiming rights, that is, if they have an initial position to bargain from, constructive discussion and compromise are more easily within reach. Thus, it is not improbable that to make bargaining and negotiation work, licences should be given more of the six characteristics, especially exclusivity and transferability.

But there is a danger here. A negotiated system can be a threat to a water-user's rights. If he is subjected to mandatory negotiation and mediation, his interest is less secure (has a lower quality of title) than if he were free to settle or fight his cases at his own initiative. Thus, a public policy of mediation and negotiaton, because it deprives a licence holder of the option of holding out defiantly for what he believes to be his rights, weakens the value of a licence as a protection for new investment or as the basis for market-oriented dispute settlement. To put it briefly, although strengthening private water rights could assist the negotiation process, the opposite is not necessarily true; a strengthened negotiation process might reduce the property-like characteristics of water licences.

This would tend to reduce private contracting, and make litigation almost impossible. This would not necessarily be a bad thing, if for example the policy was to rely on public regulation combined with negotiation. There is almost no litigation now. The chief warning to be made is that private rights and greater reliance on a semi-formal negotiation process do not necessarily build on each other.

In the absence of contracting and private pair-wise arrangements, new water problems must be dealt with by explicit and specific public processes. These may rely on negotiations (especially pollution measures) but they must be backed up by a police and penalty structure. The more the government or decentralised boards take on, the more they push out the alternative individual approach, with its reliance on ownership and trading, to accomplish the same end. What may be given up is made more explicit in the next section.

The Private-Rights, Private Market Option

In this section, I turn to the second option. Should the present system of administrative water licences be progressively developed towards the self-government of a system of private-rights owners? Here I survey some aspects of this possible course, by assuming that the decision will be made to add more characteristics to the individual rights of water users, thus reducing the environment's dependence on B.C.'s water administration. However, I assume that similar goals are to be served: resolving private disputes, reconciling public and private uses, and promoting multiple uses and integrated river-valley resource policy .

The private-rights alternative would not look so very different from an expansion of the existing public-regulation administration of river basins. There is no feasible way of dispensing with a government presence, to provide a minimum of co-ordination, enforcement and information. Of course, decentralisation of government down to a local or regional board would make a great difference, but it would not be unique to the private-rights regime, and could exist in the future under either of my alternatives.

The goal of the private-rights regime is for the owners of water rights to make *allocations* of water and other river services and functions among themselves. Thus, if irrigation were the only function of the rivers and creeks, rights owners would make re-allocations of the rights to water among themselves, register them, and dispense with most of the (very limited) government presence that now must engineer or approve these changes. As a result of these exchanges, an implicit market value of water would emerge in some regions, and the efficient transfer of water between watercourses and valleys would be assisted.

Other parts of this chapter have explained the extent to which today's licences possess, or lack, the characteristics needed for this water-trading regime. Flexibility is uncertain, exclusivity of junior licences is missing, quality of some titles is dubious, transferability is conditional and divisibility not really legal. In these circumstances, B.C.'s water users can hardly allocate water among different places and uses much better than England's millers in the late 18th century. Hence the first step in developing this alternative would be an addition to the characteristics to promote formally the licence into something more of a property interest.

As I have remarked several times, this stage may not be easy. Each addition of a characteristic might deprive some unidentified group of users of water. Furthermore, in tending to substitute formal exchange or even market pricing for today's informal procedures, it will deprive some farmer or rancher of easy recourse to political or old-boy's-network solutions to water planning. Some people will have less water and higher transactions costs. These drawbacks to the alternative should not be disregarded.

But this stage is only a beginning, hardly worth pursuing in itself. The real test of a private-rights solution is its capacity to accomodate other river users, and *new uses* as they come along. This chapter's sketch of the history of previous solutions shows that previous private-rights systems have not been flexible or comprehensive, and may be said to have failed the challenges of large technological and population changes.

We cannot know the design of system that can deal with completely unknown future demands and challenges. All we can hope is that a full set of characteristics will give the institutions and the right-holders enough resilience to accomodate say, a full-draft sustainable development policy.

Consideration suggests that if owners have transferable rights to all known river-basin functions and services, they can make a better job of allocating them than if they have full rights over some but none over others. Thus a widening of the domain of private ownership would include the following steps:

(i) *Exclusivity*: few changes would be needed so far as the consumption of water flows are concerned. What would need inclusion and definition is the degree of exclusivity of the right to change level, temperature, colour, and content. Furthermore, to cut transactions costs, title to each of these would be registered and accessible;

(ii) *Duration*: each licencee would have long or permanent tenure. This would include the right to hold water rights unused (without beneficial use);

(iii) *Transferability*: each licencee would have more freedom to assign any of the rights mentioned above for stated periods;

(iv) *Divisibility*: each owner would have more freedom to sever a particular use or service from his bundle of rights.

These characteristics are continuous, so it is possible to change the blend of characteristics now in today's licences in many ways. However, making these changes would be technically and physically difficult to define and legislate. Many water services and purposes are indivisible and essentially public goods. Thus, their transferability must be accomplished at the expense of bystanders or third parties. In other words, it may be difficult and costly in terms of transactions costs to "privatise" or grant transferable titles to all river uses and services good against third parties.

Hence, if extensive privatisation of ownership of water services would be very costly and difficult, it is necessary to see what combinations of private and public allocation and provision are possible. Considering these involves again a choice similar to that made at the outset. Should the goverment step in to guarantee, provide or enforce certain river uses or services, or should it assist private-rights holders to do so?

Assuming that, in line with the discussion so far, B.C. makes the choice that the private-rights route is to be pursued further. The big question is how public uses are to be provided for. If most of the services of the river are in private hands, what will induce them to provide, for example, such instream services as require maintained stream depth and natural water quality?

The general answer is gains in the rent of their water right. The suppliers are the owners of the private rights discussed above. All have rights exclusive and transferable enough to enable them to respond to market demand for them to give up part of what they own. The demanders are parties who buy the river services demanded, so that purposes such as fish migration, wildife habitat, waste dilution and transport, or/and navigation are satisfied. These parties cannot really tap a revealed individual market demand and so must be organized as not-for-profit agencies: societies, cooperatives, charities, trusts, crown corporations, authorities, commissions, public districts, municipalities, or bureaus of senior governments. With funds put at their disposal, they tender or bid for water-right owner behaviour that will make available a supply of the water they need. For example, a provincial trust or agency concerned with adequate bird and animal habitat and refuges could pay for the lake depths and river flows they need. The payments would compensate water owners for replacing their previous private water use (or non-use) with uses or practices that provide what the agency seeks.[68]

The general idea, on the demand side, is that if the public sector is to reserve water uses for public purposes it can do so in a universally respected way by becoming the owner of rights to these uses. The organization of the different demanders need not be uniform. Some could depend on public contributions, others on taxes, and some even on expropriation. The interests they acquire could be contractual rights, easements, profits and new kinds of licences, leases or permits. Just as a wide range of owners, from the Heritage Trust, churches and universities to homeowners and highways ministries operates together in the land market, so a wide spectrum of water demanding agencies could make up a market for the different and competing or complementary services of rivers and lakes. Obviously, there would be many problems of detail setting up these agencies and getting them financed. The theoretical version of these problems is referred to as that of the private provision of public goods. Practical versions of it crop up in urban economics, transportation economics, and the economics of health services, education, and social services. The only thing the various makeshifts and solutions have in common is the recognition that internalised government regulation or provision of a wide variety of complementary and substitute health, education, transport, planning or social services is also full of contradictions and complexities. In technical terms, the internal government organization costs, of the kind known to public administration and public finance specialists, is known to be extremely high. The external transactions costs of a set of not-for-profit agencies dealing with a set of water rights owners to provide a vector of private and public stream services may be no higher.

I will not discuss how these agencies would finance themselves. On their expenditure sides, some agency spending would be for the transactions costs of finding suppliers, assembling them, dealing with them and monitoring their supplies. Some agency payments would flow back to the government as landlord and some to the government as tax collector. But the rest of agency payments would be redistributive (transfers) compared to today's pattern—explicit net rentals to water rights owners. Attitudes to this element would vary. Most economists, for example, would explain them as the financial counterpart of the social gains from a system of water pricing, but many people would think of them as unjust enrichment or windfall gain to private-rights owners arising from private capture of social wealth. Taxation, auctioning expropriation procedures and periodic water-right renewal fees could capture some, but by no means all, of such windfalls.

---

68   The need for more ownership characteristics is evident. The holders of todays' licences could not sell this foregoing of water consumption. The agency would be not unlike Ducks Unlimited, that buys waterholes and dugouts from farmers.

It has been suggested to me that coalitions of rights owners along creeks or lakes would not only attempt to grab a windfall from the sale of, say, instream rights, but would actually combine to prevent agency acquisitions. Possibly, such formation of coalitions or organization of stubborn resistance might be easy. This is the "lack of competitive behaviour" to which doubters about market-like institutions often refer. In response, I can only remark that individual market-like response to incentives and opportunities is not confined to perfect markets. The modest reform outlined here is not to be confused with the pure-competition 100-percent-market textbook models. The model here is something like the way that agricultural land finds its way from one use to another: farm woodlot; recreational farming; dairy farming; vegetables; grain; and so forth. Such transitions do not depend on perfectly competitive markets. Indeed, land assembly by an intending user is frequently countered by strategic conditions by possible sellers. Nevertheless, better financial users do tend to wrest land from low-paying uses. I predict that the agencies I suggest would also eventually prevail in obtaining water rights from their present holders.

This has been merely a sketch of how individual rights to water, if comprehensive enough, could become the basis of a general exchange of water, leading to a preferred combination of uses. It is important to note that in this sketch the "individuals" mentioned could include the regional resource councils outlined by Fox in his chapter. Indeed, if the purpose is to integrate water use with other uses, it is difficult to think of a participant more fit to exert demand for particular water services than such a multiple-resource source of local planning and government.

Example: A Combined Water Diversion and Pollution Right

The preceding outline of how a more general system of rights to streams might be exchanged by individuals is illustrated here by considering how the present water right, treated here as a right to divert a unit of stream flow, could be broadened to include a unit right to dispose of waste in the same stream. Thus, a strictly private use and a more public demand on water would be combined.

First, a brief review of how pollution of rivers is treated now. The common law is largely ineffective on water pollution and B.C., like most other jurisdictions depends on special clean-water laws (Laurer, 1970; McLaren, 1983; Lucas, 1969). These work by banning emissions, unless a permit is obtained. A provincial statute creates the permit, which I propose to regard as another example of a rudimentary property interest, one that has even less of the six characteristics than a water licence. The procedure for granting a permit provides an opportunity for specifying conditions referred to often as guidelines. These typically set maximum effluent concentrations and call for mandatory equipment, and industrial practices.

There are also other general provincial policies regarding pollution. Furthermore, the federal Fisheries Act, forbidding the dumping of deleterious substances, complements and overlaps the provincial legislation.

Note the difference between water rights and pollution permits. Water licences are tailored to the amount of water flowing in a river. For each stream, the water licences are ranked from most senior to most junior; there are also protected in-stream water requirements. Users in the same industry get different water rights according to the watercourse, location and seniority. This is not the principle underlying the issue of provincial pollution permits. Under it users on the same watercourse get different pollution permits according to their industry and process. (Federal fishery "permissions", however, are tailored to the quality requirements of the particular watercourse.)

The question arises, whether it is possible that the water-licence system could gradually take over the pollution-permit system. The new single QWER—*Quantitative Water and Emission Right*—would not only assign a right to an amount of water to be diverted, but also a pre-determined amount of return flow. Water quality would be protected by a right to emit substances in the return flow. Both the licencee's diversion rights and emission rights would be quantitative, and issued by the same office.

The unifying of the two systems could be phased in. In the first stage, applications for new water licences would also cover proposals for the discharge of the licenced water. The Branch or its successor would have to be satisfied about all the current criteria: diversion works, appurtenancy, beneficial use, and seniority. In addition the applicant would have to satisfy the officer about plans for discharges. Both the water and the discharge would be permitted only after obtaining information about the levels and flows of the creek, the effect of the diversion on other users, the quality of the creek and the effect on it of the proposed diversion and use in relation to standards and objectives. The latter would involve a mini-environmental impact assessment. The QWER would be issued subject to requirements concerning quantity of diversion, and quality and quantity of return flow.

Once issued, a QWER would be subject to monitoring, enforcement and cancellation procedures, as now. Furthermore, there could be a stepping-up of annual fees, with brackets increasing with licenced amounts. The system would allow these fees to be linear with the amounts actually taken and discharged, effectively pricing stream use for water supply and waste disposal, and supplanting the need for enforcement of "beneficial use."

This is not a new idea for it has been proposed earlier for B.C. and Ontario, and for Michigan (Campbell, et al., 1974). Slightly different versions are already in effect in the Northwest Territories and Yukon, although the legislation there seems to permit authorizations that bypass the licencing scheme (Campbell et al., 1972; Fox and Craine, 1962; Fox, 1976).

In the second stage, government would gradually cancel water licences and replace them with QWERs. Some pollution emitters today have permits but no water licences, among them those using city water supplies, using ground water or unlicenced domestic water. There are also many waste dischargers, mostly irrigators, who have water licences but no pollution permits.

In the third stage, a QWER would be launched as a real property right, assignable with respect to its diversion and emission entanglements. As it would have been closely tailored to the capacities and needs of the watercourse, it is unlikely that a QWER could in its entirety be transferred to another position. However, a market could arise for increments or portions of its water and waste-discharge entitlements. The market prices, coupled with the annual fees, would reflect the rent of water use.

Probably a place to start would be the licences and permits of one selected activity, such as mining. Perhaps the Water Act and pollution legislation could be revised with respect to this use only, and reinforce each other. The withdrawal of a permit or licence might prove a convenient penalty for infraction of a water-use or emission standard. However, the general goals must be the *separate* achievement of water-allocation rules and water-quality standards, by *transferability* of rights and permits. When both rights are transferable, it may be administratively difficult and costly to connect water consumption to permitted emissions, because a user may be the transferee of the water and the transferor of the emission right. Who should be responsible? How much is it worth for the enforcement agency to take the trouble of connecting a person's water right and pollution permit? What should be done about polluters who use city water, or ground water, and what about water licencees who are tied in to city sewers? The connection of the two kinds of rights may cause more problems than it solves.

If water and pollution emission were both the responsibility of regional councils, it would be possible to experiment with QWERs in a particular valley or watershed. I cannot see why this combined right ever has to be general thoughout the province. My treatment here is less to be regarded as advocacy of QWERs than as an example of broadening of recruiting individuals' responsibility for their water uses by giving them rights to hold with some exclusivity in both consumption and waste disposal.[69]

Not all extensions of water-use rights would be as difficult as this one. The cost of severing the rights to strictly interdependent functions are higher than for functions or purposes that are largely independent. For these the extension of water rights as sketched in this second option may well justify the difficulties.

Acknowledgements

My chief debt is to Georgina Coustalin, primarily for participating in our reconsideration of riparian law in England. Only a little of that work surfaces here, but it flows under most of the sections. This and similar studies were started off with Michael Crommelin and Peter Pearse and all have benefitted by many

---

69 I am indebted to consideration of this proposal by Murray Rankin, who examined some of its legal ramifications.

comments from and conversations with Tony Dorcey (especially concerning this paper), Irving Fox and Andrew Thompson. Other papers on this subject have been drawn on for which I thank Betty Bono, Ruth Picha, Cliona Kimber, Jennifer Stewart and Stephen Wisenthal. At various times I have been offered great help by Sandy Clark, Linda Hannah, Mischa Gisser, Mason Gaffney, Charles Howe, Mary McGregor, Arthur Maass, Ben Marr, David Percy, and Bernadette Stale.

References

Anger, H. D., and J. D. Hornshenger. 1959 (2nd Edition). *Canadian Law of Real Property*. Toronto: Canada Law Books.

Anderson, T. L. 1983. *Water Rights—Scarce Resource Allocation, Bureaucracy. and the Environment*. Cambridge, Mass.: Ballinger, for Pacific Institute for Policy Research.

Anderson, T. L., and P. J. Hill. 1975. "The Evolution of Property Rights: A Study of the American West." *Journal of Law and Economics*. 18:163-79.

Backman, J. H. 1982. "Western Water Law and Public Land Law Reform." *Brigham Young University Law Review*. 1:1-59.

Bagnall, W. R., 1893 (Reprinted 1971). *Textile Industries of the United States*. New York: Augustus Kelley.

Bankes, N., and A. R. Thompson. 1980. *Monitoring for Impact Assessment and Management*. Vancouver: Economic Council of Canada and Westwater Research Centre.

Brajer V., A. Church, R. Cummings and P. Farah. 1984. "The Strengths and Weaknesses of Water Markets as they affect Water Scarcity and Sovereignty Interests in the West." *Natural Resources Journal*. 29(2):489-511.

Burness, H. S., and J. P. Quirk. 1980. "Water Law, Water Transfers and Economic Efficiency: The Colorado River." *Journal of Law and Economics*. 23:111-34.

Burness, H. S., et al. 1983. "Practically Irrigable Acreage and Economic Feasibility." *Natural Resource Journal*. 23:289-303.

Cail, R. E. 1974. *Land, Man and the Law*. Vancouver: UBC Press.

Campbell, R., P. Pearse and A. D. Scott. 1972. "Water Allocation in British Columbia: An Economic Assessment of Public Policy." *U.B.C. Law Review*: 247-292.

Campbell, R., P. Pearse, A. Scott and Uzelac. 1974. "Water Management in Ontario—An Economic Evaluation of Public Policy." *Osgoode Hall Law Journal*. 12(3): 475-520.

Canada, Departments of External Affairs and Northern Affairs and National Resources. 1964. *Columbia River Treaty and Protocol and Related Documents*. February 1964.

Canada, Departments of External Affairs and Northern Affairs and National Resources. 1964. *Columbia River Treaty and Protocol—A Presentation*. April, 1964.

Clark, S. D., and I. Renard. 1989. "The Riparian Doctrine and Australian Legislation." *Melbourne University Law Review*. 7:475-506.

Clark, V. S. 1916. *History of Manufactures in the United States*. Washington: Carnegie Institution.

Coase, R. H. 1937. "The Nature of the Firm." *Economica* 4:386-405.

Colby Bonnie G., Saliba and D. Bush. 1987. *Water Markets in Theory and Practice*. Boulder: Westview Press.

Colby, B. G., K. A. Rait, T. Sargent and M. McGinnis. 1989. "Water Transfers and Transactions Costs: Case Studies in Colorado, New Mexico, Utah and Nevada." Tuscon: Department of Agricultural Economics, University of Arizona.

Dragun, A. V., and V. Gleeson, 1989. "From Water Law to Transferability in New South Wales." *Natural Resources Journal*. 29(3):645-662.

Ellis, W. H. 1984. *Legal Constraints on Alberta Water Management*. Report to the Alberta Environmental Research Trust.

Fox, I. K., and L. E. Craine. 1962. "Organizational Arrangements for Water Development." *Natural Resources Journal* 2:1-44.

Fox, I. K. 1976. "Institutions for Water Management in a Changing World." *Natural Resources Journal* 16(4):743-58.

Furubotn, E., and Pejovich, S. 1974. *The Economics of Property Rights.* Boston: Ballinger Publishing.

Gaffney, M. 1969. "Economic Aspects of Water Resource Policy." *American Journal of Economics and Sociology.* 28:131-44.

Gardner, B. E., and H. B. Fullerton. 1968. "Transfer Restrictions and Misallocation of Prairie Water." *American Journal of Agricultural Economics.* 50(3):556-71.

Gibb, G. 1950. *The Saco-Lowell Shops: Textile Machinery Building in New England 1813-1941.* Vol XVI. Harvard Studies in Business History.

Gisser, M. ,and R. N. Johnson. 1983. "Institutional Restrictions on the Transfer of a Water Right and the Survival of an Agency." in Anderson. 1983. *op. cit.,* 137-66.

Gossage, P. 1985. "Water in Canadian History: An Overview." Research Paper II. Inquiry on Federal Water Policy. Ottawa.

Gould, G. A. 1989. "Transfer of Water Rights." *Natural Resources Journal.* 29(2):457-478.

Haber, D., and S. W. Bergen. 1958. *The Law of Water Allocation.* New York: Ronald.

Halsbury's Laws of England. 1952 (3rd Edition). Vol. 39 *Waters and Watercourses.* London: Butterworths.

_____ 1973 (4th Edition). Vol. 49 *Navigation.* London: Butterworths.

Hannah, L. 1987. *From Abundant to Scarce Water Resources: An Evaluation of the Water Allocation Process and the Place of Instream Uses in British Columbia.* Unpublished MA Thesis, Dept. of Geography. University of Victoria.

Hirshleifer, J., J. C. DeHaven and J. W. Milliman. 1960. *Water Supply.* Chicago: University of Chicago Press.

Horowitz, M. J. 1977. *The Transformation of American Law 1780-1860.* Cambridge: Harvard University Press.

Howay, F. W., and E. O. Schofield. 1914. *British Columbia from the Earliest Times to the Present. Volume I,* Vancouver: Clarke.

Howe, C. W., C. Boggs and P. Butler. 1990. "Transactions Costs as Determinants of Water Transfers." 61 *Colorado Law Review.* 393

Hughes, J. R. T. 1977. *The Governmental Habit.* New York: Basic Books.

Hunter, L. C. 1979. *A History of Industrial Power in the United States.* University of Virginia Press.

Hutchins, W. 1928. "The Community Acequia: Its Origins and Development." *South West Historical Quarterly.* 31: 261.

Hutchins, W. A. 1957. "The Common Law Riparian Doctrine in Oregon Legislative and Judicial Modification." *Oregon Law Review.* 36:193-220.

Ingram H., and L. Weschler. 1982. "Arizona Groundwater Reform—The Forces of Change." *The South Western Review.* 2(3):13-21.

Johnson, N. K., and C. T. DuMars. 1989. "A Survey of the Evolution of Western Water Law in Response to Changing Economics and Public Interest Demands." *Natural Resources Journal.* 29: 347-89.

Krutilla, J. V. 1967. *The Columbia River Treaty.* Baltimore: Resources for the Future and Johns Hopkins Press.

LaForest, G. V. 1969. *Natural Resources and Public Property.* Toronto: University of Toronto Press.

LaForest, G. V. 1973. *Water Law in Canada: The Atlantic Provinces.* Ottawa: Canada Information.

Laurer, T. E. 1970. "Reflections on Riparianism." *Missouri Law Review.* 56:1-25.

Lucas, A. R. 1969. "Water Pollution Law in British Columbia." *U.B.C. Law Review.* 4:56.

McLaren, T. L. P. 1983. "Nuisance Law and the Industrial Revolution—Some Lessons from Social History." in F. M. Steel and Rodgers-Masnet S. (eds.). *Issues in Tort Law.* Toronto: Carswell.

MacLean, H. A. 1955. "Historic Development of Water Legislation in British Columbia." in *Eighth B.C. Natural Resources Conference Transactions.* February 23-25th, Victoria, B.C. Victoria: B.C. Natural Resources Conference.

McLeod, W. 1977. Water Management in the Canadian North. Ottawa: Canadian Arctic Resources Committee.

Maass, A., and H. B. Zobel. 1960. "Anglo-American Water Law: Who Appropriated the Riparian Doctrine?" *Public Policy.* 10: 109.

Maass, A., and R. L. Anderson. 1978. *...And the Desert Shall Rejoice.* Cambridge: MIT Press.

Miller, K. A. 1987. "The Right to Use Versus the Right to Sell." *Water Resources Research.* 23(12):2177-2174.

Nugent, J. 1944. "The Impertinent Envoy." *B.C. Historical Quarterly* 2(8):53- 54.

Nicolls, T. 1982. "Groundwater Management in B.C." Unpublished MSc Thesis. University of British Columbia.

Ormsby, M. 1971. *British Columbia, A History*. Toronto: MacMillan.

Percy, D. R. 1988. *The Framework of Water Rights Legislation in Canada*. Calgary: The Canadian Institute of Resources law. University of Calgary.

Posner, R. 1977. *Economic Analysis of Law*. Boston: Little Brown.

Randall, A. 1975. "Property Rights and Social Micro Economics." *Natural Resources Journal*. 15:729.

Rueggeberg H., and A. Thompson. 1984. *Water Law and Policy Issues in Canada*. Vancouver: Westwater Research Centre, U.B.C.

Sage, M. 1937. *Sir James Douglas and British Columbia*. Toronto: University of Toronto Press.

Sax, J. L., and R. H. Abrams. 1986. *Legal Control of Water Resources*. Minneapolis: West Publishing Co.

Scott, A. D. 1958. "Resourcefulness and Responsibility." *Canadian Journal of Economics and Political Science*. 203-15.

Scott, A. D. 1985. "The State and Property—Water Rights in Western Canada." in D. Cameron (ed.). *Explorations in Canadian Economic History—Essays in Honour of Irene M. Spry*. Ottawa: University of Ottawa Press.

Shannon, F. 1945. *The Farmer's Last Frontier, Agriculture 1860-97*. New York: Farrar & Rinehart.

Shinn, J. H. 1884. *Mining Camps—A Study in American Frontier Government*. New York: Scribners; Torchbook Edition, R.W.Paul (ed.). 1965. New York: Harper & Row.

Smith, V. 1985. "Comment—Can We Consciously Design New and Better Property Right Systems?" in Scott, A. D. et al. (eds.). *Progress in Natural Resource Economics*. Oxford Univ. Press. 414-21.

Strangway, D. 1989. *Sustaining the Living Land*. Report of the British Columbia Task Force on Environment and Economy. Victoria: B.C. Task Force.

Swainson, N. A. 1979. *Conflict Over the Columbia*. Montreal: McGill-Queen's University Press.

Thomas, G. 1920. *The Development of Institutions under Irrigation, with Special reference to Early Utah Conditions*. New York: MacMillan

Trelease, F. J. 1954. "Coordination of Riparian and Appropriative Rights to the Use of Water." *Texas Law Review*. 33:24-69.

Umbeck, J. 1981. *A Theory of Property Rights, with Application to the California Gold Rush*. Ames, Iowa: Iowa State University Press.

Wahl, R. W. 1988. "Acquisitions of Water to Maintain Instream Flows." Paper prepared for APPAM conference Seattle. mimeo. Boulder: University of Colorado Law School.

Wiel, S. C. 1911 (3rd Edition). *Water Rights in the Western States*.

Wiel, S. C. 1919. "Waters: American Law and French Authority." *Harvard Law Review*. 33(2):133-67.

Wilson, J. W. 1973. *People in the Way*. Toronto: University of Toronto Press.

Wilson. 1989. *Irrigation in the Okanagan: 1860-1920*. Unpublished M.A. Thesis, Department of Geography. University of British Columbia.

Zimmerman. 1969. "Inter Provincial Water Use Law in Canada: Suggestions and Comparisons." in Gibson D. (ed.). *Constitutional Aspects of Water Management*. Vol. II. Winnipeg: Agassiz Centre for Water Studies, Research Report.

15

Despoiling a River: Can the Law Help to Sustain the Fraser River?

Murray T. Rankin

To consider the Fraser River is to consider the Province of British Columbia as a whole. The history of this river has been the history of this Province, at least since the arrival of the Europeans. Settlement and farming occurred in the communities established along its banks, and near its astoundingly rich delta. The majority of the province's population still lives in cities and towns along the 1,375 kilometre length of the Fraser.

The economic and environmental demands placed on the Fraser River Basin are formidable. Its tributaries produce the largest natural salmon runs in the world, making commercial and sport salmon fishing a multi-million dollar industry. It is the home of some thirty-six waterfowl species, and thousands of birds winter in its estuary. It is the source of a wide variety of recreational opportunities for an increasingly urban population as well—birdwatching, boating, fishing, photography, hunting, and hiking are available. Yet its waters are also used for the transportation, storage and sorting of logs for sawmills and pulp mills. Its harbours receive cargoes from around the world. Pollution of its waters by industrial sources, urban runoff, sewage, soil erosion, pesticides, and other causes have taken their toll. The relentless growth of population, particularly in the lower reaches of the Fraser valley, has alienated thousands of hectares of arable land and wildlife rearing habitat.

Can the demands placed upon the Fraser River and its valley be sustained? Especially in light of the exponential growth of the communities along parts of its shoreline, what future can there be for this river, the veritable lifeblood of British Columbia? What, if anything, can the legal system contribute to a tenable policy response to these challenges?

Sustainable Development and the Law

As in other parts of the developed world, environmental law perhaps represents Canada's fastest growing body of legislation. Most of this regulatory law is what the World Commission on Environment and Development (the Brundtland Commission) termed "the effects-oriented 'standard agenda' that has tended to predominate as a result of growing concerns about the dramatic decline in environmental quality that the industrialized world suffered during the 1950's and 1960's" (WCED, 1987:310-11). As has been noted, this 'standard agenda' has not been terribly successful for a variety of reasons, including the lack of sufficiently trained legal and scientific personnel, equipment and refined procedures, as well as a certain degree of resistance on the part of existing institutions (Robinson, 1989). Some of its deficiencies will be examined below, in the context of the management approaches deployed to regulate pollution of the Fraser River. Alternative approaches to this 'standard agenda' are offered, and different tools for securing compliance with these 'first generation' laws are offered. Then, in the spirit of sustainable development, reform suggestions will be advanced, in an effort to integrate market forces and environmental imperatives more fully.

Whatever policies are considered appropriate for the Fraser, realistic techniques must be found to ensure adherence to these policies: compliance must be seen as part and parcel of "sustainable development". The term "sustainable development" has been used in so many ways that many in the environmental community have become cynical about its import. The origins of the term can be traced to the Brundtland Commission, which demonstrated that the global community will be unable to provide for the well-being of future generations with present growth patterns based on increasing material and energy inputs and waste production. Nowhere is this seemingly inescapable conclusion more evident than in the case of the Fraser River. If there is to be a solution to this shared dilemma, it may lie in the concept of sustainable development, a central component of which is the more explicit integration of environment and economics. The following set of principles may serve as bench marks to measure progress toward the goal of sustainable development:

(i) Integrating environmental priorities into economic policies and strategies; anticipating and preventing environmental problems, rather than reacting to and curing symptoms;

(ii) Incorporating environmental costs fully into prices, accounting systems, and discounting practices;

(iii) Living off the interest of natural assets, and learning how to do better with less; and,

(iv) Stressing the quality of economic development rather than the quantity or rate of economic growth.

The Brundtland Commission has argued persuasively that we must resist the prevalent approach of hiving off issues of environmental quality from issues of resource development and management. The Commission reminded us that everything is linked; sustainability of the natural system of a river basin like the Fraser means that nature's limits must be taken into account explicitly at all levels of government decision-making. It is in this context that several reform proposals addressing the Fraser River will be considered below.

The Legal Status Quo

Constitutional Considerations

Any legislative response to the problems of the Fraser is hampered by the division of authority under the Canadian constitution. When the *British North America Act* (1867) was proclaimed as an important part of the Canadian constitution well over a century ago, "the environment" was not perceived as a coherent subject for legislators' attention. In the division of powers that was set out in that British statute and now found in the Constitution Act, 1982, governmental jurisdiction for the protection and enhancement of environmental quality is not explicitly addressed. Separate and apart from the jurisdiction to legislate is the issue of ownership of the lands and waters in British Columbia, which is also split between the two senior levels of government (Gibson, 1983). Both ownership and the jurisdiction to enact laws respecting the Fraser are primarily provincial in nature. Certain aspects of environmental regulation are granted specific attention in the Constitution Act, such as "sea coast and inland fisheries", a federal "matter" for lawmaking purposes, and "public lands" and "lands, mines, minerals and royalties", which are provincial matters.

However, there is still a considerable degree of ambiguity surrounding the question of which level of government may legislate with respect to many environmental concerns, with a resulting difficulty in coordination. The federal government is responsible for making criminal laws; the provinces are responsible for legislation with respect to matters coming within the class of subjects labelled "property and civil rights". A coherent response to the issue of pesticides, for instance, will be an important aspect of any response to the pollution of the Fraser, and to the destruction of the wetlands that sustain such an abundant variety of wildlife on its shores. Pesticide regulation is an example of a split jurisdiction, with the federal government generally responsible for determining what "pest control products" may be sold across Canada, and the province determining the conditions under which these federally licensed products may be applied on provincial lands. Therefore, any legislative response to this aspect of the despoilment of the Fraser River must involve both senior levels of government.

Recently, the Supreme Court of Canada determined that the introductory language to the list of federal powers set out in the Constitution Act, 1867, namely the "Peace, Order and Good Government" clause, provides sufficient jurisdiction for Ottawa to enact Part IV of the Canadian Environmental Protection Act (CEPA), formerly the Ocean Dumping Control Act. Marine pollution was determined to be a sufficiently distinct and indivisible subject matter to constitute a proper subject for federal legislation. It is expected that the control of highly toxic, persistent substances will also meet this test and thereby sustain the constitutionality of the key parts of the CEPA which deal with toxic substances. However, it remains unclear just how far this jurisdiction extends: if marine pollution is a federal matter of "national dimension", what other environmental issues have likewise achieved this stature in the eyes of the courts?

As a result of this constitutional uncertainty, a number of executive agreements have been negotiated between the federal and provincial governments. For example, the enforcement of the water pollution provisions of the Fisheries Act was delegated to the Province of British Columbia in certain situations. So-called "equivalency agreements" pursuant to the CEPA are soon to be negotiated, under which regulations enacted under that Act would not apply in British Columbia if a written agreement was reached to the effect that provincial pollution laws and enforcement practices were "equivalent" to, or more stringent than, CEPA regulations. Although CEPA regulations would still apply to federal Crown property and Crown activity in British Columbia, if such an equivalency agreement were concluded, greater flexibility would be possible in achieving compliance with CEPA regulations, with the B.C. Ministry of Environment playing the critical enforcement role.

Basic Legislative Approaches

Generally, environmental regulators have four options to consider in addressing the problem of water pollution in the Fraser River. The most basic of all is often the most politically expedient: simply to *prohibit* the offending pollution. The best example is section 36(3) of the federal Fisheries Act. It simply provides as follows:

> No person shall deposit or permit the deposit of a deleterious substance of any type in water frequented by fish or in any place under any conditions where the deleterious substance or any deleterious substance that results from the deposit of the deleterious substance may enter any such water.

"Thou shalt not pollute": it is very simple. The Fisheries Act has been the source of the lion's share of prosecutions with respect to pollution of the Fraser River and its tributaries. There are similar prohibitory sections found in the Criminal Code, creating offences for criminal negligence, public mischief, common nuisance and the like that could well be enlisted for particularly egregious conduct in the environmental sphere.

A second, slightly more advanced technique is to *licence* the polluting activity. The theory of the B.C. Waste Management Act, for example, is that no corporation or individual may introduce waste into the environment unless the industry, trade, or business in question is covered by a "permit, approval, order, or the regulations, or a waste management plan approved by the minister". In other words, a firm or municipality with a waste management permit is free to discharge effluents into the Fraser River up to the maximum quantities stipulated in that permit, but not a drop more is legal. The theory is that the ambient environment can only sustain effluents up to the permitted level; beyond that, an offence has been committed, and in theory, an enforcement action will lead to a huge fine and other penalties. As will be demonstrated, however, there has been a very considerable gap between the theory and the reality in this province, which in part has contributed mightily to the despoilment of the Fraser.

A third approach is to provide *economic incentives* to companies and municipalities in an effort to get them voluntarily to take the necessary steps to reduce or curtail their polluting activities. A Canadian example is the accelerated capital cost allowances available under the Income Tax Act or, in British Columbia, the exemptions on real property taxation for "improvements or land used exclusively for control of abatement of water, land or air pollution". There is an amazing variety of such economic incentives deployed in the United States, some of which will be examined below (Stewart, 1985; 1988).

The fourth major legislative technique is designed to avoid many of the problems associated with polluting activity in the first place: *environmental planning and impact assessment.* By planning and siting the facility with care, the objective is to anticipate and minimize the problems that are foreseeable. In this regard, the federal level features the Environmental Assessment and Review Process, perhaps to be supplanted by the Canadian Environmental Assessment Act (EARP), while British Columbia has several such processes, mostly non-legislated in nature, addressing various kinds of developments. The most recent of these provincial processes for environmental impact assessment is the Major Project Review Process.

The Problem of Non-Point Sources

For most of the stationary sources of pollution on the Fraser River, the standard regulatory approach that has been taken is a combination of the prohibition and licensing models. However, there is another major source of pollution of the Fraser which has largely escaped standard regulatory responses. Some of the main sources of pollution of the Fraser River are so-called "non-point sources". Most standard environmental regulation deals with stationary sources, such as industries and sewerage facilities. Permits are required for such effluents; penalties for unauthorized discharges are readily available. However, a more subtle and less traceable form of water pollution arises out of collective activities such as failed on-site waste disposal systems, overgrazing, waste oil dumped into storm drains by householders, or soil and debris pushed into a watercourse. Traditional methods of pollution control simply cannot address such nonpoint pollution.

Water quality objectives may be established for fresh and marine waters, like the Fraser River, but a single-minded concentration upon point sources will be ultimately unsuccessful in achieving these objectives without tackling the nonpoint sources (see Canadian Water Quality Guidelines, 1987). For example, fecal coliform bacteria live in the intestinal tract of warm-blooded animals. Their presence in water indicates the presence of animal wastes and the possible presence of disease-causing bacteria or viruses. Even if the Greater Vancouver Sewerage and Drainage District, for example, were in complete compliance with its Waste Management permit for the discharge of sewage and effluent from its facility on Annacis Island into the Fraser (something that it has notoriously failed to achieve), nonpoint sources of fecal coliforms from failed septic fields, waste from animals grazing near tributaries or shorelines, overflows from combined sewage/storm sewer water systems, and the combined effects of agricultural, forestry and mining operations could still thwart efforts to reach these goals.

Turbidity, caused by suspended solids, is increased when eroded soils are added to the river during rainstorms. If protective ground cover is adequate, the rain will sink into the ground and be released slowly, with little runoff or flooding. If the groundcover is stripped away, suspended soil settles to the bottom of streams, and bottom-dwelling plants and animals are smothered, together with the eggs of salmon and trout. Fine silt in an estuary can also smother shellfish. Light needed by plants to produce oxygen is reduced. Likewise, the temperature of the water may be increased by the loss of shade along the river or its tributaries, as a result of logging, land clearing and agriculture. Fish such as juvenile salmon and trout, may suffer stress as a consequence of the increased temperature. Dissolved oxygen, necessary to sustain plants and animals in surface water, may be reduced by inorganic waste, causing an explosion of bacteria, fungi and other organisms that use this waste as food.

Inorganic nutrients such as those associated with fertilizers, stimulate plant growth in water. If excessive quantities are applied, or if applied during rainy periods, they may wash into the tributaries of the Fraser and cause eutrophication. The algae and other plants produced likewise deplete oxygen and may also impart a foul smell and taste to the water. Toxic substances from automobiles and road drainage may contribute lead, oil, grease, and complex hydrocarbons which find their way down storm sewers. These sewers in industrial areas of the shoreline have contributed heavy metals and organic compounds as well, while agriculture and forestry produce pesticides and herbicides which have also been discovered in the groundwater flowing into the Fraser, as well as in the water, sediments, plants and animals of the Fraser River itself.

There are no simple solutions to the serious pollution generated by such nonpoint sources. They represent what economists term "negative externalities" (Schrecker, 1984). The disposal of wastes as the by-products of other activities carries no price; it is a free good (Ayres and Kneese, 1969). Many people contribute to the problem; most are "free riders", not motivated to curb their polluting behaviour, acting in the hope that others will curb their behaviour instead. Identifying each source in the Fraser River Basin would be very costly and technically it would be very difficult to acquire the data with which to establish baseline emission levels. The efforts of some citizens' groups in the Lower Mainland to paint pictures of fish on sewer grates may deter some from thoughtlessly dumping waste oil. Explaining to farmers in the Fraser Valley the correct amount and conditions for applying pesticides and herbicides is also crucial, particularly since there is no permit requirement under the B.C. Pesticide Control Act for such users.

Such educational efforts are key. Ultimately, prevention, or, at least, reduction of nonpoint sources of water pollution is the best answer. However, in some jurisdictions, more aggressive approaches to this problem have been attempted (Project 88, 1988). For example, in Colorado's Dillon Reservoir, which is the major source of drinking water for the city of Denver, nitrogen and phosphorous loading was causing eutrophication, even though the point sources of pollution were under control. A kind of trading approach was implemented to reduce nonpoint pollution, primarily from nonpoint urban and agricultural sources. The publicly owned sewage treatment plant was permitted to finance the control of nonpoint sources, in lieu of having to upgrade its own treated effluent. As a result of this trading program, the cost per pound of phosphorous removed was $67, rather than the $824 per pound cost for the cheapest alternative available. A 2 to 1 ratio on trades was used, so that the sewage facility was required to control over a minimum of two pounds of nonpoint phosphorous for one pound of credit for the point source. The U.S. Environmental Protection Agency has estimated that the plan has made aggregate savings of over $1 million annually. Imaginative programs like this one might well be applied to the problem of the pollution of the Fraser by nonpoint sources.

The Issue of Compliance

In analysing the legal response to most stationary sources of pollution, Nemetz has described Canadian environmental legislation as "a relatively closed, consensual and consultative approach with a small number of prosecutions" (Nemetz, 1986). Others have agreed that the "command/penalty" model of regulation scarcely applies in the Canadian environmental context. Instead, negotiation and persuasion are said to be the main techniques employed to achieve compliance, with enforcement being very much a secondary strategy (Thompson, 1980). The weak persuasion model that has been observed may be contrasted with the stronger negotiation model that has been posited by some critics as a contract model of pollution control (Barton, Franson and Thompson, 1984). Research conducted by Brown and the author suggests that a consensual compliance strategy featuring persuasion is indeed the strategy utilized primarily by the British Columbia Waste Management Branch (WMB), which was recently renamed the Environmental Protection Division of the Ministry of Environment (Brown and Rankin, 1990). In this part of the chapter, the results of this research are summarized.

Where a person contravenes the terms of a waste management permit, whether for ordinary waste or special waste, he or she is subject to a fine. In the research conducted by Brown and the author, an attempt was made to demonstrate that the theoretical resort to prosecution under the Waste Management Act is most unlikely to achieve compliance in practice. The search for alternative approaches to securing compliance was recommended as an urgent priority. The authors examined all waste management files in the WMB's database for the Northern Region and the Vancouver Island Region for the period between January 1st, 1985 and May 31st, 1987. The research involved a comparison between the way in which the Waste Management Act was enforced during that period with the way in which the Workers' Compensation Act was enforced—two B.C. statutes often regulating the same firms, during the same economic and political climate in the same province.

It was concluded that many habitual offenders in British Columbia were virtually immune from punishment during the period under study. It seemed that the administrative penalties utilized by the Workers' Compensation Board have proven to be better enforcement mechanisms to meet this challenge than criminal prosecutions, which are usually the sanction of last resort for the WMB, the front line regulatory agency for water pollution in the Fraser River Basin.

Politicians made much political mileage when the Waste Management Act was amended to provide substantial penalties for pollution in contravention of a permit; a fine of up to $1 million dollars became possible for each day that non-compliance persisted and $3 million if conduct approaching intentional pollution can be proven. Presumably, this will also be one of the amendments that will enable the B.C. legislation to achieve "equivalency" with the new Canadian Environmental Protection Act. The empirical research demonstrated that the number of employers penalized by the Workers' Compensation Board for health and safety infractions far exceeded the number of firms prosecuted for environmental offences. Even repeat offenders were not singled out for prosecution under the Waste Management Act. Moreover, as will be noted below, the amount of the fines that in practice have been levied in the rather unlikely event of a prosecution, have also has been extremely low, at least until very recently.

Until very recently, the WMB has rarely prosecuted offenders. In a highly publicized report of the 1980 Task Force established to investigate pollution in the Fraser River, several critical observations on the Branch's enforcement practice were made.

> Enforcement of permits and orders was lacking on many occasions and this proved to be a serious problem when the Task Force came to investigate the company. Although a company would be in violation for, in some cases, two or three years, no legal action had taken place by the Waste Management Branch (Ackerman and Clapp, 1980).

The Task Force recommended that "the Ministry make a major attempt to change the past philosophy of the Branch from "non-enforcement" to "enforcement" and that "the practice of amending Pollution Control Permits to justify or legalize discharges in excess of present permits be stopped" (Ackerman and Clapp, 1980). This research suggests that despite these strong recommendations, the enforcement practices of the Branch did not change appreciably in the intervening years.

The WMB monitors permittees in three principal ways:

(i)   The concentrations of pollutants around the discharge are monitored;
(ii) The results of samples taken and tested by the discharger are reviewed by the WMB; and, lastly,

(iii) The premises of the discharger are inspected and samples sometimes taken by WMB technicians.

Most types of surveillance are intermittent, so that emission data are provided only on the specific days on which inspection occurs. Inspection visits are rarely unannounced. As a consequence of this normal pattern of announced surveillance, the WMB records that were reviewed likely understate the extent of non-compliance in British Columbia.

A substantial number of firms habitually violate environmental and occupational health and safety regulations, committing the very same offence time after time. These firms are impervious to persuasion. The research demonstrated that many of these habitual offenders were never punished; many habitual offenders in British Columbia were virtually immune from punishment. The striking disparity between the Workers' Compensation Board and the WMB in the number and magnitude of sanctions appears to make a strong case for administrative penalties. By way of illustration, only nine convictions were registered under the Waste Management Act in 1986, with a mean fine of approximately five hundred dollars. In the same year, the Workers' Compensation Board handed out over three hundred administrative penalties. The mean penalty during the last half of 1986 was almost five thousand dollars. It was argued that the huge gap separating the enforcement activities of these two agencies is largely attributable to the type of sanction that each utilizes. An agency empowered to impose administrative penalties is much better equipped to reduce the enforcement deficit than one that must rely upon prosecutions, because the criminal process often fails to identify offenders deserving of punishment and rarely culminates in a sanction capable of deterrence.

It was assumed that penalties do deter regulatory offenders, moreover, it should be noted that there is reason to expect that deterrence is more effective for such offences than for "expressive" crimes such as murder and illicit drug use. Even if not committed in the deliberate pursuit of profit, regulatory violations are committed by corporations for which one important goal is profit-making. These violations are likely to be deterred by the threat of a negative profit contingency in the form of a monetary penalty (Chambliss, 1967). It was recognized that threatening corporate profits does not deter those violations that are committed by managers whose personal goals conflict with corporate goals and who cannot be controlled by their employer. But even with this caveat, deterrence holds great promise in the regulatory context. The limited empirical evidence suggests that regulatory offenders are deterred by penalties. For example, a study of the Occupational Safety and Health Administration in the United States found a statistically significant, negative association between penalties and violations (Bartel and Thomas, 1985).

Persuasion clearly is utilized as the primary method to seek compliance in the WMB. The research indicated that in neither region studied had there been a single case in which a penal sanction was contemplated solely as a result of a firm exceeding its permit specifications. Instead, the files revealed that even where a firm was consistently out of compliance for the entire period of over two years that was examined, the most stringent corrective action apparently taken was the scheduling of a meeting with the permittee. In some instances, appropriate pollution abatement equipment was installed during the period under question, thereby bringing the firm into compliance. It is of course difficult to assess whether or not such corporate decisions could be attributed to the use of this persuasion strategy.

Prosecution and the Alternatives

Enforcement of the Waste Management Act

Prosecution is the sanction of last resort for the WMB, just as for almost all regulatory agencies in Canada. The Workers' Compensation Board uses administrative penalties and they are used in federal legislation as well. It was concluded that administrative penalties are more effective than criminal sanctions in reducing the enforcement deficit. It was assumed that the threat of punishment does deter regulatory offenders and that the degree of deterrence is a function of the certainty and severity of punishment as perceived by potential offenders.

The Workers' Compensation Board resorts to administrative penalties much more often than the WMB initiates prosecutions, and the penalties levied by the Board are much larger than the fines typically imposed by the courts for environmental offences. The Workers' Compensation Act allows for penalties against employers who violate safety standards. Unlike the ticketing measures in the Waste Management Act, there is no resort to the courts with respect to these administrative penalties. Moreover, tickets issued by the WMB are generally for very small sums. The fines or penalties are only levied after repeated offences and warnings. If deterrence is a function of the certainty and probability of punishment, the administrative penalties meted out by the Board provide much greater deterrence than the Branch's use of criminal prosecutions.

Charges under the Waste Management Act have only rarely been laid for the habitual violation of permit specifications. A review of prosecution files reveals that prosecutions are sometimes initiated for discharges without a permit and isolated major spills, but not for persistently exceeding the limits imposed in a permit. The Branch laid twenty-two charges in 1984, fifty-eight in 1985, and fifty-three in 1986. The number of convictions registered in each of these years was nine, twenty-seven and twelve respectively. The average fine between 1984 and 1986 was $565. The 1986-87 Ministry Annual Report notes that nine convictions were registered under the Waste Management Act during that fiscal year; a total of $4900 in fines were collected. It has been reported that in the last five years, 201 polluters were fined a total of $145,300 under the British Columbia Waste Management Act (*Province*, September 3, 1989). Of those ticketed or convicted by the courts between January 1, 1984 and June 19, 1989, the average fine was $723, with most in the order of between $100 and $200. In the face of these statistics, it is difficult to believe that the prospect of a conviction would provide much of a deterrent effect.

Nevertheless, recent improvements to the enforcement stance of the Ministry of Environment may go some distance to improving this situation. It was announced on December 12, 1990 that a total of 176 charges were laid under the Waste Management Act during a six month period during 1990, representing a 43 per cent increase as compared to the same period during the preceding year, which represented a considerable increase over the same period in 1988. Although most of these prosecutions resulted in "tickets" and fines for amounts less than $300, there have been some noteworthy developments. In December 1990, a fine of $275,000 was levied against a pulp and paper mill at Quesnel for the discharge of about eight hundred thousand litres of toxic "white liquor" into the Fraser River (*Vancouver Sun*, December 14, 1990). In addition, orders under the Waste Management Act may lead to the temporary closure of a pollution source, or to a facility "voluntarily" shutting down, rather than facing a possible prosecution.

In contrast to the pattern of the WMB, the Workers' Compensation Board assessed just over three hundred administrative penalties against employers in 1986. Although the Board may also initiate prosecutions, there were only two criminal proceedings in 1985 and none in 1986; the Board's clear preference is for administrative penalties. The Workers' Compensation Act specifies neither a minimum nor a maximum penalty. The amount of penalty recommended varies with the severity of a violation, the imposition of a previous penalty, and the size of an offender's payroll. In the case of first penalties for less serious violations, the amount ranges from $1,500 to $4,000, depending upon a firm's payroll. First penalties for more serious violations range from $3,500-$15,000, again depending upon a firm's payroll. A second sanction for a more serious violation within five years of the first, or a second sanction for a less serious violation within three years of the first, results in a doubling of the penalty. The actual amount of the penalty in any case may vary from these recommended amounts where warranted by the facts of a particular case. During the last half of 1986, after a new schedule was implemented, the mean penalty was $4,885.

Not only does the Workers' Compensation Board resort to formal sanctions much more often than the WMB, the administrative penalties assessed by the Board are much larger than the fines levied by the courts for pollution offences. These differences in enforcement activities may be partly attributable to the different kinds of sanction utilized by these two agencies. This is not to deny that other factors may explain some of the difference between these agencies in the level of enforcement; the costs to the firm for pollution control measures may differ from the costs of health and safety precautions; there may also be differences in the degree of organization among those exposed to occupational hazards as opposed to environmental risks; the general public may feel differently about occupational and environmental regulation. These economic and political factors probably influence the level of enforcement. But such economic and political differences should not be exaggerated. Both of the agencies under study were operating in the same province during the same period. Almost all of the enterprises regulated by the WMB as permittees are also employers regulated by the Workers' Compensation Board, although employers in some industries are not permittees. In other words, these two agencies were subject to the same general economic and political forces, not only at the provincial level, but also at the industry level in many cases. As will be detailed below, it is therefore recommended that the Ministry of Environment consider amending the Waste Management Act to provide for administrative penalties. Some additional justifications for this recommendation follow.

Risk vs. Harm

Although some health and safety and environmental infractions are detected only after they have caused actual harm to people or to the life systems upon which people depend, many violations are detected before any injury occurs. If punishment is to be meted out in this setting, it must be for creating risk, not for doing harm. Different types of legal actors are likely to differ in their reaction to risk. As the major objective of sanctions is to enhance compliance with regulatory requirements, offenders should be penalized for creating the risk that regulatory standards are designed to avoid. The larger the risk of harm associated with a violation, the greater the need for a penalty designed to prevent this harm. The occurrence of harm ought not to be a necessary condition for a penalty. If one believes in retribution, the case for punishment is even stronger when harm occurs.

Pollution officials in British Columbia complain that judges show little concern about permit violations that do not cause harm. Although it was ultimately overturned on appeal, one County Court judge even held that actual environmental degradation is a necessary element of an offence under the Waste Management Act, and that a mere risk of a substantial impairment of the environment is not enough to constitute an offence.

"Due Diligence", the Charter and the Standard of Proof

The criminal standard of proof, the due diligence defence and the problem created by the court's general reluctance to consider previous infractions except at the stage of sentencing all pose difficulties. The prosecution must prove beyond a reasonable doubt that a polluting firm failed to take reasonable precautions to ensure compliance. The criminal burden of proof also poses problems in proving sub-lethal deleterious effects in environmental cases. Stringent procedures must be followed in the gathering, custody, transfer, analysis and production of evidence. The criminal standard of proof resolves any reasonable doubt by protecting corporate treasuries rather than deterring hazardous activities. The civil standard of proof that is applied in administrative proceedings is more appropriate because it reverses this ranking of priorities. In recent case law, difficulties in securing convictions have increased, at least in the strictly criminal context. For example, the Ontario Court of Appeal has recognized the defence of "officially induced error of law" as a defence in regulatory matters. Where an accused has reasonably relied on the erroneous legal opinion or advice of the appropriate government official, a defence may be available which is distinct from the defence of due diligence. In a more recent case, the Ontario Court of Appeal held that an onus placed by statute upon the accused to show that he or she acted with due diligence violated section 11(d) of the Charter of Rights and Freedoms. Obviously, this line of authority will only make it more difficult for the Crown to secure convictions in environmental prosecutions.

Persuasion does not appear to work. The public demands new approaches. Simply threatening a charge in the Provincial Court may not be much of a deterrent. A substantial number of firms habitually violate regulatory requirements, many of them with impunity. An enforcement deficit may indicate a lack of determination to enforce the law on the part of regulators and their political masters. But the political will to get tough is not enough to make a noticeable dent in a deficit so large. Regulators must be provided with a sanctioning mechanism that is implemented by qualified specialists, treats risk and previous infractions as important criteria in determining which offenders should be punished, offers monetary penalties capable of deterrence, avoids undue stigma, and entails minimal costs. Criminal prosecution, the most common sanction of last resort among Canadian regulatory agencies, scores poorly on all of these counts. Much more appropriate are the administrative penalties imposed by the Workers' Compensation Board and by other regulatory agencies in several other jurisdictions.

The most important point is that the use of criminal sanctions severely restricts the number of enforcement proceedings launched, as well as influencing their disposition. A disdain for the disruption to their routine work occasioned by court appearances may lead field staff, the gate keepers of the enforcement process, not to recommend prosecutions in the first place. Senior officials may shun time consuming prosecutions because they believe that the energy of field staff is better spent conducting inspections. Just as the high cost of criminal proceedings may be a disincentive to laying charges, so too may low fines, the stigma of conviction and the deficiencies of the criminal process in identifying offenders who should be punished.

Some Alternatives

It is essential to note that the pursuit of compliance with environmental legislation and policy involves much more than "command and control", that is, simply setting out a standard or rule and then stipulating a penalty for its violation. Merely enacting more environmental offences, punishable by bigger and bigger fines is very unlikely to improve environmental quality. Instead, it is argued here that what is needed is a wider range of enforcement options to tailor the compliance and enforcement response to the level of culpability in a particular situation. In particular, British Columbia should examine the wide array of instruments that are available to provide economic incentives for compliance.

Administrative Penalties and the Oregon Experience

Oregon has developed an innovative approach to dealing with the demands of the federal EPA by establishing a civil penalty scheme. Rather than choosing between either putting environmental offenders through an overcrowded court system or not taking any legal action due to the cost or delay of the court process, Oregon uses a civil penalty system. Although this scheme has been in place there for the past fifteen years or so, criticisms of unpredictability and subjectivity have prompted some recent changes to the civil penalty rules. Environmental offenders vary greatly. At one end of the spectrum there are ordinary citizens, perhaps applying pesticides to their property without a permit, while at the other end there are the "midnight dumpers", who knowingly release prohibited and often extremely dangerous substances into the environment because they are unable or unwilling to dispose of them properly. Somewhere in between are corporations and small private companies, as well as many others. Potential offenders vary in motivation, information and financial resources and so must be dealt with differently in regards to deterrence and enforcement.

Instead of simply stipulating a minimum and a maximum amount, more guidance is offered to the Director of the Oregon Department of Environmental Quality in setting fines. Two grids have been established, one for offences which carry penalties up to $500, the other for offences with maximum fines of $10,000. The minimum civil penalty in both cases is $50. Descriptions of precisely which offences are to be included in each grid accompany the grids. The grids show 'Class of Violation' along the 'y' axis, and 'Magnitude of Violation' along the 'x' axis. There are three classes of offence, ranging from Class One, the most serious, to Class Three, the least serious. Lists included in the rules indicate which offences fall into each class, including how many repeat offences in other classes will justify a more serious classification, despite a less serious nature of the offence in question. The magnitude of violation refers to whether the spill or release is minor, moderate or major. Again, lists are included in the rules to provide guidance when categorizing an offence.

Nine squares make up the matrix, each containing a base penalty for the combined class and magnitude of violation. Once a base penalty has been determined, a formula is applied to give the actual amount of the fine. The formula used is

$$BP + [(.1 \times BP)(P+H+E+O+R+C)].$$

Each letter in the formula is assigned a numerical value depending on the circumstances of the offence and the offender. Again, a list is provided which indicates what values are to be assigned in particular circumstances. The letters in the formula stand for the following factors:

'P' - prior violations of environmental statutes, rules, permits, etc.

'H' - past history of the respondent in taking steps necessary or appropriate to correct any prior violations.

'E' - the economic condition of the respondent.

'O' - whether the violation was a single occurrence or was repeated or continuous.

'R' - the cause of the violation; was it an unavoidable accident or a negligent or intentional act of the respondent.

'C' - the violator's cooperativeness in correcting the violation.

Some factors can never be assigned a mitigating score, such as when there is a lack of prior offences, for example. Others, such as cooperativeness, can be calculated as having either a mitigating, neutral, or an aggravating factor, depending on the value assigned.

The formula obviously allows considerable variations in the size of the civil penalty assessed. As in the B.C. legislation, the penalties can also be increased to make them commensurate with the economic gain received by the firm as a result of the violation, provided the final amount does not exceed the maximum permitted by the rule or the statute. Once a penalty has been calculated by Department staff, the file is passed to the Director to approve. The Director personally reviews all assessments before violators are notified. Respondents are notified in writing of the penalty which has been assessed against them and the assessment becomes payable upon receipt of the notice.

Unless the respondent declares otherwise, the Commission may assume that it is able to pay the assessed penalty. Offenders have 20 days in which to file a request for a hearing to have their penalty mitigated. Hearings take place in front of the Department of Environmental Quality Commission Hearing Officer, and are usually scheduled from 30-60 days after the request is filed, to allow time for informal discussions to occur and perhaps settle the matter. Approximately 90% of contested penalties are settled before the hearing occurs. If the respondent can provide information to the Commission, either through discussions or at a hearing, which was not included in the initial assessment, such as financial hardships for example, the amount can be reduced. Settled penalties can still be substantial; a violation involving asbestos has been settled at $56,000, where the original penalty assigned was $80,000.

Officials from Oregon have pointed out that many offenders are not corporations but are private citizens with wood burning stoves, and the like, who unknowingly exceed the maximum allowable emission levels. Applications to mitigate civil penalties usually stem from private citizens who, given their income, are in no position to pay a stiff penalty. Corporations and businesses are more strictly scrutinized and claims of financial hardship from viable businesses are generally not well-received. Past tax records can be used to confirm these claims if necessary, or the Oregon Fiscal Office can be called upon to give a professional opinion regarding the financial status of a business and its ability to pay a particular penalty.

The civil penalty system seems to be effective against many different types of polluters due to the flexibility inherent in the grid and mitigation combination. In addition, penalties are predictable and substantial enough to operate as a deterrent to would-be offenders. The system is also very efficient, as formal action in the form of a civil penalty is always applied within 45-60 days of when the violation was discovered and sometimes as soon as two weeks to a month afterward. This compares very favourably with the average 6 month time span that it would take the same cases to proceed through the Oregon criminal system. These penalties are not damages; the right to pursue offenders in either criminal or civil proceedings continues to exist. When such proceedings are launched, the argument of "double jeopardy" has not succeeded. Oregon officials pointed out that the civil penalty system is very helpful in processing offenders who would not otherwise have criminal proceedings initiated against them, not because they did not commit an offence, but because District Attorneys are simply too busy trying rapes, murders, and other violent crimes to bother with environmental crimes which are classed as 'Class A' misdemeanors.

While most civil penalties paid in Oregon go into the state treasury, some are assigned to particular departmental accounts. Environmental groups have suggested that trust funds could be established into which air or water penalties could be paid. State environmental officials seem amenable to this suggestion, however there is some question whether the state is dependent on the income from these penalties.

Suggestions for British Columbia

It is recommended that the Waste Management Act be amended to permit administrative penalties up to $10,000 for exceeding waste permits. Such penalties could be levied almost automatically if a permittee's monitoring data revealed that it was exceeding its permit by a stipulated amount. The Act already allows for appeals of certain matters to the Environmental Appeal Board. It is suggested that appeals against such penalties should be made available to the Environmental Appeal Board, thereby avoiding many of the perennial problems identified with resort to the courts, but affording natural justice to permittees. Substantial changes to the composition and procedures of the Environmental Appeal Board would also be necessary.

This is not to suggest that administrative penalties should be the exclusive form of punishment for environmental offences. Flagrant offenders should attract the full force of a revised Criminal Code, in addition to prosecutions under the Fisheries Act, the Waste Management Act and other statutes. Given the severe penalties that are now available for environmental offences, however, it might be preferable for environmental cases to be heard not in Provincial Court, where judges are not accustomed to levy fines in the order of magnitude now contemplated, but instead in the Supreme Court of British Columbia. However, a few recent sentences exacted by Provincial Court judges involving fines exceeding one hundred thousand dollars may suggest that this transfer of jurisdiction to the Supreme Court is not warranted.

Generally low fines in the criminal process may be offset by the stigma associated with convictions. People respond to the threat of legal sanctions partly because they do not like to be publicly stigmatized as lawbreakers, regardless of the amount of money involved. Indeed, there is reason to believe that these non-pecuniary concerns may rival the monetary impact of a penalty. Some empirical studies of deterrence found that "informal sanctions", defined as loss of respect among personal acquaintances and the community at large, have a greater deterrent effect than "formal sanctions", including arrest and jail. Two studies of the enforcement of routine water pollution offences in Britain concluded that adverse publicity was a more effective deterrent than very low criminal fines (Hawkins, 1984; Brittan, 1984).

Enhancing the Prosecution Model

A fine imposed by a criminal court, even for a regulatory offence like those under Ministry environmental statutes, may be perceived by most people as indicating greater moral turpitude than an administrative penalty. This perception may exist because judicial pronouncements are seen as more authoritative than administrative rulings, or because the judiciary is associated with more serious crimes. One way to better tailor the use of the prosecution option to the specific offender is to provide differential fines by statute. One example is found in Manitoba. Under Manitoba's Environment Act of 1988, corporate offenders are liable to a fine of up to $100,000 for a first offence, and $200,000 for each subsequent offence. However, for individuals, the maximum fines are set at $5,000 and $10,000 respectively. In the case of individuals, imprisonment for up to one year is also possible for repeat offenders. For both individuals and corporations, the Act specifically empowers the judge to suspend or revoke all or part of their environmental permits or licences.

Another way that has been suggested to improve the prosecution option in British Columbia legislation is to promote private prosecutions. The threat that individuals or public interest groups might themselves initiate prosecutions, without government support, might induce firms to comply. One incentive, already found under Regulations to the federal Fisheries Act, is to allow private citizens who successfully prosecute an offender to keep half of the fine imposed. This incentive has already prompted a member of the Fraser River Coalition to initiate a prosecution of Crown Zellerbach Properties Ltd. under the Fisheries Act and to keep one half of the $28,000 fine levied by the court (Webb, 1988). The disadvantage of such a scheme is that it interferes with the exercise of government discretion—losing control over the timing of a prosecution, forcing government to abandon negotiations prematurely, and so on. However, the Attorney General can always stop a private prosecution, so the government retains final control over this enforcement technique.

(i) *Sentencing Options.* A variety of sentencing options are available to a judge when a conviction is entered.
- A firm's property can be forfeited;
- Where a cleanup is undertaken by the Crown or a public agency on behalf of or in default of the person responsible, costs may be charged to the person responsible, and a suit may be initiated to collect the debt;

- Imprisonment is also an option. Already in Ontario and in the United States, corporate officers have been imprisoned, usually for the willful contempt of a court order;
- Probation orders may be made, even for corporate or municipal officers;
- Restitution and compensation may be ordered by the judge as part of the penalty.

With full recognition and use of the variety of possibilities inherent in prosecution, this technique will always remain a vital component of an enforcement strategy.

(ii) *Suspension or Cancellation of Permits.* A very practical way to enforce a regulatory scheme is merely to suspend or cancel the permit for non-compliance. This option is provided in section 20 of the Water Act and in section 23 of the Waste Management Act. To suspend a permit would obviously have a dramatic impact on the permittee, since without a permit, approval or licence, the firm would have no legal authority to carry on business. However, in practice this option is rarely used, since the drastic step of closing down a business is obviously not an easy one for a regulator, or a politician, to take, since the consequence might well be to close down the main employer in a community.

(iii) *Injunctions and Restraining Orders.* Another civil remedy—that is, one that is not enforceable in the criminal courts—is the injunction or restraining order. This remedy enables the Minister to proceed in the Supreme Court of British Columbia to prevent the permittee or any other person from carrying on activities contrary to statute or the common law. Specific statutory authority is often given as well to restrain certain activities. For example, in section 24 of the Waste Management Act, the Minister is empowered to seek a restraining order in respect of certain activities involving special wastes. In addition, even without statutory provisions, the Minister may apply to the court under common law causes of action for damages incurred as a result of pollution. An interesting example of this approach was the "Tilbury Slough Order", made in 1977. After reviewing the plans received from the British Columbia Development Corporation for landfilling and construction in the Tilbury Slough area of Delta, the federal Minister of Fisheries used the authority granted to him under section 37(2) of the Fisheries Act simply to prohibit the activity.

Economic Incentive Instruments

The Status Quo of "Command and Control"

Unless provincial and federal regulators have the political will to enforce the standards that are established by legislation and set out in the permits and licences of regulated undertakings, even the most progressive of laws will be irrelevant.

The entire premise of "command and control" measures enacted for environmental protection is that there will be an enforcement proceeding taken if the stipulated level of discharge is exceeded. Otherwise, what is the point of setting any standards? Canadian environmental laws will be "full of sound and fury and signifying nothing". They will be purely cosmetic in nature, with at best symbolic value. Of course, the standards that are set in permits must be specific enough for enforcement actions to be possible. If vague language is used, no court or regulatory authority will ever be able to demand compliance.

There are many equally serious deficiencies that have been identified with a "command and control" approach to enforcement. Several of these drawbacks are analyzed in a report prepared for the Ontario Government (Peat Marwick, 1983). Some of the deficiencies it identified were as follows:

(i)   Where costs of control or abatement are large, firms and even government agencies (such as municipal and regional governments) face powerful economic incentives to continue polluting rather than to comply. The least-cost alternative is often followed, even though it will result in permit violation.

(ii)   There are no incentives for further reductions after specific emission objectives are reached. For example, if a permit stipulates that 100 units of substance X per day may be emitted, it makes no difference to the firm whether it is emitting 99 units or 1 unit per day. If a production change could be made at a very small cost, it would be irrational to spend any money in making the change, even though the environment would be improved as a result.

(iii)   There are no incentives to ensure that industrial or municipal treatment facilities will be operated in the most effective and efficient manner. Even after the abatement technology is installed, firms may be able to save money by not hiring full-time operators, by improper operation or maintenance of the equipment, and the like. Only if enforcement measures are initiated or the firm can be persuaded to comply will poor operating procedures be curtailed. If there is little or no monitoring or inspection carried out by the regulatory officials, these problems are only exacerbated.

(iv)   A recalcitrant polluter can use appeal mechanisms in the legislation to defer enforcement indefinitely.

(v)   To the extent that uniform standards and objectives are imposed on firms, unnecessarily high costs can be imposed. Firms with high abatement costs pay much more than firms with lower abatement costs. The total costs to achieve compliance and to meet ambient objectives may be much higher than if the firms with lower costs were given economic incentives to comply and the firms with higher costs paid an appropriate fee.

(vi) Command and control regulations cannot easily accommodate economic growth and still maintain environmental quality. If new firms move into an area, the Ministry must continuously revise discharge objectives involving other firms, requiring the re-opening of negotiations between the firm and the Ministry. There is no automatic mechanism to induce existing firms to adjust their emissions if new sources are established.

(vii) The current regulatory system can be very time-consuming and offers polluters many seemingly legitimate opportunities for delay in achieving compliance. For example, strikes, financial hardship, technical problems, investigating new technology, or economically impractical technology have all been accepted as excuses for non-compliance and delay in the past.

(viii) Prosecutions and injunctions cannot easily be adjusted according to the severity of the violation or to temporary economic conditions. Especially in tough economic times, often the only options for non-compliance are to prosecute on the one hand or to enter into negotiations for extensions and the like on the other. There may not be a middle ground response option available to the Ministry, so that some reasonable penalty or incentive is provided to the firm.

(ix) Litigation and fines are generally counter-productive to the goal of environmental protection. The focus on technical and legal issues usually has little to do with the pollution problem at hand. Even steep fines, which are exceedingly rare in British Columbia, amount to only a fraction of compliance costs. In any event, the legal process only diverts the money and energy of the firm and Ministry away from abatement measures.

Some Kinds of Incentives

A variety of more explicitly economic approaches may be contemplated.

Surety bonds

By this technique, a polluting firm or municipality would be obliged to deposit a sum of money with the Ministry or with a bank at the time an abatement program is agreed upon. The amount deposited in the account can be 100% or less of the estimated cost of the program. The money could be invested in interest-bearing notes. As the firm completes its program, the money is refunded until it is paid back in full. Failure to meet deadlines or to achieve the specific results indicated can result in the deposit being forfeited. Non-refundable surety bonds can also be set up to provide funds to repair facilities, pay compensation to damaged parties, to maintain the facility after closure or to maintain the facility if the original operator closes down for any reason.

Precedents for such surety bonds are found in the B.C. Mines Act where they are used to guarantee mine reclamation and the waste disposal of the mines. There are also provisions in Ontario's Environmental Protection Act and the federal

Northern Inland Waters Act authorizing the use of similar performance bonds. Here again, the regulated firm provides a security as an assurance that it will carry out certain obligations. If these requirements are met, the security is returned; if not, the security is expended to carry out the obligations.

Emission and Effluent Charges

Under this scheme, a polluting firm would pay the Ministry an annual amount equal to the total quantity of a designated pollutant (computed as 'volume' x 'concentration' x 'time') being discharged, multiplyed by a unit price or charge rate. As the quantity of the pollutant increases or decreases, the charge payment will vary accordingly, down to zero emissions. If the total emission charge without any abatement is lower than the costs of compliance, the firm would likely elect to pay the charge and not implement the control measures. Each firm would make its own economic choice, based on its costs of abatement. The goal is not to raise revenues but to provide a strong and immediate economic incentive to reduce emissions. Metering technology to measure the amount of pollution discharged would not seem to pose a problem. Indeed, the firm's own monitoring data could be used as the basis for the effluent charge.

This scheme would eliminate the economic incentive to delay; it would become more costly to pollute than to abate. The charges would provide an automatic, ongoing incentive to reduce emissions or effluent. Incentives would be generated for a firm to undertake research and development to find cleaner and more efficient production processes and treatment methods. There are already examples of this scheme in sewer surcharges in several Ontario cities, where industrial discharges of certain contaminants into municipal sewers cost firms additional money, and several European countries have charge systems in place for waste-water effluents. Ideally, the goal is not to raise revenues but to provide a strong and immediate economic incentive to reduce emissions.

The B.C. Waste Management Act Permit Fees Regulation, which became effective on September 1, 1987, allows annual fees for permits. It appears that these fees, which are based on categories of industry and capacity, are very low. For example, pulp and paper mills pay a maximum fee of $12,000 for their air permits and $9,000 for their effluent permit. At present, these fees are largely administrative in nature. By a simple amendment to these regulations, there could be a considerably larger fee established, which could vary directly with the amount of discharge: "The more you pollute, the more you pay". The amount of the fee would vary with the effluent in question, and might be set in a non-linear way; in other words the more of certain effluents you emit, the more you pay per unit. It should be noted the April 1990 Budget promised that effective April 20, 1990, the discharge fees under the existing regulation would also apply to municipalities. They would be "encouraged to recover this revenue by increasing user fees, such as tipping fees at landfill sites and charges on industrial effluent introduced directly into municipal sewage systems." In addition, the 1990 B.C. Budget stated that effective January 1, 1991, all discharge fees will be increased and the basis on which they are calculated will be revised to take into account both the volume and toxicity of waste discharged (B.C. Budget, 1990). Revenues generated will be placed into the Sustainable Environment Fund and targeted to waste management initiatives.

Delay Penalties and Financial Incentive Schemes

Several options have emerged particularly in the United States, specifically to address the problem of delay in achieving compliance. Under such schemes, ambient quality objectives and emission reduction requirements would be established by the Ministry in the usual way. Schedules and deadlines would also be agreed upon as well. Prosecutions, fines, and the like would also still be available. Firms would be liable for predetermined administrative penalties or assessments if they miss deadlines, allowable emission levels are exceeded or monitoring or reporting requirements are breached. Such administrative penalties or assessments could be levied by the Ministry, not the courts. The amounts could be calculated on the basis of costs of abatement or the cost savings that have accrued by avoiding or delaying the abatement program.

Some U.S. statutes like the Clean Air Act contain mandatory penalty requirements; there is no discretion and the stipulated penalties must be imposed. Under the Connecticut Civil Penalties Program, a non-compliance penalty is levied equal to the firm's cost savings and profits made as a result of these cost savings. The regulations set out elaborate steps in determining this figure. In 1989, the British Columbia Waste Management Act was amended to provide a similar measure. It allows for an additional fine where the polluter has acquired any monetary benefits as a result of the offence. This provision, derived from a similar provision in the Canadian Environmental Protection Act was widely heralded.

Another scheme proposed by economists in the Ontario Ministry of the Environment and the Economic Council of Canada is the "pollution control delay penalty". Under this scheme, each permittee would be given a schedule specifying the maximum allowable emission of a pollutant, which would decline over time. The schedule would set out the initial allowable discharge, the rate of reduction, and the ultimate objectives for a firm. If a firm unduly deviated from its schedule so that its pollution exceeded the allowable amount in any period, an automatic penalty would be imposed. The size of the penalty would be such that large excess discharges would be penalized proportionately more than smaller ones. The goal would be to make the total penalty rate high enough to make delays in complying with the schedule unprofitable. Penalties in the form of effluent or emission charges are levied on firms that do not meet agreed-upon deadlines. The charge would be applied to emissions that exceed the objectives stipulated in a control order. A formula is established for calculating the charge rate which reduces the total penalty charged as actual discharges become closer to the deadline objective discharge levels.

Other Tax Incentives

Under the Income Tax Act, accelerated capital cost allowance is allowed for firms that install pollution abatement equipment. "Rapid write-off" of such capital equipment gives a firm a tax break, and a clear incentive to install new technology. However, changes in a firm's production processes that achieve the same result are not rewarded. Similarly, under the B.C. Municipal Act and the Taxation (Rural Area) Act, certain pollution facilities and equipment are likewise exempt from property taxation, thereby providing an incentive to acquire such property without fear that it will attract taxation.

Other Efforts to Harness Market Forces

The Environmental Choice Program

A variety of "good housekeeping seals of approval" may be given by the government in order to reward environmentally appropriate goods or technology. In 1989, for example, Environment Canada launched the Environmental Choice Program, which is the so-called "environmentally friendly goods" campaign. Firms that produce goods that are less environmentally deleterious will be entitled to display the environmentally friendly logo on their products. The thought is that environmentally sensitive consumers will reward such innovations by purchasing such products. The Environmental Choice Board, consisting of citizens drawn from outside government and who represent various interests and regions, awarded the certification to some eighteen products during 1990. In order to carry the EcoLogo, however, these products must meet guidelines which require the applicant to provide verification that it has complied with applicable regulatory standards. Therefore, a company that enjoys the benefits of certification by the Program will lose its certification if it is out of compliance with environmental laws.

Government Procurement Policies

Similarly, government procurement policies may also provide direct incentives to firms that are producing environmentally appropriate goods. For example, if the British Columbia government was required to meet some or all of its paper requirements by the purchase of recycled or unbleached paper, a major boost would be provided to a fledgling, though environmentally critical industry. Although the B.C. Purchasing Commission does have an Environmental Purchasing Policy, it does not meet these goals. Its policy of increasing supply and demand of environmentally advantageous products only where it can be shown to be effective and practical shows very little commitment to this central theme. Its position of continuing to evaluate purchase decisions on the basis of overall value to the province fails to account adequately for future environmental costs. The present policy has no force of law; it can be changed at the whim of policy-makers. By legislating preferential treatment, the Commission could avoid charges of discrimination from unsuccessful suppliers. The legislation would also ensure that the policy is not quietly discarded when environmental issues are less prominent.

Moreover, it has been recommended that price preference be given to appropriate environmentally friendly products. In this way, the government could take into account that seemingly "cheaper" products often have a hidden and unaccounted for environmental cost. Such preferential pricing would also help alter market dynamics in favour of environmentally beneficial products. For example, the State of Oregon has legislated a price preference of 5% for recycled paper. California, New York and Maryland have procurement programs for secondary materials and have provided a market for recycled paper using price preferences, as well as minimum content standards, "set-asides", allowing a specified amount of paper purchases to be recycled paper without consideration of price.

Conclusion

The central message of the Brundtland Commission's analysis is that the environment must be turned into a mainstream economic issue and that a subordinate role for ministries of environment is no longer adequate, if "sustainable development" is to be any more than ironic rhetoric. Like other jurisdictions committed to implementing the principles of sustainable development, Canada and British Columbia must resist the prevalent approach of hiving off issues of environmental quality from issues of resource management and even resource allocation in addressing the challenge posed by the Fraser River. As the Brundtland analysis demonstrated, everything is linked; sustainability of the natural system means that nature's limits must be explicitly taken into account at all levels of government decision-making.

The Canadian Environmental Advisory Council has stated that sustainable development has to be "the central theme for the planning and undertaking of virtually all social and economic activities" (Canadian Environmental Advisory Council, 1989). The National Task Force on the Environment and Economy, endorsed by the First Ministers of Canada, has stated that governments

> must integrate environmental input into decision making at the highest level. Environmental consideration cannot be an add-on and afterthought. They must be made integral to economic policy making and planning and a required element of any economic development proposal (CCREM, 1987:6).

The despoilment of the Fraser River raises in microcosm many of the central legal problems that must be faced in the pursuit of sustainable development in British Columbia. A key aspect of any reform is to ensure compliance with policy measures that are enacted; indeed, compliance and enforcement is the very bedrock of sustainable development. A variety of options for securing compliance with such standards—both "carrots and sticks"—are available and have been assessed above. Another central concern in any effective management strategy is the need to better harness market forces. A number of tools are now available, and some of them have likewise been canvassed above. The despoilment of the Fraser is hardly a new problem; the time has come for action.

References

Ackerman, A., and B. Clapp. 1980. *Fraser River Task Force.* Victoria: Ministry of Environment, unpublished.

Ayres, R., and A. Kneese. 1969. "Production, Consumption and Externalities." *American Economic Review.* 59:282.

Barton, F., and A. R. Thompson. 1984. *A Contract Model of Pollution Control.* Vancouver: Westwater Research Centre.

B.C. Budget. 1990: Appendix I, "Towards a Sustainable Environment." (April 22, 1990).

Bartel, A., and L. Thomas. 1985. "Direct and Indirect Effects of Regulation: A New Look at OSHA's Impact". *Journal of Law and Economics.* 28.

Brittan, Y. 1984. *The Impact of Water Pollution Control Legislation: A Case Study of Fifty Dischargers.* Oxford: Centre for Socio-Legal Studies.

Brown, R., and M. Rankin. 1990 "Persuasion, Penalties and Prosecution: Administrative Penalties v. Criminal Sanctions." in Friedland, M. L. *Securing Compliance: Seven Case Studies.* Toronto: University of Toronto Press.

Canadian Environmental Advisory Council. 1989. *Preparing for the 1990's; Environmental Assessment, An Integral Part of Decision Making.* Ottawa: Environment Canada.

Canada: Environment Canada. 1987. *Canadian Water Quality Guidelines.* Ottawa: Environment Canada.

CCREM. 1987. *Report of the National Task Force on Environment and Economy.* Ottawa: Canadian Council of Resource and Environment Ministers.

Chambliss, W. 1967. "Types of Deviance and the Effectiveness of Legal Sanctions." Wisconsin Law Review. 703.

Environmental Assessment and Review Process Guidelines Order, SOR/84-467. June 22, 1984. (to be replaced by the *Canadian Environmental Assessment Act*).

Gibson, D. 1983. "Constitutional Arrangements for Environmental Protection and Enhancement under the Canadian Constitution." in Beck, S., and I. Bernier (eds.). *Canada and the New Constitution* Volume 2.

Hawkins, K. 1984. *Environment and Enforcement.* Oxford: Clarendon Press.

Nemetz, P. 1986. "The Fisheries Act and Federal-Provincial Environmental Regulation: Duplication or Complementarity?" *Canadian Public Administration* 29:401.

Peat Marwick and Partners. 1983. *Economic Incentive Policy Instruments to Implement Pollution Control Objectives in Ontario.* Ontario Ministry of Environment. Unpublished.

Project 88. 1988. *Harnessing Market Forces to Protect our Environment.* Washington, D.C. An unpublished public policy study sponsored by Senators T. Wirth and J. Heinz.

Robinson, N. A. 1990. "A Legal Perspective on Sustainable Development." in Saunders, J. O. (ed.). *The Legal Challenge of Sustainable Development.* Calgary: Canadian Institute of Resources Law.

Schrecker, T. 1984. *Political Economy of Environmental Hazards.* Ottawa: Law Reform Commission of Canada.

Stewart, R. 1985. "Economics, Environment, and the Limits of Legal Control." Harvard. Environmental Law. Review 1:1.

Stewart, R. 1988. "Controlling Environmental Risks through Economic Incentives." 13 *Columbia Journal of Environmental Law.* 153:13.

Thompson, A. R. 1980. *Environmental Regulation in Canada: An Assessment of the Regulatory Process.* Vancouver: Westwater Research Centre.

Webb, K. 1988. *Pollution Control in Canada: The Regulatory Approach in the 1980s.* Ottawa: Law Reform Commission of Canada.

World Commission on Environment and Development (WCED). 1987. *Our Common Future.* Oxford: Oxford University Press.

16

Water Pricing and Sustainable Development in the Fraser River Basin

Roger C. McNeill

The theory of public utility and natural resource pricing shows that optimum prices can be defined that will result in maximum net benefits from water use. This theory has generally been developed based on an objective function which maximizes benefits using traditional economic measures such as consumer and producer surplus. The theory has not generally incorporated sustainable development objectives into the maximization problem. Fortunately, water pricing has the capability to improve both economic efficiency of water use and to improve sustainability of the economy and natural ecosystems. There is considerable potential to improve water pricing in the Fraser River Basin where current pricing practices, more often than not, lead to both economic inefficiency and decreased sustainability of the ecosystem.

The purpose of this paper is to assess the potential of water pricing as an instrument to improve the sustainability of the economy in the Fraser River Basin. Two different interpretations of sustainability are considered in the analysis.

Interpretations of Sustainable Development

The two interpretations of sustainable development used in this paper are:

(i) An economy where environmental concerns are taken into account at all levels of economic decision making and planning.
(ii) An economy where resource extraction (in this case water) does not exceed sustainable levels. The defenition of sustainable levels includes both the sustainability of extracted water flows over time and the sustainability of the ecosystem dependent on natural flows.

Using definition (i), instream flows, water withdrawals and water prices are determined simultaneously, while under definition (ii), instream flows are predetermined, and the withdrawals and prices are then calculated. The first definition places water pricing and sustainable development in a traditional resource/welfare economic framework where an accounting solution based on benefits and costs is used to determine prices and allocate water. It is important to note that the correct solution under the first definition does allow for values placed on environmental conservation. The second definition puts highest priority on a sustainable ecosystem, however defined, and overrides the accounting solution of benefits and costs.

Definition (i) is a general interpretation of sustainable development as was discussed in the report of the World Commission On Environment and Development (1987). This general interpretation, while not explicitly recognized as a policy of the Canadian government, has been widely distributed to federal employees involved in environmental planning. It has therefore been selected as one definition of sustainable development to be used in the analysis of water pricing in the Fraser River Basin.

The first definition can be considered in the context of traditional resource economic theory, which recognizes that environmental concerns are often not taken into account in market decisions because of externalities and common property characteristics of natural resources. Water pricing can be used as an instrument to account for externalities, thus resulting in a more beneficial allocation of water among multiple uses, including instream uses.

This definition of sustainable development is quite general, since it does not predefine the weights that are given to environmental values. These weights could be estimated using techniques of non-market evaluation, and then entered into the water pricing process. Instream flows for ecosystem protection are then determined simultaneously with water withdrawals and prices. However, environmental values would be expected to vary widely throughout the geographically diverse Fraser River Basin, meaning that non-market evaluations would have to be carried out on a highly disaggregated basis. While not an impossible task, this would present many operational difficulties.

Definition (i) is also a weak definition in regards to sustainability of ecosystems. It implies that some ecosystem loss may be acceptable as a trade-off against demand for water for consumptive and productive uses. The amount of acceptable ecosystem loss depends on the relative values placed by the population on environmental conservation versus water consumption. Ecosystem losses will continue over time until the scarcity of natural environments or ecosystems results in an increase in their marginal value to the point equal to the marginal value of water for consumptive uses. At this equilibrium point, no further ecosystem deterioration would occur, and a sustainable level of development would have been achieved.

Definition (ii) accepts pre-imposed limits on the amount of water that can be extracted at any time in order to achieve sustainability of the ecosystem. Given the existence of such limits, the paper describes the use of water pricing to constrain water use to these levels. The determination of pre-imposed levels of water withdrawal consistent with this definition of sustainable development is not attempted in this analysis. The actual determination could be based on biological or political criteria rather than on an economic accounting of consumptive versus instream values. Once the pre-imposed limits have been determined, the definition is quite operational as the correct prices could be directly established, given knowledge of demand curves for water in different reaches of the basin.

The second definition, while still quite general, allows a strong interpretation of sustainability to be imposed on the water allocation process. For example, policy makers might accept the philosophy of no-net-loss, where further degradation of ecosystems from current levels is not acceptable. Under this criterion, adequate instream flows would have to be ensured to maintain the current populations of fish and other aquatic and riparian communities. No further trade-off between instream flows and consumptive use would be considered.

A final note is that the two definitions may result in the same solution. This would occur if the values on the ecosystem estimated by non-market evaluation techniques under the first definition were consistent with the biological and political criteria used to determine the imposed level of water flows in the second definition.

Setting Water Prices to Take into Account Environmental Concerns

Many water utilities and water works in the Basin (see below) charge a flat rate for water that does not vary with the amount of water consumed. The marginal price of water under this system is zero, and customers will use water until the marginal value is zero (Qf in Figure 16.1). The economically efficient price for water is at the point where the demand curve and the marginal cost of water supply intersect. This price results in a significant drop in water consumption, from Qf to Qm in Figure 16.1. Thus, even without consideration of environmental concerns, marginal cost pricing reduces water use and contributes towards sustainability.

If we assume that environmental concerns can be quantified in measurable economic terms then a new optimal price can be defined. The loss in environmental value from water withdrawal is incorporated into the marginal cost curve of water supply and a new equilibrium price, Pe, is chosen (Figure 16.2). Adoption of this price results in a further reduction in water use from point Qm to Qe.

Because of the geographical diversity of the Fraser River Basin, the methodology described above will have to be carried out on a disaggregated basis, breaking down the Basin into a number of reaches. Estimates of the water demand functions will be required in the different reaches. Within each reach, a single aggregate water demand function could be estimated, or alternatively a number of demand curves could be estimated for different classes of users. The advantage of disaggregating demand by user class is that the optimum allocation between user classes could then be determined. The major difficulty and sources of error will

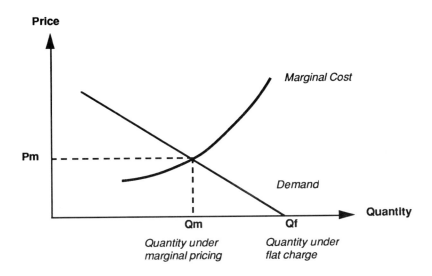

Figure 16.1: Demand for Water Under Flat Charges and Marginal Cost Price

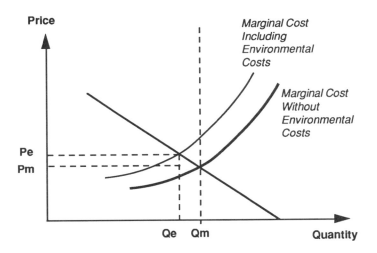

Figure 16.2: Marginal Cost Pricing Including Environmental Cost

probably be in assigning values to instream uses and ecosystem effects of reduced water flows. Although techniques do exist for this type of valuation, substantial economic and biological information is required. For a basin the size of the Fraser, this would involve a major research commitment.

Pricing to Achieve Sustainable Levels of Water Supply

Given predefined limits on water supply, it is a fairly straight-forward process to set prices, such that these limits will not be exceeded. In order to maximize economic returns subject to withdrawal limits in any specified reach of the Basin, a common price should be charged to all users, such that the limits are just reached (Figure 16.3). Again knowledge of the demand curve(s) for water in each reach will be required.

Determination of the acceptable limits on water withdrawal could be done on a consultative basis between interest groups. The acceptable limits will vary across regions because of the geographical variation in the Basin. It is possible that this process may require less research effort than the alternative process of quantifying environmental concerns required under our first definition of sustainable development. The consultative process to set withdrawal limits also has the advantage of incorporating ethical or non-measurable values into the analysis. The

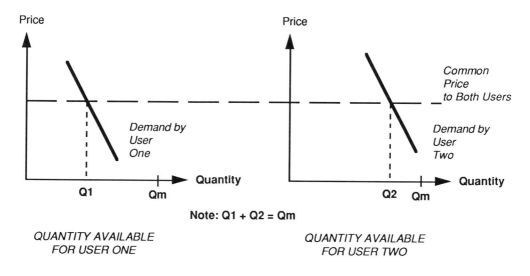

Figure 16.3: Pricing Subject to Limits on Water Withdrawal.

ethical values are supplied by the groups involved or the policy makers, rather than relying on the imperfect concepts of economic welfare implicit in much applied economic analysis. The disadvantage of the consultative process is that it may result in an allocation that reflects only the political influence of the various interest groups involved. There is no guarantee that broader social ethical values will be incorporated into the allocation process.

Current Water Pricing Practices in the Fraser River Basin

At the basic extraction level, surface water is allocated through a system of licences that act to ration quantities. These licences have generally been granted on a "first come, first served" basis, with new licences issued on demand, as long as sufficient water exists in the particular water body. Groundwater extraction is not subject to licencing and is subject only to land ownership constraints. Relatively small provincial tariffs, based on the amount of water extracted, are also charged. In general, at the extraction level, pricing is not a major factor in the allocation of water between users.

No consistent water pricing policy for final users of water exists in the Basin. Final users of water may be self-supplied or may be supplied by irrigation districts, local water works or municipalities. Among each of these categories varying pricing policies exist. Self-supplied users always meet at least part of their own costs of water supply through implicit volumetric costs. Users who are supplied by a waterworks are sometimes charged a volumetric price but are often only charged a flat rate that offers no incentive to conserve. A sectoral analysis of water pricing, discussed below, enables us to make some inference about the extent of different pricing regimes.

Municipal Water Pricing

Municipal water use (excluding manufacturing) accounted for 39% of the total water withdrawal in the Basin according to Environment Canada estimates reported in Pearse et al., (1985). This category includes domestic use, commercial use and public use including parks, firefighting and public buildings, but does not include manufacturing water use supplied by municipal water utilities. A rough estimate (see below) is that about 40% of municipal water use is subject to some sort of volumetric tariff at the final consumer level and 60% is subject to flat rates only.

The majority of the municipal water use takes place in the Lower Mainland and is supplied by the Greater Vancouver Water District. The waterworks supplies member municipalities using a single volumetric price sufficient to meet budgeted costs. However, these costs are passed on to the residential customer in the form of flat rates. Larger industrial and commercial customers are metered and are charged based on the amount used.

Using the municipality of Vancouver as an example, the volume of water (excluding water for manufacturing industries) subject to metering and volumetric charges in the Lower Mainland can be inferred. Vancouver consumed about 122 million cubic meters of water in 1988. It is estimated that about 25 million cubic meters of this total went to manufacturing industries and is therefore subtracted from the total giving 97 million as a gross municipal consumption figure, excluding manufacturing. Municipal records show that about 65 million cubic meters were supplied to customers with water meters. This category includes all industries and most service establishments. Subtracting the 25 million used by manufacturers, leaves a total of about 40 million cubic meters that were supplied to non-manufacturing metered customers. This represents about 41% of the gross municipal consumption excluding manufacturing industries.

In general, other municipalities in the Fraser River Basin have pricing policies similar to the Lower Mainland. Environment Canada pricing surveys show that five out of the eleven municipalities in the Fraser Basin (excluding the Lower Mainland) charge flat rates for residential consumers. The remaining municipalities charge a mixture of flat rates and volumetric rates. It is believed, however, that most residential customers in the communities with mixed rates are subject to flat rates only. Non-residential customers are usually charged a volumetric price, although there is one community that charges only flat rates for all customers. Because these practices are similar to those in the Lower Mainland, it would be reasonable to assume that the 60/40 ratio between flat charges and volumetric charges at the final consumer level would be approximately correct for municipal consumption (excluding manufacturing) in the Basin.

Municipal water utilities are subject to provincial water tariffs that are applied on a per volume basis. All public waterworks in the province pay a standard charge of $60 for the first 10 million gallons (945,455 cubic meters) with an additional charge $0.60 for each additional 100,000 gallons. The marginal price of the water tariff works out to be only $.0013 per cubic meter, accounting for only a small fraction of the total costs to utilities of supplying water. In the case of the Greater Vancouver Water District, for example, provincial water taxes accounted for only 2.8% of the total costs of supplying water in 1988. Furthermore, the cost of the water tariffs are not generally passed on to the consumer in the form of volume based prices. Thus, in general the provincial water taxes do not significantly affect volume based prices and conservation of water by municipal customers.

Rural Residential Water Pricing

Rural residences account for about two percent of the total water withdrawal in the Basin. Based on communications with local waterworks, it is estimated that practically all of this use is subject to flat rate charges rather than volumetric pricing.

Industrial Water Pricing

Industrial water use, which includes manufacturing and resource extraction, accounted for about 33% of the water withdrawals in the Basin in 1985 (Pearse et. al., 1985). Most industrial establishments in the Basin are subject to explicit volumetric charges by water utilities, or are self-supplied and therefore subject to implicit volumetric costs. Self-supplied users are also subject to provincial water taxes, which are applied on a volume basis. These taxes again are low (Table 16.1), and therefore, in most cases are only a minor component of the cost of water supply.

Table 16.1: Water Taxes on Industry: Selected Categories

Category	Unit of Measure	Annual Rental (dollars)	Water Tax (dollars per cubic metre)
Pulp Mills	cubic ft. per second	235.00	0.00026
Sawmills, Manufacturing and Food Processing	First 20,000 gallons per day	23.50	0.00070
	Next 10,00 gallons per day	8.00	0.00048
Commercial and Service	First 2,000 gallons per day	23.50	0.00700
	Next 1,000 gallons per day	12.00	0.00740
Ore Processing	Each 100,000 gallons per day	220.00	0.00130

The above taxes are in the same order of magnitude as paid by public waterworks ($.0013 per cubic meter). Since the charges are granted on the basis of flows, rather than total amount, the average fee per volume used in a year cannot be calculated exactly without some assumptions as to continuity of water usage. Under most scenarios, the cheapest rates are for pulp mills, followed in order by sawmill-manufacturing, ore processing and commercial-service. The rates seem to be biased in favour of large users, such as pulp mills, who pay considerably less per unit of water than small commercial-service enterprises. No regional or seasonal variation occurs in the rates. Provincial water taxes, although minimal, may in some cases reflect some or all of the instream values lost due to industrial water withdrawal. They are not, however, applied on a regional basis and therefore fail to reflect regional differences in the value of water for instream purposes. Given their low values for most uses, there is considerable potential to increase them to reflect local values of instream water use.

On the whole, industrial water pricing appears to be much more efficient than municipal or agricultural water pricing. Almost all users face implicit volumetric water costs or volume based tariffs from utilities, compared to only 40% for municipal water use.

Agricultural Water Pricing

Agricultural water use accounted for about 26% of the total water withdrawal in the Basin in 1985 (Pearse et. al., 1985). Explicit volumetric charges are not applied for most water use. Irrigation districts generally charge on the basis of area irrigated, rather than the amount of water actually applied, thus offering no incentive to conserve. Many individual agricultural operations are self-supplied, drawing directly on surface or ground water for irrigation and stock watering. These users face their own costs, which are related to the amount of water used, and thus have an economic incentive to conserve water. In some cases self-supplied agricultural water users may receive the benefits from existing infrastructure for flow regulation. An example of this is the Nicola Lake outlet control structure, which improves flows downstream in the drier summer months, enabling individual operations to draw sufficient water when required.

Self-supplied users and irrigation districts are also subject to provincial water taxes as shown in Table 16.2.

Table 16.2: Water Taxes on Agriculture

Category	Unit of Measure	Annual Rental (dollars)	Taxes (dollars per cubic metre)
Irrigation conveyed by Public Authority	First 50 acre feet	12.50	0.00020
	Each additional acre foot	0.30	0.00024
Private Irrigation	First 50 acre feet	23.50	0.00038
	Each additional acre foot	0.25	0.00020

These taxes are again very low and as an incentive to conserve water for instream uses their effect would only be minimal. They do not vary according to regional conditions and therefore do not reflect regional environmental values.

Improving Water Pricing Practices in the Fraser Basin

Given the present water pricing practices in the Basin, considerable potential exists for revamping pricing systems to achieve a reduction in water use. In particular, municipal water pricing practices have room for improvement. As discussed above, an estimated 60% of municipal water use (excluding water used by manufacturing firms) is supplied at flat rates. Almost all residential use, both urban and rural, is supplied at flat rates. Agricultural water, when supplied by organized systems, is almost universally supplied at flat or per acreage rates. Industrial water use, in contrast, usually has some volumetric charges associated with it. It is unknown whether or not these charges reflect marginal supply costs or marginal environmental costs.

Provincial water taxes theoretically could serve as an instrument to internalize environmental losses in the price. At present, these taxes are very low compared to costs of withdrawing, treating and delivering water. Because they are applied on a provincial basis, and do not reflect regional differences, they cannot realistically reflect instream values. In many cases, the taxes are not passed on to the consumer in a form that will encourage conservation. Thus, several modifications to the rates would have to be undertaken in conjunction with a change in final consumer pricing.

A two tiered approach to revising water rates would be necessary under both definitions of sustainable development used in this paper:

(i)   Apply a volumetric charge at the final user level based on the marginal costs of water withdrawal, treatment and delivery. This system would be in effect for all organized water supply systems.
(ii)   Apply a provincial water tax that reflects instream values of water or sustainable limits of water withdrawal to all organized systems or self-supplied users.

This two tiered system would insure that all users are charged a volume based price that reflects both marginal costs of supply and environmental values. The provincial water taxes should be applied based on regional conditions. The water tax can be set at rates based on either definition of sustainable development used in this paper.

The first step of universal volumetric pricing would reduce water withdrawals significantly in the Basin, even without additional charges for environmental costs. A number of case studies confirm the reduction in water use that occurs when municipal systems move to metering and volume based pricing. A survey of such studies (McNeill and Tate, 1990) showed that significant water reductions occurred following meter installation in all thirteen of the areas studied. The reductions ranged from 10 to 50% of pre-metering levels. There is no reason to believe that similar reductions would not take place in the Fraser River Basin with the exact level of reductions dependent on the actual prices charged. These levels of reduction would probably result in significant environmental benefits, particularly in the drier interior of the Basin.

Further reductions in water use would result from the implementation of regionalized water taxes. The level of such taxes will vary significantly between regions, depending on the current level of water withdrawals and the local sensitivity of the environment. As discussed earlier, a major research commitment would be required to determine the environmental value of instream water use or sustainable development limits on water use. This work would form the basis for the regionalization of the provincial water tax.

Problems in Implementing Volumetric Charges

Implementation of volume based pricing requires acceptance both from the public and utility managers. A lack of information or misunderstanding of the costs of metering and the effects of volume based pricing have hindered the adoption of more efficient pricing practices. The perception that water is plentiful in British Columbia and the Fraser River Basin has also impeded conservation efforts. The present inefficient pricing practices are evidence of these attitudes.

In the Lower Mainland, predominantly served by the Greater Vancouver Water District, average prices paid for water are, to the author's knowledge, among the lowest in Canada. A survey of local municipalities showed the average price paid to be about $0.11 per cubic meter. This is considerably lower than the provincial average of $0.21 and the national average of $0.26. This low price reflects the natural advantages of the area's water supply: gravity fed primary distribution and high natural water quality. The low prices reinforce the concept of water as an abundant good available at minimal cost.

Most customers of the Greater Vancouver Water District who have faced very low flat rate prices for many years, while observing first hand the high winter rainfall, are not likely to be strong supporters of water conservation measures. Before such customers will accept metering and volume based prices, a number of facts will have to be made clear. First, despite high winter precipitation, summer rainfall in the Lower Mainland is very low compared to many other North American cities. Peak summer demands during periods of natural low flow require storage reservoirs and storage management. As population expands, high capital expenditures on storage and distribution will be required. Work by Renzetti (1990) indicates that the cost of future capacity expansion has not fully been factored into the present cost of water by the Greater Vancouver Water District. Furthermore, the construction and expansion of mountain reservoirs has effects on the quality of the environment. The loss of natural spawning habitat on the Capilano system after construction of the reservoir is evidence that environmental costs do occur, even in areas with high natural run-off.

Public perception that metering will lead to a higher water bill may have impeded acceptance of volumetric pricing. The total and average water bill per household will in fact be lower using a marginal cost pricing than it will be with a flat charge. This is because the volume based price will reduce overall consumption and, thus, total costs. Furthermore, marginal cost pricing is likely to be more equitable than flat charges, since customers who have smaller homes and water demands will pay proportionately less than owners of large homes. These advantages of metering and volume based pricing must be sold to the public before widespread acceptance will occur.

The cost of installing and reading meters is also an impediment to wider scale adoption of volume based pricing. Based on the number of dwellings in the area and using cost data reported by Tate (1988), installation of universal residential metering would cost over \$80 million for the Fraser River Basin. Given the size of the capital expense, utilities are going to require benefit cost analysis of their investment before installing meters. Based on existing data (see below), it is the author's opinion that installation of meters with volume based pricing would be a feasible investment for most waterworks in the Basin.

Previous studies of metering in North America and Australia indicate that the benefits generally outweigh the costs. In a survey of studies on metering, McNeill and Tate (1990) report that four out of five studies examined reported positive net present values for metering. A recent study for the Greater Vancouver District by Renzetti (1990) reported that the benefits of metering outweighed the costs under most of the scenarios analyzed. This result is interesting because Vancouver has particularly low water supply costs. In other areas of the Basin, supply costs will usually be greater resulting in a higher benefit cost ratio of metering.

Conclusions

In theory, water pricing is capable of improving both economic efficiency and sustainability. Theoretical models of water pricing exist that can achieve a sustainable economy using the two divergent definitions of sustainable development described in this paper.

Current pricing practices in the Fraser Basin lead to economic inefficiency and over-consumption of water, leaving considerable potential to improve water conservation through a revamping of the pricing system. Residential water pricing, both urban and rural, is particularly inefficient, with virtually all of the population subject to flat rate charging. Organized waterworks supplying agriculture also have inefficient pricing systems. Pricing systems in place for industry are generally more efficient, as most industries are charged for water on a volumetric basis or are self-supplied.

Institutional arrangements now exist for implementation of improved water pricing practices. The water tariffs administered under the provincial Water Regulation Act could be revised to reflect regional differences in environmental losses occurring from water withdrawal. Increased revenue from this source could be used in the promotion of metering and water pricing by utilities and irrigation districts. At the final consumer level, all water works have the authority to implement volume based charges that fully reflect the marginal costs of supply. While some impediments exist, such as the cost of metering and the public perception of water as a free good, these can be overcome with the provision of adequate information to the public and to utility managers.

References

Greater Vancouver Districts. 1989. *Provisional Revenue and Expenditure Budgets - Year Ending December 31, 1989.* Greater Vancouver Regional District.

McNeill, R. C., and D. Tate. 1990 (forthcoming). *Municipal Water Pricing Guidelines.* Ottawa: Environment Canada, Inland Waters.

Pearse, P. H., F. Bertrand and J. W. MacLaren. 1985. *Currents of Change,* Final Report, Inquiry on Federal Water Policy. Ottawa.

Province of British Columbia. 1988. *Water Regulation.* Order in Council 889, Victoria: Queen's Printer.

Renzetti, S. 1990. *The Economics of a Seemingly Abundant Resource: Efficient Water Pricing in Vancouver.* Canada. PH.D. Thesis, University of British Columbia, Department of Economics.

Tate, D. 1988 *Water Demand Management in Canada, A State of the Art Review.* Ottawa: Environment Canada, Inland Waters.

World Commission On Environment and Development (WCED). 1987. *Our Common Future.* Oxford: Oxford University Press.

17

Economic Instruments for Sustainable Development of Water Resources

Peter H. Pearse and Donald M. Tate

Most people think of Canada as a country with abundant water. The common perception is one of a land of great rivers, countless streams, endless lakes and marshes, and expanses of snow and ice. This impression is supported by statistics showing that Canada contains the largest area of water of any country in the world; it includes several of the world's largest lakes; it accounts for a significant fraction of the world's stock of freshwater (Pearse et al., 1985). With roughly nine percent of the world's annual renewable freshwater supply and less than one percent of world population, it is not surprising that Canadians take it for granted that they have more than enough water to meet all their needs.

Recently, however, we have had to qualify this generalization. Closer examination reveals that over half of the water runoff in Canada flows north, away from the centres of population and industry, leaving scarce supplies in some southern regions. In developed areas, pollution has significantly impaired the natural quality of the resource. And nature's abundance has not prevented the cost of collecting, storing and distributing water to where it is needed from rising dramatically. Thus, although Paul Samuelson's *Economics*, the textbook read by a generation of North American economics' students, refers to water as one of nature's "free goods", this characterization is obsolete.

Canada's emerging problems of water management are well illustrated in the basin of the Fraser River. This great river rises in the Rockies, flows through the mountainous interior and the rolling southern dry belt to the humid west coast. Its annual flow is the third largest among Canada's rivers. It provides migration channels and spawning grounds for huge stocks of Pacific salmon. At the same time, it is the spine of British Columbia's transportation and communication networks, connecting the province's main centres of population and commerce.

The Fraser River supplies much of the water needed for British Columbia's industrial, agricultural and domestic needs. Its lower reaches form a major navigation route that has been extensively dredged, dyked and channelled. And its estuary has been substantially altered and developed, and includes a major port.

The diverse uses of the river often conflict. In some interior areas, notably in the Thompson-Nicola sub-basin, the demand for water and for irrigation and municipal needs threaten fish spawning habitats. Substantial hydroelectric potential on the river's mainstream has repeatedly tempted governments to sacrifice the salmon that depend on the uninterrupted flow. Throughout its course, the river is a receptacle for industrial, municipal and agricultural wastes, causing local pollution and impairing water quality for downstream users. With growth and development, these conflicts are increasing.

Thus the Fraser illustrates the conflicts that must be resolved, the trends that must be reversed, and the obstacles that must be overcome if sustainable development is to be achieved in an advanced industrial economic environment.

Nevertheless, the Fraser, in contrast to many of the other great rivers of the world, is a healthy river. Certainly it has suffered from human pressures, but its main stem has never been dammed and, over most of its length, it has never been significantly altered. It remains the world's greatest salmon river. Though pollution can be found in industrialized, mainly downstream areas, and in the estuary, the quality of its water remains generally high. Thus the challenge of sustainable development (which often implies a need to restore degraded ecosystems) in the Fraser River context means mainly protecting, maintaining and enhancing the natural quality and productivity of the waterway.

This chapter uses the example of the Fraser River to illustrate the challenge of sustainable development with respect to water resources. More specifically, it examines how economic decision-making of water users bears on sustainable approaches to resource development. It focuses on the bias of economic forces that lead to wasteful use and degradation of such non-marketed resources. This leads to an exploration of opportunities for developing economic instruments for improving water management and use.

The discussion begins with a commentary on the concept of sustainable development and its implications for water management, thus identifying the changes needed in water policy. It then examines the growing problems of excessive water use, waste discharge and degradation of water quality, arguing that these are the result, in large part, of insulating water from the market forces that ration other resources among users, encourage consumers to use them frugally, and induce suppliers to protect and conserve them.

The argument develops as follows. For mainly historical reasons, water and most other environmental resources are excluded from the market arrangements governing the use of resources that provide raw material for production, such as minerals and timber. With few exceptions, users of water have neither title to nor exclusive rights to use it, and water is isolated from market pricing responsive to supply and demand. As a result, water and its waste assimilative capacity are treated as free goods, and no one has either the incentive or the right to manage, conserve and enhance them. The task of protecting them from over-use and abuse falls to the government, which has resorted historically to regulation to restrain the powerful economic incentives of private users.

This leads to the proposition that our present economic organization is biased against so-called environmental resources such as water. Experience in Canada and elsewhere suggests that this bias can be corrected most effectively not by ever-increasing regulation of economic activity, but by embracing these resources within the economic system, thereby bringing market incentives to bear on their protection, conservation and development. Engaging market forces in this way is seen as one means, among many others, of integrating environmental goals with economic progress.

The final sections of the paper discuss practical means of bringing about the needed changes, through pricing, improvements in the form of property rights held by water users, and other policies. Drawing on experience in other countries, a variety of practical measures to promote sustainable water management are suggested.

Water and Sustainable Development

Sustainable development, as popularized by the recent report of the World Commission on Environment and Development, *Our Common Future*, means economic growth and development today without impairing the capacity of future generations to grow and develop (WCED, 1987; also known as the Brundtland Commission report). In emphasizing the capacity of future generations to continue to improve living standards, the commissioners focused on the natural environment, the importance of protecting the health of the biosphere and the need to maintain the productivity of natural resources to support continuing economic improvement.

The Brundtland Commission asserted that economic growth and environmental improvement are not only jointly possible, but each is essential to the other. This reassurance about our opportunity to enjoy both economic and environmental improvement, without having to sacrifice one for the other, undoubtedly accounts for the popularity of the sustainable development idea. But as a feasible social objective, it is simply asserted; it is not supported with careful analysis of the interdependence of the economy and the environment, nor by historical inference. And it ignores more than two centuries of scholarly investigation by the world's leading economists and philosophers leading to the opposite conclusion.

This is not the place to trace the development of theories about how limited land and resources constrain economic growth, but long before Thomas Malthus reasoned that unrestrained population growth would be held in check by the limited amount of food producing land, Adam Smith and the Phisiocrats of eighteenth century France had argued that all wealth ultimately came from the land and so the limits of land would limit production. This theme recurs in economic doctrine through the Victorian period, the Conservation movement and today's environmental movement (Scott and Pearse, 1988). A prominent recent example is the Club of Rome's *Limits to Growth*, which predicted, in the 1970's that if economic activity continued to expand the world would deplete its supplies of all basic natural resources and food within a decade (Meadows et al., 1972).

Yet experience has not confirmed these gloomy predictions; indeed, trends have been quite the opposite. World production and consumption of natural resource commodities have continued to expand, even at an accelerating rate. At the same time, their costs and prices have actually declined in real terms (Barnett and Morse, 1973). Since Malthus' time, the world's population has increased more than five-fold, yet standards of living, far from declining, have improved. To this extent, the optimism of Brundtland has more historical support than the pessimism of Malthus and the Club of Rome.

But this is an oversimplification. The Malthusian tradition and its modern extensions deal with the limitations of agricultural land and natural resources, and the increasing scarcity of food and industrial raw materials as populations and economies expand. Historical experience suggests this concern has been misplaced. The threat to continued improvement in standards of living is not depletion of the natural resource materials needed to expand production. Rather, the central concern is the accelerating degradation of unmarketed environmental resources such as air and water, which endangers whole ecosystems and hence also the economic and social structures that depend on them. In spite of continuing growth in material consumption, environmental deterioration threatens the productivity of natural systems, the quality of life, human health and perhaps survival.

This distinction is important, because it implies a fundamental redirection of traditional concern about the limits to growth. Much of the world, and certainly Canada, has escaped the Malthusian trap of scarce land and resource materials needed for production. But, in doing so, we have begun to threaten ecological life support systems. Sustainable development implies, if nothing else, avoiding the destruction of natural systems on which life on earth depends.

The apparent triumph over scarcity of land and natural resource materials in modern industrial economies is instructive in our search for solutions to environmental problems. The key has been technological advance. On the supply side, the progression of technology has vastly increased the resources available, through discovery of new reserves and stocks of everything from petroleum to fish. Supplies have been expanded even more by advances in technologies that have enabled the use of less accessible resources, lower qualities, and lesser concentrations. Even land, though limited in the spatial sense, has been augmented enormously in its capacity to produce crops.

On the demand side, technology has progressively reduced and eliminated our dependence on particular resources for particular purposes, broadening the range of materials available to producers, and improving the suitability among them. Timber is no longer needed to construct buildings and ships because there are now a dozen new materials to choose from. Societies no longer need copper to transmit energy and messages because materials like aluminum and fibre optics, made of much more ubiquitous raw material, will do the same job. Indeed, no materials at all are needed to connect senders and receivers of electronic messages, because they can be transmitted without them.

All this innovation has more than offset the depletion of resources through consumption. Notwithstanding the enormous economic growth of the past century, the demand for almost all natural resource commodities and food has risen more slowly than the supply. As a result, the real price of natural resource products— that is, the cost relative to manufactured goods, or to all goods and services taken together—has gradually declined.

For present purposes, it is important to understand the forces driving all the creative technological effort that has overcome the limits of nature's endowment. Owners of land and natural resources are constantly striving to generate the greatest possible value from them, so they search for new reserves, find ways of extracting more from them, protect and if possible enhance them, make more valuable products from them, and so on. And those who need these resource commodities are constantly searching for cheaper sources of supply, alternative materials that are less costly, and ways of using them more efficiently. Both suppliers and demanders, driven by financial incentives created by resource commodity markets, direct their creativity toward overcoming scarcity. Their collective effort is obviously successful.

But why haven't these same forces succeeded in preventing the depletion of our so-called environmental resources? The answer is that they have not been at work on this problem. The economic incentives to do so have not been felt by the suppliers or the demanders. The suppliers, or owners of the water, air, flora and fauna are often difficult to identify; they may be common property owners or governments. They rarely have either the motivation or the means to maximize the value of these assets, and they typically do not even charge prices for their use. And the demanders, having access to these environmental resources without charge, have no incentive to treat them as valuable and costly resources, or to economize on their use of them. There is no market mechanism to balance demand with the available supply, so demands are often excessive. And there are no economic incentives directing technology toward increasing supplies and reducing demands. In consequence, economic growth leads inexorably to overuse, depletion and degradation of these unmarketed environmental resources, creating the challenge of sustainable development.

This contrast between the natural resource commodities used as raw materials in production and environmental resources which are not bought and sold in private markets is well illustrated in the Fraser Basin. The progression of mineral development, from the 1858 Gold Rush that opened the whole region for settlement to the modern open-pit copper mines, reveals remarkable progress in exploration, development and utilization of minerals, and an enormous expansion of supplies. Reserves of timber have similarly been increased as technology has made accessible and useful the more remote forests, the lower quality trees and the previously unusable species. Developments in fish canning and other forms of processing have greatly expanded the river's useable fish resources. Recently, attention has turned to opportunities for expanding both forest and fisheries resources through investment in enhancement and the potential appears impressive.

At the same time, food production has expanded sharply and the productivity of agricultural land continues to improve.

In contrast, water resources are deteriorating; flows are overused in some areas, and pollution is evident in many more. These problems of overuse and pollution are a direct result of the exclusion of environmental resources from the economic system. In other words, the economic system is biased against resources that are excluded from the market process. Far from encouraging users to economize on their demands, to use them efficiently and to enhance them, as it does with marketed raw materials for industrial production, the system invites wasteful use and depletion of non-marketed environmental resources.

Regulation, Market Processes and the Role of Property Rights

If public policy is to be directed toward sustainable development, which means protecting environmental resources from progressive degradation as pressures on them increase with economic growth, two general strategies are available. One is the regulatory approach, or what American economist Charles Schultze has called the "command and control" system, which depends on legal proscriptions, regulations and bureaucratic controls to restrain unwanted tendencies of market processes (Schultze, 1977). The other involves and cultivates market forces to harmonize economic incentives with the public interest, in this case the public interest in protecting environmental resources.   A fundamental issue of economic organization is the division between the two: what should be left to market forces and what should be managed by governmental regulation.

The major disadvantage of the regulatory approach is that it offers no incentives for suppliers to develop new technologies for augmenting supplies or for demanders to conserve, reduce their demands, and find substitutes. The long-run effect is well illustrated in the use of water resources in British Columbia, where water supply systems are typically governmental; the product is supplied free or below cost, it is used inefficiently and wastefully, and technologies are unsophisticated.

However, the market approach can be relied upon to allocate resources efficiently only to the extent that their use can be controlled by people holding suitable property rights over them, among other things. Where rights to resources are well-defined, exclusive and tradeable, the market affords a feasible means of ensuring efficient use, as in the cases of most farmland, forests and minerals, described earlier. But when the rights are ill-defined, non-exclusive and non-transferable, as are those of many users of water, recourse must be taken in regulation.

The degree to which well-defined property rights extend over natural resources is a matter of public choice, however. The predominant theory about the origins of property suggests that exclusive property rights emerge from an original situation of no property or common property when resources become valuable and demands press on the available supply to such a degree that the absence of an allocation system results in users interfering with each other, causing costly inefficiencies. Eventually these costs, or losses, become so great that it is worth the expense, trouble and dislocation to organize a system of allocating rights among users (Demsetz, 1967). In other words, when resources are abundant and demands on them are light, systems of property are crude, and appropriately so. But when resources are valuable and demands exceed the available supply, we can expect property rights to emerge so that users can gain the control they need to get the most out of the available resources (Scott, 1984; see also Scott's chapter in this volume).

This theory is well supported by the evolution of property rights in natural resources in Canada. The first settlers found all natural resources so abundant that there were more than enough for everyone, so they did not bother about property and allocation systems. But, as the frontier receded one resource after another became scarce and valuable and needed to be allocated. In the Fraser basin, which was always the focus of development in what is now mainland British Columbia, property rights were developed first for fur-bearing animals, then gold deposits and, in succession, land in settlements, agricultural lands, timber, other minerals, petroleum and so on. The rights available to users of some resources are still rudimentary, such as those over fish, wildlife, water and the waste assimilative capacity of water (Pearse, 1988). It is no coincidence that it is these resources, available to users under weakly-defined and typically non-exclusive rights, that are generally deteriorating and manifesting the environmental problem.

Reflection on the historical pattern of development of property rights in natural resources suggests that the unprecedented pace of economic growth and technological advance in recent decades has expanded the range of resources that are valuable, scarce and in need of allocation, but the development of new forms of property rights has not kept pace. What is needed is a deliberate policy to accelerate this process if market forces are to be brought to bear on their protection and management of these threatened resources.

This is not to say, of course, that markets can be relied upon to allocate resources efficiently and equitably in all cases. There are so many imperfections in markets, especially those for natural resources, that there will always be plenty of scope for beneficial intervention. However, to the extent that property rights and economic incentives function to protect, conserve and enhance environmental resources, they can reduce the burden on regulatory controls by helping to reconcile the environment and the economy, thus advancing the objective of sustainable development. In other words, environmental management can benefit from the development of economic instruments.

Economic Costs of Water Use

Before turning to some of the opportunities for bringing market forces to bear on the conservation and management of water resources, it is helpful to identify clearly how the concept of economic scarcity applies to water use. This is fundamental to an understanding of the cost of using water, and hence also of how instruments for water management must be designed to achieve the desired results.

At the outset we must recognize the two basic dimensions of water resources: their quantity and quality. Correspondingly, water is valuable to man both for its physical quality or flow, and for its capacity to assimilate wastes. Both dimensions are limited and specific to each waterway. They are related, of course, because the greater the flow the greater the waste absorbing or assimilative capacity of a watercourse, but they are used in different ways by different users, and so require separate management attention.

The management task with respect to flows consists mainly of allocating the available quantity among all its potential uses, including in-stream as well as withdrawal uses. If the natural supply is sufficiently great relative to the demand so that water allocated to one use does not impinge on any other, the resource is not "scarce" in the economic sense; since using it imposes no sacrifice, its real economic cost is zero. These circumstances prevail in many reaches of the Fraser system.

However, in some tributaries, water demands exceed the available flows, so that one use or user does impinge on others. In the Fraser Basin, ranchers' demands for irrigation water along rivers and streams of the dry interior compete with each other and with in-stream fish habitat requirements. The real economic cost of using water in these circumstances is its value in alternative uses foregone; that is, its *opportunity cost*. This cost applies to the water withdrawn by a user net of return flows, referred to as water consumption.

The same concept applies to the waste assimilative capacity of water resources. The management task involves determining the balance between maintaining the natural quality of the waterway and utilizing its capacity to assimilate wastes and, where demands exceed the available capacity, rationing it among users. Thus a real economic cost, or opportunity cost, is incurred whenever the demands for the flows or waste assimilative capacity of a watercourse exceeds its available supply, as indicated in Table 17.1.

Table 17.1: Water Resources and Components of the Real
Economic Cost of Using them

	Dimensions of Water Use	
Scarce Factor	**Flow**	**Water Assimilative Capacity**
Natural Resource Supply	Opportunity Cost of Water	Opportunity Cost of Assimilative Capacity
Infrastructure	Cost of Water Supply, Treatment and Delivery System	Cost of Waste-Water Collection and Disposal System

Pollution control objectives may call for zero discharges of certain toxic and persistent substances, in which cases outright prohibitions are the appropriate control method. The problem of allocating assimilative capacity arises in connection with the more common wastes which can be safely dispersed or broken down by natural processes within acceptable limits of water quality. Thus assimilative capacity is a limited resource available for use, as is the available flow. The amount of both must be determined with reference to the natural character of each waterway and the quantity and quality of the water to be maintained in it. Given those objectives, the task is to allocate flows and assimilative capacity to their most productive uses.

In addition to the value, or opportunity cost, of the water itself, account must usually be taken of the cost of facilities required to make it accessible to users. To meet demands, infrastructure must be constructed and serviced, so the cost of a particular use is the additional demands it puts on the infrastructure. This cost includes both the capital costs associated with providing infrastructure capacity and the operating and maintenance costs associated with using it. As Table 17.1 implies, these infrastructure costs are additional to the cost of using the natural water flow or its waste assimilative capacity. Their relative importance varies greatly. For municipal water uses on the Fraser, for example, infrastructure costs typically dominate, and the opportunity cost of the water itself may be close to zero. For agricultural uses in arid regions, the reverse is likely.

For present purposes, it is important to emphasize that economic growth and increasing demands on water resources drive up both categories of costs disproportionately to the growth in demand itself. Growth tends to increase all forms of demand on waterflows and their assimilative capacities, with the result that the opportunity costs of using water increase and multiply. And infrastructure costs are forced upward by the need to tap progressively less accessible and hence more costly sources of supply and to spread the network of delivery and collection systems.

Economic Instruments for Managing Water

Hitherto, in British Columbia and throughout Canada, water users have been insulated from most of these costs. Water management has been a process of progressively harnessing water resources to meet growing demands, with little or no attempt to manage the demand itself. This approach has become known as *supply management* (Pearse et al., 1985).

A predictable consequence of this approach is profligate use of water. Table 17.2 shows that per capita water consumption in Canada exceeds that of all the other western industrial countries listed by a considerable margin. The exception is the United States where, as in Canada, domestic users are commonly supplied with water at little or no charge, and where technology, income levels and lifestyles encourage heavy water use in lawn and garden irrigation and in household appliances. In British Columbia, where domestic water prices are

Table 17.2: Domestic Water Use: An International Perspective

Country	Water Use Per Capita (cubic metres per day)
United States	0.43
Canada	*0.36*
Sweden	0.20
United Kingdom	0.20
West Germany	0.15
France	0.15
Israel	0.14

among the lowest in Canada, per capita use is above even the Canadian average, as shown in Table 17.3. (Tate, 1989).

Recently, the deficiencies of this passive response to demands for water have drawn attention to the considerable opportunities in *demand management*, which refers to pricing and other measures to restrain water use (Tate, 1990). Thus, the recent Inquiry on Canada's Federal Water Policy recommended increased attention to demand management, to balance and supplement the traditional emphasis on supply management (Pearse et al., 1985).

Table 17.3: Municipal Water Use in the Fraser Basin

	Fraser Basin	All British Columbia	All Canada
Population Served by Water Systems (thousands)	501	2,478	20,367
Domestic Water Use:			
total (thousand m^3/ d)	201	1,109	7,518
per capita (m^3 /d)	0.401	0.447	0.368

Source: Tate and Lacelle (1990).

A wide variety of techniques can be used to restrain demands for water and its waste disposal capacity to their available supplies. They include technological controls, in the form of prescribed water conserving equipment on consumer goods such as shower heads, and in industrial plants, such as recycling systems;

prohibitions on certain uses, such as agricultural, irrigation and lawn-watering, during dry periods; regulations about such things as water treatment and waste disposal; public appeals to conserve water and avoid pollution; and many others. Here, we draw special attention to *economic instruments*; that is, techniques that generate economic incentives to restrain demands on water and its waste assimilative capacity.

The main types of economic instruments for managing water are listed in Table 17.4, roughly in order of their dependence on market forces. The first, *regulations and penalties*, is not primarily economic; these devices provide economic incentives only in the negative sense of economic penalties for failure to comply with regulations. To the extent that regulation objectives are achieved, the cost is borne, in the first instance, by the water users, though in a competitive environment producers can be expected to shift such costs to the consumers of their products and the suppliers of other inputs. This approach provides no incentive to economize on water use or waste disposal within the regulatory limits. Nor does it capture any resource value or generate any revenue.

Subsidies are another common device for achieving water management objectives in Canada. These take the form of federal or provincial assistance to municipalities for water supply and water treatment facilities; tax write-offs, soft loans and grants to private companies for installing water conserving and anti-pollution equipment; and tax incentives for water conservation projects. These techniques shift the costs to taxpayers, and by shielding users from the cost of their water use tend to aggravate excessive demands and waste of both water resources and infrastructure.

In contrast, *prices* for water and for waste discharges into water direct the cost to the users, generating incentives to reduce demands. As a result, pricing can be a powerful technique for restraining water use, as discussed further below. Prices are consistent with the "user pay" principle, but again it is important to recognize that producers will normally shift the costs onto others.

Property rights refer to water rights in the form of title, licenses and permits, and to waste discharge rights. Where water users are not served by collective water supply systems but withdraw water and discharge waste individually, well designed, transferable rights can provide economic incentives similar to prices. The value of such rights encourages water users to allocate resources efficiently and provides them with appropriate incentives to use reserves conservatively. This technique is also examined further below.

Finally, Table 17.4 includes *privatization* among the economic instruments for water management because under suitable arrangements, private enterprises supplying water and treating waste can be expected to recoup their costs from water users, by means of charges. Thus private enterprise can be regarded as a mechanism for ensuring that water users bear the cost of their demands for water through prices, discussed above.

Table 17.4: Economic Instruments for Water Management

Management Approach	Instrument	Initial Distribution of Cost[1]	Efficiency Effects
Regulations and other penalties	Legal prohibitions and controls with penalties for offenders	Users	No incentive for efficiency other than minimum compliance
Subsidies	Government-funded water-works and services, or assistance to private providers or users	Taxpayers	Encourages excessive use and economic waste
Pricing	Prices charged for water use and waste discharged, based on metered use	Users	Promotes conservation and efficient use: more the closer the price to marginal cost including resource rent
Property Rights	Title, licenses or permits for water and waste disposal	Users	Promotes efficient use and allocation if transferable
Privatization	Private enterprise water utilities and pricing	Users	Promotes efficient use: more the closer the price to marginal cost

Notes:
1   In the long run, the costs can be expected to be shifted from these initial payers forward onto consumers and backward onto resource owners

Present water management in the Fraser basin takes little advantage of economic incentives to encourage conservative use of water and its waste assimilative capacity. As we note below, domestic water users are supplied with water and sewage treatment at no direct cost or at nominal fixed rates, regardless of the amount they use. Industrial water charges are unrelated to the opportunity cost of the resources in different waterways and are not well designed to encourage efficient use. No charges are levied for industrial waste discharges other than penalties for exceeding authorized effluent limits. To control pollution, heavy reliance is put on technological regulations and controls based on concentrations of effluents, while the wide variation in the capacity of waterways to dilute and assimilate pollutants is only crudely recognised. Senior governments have provided substantial subsidies for municipal water and wastewater systems, especially the capital costs of these facilities, though this support has recently diminished. Private enterprise and marketing of water is found only rarely, and in insignificantly small communities. And the property rights of water users are not designed to generate financial incentives to economize on water demands.

The remainder of this paper focuses on the two types of economic investments that seem to offer the greatest opportunity for promoting sustainable development of water resources in the Fraser system: pricing in the context of municipal water and wastewater systems, and property rights in the context of individual water supply and disposal works.

Pricing

Economic theory explains that the "right" price for water delivered to a user is the opportunity cost of the water itself, if any, plus the cost of delivering it. This corresponds to the sum of the two components of the cost of water use described earlier and indicated in Table 17.1: the resource cost and the infrastructure cost.

It is important to note that the relevant costs in this context are *long-run marginal costs*. Marginal refers to the water at the margin of use; that is, the cost of supplying an additional cubic meter of water to the system. Long-run means that the capital costs of expanding infrastructure to accommodate the additional use is included. The long-run marginal cost price is thus the sum of:

• The marginal opportunity cost of water;
• The marginal capital cost of infrastructure capacity;
• The marginal cost of operating and maintaining the infrastructure.

This price corresponds to the price that could be expected to emerge in a competitive market.

The long run marginal costs of water and infrastructure are likely to be higher than their average costs because, as noted earlier, costs per unit of water usually rise disproportionately as water systems are expanded, since the lowest-cost sources are exploited first (Hirschleifer et al., 1960). It follows that a price equal to long-run marginal cost will yield revenues in excess of costs. The resulting profit can generate public resistance, especially where the supplier is a monopoly utility (as illustrated in B.C. Hydro's current effort to raise electricity prices closer to its long-run marginal cost).

However, the economic rationale for pricing at long-run marginal cost is that such prices guide users to utilize water efficiently. Users, whether domestic consumers or industries, use water as long as its value to them exceeds its cost or price. Any price less than the full long-run marginal cost will encourage use beyond the level at which the value of water to users is equal to or greater than the cost of providing it. If the price of additional water is zero, as in the case of flat-rate pricing formulae, users can be expected to demand it as long as it has any value to them at all. This is likely to be substantially more than the amount that would be demanded at a price equal to the marginal cost. A price equal to the full long-run marginal cost of supplying water, levied by a supply utility without discriminating among users, will thus encourage efficient water allocation and use, and provide incentives to conserve and recycle water to the appropriate degree.

Ideally the price of water would vary among seasons, or even different times of the day, responding to regular changes in supply and demand. Water systems are designed to meet demands on capacity during peak demand periods, so that capital costs are appropriately charged against users during these periods. This suggests higher prices during periods of peak demand, as explained in the paper by McNeill in this volume. Such demand-sensitive pricing is commonly adopted by electrical utilities, but not by water supply utilities in Canada.

Similarly, the opportunity cost of water may be significant only during certain seasons of low flow or high demand, and is appropriately deleted at other times. In practice a variety of simple formulae can be adopted to recognize the higher costs associated with using water at certain times.

The components of the long-run marginal cost of water use, described above, imply a different price for each water supply system, because both the cost of water and of infrastructure are unique to each set of circumstances. They imply the same price for all users of a system, (unless the supply cost varies among them).

In the Fraser Basin, water pricing is rudimentary at best, and incorporates none of the principles of marginal cost pricing. Most municipalities charge flat rates for domestic water; that is, the householder is supplied with unlimited quantities of water and waste treatment for a fixed annual or periodic payment, averaging a little more than $7.00 per month (Tate and Lacelle, 1990). In British Columbia as a whole, the average monthly water bill for residential consumers in 1989 was $11.89, the second lowest among all provinces. The Canadian average was $20.88.

Charges for water in the Fraser Basin are thus conspicuously low. More important, they are levied as flat rates, which mean that the cost a user incurs for additional water is zero. Not surprisingly, such systems show considerably higher use per capita than systems that meter use and charge accordingly. A recent national survey of municipal water rates showed that municipalities in the Fraser Basin that charge flat rates use 32 percent more water per capita than those that base charges on the quantity used (Tate and Lacelle, 1990). A 1970 study found that residential water use per capita in Calgary, which was unmetered, was twice as high as in Edmonton, which was fully metered (Kellow, 1970). This contrast between two cities of comparable size and climate was confirmed by the 1989 federal survey, and it provides an especially graphic example of the impact of water pricing according to use.

These statistics illustrate the responsiveness of water demand to price, and in this respect is consistent with the findings of many other studies. Bearing in mind the fact that, even in the cases of metered municipalities, the charges per unit of water use are well below the full long-run marginal costs of water systems, these survey results reveal the considerable scope for managing water demands by means of appropriate pricing policies.

Most industrial and commercial enterprises in the Fraser Basin take their water from municipal systems. However, some have independent supply systems, so they bear their own costs of intake, waste treatment and recycling facilities (see Table 17.5). In these cases, the scope for public water pricing is limited to charges for the water itself, excluding the infrastructure.

Table 17.5: Water Related Costs by Industry Group in the Fraser Basin[1]

| Industry | Cost Category | | |
	Intake[2]	Recycling	Waste Treatment
	(annual cost in thousands of dollars)		
Food and Beverage	1,261	80	503
Wood Products	500	161	35
Paper and Allied Products	5,552	430	5,092
Petroleum Products	683	1,047	714
Chemical Products	153	50	23
Other Manufacturing	579	84	815
Total Manufacturing	8,728	1,852	7,182
Mineral Extraction	4,014	1,541	125
Thermal Power	357	—	—
Total	13,099	3,393	7,307

Source: Inland Waters Directorate, Environment Canada, unpublished results of 1986 survey of industrial water use. For a national and provincial summary of this survey, see Tate and Scharf (1990).
Notes:
1   Excludes capital costs. 1986 data.
2   Includes payments to municipal utlilities, costs of water licenses, and operating and maintenance costs for water intake facilities and treatment prior to water use. 1986 data.

Like other provinces, British Columbia charges annual rentals for water drawn from surface sources (the legislation that applies to groundwater has never been proclaimed, so is not in force) and for in-stream uses (RSBC, 1979). The rentals are in the form of annual license fees based on estimates of daily water use, as indicated in Table 17.6. These price formulae fall short of marginal cost pricing in important respects. First, they apply throughout British Columbia, thus ignoring differences in the value of water on different waterways. Second, they discriminate among industries, though the marginal cost of water is not likely to differ correspondingly. Third, they prescribe lower prices at higher levels of use, even in the same industrial sector, in conflict with the rule for consistent marginal cost prices. One result of the declining block rates is a bias against smaller users, which obviously weakens financial incentives to conserve and recycle.

Current industrial water prices thus tend to distort efficient water use in two ways. One is the distortion that results from pricing at the wrong level—that is, above or below long-run marginal cost. To the extent that the price borne by the

Table 17.6: Annual Charges for Industrial Users in British Columbia

Industrial Use	Units of Measurement	Range of Daily Use	Annual Charge	
	(m³/day)	(units)	($ per unit)	($ per m³)
Pulp Mills	2,445	all units	200	0.08
Sawmills, Food Processing, Other Manufacturing, Sand and Gravel Washing	45.4	first 50	8	0.18
		next 50	4	0.09
		over 100	2	0.04
Industrial Cooling	45.4	first 40	4	0.09
		next 50	2	0.04
		over 100	1	0.02
Hydraulic Mining	2,445	all units	20	0.008
Coal Washing	2,445	all units	200	0.08
Ore Processing	454	all units	200	0.44
Bulk Export[1]	1,234	all units	15	0.012
Hotels, Motels, Trailer Parks, Restaurants, Service Stations	4.5	all units	10	2.20
Bottled Water	0.45	first 5	8	17.80
		over 5	2	4.40

Source: Environment Canada (1986). Water Licenses in B.C. are written in Imperial Units and have been converted here to metric equivalents. Annual charges are set out in the licensing regulations in terms of the units indicated in column 1. Column 4 shows annual charges in terms of a common unit (cubic metres) for comparative purposes.
Notes:
1   Bulk export licenses are written in terms of volumes used, not daily flows.

users at the margin falls short of the long-run marginal cost of water use, water can be expected to be used excessively; the real costs of both the water and the capital and operating costs of supplying and disposing of it will be excessive, and inadequate effort will be put toward water conservation and recycling. Table 17.5 shows that the water-related costs of the major industries in the Fraser Basin totalled $23.8 million in 1986. This was less than one percent of the value of shipments, providing weak incentives for water conservation. The other distortion is that resulting from misallocation of water among users; wherever water use must be rationed, too much will be used by those charged low prices at the margin and too little by those bearing high prices.

The principles of marginal cost pricing apply equally to waste discharges. In this case, the scarce natural factor is the assimilative capacity of the particular waterway, and the opportunity cost of using it is its waste disposal value that is consequently foregone by other potential users. The infrastructure costs correspond to those associated with water supply.

The regulatory task is to limit the discharge of contaminants so that ambient concentrations do not exceed the assimilative capacity or quality standard set for the particular receiving water. This implies pricing according to the amount of contaminants discharged (not their concentration in discharges or the volume of effluent discharged, but the product of these two variables). And because standards of water quality apply to a variety of polluting substances ranging from sediments to toxic chemicals, it implies separate pricing arrangements for each.

For practical purposes, the number of contaminants subject to separate pricing can be reduced. Discharges of many hazardous substances and persistent toxic chemicals are completely unwanted, and can simply be prohibited. Others, for which some assimilative capacity is ascribed, can be reduced to a few broad categories or indices such as suspended solids, biochemical oxygen demand and portion of the quality control problem. Inevitably special arrangements will be needed for special pollutants and circumstances.

A sophisticated pricing system for waste discharges presents as formidable a monitoring task as it does in an effective regulatory system; the volume of effluent and the concentration of each contaminant in it must be measured. As well, the timing of discharges may affect its cost implications, as in the case of water use. In practice, it may suffice to employ a single price for broad categories of waste discharge, such as domestic sewage, applying an extra-strength sewage surcharge for discharges having concentrations of contaminants above a designated level. Such a surcharge can recognize, in a rough way, the extra burden highly concentrated discharges put on the assimilative capacity of natural water systems and provide incentives to reduce contaminants in effluents.

Present water quality control policy in British Columbia involves no pricing for use of the assimilative capacity of waterways. Instead, reliance is put on legal prohibitions such as those in the federal Fisheries Act, the provincial Waste Management Act and other statutes; technological requirements such as equipment for recycling water and abating pollution in industrial plants; water discharge permit requirements to regulate waste discharges into waterways; and municipal water and sewage systems (see the chapter by Rankin in this volume). None of these mechanisms offers incentives to reduce polluting activities below permitted levels. Nor do they ensure that the limited assimilative capacity is allocated to its most valuable uses. (Pearse et al., 1985:93).

However, encouraging experience in pricing water discharges has been accumulating in some European countries, notably France, Germany and the Netherlands. The German system, for example, recognizes settleable solids, organic content, mercury, cadmium and toxicity to fish in assessing fees for municipal and individual industrial outfalls. Measures of the pollutants in industrial discharges are combined to determine the number of "units" of pollution emitted by each plant, and a charge per unit determines the fee paid by each plant. Though far from an ideal formula for discharge fees, this German system has succeeded in improving water quality control, and in demonstrating the opportunities for strengthening water management through simple discharge pricing (Brown and Johnson, 1984).

To provide the desired market signals and incentives described above, prices for water and waste discharges must be borne directly by the users. This calls for means of metering and billing each user by municipal water utilities, irrigation districts and other collective systems, and by the government for self-supplied users. Water use and waste discharges must usually be treated separately, as explained above, but for some users, such as households, the relationship between water intake and outflow is fairly fixed, in terms of both quantity and quality. This allows further simplification of pricing systems by merging the metering and pricing of water use and waste discharges.

Property Rights

Where individual water users are not served by collective water utilities, marketable *rights* to withdraw specified quantities of water from waterways can be equally effective in generating economic incentives to use water conservatively and efficiently. As long as there are sufficient demanders and holders of such rights on a waterway, the rights will take on a market value, and the price of a right will reflect its value to other users, or its opportunity cost as described earlier. Transferability of rights will ensure that, over time, they will be acquired by those who make the most valuable use of the water, and therefore pay the most for it. The more easily transferable, divisible and combinable these rights are, the more they will encourage efficient allocation and use (Scott, 1984; and this volume).

An ideal system of water rights requires the regulatory authority to establish first the minimum levels or flows it wants to maintain in the relevant waterway (a task required of any regulatory scheme). The flows in excess of this minimum, plus any return flows, provide the scope for allocating water rights, which is likely to vary seasonally. Water withdrawal rights can then be issued which apply to particular points or reaches of the waterway, and some of which may be exercised only during specified periods. Over time, free transferability will ensure that the rights are acquired by the highest users, their value will provide the incentives to avoid waste and to use water only to the extent that it generates at least that much value in use, and the market for them will enable the regulatory agency to adjust standards in response to changing conditions by purchasing discharge rights or allocating more.

However, the market price for water rights will reflect only its value to other potential users of those withdrawal rights; it cannot be expected to recognize the value the water might generate for instream uses, or the external costs and benefits of water withdrawals. These considerations inevitably fall to the regulatory authority in deciding upon the appropriate levels and flows in the first place.

Many agricultural and other users of water outside municipalities on the Fraser system hold individual water withdrawal rights. Water rights issued under British Columbia's Water Act may be transferred with the Minister's consent, which is normally granted. However, the system is encumbered by provisions that restrict divisibility, use and certainty of marketability, all of which limit the system's effectiveness in promoting efficient water use (Campbell et al., 1972; see also the chapter by Scott in this volume).

Rights to discharge contaminants into waterways offer corresponding opportunities to efficiently regulate use of waste assimilative capacity and to encourage users to abate pollution (Dales, 1968). To take advantage of these possibilities, the present discharge permits would have to be replaced with rights that specify quantities of specific contaminants permitted to be discharged into the watercourse, and providing for their divisibility and transferability.

Conclusion

Sustainable development remains only vaguely defined, and much clarification is needed before it can be operational in any particular set of circumstances. This chapter has emphasized the importance of reconciling economic processes with nature's endowment, and bringing market forces to bear on our environmental problems; others argue that sustainable development calls for more fundamental change in our perception of man's place in the natural world and in our prescriptions for economic improvement (Underwood and King, 1989; see also Dorcey, this volume). Scott (this volume) points out that we ought not to attempt to define sustainable development for a region like the Fraser Basin in isolation, because the global dimensions of the problems it addresses call for integration and trade-offs with other regions.

Nevertheless, whatever form sustainable development will ultimately take, it will require means of ensuring that economic activity does not erode the health and productivity of natural environmental resources. This paper has examined the existing means and some alternate approaches with specific references to the water resources of the Fraser Basin.

At present, our policy framework for managing water and the quality of natural waterways depends almost entirely on direct regulation—the "command and control" approach to reconciling private activity with the public interest. It does almost nothing to bring market incentives to bear on the conservation, protection and enhancement of water resources. Indeed, subsidies to water users aggravate tendencies to overuse both flows and the waste absorbing capacity of waterways. The limitations of this approach are reflected in increasing conflicts over flows and deterioration of water quality in the Fraser system and elsewhere.

Present trends, and the inevitability of increasing pressures on water resources, suggest that a reassessment of this dependence on regulation is called for in the interests of sustainable development. The goal of harmonizing economic activity with the capacities of the natural environment calls attention to opportunities for directing market forces to the task of managing water resources. All the evidence, and experience elsewhere, suggests that water pricing and well designed water rights are potentially powerful policy instruments for improving water management.

This is not to say, of course, that market processes can resolve all our management problems. There are so many ways in which markets fail, are not permitted to work, or yield distorted results, especially for environmental resources, that there will always be plenty of scope for regulation.

> Markets are a means by which society, establishing its environmental values, may achieve its goals. Markets are one instrument of policy among many that can be used to meet the environmental challenge. To treat them in any other way is to invite either their aggrandizement, relative to the problems, or their dismissal, as part of the solution. Neither extreme is a constructive approach to this process. (Kierans, 1990:128)

Our intent is only to suggest that, in ignoring the potential role of market incentives in our water policies, we may have put too heavy a burden on direct regulation, and we should re-examine the balance we have struck between compulsive regulation and incentives.

Nor do we mean to imply that the water resources of the Fraser system are in such dire condition that abrupt, wholesale reform is necessary. As in so many other waterways in Canada, the task is to begin to put into place a regulatory framework that can forestall deterioration as demands and pressures grow. Our review suggests that we should begin by creating the elements of a water management system that will generate economic incentives for users to conserve water, protect its quality and use it efficiently. The first steps include elimination of subsidies to water users, introducing water and wastewater metering, and adoption of the user-pay principle. The complications of long-run marginal cost pricing, the design of water rights and other economic instruments can then be addressed as needs develop.

References

Barnett, H. J., and M. C. Morse. 1973. *Scarcity and Growth: The Economics of Natural Resource Availability*. Baltimore: Johns Hopkins University Press.

Brown, G. M. Jr., and R. W. Johnson. 1984. "Pollution control by effluent charges: it works in the federal republic of Germany, why not in the U.S?". *Natural Resources Journal*. 24:929-966.

Campbell, R. S., P. H. Pearse and A. D. Scott. 1972. "Water Allocation in British Columbia: An Economic Assessment of Public Policy." *University of British Columbia Law Review*. 7(2).

Dales, J. H. 1968. *Pollution, Property and Prices*. Toronto: University of Toronto Press.

Demsetz, H. 1967. "Toward a Theory of Property Rights." *American Economic Review*. 57:347-59.

Drucker, P. 1986. "The Changed World Economy." *Foreign Affairs*. 768-791

Environment Canada. 1986. *Water Charges to Industry (excluding hydro-electric generation), Canada. 1986.* Ottawa-Hull: Inland Waters Directorate.

Hirschleifer, J., J. C. de Haven and J. W. Milliman. 1960. *Water Supply: Economics, Technology and Policy.* Chicago: University of Chicago Press.

Kellow, R. L. 1970. *A Study of Water Use In Single Dwelling Residences In The City of Calgary, Alberta.* Edmonton: University of Alberta, Department of Economics and Rural Sociology. Unpublished Master's thesis.

Kierans, T. E. (ed.). 1990. *Getting It Right: Policy Review and Outlook 1990.* Toronto: C. D. Howe Institute.

Kindler, J., and C. S. Russell. 1984. *Modelling Water Demands.* Toronto: Academic Press.

Meadows, D. H., D. L. Meadows, J. Randers and W. Behrens. 1972. *The Limits to Growth.* New York: Universe Books.

Organization for Economic Cooperation and Development (OECD). 1989. *Economic Instruments for Environmental Protection.* Paris.

Pearse, P. H. 1988. "Property Rights and the Development of Natural Resource Policies in Canada." *Canadian Public Policy.* 14(3): 307-320.

Pearse, P. H., F. Bertrand and J. W. MacLaren. 1985. *Currents of Change: Final Report of the Inquiry on Federal Water Policy.* Ottawa: Environment Canada (Catalogue No. En 37-71/1985-1E).

Postel, S. 1985. "Conserving Water: the Untapped Alternative." *Worldwatch Paper* 67 (September 1985).

Schultze, C. W. 1977. The Public Use of Private Interest. *The Godkin Lectures.* Cambridge, Mass.: Harvard University Press.

Scott, A. D. 1984. *Does Government Create Real Property Rights?: Private Interests in Natural Resources.* Discussion Paper 84-26. Vancouver: Department of Economics. University of British Columbia.

Scott, A. D., and P. H. Pearse. 1988. *Natural Resources in a High-tech Economy: Scarcity Versus Resourcefullness.* Discussion Paper 88-XX Vancouver: Forest Economics and Policy Analysis Research Unit. University of British Columbia.

Tate, D. M. 1989. *Municipal Water Rates in Canada: Current Practices and Prices.* Ottawa-Hull: Environment Canada, Inland Waters Directorate, *Social Science Series,* #21.

Tate, D. M. 1990. *Water Demand Management in Canada: A State of the Art Review.* Ottawa-Hull: Environment Canada, Inland Waters Directorate. *Social Science Series* #23 (forthcoming).

Tate, D. M., and D. M. Lacelle. 1987. *Municipal Water Use in Canada, 1983.* Ottawa-Hull: Environment Canada, Inland Waters Directorate. *Social Science Research Series,* 20.

Tate, D. M., and D. M. Lacelle. 1990. *Municipal Water Use in Canada, 1983.* Ottawa-Hull: Environment Canada, Inland Waters Directorate, *Social Science Research Series,* forthcoming.

Tate, D. M., and D. N. Scharf. 1989. *Water Use in Canadian Industry: 1986.* Ottawa-Hull: Environment Canada, Inland Waters Directorate. *Social Science Series* #24, forthcoming.

Underwood, D. A., and P. A. King. 1989. "On the Ideological Foundations of Environmental Policy." *Ecological Economics.* 1(1): 315-334.

World Commission on Environment and Development (WCED). 1987. *Our Common Future.* New York: Oxford University Press.

18

The Ecological Basis for Sustainable Development in the Fraser Basin

William E. Rees

This paper discusses the prospects for sustainable development in the Fraser River Basin from an ecological perspective interpreted in a global context. The overall purpose is to contribute to the development of a scientifically credible framework for sustainable regional development. My thesis is that nature imposes certain inviolable conditions on development and that without a realistic model of biophysical reality, sociopolitical and institutional mechanisms attempting sustainable development can only fail.

There are, of course, many definitions and interpretations of sustainable development reflecting the differing values and political ideologies held by various interest groups in society.[1] Some would argue that on the face of things, each of these has equal merit, that the socioeconomic and ecological characteristics of sustainable development are largely a matter of belief and opinion. From this perspective, society will ultimately arrive at a politically "practical" interpretation of sustainable development for purposes of public policy, through the usual "democratic" processes of power brokering, negotiation, and compromise.

Certainly it cannot be denied that many dimensions of development are open to debate. As Peter Boothroyd argues eloquently elsewhere in this volume, some forms of sustainable development might help reduce economic disparities between the rich and poor, while others might well exacerbate existing relative poverty. However, this paper develops the position that certain basic elements of sustainability are not negotiable. I argue that industrial society is constrained by certain biophysical realities which, in effect, establish a set of absolute, objective requirements for sustainability. While not sufficient in themselves, these biophysical criteria are a necessary condition for sustainable development whatever its political and socioeconomic character.

---

1   See Rees (1989) for a comprehensive working definition incorporating ecological, social, and economic factors, and a sample of other definitions from the literature.

The Ecosphere as Independent Variable

Acceptance of the foregoing argument would put a fundamentally different complexion on the face of development. Historically, the economy has always been considered the independent variable and environmental quality the dependent variable in the development equation. From this perspective, maintaining a "healthy" environment is seen largely in terms of society having to choose between certain ill-defined aesthetic and other intangible values on the one hand and measurable material economic gains on the other. When the problem is framed this way, ecological factors are generally "traded off" against economic growth in the belief that the resultant tangible economic benefits exceed any likely ecological costs.[2] Even today, critical ecosystem functions are unrecognized or discounted. Many resource economists treat the appropriate level of environmental quality largely as a matter of mere public choice (see Baumol and Oates, 1988).

By contrast, I argue that we have reached a stage in the "development" of Earth where we must recognize that the environment has become the independent variable and the economy the dependent one. The last significant trade-offs have been made. This approach acknowledges that it is the productivity of the ecosphere that ultimately determines the potential level of economic activity, whatever the current level of technological sophistication. From this perspective, the sustainability of 21st century civilization depends on the development of governance and management practices whose "practicality" will be based more on functional biophysical reality rather than on arbitrary public preference.

The Global Context

While the emphasis in this volume is on regional governance, the use of more global terms in the previous paragraph is deliberate. It reflects the fact that development in the Fraser Basin may produce impacts well beyond its borders. Similarly, events outside the Fraser Basin can affect the potential for development within the region *however "undeveloped" the region's own resources might appear to be.*

I am not referring to the usual economic factors such as the strength of external markets for Fraser Basin products, but rather to the cumulative ecological impacts of global economic activity. Such global trends as ozone depletion and increasing atmospheric carbon dioxide are a direct consequence of the widespread application of ecologically unsophisticated technologies and the five-fold increase in world economic activity since the Second World War. Unprecedented growth during this period has produced an increasingly integrated world economy whose scale now approaches that of the ecosphere itself. Consequently, the global economy has begun to undermine the integrity of ecological processes upon which

---

2   There is an unspoken assumption here that humankind is functionally independent of, and the economy materially indifferent to, the functional state of the ecosphere. This implies that, in a materialist society, the marginal benefits of economic exploitation may be perceived as always exceeding the marginal costs of ecological damage. We are free to degrade the environment indefinitely without additional penalty if we choose to do so for material gain.

the entire enterprise is itself dependent. Persistent negative global trends carry the threat of irreversible ecological disruption and attendant geopolitical chaos.[3] It is therefore a central premise of this paper that neither the trends nor the pattern of development that produced them are sustainable.

The erosion of ecospheric processes is both the cumulative product of previous "development" and a constraint on potential future development all over the planet. Global sustainability means that decisions affecting development in individual regions can no longer be taken in isolation of political or ecological events elsewhere in the world. The bad news for residents of the Fraser region is that they may find themselves both morally and ecologically obliged to constrain certain perceived economic opportunities that might otherwise be available. The good news is that if every economic region can be persuaded (if only by enlightened self-interest) to conduct itself similarly, the aggregate effect would be ecological security and geopolitical stability for all.

Defining Sustainable Development

"Sustainable development" has become the rallying cry of dedicated environmentalists and trenchant industrialists alike. With key global ecological trends steadily worsening, any concept that implies we can eat our developmental cake and have the environment too naturally inspires enthusiasm on all sides of the debate. "Sustainable development" is one oxymoron whose time had come!

As noted, the apparent unity over sustainable development is illusory. There is no general agreement on the meaning of the concept. Environmentalists and those on the political left emphasize the "sustainable" part. They see a need to put Earth first, to return to community values, and to devise ways to share the world's wealth more equitably. The political centre and those to the right warm more to the "development" component. From their perspective, development, defined as economic growth, remains the key to both ecological and social security.

Given this divergence of views, some have argued that it is futile to debate the meaning of sustainable development, that we should simply get on with it. However, this recalls the caterpillar's chiding of the much disoriented Alice: if you don't know where you are going, it doesn't much matter which road you take. By contrast, if there is anything new and distinctive about "sustainable development," it very much matters which road we take. This paper is dedicated to identifying some of the landmarks of sustainable development. If we learn to recognize the place, we might avoid entrapment in one of the attractive cul-de-sacs along the way.

---

3   The mid-East crisis in early 1990 is perhaps an early example. The Persian Gulf war was very much rooted in defence of the profligately unsustainable oil-based lifestyles of western democracies. Had we adopted strong conservation measures and greater emphasis on energy efficiency, and promoted more investment in ecologically benign solar technologies in the 1980's in response to rising energy prices and early warnings of atmospheric change in the 1970's, we would be facing an oil glut in the 1990's. This would have reduced not only the destabilizing inter-regional dependencies that led to war but also the threat of global warming.

The View from the Mainstream

The concept of sustainable development has deep roots in the theory of renewable resource management but has only recently been popularized by *Our Common Future*, the 1987 report of the World Commission on Environment and Development (The Brundtland Commission). The Brundtland Commission defined sustainable development as "development that meets the needs of the present without compromising the ability of future generations to meet their own needs" (WCED 1987:43). This innocuously skeletal definition gave something to everyone, and academe, governments, and non-governmental organisations have been striving ever since to flesh it out, each in its own image.[4]

Something for Everyone

The commission was itself curiously ambiguous in elaborating its own definition. *Our Common Future* defines "needs" as the "essential needs of the world's poor, to which over-riding priority should be given." It also acknowledges the "limitations imposed by the state of technology and social organization on the environment's ability to meet [those needs]" (WCED, 1987:43). To people concerned about ecology and social equity, such words seemed at last to be a plea for political recognition of global economic injustice and limits to material growth.

But there is another side to *Our Common Future* that guaranteed its message would be just as enthusiastically received in corporate boardrooms everywhere. The report reassuringly asserts that "sustainable development is not a fixed state of harmony, but rather a process of change in which the exploitation of resources, the orientation of technological development, and institutional change are made consistent with future as well as present needs" (WCED, 1987:9). In effect, the World Commission equated sustainable development with "more rapid economic growth in both industrial and developing countries" on grounds that "economic growth and diversification...will help developing countries mitigate the strains on the rural environment..." (WCED, 1987:89). Consistent with this interpretation, the commission suggested that "a five to tenfold increase in world industrial output can be anticipated by the time world population stabilizes some time in the next century" (WCED, 1987:213). All this to be achieved while we "conserve and enhance" the resource base, of course (WCED, 1987:57).

Canadian Orthodoxy

In Canada, the closest thing to an official position on sustainable development is the *Report of the National Task Force on Environment and Economy*. The task force was established by the Canadian Council of Resource and Environment Ministers (CCREM) in October 1986 as a follow-up to the Brundtland Commission's visit to Canada.

---

4   Daly and Cobb (1989) suggest that the Brundtland Commission's vague definition of sustainable development may have been purposeful and politically astute. It guaranteed there would eventually be serious debate of a full spectrum of possible interpretations (e.g., Rees, 1989).

Taking its cue from Brundtland, the task force defined sustainable development as "development which ensures that the utilization of resources and the environment today does not damage prospects for their use by future generations." Ignoring the obvious difficulty posed by the consumption of non-renewable resources in any generation, the task force report goes on: "At the core of the concept...is the requirement that current practices should not diminish the possibility of maintaining or improving living standards in the future." Perhaps most revealing is the assertion that: "Sustainable economic development does *not* require the preservation of the current stock of natural resources or any particular mix of human, physical and natural assets. Nor does it put artificial limits on economic growth provided such growth is both economically and environmentally sustainable" (CCREM, 1987:3, emphasis added).

Certainly no one can accuse this task force of confusing sustainable development with any "fixed state of harmony!"

Can the Solution be Found in the Problem?

Both the Brundtland Commission and the National Task Force reflect the mainstream interpretation of sustainable development in industrialized countries. Governments and industry increasingly acknowledge that present development practices do produce significant environmental and socioeconomic stress. However, without pausing to examine its systemic roots, both reports argue that the solution to the global ecological crisis resides within the same socioeconomic structures that seem to have created it in the first place.[5]

Most important, both documents advance sheer economic growth as the principal vehicle for sustainability in the belief that the resultant economic surpluses will be used for ecosystems maintenance. Tenuous assumption aside, many people find this continuing reliance on growth to be the most troubling aspect of the mainstream prescription for sustainable development.[6]

It is particularly significant that neither the Brundtland Commission nor the National Task Force distinguish between *growth*, which "should refer to quantitative expansion in the scale...of the economic system," and *development* which "should refer to the qualitative change in a physically non-growing economic system in dynamic equilibrium with the environment" (Daly and Cobb, 1989:71). By these definitions, sustainable growth in a finite environment is a logical impossibility but sustainable development contains no self-contradiction. This simple distinction between mere growth and true development is essential to rational debate on developing sustainability, *but has scarcely entered the discussion!*

---

5   One participant in "Globe '90" (a major conference and trade show for the environment industry held in Vancouver in March 1990) observed that sustainable development had apparently come down to "business-as-usual with a treatment plant!"

6   Nikiforuk (1990) condemns sustainable development as "dangerous words now being used... to mask the same old economic thinking that preaches unlimited consumption in the crusade to turn more land into glorified golf courses, deadly suburban ghettos, and leaking garbage holes (so-called landfill sites)". Similarly, Nelson (1990) sees industry's enthusiasm for sustainable development as a dangerous "corporate takeover" and the accompanying green rhetoric as little more than public relations "ecobabble."

The fixation on growth *per se* should come as no surprise. Our "largely uncritical worship of...economic growth is as central to [capitalism's] nature as the similar veneration of...divine kingship or doctrinal orthodoxy has been for other regimes" (Heilbroner, 1989:102). Indeed, some economists believe "not only in the possibility of continuous material growth, but in its axiomatic necessity" (Georgescu-Roegen, 1977).

There is an important historical rationale. Economic growth has long been the principal instrument of social policy in capitalist societies. The promise of an ever-increasing economic pie holds out hope that even the poor will eventually get an adequate share. The expectation of a better future therefore reduces popular pressure for policies aimed at more equitable distribution of income (see Boothroyd, this volume).

While morally bankrupt, this "solution" to social inequity posed no physical threat to society as long as the economy was small relative to the scale of the ecosphere. This is clearly no longer the case, but in advancing growth-as-solution once again, our authors make no attempt to weigh the anticipated future scale of the global economy against the finite productive capacity of the ecosphere.

Part of the problem here is that our present economics cannot even pose the right question. *Macro-economic theory has nothing to say about the appropriate scale of the economy* (Daly, 1989). The idea of continuous growth is so firmly entrenched that the issue of scale has apparently not been considered relevant! By contrast, from the ecological perspective, it is very much an open question whether it is possible to expand industrial production by a factor of five to ten while simultaneously "guaranteeing the sustainability of ecosystems upon which the global economy depends." (WCED, 1987:67). How the world's dominant economic paradigm has drifted so far from what seems to be self-evident reality is the focus of the following section.

The Mechanical Economy

The internal contradictions of prevailing economic thinking can be traced to certain fundamental assumptions of neoclassical theory. The 19th century founders of the neoclassical school, impressed with the successes of Newtonian physics, strove to create economics as a sister science, "the mechanics of utility and self-interest" (Jevons, 1879; cited in Georgescu-Roegen, 1975).

The decision to develop a mechanical rather than biological metaphor for the economy was critical. While economics is (or should be) a branch of human ecology, the central assumptions of modern economic theory are uninformed by ecological principles. Three closely related assumptions of the model are critical to any consideration of theory for sustainable development.

First, industrial society perceives the human enterprise as dominant over and and essentially independent of nature. Thus, we act as if the economy is somehow separate from the rest of material reality. This perception derives in part from the Cartesian subject-object dualism at the heart of western scientific materialism. In effect, the idea of a separate "environment" is a social invention reflecting the

Cartesian worldview. The very word becomes its own pejorative, alluding to whatever surrounds some other thing of greater value—environment "diffidently declares itself to be peripheral, unimportant, not to be taken seriously" (Rowe, 1989). The economy may use the environment as a source of resources and sink for wastes (Herfindahl and Kneese, 1974), but beyond that it is perceived as a mere static backdrop to human affairs.[7]

Second, economists have adopted the circular flow of exchange value as the starting point for analysis rather than the one-way entropic throughput of energy and matter (Daly, 1989). The major consequence is an entrenched view of economic process as "a self-sustaining circular flow between production and consumption". By this perception, "everything...turns out to be just a pendulum movement... If events alter the supply and demand propensities, the economic world returns to its previous position as soon as these events fade out." Most important, "*complete reversibility* is the general rule, just as in mechanics" (Georgescu-Roegen, 1975:348, emphasis added). Indeed, by inventing a perpetual motion machine, economics seems to have done mechanics one better!

Third, we have come to believe that resources are more the product of human ingenuity than they are of nature. According to neoclassical theory, rising market prices for scarce materials encourage conservation on the one hand and stimulate technological substitution on the other.[8] It is part of the conventional wisdom of many economic planners that these factors have indeed been more than sufficient to overcome emerging resource scarcities (Victor, 1990).

While standard neoclassical texts conclude almost conservatively that "exhaustible resources do not pose a fundamental problem" (Dasgupta and Heal, 1979), the most ardent (and influential) disciples of the substitutability principle are moved to idealistic, almost surreal, extremes.[9] Gilder (1981) argues that we "must overcome the materialistic fantasy: the illusion that resources...are essentially things, which can run out, rather than products of the human will and imagination which in freedom are inexhaustible" (Gilder, 1981:232; cited in Daly and Cobb, 1989:109).[10] Similarly, Simon (1982:207) remarks: "You see, in the end copper and oil come out of our minds. That's really where they are." So pervasive is this doctrine that Block (1990:304) even uses it to argue for further population growth on grounds that people "create the wealth they need to maintain themselves and more, thanks to free markets and technological progress."

To summarize, economic theory *necessarily* contains a model of nature. The anthropocentric assumptions of the contemporary model range from mechanical dualism on one extreme to metaphysical idealism on the other. Given its apparent

---

7   Indeed, Descartes viewed the external world "as a machine and nothing but a machine. There was no purpose, life, or spirituality in matter" (Capra, 1982:60). He even extended this mechanistic view to living organisms: "...I do not recognize any difference between the machines made by craftsmen and the various bodies that nature alone composes" (Descartes, cited in Capra, 1982:61).

8   For example, coal replaced wood and petroleum gradually displaced coal as the dominant form of commercial energy.

9   This reflects the Kantian argument that the human mind is not passive in its experience. It actively creates its own reality. "In fact, anything we can speak of...is in some sense a product of the human mind" (Daly and Cobb 1989:108).

10 He adds for emphasis: "Because economies are governed by thoughts, they reflect not the laws of matter but the laws of mind," thus revealing the Cartesian roots of his idealism.

success in the industrial age, society everywhere now finds this modified neoclassical model a more compelling guide to economic policy and behaviour than is the biophysical reality from which the model was abstracted. As with all models, its internal logic "heighten[s] the tendency to prize theory over fact and to reinterpret fact to fit theory" (Daly and Cobb 1989:38).[11]

Real-World (Ecological) Economics[12]

This section re-examines the "internal logic" of neoclassical economics in light of ecological theory. My premise is that it is futile to seek solutions to the global ecological crisis through conventional analyses. The dominant models are self-referencing systems fatally flawed by limited content and false assumptions. Society must recognize that "we cannot regulate our interaction with any aspect of reality that our model of reality does not include...because we cannot by definition be conscious of it" (Beer, 1981).[13]

Economics as Human Ecology

From the relative objectivity of scientific ecology, there is little to distinguish humankind functionally from the millions of other species with which we share the planet. Like other organisms, we survive and grow by extracting energy and material resources from the ecosystems of which we are a part. Like them we "consume" these resources before returning them in altered form to the ecosphere. Thus, *far from existing in splendid isolation, the human economy is and always has been an inextricably integrated, completely contained, and wholly dependent sub-set of the ecosphere.*

While politicians and businessmen call for "environment-economy integration" as the solution to our environmental crisis, it is actually the present form of integration that is the cause of the problem. It follows that since we cannot separate the economy from the ecosphere, we must restructure the relationship to conform to ecological reality rather than to simplistic assumptions. Only in this way can economics finally become good human ecology.

The Second Law: Economy as Consumption

Contrary to conventional wisdom, the ecologically relevant flows through the material economy are not circular but unidirectional. This is because *the ultimate regulator of the economy is not mechanics but the Second Law of Thermodynamics* (the entropy law): in every material transformation, available energy and matter are continuously and irreversibly degraded to the unavailable state (see Georgescu-Roegen, 1975, 1977). Economic activity therefore necessarily

---

11   Daly and Cobb (1989) refer to this general problem as the "fallacy of misplaced concreteness" and provide several additional examples.
12   Based on Rees, 1990a,b,c.
13   Alternatively, "...the regulation that the regulator can achieve is only as good as the model of reality that it contains" (Beer, 1981:9)

contributes to a constant increase in global net entropy (disorder) through the continuous dissipation of energy/matter into the ecosphere.[14] Without reference to this entropic throughput "it is virtually impossible to relate the economy to the environment," yet the concept is "virtually absent from economics today" (Daly, 1989:1).

In effect, thermodynamic law dictates that all material economic "production" is actually consumption. Herein lies the essence of our environmental crisis. *Since our economies are growing and the ecosystems within which they are embedded are not, the consumption of resources everywhere has begun to exceed sustainable rates of biological production.*

We now have the basis for a thermodynamic definition of sustainable development as development that at least minimizes the increase in net global entropy. By contrast, our present emphasis on material growth maximizes consumption and resource use, thereby maximizing entropy.

Obligate Dependency and the Ultimate Market Failure

Wishful thinking aside, humankind remains in a state of obligate dependency on many critical products and processes of nature. Moreover, while market mechanisms may be effective at setting prices and finding substitutes for valued non-renewables such as copper or oil, they are an inadequate solution to the depletion of bioresources on several grounds:

(i) Price- or scarcity-induced substitution may occur too late to permit the recovery of renewable resources that have been over-exploited;

(ii) Substitution does nothing to repair the pollution damage caused by the dissipated by-products of previously depleted resources;

(iii) Some renewable resources for which there are markets (e.g., agricultural products) are dependent on material or process resources (e.g., soils and soil-building processes) for which there are none; and,

(iv) Other material (e.g., the ozone layer) and process resources (e.g., photosynthesis, climate stabilization) have not been recognized as resources at all.

These last two factors are particularly important. Markets are silent on the state of many ecologically critical materials and processes despite their immeasurable economic value. The primary scarcity indicator offered by the neoclassical school—pricing—fails utterly when the assumptions under which it operates do not prevail (Victor, 1990). *Consumption and pollution are therefore destroying ecologically essential resources with no signal from the marketplace that the very basis of survival is being irreversibly eroded. Moreover, there are no technological substitutes.*

---

14 For example, a finished automobile represents only a fraction of the energy and material (typically 25 metric tons) that has been permanently dissipated (as pollution) in the manufacturing process. Similarly, modern energy-subsidized agriculture consumes up to 10 fossil calories for every calorie of food energy produced.

The Self-Producing Ecosphere

Fortunately, the ecosphere has the capacity to recover. Unlike economic systems, ecosystems are inherently self-sustaining, and contribute continuously to reducing global net entropy. The ecosphere therefore appears to defy the entropy law: "...[the system] is in many respects self-generating—its productivity and stability determined largely through its internal interactions" (Perry et al., 1989).

The organizational property which enables living systems to produce themselves is known as autopoiesis (Maturana and Varela, 1988). Autopoiesis is a product of the complex, interdependent relationships (energy, material, and information flows) linking the system's major components. *The structural integrity of these relationships is essential not only to the functioning of the system, but also for the production and maintenance of the participating components themselves.* Human disruption of these relationships on a global scale would severely compromise the possibility of achieving sustainable development.

Autopoeisis is possible only because ecosystems, unlike economic systems, are driven by an *external* source of free energy, the sun. In thermodynamic terms, *photosynthesis is the most important productive process on Earth and the ultimate source of all ecological capital (renewable resources) used by the human economy.*[15]

Since the flow of solar radiation is constant, steady, and reliable, ecosystem production is potentially sustainable over any time scale relevant to humankind. Productivity is limited, however, by the availability of finite nutrients, photosynthetic efficiency, and ultimately the rate of energy input (the "solar flux") itself. Ecosystems therefore do not grow indefinitely. Unlike the economy which expands through dominant positive feedback, they are held in dynamic, far-from-equilibrium "steady-state" by negative feedback.

The Ecology of Sustainable Development: Maintaining Natural Capital

Global resource depletion and pollution provide evidence of the inadequacy of neoclassical theory on the one hand and of the operation of thermodynamic law on the other. Existing data suggest that the present rate of economic throughput already exceeds the rate of ecospheric (self-)production in important ways. Encroaching deserts (6 million ha/year); deforestation (11 million ha/year); acid precipitation and forest dieback (31 million ha damaged); toxic contamination of food supplies; soil oxidation and erosion (26 billion tonnes/year in excess of formation); draw-down and pollution of water tables; species extinction (thousands per year); fisheries exhaustion; ozone depletion (3% worldwide in 1989); greenhouse gas buildup (25% increase in atmospheric CO_2 alone); potential climatic change (1.5 to 4.5°C mean global warming expected by 2040); and rising

---

15   The human enterprise already appropriates about 40% of terrestrial photosynthetic activity (Vitousek et al., 1986). Note that in a finite ecosphere, expansion of human populations and the material economy can only increase this ratio at the expense of other species.

sea-levels (1.2 to 2.2m by 2100) and like trends are the result of either excess consumption or the thermodynamic dissipation of toxic by-products of economic activity into the ecosphere. Both factors threaten to undermine autopoiesis, the self-producing capacity of the ecosphere.

This global-scale ecological deterioration is forcing recognition that sustainable development based on prevailing assumptions and existing patterns of resource use is simply not possible. Present economic logic and development approaches compromise our own potential and "shift the burden of environmental risks to future generations" (Pearce et al., 1989). A new model of reality is required that includes the biophysical and thermodynamic parameters missing from existing economic and management models.

Various authors have begun to emphasize the need to develop better ways to evaluate ecological resources; the need to extend the time horizon for economic policy into the long term; and the need to elevate both intra- and inter-generational equity to a place of prominence in developmental decision-making. Pearce et al. (1989) integrate these objectives through the proposition that *"future generations should be compensated for reductions in the endowments of resources brought about by the actions of present generations"* (1989:3, original emphasis). In short, today's generation should leave the next generation a stock of productive assets undiminished from that which we originally inherited. There are two possible interpretations of this "constant capital stock" idea:[16]

(i)   Each generation should inherit an aggregate stock of human-made and natural assets no less than the stock inherited by the previous generation. This corresponds to Daly's (1989) conditions for "weak sustainability";

(ii) Each generation should inherit a stock of natural assets *alone* no less than the stock of such assets inherited by the previous generation.[17] This is a version of "strong sustainability" as defined by Daly (1989).

The first interpretation reflects the neoclassical assumption that human-made and natural assets are perfect substitutes and that biological assets can rationally be liquidated through "development" as long as subsequent investment in manufactured capital (e.g., factories and machinery) provides an equivalent endowment to the next generation.[18]

The second interpretation reflects the ecological principles advanced in this paper. It recognizes that because of the unique and essential services provided by ecological capital, we cannot risk its depletion. By this interpretation, manufactured and natural capital "are really not substitutes but complements in most production functions" (Daly, 1989:22).

In effect, strong sustainability places infinite value on maintaining a basic stock of key biophysical resources and systems *in place*. It therefore overturns the

---

16 Both interpretations imply constant capital stock per capita. If populations are growing or material standards are increasing, the total stock of productive capital will have to be increased accordingly.

17 "Natural assets" encompasses not only material resources (e.g., ozone, forests, soils) but also process resources (e.g., waste assimilation, photosynthesis, soils formation).

18 "Equivalent endowment" would be defined in terms of monetary value, wealth generating potential, jobs, and similar economic criteria.

conventional wisdom that "sustainable economic development does not require the preservation of the current stock of natural resources or any particular mix of human, physical and natural assets" (CCREM, 1987:3).

Conceptually, strong sustainability also satisfies the basic requirements for autopoiesis without which sustainable development is impossible. Humankind cannot exist indefinitely in a thermodynamically far-from-equilibrium world unless the ecosystems upon which we depend are capable of continuous self-organization and production. Only by adopting "strong sustainability" can we be assured of achieving our objectives of long-term ecological security and inter-generational equity.

Ecology's Bottom Line

The ecological bottom line for sustainable development should by now be apparent: humankind must learn to live on the interest generated by the remaining stock of living natural capital. Any human activity dependent on the consumptive use of ecological resources cannot be sustained indefinitely if it consumes not only annual production (interest), but also cuts into the standing stock (natural capital). Beyond a certain point, additional growth is "uneconomic growth that impoverishes rather than enriches" (Daly and Cobb, 1989:2).

While "development" defined as qualitative change is in no way impeded by this constraint, having to "live on the interest" challenges all prevailing assumptions about continuous material growth.

Implications for Sustainable Development of the Fraser Basin

This section explores a framework for sustainable development in the Fraser Basin based on the constant natural capital requirement. It assumes a decentralized system of governance that devolves effective control over resource management to regional authorities (c.f., Fox, this volume).

The logic of this framework has much in common with that of bioregionalism, "a teaching which helps people both to describe the bioregion where they live and then to live within its natural capacity to support life on a sustainable basis by ecological laws" (Aberley, 1985:145). To the modern mind, high on the rhetoric of mainstream global expansionism, bioregional thinking may appear quaintly naive and simplistic. However, bioregionalism has conceptual strengths absent altogether from conventional analyses. For example, bioregionalism addresses the concept of scale (ignored entirely by macroeconomics) as "the single critical and decisive determinant of all human constructs..." (Sale, 1985:54):

> The only way people will...behave in a responsible way is if they have
> been persuaded to see the problem concretely and to understand their
> own connections to it directly—and this can be done only on a limited
> [spatial] scale. It can be done where the forces of government and

society are still recognizable, where relations with other people are still intimate, and where the effects of individual actions are visible...Then people will do the environmentally 'correct' thing not because it is thought to be the *moral*, but rather the *practical*, thing to do (Sale, 1985:53, original emphasis).

Thus, bioregionalism provides an entirely appropriate sociopolitical context for "thinking globally but acting locally."

The proposed framework is also more firmly rooted in biophysical reality than are mainstream approaches to development. It recognizes that for all our technological wizardry, humankind remains dependent on a constant flow of energy, material, and services (known and unknown) from the biosphere. Sustainable regional development depends on maintaining, indeed enhancing, the natural capital stock that produces these flows.

Emphasizing natural capital as the key to development requires that each designated bioregion recognize both its contribution to, and dependency on, global resource flows. Historically, regional "development" in B.C. has been largely based on the liquidation of natural capital stocks such as fish, forests, and agricultural soils. While this has contributed to the accumulation of manufactured capital in our metropolitan areas and elsewhere, it ignores such things as the contribution of our mature forests (e.g., as carbon sinks) to global climate stabilization and assumes people of the province will always have access to the productivity of natural capital outside the province.

If all developing regions followed this practice the resultant pattern of global development would not be sustainable. (In fact, this pattern is at the root of the present global ecological "crisis.")[19] Instead, each region must plan its future development so that individual regions make no net contribution to global deterioration. This requires that every region balance consumption with production. For many overpopulated regions this will in turn require inter-regional negotiations to establish dependable mechanisms for the importation of sustainability factors beyond the usual requirements of voluntary exchange. In effect, we must come to terms on how to share global "carrying capacity" on a regional basis.

Regional Human Carrying Capacity[20]

For most species, carrying capacity is the maximum population that can be supported indefinitely in a given habitat without permanently damaging the ecosystem. In the present context, therefore, human carrying capacity can be defined as the maximum rate of resource consumption and waste discharge that

---

19   By the "constant natural capital" criterion, present human populations, material standards, and technologies already exceed the long-term carrying capacity of the earth. For example, the biosphere has the capacity to absorb 12 billion tons of CO_2 per annum (a resource of great positive economic value). However, human activity presently generates 24 billion tons of CO_2 annually. The resultant accumulation of excess CO_2 in the atmosphere threatens to destabilize global climate exposing humanity to incalculable economic costs and ecological risk (Rees, 1990d).

20   For opposing views of the utility of this concept, see World Bank (1985).

can be sustained indefinitely in a distinct planning region without progressively impairing ecological productivity and integrity (Rees, 1988.)

The corresponding maximum human population for the region is clearly a function of *per capita* rates of resource consumption and waste production (system capacity divided by *per capita* demand). These are in turn affected by average material standards and the level of technological sophistication. For example, the population could increase without violating carrying capacity (i.e., without reducing natural capital) if average material standards were lowered or if the efficiency of resource use or waste management technology were improved. (In general, however, this analysis supports policies to reduce populations. Ecological trends suggest that the present human population already exceeds the long-term carrying capacity of the planet. Thus ecological processes in some seemingly underpopulated regions are actually supporting people living in overpopulated regions elsewhere.)

Working within regional carrying capacity obviously does not preclude some environmental damage in the course of development (buildings and roads must occupy some space); nor does it preclude using renewable resources and nature's services (e.g., organic waste processing and recycling) to capacity. It does mean, however, that long-term ecological factors rather than short-term market forces would be the primary determinants of land use and resource management decisions as limits to the region's productivity are approached.

Markets would be recognized as the most efficient way to allocate available material and process resources. However, the actual quantity of resources to be made available is an ecological, not an economic question. In short, the appropriate scale of economic activity for the Fraser Basin would be based on ecological considerations designed to ensure that sufficient stable natural capital remains permanently in place to support the anticipated dependent population indefinitely at an acceptable standard of living.

It should be understood that while human society depends on many ecological resources and functions for survival, *carrying capacity is ultimately determined by the single vital resource or function in least supply*. On the global scale, loss of the protective ozone layer *alone* could do us in and substantial greenhouse enhancement (from accumulating carbon dioxide and other greenhouse gases) would *itself* be catastrophic (Rees, 1990d).

Regional Resource Inventory and Systems Monitoring

Maintaining sustainable levels of economic activity within the Fraser Basin will require more ecologically rigorous approaches to regional resource planning than are used at present. The relevant planning authority would have to develop an accurate, comprehensive inventory of lands, water, and associated resources, and implement a resource systems monitoring program. The inventory would provide the basis for economic resource extraction while systems monitoring would allow for cumulative ecological effects assessment. Both are essential to track the region's position relative to developmental limits imposed by carrying capacity.

(Given the global context, persistent deterioration in key ecological variables—stocks, flows, capacities, contaminants—at the regional scale can no longer be tolerated. Moreover, whether such trends are driven wholly by local activity or are the result of more global factors, the necessary corrective action must ultimately be implemented locally.)

Monitoring regional carrying capacity also provides the missing context for project-specific environmental assessments. Knowing regional carrying capacity enables new development proposals to be evaluated, as they should be, in light of preceding development, opportunity costs, and the remaining capacity of biophysical and social systems to cope with stress. Project-specific assessments would in turn provide data for the on-going regional monitoring/cumulative assessment program and an opportunity to test specific hypotheses on environment-development relationships (Rees, 1988).

A Complication: Inter-Regional Trade

While the notion of carrying capacity is conceptually simple, various factors make it difficult to put into practice. For example, inter-regional flows and commercial trade in ecological goods and services, obscure the immediate people-land relationship. This includes the movement of air and water in natural cycles throughout the ecosphere, and trade in fisheries, forestry, and agricultural products. Because natural products can be imported, the populations of many regions today unknowingly exceed their local carrying capacity with impunity *while importing sustainability from elsewhere.* Some regions and nations with admirable excellent economic accounts (e.g., Japan) are ecological black holes that would be unviable as isolated units.

In the absence of feedback from the land on their life-styles or economy, there is no direct incentive for such populations to practice sustainable management of local resources. The psychological effect further distances people from the ecosystems that support them. They forget their obligate dependency on the natural environment. Why should the citizens of the Fraser Basin region be concerned about the urbanization of their limited agricultural land when they can always import food from southern California?

The problem is, that as one region's population undermines its own environment, it becomes dependent on apparent excess carrying capacity "imported" from other regions over which it has no direct management control. In these circumstances, the populations of some of the world's "surplus" regions may not be able to rise to the level of their own regional carrying capacity without compromising people in dependent import regions. The relationship becomes more complicated—and unsustainable—if management practices in the export regions are undermining ecosystems there as well.

We should also acknowledge the ecological inequity that sometimes arises from the inequity in the distribution of the world's wealth. The perceived need for foreign exchange (often to pay off so-called development loans) drives some impoverished developing regions and nations to export *non-surplus* carrying capacity in the form of cash crops to wealthy industrialized regions, thereby jeopardizing staples production and harming their own people. This situation is not sustainable.[21]

In neither of the above situations is there generally a permanent commitment by export regions to dependent regions. However, as various countries adopt ecologically-based approaches to sustainable development, inhabitants of significant trading regions might prefer to enter formal contractual relationships to ensure mutual compliance with required management principles.

The necessary negotiations would be oriented to creating a morally and politically acceptable basis of exchange and serve a valuable educational function. Documenting the nature of inter-regional dependencies would both increase public awareness of ecological realities and contribute to inter-regional equity. For example, importers might have to pay a surcharge for reserving and maintaining the productivity of extra-territorial carrying capacity. At present, the residents of developed countries are not even aware of the negative impacts their imports of luxury crops have on such factors as local food production, land use and ownership patterns, and ecological conditions, in exporting developing counties.

Similarly, global CO_2 production should be reduced by about 50% to achieve atmospheric stability. One possible solution would involve the international allocation of sustainable atmospheric capacity to various nations in proportion to population. Since Canadian production of CO_2 is presently four times the world average *per capita*, our quota would be 1/8 of current levels. Thus, to take us through the transition to sustainable solar technologies, we (and other industrial regions) would have to purchase additional CO_2 rights from developing nations who don't need them. The latter could use the resultant revenues to bypass the hydrocarbon economy and move directly to more sustainable (solar-based) energy forms.

Although inter-regional trade reduces the incentive to husband local ecosystems, making it politically more difficult to implement sustainable regional development, trade *per se* is not at fault. If by adopting an ecological development paradigm, the population of each planning region were to achieve intra-regional stability (i.e., constant natural capital and no progressive environmental degradation) *regardless of its trade balance*, the net effect would be a sustainable level of development within a global carrying capacity.

Principles for Sustainable Regional Development[22]

The following principles are suggested as a guide to a form of sustainable development in the Fraser River Basin that would be consistent with the foregoing analysis. While many of the principles relate to global issues, it should be clear that corresponding policy and program implementation will take place at the local and regional levels. Indeed, the constant natural capital criterion for sustainability is particularly relevant to rural resource-based regions whose economies have

---

21 Ecological trade is a zero-sum game that can relieve imbalance but not overall scarcity.
22 Based on Rees (1990 a,b).

heretofore been based on the liquidation of natural capital. As has been emphasized many times in the present debate, sustainable development very much depends on thinking globally and acting locally.

- The economy is an integral *dependent* sub-set of the ecosphere. The future of society therefore rests on our ability to restore and maintain the self-producing structure and functional relationships of the ecosphere (autopoiesis).

- The maximum sustainable level of global economic activity is limited by the productivity of stocks of ecological capital which are currently in decline. Development planning in individual regions must recognize the constraints this imposes on future development and the fact that negative global trends are the cumulative result of local activities.

- Harvest rates in the renewable resources in the Fraser Basin must be held to average rates of production and not be responsive to ever-increasing market demand. Maximizing economic return often encourages the liquidation of ecological capital stock (fish, forests, soil, etc.) (Clark, 1973). By contrast, sustainable development requires that society live on the "interest" of our ecological endowment. *This is not an option but a necessity if we are to have a sustainable future.*

- *Historic levels of profits generated by resource exploitation in the Fraser Basin may not be compatible with sustainable development.* Forestry and other resource corporations should be required to demonstrate adequate maintenance of the resource base (natural capital stocks) before declaring a dividend.

- Society will have to pay the true costs of goods production. In general, market prices should reflect producers' costs for ecosystems maintenance (e.g., forest restocking, soils rehabilitation, wastewater treatment).

- Where serious damage has already been done, society may have to devote substantial resources to ecosystems rehabilitation. Entropy taxes may have to be imposed to provide public funds for common property systems maintenance. (For example, an entropy tax on fossil fuels could be used to rehabilitate commercial forests and plant carbon sink forests to help stabilize atmospheric CO_2 levels.)

- If adequate material standards are to be extended to all the world's people natural capital depletion must be reversed. The rehabilitation of ecological capital *everywhere* is important to global ecological security.

- Rates of waste discharge (including pesticide use) in Fraser Basin water and airsheds must be limited to the rate at which local ecosystems can absorb and denature the wastes. Exceeding regional capacities assumes excess capacity is available elsewhere.

- Significant natural waste processing capacity generally exists only for ecologically benign organic waste and nutrients. In the case of carcinogens and similar dangerous compounds, zero tolerance is warranted.

- The maximum sustainable human population of the region is a function of bioproductivity, quality of economic activity, technological sophistication, mean *per capita* consumption (material standard of living), and import-export relationships. All these factors are subject to public policy adjustment. In the long run, any population growth beyond regional carrying capacity can only be justified by improved technology or productivity, assured (formalized) access to extra-regional carrying capacity, or be accompanied by a proportional decline in standard of living.

- Residents of the Fraser Basin may have to recognize that seemingly under-developed ecological assets may actually be performing vital non-market functions that are already being fully utilized by the world economy. While forests are currently valued for wood-fibre, it is conceivable that their most economically significant role is actually in atmosphere and climate stabilization. This may impact the economics of forestry in coming decades.

- When the carrying capacity of the Fraser Basin or any other region has been reached, ecological factors must necessarily override economic considerations. The next project cannot be built (unless extra-regional capacity has been negotiated). The point is that if each nation or management region achieves (net) ecological stability, the overall effect would be global stability. Conversely, if most regions exceed their carrying capacities, global destruction is assured.

- If well-documented global ecological trends such as atmospheric change, ozone depletion, deforestation, and falling *per capita* food production persist, residents of the Fraser Basin and other industrialized regions may well have to lower their material expectations and even accept a decline in material standards to achieve global sustainability.

- Global sustainable development demands new forms of international cooperation and regulation to foster increased efficiency and reduced consumption and the rehabilitation of natural capital, and to ensure orderly trade in surplus capacity. This is contrary to the current emphasis on competition, exploitation of comparative advantage, and deregulation as means to stimulate world economic growth.

- New systems of national economic-ecological accounts are being developed to account for defensive (pollution control) expenditures and the depreciation of natural capital. A parallel system of regional ecological accounts should be developed to monitor the Fraser Basin's natural capital stocks and the region's balance of trade in ecological goods and services. The factors to be monitored might include key nutrients, soil conditions, air and water quality, and net primary production (photosynthesis).

- Shifting to sustainable development may force significant restructuring of national economies in the developed regions (for example in the petroleum and automotive sectors). This may require new forms of social safety nets to catch and retrain workers displaced from ecologically unsustainable employment. At the same time, *new jobs will be created in developing and producing the alternative energy and materially efficient products and technologies of the future.*

- Socially sensitive interpretations of sustainable development emphasize the opportunity to reassert community values, local control over resources, community-based development, and other forms of decentralized governance. These elements challenge current trends toward concentrated economic power and centralized political decision-making.

- Sustainable development represents an opportunity to shift the emphasis from quantitative to qualitative considerations. We might rediscover that development has more to do with community relationship, self-reliance, and personal growth (qualitative improvements) than it does with increased economic capacity (quantitative growth).

References

Aberley, D. 1985. *Bioregionalism: A Territorial Approach to Governance and Development of Northwest British Columbia.* Unpublished M.A. Thesis. Vancouver: University of British Columbia, School of Community and Regional Planning.

Baumol, W., and W. Oates. 1988. *The Theory of Environmental Policy* (second edition). London: Cambridge University Press.

Beer, S. 1981. "I Said, You Are Gods." *Teilhard Review* 15(3):1-33.

Block, W. 1990. "Environmental Problems, Private Property Rights Solutions." in Block, W. (ed.). 1990. *Economics and the Environment: A Reconciliation.* Vancouver: The Fraser Institute

Capra, F. 1982. *The Turning Point.* Toronto and New York: Bantam Books.

Canadian Council of Resource and Environmental Ministers (CCREM). 1987. *Report of the National Task Force on Environment and Economy.* Ottawa: Canadian Council of Resource and Environment Ministers.

Clark, C. 1973. "The Economics of Overexploitation." *Science* 181:630-634.

Daly, H. 1989. "Sustainable Development: From Concept and Theory Towards Operational Principles." (Hoover Institution Conference). Manuscript prepared for special issue of *Population and Development Review.*

Daly, H., and J. Cobb. 1989. *For the Common Good: Redirecting the Economy Toward Community, the Environment, and a Sustainable Future.* Boston: Beacon Press.

Dasgupta, P., and D. Heal. 1979. *Economic Theory and Exhaustible Resources.* London: Cambridge University Press.

Georgescu-Roegen, N. 1975. "Energy and Economic Myths." *Southern Economic Journal* 41:3:347-381.

Georgescu-Roegen, N. 1977. "The Steady State and Ecological Salvation: A Thermodynamic Analysis." *BioScience* 27:4:266-270.

Gilder, G. 1981. *Wealth and Poverty.* New York: Basic Books.

Heilbroner, R. 1986. *The Nature and Logic of Capitalism.* New York: W.W. Norton.

Herfindahl, O., and A. Kneese. 1974. *Economic Theory of Natural Resources*. Columbus, Ohio: Charles E. Merill.

Jevons, W. 1879. *The Theory of Political Economy* (2nd ed.). London: Macmillan.

Maturana, H., and F. Varela. 1988. *The Tree of Knowledge*. Boston: New Science Library.

Nelson, J. 1990. "Deconstructing Ecobabble: Notes on an Attempted Corporate Takeover." *This Magazine*. 24:3:12-18.

Nikiforuk, A. 1990. "Sustainable Rhetoric." *Harrowsmith*, October 1990:14-16.

Pearce, D., A. Markandya and E. Barbier. 1989. *Blueprint for a Green Economy*. London: Earthscan.

Perry, D., M. Amaranthus, J. Borchers, S. Borchers and R. Brainerd. 1989. "Bootstrapping in Ecosystems." *BioScience* 39:4:230-237.

Rees, W. 1988. "A Role for Sustainable Development in Achieving Sustainable Development." *Environ. Impact Assess. Rev.* 8:273-291

Rees, W. 1989. "Defining Sustainable Development." CHS Research Bulletin, May 1989. Vancouver: UBC Centre for Human Settlements. (Originally prepared as a background paper for *Planning for Sustainable Development*, a Symposium organized by the UBC School of Community and Regional Planning, 25-27 November, 1988.)

Rees, W. 1990a. "Sustainable Development and the Biosphere: Concepts and Principles." *Teilhard Studies* 23. American Teilhard Association.

Rees, W. 1990b. "The Ecology of Sustainable Development." *The Ecologist*. 20:1:18-23

Rees, W. 1990c. "Why Economics Won't Save the World." Presented to: *The Ecological Economics of Sustainability*, a conference sponsored by the International Society for Ecological Economics. Washington, DC: The World Bank (21-23 May 1990).

Rees, W. 1990d. "Atmospheric Change: Human Ecology in Disequilibrium." *International Journal of Environmental Studies*. 36:103-104.

Rowe, S. 1989. "Implications of the Brundtland Commission Report for Canadian Forest Management." *The Forestry Chronicle*, February 1989: 5-7.

Sale, K. 1985. *Dwellers in the Land: The Bioregional Vision*. San Francisco: Sierra Club Books.

Simon, J. 1982. Interview with William F. Buckley, Jr. *Population and Development Review*. March: 205-218.

Simon, J., and H. Kahn (eds.). 1984. *The Resourceful Earth: A Response to Global 2000*.

UNEP/World Bank. 1988. *Report of the Joint UNEP/World Bank Expert Meeting on Environmental Accounting and the System of National Accounts*. Paris, 21-22 November 1988.

Victor, P. A. 1990. "Indicators of Sustainable Development: Some Lessons from Capital Theory." A background paper prepared for a Workshop on Indicators of Sustainable Development. Ottawa: Canadian Environmental Advisory Council.

Vitousek, P., P. Ehrlich, A. Ehrlich and P. Matson. 1986. "Human Appropriation of the Products of Photosynthesis." *Bioscience* 36:368-374.

World Commission on Environment and Development (WCED). 1987. *Our Common Future*. Oxford: Oxford University Press.

World Bank. 1985. "Rapid Population Growth and Human Carrying Capacity." Staff Working Papers #690 (Population and Development Series, #15). Washington: The World Bank.

19

Distribution Principles For Compassionate Sustainable Development

Peter Boothroyd

[A] recent Canadian Press story...defined the top 20 per cent of [Canadian] households as rich. What was left unsaid was that this broad definition includes about two million households with an average annual pre-tax income of $92,000—surely a far cry from what most people view as 'the rich'." (Grant Reuber, former President of the Bank of Montreal, Vice-President of the University of Western Ontario, Deputy Minister of Finance for Canada. *The Globe and Mail*, February 11th, 1991.)

Developing Sustainably and Compassionately: The Combined Challenge

Development can be sustainable in a way that reduces disparities between the rich and poor or in a way that increases disparities. Both the Caribbean slave plantations and the communes of Maoist China were ecologically sustainable: in the former, a few rich owners lived off the backs of many poor; in the latter, whatever the political and organizational shortcomings, people shared and lived at about the same standard of living. Today, as we seek ways to develop the Fraser River Basin so that its forests, fisheries, farms and settlements are sustainable, we must remember that the ways we choose may either exacerbate or alleviate current disparities in standards of living, access to services, and quality of life—both within the Basin and between the Basin and other regions.

The starting point for this paper, and the fundamental value underlying the discussion throughout, is that reducing *intra*-generational disparities in the Fraser Basin, as elsewhere, is a social goal equal in importance to the goal of achieving *inter*-generational sustainability. The paper holds that nobody in the Basin, or outside, should suffer for lack of access to resources while others live luxuriously on $92,000 a year or more.

It has been hard to settle on an appropriate name for this value. Like others, I have sometimes used the term "fair." (Boothroyd, 1990b). But "fair" denotes procedural impartiality rather than substantive equality of outcome. "Fair" does not necessarily mean redistribution from the rich to the poor, as usage of the word in discussions of sustainable development by the Brundtland Commission (WCED, 1987) and the B.C. Round Table on the Environment and the Economy (B.C., 1990) shows. To many people, it would be fair for the various classes of society to maintain their current shares of wealth and income as we move to a sustainable economy, regardless of whether the economy is growing or contracting.

"Equity" and "justice" are, as individual words, close synonyms of "fairness" and therefore present the same problem. While "economic justice" and "distributive justice" have venerable histories in referring to equality of outcome, as C. B. MacPherson points out in a recent essay (1987), those terms are esoteric in today's society as well as being cumbersome.

The simple word "equality" is too absolute and refers to an end state rather than a process or perspective. "Humanitarianism" and "humaneness" are not specific enough to the issue of disparity. "Altruism," "benevolence"," and "charity," suggest disparity is to continue. "Love", or indeed "agape" would suit certain contexts but, for general purposes, those terms are respectively confusing and arcane.

In the end, I have settled on the word "compassion" because of the intensity of feeling it denotes, its clarity, its close synonymity with "agapic love", and its connotation of an impulsion to act. To a degree, "compassion" has the same limitation as "altruism," "benevolence, and "charity," but it is a little better than those terms in connoting the feelings of sadness, outrage, and often impotence, that many people like myself feel when beholding poverty juxtaposed with luxury and conspicuous consumption at both local and global levels.

Development of the Fraser Basin, then, can be posed as presenting a challenge to achieve both sustainability and *compassion*. The challenge of compassionate sustainable development is to eliminate current poverty within the Basin, to create cultures, settlements, and productive enterprises that husband the Basin's resources for future generations, and to use the Basin's resources generously and effectively for the immediate and long-term alleviation of poverty elsewhere.

Purpose and Outline

In this paper, I explore the general implications for regional development of accepting the challenge of compassionate sustainable development. The exploration begins with a discussion of growth-with-trickle-down as the commonly proposed approach to sustainable development, an approach which requires no significant departure from the dominant development paradigm of the past four decades. This approach assumes that through better engineering the environment can be protected while growth is sustained, and that through growth poverty can be reduced while disparity continues. The growth-with-trickle-down approach is rejected in this paper as being neither sustainable nor compassionate. It is argued that it is already making life harder for more and more people.

The exploration continues with the identification of seven principles that guide distribution of resources and their products in our current growth-oriented, distribution-maintaining welfare states. Their evolutions and implications are presented. Seven alternative distribution principles are proposed as necessary for the achievement of compassionate sustainable development. Adoption of these principles by the mainstream of our society would involve radical changes in our institutions and in the functioning of the state. But examples drawn from the Fraser Basin are provided to show that the alternative distribution principles are increasingly reflected in the practice of significant portions of our society, particularly in the development of community-level institutions, and that the necessary radical change is not only possible, but occurring.

The Growth-With-Trickle-Down Approach to Sustainable Development Versus Compassionate Sustainable Development

Development agencies and theorists now commonly agree that development planning must be oriented to sustainability. They also agree that equity in some sense must be simultaneously considered. Subscribers to this apparently new orthodoxy range from the Brundtland Commission (WCED, 1987) and the World Bank (IBRD, 1990) to the Canadian International Development Agency (CIDA, 1987) and Canada's federal and provincial "Round Tables" on the environment and the economy (e.g., B.C., 1990).

The common approach to dealing with the sustainability imperative and its equity implications is to seek ways to increase the efficiency of resource use and human labour without polluting the environment, and to seek ways to ensure the poor benefit from growth without changing the distribution systems that create the poor in the first place. This non-compassionate approach to sustainable development simply adds environmental considerations to the growth-with-trickle-down policies that have guided national and international development for two centuries.

Few seem to appreciate the radical implications of a commitment to development which is truly sustainable or to take a truly compassionate view of equity. That is to say, few seem willing to accept that a move to sustainability means ending growth in overall material and energy consumption, and that a move to compassionate sustainability, therefore, means that those of us who are richer will have to do with less in order that those who are poorer can not only survive but live in decency.

The Meaning of Growth-With-Trickle-Down

Economic growth can mean many things. To the mercantilists it meant accumulation of gold; to the physiocrats, increased agricultural output; to the classical liberal economists, increased labour productivity through free markets and capital investment; to Marxists, increased labour productivity through social organization and capital investment; to neoclassical economists, increased purchased consumption, investment for future consumption, and consumption of government services, usually as measured by equivalent growth in the market value of goods and services produced; to steady-state theorists (e.g., Georgescu-Roegen, 1971; Daly 1971, 1973; Meadows et al., 1972; and Brown, 1981), life-threatening increases in entropy and pollution (in such forms as atmospheric change, soil degradation, contamination, and species extinction) as a result of increases in closed-system "throughput" of fossil fuels and minerals and in renewable resource practices that are ecologically destructive (see chapter by Rees, this volume.)

When I say non-compassionate sustainable development continues the growth-with-trickle-down paradigm, I am referring simultaneously to the growth in consumption that steady-state theorists are concerned about and neoclassical economists promote and measure through their indicators of gross domestic or national product (GDP or GNP). The steady-state theorists and neoclassical economists are talking about different sides of the same coin. Given the structure of the world economy and its national components, growth in throughput and the accompanying increase in habitat deterioration are the bases for most of our growth in market-valued consumption.

GDP as an Indicator of Growth

It is well understood that growth in the GDP (or GNP) indicator does not necessarily mean overall quality of life is improving today, let alone that life will continue to get better. The indicator ignores self-help and non-monetary transactions; it says nothing about equity or about how hard people are working; it ignores natural resource depletion and degradation; and it values equally all consumption, investment and government expenditures regardless of their environmental or social consequences.

But GDP does, of course, measure well levels of consumption in the formal (i.e., measurable cash-based) economy. In an economy like Canada's which is dominated by the formal economy and in which people largely measure their quality of life by how much they can buy in the market or have provided to them by government employees, the GDP indicator does what the neoclassical economists claim: it tells us how big the pie is that most of us rely on for most of our essentials and luxuries. If the pie grows faster than the number of eaters, those who can at least maintain their share enjoy more economic security, comfort and fun. (As I will discuss later, generally speaking people did maintain their shares of Canada's fast growing per capita GDP in the 1950's and 1960's.) If the pie grows just as fast as the number of eaters and each keeps his/her share, consumption is at least stable whether or not it is fair, lower than desired, or requires more work. (As I will discuss later, in the 1970's and 1980's, the rate of GDP growth slowed to the point that it now approximates population growth, and would have been much lower were it nor for more women taking jobs; still, income distributions have remained roughly constant though with a slight shift from the middle-income to the rich.) If the pie shrinks and people keep their shares, anxiety increases for all and the poor become malnourished and exhausted. (As I will also discuss later, this scenario is likely to be the best real outcome of present policies that promote growth-with-trickle-down, even those billed as sustainable development policies; at worst, the middle and poor could suffer more than their "fair" share.)

Because GDP is an effective measure of consumption, it is also an effective indicator of the *un*sustainability of our development. Given the current structures of our economies, in particular their continuing dependency on fossil fuels (see Tables 19.1 and 19.2, for example), rising GDP indicates that entropy and ecological deterioration are increasing. Therefore, GDP growth today signals GDP declines, and therefore consumption declines, tomorrow. Indeed, even GDP

Table 19.1: 1987 Energy Consumption Distributed, by Source

	Energy Consumption Distributed, by Source (% of total consumption)				
	Oil	Natural Gas	Coal	Hydro-electr.	Nuclear
World	38	20	30	7	5
U.S.A.	41	23	24	4	7
China	15	2	79	4	—
Canada	30	18	14	31	7

Source: British Petroleum Company (presented in *The Canadian World Almanac and Book of Facts 1990.* Agincourt, Ont. Global Press.)

Table 19.2: Percentage Increases in Energy Consumption 1984-87, by Source

	Oil	Natural Gas	Coal	Hydro-elec.	Nuclear	All Sources
World	3.4	10.4	9.5	8.0	43.3	8.5
U.S.A.	5.4	-5.7	4.4	-18.9	39.3	2.7
China	20.9	18.5	18.4	27.7	—	19.0
Canada	2.8	-13.8	3.4	21.6	32.8	5.5

Source: British Petroleum Company (presented in *The Canadian World Almanac and Book of Facts 1987, 1990.*)

stability probably indicates decline tomorrow. GDP must decline sooner or later. The sooner it declines to an ecologically sustainable level, the higher this level can be.

The idea that consumption must decrease in order for there to be sustainability is not new. It was made famous, if unconvincing, by the book *Limits to Growth* (Meadows et al.) in 1972, and has been the central theme of the steady-state theorists for two decades. What is not so clearly stated by the steady-state theorists is that GDP must decline in order for there to be sustainability. They have been bedevilled by the the neoclassicists' claim that GDP can infinitely grow as consumption and production are shifted to non-destructive forms, and that it will, thanks to the wisdom of consumers, capitalists, and technocrats. Because GDP is a promiscuous indicator which values all processes equally, they say, it can just as well reflect a growing economy that is ecologically benign as one that increases entropy.

The neoclassical economists make several arguments. First, they argue that GDP will grow through continuing growth in the efficiency of machines. The steady-state theorists counter, effectively, I would say, that machine efficiencies may be offset by the growing costs of resource depletion and human settlement growth, forcing us, like addicts, to engage in more and more entropifying and polluting activity in order to maintain a given level of final consumption; farmers will become dependent on increasing applications of fertilizers, commuters will drive cars farther and farther to work. Increasing machine efficiencies, in fact, induces overharvesting.

More troubling for the steady-state theorists is the neoclassical prediction that growth in services will continue to outpace growth of goods. I would argue not only that goods will always make up a large part of the world economy, but that services will always require associated transportation, space heating, construction, and tools, and will involve, therefore, resource consumption. (Many would also point out that service-led growth, like material growth, does not necessarily reflect improved well-being: jailers, social workers, commodity brokers, and bailiffs come to mind as servicers who, like arms makers and industrial farmers, do not represent human progress.)

Table 19.3: United States Energy Consumption per GNP, in 1982 dollars

Year	Energy Consumption per GNP (thousands of Btu's)
1970	27.8
1980	23.8
1988	19.9
1989 (estimated)	19.6
1990 (forecast)	19.4

Source: Oil and Gas Journal. Jan. 29, 1990.

Over the last two decades, thanks to efficiency improvements and growth of the service sectors, GDP (or GNP) growth in the rich countries has indeed been achieved with decreasing "energy consumption" per dollar of output (Table 19.3).

Yet, overall economic growth, even in the low-growth 1980's, has still involved some increases in energy consumption. In the United States, to take a significant example, total energy consumption was at consecutively record levels in 1988, 1989, and 1990, even though there were short periods of decreasing energy consumption in the early 1970's and early 1980's (Tables 19.4, 19.5).

Table 19.4: Mean Annual United States Energy Consumption

Year	Mean Annual U.S. Energy Consumption (quadrillions of Btu's)	
	Fossil Fuels	**Total**
1960	42.1	43.8
1970	63.5	66.4
1980	70.0	76.0
1988	71.4	80.1
1989 (estimated)	n/a	81.1
1990 (forecast)	n/a	82.9

Sources: U.S. Energy Information Administration, *Annual Energy Review*, 1988 (presented in *The World Almanac and Book of Facts.* New York, Pharos 1990.); *Oil and Gas Journal.* Jan 29, 1990.

Table 19.5: Mean Annual Growth in United States Total Energy Consumption

Year	Energy Consumption (Mean annual percentage growth)
1960-69	4.3%
1970-79	2.1%
1980-89	0.3%

Sources: U.S. Energy Information Administration, *Annual Energy Review*, 1988 (presented in *The World Almanac and Book of Facts.* New York, Pharos 1990.); *Oil and Gas Journal.* Jan. 29, 1990

The most sophisticated neoclassical argument for the possibility of ecologically benign GDP growth posits a scenario of renewable resources replacing non-renewables as the basis for our economy. There are two problems with this argument. First, our consumption may soon, if it has not already, exceed the sustainable productive capacity of renewable resources. The evidence is mounting that this is true for forests and fisheries. Secondly, a shift in economies to ecologically appropriate forms of renewable resource production would likely involve labour-intensive inputs replacing current high fossil fuel inputs, thus lowering GDP per capita.

The only physical processing activities that could be increased from current levels with increased output but without ecological damage is the more effective harnessing of solar energy (including wind and wave power) and perhaps geothermal and tidal energy. Until the physical limits to solar energy use are reached, cash-based activity to increase its use (e.g., through utilities, retrofitting) will indeed contribute to GDP without direct ecological damage.

We may be able to learn how much GDP growth reflects ecological deterioration from current intellectual effort to develop "satellite" systems of national accounts that modify GDP to take into account losses in natural capital and the costs of fighting pollution (see for example, Repetto et al., 1989; UNEP, 1988). If such effort is successful, politically and technically, we may well discover that in the past, fully netted domestic products were falling as gross domestic products rose, that economic growth as conceived, promoted, and measured by the neoclassicists was not sustainable.

In the near future, we will likely see the rate of GDP growth continue to slow then turn negative, while the satellite accounts portray an ever worsening decline in domestic products after they have been fully netted to take into account environmental deterioration. That is to say, we will see that even current levels of neoclassically defined economic activity are not sustainable. By this, I mean that modern society has probably exceeded the limits to *its* growth, not that world population has necessarily exceeded the earth's carrying capacity which is a function of our wants, organization, and technology.

Maintenance of the energy component of, and basis for, our current consumption will be particularly problematic. Sooner or later, because of depletion and/or pollution, the world will no longer be able to depend on fossil fuels for seven-eighths of economically measured energy consumption. The alternatives all have their limitations. Hydroelectricity projects, though long-lived, are also finite sources of energy: reservoirs fill up. Moreover, hydro projects create their own type of ecological damage. Nuclear fission depends on finite uranium and poses a constant threat. Fusion, hot or cold, remains at best a very distant prospect. Formal-sector solar energy harnessing, even though a potentially significant contributor to GDP, could probably not replace the current levels of consumption we enjoy by using fossil fuels.

In short, current levels of consumption, and therefore of GDP, let alone growth in those levels, are not sustainable. The sooner we see GDP as an inverse indicator of progress and begin to *plan* the reduction of consumption instead of trying to swim against the tide, the more we will be able to have in our future and be able to leave to our descendents.

The Buddhist Alternative to Growth

With planning, declines in GDP could represent not only lower consumption today in order to save for tomorrow, but also the conversion of our economy to user-harnessed (as opposed to utility-harnessed) solar energy, to more labour-intensive but more fulfilling community production for use, value and management of renewable resources, and to lifestyles that are less consumptive of fuels and materials.

Development in this direction was correctly identified by Schumacher in 1973 as development based on Buddhist principles. Over the last decade, some Buddhist rural and urban leaders in Thailand have shown that this form of development can be effective and appealing to many people (Pongphit 1986, 1989; Roberts, 1990), as have aboriginal or experimental minorities who base their work on their own, Buddhist-like principles.

The Buddhist approach to development still seems very peculiar to the mainstream of Western society, however. The mainstreams of virtually all countries have "modernized" and have embraced Western consumption values, economic systems that reinforce these values (by rewarding producers of consumables and stimulators of consumption by increasing their own consumption power), and have adopted neoclassical concepts of economic management. Many more people have come to believe that individually-organized consumption of materials or personal services is the purpose of life: to develop insatiable tastes in housing, appliances, clothing, recreation, and exotic foods. Ironically, many of these same people now find themselves feeling more insecure than those who have rejected these values and turned to spiritual or social sources of satisfaction.

Buddhist development of course involves growth: growth in human activity directed to working with, rather than against, nature and the sun; growth in appropriate technology; growth in satisfaction from meaningful work; growth in community organization. This perspective on growth is fundamentally different than that of the high-tech-oriented neoclassicists who claim that because of human ingenuity, because of the unlimited potentials for resource substitution, and because of increased efficiency of resource use, there are no limits to consumption. But it is the neoclassical perspective that still dominates thinking about growth, and unfortunately, sustainable development.

The word "growth" in its economic sense, has been appropriated by the neoclassicists, not to mention their Marxist cousins and by the steady-state critics, to refer to the kind of growth measured so well by GDP. Accordingly, when I say I am arguing against growth-with-trickle-down as an approach to sustainable development and am calling for more compassionate forms, I mean, to put it most simply, that I am against GDP growth, and for Buddhist development.

Trickle-Down

Just as sustainable development thinking is dominated by the neoclassical view of growth, so it is dominated by the neoclassical idea of how distribution does and should occur. The idea is captured by the evocative phrase "trickle-down". The idea is that the poor can receive some of the benefits of growth, their "fair share", without the rich being required to redistribute any of their own relative consumption power. The assumption is that consumption and investment at the top will create jobs and thus consumption-power at the bottom. The concept of trickle down justifies there being a top and a bottom. It justifies the maintenance by the classes of their relative shares of wealth and income. It enables the rich to justify inequality on the pretext of helping the poor.

Approaches to Trickle-Down

The concept of trickle-down can justify subsidizing the rich, laissez-faire policies, or the welfare state. Subsidies to the rich are justified by two formulations of the trickle-down concept:

(i)   As the rich invest or consume their incomes they create jobs for the poor;
(ii) As the richer move "up" (housing being the usual example) they leave places behind them for the less rich to fill.

Laissez-faire systems can be justified with the same two formulations.

The rapid increases in wealth, combined with instabilities and gross inequalities, that were produced in the 19th and early 20th century economic systems employing various combinations of laissez-faire and subsidization policies, led to these approaches evolving into welfare states in the middle of this century. The welfare state's approach to trickle-down has been to intervene in an essentially laissez-faire economy not only to provide subsidies to the rich but also to ensure that there is indeed trickle-down: to ensure that income, social product, and resources do flow from the rich down to the poor, but also to ensure, through the maintenance of private property, capital accumulation, and employer rights, that there are rich and there are poor.

Similarly, in the international welfare system which evolved after World War II, there has been international trickle-down of "overseas development assistance" from rich countries to poor countries; but, by controlling capital, international financial institutions, the terms of trade, and, sometimes, the governing elites of poor countries, the rich welfare states have ensured that they stay rich and, in effect, that the poor stay poor.

Distribution Indicators

The most commonly monitored indicators of consumption-power distribution are based on computations of pre-tax cash income. The Gini coefficient of income distribution is often referred to in the international development literature. Like GDP, it is attractive in that it provides a one-number indicator. This feature also limits its usefulness: it does not tell us which classes receive a disproportionate share nor by how much.

Domestically, analyses of welfare state consumption-power distributions often refer to the distribution of pre-tax income among quintiles. In these terms, the welfare state's trickle-down approach has shown itself to be remarkably effective in maintaining the relative consumption-power of the various classes. In middle-of-the-road Canada, for example, the poorest fifth of households (families and unattached individuals) have consistently received about 4% of the income over the

Table 19.6: Income Shares of Families and Unattached Individuals in Canada

Year	Income Shares in Canada (% of total income)		
	Lowest Quintile	Middle Quintile	Highest Quintile
1951	4.4	18.3	42.8
1961	4.2	18.3	41.3
1971	3.6	17.6	43.3
1981	4.6	17.6	41.7
1989	4.8	16.9	43.2

Sources: Statistics Canada. 1980. *Perspectives Canada III.*; Statistics Canada. 1990. *Income Distributions by Size in Canada 1989* (Catalogue 13-207 Annual).

last four decades; the richest fifth, a little over 40% (Table 19.6). Income distribution is the same in the United States.

Household pre-tax income distribution data are only rough indicators of comparative living standards, however. They do not tell us about the amount or kind of work people do to make income. Nor do they tell us about the relative income risks faced by the various classes, about comparative taxation levels, or about the distribution of living conditions and income-in-kind, particularly the distribution of public benefits (a major source of income-in-kind) that taxes pay for. Net distributions of consumption-power are difficult to compute, but there is good reason to believe that the rich do better than the pre-tax income distribution indicates, and that their relative position has been improving in recent years.

The rich are clearly favoured in any comparison of income risks. Bankruptcy judgements, for example, take into account the bankrupt's standard of living in determining what s/he can reasonably be asked to pay to creditors. Layoffs have always been a normal, but stressful, part of life for wage-labourers—and they do not include golden handshakes. Renters, constituting 60% of Canadian families defined as "low-income" by Statistics Canada, have little control over the largest component of their cost of living.

Data on wealth distributions, which also affect income risk, are not as readily available as income distribution data, but it seems reasonable to suppose that wealth disparities are even greater than income disparities. After all, privilege started Canada off (Myers, 1914). One estimate is that the richest 10% of Canadians own 58% of all wealth; a 1983 study estimated that the Gini coefficient for wealth distribution in Canada was 0.69, compared with a less unequal 0.39 for income distribution (MacDonald, 1985). Under current conditions of inflation and high real interest rates, disparities in wealth are likely increasing.

The tax system (income, sales, excise, property, etc.) also favours the rich (Canada, 1971; NCW, 1976). This has been known by many Canadians since the Carter Commission's 1966 report. The introduction of partial capital gains taxes in the 1970's might have evened matters somewhat had this improvement not been offset by the abolition of estate taxes. In the 1980's, Registered Retirement Savings Plan contribution increases, capital gains tax limitations, and the Goods and Services Tax have all been regressive: at worst, they have provided taxation advantages to the rich; at best they have diluted the impacts of the theoretically progressive income tax.

To compare the benefits of public services accruing to the various classes is so difficult that to my knowledge no one has tried to do so in Canada. How do industrial subsidies compare to public assistance, and what is the chain of benefits in either case? Who benefits most from roads or from rapid transit that brings workers to downtown offices. Who do the police most protect? While such calculations are difficult to make, the trends in public services are apparent.

In the 1950's and 1960's, when GDP growth was strong, a portion of the rising income was allocated by the evolving welfare state to improving universal social programs (medicare, university and college expansions, recreation) and to increasing income security for the poorest through transfer payments (family allowances, pensions). This allocation enabled the various classes to maintain their share of the growing pie.

In the 1970's, when growth weakened, growth in social programs ceased—the widely expected universal denticare and medicare programs never materialized—although most income security schemes were indexed to inflation. Through the 1980's, public funding for health and education was reduced and income became less secure. Waiting lists for elective surgery lengthened, university tuition fees rose in real terms. Total funding for income security remained high, because of the high unemployment rates and aging population, but individuals' benefits were reduced: qualifications for unemployment insurance (no longer a self-funded system) became more stringent, pensions were no longer fully indexed to inflation, and levels of public assistance ("welfare"), the last resort for the very poor, declined steadily in real terms. Food banks which were organized in the early 1980's as temporary measures became permanent fixtures.

In sum, the Canadian welfare state's distributive policies on taxation, services and income security programs seem to have maintained the inter-class distribution not only of pre-tax incomes but also of resulting standards of living through the booming 1950's and 1960's. But as the economy increasingly has faltered in the 1970's and 1980's, the policies may be decreasingly mitigating, and in some cases exacerbating, the effects of a relatively constant pre-tax income distribution.

Indeed, the cut backs are so great and the tax increases so regressive that it may be we are seeing an end to the welfare state's distribution-maintaining approach to trickle-down. At the beginning of the 1980's, Thatcher, Reagan, and their equivalents explicitly excoriated the distribution-maintaining trickle-down policies of the welfare state, and called for a return to laissez-faire or even subsidization (e.g., military contracting) trickle-down policies favouring the rich. Subsequent leaders have been less explicit about their contempt for the welfare state, but their policies have continued to undermine it.

As economies continue to decline, the political pressure from all classes will be directed to at least maintaining their respective shares of the pie. The richer and more powerful classes will be best able to protect their interests, however. As the ideological revival of new-right anti-welfare-state rhetoric in the 1980's indicates, the richer classes may actually be able to capitalize on the *sauve-qui-peut* panic induced by economic decline, by convincing the poorer classes that their interest too will be served by an end to the "unproductive" and "debt-ridden" welfare state. The relative standard of living for the poor, as indicated by after-tax income and availability of public services, whether or not by pre-tax income, might not only decline proportionately to the shrinking of the pie but at a faster rate. In either event, decline in standard of living for the poor will not only be stressful, as it will for all classes, but will increasingly affect physical health.

Lacking widely-accepted hard distribution indicators other than those for pre-tax income, just as we lack alternatives to GDP as a measure of overall economic output, policy makers fail to see, or attempt to disguise, the growing extent of poverty during this incipient decline. Seeing, or claiming to see, no alternative to trickle-down, in any of its forms, as a mechanism to distribute income, social product, and resources, policy makers continue to reinforce non-compassionate development.

Growth and Trickle-Down: A Useful Fit

The neoclassical concepts of growth and trickle-down fit well together to form a development paradigm which is attractive to welfare states and the international agencies they dominate. The paradigm simultaneously supports the rich and gives hope to the poor, even if, as often happens (Oshima and Mizoguchi, 1977, cited in Lo and Salih, 1981) disparity increases with growth. To mix the metaphor, the growth-with trickle-down paradigm gives comfort in the notion that a rising tide floats all ships.

The Growth-With-Trickle-Down Approach to Sustainable Development

The recent widespread endorsement of "sustainable development" reflects not the emergence of a new dominant paradigm in policy circles but rather a continuation of the growth-with-trickle-down paradigm. Indeed, many business and political leaders now use the terms "sustainable growth" and "sustainable development" interchangeably.

This view of sustainable development is held not only by those who see their sole task as stimulating growth but also by many of those who see their task as alleviating poverty. Most national and international development agencies have implicitly or explicitly defined sustainable development as sustainable growth, rather than as living within our means, and poverty alleviation as a matter of insuring that the poor receive some benefits from this growth, rather than as a process of redistributing consumption-power from the rich to the poor.

Indeed, the Brundtland Commission's report (WCED, 1987), which perhaps more than any other document has been responsible for making sustainable development a household word, calls for continuing growth in both poor *and rich* countries. The report cautiously hints at the need for redistribution within poorer countries but not between nations.

> While attainable growth rates will vary [among Third World countries], a certain minimum is needed to have any impact on absolute poverty. (WCED, 1987:50)

> Growth must be revived in developing countries...Yet developing countries are part of an interdependent world economy; their prospects also depend on the levels and patterns of growth in industrialized nations. The medium-term prospects for industrial countries are for growth of 3-4%, the minimum that international financial institutions consider necessary if these countries are going to play a part in expanding the world economy. Such growth rates could be environmentally sustainable if industrialized nations can continue the nations' recent shifts in the content of their growth towards less material and energy-intensive activities and the improvement of their efficiency in using materials and energy...for all developing countries high export growth, especially of non-traditional items, will also be necessary to finance import...(WCED, 1987:51-52)

> ...rapid economic growth combined with deteriorating income distribution may be worse than slower growth combined with redistribution in favour of the poor. (WCED, 1987:52)

Similarly, the World Bank, which has been forced to respond to severe and cogent criticism of its development approach by environmentalists, has begun to take environmental impact assessment more seriously, but still promotes growth and downplays the need for fundamental inter- as well as intra-national redistribution.

> Effective action to help the poor involves some costs for the non-poor in both developed and developing countries. But these costs are modest even in the short term...(IBRD, 1990:143)

Canada's published strategy for Canadian Official Development Assistance (CIDA, 1987) is to be credited for placing highest priority on programs that directly alleviate poverty and for not explicitly calling for growth. But, of course, the strategy does not reject growth, nor does it mention national or international redistribution actions and systems (e.g., debt forgiveness, resource sharing, land reforms, reduced consumption by the rich) that would be much more effective in alleviating poverty than trickle-down aid to the poor from or within welfare states.

The Meaning of Compassionate Sustainable Development

In contrast to conceptions of sustainable development that simply add to the growth-with-trickle-down paradigm by calling for increased efficiency and attention to pollution, *compassionate* conceptions of sustainable development assume that because the limit to the earth's capacity to support material throughput by human beings has already been reached, that total material consumption will sooner or later have to be stabilized if not indeed reduced, that the longer we wait to reduce consumption the more we will have to do so, and that the poor will grow in numbers and suffer even more if there is no redistribution of consumption power from the rich to the poor.

The compassionate sustainable development critique of growth-with-trickledown is that it reduces the earth's carrying capacity and exacerbates poverty. The challenge of compassionate sustainable development is not only to find ways to use natural and human-made wealth efficiently to meet basic human needs, but also to equalize living and working conditions produced by that wealth, and to replace desires for material consumption with non-consumptive social and spiritual values; it is a matter, as Hazel Henderson put it in one of her famous epigrams, of "sharing smaller pies."

While the morality of compassionate distribution stands even if we assume a growing pie (i.e., the argument for equality stands independently of assumptions about growth) the need for redistribution can be seen as more urgent if we assume growth has come to an end. Trickle down cannot even be considered as a solution to poverty if there is less and less to trickle.

Challenges to Growth-With-Trickle-Down in the 1970's: The Theoretical Roots of Compassionate Sustainable Development

The theoretical basis for compassionate sustainable development was originally laid at the beginning of the early 1970's, a time of rising commodity prices and economic instability which seemed to reflect resource limitations and localized pollution. Proponents of what I am calling compassionate sustainable development employed such terms as "the steady-state economy" and the "distributist state" (Daly, 1973), "global equilibrium" (Meadows et al., 1973), and "Buddhist economics" (Schumacher, 1973), all of which terms suggested the parallel requirements for conservation and income redistribution. In Canada, "conserver society" was a term in good currency in the mid-1970's (GAMMA, 1976; Science Council, 1977); several writers on the conserver society discussed the distribution implications of "doing less with less" (Arnopoulos, 1976; Chodak, 1976).

International development theorists in the 1970's also began to write of the need to substitute meeting basic needs for stimulating growth-with-trickle-down as the objective of planning. (Seers, 1969; ILO, 1976; Friedmann and Weaver, 1979; Stohr and Taylor, 1981.)

For the most part, the writers of the 1970's who addressed both conservation and distribution issues saw the need for *re*distribution—redistribution of consumption-power in favour of the poor through redistributions of wealth, after-tax income, perquisites, public expenditures, and/or amenities. The exceptions, Garrett Hardin (1968, 1977, 1980) perhaps being the best known, promoted, as an ethical alternative to redistribution, peacetime "triage"—the sorting of people, even nations, into three categories according to whether they would be likely to survive without aid, could survive with it, or needed aid to survive. Whether redistribution or triage was proposed—if one foresaw a very gloomy future, one could call for both redistribution and triage, but I am not aware of such a position having been taken—there was a widespread awareness among the theorists of scarcity in the 1970's that the current international distribution system, and most national systems, could not be morally maintained.

Eclipse of the Compassionate Sustainable Development Perspective in the 1980's

In the early 1980's, interest waned in the ecological questions raised in the 1970's, and in answers such as solar energy that had begun to be actively promoted. To a large degree, this waning was due to the severe and protracted (18 month-long) recession which was induced in 1981-82 by the central banks of most welfare state economies as a response to the inflation of the 1970's.

Rising prices in the 1970's reflected the continuance of welfare state growth-with-trickle-down policies, which had worked in the 1950's and 1960's when resources were abundant and demands relatively low, but which led to increasing budgetary deficits and inflation as the limits to growth were being reached. The approaching of the limits to growth was suggested by widespread shortages of agriculture, forest, metal, and fossil fuel commodities.

Under the cold-turkey treatment for inflation administered by the central bankers in the early 1980's, growth was temporarily stopped. Unemployment replaced inflation as society's chief worry. Commodity prices collapsed. For instance, consumer heating oil prices in Canada, which had been rising at a double-digit rate from 1973 to 1980, and had spiked up 44% in 1981, rose at a declining rate until 1986 when actual prices declined then stabilized. Grain prices fell sharply in real terms in 1981, and stayed low.

Workers and speculators having learned their lesson, money supplies were loosened in 1983, and a sustained period of slow but steady growth in GDP ensued until 1990. The conversion of the GDP-measured economy from recession to sustained recovery without a revival of commodity price inflation, led mainstream economists, politicians and publics to see themselves as vindicated in their dismissal of the "limits-to-growth", "closing circle", "steady-state" theorists of the 1970's as "neo-Malthusians" and "prophets of doom."

The basis for this self-vindication is illustrated well by the outcome of a bet between ecologist Paul Ehrlich and economist Julian Simon. Just as the 1980's began, Simon, who has become famous for unequivocally stating (1981) that "natural resources are not finite," issued a challenge "to all Malthusians" to bet against his prediction that minerals and other natural resources would become cheaper in real terms over the coming decade, and by implication, forever. With colleagues, Ehrlich accepted the bet and specifically proposed that the real 1990 prices of chrome, copper, nickel, tin, and tungsten would be higher than those in 1980. Ehrlich lost (Tierney, 1990).

The eclipse of the compassionate sustainable development thought that had begun to emerge in the 1970's by a revival of growth-with-trickle-down apologies in the 1980's was not only due to the reappearance of apparent evidence that resources pose no limits to growth. It was simultaneously due to the anxiety created by the 1982 collapse and the resulting widespread desire by many people in all income classes to recoup their losses through a growing economy that rewarded individual effort with personal gain. The need to cope with the recession and collapse diverted attention of many people, including many scholars, away from long-term economic problems.

When the unavoidable environmental threats became apparent again in the late 1980's, the taste of what stopping growth could mean still lingered from 1982, and thinking quickly focussed on how to solve environmental problems without sacrificing growth or redistributing consumption power. The casting of sustainable development as growth-with-trickle-down was the result.

Growth seemed potentially limitless to many in the 1980's, but this was because they ignored some fundamental economic problems and pressures that were being exacerbated by that very growth.

Indicators of Fundamental Economic Problems

Some fundamental current economic problems are revealed by an analysis of the terms and outcome of the Ehrlich-Simon bet. Ehrlich predicted prices would rise as a result of supply depletion combined with rising demand from population growth; Simon predicted that human ingenuity as "the ultimate resource" (1981) would produce the necessary innovations to increase resource use efficiency faster than population growth. Neither seemed to have considered that the relationship between commodity prices and standards of living depends on fiscal, monetary and distribution policies, that falling commodity prices can be associated either with resource abundance and growing affluence or with growing poverty and lack of effective demand.

Ehrlich's mistake, I would argue, (in hindsight, having lost similar bets) was not to recognize that the "immiseration" he had been predicting since 1968 had already begun by 1980 and that some people around the world would be consuming less in the 1980's—partly because of increased efficiencies, but also because of poverty which, in its immediacy, was induced by new tight-money policies of the welfare state central bankers in 1981, and which in the long term reflected resource constraints and the limitations of trickle-down in a non-growing economy. Ehrlich also apparently failed to recognize that for many reasons producers would lag in cutting back their production from the booming 1970's. Producers lagged in cutting back production, in part, because they made the same bad bet as Ehrlich; in part, because they were individually driven to grow in order to achieve economies of scale and dominate markets; in part, because as Simon predicted, they were able to lower their costs through increased efficiency; in part, because they did not have to pay the full cost of their environmental impacts; in part, because many were encouraged to produce by direct government subsidies.

The growth in GDP during the 1980's that was permitted by cheap oil and gas, metals, forest products, and foods, was enjoyed by the rich but masked rising deficits despite cutbacks in public services, high unemployment, especially among the young, and inflation at a rate lower than in the 1970's but higher than the rate of previous decades.

One sign of the malaise is provided by what came to be called in the 1970's "the discomfort index". The discomfort index is simply the sum of the inflation and unemployment rates. This sum was relatively constant in industrial countries during the 1950's and 1960's, as indeed Phillips (1958) had found it to be in the United Kingdom over the previous century.

In the 1970's and early 1980's, the discomfort index rose markedly, giving rise to the neologism "stagflation" It fell somewhat during the late 1980's but not to the earlier stable level. By 1990, it was rising again. On a decade-to-decade basis, the index has been steadily rising (Table 19.7).

Table 19.7: Canadian Discomfort Index (Unemployment + Inflation)

Years	Canadian Discomfort Index (mean annual rate)		
	Unemployment Rate %	Inflation Rate (Change in CPI)	Discomfort Index
1961-70	4.9	2.7	7.6
1971-80	6.9	8.1	15.0
1981-90	9.5	6.0	15.5

Sources: Canada, Department of Finance. 1981. *Economic Review*; Canada, Department of Finance. 1985. *Economic Review*; Canada, Department of Finance. 1990. *Quarterly Economic Review: Annual Reference Tables.*; Statistics Canada.

A static discomfort index indicates that unemployment can only be reduced by increasing inflation and inflation reduced only by increasing unemployment. The rising discomfort index in our present economy suggests that unemployment can be reduced only at the cost of *increasingly* increasing inflation—the policy approach of the 1970's—or that inflation rates can be reduced only at the cost of *increasingly* increasing unemployment—the policy approach of the 1980's. To put it another way, the trade-off curve between inflation and unemployment which

Phillips identified on his famous graph has been spiralling out toward higher rates of both ills. A reasonable explanation for this is that overall scarcity (i.e., our bumping up against the limits to growth) has made economic growth (i.e., increasing resource throughput) an obsolete goal and that policies directed toward this goal must exacerbate both inflation and unemployment. Effective economic management can no longer mean careful alternation between low rates of inflation and unemployment on a steady growth path. It now must mean changing the path and fine-tuning our way to reduced consumption.

Reflecting the rising discomfort index in the 1970's and 1980's were the real declines in the rates of personal income growth during these decades. Real family incomes, for example, rose at an average (non-compounded) annual rate of 4.6% from 1961 to 1971, 2.6% from 1971 to 1981, and 0.9% during the eight years from 1981 to 1989. (The full 1981-1991 rate will be even lower: a recession began in April, 1990.) That this decline is not just attributable to declining family size is indicated by the fact that per capita family income followed a similar pattern. The decline in growth of GDP was much less precipitous (Table 19.8).

Table 19.8: Mean Annual Growth in Real Family Income and Real GDP, Canada

| Year | Mean Annual Growth (Mean annual % increase) | | |
	Gross Family Income	Per Capita Income	GDP
1951-61	3.28	2.74	2.77
1961-71	4.60	5.30	5.45
1971-81	2.61	4.19	4.39
1981-89	0.89	1.25	3.20

Sources: Statistics Canada. 1990. *Income Distributions by Size in Canada 1989* (Catalogue 13-207 Annual); Statistic Canada GDP data presented in *Canadian World Almanac and Book of Facts 1990.* Agincourt, Ont.: Global Press. (GDP data source)

Such increases in family income as there were in the last two decades were due in large part to unsustainable debt financing by government and to the increased participation by women in the labour force.

Canada's federal government deficits (and therefore the cumulative national debt), as a percentage of GDP, rose exponentially through the 1970's and 1980's (Table 19.9). This delays but also exacerbates the precipitous decline in real personal income which must come when we can no longer keep borrowing from others and our own future.

The percentage of women working outside the home rose from 39% in 1971 to 58% in 1989 (Table 19.10). This has been a satisfying development for many women, of course, but it has come at the cost of considerable stress for some families and increased expenditures for child care, transportation, and fast food.

Table 19.9: Mean Federal Government Deficit as Percentage of GDP

Years	Mean Federal Govt. Deficit as % of GDP
1960-69	1.27
1970-79	2.38
1980-88	6.12

Source: Canada, Department of Finance. 1990. *Quarterly Economic Review: Annual Reference Tables.*

Table 19.10: Labour Force Participation Rates, Selected Years

| Year | Labour Force Participation Rates (percentage of eligible population in labour force) | |
	Female	Male
1966	35.4	79.8
1971	39.4	77.3
1981	51.7	78.4
1989	57.9	76.7

Source: Canada, Department of Finance. 1990. *Quarterly Economic Review: Annual Reference Tables.*

A double income is now seen as a necessity rather than as a way to afford luxuries or as a reflection of increased options for women. Statistics Canada's low-income rate for two-parent one-earner families rose during the 1980's from 16% to 18% of all such families (Table 19.11). The low-income rate for female single-parent families was 51% in 1989.

Table 19.11: Low-income Rates by Family Categories

| Year | Low-income Rates by Family Category (percentage of families in category who are defined as "low-income") | | | |
	Young (head under age 25)	Two-parent, One-earner	Two-earner	Three-earner
1980	19.5	15.8	5.3	3.1
1989	25.1	18.2	5.2	2.3

Sources: Statistics Canada. 1980. *Perspectives Canada III*; Statistics Canada. 1990. *Income Distributions by Size in Canada 1989* (Catalogue 13-207 Annual).

The secular upwards trend of the discomfort index, and the declining growth in real family income despite increasing participation of women in the labour force and growing national debt, indicate fundamental economic problems that reduce current quality of life for many people, particularly the poor, and foretell greater problems in the future for welfare states such as Canada.

The situation in many poorer countries is worse. While standards of living for many people have been improving in East and Southeast Asia over the last few decades, the economies of many African, Latin American, Caribbean, Eastern European and South Asian countries have been deteriorating rapidly. Economic deterioration in many areas such as Bangladesh, the sub-Sahara, Southern Africa and Central America can be directly attributed in large part to ecological destruction. The extent of such destruction is perhaps the most apparent indicator of fundamental economic problems in poor countries.

Destruction of forests, soils and fisheries in these countries, and in the rural regions of the better-off countries, has been motivated by the need to provide raw materials not only to growing domestic populations but also to the increasingly consuming rich countries on which the poor countries have become technologically reliant and to which, as a result, they have become deeply indebted, and has been encouraged by First-World-dominated international agencies such as the World Bank. (See volumes of *The Ecologist*).

Compassionate Sustainable Development: The Only Solution

To try to solve the economic problems of the high-consumption welfare states or the poor countries by stimulating further growth in the former, as the Brundtland Commission and many others propose, will exacerbate problems for both rich and poor countries. Even the stimulation of growth in the poor countries will be counterproductive unless the growth is oriented toward solar energy and is based on ecologically sound renewable resource production.

To attempt to deal with international disparities by trickling aid from growth-stimulated rich countries to poor countries will at best be insufficient to reduce those countries' poverty; at worst, such an approach increases their dependency on technology and oil, deepens their debt, and leads to more ecological destruction. If we in the rich countries are to help those in the poor, we must reduce our own consumption, in other words, we must renounce growth. Whether or not such a path is sufficient to move toward global equality, it is necessary.

Similarly, trickle-down within welfare states will no longer even minimally serve the poor. The welfare state approach of continuously increasing at the same rate the consumption-power of all classes is no longer viable now that we have reached the limits to growth as indicated by the rising discomfort index and the slowing of family income growth. By attempting to maintain this approach, we dig ourselves in deeper. This is well perceived by those on the economic right. They are forthright in calling for an end to the welfare state's attempt to maintain standards of living for the poor, though they seem not to dare to consider that limits to growth rather than generosity are to blame for budget deficits. They are successfully calling for welfare state growth-with-trickle-down to be replaced by the laissez-faire variant. Those on the left of centre, who continue to advocate welfare state growth-with-trickle-down policies, are fighting a rearguard action. At best, they slow reductions in the standards of living of the poor. They will continue to be on the defensive until they recognize that sooner or later growth will cease, that the longer we wait to plan for this cessation the worse conditions will get, and that redistribution from the rich to the poor rather than trickle down is required if suffering for the poor is not to increase. In short, those on the left will be on the defensive and will be ineffective until they recognize the need for compassionate sustainable development.

Distribution Principles for Compassionate Sustainable Development

Resource Distribution Questions Pertaining to the Compassionate Sustainable Development of the Fraser Basin

If we accept the above argument for *compassionate* sustainable development, then questions such as the following come to mind regarding distribution of resources in and from the Fraser Basin:

Who owns the water, trees and other resources in the Fraser Basin? Who should have the right to use them and the products of their use? Who should have the right to manage them? What should be the principles guiding use and management rights in the Fraser Basin and its sub-basins? How can/should these principles be put into practice? Are per capita formulas for distributions of resources and government programs compassionate? Whose heads should be counted in applying per capita formulas?

How can the apparent conflict between local control and national/international responsibilities be resolved? Should California have a right to some of the water? Does sub-Saharan Africa have a right to some of the trees? Do the worldwide poor have prior rights to benefit from the resources? Do would-be immigrants have a right to come here? Do producers who reduce contributions to the greenhouse effect (e.g., vegetable growers) have a prior right over mills and thermal electric plants?

Particular questions such as the above can be generalized as follows:

- Who should control and benefit from resources?
- How should goods and services be exchanged?
- To what ends should collective action be directed?
- How should collective decisions be made?
- What should be our responsibility to each other?
- Who should have decision-making rights?
- What should be the relationship of social rewards to contributions?

The remainder of this chapter attempts to achieve the following:

(i) Show the increasing relevance of distribution questions for river basin planning as limits to growth are approached and resource allocation tradeoffs become increasingly difficult;

(ii) Identify the principles which have been invoked by academics, policy-makers and publics in our welfare state society to answer the seven general distribution questions listed above;

(iii) Show the inadequacy of those welfare state principles for compassionately guiding distribution at a time when world consumption needs to be reduced; and,

(iv) Suggest an alternative set of distribution principles which would lead us to compassionate sustainable development.

River Basin Resource Distribution: Trade Offs and Limits

Each type of region presents a unique set of choices and trade offs which have to be made in determining resource distributions. In distributing the resources of a region defined as a river basin, the determination of trade offs in water use and management rights is crucial.

Water allocations affect relationships among and within the forest industry, agriculture, fisheries, manufacturing, and settlements. For example, in southern Alberta, the tradeoffs have been determined to be essentially between irrigationists and others with water use intentions: fishers, recreationists, industries, municipalities, hydro-electricity generators (whose flow requirements differ from irrigationists) and upstream ranchers (whose land would be flooded to create reservoirs for irrigation waters). In northern Alberta, the trade off is seen not only as between pulp mills and fishers, but also as between old mills and newer, cleaner mills that would nevertheless add to pollution levels.

In the Fraser Basin, maintenance of the highly productive salmon fishery may have to be traded off against various fish-threatening activities such as: hydroelectric projects (the Kemano completion project); transportation systems (such as the twin-tracking of the Canadian National Railroad in the Fraser canyon); municipal water consumption and waste disposal; fertilizer-intensive farming; clear-cut logging; industries such as pulp mills and the proposed Hat Creek thermal coal project that use water in processes or for coolants; and, perhaps, would-be future exporters or inter-basin transferers of water from this third largest Canadian river basin (in terms of discharge). Within these competing interests there are second order trade offs (e.g., among competing fishing interests: upstream-downstream, commercial-sports, Native-non-Native).

The concept of trade off implies limits. Until limits to the total amount of activity rivers could support began to be approached, there was little thinking about trade offs among competing water uses and users. As the limits were approached, increasing attention was paid to finding win-win solutions to problems posed by competing demands and claims. Multi-objective river basin planning evolved. As development pressures have increased with economic growth, and the impacts of superficially win-win solutions been observed, awareness has grown that multi-objective planning does not obviate the need to make difficult allocation decisions (i.e., to make trade offs). This awareness of the limits to growth in water consumption—all forms of consumption—is necessary for non-growth oriented sustainable development planning to begin. For such planning to be compassionate as well, awareness of limits to growth must be supplemented with awareness of the inadequacies of trickle-down, particularly in non-growth times, as an approach to helping the poor.

To look at the Fraser Basin from a compassionate sustainable development perspective is to look through a lens that brings the resource allocation issues posed by limits into focus. What is seen through the lens is the need to come to terms with limits by reducing resource consumption proportionately to people's abilities to afford reductions. The sooner we begin to plan development from this perspective, the less painful will be the transition from a growth-based economy to one that is sustainable.

While determining tradeoffs among water users is central to the management of a river basin, such management must also address the distribution of many other resources (e.g., air pollution rights and timber access) as well as distribution of the wide range of goods and services produced by, or purchased with, these resources.

River basin resource distribution issues, then, are quite complex. They cut across various resources, sub-basins, economic sectors, and citizenship categories. Rather than attempting to discuss the relative desirabilities and possibilities of various mixes and distributions of Fraser Basin resource uses, or to propose solutions to the trade off problems presented by the growing competing demands for the finite resources of the Fraser Basin, the following sections of this paper discuss how use and user allocation issues associated with the natural wealth of the Basin ecosystem might be conceptualized and addressed as distribution issues in resource management planning.

Resource management issues have moral and strategic dimensions. Accordingly, before being addressed in their basin-specific particularities, they should be approached generically as societal distribution issues whose resolution depends on which fundamental principles are posited as morally and strategically most desirable. The welfare state rests on a certain set of principles; the exigencies and desiderata of compassionate sustainable development demand an alternative set.

Distribution Principles On Which Welfare States Operate

Welfare states such as Canada, and sub-states such as British Columbia, determine the allocation of rights to natural resources, such as Fraser Basin water and timber, on the basis of fundamental principles which are assumed to be widely held. Observation of resource allocation laws and practices suggests that depending on the times and resource, governments variously base their decisions on one or more of seven principles. The seven principles reflect, and can be named after, the following institutions or values: property, the market, public interest, political pluralism, altruism, citizenship, and individual achievement. Each principle incorporates a specific conception of distributional equity, or fairness, and holds specific implications for state operations. (Thurow, 1975, discusses a somewhat similar, but condensed set of principles.)

The Property (or first-come-first-served) Principle

Under the property principle, fair is keeping what you have. This principle is fundamental in determining the allocation of resources within Canada and between Canada and the rest of the world. More than any other principle, it structures our concept of equity and our distribution practices.

In aboriginal societies, property was and is conceived as a bundle of communal use rights and management responsibilities integrated with the kinship system (Hobhouse, 1915, 1922) (see also chapter by Kew and Griggs in this volume). In modern Europeanized Canada, property is conceived as private property, i.e., as a bundle of *exclusive* rights (e.g., to use, to restrict access, to buy and sell), and of responsibilities (e.g., to maintain safety, to limit pollution) that are assigned to the individual property holder (a person or a corporation) by the Canadian state in its federal and provincial forms. (MacPherson, 1978; Hulchanski, 1988). The state determines, according to evolving criteria, who has rights to what property (i.e., who legally, not necessarily actually, came first and what the rights and responsibilities are). The state adjudicates disputes over property and enforces its laws and decisions: it "protects property" (see chapter by Scott in this volume).

Examples of the property principle in operation include the identification in the treaties of Indian rights to wildlife, the allocation of homesteads to settlers, the payment of compensation to land owners when their property is expropriated, the institutionalization of precious metal mineral claims and staking, the recognition of wills of deceased persons, and the evolution of housing tenants' rights (i.e., property-renting rights in such areas as privacy, eviction notices, rent controls, etc.). In terms of water use, the property principle has underlain the acceptance of first-come-first-served water usage by farmers, factories, and municipalities, at least until the time the limit of water quantity/quality is reached, and often, as is shown by the case in Northern Alberta where proposed new pulp mills are being required to be cleaner than mills already in operation, *after* the time that water limits are reached.

Competing views on private property lie at the heart of modern ideological debates. Most fundamentally, the debates are over the morality, desirability and legitimacy of the institution. From the beginnings of the enlightenment, conservatives such as Edmund Burke have found it necessary to justify private property as the basis for social order and civilization; liberals, such as Locke, have argued that private property is the basis for individual freedom and progress. Anarchists and socialists have argued that private property is in Pierre Proudhon's (1840) pithy phrase, "theft", that its general and specific origins and continuance lie in the domination and exploitation of some by others.

Within the Canadian welfare state, debate for the most part focusses on less fundamental property issues: what specifically should be the individual property holder's rights vis-a-vis the rights of others. The property principle itself is not questioned. The institution of private property, the rights to keep what one already has and to do with one's property whatever one wants, are virtually sacred. The possibility of a wealth tax, for example, is not even considered in Canada; inheritance taxes have in fact been abolished. Provided they do not pollute other properties, farmers may do with their land as they wish. Homeowners may build houses as big and inefficient as they like. Laws against high-grading mineral resources are one of the few restrictions. Private property rights may, for reasons of strong collective need, be chipped away (e.g., through the establishment of B.C.'s agricultural land reserve) and individual properties may be expropriated (e.g., for powerlines or highways) with compensation. But the individual's right to maintain and accumulate unlimited property through luck, hard work or inheritance, and to unlimited benefits from property so long as the rights of others and the collective are not impaired, is entrenched in our culture and the law.

The property principle is applied equally to international and intra-national distribution. Canada's claims to its various territories having been established in international law and consciousness by virtue of exploration, settlement, exploitation, conquest, and inheritance from Great Britain, we are loath to consider any other claims to the fruits of this territory. We, it has been decided were here first (well, almost first) and we therefore have the right to all the benefits this land can provide.

Because it is so deeply embedded in our consciousness and legal systems, because it is continuously and actively reaffirmed by the powerful who derive their power from it, and because it rejects any distribution principle which threatens its supremacy, the property principle is the greatest barrier to compassionate sustainable development. It still seems, to use the words of Lewis H. Morgan (1877), the anthropologist who strongly influenced Frederick Engels (1884), "an unmanageable power."

The Capitalist Market Principle

Under the capitalist market principle, fair is having the opportunity to compete as buyer and seller in a free market, to make as much profit as your luck and skill permit in buying low and selling high, and being able to expect people to keep their end of a bargain. While the market principle is closely associated with the property principle in liberal societies, the two principles can be dissociated: conservative societies have supported property but not markets; postwar Yugoslavia has been an example of a society which supported markets but not private property.

The state operationalizes the market principle by enforcing contracts made in the market, by facilitating markets, and by auctioning off its properties, such as water, to the highest-bidder.

Only within the last few centuries have societies made the "great transformation" to a system that puts the market in a predominant position (Polanyi, 1944). In this period, application of the market principle has progressively expanded. User-pay concepts—use is offered at what ultimately has to be an attractive price to users—and polluter-pay concepts related to public facilities and public resources are based on market principles, as are concepts of transferable pollution rights and urban land development rights (see the chapter by Pearse and Tate in this volume). The auctioning of hydrocarbon mineral exploration rights is based on the market principle, in an interesting contrast to our approach to hardrock mining.

The Public Interest Principle

Under the public interest principle, which neoclassical economists call the "welfare principle", fair is what the state determines is in the people's *overall* interest. The state operationalizes this principle through technocratic determinations of greatest *aggregate* public good. It relies on such concepts and techniques as Pareto optimality and cost-benefit analysis (Mishan, 1975; Davis, 1990). The public interest principle is invoked, with various degrees of explicitness, in determining the desirability of proposed public works, such as reservoirs, and in the allocation of rights to resource use, such as forest-harvesting. Debates among those supporting the public interest principle focus on the adequacy of monetary units as the basis for measuring costs and benefits, the treatment of intangibles, bases for predicting outcomes and assessing risk, and the treatment of externalities. Internal distribution of benefits and costs is not considered in applying the public interest principle (hence, the evolution of social impact assessment over the last fifteen years).

The Pluralism Principle

Under the pluralism principle, fair is achieving the highest degree of satisfaction by all parties in the resolution of contending interests. The state operationalizes this concept through the formal political process (elections and parliamentary debate), the informal political process (lobbying, campaign contributions, protests, the media), and increasingly through the development of mandated negotiations and mediation approaches to conflict resolution (Dahl and Lindblom, 1953; Dahl, 1956, 1971; Lindblom, 1959, 1965, 1977). The most fundamental and general assumption underlying this principle is that society is a cauldron of competing interests (Lijphart, 1968; Goodwin, 1987). Politics thus becomes, as F.D. Roosevelt put it, "the science of the adjustment of conflicting group interests." (Nicholls, 1974).

As with other distribution principles, there are many bases for debate among supporters of the principle. Most basic is the debate between those favouring the formal political processes (most notably, the politicians themselves) and those favouring negotiated settlement outside the formal and informal political processes. Many planning theorists, including interest-based planners, resource negotiation specialists, mediation specialists, and public participationists, have advocated mandated negotiation, in the most general sense of the term, as the appropriate approach for allocating resources. Among those favouring mandated negotiation, one of the central debates is over the relative legitimacies of *vested* interests versus *public* interests. (This point is relevant to the chapter by Fox in this volume.) Another is over the appropriate relationship between elected politicians and participants in negotiation processes: Should politicians have the final say? Should they be part of the negotiations? Should their bureaucrats? Other questions arise over issues of defining interests, selecting representatives to negotiate, and structuring the negotiation processes.

The formal and informal political processes have of course been the ultimate basis for allocating resources throughout B.C.'s history. Interest in mandated negotiations is more recent. They have been experimented with in various public participation exercises (e.g., in the Nechako completion project in the 1980's and less formally in the Okanagan Basin planning exercise of the 1970's) and in some forest management planning, but always with elected representatives and their public servants regarding the negotiation product as one of many inputs to consider in decision-making.

The Altruism Principle

Under the altruism principle, fair is when each contributes according to ability and receives according to need. Fair is some people getting more than others because of physical, family responsibility, or other need. States ruled by communist parties have held the altruism principle ("the higher stage of communism") as an ideal, seeing it to be operationable fully only once great material prosperity has been achieved through application of the achievement principle (in the socialist or "lower stage" of communism). Still, such states have invoked this principle to effect in calling for sacrifice for the common good, a call which is particularly effective when altruism is strong during and immediately after a revolution. Recently, we have seen a rapid diminution in the respectability of altruism as a distribution principle in Communist countries, and to the delight of cynics, a resurgence of property and market principles.

Capitalist and emergent-feudal countries have operationalized the altruism concept through relief to the poor (the generosity of which has waxed and waned with society's wealth and mood), progressive income tax, "free" and "subsidized" provision of public services such as transit (which only the poorer use), and income maintenance programs. One of the periods in which the altruism principle was most intensely invoked was in the refinement of the welfare state in the two decades after World War II under banners of "cradle-to-grave security," "war on poverty," and "the just society".

Despite the redistributist ring to some of the welfare state slogans, and the potential of many welfare state programs (e.g., progressive income tax) to be redistributionist, application of the altruism principle in the welfare state has in fact turned out overall only to modify laissez-faire trickle-down approaches to distribution. The altruism principle has been applied in ways that ensure that the poor receive their "fair" (i.e., proportionately constant) share of growth. As growth comes to an end, application of the altruism principle in this trickle-down form creates increasing difficulties for the poor.

The Citizenship Principle

Under the citizenship principle, fair is individuals getting what they deserve on the basis of a status ascribed by the welfare state, usually at birth. Distribution according to status was characteristic of pre-industrial societies, but status was differentiated according to class as well as territorial dimensions: nobles had more rights than peasants. Within the modern welfare state, class is not a formal consideration in determining status. All citizens in certain categories (of age, residency, etc.) enjoy equal rights. They are entitled to equal amounts of prescribed benefits from the state (e.g., free, indeed compulsory, basic education), to equal participation in basic democratic processes, and to equal protection in legal and judicial procedures. Citizens are also required to provide equal service to the state when called upon to be soldiers or jurors.

Citizenship is exclusionary. The concept of citizenship is inextricably bound up with the concept of a sovereign territorial state which has absolute control over and right to resources within the territory, as well as absolute control over people within the territory. Citizens have designated rights within the state and to the resources. Only citizens have rights to participate in the decision-making of the state, including decision-making that could affect outsiders. Non-citizens are seen as having no fundamental right of access to resources lying within the territory of the state.

The Individual Achievement Principle

Under the individual achievement principle, fair is individuals getting rewarded for what they have achieved through talent, aggression, or effort in production competitions. Distribution according to achievement runs through all societies: hunters have been rewarded with special cuts of meat, warriors with lands, clever bargainers with profits, hard workers with extra pay.

Along with the property, market, public interest, pluralist, altruism and citizenship principles, our welfare state accepts the achievement principle as a basis for distributing natural resources and their products. Differentials in wealth created by differential achievement within the rules enforced by the state are not only accepted but encouraged in the interest of productivity and growth.

In liberal laissez-faire systems, the citizenship and achievement principles combine to yield the "equality of opportunity" concept: ostensibly provided as a birthright with the necessities and freedom to competitively achieve, we are encouraged to pursue any opportunities opened up by our wits and good luck. In the welfare state, the equality of opportunity concept is modified by applications of the altruism principle. People with politically recognized handicaps are given a "head start" in the competitive market. If they achieve, they are rewarded; if they pull out ahead of others, they are rewarded even more.

In both liberal and welfare state systems, the conservative view of achievement as reflecting intrinsic merit continues. Even though the concept of merit does not fit well with the equality of opportunity concept or the notion that people with handicaps should be assisted to get a head start, individual achievement based on merit is generously rewarded in welfare states—primarily, through subsidized career-oriented education.

The Welfare State Distribution Principles Synthesized

In recent decades, there has been a world-wide convergence of societies toward a common mix of the welfare state distribution principles identified above. The welfare state institutional form crosses hitherto boundaries between socialism and capitalism. The welfare state assumes there are no limits to economic growth and blends property, market, public interest, pluralist, altruism, citizenship and achievement principles in ways that reinforce each other in supporting tickle-down approaches to distribution of resources, social products and personal income.

Private property is protected by the state with no limits on the amount individuals can hold or profit from. The market not only allocates wealth but becomes the chief mechanism for accumulating private property. The public interest is served by providing infrastructure and stimulating growth. Pluralism primarily involves competition over self-interests. Altruism is restricted to slowing the worsening conditions of the poor; it is not directed to redistribution. Citizenship is carefully guarded: the state dedicates ever increasing energies to maximizing benefits from its territorial resources for its citizens, and to minimizing access to citizenship by economic refugees from poorer countries. Achievement is defined as success in the market. It is seen as reflecting individual talent and as deserving of individual rewards; it is encouraged in the interest of growth.

Inadequacies of Welfare-State Distribution Principles for Achieving Compassionate Sustainable Development

The welfare state distribution principles exacerbate the decline in the standard of living being experienced by most people. Their applications at a time when limits to growth are being approached contribute neither to sustainability nor to equality.

The Property Principle

With the end of the frontier, property as a distribution principle no longer serves to enable the majority to better themselves. Compared to the past, including the very recent past, the absolute quantity of potential real property is now fixed. There are virtually no unused lands to farm, oil reserves to discover, forests to cut, or rivers from which to irrigate. Indeed, erosion, mismanagement, depletion, and overcutting are reducing the resource stocks. Those who own a lot already have an increasing edge over those who own only a little. This growing disparity is exacerbated by economic policies which increasingly favour property-holders (high interest rate policies) over income-earners who are attempting to become property holders. The property principle thus produces a system of positive feedback loops which creates an anxiety among more and more people to produce more in order to acquire more in order to stay ahead of the game. Garrett Hardin's argument (1968) that recognition of private and national property rights permits resource husbandry and avoidance of the "tragedy of the commons" does not apply in the context of a market. In that context, the property principle fosters growth rather than sustainable development.

The property principle serves to maintain inequality in all its aspects: inequality of opportunity, of social benefits, and of condition. Even when economies are growing and wealth is trickling down, ownership confers competitive advantages to owners. Wealth begets wealth; those who have, get. As economies approach the limits to growth, the advantages to owning property become even more invidious. The property principle is thus not an appropriate basis for determining allocations of the waters or other resources of the Fraser Basin, or the products derived from these resources, if either sustainable development or compassion is our goal.

The first-come-first-served principle has been the law of the river, but gradually awareness of the inequities from a public-good or a relative-need perspective have led to a diminishment of acceptance by policy-makers and publics of this principle in determining use rights. Claims to pollution rights based on original occupancy are becoming less acceptable, as current debates about pulp mills show clearly. Still, the property principle is fundamentally respected. Welfare states accept it as a given.

The Market Principle

The market principle similarly works to foster growth and inequality for reasons that are accepted by both market apologists and critics. The requirements for successful competition are capital investment to increase efficiency, expansion to derive economies of scale, and encouragement of consumption. By definition, in every competition some win, some lose. This spurs everyone to compete harder and produce more. Sustainable development requires us to reduce consumption; compassionate sustainable development requires mitigation of the market as a distribution principle.

The Public Interest Principle

Welfare state operationalizations of the public interest principle assume that growth is good; growth (i.e., increased throughput) is always considered as a benefit in public policy analysis. Public interest accounting currently also works against sustainable development by discounting the future, and works against *compassionate* sustainable development by disregarding distributional issues.

The Pluralism Principle

Pluralism, in the context of a society which also favours property, the market, and growth-oriented non-distributive conceptions of the public interest, leads to asymmetrical power struggles over how to slice the pie and to deceptive win-win solutions based on assumptions that the pie will continue to grow. Hence, we settle on measures which lead to resource depletion, monetary inflation, and the debt crisis: what appears to have been win-win turns out to be lose-lose for all but the very rich.

The Altruism Principle

The altruism principle, when applied in a redistributionist sense, does contribute to sustainability and justice. It encourages pluralist negotiations to focus on how to share smaller pies while relieving both poverty and the very understandable anxiety of the poor that the end of growth will mean their personal ends. The altruism principle leads the richer to accept the reality that significant sacrifice is necessary and desirable. In the context of the modern welfare state, however, altruism, as has been noted, takes a trickle-down form. It is seen as a principle that ensures the poor maintain their smaller share.

In the welfare state, redistributive altruism is seen as made unnecessary by growth. Altruism has waxed and waned in sympathy with economic growth cycles, rather than counter-cyclically as required. Higher taxes are imposed "when we can afford them" rather than when poverty demands them.

The Citizenship Principle

The citizenship principle (which welfare state policy analysts chauvinistically term the "universality" principle) has been applied primarily to legitimize distributions of new-found wealth, or expected wealth (i.e., the proceeds of growth, among all citizens of a welfare state). When, in recent years, states have found it necessary to cut back on their services and income security programs, or to increase taxes, user fees, or interest rates, the citizenship principle has been seen as requiring that the cutbacks or cost increases be proportionately distributed. Proportionate distributions of decline impact the poor harder than the rich which in turn adds to the pressure to attempt to maintain growth (i.e., in reality, to defer and increase the magnitude of the inevitable cut-backs). The poor press for growth in order to save their standard of living, the rich press for growth to buy off the poor.

Because of the relatively greater impacts on the poor, a social consensus to cut back is much harder to achieve than a consensus to grow at equal rates. The objections of the poor to cut-backs in social welfare are not only based on the relatively greater hardship to them but also on the fact that, because of the property and market principles, net (of taxes) social welfare benefits from the state are a major part of poor people's incomes but less significant to the rich who benefit more from property and profit-based incomes. The solution to the needs and objections of the poor is to cut the rich back at a faster rate (e.g., through very progressive taxation rates on incomes and property, a solution which the rich are usually very successful in fighting). The rich have in the past successfully appealed to property, market, and even public interest and pluralism principles. Now, they also appeal to altruism principles ("we shouldn't need to cut back, we should make the economy grow so we can give more") and citizenship principles ("if we really do have to cut back, we should all be cut back by the same amount, and only in terms of welfare and taxation flows from and to the state, not in terms of wealth stocks and the many non-taxed profit-making opportunities").

The Achievement Principle

Application of the welfare state achievement principle strongly encourages those who live by profit or wages (i.e., most of us) to contribute to growth through production. Application of the principle also exacerbates inequality because of differences in opportunity, starting resources, and innate ability. The rich get richer and the poor get poorer. The world-wide convergence toward a materialist culture emphasises achievement in terms of making money and buying things within it. Achievement becomes identified with high levels of consumption. Achievement in terms of making things and selling things is emphasized, not in terms of such alternative goals as friendliness, gardening ability, or musicality, unless these have market values which can be translated into more resource throughput in terms of travel, fertilizer, recordings, etc., at the production end, or bigger homes, cars and vacations for the rewarded producers at the consumption end.

Inadequacies of Welfare State Distribution Principles: Summary

In sum, the property, public interest, pluralism, altruism, citizenship, and merit principles which guide distribution in the welfare state encourage growth rather than sustainability and disparity rather than compassion. In essence, the welfare state maintains current distributions of wealth while promoting growth.

Compassionate Sustainable Development Distribution Principles as Alternatives to Welfare State Distribution Principles

For compassionate sustainable development to be achieved, the seven principles which guide distribution of resources in our current unequal growth-oriented welfare states need to be replaced with principles directed to reductions rather than increases in overall resource consumption and to compassion and equality in distributing the fruits of resource use. Such normative principles would address the same distribution questions as the seven normative welfare-state principles:

Who should control and benefit from resources? How should goods and services be exchanged? To what ends should collective action be directed? How should collective decisions be made? What should be our responsibility to each other? Who should have decision-making rights? What should be the relationship of social rewards to contributions?

The Stewardship Principle

The property principle should be converted to a *stewardship* principal. Instead of the state granting individuals rights to exclusive possession, unlimited accumulation, and commodification of resources, society at various levels should grant social subsystems use rights to a place in exchange for a commitment to the sustainable development of that place. Existing users of resources should have a first claim to continued usage, but not the sole claim. Their management claim should be judged not only on the basis of their being first in line but also on the basis of their commitment to sustainable development and to distribution of surpluses as indicated by their track records and their intentions. The possibilities for operationalizing the stewardship principle are indicated in the United States by the growing interest in community land trusts (ICE, 1982, 1990; Swann, 1989), and along the West coast of North America by the growing interest in fisheries "co-management" (Pinkerton, 1989; Dale in this volume.) Under co-management arrangements, communities are granted partial management and harvesting rights over the territory they use, but the state retains ultimate control to ensure sustainable management and fair distribution. Various experiments in co-management are planned or underway along the B.C. coast and in the Skeena basin. Indian communities, because of their historical claim to the fisheries, play a central role in all cases. In the Fraser Basin, the Shuswap Nation has taken a leadership role in protecting fish habitat in its territory (Gordon, 1990).

The granting of tree-farm licences to communities can also be seen as a form of co-management. An example of such co-management is provided by the Stuart-Trembleur Band, in the northern reaches of the Fraser Basin, which has successfully operated a treefarm under licence from the B.C. government.

To achieve compassionate sustainable development, the stewardship principle needs to be extended beyond its application to state-community co-management experiments. Co-management relationships between states and international organizations are required; states must be willing to give up some of their sovereignty. At the other end of the spectrum, co-management relationships between communities and individual members are required; individuals must permit some community control over the way resources are used and distributed (see the chapter by Gardner in this volume). The cause of compassionate sustainable development would be greatly advanced if Canadians learned from First Nations experiences in institutionalizing cooperative relationships in resource management at the community level. The Gitksan Wet'suwet'en in the Skeena Basin are particularly active in redeveloping their house and clan system and applying it to the stewardship of their territory (Gitksan-Wet'suwet'en, 1989; see also Kew and Griggs, this volume.)

The Social Exchange Principle

The capitalist market principle must be replaced with a *social exchange* principle in which efficient and mutually beneficial distribution, freedom of choice, and socially responsible entrepreneurship would replace profit maximization and accumulation as the primary motivations.

Local Exchange Trading Systems (LETS), which are multilateral bartering systems successfully operating in several B.C. towns, are examples of institutions which operate on exchange principles without focussing on profit (Ross and Usher, 1986; Davis and Davis, 1987). They serve to distribute surpluses and recycle no-longer needed goods. Because they operate within communities, fair rather than maximum prices are sought by sellers. A drive for growth in personal wealth is not a motivating force in these these markets. LETS facilitate local trade and reduce community dependence on international markets and national monetary policies.

There are many other examples of social exchange to show that capitalist markets are not essential to healthy economies, even though they have come to dominate most societies. Most families divide labour and exchange services without any quantification of the worth of their services. Their scarce resources of space and family time are allocated without the need for market pricing. Scholars freely collaborate on books and exchange ideas, only rarely feeling their ideas have been stolen in the process. Volunteers in social agencies, churches, and chambers of commerce, distribute and carry out tasks without financial reward. They also allocate scarce goods, be they Christmas hampers or meeting hall space without taking bids from recipients or users. Even nations sometimes exchange services without resorting to market pricing (e.g., they participate in joint projects ranging from space programs to the Great Lakes cleanup). To the degree there is a feeling of community, people avoid, and do not need, the cash nexus. To the degree we build that feeling, we create the possibility of compassionate sustainable development.

The Basic Needs Principle

The public interest principle, which involves the computation of benefits and costs as aggregates of individual interests without regard to distribution, should be replaced by a *basic needs* principle that holds some needs to be more important than others and, therefore, that benefits for some (the poor) are of higher priority and costs for some (the poor) of greater significance. In its broadest form, the basic needs principle says simply: look after the poor first. It rejects the notion that overall economic efficiency need be the only social goal and that benefits inevitably trickle down from the rich to the poor. The basic needs principle should be applied to the assessment of international as well as intranational distribution of benefits and costs, and to intergenerational as well as intragenerational distributions. The perspectives of ecologists, as well as economists and social scientists, are required to apply the basic needs principle in policy analysis and impact assessment.

International development assistance approaches based on the basic needs principle arose in the mid 1970's as it became increasingly apparent that growth-promotion trickle-down strategies were failing to alleviate poverty. The basic needs principle has been established in many international development programs. For example, it underlies the current policy of the Canadian International Development Agency.

To achieve compassionate sustainable development, Canadians now need to domesticate the basic needs principle and apply it in all planning and policy areas: urban design, housing, energy strategies, agriculture, forestry, fisheries, etc. Just as environmental impact assessment has become an accepted component of project planning, and most recently even of policy making, the basic needs principle can be integrated into decision-making from the regulatory to the policy-making levels.

The Consensus-Seeking Principle

The pluralism principle, which promotes competition among contending interests on the assumption that such competition produces fair and sound political decisions, should be replaced by a *consensus-seeking* principle that promotes exchanges of views on how to develop compassionately and sustainably (see Dale, this volume). Pluralist ideology assumes all interests are equal in value, whether these be narrow self-interests or broad collective interests. Doctors lobbying for higher fees are the same as environmentalists arguing for reduced CO_2 emissions. Bargaining over whose private property or income interests should have priority is the same as debate over effective strategies to reduce regional disparity.

Consensus-seeking begins when people see they have a common problem to address and thus a collective interest in finding win-win solutions. Political struggles to wrest the most from decision-makers are converted into processes to find fair solutions to resource allocation problems. Debates over public strategies are changed from attempts to prove intellectual superiority to processes involving mutual learning.

The desire to see consensus-seeking as a replacement for competitive pluralism is found in the recent widespread rejection of Roberts' Rules of Order, in the rejection of mob-inducing public meetings as approaches to public involvement in planning and their replacement by deliberative task forces such as the Environment and Economy Round Tables, and in the growing interest in negotiation techniques oriented to finding mutually satisfactory solutions.

To serve the goal of compassionate sustainable development, consensus-seeking planning, policy-making and negotiation processes must empower those "interests" that are unable to compete effectively in our pluralist society. Such empowerment is not a matter of creating a "level playing field," or even indeed of "giving an edge" to the poor, the small communities, the environmentalists, and others who have been "disadvantaged interests". Empowerment is a matter of creating processes to enable all people affected by the outcomes, including people hitherto regarded as foreigners who have no standing, to be respected partners in problem-solving. The Yukon 2000 process, which involved wide participation in that territory's economic planning, is an example of the consensus-seeking process innovations which are possible if there is a commitment to developing them (Boothroyd, 1988).

For the foreseeable future, the most important problems to be solved will be the need to find ways to reduce disparity, destruction and desires for high levels of consumption and personal power. Consensus-seeking processes will need to be seen as ongoing experiments in social learning about living decently within our planetary means. Compassionate sustainable development pluralist processes will have to be open to all parties, including parties with resource claims (based on new conceptions of property, achievement, altruism, status and the public interest) who hitherto have been excluded as foreigners.

The Shared Responsibility Principle

The altruism principle, which stems from people's feelings of guilt about their relative prosperity, should be replaced by a *shared responsibility* principle that is based on a recognition that with more of us "sharing smaller pies" for a long time, we must equalize the slices. We need to restructure our current production and distribution systems that are so wasteful of both human talent and natural resources into systems that are fair in terms of using people's energies and distributing the fruits of those energies. "From each according to his or her ability, to each according to his or her need" may seem like a quaint, hopelessly utopian, slogan by liberals and socialists alike, but it in fact expresses the quintessence of the compassionate sustainable development ideal. Its limitation is that it does not identify the mechanisms by which people offer their labour or receive products. In a society committed to compassionate sustainable development, such mechanisms must be developed.

Altruism within a competitive liberal system or within a fair-wage socialist system produces neither effective compassion nor sustainability because both liberalism and socialism are structured to provide incentives to individuals to contribute to growth by establishing differentials between those who so contribute and those who do not. Rather than the altruistic food banks of liberal systems, or the altruistic income-maintenance of welfare states, or the altruistic full-employment commitments of centralized socialist states, we need stable, productive, supportive, democratically controlled enterprises in which people can earn a decent living by contributing the full range of their talents and energies. Actual Canadian examples of such enterprises are described by Coady (1939), MacLeod (1986), and Melnyk (1985), among others.

The CRS workers' cooperative in Vancouver, which operates a bakery and food wholesale operation, provides an example of an enterprise based on the shared responsibility principle. The some four dozen worker-members are remunerated not only according to hours contributed but also to numbers of dependents they must support.

Indian communities in the Fraser Basin provide many examples of the shared responsibility principle at work. The ethic of "caring and sharing" still permeates many of the communities. It not only underlies the organization of hunts and fishing trips and the distribution of the catch, but also modern housebuilding, forestry, farming and other types of enterprises. The Li'l Wat Nation at Mount Curry has organized its child welfare system on the basis of traditional joint responsibility principles.

The Human Rights Principle

The citizenship principle, which restricts claims on distribution to those holding territorially defined membership status, should be replaced by a *human rights* principle that identifies all people as holding a basic set of rights. Over time it has been increasingly accepted that basic human rights should be seen as independent of the decisions of particular states. This acceptance is encoded in the United Nations declaration of Human Rights (1948) and operationalized by the work of various international agencies and non-governmental organizations such as Amnesty International.

Widely recognized political rights include rights to protection by the state (e.g., against slavery) and from the state (the liberal freedoms of speech, etc.), and rights to participation in the state (the democratic rights) (MacPherson, 1987). Recognized economic rights include rights to make a living and to have basic needs met (such as food and shelter).

Compassionate sustainable development will depend on the continuing recognition of political rights. People must have the right to participate at various levels in consensus-seeking processes, and to enjoy protection from coercion and threats as they do so. States which organize their decision-making around consensus-seeking processes will, like loving communities (Peck, 1987), respect different views and encourage their expression. Until that distant time when the whole world is on a compassionate sustainable development path, Amnesty International and other organizations will have to be very active in monitoring the treatment of citizens by their states. Compassionate sustainable development of and through the Fraser Basin, then, depends on flourishing local chapters of Amnesty International, Oxfam, the B.C. Civil Liberties Association, the Centre for Investigative Journalism and other organizations dedicated to preserving and extending political rights.

Compassionate sustainable development also depends on the recognition of economic rights. While political rights are widely respected and at least some of the implications generally understood in Canada, this is not true for economic rights (Echenberg and Porter, 1989). If economic security is to be a fact for all people in B.C. and in the rest of the world, then the resources of the Fraser Basin and other regions must be seen as belonging to all humans, not just those who have a claim to them by virtue of local, provincial or national citizenship. Urban land in the City of Vancouver is not just a resource for residents of the city; provincial coffers should not have sole claim to royalties on minerals found in B.C.; Canadians should not have sole jurisdiction over the resources found within Canada's borders.

Ways have to be found to balance the various human rights claims of peoples throughout the world to resources inside the borders of particular states. For there to be compassionate sustainable development, communities and states will have to accept requirements to share the resources over which they exercise stewardship. People living in rich areas such as the Fraser Basin will have to recognize that they have a collective obligation to cut back on resource consumption and to open up decision-making to outsiders for whom our resource use poses an opportunity cost.

Municipalities in the Regional District of Greater Vancouver, for example, could be mandated to provide for a certain portion of the region's population growth; internally, in the larger municipalities, neighbourhoods could be assigned population quotas. A portion of the Fraser Basin trees, fish, minerals and water could be designated to benefit the neediest people not living here—not necessarily people in California. The size of the portion could come through decision-making involving all accepted "stakeholders", the number and location of which being broader than we presently concede. Initially, the portion might be very small, but even a very small portion would be symbolically important in showing a commitment to converting the citizenship principle of distribution into a human rights principle.

The Management Rights Principle

The individual achievement principle, which assumes people should be rewarded by society for their distinction in intellectual, political or economic competitions, usually through increases in their consumption power, should be changed to a *management rights* principle that recognizes collective achievement in restructuring society to be more compassionate and sustainable. Under a management rights principle, rewards would not be in the form of increased consumption but in the form of increased management rights and political autonomy. For example, a community that minimized entropy and disparity, while maintaining human rights, within its borders, and contributed to world-wide compassionate sustainable development in proportion to its resources, would be granted more autonomy to make decisions within its own consensus-seeking processes and would be less constrained by regional co-management processes than a community which had not yet proceeded very far along the path to compassionate sustainable development. Similarly, the more a region developed itself to be compassionate and sustainable, the more it would be granted autonomy by the state; likewise for the state vis-a-vis international bodies.

At the level of the individual person, more resource management rights would be extended by the community to those who recycle, garden, tap solar energy, volunteer, share, organize, etc., than those who do not.

The granting of management rights throughout the various social systems levels would involve less political totalitarianism than present systems of social controls and rewards. Under the present system, the centralized state not only retains all ultimate power but uses that power to intervene directly in a vast range of local affairs. It settles domestic disputes, determines fishing regulations, and establishes rules for receiving public assistance (Boothroyd, 1990a).

Compassionate Sustainable Development Principles: Summary

In sum, compassionate sustainable development principles of distribution would replace the welfare-state principles by incorporating values of long-term commitment, compassion, and system awareness. Most specifically, a sustainable development principle would separate consumption rights from management rights. Consumption rights would be allocated on the basis of need, management rights on the ability to manage in the interests of sustainable development. Resource management would be seen as a production function, managers would be seen as producers. The answer to the question "what is fair?" would be seen as this: fair for managers is being encouraged to work toward compassionate sustainable development; fair for consumers is being recognized as having rights to resources by virtue of world citizenship.

The specific differences between welfare state and compassionate sustainable development principles are summarized in the Table 19.12.

Applications of Compassionate Sustainable Development Principles to the Fraser Basin

How could the set of compassionate sustainable development distribution principles be operationalized in the Fraser Basin?

New forums and processes would have to be created to enable consensus-seeking to work effectively (Boothroyd and Eberle, 1990). An extension of the Fraser River Estuary Management Program, for example, might serve the whole Basin. This forum would continuously determine the public interest with the aid of appropriate scientific expertise. On the basis of newly conceptualized human rights, management rights, shared responsibility, and stewardship principles, forum membership could be extended to representatives of contributing and needy peoples outside the basin (e.g., through western U.S.A. agencies, Organization of American States, United Nations, international non-governmental organizations).

Stewardship rights of communities in the Basin would be recognized so long as they acted within the compassionate sustainable development principles which were itemized above and which would be interpreted by the Fraser Basin Forum. These stewardship rights would include aboriginal community rights to land, water, fish, wildlife, forests and minerals currently being negotiated as "land claims".

Table 19.12: Summary: Welfare State Principles and their Compassionate
Sustainable Development Alternatives

Distribution Question: *What should be the basis for*	Welfare State Principle	Compassionate Sustainable Development Principle
Controlling and benefiting from resources?	Property (ownership)	Stewardship (by locals with outsiders) and Security of Tenure
Exchanging goods/sevices?	Capitalist Market (profit maximization)	Social Exchange (non-profit oriented)
Taking collective action?	Public Interest (as aggregate of individual interests)	(meeting) Basic Needs
Making collective decisions?	Pluralism (of competing unequal self-interests)	Consensus-seeking
Helping each other?	Altruism (rich giving some to poor)	Shared Responsibility (aiming for equality)
Claiming resources and decision-making role	Citizenship (as exclusively defined by state)	(universal) Human Rights
Recognizing achievement	(tangible rewards for) Individual Achievement	Management Rights (for collective responsibility)

Communities would be supported in their own local-knowledge-based planning
oriented to compassionate sustainable development.

Social exchange on the LETS model could form the basis of resource allocation
and product distributions within, and possibly among, communities of the Basin.
Values and prices within the LETS model could be determined not only by supply
and demand variables but also by considerations of the shared responsibility and
management rights principles. For instance, the presently poorest could be given
extra credits, low-entropy-producing activities such as canoeing could be costed
lower than high-entropy-producing activities such as reservoir construction.

By moving toward such new institutions and processes, or even by facilitating
their public consideration in the light of new distribution principles which
recognize rights to Fraser Basin resources by future generations around the world,
British Columbia and Canada could show leadership in responding to the
sustainable development imperative.

Conclusion

Assuming there is a limit to the material throughput human beings can create and
benefit from (i.e., assuming the total annual worldwide material consumption pie

will have to be stabilized if not indeed shrunk, and that therefore for many decades the per capita slice will be thinner), then the question of distribution cannot be answered by the comforting thought that a rising tide floats all ships. The compassionate sustainable development challenge has to be addressed by putting an emphasis on finding ways to redistribute and use wealth efficiently, not on finding ways to create more.

If we are to plan with regard for limits of resources such as Fraser Basin water (i.e., plan for sustainable development) and if we are to plan compassionately, then we must plan the distribution of resources. Modern societies have planned distribution, regardless of ideology, along the left-right scale, on the assumption that we could generate ever more wealth. It is true that within this country, we have indeed been able to increase the wellbeing of most citizens without requiring a redistribution of wealth. The rich in this country have never had to reduce their standard of living in order to support the standard of living of others.

If however, as this paper assumes, the pie stops growing, or indeed starts shrinking, as already is happening in many countries, and worse still if the pie has to be shrunk even faster today to preserve something for tomorrow (a process totally contrary to the accumulation-investment-growth ethic which has been fundamental to modern economies) then distribution questions will centre not on how to distribute new surpluses but on how to distribute reductions in wealth. There are many possibilities for distributing reductions, for example, redistributing wealth from the rich and/or the middle class to the poor in order to prevent extreme hardship for the latter, enabling the middle class to hold its own by reducing direct and indirect benefits to the poor and/or heavily taxing the rich, requiring the poor to take the brunt of the reductions, accepting that the rich will gain at the expense of all others, and so on.

To refer again to the Ehrlich-Simon bet, I would say that a good bet for the 1990's is that regardless of whether real commodity prices rise or fall, poverty and inequality will increase because growth-with-trickle-down policies, most likely of the Thatcherite rather than welfare-state genus, will persist despite increasingly immediate resource constraints. Depending on central government economic policies, rising poverty and inequality will be reflected in rising unemployment, or inflation, or both.

I would also bet that in response to policies that exacerbate economic instability and inequity, there will be growing local interest and experimentation in the buffering and stabilizing of sustainable, less-consuming community and regional economies and in the evolution of institutions that reflect the compassionate distribution principles discussed in this paper (Boothroyd, 1990a). In other words, I would bet that effective compassionate sustainable development will continue to be a bottom-up process.

References

Arnopoulos, P. 1976. "Political Aspects of the Conserver Society." in *GAMMA*, 1976, Vol. 3, Study No. 11.

Boothroyd, P. 1990a. "Community Development: The Missing Link in Welfare Policy." in Kirwin, W. (ed.). *Ideology, Development and Social Welfare: Canadian Perspectives.* Toronto: Canadian Scholars Press.

Boothroyd, P. 1990b. "On Using Environmental Assessment to Promote Fair Sustainable Development." in Jacobs, P. and B. Sadler (eds.). *Sustainable Development and Environmental Assessment: Perspectives on Planning for a Common Future.* Ottawa: Canadian Environmental Assessment Research Council.

Boothroyd, P., and M. Eberle. 1990. *Healthy Communities: What They Are, How They're Made.* Vancouver: University of British Columbia, Centre for Human Settlements.

Boothroyd, P. 1988. "The Yukon 2000 Project: A Study in Democratic Planning." *Northern Perspectives* 16(2):19-22.

British Columbia Round Table on the Environment and the Economy. (B.C.) 1990. *A Better Way: Creating a Sustainable Development Strategy for British Columbia.* Victoria.

Brown, L. 1981. *Building a Sustainable Society.* New York: Norton.

Canada. 1971. *Poverty in Canada: Report of the Special Senate Committee on Poverty.* Ottawa

Canadian International Development Agency (CIDA). 1987. *Sharing Our Future.* Ottawa.

Chodak, S. 1976. "Property-Rights and Income Distribution in a Conserver Society." in *GAMMA*, 1976, Study No. 8.

Coady, M. M. 1939. *Masters of Their Own Destiny.* New York: Harper & Row.

Dahl, R. A. 1956. *A Preface to Democratic Theory.* Chicago: Chicago University Press.

_____ 1971. *Democracy in the United States: Promise and Performance.* (3rd ed.) Chicago: Rand McNally.

Dahl, R. A. and C. E. Lindblom. 1953. *Politics, Economics and Welfare: Planning and Politico-Economic Systems Resolved into Basic Processes.* New York: Harper and Brothers.

Daly, H. E. 1971. "The Stationary-State Economy: Toward a Political Economy of Biophysical Equilibrum and Moral Growth." University of Alabama *Distinguished Lecture Series* No. 2. (reprinted in Daly, 1973).

Daly, H. E. (ed.). 1973. *Toward a Steady-State Economy.* San Francisco: W.H. Freeman and Co.

Davis, H. C., and Davis, L. E. 1987. "The Local Exchange Trading System: Community Wealth-Creation within the Informal Economy." *Plan Canada.* 27(9):238-45.

Davis, H. C. 1990. *Regional Economic Impact Analysis and Project Evaluation.* Vancouver: University of British Coloumbia Press.

Echenberg, H., and B. Porter. 1989. "The Case for Social and Economic Rights." *Canadian Housing.* 6(1):26-29.

Engels, F. 1884. *The Origin of the Family, Private Property, and the State.* New York: International Publishers (1942).

Friedmann, J. and C. Weaver. 1979. *Territory and Function: The Evolution of Regional Planning.* Los Angeles: University of California Press.

Georgescu-Roegen, N. 1971. "The Entropy Law and the Economic Problem." University of Alabama *Distinguished Lecture Series* No. 1. (reprinted in Daly, 1973).

Gitksan-Wet'suwet'en (Office of the Hereditary Chiefs of). 1989. *Vision Statement.* Gitanmaax, Gitksan Territory.

Goodwin, B. 1987. *Using Political Ideas.* (2nd ed.) New York: John Wiley & Sons.

Gordon, C. 1990. *Telling Our Stories/Assessing the Future: A Report on the B.C. Healthy Communities Network Meeting and the Healthy Communities' Showcase.* Vancouver: B.C. Healthy Communities Network Steering Committee.

Group associe Montreal-McGill pour l'etude de l'avenir (GAMMA). 1976. *Conserver Society Project Report on Phase II.* Montreal: GAMMA, Universite de Montreal, McGill University.

Hardin, G. 1968. "The Tragedy of the Commons." *Science.* 162:1243-48

_____ 1977. *The Limits of Altruism: An Ecologist's View of Surival*. Bloomington: Indiana University Press.

_____ 1980. *Promethean Ethics: Living with Death, Competition and Triage*. Seattle: University of Washington Press.

Hobhouse, L. T. 1915. "The Historical Evolution of Property in Fact and in Idea." in (no ed.) 1915. *Property: Its Duties and Rights*. London: MacMillan.

_____ 1922. *The Elements of Social Justice*.

Hulchanski, D. 1988. "The Evolution of Property Rights and Housing Tenure in Postwar Canada: Implications for Housing Policy." *Urban Law and Policy*. 9(2):135-156.

Institute for Community Economics, Inc. (ICE) 1982. *The Community Land Trust Handbook*. Emmaus, Pennsylvania: Rodale Press.

_____ 1990. *Community Economics*. No. 21. Springfield, Maine.

International Bank for Reconstruction and Development/The World Bank (IBRD). 1990. *World Development Report*. New York: Oxford University Press

International Labour Office (ILO). 1976. *Employment, Growth, and Basic Needs*. Geneva.

Lindblom, C. E. 1959. "The Science of Muddling Through." *Public Administration Review*. 19(2):79-99.

_____ 1965. *The Intelligence of Democracy*. New York: Free Press.

_____ 1977. *Politics and Markets: The world's political-economic systems*. New York: Basic Books.

Lijphart, A. 1968. *The Politics of Accommodation: Pluralism and Democracy in the Netherlands*. Berkeley, Ca.: University of California Press.

Lo, Fu-chen, and K. Salih. 1981. "Growth Poles, Agropolitan Development, and Polarization Reversal: The Debate and Search for Alternatives." in Stohr, and Taylor, 1981.

MacDonald, M. 1985. "Capital and Wealth." *The Canadian Encyclopedia*. Edmonton: Hurtig. 286-7.

MacLeod, G. 1986. *New Age Business Corporations that Work*. Ottawa: Canadian Council on Social Development.

MacPherson, C. B. 1978. *Property: Mainstream and Critical Positions*. Toronto: University of Toronto Press.

_____ 1987. *The Rise and Fall of Economic Justice and Other Essays*. Toronto: Oxford University Press.

Meadows, D. H. et al. 1972. *The Limits to Growth: A Report for the Club of Rome's Project on the Predicament of Mankind*. New York: Universe Books.

Melnyk, G. 1985. *The Search for Community: From Utopia to a Co-operative Society*. Montreal: Black Rose Books.

Mishan, E. J. 1975. *Cost Benefit Analysis*. (2nd ed.). London: George Allen & Unwin.

Morgan, L. H. 1877. *Ancient Society, or Researches in the Lines of Human Progress from Savagery, through Barbarism to Civilization*. London: MacMillan & Co.

Myers, G. 1914. *A History of Canadian Wealth*. (Republished, 1972). Toronto: James Lewis and Samuel).

National Council of Welfare (NCW). 1976. *The Hidden Welfare System: A Report by the National Council of Welfare on the Personal Income Tax System*. Ottawa.

Nicholls, D. 1974. *Three Varieties of Pluralism*. New York: St. Martin's Press.

Oshima, H. T., and T. Mizoguchi. (eds.). 1977. *Income Distribution by Sectors and Over Time in East and South Asian Countries*. Tokyo: Council for Asian Manpower Studies.

Peck, M. S. 1987. *The Different Drum*. New York: Simon & Schuster

Phillips, A. W. 1958. "The Relation Betwen Unemployment and the Rate of Change of Money Wage Rates in the United Kingdom, 1861-19 7." *Economica*. 25(100). (Nov. 1958).

Pinkerton, E. (ed.). 1989. *Co-operative Management of Local Fisheries: New Directions for Improved Management and Community Development*. Vancouver: University of British Columbia Press.

Polanyi, K. 1944. *The Great Transformation*. Boston: Beacon Press (1957).

Pongphit, S. (ed.). 1986. *Back to the Roots: Village and Self-Reliance in a Thai Context*. Bangkok: Rural Development Documentation Centre.

Pongphit, S. 1989. *Development Paradigm: Strategy, Activities and Reflection*. Bangkok: Thai Institute for Rural Development.

Proudhon, P. J. 1840. *What is Property: An Inquiry into the Principle of Right and of Government.* (tr. Tucker, Benjamin R. 1890, New York: Humboldt. Reprint: 1970. New York: Dover.

Repetto, R., et al. 1989. *Wasting Assets: Natural Resources in the National Income Accounts.* Washington: World Resources Institute.

Roberts, A. 1990. "Making Sacrifices, Not Promises." *Globe and Mail.* Oct. 8.

Ross, D. P., and Usher, P. J. 1986. *From the Roots Up: Economic Development as if Community Mattered.* Ottawa: Canadian Council on Social Development.

Science Council of Canada. 1977. *Canada as a Conserver Society: Resource Uncertainty and the Need for New Technologies.* Report No. 27. Ottawa.

Schumacher, E. F. 1973. *Small is Beautiful: Economics as if People Mattered.* London: Abacus.

Seers, D. 1969. "The Meaning of Development." *International Development Review.* 2-6 Dec.

Simon, J. L. 1981. *The Ultimate Resource.* Princeton: Princeton University Press.

Stohr, W. B., and D. R. F. Taylor (eds.). 1981 *Development from Above or Below: The Dialectics of Regional Planning in Developing Countries.* New York: John Wiley.

Swann, R. 1989 "Community Stewardship of Land and Natural Resources." in Morehouse, W. (ed.). *Building Sustainable Communities: Tools and Concepts for Self-Reliant Economic Change.* New York: The Bootstrap Press.

Thurow, L. C. 1975. *Generating Inequality: Mechanisms of Distribution in the U.S. Economy.* New York: Basic Books.

Tierney, J. 1990. "Betting the Planet." *The New York Times Magazine.* Dec. 2.

United Nations Environmental Program (UNEP). 1988. *Report on the Joint UNEP/World Bank Expert Meeting on Environmental Accounting and the SNA [System of National Accounts]: Paris, 21-22 November 1988.*

World Commission on Environment and Development (WCED). 1987. *Our Common Future.* New York: Oxford University Press.

20

Aboriginal Rights and Sustainable Development in the Fraser-Thompson Corridor

Andrew R. Thompson

The historical land use of the Fraser River Valley by the Indian Tribal Nations has been described by Kew and Griggs (this volume). The purpose of this chapter is to explain how this history is reflected in the modern day Canadian legal system and how it may impact on "sustainable development" issues.

As I understand their perspective, the impact of Native claims on these issues is often irrelevant because they are still at the stage of defining and legitimizing their basic position in relation to the non-native society—aboriginal title and self-government. They can little afford to worry about such abstract concepts as "ecosystem integrity" when they are maintaining roadblocks to protect their burial grounds. Nor can they find comfort in "sustainable development" that portrays their future so meanly as treading "a fine line between keeping them in artificial, perhaps unwanted isolation and wantonly destroying their life styles." (WCED, 1987:116).

For the Native peoples of Canada, definitions of sustainable development are usually infected with the values and ideologies of non-indigenous societies. Rather than adding to these definitions, this paper will describe current legal and political events that are shaping aboriginal relationships within the Fraser watersheds. These relationships will be analysed to identify what they imply for the governance systems in British Columbia that must come to terms with sustainable development principles.

Confining this study to the Canadian legal system is not to say that aboriginal peoples have no independent standing under international law. Rather, the claims of Indian Nations in Canada to self-determination and sovereignty under rules of international law are another story. It is the position of aboriginal rights under Canadian law that is the preoccupation of this chapter.

For several tribes and nations of Indian people, from time immemorial, the Fraser River system provided a home land—a place to hunt and fish and a means of travel and trade, as well as places for village sites and cultivation. This use and occupation provides the basis for legal recognition of aboriginal rights.

Aboriginal Rights as Sources of Legal Rights

Aboriginal rights derive their legal foundation from the rules that western European nations developed to resolve their competing claims to sovereignty and colonization of "newly-discovered" territories (Canadian Bar Association, 1988). These rules culminated for Great Britain's colonies in North America in the Royal Proclamation of 1763 which provided in part:

> ...that the several Nations or Tribes of Indians with whom we are connected, and who live under our protection, should not be molested or disturbed in the possession of such parts of our dominions and territories as, not having been ceded to or purchased by us are reserved to them, or any of them, as their hunting grounds...

The essence of the rules that are distilled as part of the modern law of Canada is that the rights of possession and use of lands enjoyed by their ancestors before British settlement are to be retained by Indian tribes and nations in Canada without disturbance unless and until these rights are surrendered to the sovereign authority by agreement or unilaterally extinguished by clear and plain sovereign intent.

In the United States, judicial recognition of these rights at the highest level was afforded early in the last century when Chief Justice Marshall in two landmark decisions of the United States Supreme Court laid down the basic law relating to Indian title.

In Worcester v. Georgia[1], Chief Justice Marshall stated that the European discoverer would gain the sole right as against other European sovereign states of acquiring the soil in the newly discovered land, but this right was not:

> one which could annul the previous rights of those who had not agreed to it. It regulated the right given by discovery among the European discoverers but could not affect the rights of those already in possession, either as aboriginal occupants, or as occupants by virtue of a discovery made before the memory of man.

In Johnson v. McIntosh[2] Chief Justice Marshall described the right of aboriginal occupation as follows:

> They were admitted to be the rightful occupants of the soil, with a legal as well as just claim to retain possession of it, and to use it according to their own discretion, but their rights to complete sovereignty, as independent nations were necessarily diminished, and their power to dispose of the soil, at their own will, to whomsoever

---

1   31 U.S. (6 Pet.) 515 (1832).
2   (1823) 8 Wheaton 543.

they pleased, was denied by the original fundamental principle that discovery gave exclusive title to those who made it.

That aboriginal rights to land of this nature still exist as part of the modern law of Canada has gained only belated recognition, with the detailed definition of these rights still far from complete. As the Supreme Court of Canada has said in 1990 in R. v. Sparrow:[3]

> For many years, the rights of the Indians to their aboriginal lands— certainly as legal rights—were virtually ignored.

Treaty Making in Canada

The earliest formal recognition of aboriginal rights in Canada occurred in the form of treaties between various aboriginal peoples and the Crown, beginning with 18th and 19th century treaties in Quebec and Ontario, and later extending to numbered treaties covering northern Ontario, the Prairie Provinces and portions of British Columbia and the Northwest Territories, as treaty-making became a systematic method for opening Crown lands to settlement or to oil or mineral development. The last of these serial treaties was Treaty No. 11 covering part of the Mackenzie River Valley in the Northwest Territories.

Not all treaties operated as a surrender of aboriginal rights. Some were treaties of peace and friendship. However, the serial treaties all followed a pattern whereby, in exchange for the government's promises, the Indian people ceded and surrendered their aboriginal rights to land. While, in some individual situations, Indian people challenge the legality of the treaties or their effectiveness in extinguishing aboriginal rights to land, the legal position seems clear that, where a validly made treaty contains clear language of cession and surrender, the result is that the aboriginal rights to the lands covered by the treaty have been extinguished by agreement.

Significantly, all of British Columbia west of the Rocky Mountains escaped this post-confederation treaty-making process. Only in portions of Vancouver Island can it be argued that aboriginal rights to land were extinguished by treaty. The treaties in question were made by Governor Douglas in pre-confederation times when British Columbia retained colonial status. The outcome is that no treaties were made with the Indians of the Fraser River Basin.

The Department of Indian Affairs and Northern Development (DIAND)

The Canadian constitution of 1867 recognized the special relationship between the Crown and aboriginal peoples by allocating "Indians and Lands Reserved for Indians" as exclusively a subject matter for legislation by Parliament.[4] Parliament

---

3   (1990) 4 W.W.R. 410.
4   Constitution Act, 1867, s.91(24).

enacted the Indian Act[5] to provide the authority for managing Indian affairs. DIAND is the federal government department assigned the task of exercising this statutory authority. The Act employs a system of land reserves and Indian status which some describe as intended to maintain Indian people in isolation and dependency. For example, the Indian Act empowers Indian bands to enact by-laws regulating activities on reserves, but these by-laws require the approval of the Minister of DIAND and may be overridden by regulations made pursuant to the Act.

Judicial Recognition of Aboriginal Rights

Judicial recognition of an aboriginal rights doctrine in Canadian law came as recently as 1973, when six of the seven judges in the Supreme Court of Canada held in the Calder Case[6] that aboriginal rights are part of the law of the land. This decision left much to be decided in the future, for there was no explicit definition of the legal nature of these aboriginal rights, and the six judges split evenly on the question of whether these rights had been extinguished in the particular circumstances of the case.

Nevertheless, the fall-out from Calder included a re-evaluation of federal policy relating to aboriginal lands, out of which emerged both a "specific claims" policy and a "comprehensive land claims" policy. The former policy dealt with cases where disputes had arisen between governments or third persons and Indian bands concerning questions of title to and boundaries of reserves. In these claims, Indians usually asserted that their land rights had been violated by improper surrender procedures or just plain trespass. In the Fraser-Thompson corridor there were scores of past incidents which, in the minds of Indian people, amounted to confiscation of their land rights by highway authorities and railway and pipeline companies.

The comprehensive land claims policy was explained in a 1981 document entitled "In All Fairness" (DIAND, 1981). It stated the commitment of the federal government to enter into negotiations with aboriginal peoples who had not previously surrendered their aboriginal rights through the treaty process. Indeed, the comprehensive land claims policy could best be explained as the continuation in modern day terms of the historic treaty-making process.

Initially, six claims were accepted for negotiations. Of these, the James Bay and Northern Quebec Agreements of 1975 and 1978 and the Inuvialuit Final Agreement of 1985, covering the western Arctic, have been concluded. As well, Umbrella Final Agreements have been signed (but not yet ratified) dealing with the Yukon Final Settlement, the Dene-Metis Final Settlement in the MacKenzie Valley and the claim of the Inuit in the central and eastern Arctic. The sixth claim, involving the Nish'ga people of British Columbia, who were the plaintiffs in the Calder Case, continues to be negotiated.

---

5   1989 R.S.C. c. I-5.
6   (1973) S.C.R. 313. The 1888 decision of the Privy Council in St. Catherines Milling and Lumber Co. v. R., 14 A.C. 46, left much uncertainty on the subject.

Difficulties encountered in these claims led to a study and report by the Coolican Task Force (TFRCCP, 1985) recommending important changes in both the content of settlements and the process for negotiation. But unanswered are the complaints that if the federal government persists in its policy of negotiating only six comprehensive claims at a time, the completion of the twenty or so outstanding claims will take 200 or more years!

Nor do these comprehensive claims include the hundreds of specific claims that aboriginal peoples may assert with respect to reserve lands and to other lands whose history is fraught with ambiguities as to how native use and occupation rights were terminated. That such claims may emerge as testing grounds for Canada's resolve to "do justice" in relation to aboriginal peoples in the 1990's has been shown by the recent barricade events at Oka in Quebec and on the Duffey Lake Road in British Columbia.

Extinguishment of Aboriginal Rights Other than by Treaty

The rights of the Nish'ga people, represented by Chief Calder, had clearly not been extinguished by treaty. The argument on behalf of the government of British Columbia in Calder was that aboriginal rights could be extinguished other than by treaty-making. The government pointed to the policies of the colonial government in British Columbia respecting the establishment of reserves for Indians and the enactment of laws providing for land grants, mineral claims and forest licences as being inconsistent with the continuation of aboriginal rights and therefore impliedly extinguishing them.

Since this even split of the Supreme Court of Canada in 1973 on the question of implied extinguishment, this issue has featured largely in aboriginal rights cases before Canadian courts. For example, the arguments before Chief Justice McEachern in the current case to determine land ownership in the vast region of British Columbia occupied historically by the Gitksan Wet'suwet'en Indian people have centered on the issue of implied extinguishment. Meantime, the Supreme Court of Canada in Sparrow in 1990 seems to have closed the door on implied extinguishment by a ruling that "the test of extinguishment to be adopted, in our opinion, is that the sovereign's intention must be clear and plain if it is to extinguish an aboriginal right."

Obviously, much was undefined and uncertain concerning the nature and effect of these aboriginal rights. Such was the situation leading to the enactment of the 1982 Constitution of Canada.

Constitutional Recognition of Aboriginal Rights

Through the period of constitutional reform and repatriation in the 1970's, native people were concerned that their status and rights as aboriginal peoples would be imperilled. Native support for the new constitution was gained on the basis that it would contain an express provision recognizing aboriginal rights and that constitutional conferences would be held for the purpose of defining aboriginal rights, and, in particular, rights of self-government.

Consequently, section 35(1) of the Constitution Act, 1982 enacted that:

> The existing aboriginal and treaty rights of the aboriginal people of Canada are hereby recognized and affirmed.

Section 35(3) declared that modern comprehensive land claims settlements would be included as "treaty rights", and section 52 made any legislation inconsistent with a provision of the Constitution ineffective.

While the required constitutional conferences were held in 1985, 1986 and 1987, no agreement was reached. The definition of the legal nature and extent of aboriginal rights to land remains to be accomplished and a constitutionally guaranteed right to self-government continues to be a main goal of aboriginal peoples. But for what it was worth, the "existing" aboriginal rights of aboriginal peoples, though not defined, were "recognized and affirmed". Only future court decisions could determine how much aboriginal peoples had gained by the inclusion of section 35 in the 1982 Constitution.

Effect of Sparrow Decision on Aboriginal Rights

With the 1990 decision in Sparrow, the Supreme Court of Canada set about the task of giving content and meaning to section 35. The case involved charges laid under the federal Fisheries Act for illegal fishing by Sparrow, a Musqueam Indian, who was using a drift net to catch salmon in the mouth of the Fraser River. Sparrow's net exceeded the length specified in the Musqueam Band Indian Food Fishing Licence issued pursuant to Fisheries Act regulations. Sparrow's defence was a claim that he was exercising his aboriginal right to fish and this right overrode the restrictions of the licence.

The judgment begins with an analysis of the meaning of the "existing" aboriginal rights that are recognized and affirmed by section 35(1). The Court decided that the word "existing" makes it clear that the rights to which section 35(1) applies were those in existence when the Constitution Act, 1982 came into effect. Rights that had previously been extinguished by clear and plain intent were not revived. Those that had not been extinguished, and therefore continued to exist, were not frozen in time in the sense of incorporating the specific manner in which they were regulated in 1982. To the contrary, the phrase "existing aboriginal rights" was to be interpreted flexibly, so as to permit the evolution of aboriginal rights over time and in contemporary form.

As to the nature of Sparrow's aboriginal right to fish, the Court found its substance to be the fact that the Musqueam had lived in the area as an organized society long before the coming of European settlers and that the taking of salmon was an integral part of their lives and remained so today. This right had not been extinguished merely because it had been closely regulated as a food fishery for over 100 years under the Fisheries Act, and the Act contained nothing that demonstrated a clear and plain intention to extinguish the Indian aboriginal right to fish for food and social and ceremonial purposes. The question whether the aboriginal right to fish would extend to fishing for commercial or livelihood purposes was not an issue before the Court and therefore would have to be decided in a future case. The Court did comment, however, that the nature of government regulation could not delineate the aboriginal fishing right and therefore the fact that the Fisheries Act regulations had restricted Indian fishing to food purposes would not, by itself, rule out fishing for commercial or livelihood purposes.

With respect to the legal effect of section 35(1) in recognizing and affirming aboriginal rights, the Court commented that the words are to be construed in a purposive way, receiving a generous, liberal interpretation in favour of aboriginal people. They would afford aboriginal people constitutional protection against provincial legislative power and, while federal legislative powers respecting Indians pursuant to section 91(24) of the Constitution Act, 1867 would continue, federal legislation restricting aboriginal rights would, since 1982, have to be justified as a way of reconciling the inherent conflict between the constitutionally affirmed aboriginal rights and federal constitutional powers. Underlying these determinations, the guiding principle for section 35(1) would be the government's responsibility to act in a fiduciary capacity with respect to aboriginal peoples. The relationship between the government and aboriginals was to be trust-like rather than adversarial.

The Court completed its decision by laying down a process for determining whether or not an interference with aboriginal fishing rights would be justified. The first step in this process is to determine whether fishing rights have been interfered with such as to constitute a prima facie infringement of section 35(1). The onus of proving this prima facie interference with aboriginal fishing rights would lie on the individual or group challenging the interference. Certain questions would be asked: Was the limitation unreasonable? Does the regulation impose undue hardship? Does the regulation deny to aboriginals their preferred means of exercising the aboriginal right?

The second step deals with justification. Here the Crown must prove that the prima facie interference is justified. While not an exhaustive list, questions to be asked are: Is there a valid legislative objective?—an objective aimed at preserving section 35(1) rights by conserving and managing a natural resource would be valid, as would objectives of avoiding public harm or other compelling and substantial purpose. Are the restrictions consistent with allocating the right to take fish, so as to give priority to the aboriginal right to fish for food? Is there as little infringement on the aboriginal right as possible? In situations of expropriation, is fair compensation available? Has the aboriginal group in question been consulted with respect to the conservation measures being implemented?

Finally, if there is a valid legislative objective, the legislation will nevertheless not be justified if it offends the guiding principle that the honour of the Crown and the special trust relationship of the government vis-a-vis aboriginals are the first considerations.

Summing up re Sparrow

Sparrow dealt with fishing in the mouth of the Fraser River. It is a final and binding determination of the law that aboriginal peoples have the right to fish subject only to justifiable regulation. Hence, it applies anywhere in the Fraser River Basin where Indian people have fished from time immemorial and continue to fish today. At present, the law is settled only with respect to Indian food fishing. But the door is not closed on an extension of the aboriginal right to include fishing for commercial and livelihood purposes.

This aboriginal fishing right is a constitutional right stemming from section 35(1) of the Constitution Act, 1982. It cannot now be affected by provincial legislation. While it is constitutionally protected, it remains subject to federal regulation. But if this regulation interferes with exercise of the aboriginal fishing right, it must be justified according to objectives and protections specified by the Court.

Therefore, finally in 1990, the Indian people of the Fraser River Basin have gained the legal and constitutional right to fish that they have staunchly asserted from the beginning of European settlement. As precedent, this decision can be extended to cases of use and occupation of land other than for fishing where Fraser River Indian peoples can prove this use and occupation from time immemorial. Obviously, a new era has dawned. Even the federal Department of Fisheries and Oceans (DFO), which historically has been the implacable foe of Indian assertions of fishing rights, has recognized that the old order must change.

The rest of this chapter will identify some of the Indian concerns regarding sustainable development in the Fraser River Basin and more specifically, in the Fraser-Thompson corridor.

Indian Concerns in the Fraser-Thompson Corridor: The Pasco Case

Indian grievances concerning encroachments on land allotted to them as reserves in the Fraser-Thompson corridor are as numerous as they are long-standing. Most deal with railways, highways, pipelines and hydro-electric transmission lines. Those that are being dealt with under the specific claims policy of DIAND number in the hundreds. In some cases, Indian people are resorting to blockades to gain attention to these grievances. In others they are seeking remedies in the courts. A recent example is the case of Harper Valley Ranch Ltd.[7] where the Kamloops Indian Band was successful in obtaining an interim injunction restraining the building of a golf course on lands they had claimed from before the turn of the century.

A case that illustrates the many facets of Indian concerns in the corridor is Pasco v. Canadian National Railways (CNR).[8] The Indian people applied to the Supreme Court of British Columbia for an interim injunction restraining CNR

---

7   Vancouver Registry: CA010911; (1990) B.C.J. No. 1268.
8   Pasco v. CNR, (1986) 1 C.N.L.R.

from proceeding with a twin-tracking construction project along its mainline in the Fraser-Thompson corridor. The particular section under attack was an eight-mile stretch of the Thompson River between Spences Bridge and Ashcroft. This stretch ran by the Oregon Jack Creek Indian Reserve No. 5. The allocation of this reserve included a salmon fishery on both sides of the river for a distance of two miles.

The complaint of the Indians was that the dumping of rock on the river side of the mainline to form a bed for the second track would encroach on their reserve lands and interfere with their fishing rights. In particular, Indian concerns focussed on (i) their exclusion from any effective participation in decision-making concerning the project; (ii) the uncertainty and confusion surrounding government/railway jurisdiction over the project; (iii) the unwillingness of DIAND to support the Indian position; and (iv) the general indifference that CNR and the governments exhibited towards Indian interests.

Exclusion of Indians from Decision-Making

Prior to Pasco, there was no place for Indians in any decision-making concerning planning and development of the use of the Fraser-Thompson corridor. They were not included in the working group which was established by the CNR and government to deal with the technical aspects of the twin-tracking project. Nor were they participants in the steering committee that decided policy matters. Rather, the historic pattern of development in British Columbia was being followed. Indian people would be ignored except to the extent their reserve lands were needed for non-Indian purposes. Then the procedures would be initiated for surrendering Indian lands to the government so that they could be granted to developers. If Indians objected, they were confronted by the full authority of government, with expropriation an outcome if all else failed. Certainly, DIAND was not an advocate on their behalf.

The CNR twin-tracking project had a unique beginning. While the Trudeau government mandated the project as a matter of major public importance, and thereby ensured that there would be no obstruction by government departments, the project was referred to an environmental impact assessment panel (EARP) to recommend measures that would reduce negative environmental impacts. A panel was established that included Robert Pasco, Chief of the Oregon Jack Creek Indian band. Funding was provided to affected Indian bands to enable their participation in the panel process. In consequence, their submissions to the panel, particularly with respect to the effects of the project on salmon fishing, constituted a major portion of the public contribution received by the panel.

The insignificance of the panel process came to light when the CNR announced that it would proceed with construction of the Ashcroft section of the twin-tracking notwithstanding that the panel report was not yet completed. Faced with this contempt of the EARP process, Chief Pasco resigned from the panel and the Indians of the region initiated a lobbying effort in Ottawa to stop the CNR. The threat of blockades of the main line brought a federal cabinet response that laid down requirements that the CNR must meet to deal with the objections of the Indians. As well, the cabinet appointed the author as a facilitator to encourage a negotiation process between the CNR and the Indians.

The particular complaints of the Indians concerned interference with the traditional places they fished, obstruction of access routes to reach these fishing places and threat to the maintenance of the fish stocks in the Fraser-Thompson system. DFO would listen to them only with respect to the conservation issue, asserting their traditional position that their concerns are management of the fishery as a whole and do not extend to protecting fish sites or fish stocks on behalf of particular individuals or groups. Neither they, the CNR, nor any other government department assumed any responsibility with respect to the exercise of Indian fishing rights.

With no one taking responsibility, and with the EARP process discredited, there was no forum for Indian participation in decision-making. They therefore turned to lobbying the federal cabinet ministers.

The facilitation process established by the ministers provided the Indians a voice in decision-making for a short period of time, but this process proved a failure once it became plain that the CNR would not consider relocation of the track or other costly measures to minimize interference with fishing. On their part, the Indians decided that they could not accept construction methods that would, from their perspective, destroy a heritage which rightly belonged to their children and grandchildren.

At this point in time, the Indians made a successful application to the court for an interim injunction. In effect, the court provided the only opportunity available to Indian people to play a part in decision-making concerning the fate of the Fraser-Thompson corridor.

Government Uncertainty and Confusion

The Pasco case revealed startling uncertainties and confusion on the part of governments concerning their jurisdiction and roles in the Fraser-Thompson corridor. At the federal level, the CNR was treated as if it were a government department, itself. Its representatives chaired both the working group and the steering committee. It hired the consultants who prepared project studies. It was unclear that the CNR would accept directives from DFO concerning fisheries management and the application of its "no net loss" policy whereby it would require the replacement of spawning grounds lost to the project. As to DFO, it was without experience or data to predict the impacts of the twin-tracking on salmon stocks. The channelling effect of the rip-rapping of the banks (i.e., lining the banks with large boulders) would accelerate river currents with unknown effects on the energy budgets of migrating salmon and potential destruction of resting and rearing places for juvenile salmon along the river banks.

There was a dispute between federal and provincial authorities over management of the river itself The provincial Water Management Branch considered the river to be under its licensing jurisdiction with respect to engineering works affecting the banks or bed of the river, citing the provisions of the provincial Water Act. The CNR refused to recognize this assertion of jurisdiction, with the backing of DFO, the Department of Transport and the Department of Environment. In these circumstances, the provincial authorities faded from the scene, satisfied to be given the opportunity to participate in the efforts of the working group and the steering committee.

The Indians, too, were offered and accepted participation in the working group and the steering committee as a result of efforts by the facilitator to encourage cooperation and negotiation among the participants.

This technique of resorting to interdepartmental committees to paper over defects in jurisdiction and gaps in responsibility is an often-used device on the part of federal and provincial governments in Canada. It has the effect of prolonging the status quo without accountability, and responsibility can be evaded by laying the blame on the inadequate or inconsistent mandates of others assembled at the table. It can hardly be expected to fulfil the expectations of Indian peoples toward self-government, including a clear and effective role in planning and decision-making regarding development projects that interfere with their aboriginal rights.

Unwillingness of DIAND to Support Indian Position

Despite judicial rulings that the government owes a fiduciary duty to aboriginal peoples with respect to their rights, the department of the federal government charged with responsibility for Indians—DIAND—made no effort to assist them. This non-involvement of DIAND is the customary stance of the department in contests like that between Pasco and CNR. This lack of support has the effect, from the Indian perspective, of casting the entire Canadian government in an adversarial role with respect to aboriginal peoples. This is particularly so when the only DIAND policy that comes close to dealing with an event like CNR's twin-tracking is its Specific Claims Policy whereby, through a legally oriented process, Indian people must prove a specific grievance as a legal claim against the Crown in order to obtain redress.

General Indifference Towards Indian People

All of these shortcomings of government signify to Indians that there is a general indifference in Canada toward the complaints of Indian people. We see their response to this indifference in events like Oka and in the spate of blockades in British Columbia and elsewhere in Canada. These grievances are, in most cases, founded on aboriginal rights which increasingly are being recognized by the courts in Canada. The contrast between the judicial decisions and the political reality is disturbing. It suggests that the Canadian public has further affronts to endure before reconciliation between national interests and aboriginal rights will be achieved.

Implications for Development in the Fraser River Basin

Sparrow makes clear what hitherto has been speculation—that aboriginal people have rights which must be reckoned with in terms of the management and use of natural resources and their sustainable development in the Fraser River Basin. The considerable scope of these rights is foreshadowed in Pasco, and the recent British Columbia Court of Appeal decision in Saanichton[9] reveals their potential force in controlling development activities.

Sparrow makes illegal any activity that interferes with the exercise of an aboriginal right, unless the interference is justified according to principles laid down by the Supreme Court of Canada. With respect to fishing, this illegal interference can be a licensing requirement of DFO which cannot be justified for a conservation or public safety purpose.[10] It could be an activity that impairs fish stocks or catch opportunities so as to deprive Indians from enjoying their priority right to catch sufficient fish for food and ceremonial purposes. This priority right may be extended to cover fishing for commercial or livelihood purposes. It can also be extended by analogy to cover hunting, trapping and food gathering activities.

Pasco shows that, in addition to aboriginal rights to fish, Indians living along the rivers have rights to reserve lands and to allotted fisheries that may include ownership of the banks and beds of the rivers and of the right to fish, similar to real property rights recognized by the common law.

If the interim injunction against the CNR in Pasco is confirmed by a final and permanent injunction, it will mean that this Indian ownership of reserve and fishing rights can thwart corridor developments such as railways, roads, pipelines and transmission lines unless Indian agreement is reached or expropriation procedures are successful.

Saanichton demonstrates that the courts can reinforce these aboriginal and reserve rights by ensuring that Indian people have rights of access to exercise these rights and rights to protect the environment in which they are enjoyed. In this case, the British Columbia Court of Appeal permanently restrained the construction of a marina where it was shown that this development would interfere with traditional fishing in places where the Saanichton people were accustomed to fish. The court made it plain that the protected fishery would include protection of the eel-grass beds where the fishing took place and protection of the means of access used by the Indians to exercise their rights.

To this arsenal of legal rights must be added the right of Indian bands to enact by-laws pursuant to the Indian Act, which regulates activities on reserve lands. This Indian Act power includes the right to regulate fishing. The courts have said that a validly-enacted band by-law regulating fishing will override provisions of the Fisheries Act.[11] Hence, reserves along the rivers have the potential to provide

---

9   Saanichton Marina Ltd. v. Claxton (1989), 57 D.L.R. (4th).
10 R. v. Richardson No. 1793C, Masset Registry.
11 R.S.C. 1989. Note, however, that a regulation made pursuant to the Act may, in turn, override a provision of a by-law.

a base for planning and regulating developments along the river that may affect fishing and other aboriginal rights.

While these rights and powers are no more extensive than those enjoyed by other land owners under Canadian law, their potential for underpinning a governance role in the Fraser River Basin by the Indian bands and tribal councils assumes major significance when it is realized how strategically-placed are the reserves along the River, how many there are, and that Indian people have communal traditions that could lead to cooperative planning and regulation of corridor developments.

So far as sustainable development is concerned, the Kew and Griggs study (this volume) identifies traditional Indian values as being attuned to the environment. In modern day terms, the numerous injunction applications before the courts reveal Indians in the role of seeking to restrain forest and mineral developments that impact adversely on renewable resources.[12] In Pasco, the conflict of values that took the parties to the courts was the railway's determination to minimize the cost per mile of track as opposed to the Indian's sense of duty to preserve the valley for their children and grandchildren. The fear may well be that the Indian people are so preservationist that sustainable development will be indiscriminately thwarted by their activities in pursuit of aboriginal rights.

However, recent comprehensive land claims agreements like the Yukon Umbrella Final Agreement[13] belie this fear. While it is often misleading to assume that the experience of one aboriginal people can be applied to other aboriginal people, a sense of what is in store for the Fraser River Basin can be gained by treating terms and provisions of this agreement as a model.

Applying the model to the Fraser River Basin, the Indians would bargain for a water licensing system that would give priority to traditional uses so that there could never again be a dedication of the entire flow of a river system to a single development enterprise such as occurred in the case of the Alcan hydroelectric development on the Nechako and Kitimat Rivers. Those Carrier-Sekani Indian people who were displaced without agreement and with scarcely any notice by the flooding of Alcan's reservoir in the 1950's would not accept any future river management system that excludes them as participants.

Indians would also expect to be co-managers of water quality in the Fraser River Basin. As well, they would expect a management role in relation to land use planning, the exercise of access and surface rights, and the assessment of the social and environmental effects of development projects. Under the Yukon Umbrella Final Agreement, the Indian role in management is assured by the establishment of agencies or boards that have equal participation in decision-making by Indians and non-Indians with an independent chairperson. These new institutions along with the terms of the Umbrella Final Agreement are to be ratified by legislation on the part of the federal and territorial governments. Their terms and conditions will

---

12 e.g. The Meares Island Case.
13 The Yukon Umbrella Final Agreement was initialled on March 31, 1990. When Yukon First Nation Final
    Agreements are signed and all the Agreements are ratified by First Nation assemblies and by Parliament, the
    Yukon Indian land claims will be finally settled.

qualify as existing aboriginal rights under section 35 of the Constitution Act, 1982 and thereby become part of the constitution of the country.

What would not be accepted, except as an interim response, is participation in an advisory body like the Fraser-Thompson Transportation Environmental Steering Committee established in 1988 by the federal and provincial Ministers of Environment, for the clear implication of an advisory role is that someone else is in charge of decision-making.

Conclusion

While the emerging status of aboriginal people as participants in water management in the Fraser River Basin may contribute little to the abstract definition of sustainable development, it will have a good deal to say about the governance of the system. To the extent this system must rest on agreement, the aboriginal people will expect to be full partners. At the present time, their preoccupation is to establish the legal basis for such partnership.

Should they succeed (and what this means is convincing the non-native society to accept them as partners), certain predictions may be made about their management contribution. It will be both consensual in style and community-based, reflecting values that the Brundtland Report identifies as contributing to "sustainable development". It will likely be preservation-oriented, though this trait may be more evident when their claims are contested than when they are managers.

Finally, it may be merely a non-native pipedream to assume that the aboriginal people of the Fraser River Basin will want to participate in the elaborate planning and management systems that their non-native partners have constructed. Maybe they can show us a better way!

References

Canadian Bar Association. 1988. *Report of the Special Committee of the Canadian Bar Association: Aboriginal Rights in Canada: An Agenda for Action.* Ottawa.

Department of Indian Affairs and Northern Development (DIAND). 1981. *In All Fairness: A Native Claims Policy.* Ottawa:.Comprehensive Claims.

Task Force to Review Comprehensive Claims Policy (TFRCCP). 1985. *Living Treaties: Lasting Agreements. Report of the Task Force to Review Comprehensive Claims Policy.* Ottawa: Department of Indian Affairs and Northern Development: Ottawa.

World Commission on Environment and Development (WCED). 1987. *Our Common Future.* Oxford: Oxford University Press.

21

Towards Agreement on Sustainable Development in Water Management: Learning from the Differences

Anthony H. J. Dorcey

In the two concluding chapters, the implications of sustainable development principles for water management in river basins are explored in the light of the ideas in the preceeding chapters and advances in sustainable development research. The introductory chapter described an initial analytical framework that was drafted a year ago in order to guide the preparation of background papers and begin the case study analyses in the Fraser River Basin. In the intervening months, this collection of papers has been written. In addition, the case study analyses have progressed and there is a much better appreciation of what can be achieved with only existing information in the first phase of the research program. At the same time, there has been immense activity by many other people throughout British Columbia, Canada and the rest of the world on sustainable development initiatives. The concluding chapters, therefore, consider the implications of these combined developments for the analytical framework and research strategy proposed at the outset.

In general, the initial analytical framework and research strategy have served the project well. There are no significant aspects that have transpired to be seriously ill-conceived—in fact, experience so far strongly confirms their worth. Instead, the major lessons relate to ways in which our initial ideas should now be further developed. One, in particular, is perceived to be of such over-riding importance that it is a major theme in the concluding chapters.

Reaching Agreement in Sustainable Development

The critical importance and difficulty of reaching agreement on a diverse array of issues in sustainable development cannot be overstated. While this challenge was highlighted in the initial analytical framework, all of our experience since then suggests it merits even greater emphasis and attention. In diverse ways, this issue has arisen again and again with regard to the background papers, in the case study analyses of the Fraser River Basin, and in the many other settings in which Westwater has been involved in sustainable development initiatives. This includes our experience not only in British Columbia and Canada, but also in other parts of the world as varied as Europe, Australia and Nepal.

It has become common to hear people declare in exasperation: "There are as many definitions of sustainable development as there are people talking about it!" Associated with such comments are a series of issues about which agreement is sought and around which there is continuing disagreement in both academic and governance forums. They give rise to a number of questions that are important in this project:

- What is the definition of sustainable development?
- What are the implications of sustainable development for water resource management?
- What are the indicators of sustainability?
- What are the functional relations between indicators of sustainability?
- What is the present state of sustainability?
- What are the limits to sustainability?
- What kind of adaptations does sustainability require?
- How should risk and uncertainty be treated in adapting to sustainability?
- At what rate should adaptation to greater sustainability be made?
- What should be the distribution of burdens in adapting to greater sustainability?
- What institutional arrangements should be used in adapting to greater sustainability?

The two concluding chapters examine the nature of and interrelations between these questions and responses to them. This chapter focuses on the first two questions: *What is the definition of sustainable development? What are the implications of sustainable development for water resource management?* The objective is to reveal the breadth and diversity of the debate about sustainable development and suggest general strategies for moving towards agreement in exploring its implications for water management. The final chapter focuses on the remaining questions: its objective is to examine more specifically the issues that need to be explored in the case study of the Fraser River Basin and suggest a preliminary model for guiding water management in its sustainable development.

Commonly the purpose of the final chapter in a collection such as this is to summarize the conclusions in the contributed papers. The two chapters are not designed to present a summary, rather the primary purpose is to lay out a more detailed foundation for both future research and for the analytical framework that can be used in the case study. This is done by drawing on the sustainable development and water management literatures and relating the papers to them. The background papers thus make two major contributions. In the sections that follow, they contribute primarily to the development of the analytical framework for guiding future research and a preliminary model of water management in sustainable development. Then in the second volume, they make major contributions to the analysis and recommendations in diverse ways that are both conceptual and substantive.

The focus emphasised here—reaching agreement—is not founded in a naive assumption that its complete achievement is desirable, let alone feasible. Rather the assumption is that there is a preferred middle ground between the undesirable extremes of total agreement or disagreement. In an increasingly conflict-riven world, movement towards greater consensus is essential. Further, this can be done in ways that capture the great potential for learning from disagreements and the differences that underlie them. In the process of exploring the middle ground, new potentials for agreement can be identified and an enhanced appreciation of the relative merits of agreement and disagreement can be developed.

From this perspective, the capability of society's institutions to both foster agreement and cope with the turbulence of disagreement is crucial. Attention can focus on the ways in which legislative, judicial, administrative and market institutions might be better utilised and integrated in the management of water resources. However, the sustainable development debate raises much more fundamental questions about how these and other institutional arrangements can be transformed to cope better with increasing disputes and avoid slipping further into disagreement and ultimately violent conflict. Water and associated resources have often been the subject of violent conflict between both individuals and nations on a worldwide basis. This continues today with threats of escalation in various parts of the world (Vlachos and Priscoli, 1990), including British Columbia and the Fraser River Basin where there have recently been incidents of physical violence and armed confrontation (see papers by Dale and Thompson). The spectre of growing violence provides an urgent incentive to create more resilient institutions of governance that can cope with disagreements productively and peacefully.

In this context, the concluding chapters consider the challenges and strategies for moving towards agreement in both governance and academic forums. They focus on the governance system in order to examine comprehensively the role of all governmental and non-governmental organisations in water management for sustainable development. Particular consideration is given to the contribution of academic organisations because of the critical role that they can play in training people and developing knowledge which is essential for moving towards greater agreement.

In the first section of this chapter, the fundamental influence of different world views in defining sustainable development is examined. If the debate in governance and academic forums is to be productive, it is crucial to appreciate the differences in world views and schools of thought found in the disciplines. The second section examines the implications of this for water resources management. It suggests that water is a field that has been at the forefront in advancing the interdisciplinary approaches and more comprehensive principles that are necessary to sustainable development, but much more radical innovation is also required. In concluding, constraints are recognised so that attention can focus on a preliminary model of water management in sustainable development for the Fraser Basin case study. The final chapter develops this model more specifically while futher elaborating on the analytical framework.

Definition of Sustainable Development

A major achievement of the Brundtland report was its success in drawing wider attention to the interdependence of environmental, economic and social systems through its concept of sustainable development. This perspective was not entirely new in that it represented the culmination of a series of international conferences and reports going back at least to the Stockholm UN Conference on the Environment in 1972 and an evolving academic and professional literature that had been advancing along various fronts for much longer (O'Riordan, 1988). However, the vigorous debate that the Brundtland report catalysed has also revealed how the concept can be understood and interpreted very differently. In this respect, the various papers in this volume reflect the larger reality.

As indicated in the Preface, the contributing authors were asked in the first of two general requests to define sustainable development at the outset of their paper. More specifically, they were asked to make clear the extent to which they accepted the Brundtland definition, as elaborated to guide the Westwater project. While no contributor explicitly rejected the definition or its general elaboration, it is notable that their uses of it (at least implicitly and sometimes explicitly) gave it a wide variety of different emphases and interpretations.

Drawing on the literature, the project's initial approach to defining sustainable development can be further elaborated to understand these differences in the papers in terms of world views. This provides a more comprehensive frame of reference for considering the diversity of possibilities and a means for clarifying fundamental reasons for disagreement about the definition of sustainable development. The contributed papers reflect some of these differences, illustrating how they can be found in varied forms amongst particular individuals, disciplines and professional fields.

World Views

From the broad perspective of Western industrialized society, O'Riordan and Turner have suggested one way of organising alternative world views relating to the environment into two major groupings: technocentrism and ecocentrism. They divide each of these into two further sets:

(i)   *Cornucopian technocentrism*: an exploitative position supportive of a growth ethic expressed in material terms (e.g., Gross National Product); it is taken as axiomatic that the market mechanism in conjunction with technological innovation will ensure infinite substitution possibilities to mitigate long-run real resource scarcity;

(ii) *Accommodating technocentrism*: a conservationist position, which rejects the axiom of infinite substitution and instead supports a 'sustainable growth' policy guided by resource management rules;

(iii) *Communalist ecocentrism*: a preservationist position, which emphasises the need for prior macroenvironmental constraints on economic growth and favours a decentralised socio-economic system;

(iv) *Deep ecology ecocentrism*: an extreme preservationist position, dominated by the intuitive acceptance of the notion of intrinsic (as opposed to instrumental) value in nature and rights for non-human species (1983; cited in Turner, 1988).

Writing in the early 1980's, these authors saw the dominant world view of industrialised societies as being cornucopian technocentrism, a classification which they felt had not changed significantly since O'Riordan had first suggested a similar typology in 1976. Most government policy and the majority of the literature functioned within this world view, although it did not necessarily reflect the minority cornucopian beliefs of extreme technological optimists, such as Simon and Kahn (1984). The other three sets of world views were reflective of ideas that were more commonly found in the academic literature, with the deep ecologists, represented by writers such as Næss (1973), being again an extreme, minority view. At that time, the major challenge to the dominant world view was being made by the accommodators and, to a lesser extent, the communalists. In the last few years since the Brundtland report, it seems that the challenge to the cornucopians from all three of the other basic views has been accentuated and that the communalist challenge has been pressed more vigorously, although still not as strongly as the accommodators.

While these four sets of world views can be envisaged across a spectrum from extreme technocentrism to extreme ecocentrism, there is in actuality considerable variation within each of them and some writers, particularly near to margins, are characterised by beliefs drawn from more than one. The Brundtland report includes both accommodator and communalist arguments, but in such varied combinations with those of the cornucopians that it defies unambiguous classification and provides rich opportunities for criticism from all four world viewpoints (e.g., Daly, 1990).

Associating the contributed papers with particular world views also gives rise to similar difficulties. While no paper clearly reflects the extreme views of either deep ecologists or cornucopians, and while the authors variously appear to reflect elements of technocentric and ecocentric perspectives, their world views cannot always be unambiguously discerned from the present papers. Part of the reasons for this are the specific foci of the papers that they chose to write, but another part derives from their differing schools of thought.

Schools of Thought

Accompanying the articulation of the four different world views in recent years has been new interest in the academic disciplines dealing with the environment, economy and society. Separately, each of the disciplines has been growing and diversifying into specializations within its own bounds and has experienced vigorous debate between differing schools of thought. For examples, consider the disputes over diversity-stability theory in ecology, supply-side vs. demand-side theories in economics, and pluralist vs. corporatist theories in political science.

Of particular interest here, however, are the more innovative disciplinary combinations that have developed in response to explicit interest in the interactions between environmental, economic and social systems (e.g., ecological anthropology, environmental economics, environmental politics, neo-institutional economics, etc.). These are not necessarily entirely new schools (e.g., neo-institutional economics, as the prefix suggests, is a revision of an old school of political economy). Such schools also range from sub-fields within the mainstream of the discipline (e.g., environmental economics as a sub-field of neoclassical economics) through to different schools of thought that are self-contained alternatives to the mainstream (e.g., the steady state theorists that represent new perspectives within the discipline of economics or, perhaps more accurately, outside of it). Typically, these combinations entrain not only the controversies within their member disciplines but additionally those distinctive of the different world views on the issues they address. In turn, these can spawn alternative schools of thought. Consequently, the scope for disagreement is great indeed.

An appreciation of these different combined disciplines and how they are challenging dominant views can be of great assistance in better understanding the sustainable development debate and seeking opportunities to resolve disagreements, including how the concept itself should be defined. It is beyond the scope of this chapter to review and contrast all the potentially relevant disciplinary combinations and schools of thought within them. However, we can indicate some of the major new fields and we begin by briefly examining one of the most important ones, environmental economics, so as to illustrate the kind of appreciation required and the insights that this provides (also see discussion in Rees, this volume).

The mainstream, neoclassical view of environmental economics is being challenged by steady state theorists. Differences between their diagnoses, prognoses and prescriptions stem from some of the most fundamental and common bases for disagreement about sustainable development arising in both academic and governance forums—Underwood and King (1989) review each of these schools of thought in environmental economics by examining the sets of first principles shaping their theoretical development.

For neoclassicists there are two critical beliefs: (i) substitution is always possible and (ii) human nature is such that acquisitiveness and the pursuit of self-interest are fundamental determinants of rational behaviour. The first is their belief about the nature of the world (i.e., the cosmology) and the second is their belief about the determinants of human behaviour (i.e., the ontology). They summarize the essence of the neoclassical view as being that

[a]s a resource is used, the market *should* cause prices to rise naturally over time, induce the introduction of resource substitutes, bring about capital augmentation for economic growth, and assure the development of new technology...Thus absolute scarcity is relegated into a future which is effectively an infinite distance away. The belief in the power of competitive forces to create appropriate substitution is an immutable metaeconomic first principle oblivious to objective scrutiny and critique (Underwood and King, 1989:321-322, emphasis in original).

In contrast, two differing beliefs underlied steady statism as this school of thought emerged under the influence of Georgescu-Roegen (1971), Boulding (1970), and Daly (1977) to challenge the mainstream environmental economics' view: (i) the laws of thermodynamics are inescapable (the cosmology) and (ii) the interaction of people with nature is viewed as an element of species being (the ontology). The scientific basis for this cosmology is elaborated as follows (see also discussion in Rees, this volume):

The first law of thermodynamics and the Law of Conservation of Matter, together state that energy-matter cannot be created or destroyed, but only altered in form. This means that when material resources are introduced into a production process, the total mass of these inputs after production remains unaltered, i.e., it will be equal to the product plus all forms of waste including gaseous forms. The second law of thermodynamics, the Entropy Law, states that the free and unbounded energy required to perform work is irrevocably diminished as its potential is utilized. Hence, energy undergoes a transformation from an unbound, ordered and more usable state to a disordered, bound and less usable state as its internal thermal temperature reaches equilibrium with its external surroundings...[t]he conservation law and the first law of thermodynamics are associated with the problem of pollution and the second law with absolute resource scarcity (Underwood and King, 1989:323).

While recognizing the historical evidence for resource substitution (e.g,. Barnett and Morse, 1963) and making no specific claim about where the limits of technology are in the face of the entropy law, Underwood and King conclude that "to argue that absolute scarcity does not exist, or that it can be 'solved' by technological progress, is to deny the existence of the laws of thermodynamics; there are no known exceptions to these laws" (1989:328).

They also argue that the new cosmology has dictated new ontological elements—ethics and morality.

A steady state economic analysis asks the discipline and the society to transcend rational egoism as the motivating principle for the actions of homo economicus. Interestingly, Jevons, one of the architects of classical egoism, was well aware of the alternative principles of motivation:

> "A higher calculus of moral right and wrong could be needed to show how he may best employ that wealth for the good of others as well as himself. But when that higher calculus gives no prohibition, we need the lower calculus to gain us the utmost good in matters of moral indifference" (1871:32).

For proponents of the steady state, the question of sustainability is not a matter of moral indifference. It is *the* question of Political Economy, all others having only tangential importance...If limits exist, and the entropy law shows us they do, then ethical values can make claims upon economic analysis (Underwood and King, 1989:332).

Out of these two different schools of thought, reflecting different beliefs and associated world views, come markedly different perspectives on policy. While neoclassicists focus on making the market work in spite of its failures, steady statists focus on determining the limits within which the market should work. Thus while both see a role for the invisible hand, the latter sees it as secondary to the issue of setting limits to material throughputs. Questions of absolute scarcity take primacy over the neoclassicist's concern with relative scarcity and the environmental problem is viewed in its global dimensions over a longer time continuum. More fundamentally, ethical and moral judgements involving non-utilitarian values, in particular those associated with the environment, are seen to be the basis upon which choices should be made.

By elaborating these two major schools of thought in environmental economics, we illuminate more clearly some of the distinctions between the technocentric and ecocentric world views. Clearly the neoclassical school of thought is more strongly associated with the dominant cornucopian world view and, likewise, the steady statists support challenges to it. But it is not quite so obvious whether steady statism might go beyond what the accommodators seek and yet not far enough for the communalists; accommodators may not want to go so far as to give predominance to non-utilitarian values and communalists may not be satisfied without greater commitment to decentralisation in the socio-economic system. At the same time, not all steady statists would adopt the non-anthropocentric ethics of deep ecologists (Shearman, 1990).

Once again, as with regard to world views, most of the contributed papers are ambiguous or inexplicit about the economic school of thought to which they subscribe. Most of them at least touch upon the economics of the environment and six specifically address the potential for increased use of market mechanisms (Fox, Hutton and Davis, McNeill, Pearse and Tate, Rankin, Scott). In varying degrees of explicitness, some appear to be based on the assumption of a neoclassical model and others on the steady-state model. Only Rees and Boothroyd explicitly address their subscription to steady state theory. Such ambiguities about world views and schools of thought are important because they not only obscure the debate about the definition of sustainable development but also confuse the discussion of its implications for water resources management.

Implications of Sustainable Development for Water Resources Management

The second of the two general requests to each of the authors of the contributed papers was that they relate their analysis to water resources management and, in as far as possible, to the Fraser River Basin. All of the papers have related the discussion of their topic to water resources management in general and, in many cases they contribute extensive detail on their topic drawn from the Fraser River Basin. However, the manner in which this is related to sustainable development principles varies greatly, reflecting in turn differences in views on its definition and implications.

Sustainable development of water and other resources is generally perceived very differently by the three challenges to the dominant world view of the cornucopians. Indeed for most ecocentrists, the narrowly technocentric view of the natural world is epitomised by reference to it as a "resource" and the belief that it can be "managed." These words are seen by ecocentrists to reflect the narrow concern with use and the instrumental value of the biosphere. The idea that the ecosystem can be managed is perceived by ecocentrists as anthropocentric and neglecting both non-utilitarian values and the profound ignorance of ecosystem behaviour; at a minimum, this is perceived by them to be incomplete, more seriously, as arrogant and immoral (see discussion in Rees, this volume).

In the present research, the "management of water and other natural resources" is discussed because of the pervasive use of these terms and the convoluted phrasing that results from trying to avoid them. It must be stressed, however, that it should not be presumed that this implies adoption of a cornucopian technocentric view; when this is intended it is made explicit, just as for any of the other views.

Not only are disagreements with regard to the sustainable development of resources obscured by the very words central to discussion of the issue, but also there is great difficulty in differentiating between principles and practice. On the one hand, there are bodies of academic and professional literature which advance ideas about how people *should* relate to the biosphere in order to achieve specific goals; expressed in the terms commonly used, they are "natural resource management principles". On the other hand, there is the actual experience of what *is* practiced in the real world of resource management. The two are seldom the same for a wide variety of reasons. This section concentrates firstly on issues of principle and later comes to the further complications of practice.

The Disciplines of Water Resources Management

Water is a mature field of academic and professional specialization, perhaps longer established than any other relating to the natural environment. This is not surprising given the belief that life originated in water and the recognition of its essential role in supporting the existence of life. Beyond the continuing basic human interest in water for drinking, there have grown to be other interests in aquatic environments that are increasingly diverse, substantial and often conflicting: it is a source of food and means for travel; it is manipulated to avoid floods, to divert supply, to transport things around, to irrigate the land, to make power, to enjoy recreation and to flush away wastes; and it is appreciated for its intrinsic value. All of these water interests, in past, present and future forms, are at least touched upon in the contributed papers and some are considered in detail.

Reflecting such a diversity of interests, studies in the field have long involved a variety of disciplines (Saha and Barrow, 1981). River basin management studies in the twentieth century have increasingly been *multidisciplinary* in the sense of having relevant aspects addressed by a growing diversity of different disciplines (e.g., the hydrologists modelling the river flows, the fisheries biologists inventorying the fish stocks, the economists analysing the regional economy, and the lawyers assessing the institutional arrangements [see Figure 21.1a]). In earlier days the multidisciplinary approach was typified by investigators from different disciplines not directly working together and only using and referencing each others work to a limited extent in the production of component studies and publications. When an overall report was produced, it would likely involve little interaction and would have separate sections on each of the different aspects authored as separate contributions.

The water field has, however, also been a major innovator in *interdisciplinary* studies that advance greater interactions between the disciplines, perhaps one of the primary fields for such innovation (Figure 21.1b). There have been major advances in the understanding of natural resource systems, analytical techniques and policy design, which have been adopted in many other countries, as a result of interdisciplinary initiatives in the United States and Canada in the years since the Second World War (Dorcey, 1987). The Harvard Water Project in the 1950's brought together one of the early teams, including hydrologists, economists and political scientists, that began to work in a more interactive manner and made the important shift from multidisciplinary to more interdisciplinary approaches. In the early 1970's in Canada, this also began to happen as a result of the Federal-Provincial river basin studies conducted under the new Canada Water Act (e.g., the Okanagan and Saint John River Basin studies), as well as programs undertaken by the new university research centres established by the Inland Waters Directorate of Environment Canada. One of these centres was Westwater; it undertook a five year interdisciplinary study of science, policies and institutional arrangements for water pollution control in the Lower Fraser River (Dorcey, 1976; 1986).

From these innovations, however, it began to be recognised that it was necessary to develop *transdisciplinary* approaches to river basin management before further advances could be made (Saha and Barrow, 1981. See Figure 21.1c). Beyond the progress that can be made by revising the theories of individual disciplines as a result of people from each working together, is the possibility of forging new disciplines and associated theories. Drawing on

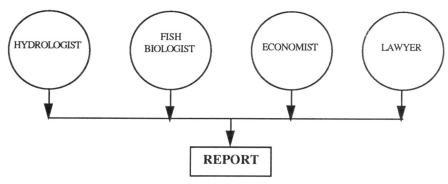

Figure 21.1a: Multidisciplinary

Figure 21.1b: Interdisciplinary

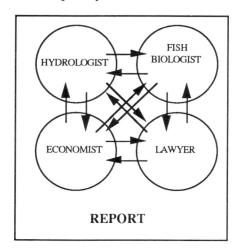

Figure 21.1c: Transdisciplinary

experience over thousands of years, as well as the more recent experience in both developed and developing countries, Saha and Barrow traced how this had already begun to happen in the water field in the late 1970's and suggested the opportunities that lay ahead.

> The idea of integrated management of land and water resources is not new. The history of irrigated agriculture can be traced all the way back to 7000 BC in Jericho. Many of the World's greatest civilisations have had close association with rivers. The Hindu-Indian, Egyptian, Chinese, and Sumerian civilisations emerged and flourished in the major river valleys of the Indus, Nile, Hwang-Ho and Tigris-Euphrates respectively. These 'hydraulic' civilisations rose to great heights of splendour because they were each successful in evolving a technology and in organising a social, economic and political system which enabled them to harness the water resources at their disposal. They flourished over long periods of history because they learnt to manage their land and water resources in a way that harmonised the pursuit of economic objectives with the integrity of their environment. Eventually they disintegrated or were subjugated by outside powers or suffered long periods of destabilisation because they used their technology and political authority to enforce social structures which became increasingly oppressive. There seems to be a moral in this broad sequence of history—a moral which present societies presently trying to rediscover the ancient art of successful river basin development can only ignore at their peril. And the moral seems to be this: *Economic development can be sustained as a continuous process only if it is ecologically sound and socially just.* (Saha and Barrow, 1981:1, emphasis added)

Anticipating ideas that have since been popularized by the Brundtland report, Saha and Barrow defined a context for water resources management emphasizing that social justice and the maintenance of ecosystem integrity are necessary for what they referred to as sustainable economic development. They concluded that this, in turn, necessitated a focus on transdisciplinary learning that would be capable of generating a new model and principles.

> A shared paradigm will take time to emerge. In the meantime, the only way the existing gaps in the information system could be bridged and the fragmentary nature of the academic knowledge base could be harmonized and made to fit in more closely with the integrated need structure of the user is to institute a system of trans-disciplinary [sic] learning. In trans-disciplinary learning, one would retain his firm roots in his own disciplinary knowledge base, but at the same time would have to display the intellectual capability of cutting through the web of special symbolisms and imageries that all disciplines tend to weave around themselves and reach out to the concept systems of

other disciplines. This 'reaching out' process need not quite reach out to the roots of the other disciplines but the contact established with the rich new flora across one's disciplinary boundary will in itself go a long way in linking up the disparate information systems into an integrated knowledge base (Saha and Barrow, 1981:33-34).

A decade later, progress in developing a new water management paradigm or model has indeed been slow, as Saha and Barrow predicted. It is now evident, however, that transdisciplinary learning is even more important and it needs to question more fundamentally the roots of other disciplines than even Saha and Barrow perceived.

Challenging the Dominant View

The principles of water resources management found in the literature today are in large part the result of the challenges to dominant views that began to be mounted in the United States and Canada in the second half of the 1960's (Dorcey, 1987). They were already widely acknowledged in Canada by the mid 1970's. The challenges to dominant views were stimulated by the growing concerns about pollution and other undesired consequences of economic development. River basin planning and impact assessment processes began to be seen as essential parts of management. Out of the earlier concepts of multiple purpose river basin development, using multiple means to pursue multiple objectives, came ideas for integrated resources management. The need to consider not only economic but also environmental and social consequences of water resources development was responded to in new valuation methods and procedures. Pricing of water use was believed to be the way to increase economic efficiency and equity. Opportunities for involving the public in impact assessment and planning were considered to be essential to the process of evaluation and a fundamental element of regional approaches to management. At the time, O'Riordan (1976) characterised these changes as a shift towards a more ecocentric world view, although he still believed that it remained dominantly technocentric.

In the second half of the 1970's and during the first half of the 1980's, the momentum of change in the dominant view and putting new water management principles into practice faltered in Canada. In part, this was a consequence of events outside the immediate water field (in particular economic problems) but it was also a result of reactions to the changes. The newly emerging economic, environmental and social elements of the model were being challenged and a decade of heightened conflict and of uncertainty about water management principles ensued.

Environmental and social impact assessment requirements for projects, planning for river basins, and public involvement processes were increasingly challenged in the late seventies, by developers and politicians, as generating more costs than benefits (Thompson, 1981). At a time when there was growing concern about cutting costs in order to improve competitiveness. these "regulatory" costs became the focus of increasing attack. One response in the late 1970's was a referral by the Prime Minister to the Economic Council of Canada to assess the costs and benefits of regulation in all aspects of Canadian governance (Economic Council of Canada, 1981). Even though their studies concluded that deregulation was not relevant to environmental regulation and that the issue was how to make regulation more productive, the report came at a time when concerns about restoring economic growth were paramount. There was a strong interest in downsizing government and increasing the use of market mechanisms, not only in Canada but also in other countries such as the United States and the United Kingdom. Associated with this has been a growing body of research founded on neo-conservative ideals including some focusing on water and environmental management (e.g., Anderson, 1983; Block, 1989). As reflected in the cornucopian world view and neoclassical schools of thought, the emphasis is on the definition of rights and duties, market mechanisms for the transfer of rights, and the use of pricing mechanisms (see discussion of these instruments of governance in the papers by Fox, McNeill, Pearse and Tate, Rankin, and Scott).

Even before these events unfolded, there were already concerns among some writers that the changes of the early seventies did not adequately address the degradation of the aquatic environment. A major focus of such concern in Canada has been water pollution in the Great Lakes (Colborn, 1990). This was the genesis of what has become known as the "ecosystem approach" to water management, with origins in the intensive research that was undertaken as a result of the Great Lakes Water Quality Agreement signed by the United States and Canada in 1972. The research focused on the urgent problem (typified by the concern that Lake Erie was dead or dying of eutrophication) resulting from excess nutrients entering the water from land based activities. Lessons learned in this research laid the foundation for a new agreement in 1978, which had a much more comprehensive objective: to restore and maintain the chemical, physical and biological integrity of the Great Lakes Basin ecosystem. To do this, it was recognised that it would be necessary to deal with the interacting components of air, land, water and living organisms, including humans, within the drainage basin.

In assessing the results of implementing the ecosystem approach over the last decade, Colborn et al., (1990), recount its considerable success in remedying lake eutrophication problems, but suggest that it is only over the next decade that it will become evident whether the increasingly serious problems in other areas that have been revealed by applying the ecosystem approach can be resolved. For example, research in the intervening years has brought to light much more difficult and serious problems relating to toxic materials, acid precipitation and climate change; problems that necessitate consideration of not only the whole basin, but also of regions outside the basin and even global systems. More fundamentally, Colborn et al. point out that the ecosystem approach is as much a philosophical concept as a management system; it implies committing to ethical principles for restoring and conserving the natural resource base so that future generations inherit it in at least no worse condition. While the authors conclude that it is the only approach to water management that is appropriate to the task, they are unsure whether this ecocentric view will be accepted widely enough to attract public support and the necessary management resources. A comparable emphasis on the need for an ecosystem approach is found in several of the background papers (see Fox, Gardner, Henderson, Kimmins and Duffy, Rees, Savard).

Again, even before both economic and environmental concerns were being loudly voiced, some people's doubts focused on the efficacy of the social aspects of the innovations of the early 1970's (see Boothroyd, Dale, Fox and Gardner in this volume and references in Gardner and Roseland, 1989a,b; Berkes, 1989; Pinkerton, 1989). Their concerns relate to varied issues in water management, but in particular to decision-making processes and questions of equity. Although public involvement processes conducted as part of project assessments, watershed planning and aquatic resources management became more common, they were perceived by some to be inadequate. There was insufficient opportunity for participation and the resulting decisions appeared to be unaffected by it. This increasingly generated a suspicion of cooptation. Others more fundamentally questioned only being consulted and not being given the opportunity to make decisions directly. For many of these people, the issue was seen as one of fairness and a question of redistributing power. Often these concerns focused on resource based communities and aboriginal peoples that were being impacted by the boom and bust cycles of economic growth and associated environmental degradation. The conclusion of many of these writers is that much more emphasis must be given to community development strategies that give local peoples greater responsibilities and opportunities to make decisions for themselves. From this broadly based communal ecocentric view, common property analysts have argued that co-management of aquatic resources, such as fish and water, is a better alternative than either solely state or private property regimes that predominate in the technocentric view. Many of these themes are developed by authors of the background papers (see Boothroyd, Dale, Fox, Gardner, Kew and Griggs, Thompson, and Rees).

Towards Agreement

By placing the background papers in the larger context of literature on sustainable development and water resources management, it is easier to appreciate why people disagree on the conclusions that they reach about the implications of sustainable development principles for water resources management. In fact, there would appear to be more common ground about the principles that should guide water resources management than the differences about sustainable development principles might at first suggest. In the next two sections the general nature of this potential agreement is suggested while exploring strategies that can be employed in beginning to move towards agreement.

Towards Agreement on a Definition of Sustainable Development

Given the value-laden nature and ethical content of the sustainable development concept, it is not surprising (and indeed, in principle, quite legitimate) that each individual has their own definition of sustainable development. In the light of this, what can be said about reaching agreement on a definition of sustainable development? What should be done to move towards this in academic and governance forums? For this project, as for many others, the Brundtland definition has been a useful starting point, but clearly more needs to be done than was suggested in the initial elaboration of it, if misunderstandings are to be avoided. In the immediate future, a general strategy for the immediate future of exploring the implications of different ethical elements explicitly and testing their application in various contexts, while searching for common ground, still makes sense and would appear to be essential.

In arriving at similar conclusions and recommendations, Shearman (1990) has argued that it is not the *meaning* of sustainability that is unclear, but the *implications* of its application in a particular context. He suggests that there can surely be no debate about the dictionary definition of sustainability—"the capability of being maintained"—paraphrasing the Oxford English Dictionary definition quoted by Brown et al., (1987).

> In the final analysis, I assert that the meaning of sustainability should not be an item for further discussion. What should be discussed are the implications of sustainability that result when it is applied as a modifier to a particular context. In other words, what are the consequences that result from seeking a sustainable society, a sustainable economic arrangement, or a sustainable ecosystem, and how are they constituted? What contradictions, if any, become apparent within each of these contexts when sustainability is sought as a goal? (Shearman, 1990:3).

Accepting this argument, the specific interest of this project is in exploring the implications of "sustainability" for the management of water in the sustainable development of large river basins. To do this it is necessary to anticipate the diversity of contexts in which the goal of sustainability might arise. In the initial analytical framework, this was done in a preliminary way by recognising the three systems—environmental, economic and social—from which they might arise separately or in various combinations. Further, in elaborating this framework it was proposed that the project should understand sustainable development as an evolving ethic relating to all three systems and including at least five ethical elements:

- Maintaining ecological integrity and diversity;
- Meeting basic human needs;
- Keeping options open for future generations;
- Reducing injustice; and,
- Increasing self-determination.

It is now evident, however, that while this framework serves well as a preliminary indication of the potential comprehensiveness of the concept of sustainable development, it needs to be further elaborated to provide a better basis for understanding why views differ and thus assist in moving towards greater agreement. In summary, a framework is needed that can be used both to make clear what is embraced in the concept of sustainable development and to clarify why and how people's views differ.

One simple way that we have found to be helpful in exploring different views of sustainable development is by drawing diagrams of the systems involved. The diagrams can be designed so as to bring out alternative views about the subsystems involved and the nature of their interrelationships. Figure 21.2a illustrates the idea that the interactions between interdependent environmental, economic and social systems should be analysed in considering sustainable development. By drawing the relations between the three systems differently, it is possible to reflect the effects of "first thinking" (e.g., Figure 21.2b) or, more strongly, the belief that one system should be considered a subsystem of another. These diagrams can be used to clarify, in relatively simple terms, whether people believe that

(i)   all three systems should be considered in their notion of sustainable development;
(ii)   one or more systems should be considered as subsystems; and,
(iii) one system should be judged to be more important than another.

The diagrams can also be drawn so as to add other systems or show different constituent subsystems (e.g., Figure 21.2c). This can be used to clarify whether people believe that

(iv)   all the systems that should be considered are included; and,
(v)   constituent subsystems should be differently represented.

When consideration is given to what people believe to be the ethical elements that should be recognised and how they view the appropriateness of the minimal five suggested above, it is almost certain to be necessary to elaborate the diagram in a more detailed form, such as that illustrated by Figure 21.2c.

However, of much greater importance than the diagrams, which are only an aid, is to follow Shearman's proposal and ask questions focussing on what needs to be clarified. This will reveal what people consider to be the *context* for sustainability and hence what they believe to be the *meaning* and *implications* of sustainable development. From our experience, a few simple questions can go a long way in clearing up misunderstandings, clarifying residual reasons for disagreement and moving towards agreements.

This is the way in which to begin to deal with what is perhaps the most serious problem in the sustainable development debate—the deafening silence about assumptions and presumptions. Even within agreed world views or schools of thought, this can cause great difficulty. However, when the debate involves challenging those that are dominant, as the debate about sustainable development does, then the problem is increased exponentially, as revealed by the ambiguities in the contributed papers. While it has been recognised that the controversy is about challenges to the dominant ideas, it does not seem that enough attention has been given to the strategies for advancing such a debate.

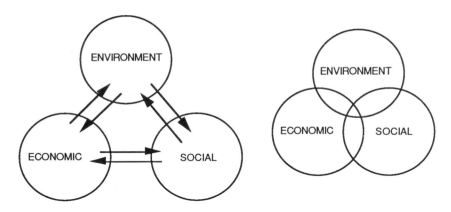

Figure 21.2a: What systems should be considered in sustainable development?

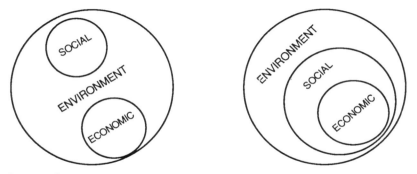

Figure 21.2b: Are some of them sub-systems?

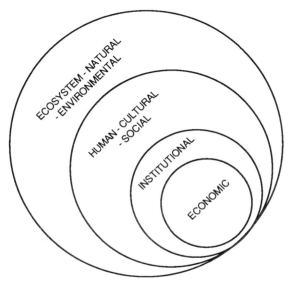

Figure 21.2c: One way of conceptualizing the analysis of sustainable development.

One strategy that can be employed is to consider actively the implications of alternative views of sustainable development and how these relate to what appear to be emerging as common elements of the challenge to the traditionally dominant view. Extending Norgaard's (1989) arguments for actively exploiting competing and contrasting methodologies in environmental economics, there might be an argument for doing the same in fostering movement towards agreement on the definition of sustainable development. A glimpse of what this might involve and yield is provided by the comparison of the neoclassical and steady state schools of thought that was made above. It is further illustrated by additional examples in the final chapter.

The deafness of disciplines and schools of thought to the ideas of others is a major source of lost opportunity. Each has an immense amount to offer that could complement the other. Too much attention is focused on accentuating the differences between the views and too little on the potential complementarities. As a result, good ideas and principles often languish in separate literatures. It is necessary to give much more thought as to how to encourage more vigorous debate of these ideas and principles, so as to test their worth and bring them forward in a more constructive fashion. Publications specifically designed to do this, such as the integrative books mentioned above (e.g., Daly and Cobb, 1989) and the recently introduced journal *Ecological Economics*, can be important elements in the strategies that are needed.

While the potential for divergence is very great, it is encouraging that some of the most vigorous critics of the dominant cornucopian view have emphasized that there is much to be offered by conventional disciplinary models which they would want to employ, albeit within the context of strategies that have different fundamentals. For example, Daly and Cobb (1989) stress that although their book on steady state theories and community development is a severe critique of the contemporary discipline of economics, this does not mean that they do not see an important role for market principles in replacing government regulation, in order to better serve many public purposes. Likewise, O'Riordan (1988) acknowledges that some of the technocentric innovations recommended by his colleague, Turner (1988), can make growth more sustainable, even though they do not address the ethical norms that he considers to be essential to sustainable development from his more ecocentric viewpoint.

Further, there is clearly a need to complement this strategy of learning from differences with one of iterating between debates in simple and more complex terms. We have seen that relatively simple questions and classifications of world views can be powerful aids in clarifying the discussion of sustainable development. But we have also shown that they inevitably obscure issues that can only be addressed by more complex analyses within and between different schools of thought. These analyses are ultimately of great assistance in revealing that disagreements about sustainable development are underlain by the most fundamental questions in the philosophy of science, morals and ethics. At the end of the final chapter, I will suggest the implications of these conclusions for future research focussed more specifically on defining sustainable development.

Towards Agreement on Implications for Water Management

The Brundtland report did not resolve the emerging challenges to the dominant view, but it did shift the debate by considering arguments emanating from all three sources of challenge and by suggesting one way in which they might be brought together in a concept of sustainable development. Although the report did not address water management in particular, a succession of subsequent studies, conferences and publications have begun to explore more specifically the implications of sustainability for water management (e.g., Golubev et al., 1988; Falkenmark, 1988; IWRA, 1988; Colborn et al., 1990). Progress to date has, however, been slow because of the difficulties encountered with the varied interpretations of sustainable development. If the general strategy that was proposed above for defining sustainable development was applied, better progress might be made in moving towards greater agreement on the implications for water resources management principles.

More fundamentally, to make exploration of the implications of sustainability in the water field more productive, it is critically important to foster greater transdisciplinary learning. This is not easy and will take time, as illustrated by the background papers and case study in the first phase of this program of research on sustainability. Critics can easily say that the contributed papers are not a product of transdisciplinary learning. In those instances where there is more than one author of a paper, they are generally not bringing together substantial differences in disciplinary views. In so far as any author brings interdisciplinary or transdisciplinary perspectives to bear, this is very much the result of what the author contributes to the task separately as a result of his or her previous research experience. Interactions among the authors of the papers have taken place, but as described in the Preface, these were limited compared with what they might be in future phases of the research. In addition, it should be noted that some of the authors came to this project familiar with literature on water resources but with relatively little previous knowledge of the literatures on sustainable development and vice versa.

To dwell on such criticism would be short sighted. These papers should be viewed as a starting point for the interactions that will lead to transdisciplinary learning. It is necessary to start slowly to be successful in attracting and sustaining the involvement of people who have significant differences in their world views, operate within competing schools of thought and bring to bear the divergent perspectives of the academic and practitioner. Likewise, it is essential to involve people who have much to offer but are initially relatively unfamiliar with literature on sustainable development or water resources management. It is, however, of the utmost importance to catalyse a constructive and searching examination of the assumptions that underlie their different views. This will be essential to eventual success in other research programs as well as this one. To bring together people who hold similar views might produce agreements more quickly, but it would not address the critical need to foster not only transdisciplinary learning in academic forums but also more productive ways to deal with the conflict over sustainability in the society at large. Besides, it is in the nature of things that there will always be many more research groups whose participants share similar views in addressing sustainability issues, than there are diverse groups.

Despite the differences in the interpretation of the Brundtland definition of sustainable development, it would appear that evolving principles of water resources management go a long way towards potentially addressing its breadth of concerns. By concentrating on what the challengers to the dominant paradigm have in common, it seems likely that there could be widespread agreement that water resource management principles should at least provide for making governance decisions

- based on the consideration of economic, environmental and social values;
- informed by research, project assessment and watershed planning;
- structured for involving stakeholders and elected representatives;
- implemented by combinations of regulatory and market mechanisms; and
- enforced ultimately by the courts.

Each of these elements can be generally found in the Federal Water Policy adopted in Canada in 1987 and they are variously advocated in the background papers. However, just as in the case of the five ethical elements of sustainable development, it is unclear how much agreement there really is until each of them is explored in the more specific terms that reveal the different designs and emphases that people have in mind. In the next chapter, these elements are examined in more detail.

References

Anderson, T. 1983. *Water Crisis: Ending the Policy Drought.* Baltimore, Md.: John Hopkins University Press.

Barnett, H. J., and Morse, C. 1963. *Scarcity and Growth: The Economics of Natural Resource Availability.* Baltimore: Johns Hopkins.

Berkes, F. (ed.). 1989. *Common Property Resources: Ecology and Community-Based Sustainable Development.* London: Belhaven Press.

Block, W. 1990. *Economics and the Environment: A Reconciliation.* Vancouver: Fraser Institute.

Boulding, K. 1970. *Economics as a Science.* New York: McGraw-Hill.

Brown, B., M. E. Hanson, D. M. Liverman and R. W. Merideth. 1987. "Global Sustainability: Toward Definition." *Environmental Management.* 11(6):713-719.

Colborn, T. E., A. Davidson, S. N. Green, R. A. Hodge, C. I. Jackson and R. A. Liroff. 1990. *Great Lakes Great Legacy?* Ottawa: Institute for Research on Public Policy.

Daly, H. E. 1977. *Steady-State Economics.* San Francisco: Freeman.

Daly, H. E. 1990. "Towards Some Operational Principles of Sustainable Development." *Ecological Economics.* 2 (1):1-6.

Daly, H. E., and J. B. Cobb. 1989. *For the Common Good: Redirecting the Economy Toward Community, the Environment, and a Sustainable Future.* Boston: Beacon Press.

Dorcey, A. H. J. 1976. *The Uncertain Future of the Lower Fraser.* Vancouver: Westwater Research Centre, The University of British Columbia.

Dorcey, A. H. J. 1986. *Bargaining in the Governance of Pacific Coastal Resources: Research and Reform.* Vancouver: Westwater Research Centre, The University of British Columbia.

Dorcey, A. H. J. 1987. "Research for Water Resources Management: The Rise and Fall of Great Expectations." in Healey, M. C., and R. R. Wallace. (eds.). *Canadian Aquatic Resources.* Canadian Bulletin of Fisheries and Aquatic Sciences. 215:481-511.

Economic Council of Canada. 1981. *Reforming Regulation.* Ottawa: Supply and Services Canada.

Falkenmark, M. 1988. "Sustainable Development as Seen from a Water Perspective." in Stockholm Group for Studies in Natural Resources Management, *Perspectives on Sustainable Development: Some Critical Issues Related to the Brundtland Report.* Stockholm: Department of Natural Resources Management, University of Stockholm.

Gardner, J. E., and M. Roseland. 1989a. "Thinking Globally: The Role of Social Equity in Sustainable Development." *Alternatives.* 16(3):26-35.

Gardner, J. E., and M. Roseland. 1989b. "Acting Locally: Community Strategies for Equitable Sustainable Development." *Alternatives.* 16(3):36-48.

Georgescu-Roegen, N. 1971. *The Entropy Law and the Economic Process.* Cambridge: Harvard University Press.

Golubev, G. N., L. J. David and A. K. Biswas (eds.). 1988. "Sustainable Water Development." Special Issue, *Water Resources Development.* 4(2):74-148.

IWRA, 1988. *Water for World Development.* Proceedings of the VIth International Water Resources Association World Congress on Water Resources, Ottawa 29 May-3 June, 1988.

Jevons, W. S. 1871. *The Theory of Political Economy.* London: Macmillan.

Næss, A. 1973. "The Shallow and the Deep, Long Range Ecology Movements: A Summary." *Inquiry.* 16:95-100.

Norgaard, R. B. 1989. "The Case for Methodological Pluralism." *Ecological Economics.* 1(1):37-57.

O'Riordan. T. 1976. *Environmentalism.* London: Pion Ltd.

O'Riordan, T., and R. K. Turner. 1983. *An Annotated Reader in Environmental Planning and Management.* Oxford: Pergammon.

O'Riordan, T. 1988. "The Politics of Sustainability." in Turner, R. K. (ed.). 1988. *Sustainable Environmental Management: Principles and Practice.* Boulder: Westview Press, Colorado.

Pinkerton, E. (ed.). 1989. *Co-operative Management of Local Fisheries: New Directions for Improved Management and Community Development.* Vancouver: University of British Columbia Press.

Saha, S. K., and C. J. Barrow. 1981. *River Basin Planning: Theory and Practice.* Toronto: Wiley.

Shearman, R. 1990. "The Meaning and Ethics of Sustainability." *Environmental Management.* 14(1):1-8.

Simon, J., and H. Kahn (eds.). 1984. *The Resourceful Earth: A Response to Global 2000.* Oxford: Basil Blackwell.

Thompson, A. R. 1981. *Environmental Regulation in Canada: An Assessment of the Regulatory Process.* Vancouver: Westwater Research Centre, The University of British Columbia.

Turner, R. K. (ed.). 1988. *Sustainable Environmental Management: Principles and Practice.* Boulder: Westview Press, Colorado.

Underwood, D. A., and P. G. King. 1989. "On the Ideological Foundations of Environmental Policy." *Ecological Economics.* 1(4):315-334.

Vlachos, E., and J. D. Priscoli (eds.). 1990. "Water, Peace and Conflict Management." Special Issue, *Water International.* 15(4).

22

Towards Agreement in Water Management: An Evolving Sustainable Development Model

Anthony H. J. Dorcey

In this chapter, the model of water resources management that has been evolving in the literature on water resources management is elaborated more specifically and related to the emerging principles of sustainable development. Drawing on a wide variety of literatures and the background papers, the analytical framework that can guide the case study in the second volume, as well as future research, is explored. In elaborating the evolving model, the objective is to define an analytical framework that is powerful in itself, but simple enough for the first stage and capable of advancement in future research.

Assessing Sustainability

To progress in any discussion of sustainability, it is essential to agree on how it is to be assessed in more specific terms than have been examined so far. As seen in the previous chapter, the consideration of sustainability in terms of world views or disciplinary schools of thought inevitably involves discussion of particular sets of variables or parameters that each perspective judges to be essential. This section examines the issues involved in agreeing on *indicators of sustainability*—indicators that are capable of addressing the differing interests of aquatic technocentrists and aquatic ecocentrists. Their different perspectives on environmental, economic and social systems have led to the development of diverse measures and associated empirical and analytical techniques. In addition, there have been growing efforts to generate indices combining economic, environmental and social indicators in ways that might permit assessment of sustainability at both the macro and micro level.

Economic Perspectives

From the outset, controversy about indicators has been a central part of the challenge to the dominant technocentric view. Growing recognition of the inadequacies and distortions inherent in using Gross National Product (GNP) as the indicator of a nation's well-being has increasingly led to the development of economic, environmental and social indicators since the 1960's. When national accounts were being developed in the 1930's and 1940's, the primary concern was the assessment of macroeconomic performance using national income as the indicator (Repetto et al., 1989). Reflecting the influence of Keynes, the accounts were primarily concerned with estimating national income and consideration of variables such as consumption, savings, investment and government expenditure. Whereas national income statements indicate the flow of income each year, national balance sheets indicate the change in the stock of assets, but in neither case do changes in natural resource flows or stocks get included, unless they are reflected in monetary transactions of the economy. Growing concerns about the distortions, underestimation and neglect of these flows and stocks, as well as the limited perspective on values provided by monetary measures, has led to a variety of innovations.

While continuing in a predominantly technocentric mold, innovations have involved adding and combining environmental and social indicators. At the macro level, this has included experimentation with both satellite environmental (e.g., Norway, France, Canada [Potvin, 1989]) and social accounts (e.g., United Kingdom, United States, Canada [Carley, 1980]), as well as adjusted national economic accounts (e.g., Japan, Indonesia [Pearce et al., 1989]). Since 1978, France has pioneered an approach to satellite environmental accounts, involving the design of four sets of physical accounts to complement the monetary accounting. The French system adds information about natural resource stocks and flows in a four part classification: type of environment (inland waters, air, soil); living organisms (fauna, flora); land (unbuilt areas); underground resources (mineral, energy). The water accounts include breakdowns of water balances, water related expenditures and revenue, and water quality conditions relative to objectives (Pearce et al., 1989). Currently there is no internationally accepted approach to extended national accounting and nowhere yet are the environmental innovations fully operational. Canada is developing an approach that uses elements of both satellite and adjusted accounts (Potvin, 1989).

With regard to social indicators, Canada now collects diverse information through its census and various governmental program activities. This information complements the economic indicators largely in the same manner as satellite environmental accounts; there has not been comparable interest in the production of adjusted social accounts.

It is in the context of these innovations that the question of indicators of sustainability has begun to be considered in the last decade. Disagreements about the definition of sustainable development have been compounded by the rich potential for disagreement in the use of indicators to measure sustainability. The choice of sustainability indicators is strongly influenced by the world view and disciplinary schools of thought adopted and the consequent selective emphases on economic, environmental and social systems.

From the technocentric perspective, the major emphasis has been on ways to adapt traditional economic indicators of well-being to take account of environmental and social costs and benefits that are neglected in measures such as GNP. For example, one of the earliest approaches of this kind was initiated by Japan in 1973 and involved estimating Net National Welfare by deducting losses due to environmental pollution and urbanization (Uno, 1988; cited in Pearce et al., 1989). Their estimates indicate the adjustment is quite substantial; instead of GNP growing by a factor of 8.3 between 1955 and 1985, the adjusted measure suggests growth by a factor of only 5.8.

Focusing on the definition and measurement of sustainable development from a relatively progressive but still predominantly neoclassical perspective, the proposals of Pearce et al.(1989) have received widespread attention. They build on the Brundtland concept of sustainable development and argue that "the prescription is to leave to future generations a *wealth* inheritance—a stock of knowledge and understanding, a stock of technology, a stock of man-made capital *and* a stock of environmental assets—no less than that inherited by the current generation" (WCED, 1989:xiv; emphasis in original). After examining the national approaches that have been tried so far in measuring sustainability they predictably conclude that those that utilise monetary measures in so far as possible (e.g., Japan) are to be preferred over those employing physical measures. They recommend beginning to make estimates of *sustainable income* (WCED, 1989:108) where

sustainable income = measured income   - household defensive expenditures
                                                                   - monetary value of residual pollution
                                                                   - depreciation of man-made capital
                                                                   - depreciation of environmental capital

While Pearce et al. only outline how this might be done, Daly and Cobb (1989) have subsequently reported on an Index of Sustainable Economic Welfare (ISEW) for the United States which follows in the same tradition but includes a broader set of indicators, reflecting their more ecocentric view. Focusing on the period from 1950 to 1986, Daly and Cobb estimated that real GNP per capita grew by 106%, but per capita ISEW only by 37%. In addition, the overall increase for the whole period masked a levelling off during the 1970's and a decline in the 1980's (1950's: 0.84%; 1960's: 2.01%; 1970's: -0.14%; 1980's: -1.26%), which they attributed to growing income inequality, exhaustion of resources, and failure to invest adequately to sustain the economy in the future (see discussion of Canadian indicators in Boothroyd, this volume).

These macroeconomic approaches to the assessment of sustainability have been accompanied by complementary innovations at the micro level of project assessment and regional planning. The innovations have been associated to a large extent with the water field in the United States and Canada (Dorcey, 1987). In the early 1970's, a system of four project accounts was developed in the United States and variations on it were applied in Canada: National Economic Development

Account; Environmental Quality Account; Regional Development Account; and Social Well-Being Account. The objective was to extend cost-benefit analyses of projects so as to go beyond the narrow focus on national income and to indicate better previously neglected environmental and social consequences. There is again a preference for expressing these accounts in monetary terms, but of necessity non-monetary indicators are often used. To assess the regional consequences of development, there have been pathbreaking research projects in the water field to link economic and environmental systems through the use of input-output analyses and simulation models. In considering project appraisal requirements in the context of their definition of sustainable development, Pearce et al. (1989) conclude that it has two specific implications for more appropriate analysis: more extensive use of improved techniques for estimating environmental values (e.g. option, existence and bequest valuation techniques) and making investment programmes subject to a sustainability constraint to ensure that environmental capital in the aggregate is not reduced.

Thus, acting within the dominant technocentric view, there have been substantial innovations in developing indicators of economic well-being which incorporate economic, environmental and social indicators and that might be used in assessing sustainability (as emphasized in papers by Hutton and Davis, and Pearse and Tate, this volume). However, not only are there major difficulties in putting these innovations into practice, as discussed in a later section, but also they are fundamentally questionable to those who come from a more ecocentric viewpoint.

Environmental Perspectives

The introduction and expansion of impact assessment requirements in the 1970's was a response to such concerns and catalysed extensive work on the design and implementation of environmental indicators. For example, in the water field, indicators of water quantity and quality became much more varied and complex as they came to be considered in increasingly comprehensive and sophisticated systems contexts (e.g., see Sheehy, 1989). The design of indicators for water stocks and flows was already well defined because of the relatively advanced state of hydrological science; this relative sophistication was the result of many years of development studies dealing with water supply, flood control, hydroelectricity and navigation; but these also were increasingly refined to provide better bases for dealing with issues relating to water shortages (e.g., instream flow requirements) and excesses (e.g., forestry impacts on runoff).

Indicators of water quality were progressively expanded from conventional parameters that had been in use for some time (e.g., temperature, colour, pH, suspended solids, dissolved oxygen, and coliforms) to those associated with the problems of growing concern (e.g., nitrogen and phosphorus because of eutrophication; heavy metals and chlorinated organics because of toxicity). Increasingly, indicators were added that went beyond physical and chemical measures of the water directly to measures of the associated biota (e.g., concentrations of toxicants in the fauna and flora; bioassays to determine lethal and acute toxicity). In addition, more attention began to be given to indices that combined the growing array of indicators into a single measure or sub-indices and indicator species that could be used in measuring the condition of the ecosystem (e.g., plankton or fish whose presence or absence would indicate the trophic status of eutrophication in lakes or degradation of contaminated streams).

Indicators were also designed for considering aquatic habitats and ecosystems more broadly. In addition to pollution, there were concerns about the physical impacts on aquatic habitats and the consequences for associated fish and wildlife populations (e.g., drainage and infill of wetlands from agricultural and urban development; stream siltation from forestry; diminished instream flows from diversions). The indicators that were introduced provided measures of the quantity and quality of the habitat (e.g., area, type and productivity of wetland plant communities; pool-riffle ratios). Attempts have also been made to link measures of habitats to the fish and wildlife populations that they support and thus exploit population indicators. An additional major impetus for the latter is the direct concern for the management of fish and wildlife populations. The problems associated with growing consumptive and non-consumptive demands for fish and wildlife have catalysed extensive efforts to develop indicators of populations and their dynamics (e.g., stock-recruitment in fisheries) (see discussions in Dale, Henderson, and Savard, this volume).

Accompanying these innovations in indicators of water quantity and quality have been unprecedented advances in the modelling of the systems involved, particularly through the use of computers (e.g., see Anderson and Burt, 1985). An immense variety of computer models has been developed for analysing the behaviour of indicators of natural systems both with and without human interventions. Some models focus on particular subsystems (e.g., dissolved oxygen in a stream), others on major biophysical systems (e.g., global climate). Depending on the specific questions being examined, they vary in the number and nature of the relationships they involve, ranging from the very simple to highly complex; the scale of application might be anywhere from the local to the global; and the time periods considered can range from seconds to hundreds of years.

In the growing concerns about sustainability, the earlier, more partial interests in indicators, driven by pollution control and resource management activities, have coalesced into a more integrated and fundamental interest in the integrity of aquatic ecosystems. This in turn, has stimulated a growing challenge to indicators and techniques employed in the more technocentric assessments of sustainability. Over the last two decades, there has been progress in elaborating the concept of ecological integrity and Canadians have been important contributors, particularly in applying the concept to water management in the Great Lakes (Regier, 1989). At a broad philosophical level, the ethical content of the concept is recognised; Regier differentiates "subjective integrity" meaning truthful, honest and wholesome, from "objective integrity" meaning unified, complete, all parts fitting together in a cohesive balance. More specifically, the concept of integrity has been elaborated in terms of ecosystem attributes including diversity (constituent variety), stability (resistance to change), resilience (ability to recover from rapid change), and adaptability (ability to change gradually). There has been a growing appreciation that the actual nature of the relationships between such attributes, that would be consistent with maintaining or increasing ecological integrity, can only be determined in a specific context (i.e., it does not necessarily follow that increasing either or any combination of them, increases integrity). Indicators of these attributes have been developed, but by far the greatest attention has been given to diversity, because it is relatively easy to measure and can be examined at all "ten levels of life": macro-molecule, organelle, cell, tissue, organ, organism, population, community, ecosystem and biome (Zonneveld, 1983). However, groundbreaking research by Canadians on the application of computer simulation models both in environmental impact assessment and renewable resource management has led to the development of analytical techniques focusing on the consideration of stability, resilience and adaptability of the systems involved in project development and stock management decisions (Holling, 1978; Walters, 1986). The development of these and other techniques of systems analysis has subsequently been advanced internationally by their application to global issues of sustainability (Clark and Munn, 1986).

In addition to these modelling activities, growing use of state-of-the-environment (SOE) reports during the 1980's has greatly expanded the variety and exploitation of indicators. In Canada, the first federal SOE report was published in 1986 (Bird and Rapport, 1986) and subsequently most provinces and territories have produced or are planning their first one (Dorcey and Rueggeberg, 1989). Quebec has already produced a first and is planning a second report (1992) and the next federal report will be released in 1991, and will include a regional case study of the Lower Fraser Valley. Over the same period, there have been various SOE reporting initiatives undertaken in other countries and by international organisations (Averous, 1989). The latter have begun to provide compendiums containing an immense variety of indicators of global environmental conditions including aquatic resources, some of which are being issued on an annual or biannual basis, so as to track trends and revise assessments (e.g., World Resources Institute, 1990). These documents typically assess sustainability by using tables and graphs of all kinds of measures, from narrowly defined specific indicators such as coliforms to broadly conceived indicators such as ecological integrity.

The potential scope for selective presentation and interpretation, with consequent disagreement, is enormous. Nevertheless, acting within the dominant technocentric view, there has obviously been immense progress in designing and applying environmental indicators that can be employed in assessing sustainability, both separately and in conjunction with economic indicators. From a more ecocentric viewpoint there would, however, be concerns that it has not progressed far enough to reflect appropriate respect for ecological integrity, and that it ignores fundamental social issues (see Boothroyd, Dale, Fox, Gardner, Kew and Griggs, Rees this volume).

Social Perspectives

Accompanying the innovations of the early 1970's in impact assessment that focused on environmental variables were comparable and associated techniques and processes focused on social issues. Information collected in operating governmental programs and through the census had already generated diverse data on the characteristics of the population and its settlement infrastructure. Use of this data in assessing the social consequences of project development led to significant advances in ideas about how such effects should be considered. There were two distinctive foci for these ideas.

One focus was on the indicators that should be used. Once again, the water field, with work in the United States and Canada, was one of the important arenas for these advances (Fitzsimmons and Salama, 1973). Treating human well-being solely in monetary, economic and demographic terms was acknowledged to be grossly inadequate. From considering the effects of both project developments (e.g., a dam) and natural hazards (e.g., floods), it was argued that social consequences have to be examined at three levels of society: the individual, the family, and the community. Attention focused on the impacts that were not reflected in economic and environmental indicators and that were usually omitted from the census and other routinely gathered governmental statistics. Instead, questions addressed human social relationships, personal lifestyle, and the culture in which people lived. It was obvious that the determination of appropriate indicators was strongly case-specific, as well as the determination of the relevant spatial and temporal scales for consideration of them.

The second focus was on the diversity of governance processes in which people use social indicators (Bankes and Thompson, 1980). Opinions differed on the relative importance of focusing on the design of the governance processes versus the specifics of indicator measurement. Within this focus, there was, at a minimum, a recognition of the need to give greater attention to the design of the process whereby people identify, measure and use indicators in reaching decisions. In addition, the difficulty of predicting social consequences in advance led to an emphasis on structuring processes that did not attempt to make all decisions in advance, but rather could monitor and respond to social consequences as they became evident.

However, this latter focus on process has to be also seen in the context of concerns about much more fundamental social issues (Utton, Sewell and O'Riordan, 1976). Beyond the pragmatic reasons for focusing on the design of processes whereby people utilize indicators are normative imperatives associated with the ideals of fairness, equity, justice and democracy. Most of the very extensive experimentation with public participation processes in the 1970's was at least justified in part in these terms. The Mackenzie Valley Pipeline Inquiry conducted from 1974 to 1977 by Justice Berger achieved world-wide recognition as a prototype in the mainstream of this tradition. It epitomized the emphasis on designing a process that would facilitate and ensure the opportunity for social issues to be addressed in terms meaningful to all the stakeholders.

Concerns about social sustainability in the last decade have elevated the original somewhat peripheral interest of impact assessment in multidimensional distributional issues and non-monetary values to major and, for some, dominant importance (Gardner and Roseland, 1989a, b). As indicated above, Daly and Cobb (1989) conclude that changes in the distribution of income are a major reason for the declining per capita ISEW in the United States in recent decades. Globally, the Brundtland report has put distributional issues front and centre with its emphasis on meeting basic human needs in the Third World and the imperative of keeping options open for future generations. The ensuing debate has increasingly recognised the fundamental ethical and moral nature of sustainability issues (see discussion by Boothroyd, this volume).

The focus on processes for including consideration of community priorities has been greatly reinforced by this perspective on sustainability (Gardner and Roseland, 1989a, b). For both practical and normative reasons, there has been increasing emphasis on greater use of community based approaches to development that can better integrate the assessment of economic and environmental consequences in an appropriate social framework, as well as strongly linking assessment to action. While the need for issues to be addressed by international and national communities is recognised, there is a much greater emphasis on local and regional communities. This has been advocated by writers addressing an incredible diversity of social issues in both the developing and developed world. Influential concepts in this tradition have been appropriate technology (Schumacher, 1973), eco-development (Sachs, 1977), the sustainable society (Brown, 1981), bio-regionalism (Sale, 1985) and sustainable livelihoods (Chambers, 1986). These ideas are frequently advanced in assessing social sustainability in resource-based communities and where there are aboriginal interests (see discussion in Boothroyd, Dale, Fox, Gardner, Kew and Griggs, and Rees, this volume).

Once again, it is evident that major advances have been made over the last two decades in advancing potential approaches to the assessment of sustainability. In the case of social sustainability, however, this has involved much greater emphasis on integration with economic and environmental assessment through the design of governance processes that can more appropriately employ indicator methods. By their very nature such process-focused innovations substantially challenge the dominant technocentric view. From the aquatic ecocentric viewpoint, the aquatic accommodators do not address the basic governance issues. In turn, the deep aquatic ecocentrists believe even the aquatic communalists fail to address the most fundamental issues of the rights of non-human species and intrinsic values.

Towards Agreement on Assessing Sustainability

In retrospect, there has been impressive progress over the last two decades in developing indicators that can be employed in assessing sustainability in more specific terms. Equally impressive is the potential for disagreement in doing this. There are two major reasons for the latter. Firstly, differing world views and associated disciplinary schools of thought see indicators and their use in varied lights. Secondly, apart from this, the use of indicators is fraught with opportunities for misunderstanding. Thus, to capitalize on the immense potential for better assessing sustainability, it is essential not only to pursue strategies for responding constructively to differing world views and different schools of disciplinary thought as discussed in the previous chapter, but also to adopt strategies for selecting and using indicators that anticipate and avoid misunderstanding.

One major element of such a strategy is to reach agreement on what constitutes a good indicator of sustainability. Faced with the need to do this in advancing the state of the art of SOE reporting for Canada, a series of studies has been undertaken to review the literature on indicators and experience with them. Based on this work it has been proposed that indicators should be feasible to obtain, scientifically credible, understandable, provide early warning detection, and enable the detection of temporal and spatial trends (Gelinas and Slaats, 1989). Each of these apparently simple characteristics is elaborated to indicate the difficult and complex trade-offs that have to be considered in each situation. Focusing on the measurement of global sustainability specifically, Liverman et al. (1988) have proposed a similar set of criteria for indicators: sensitivity to change in time, sensitivity to change across space or within groups, predictive ability, availability of reference or threshold values, ability to measure reversibility or controllability, appropriate data transformation, integrative ability, and relative ease of collection and use. By agreeing on a set of criteria, such as these, together with how they are to be applied in the particular water management situation (e.g., the Fraser River Basin), it should be possible to greatly reduce misunderstandings that arise in assessing sustainability from all perspectives. However, to be successful in doing this, it will be necessary to give much more consideration to the design of the decision making and governance processes within which such agreements are reached and implemented. Strategies for moving towards agreement on the assessment of sustainability have to be integral parts of the strategies required for taking action.

Acting on Sustainability

A multitude of decisions are involved in acting on sustainability. They include decisions about not only the definition of sustainable development and indicators and methods to be utilised in assessing sustainability, but also the policies and institutional arrangements to be used in implementing sustainable development strategies; there are decisions to be made about how to make decisions! Such decisions range from micro decisions about the choice and interpretation of a particular indicator at a specific place and time, to macro decisions about the governance system within which the plethora of judgements involved in sustainable development are to be made. There can be great differences in the perspectives that people bring to bear on these decisions which have major implications for action on sustainability.

Judgement perspectives

Perhaps more than ever before, the concept of sustainable development has starkly revealed the pervasive necessity of judgement in the science and politics of water resources management. Not only is there immense uncertainty in the relevant science, but also the decisions are heavily dependent on ethical and moral values. Ironically, the substantial progress over the last two decades in advancing indicators and analytical methods for assessing sustainability has brought a new appreciation of these more fundamental and difficult problems.

The criteria discussed above for guiding the selection, application and interpretation of indicators of sustainability make it explicit that assessment involves exercising great judgement. For example, consider the following common realms of uncertainty and consequent need for judgement:

(i)   *Functional relations of sustainability.* To be meaningful, the variables used as indicators need to be understood in terms of how they relate to other system variables. This implies understanding how relevant environmental, economic and social systems behave. Thus, for example, the stress-response model underlying the first Canadian approach to SOE reporting (Bird and Rapport, 1986) and the Great Lakes aquatic ecosystem studies (Colborn et al., 1990) differentiates between indicators of stress (e.g., pollution loadings, land use changes and resource exploitation) and ecosystem responses (e.g., changes in productivity, species composition and disease incidence). It then draws on knowledge of the functional relationships between the indicators of stress and responses in order to reach conclusions about causes and effects. In some areas of water management, this theoretical knowledge has been well developed and its application is relatively routine (e.g., BOD waste loads and the resulting dissolved oxygen levels in the stream). But the understanding of systems required to interpret the indicators being employed to assess sustainability frequently demands functional knowledge that does not exist or is highly uncertain. This has become starkly evident in recent years as issues relating to toxic materials, acid precipitation and climatic change have come to the fore. The uncertainty that pervades knowledge of the behaviour of biophysical systems is also characteristic of economic and social systems. This is most strikingly evident when interactions between the three need to be comprehended (see discussion of energy by Chapman, fisheries by Dale and Henderson, forestry by Kimmins and Duffy, and of erosion by Slaymaker).

(ii) *State of sustainability.* Beyond the uncertainty imposed by deficiencies in functional knowledge is uncertainty in particular situations about the state of environmental, economic and social systems, as a result of the lack of appropriate data. Sustainability concerns have generated a need for data on variables that may well not have been previously observed or, at least, not in the locations, nor for the time periods, nor by the methods that have become relevant (e.g., dioxin contamination or precipitation). The use of historical data typically brings with it a host of uncertainties about the qualifications that have to be placed upon them. For example, in the Fraser Basin, assessing the state of the salmon resource and fisheries is clouded by all these uncertainties (see chapters by Henderson and Dale, this volume).

(iii) *Limits to sustainability*. Ideas about limits are fundamental in using indicators to assess sustainability. Sustainable development is fundamentally about the limits within which environmental, economic and social systems can operate while meeting desired objectives, in particular, keeping options open for future generations. Again, in some areas of water resources management, the theoretical and empirical knowledge of limits is relatively well developed (e.g., the limits on dissolved oxygen depression before salmon are affected). But usually there is considerable uncertainty about such limits. Concepts of carrying capacity are highly relevant and often advanced (see chapter by Rees, this volume) but they present great difficulties in practice because of the measurement problems involved. More macro indicators of systems' properties such as diversity, stability, resilience and adaptability are highly appropriate in principle, but there are still very considerable theoretical and empirical difficulties in putting them into practice, particularly in extending such ideas from biophysical to socioeconomic systems.

Uncertainties such as these are endemic in assessing and acting on sustainability. The more it is realised that new and different information is required to address an increasing diversity of systems and their interactions, at scales that range from the local to the global, and across time dimensions that reach back thousands of years and forward through future generations, the more pervasive and serious the uncertainties become (e.g., see discussion of sedimentation in Slaymaker, and forestry in Kimmins and Duffy, this volume). Compounding these difficulties is the realization that many of these deficiencies cannot be easily resolved; long lead times are required, large costs are involved and, more fundamentally, the nature of the systems may be essentially unpredictable in any practical sense (Holling, 1978).

Confronting these judgement dilemmas in sustainable development, Costanza (1989) has used the game theoretic concept of a pay-off matrix to consider the outcomes under alternative policy choices and assumptions about technological optimism (Figure 22.1). Within the framework of game theory and Constanza's assumptions about the payoffs, the optimal policy if a MaxiMin strategy is adopted is to follow the technological pessimist policy, since this gives the least of the worst possible outcomes (i.e., a tolerable outcome is preferable to disaster). Costanza's concept of technology can be usefully broadened to include research and the "softer technologies" whereby society governs itself. The analysis then reflects why challengers of the dominant technocentric view, particularly the aquatic ecocentrists, believe judgements about sustainable development should be conditioned by more conservative policies. This perception is among the major reasons for the types of sustainable development policies commonly advanced by the challengers, as is described in the next section. The analysis, however, also brings out the value judgements that are intimately involved in assessing and acting on sustainability at both the macro level of global decisions and the micro level of specific decisions in water resources management. This has major implications for the design of the governance systems that are responsible for making these decisions, as is discussed below.

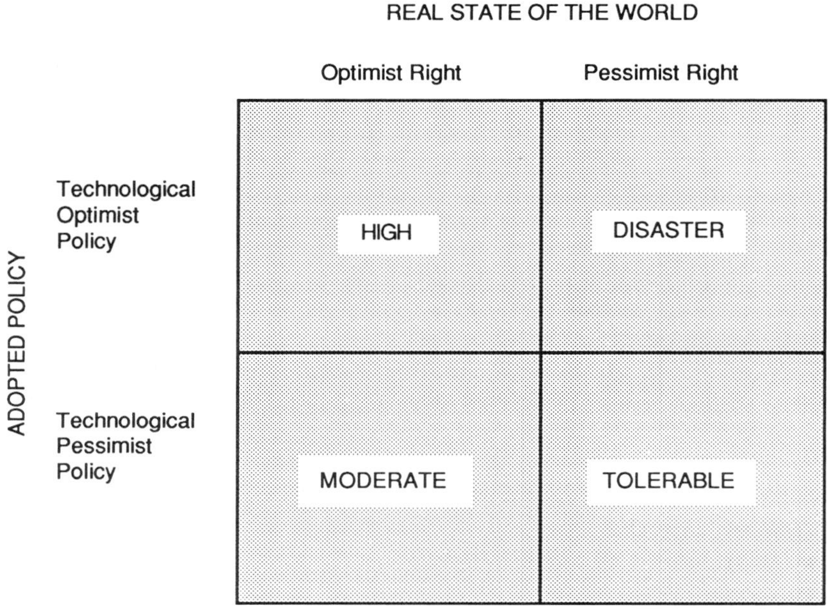

REAL STATE OF THE WORLD

Figure 21.1: Payoff Matrix for Technological Optimism Versus Technological Pessimism (After Constanza, 1989).

Policy Perspectives

Associated with each of the aquatic world views are different policy imperatives that reflect their varying judgements about the nature and extent of the adaptations required for greater sustainability. As described above, principles of water resources management have advanced significantly and become more comprehensive over the last two decades, in response to the increasing challenges to the prevailing cornucopian views. Today, there is considerable agreement *in principle* among the technocentrists about the nature of the comprehensive considerations and adaptations that are required for greater sustainability in water resources management. Variations in views between the cornucopians and accommodators relate more to the extent and rate of adaptation. Thus, for example, many technocentrists would generally agree that policies for :

(i)   *Water supply management* should be comprehensive in consideration of the diversity of water uses (consumptive and non-consumptive; instream and withdrawal), the hydrological system (precipitation, evaporation, surface water and groundwater) and opportunities for conservation and development of supply. Differences in view would include judgements about the reliability of the supply, its allocation among uses, the emphasis on supply development versus demand management, how quickly to change allocations, and what are the most cost-effective means of implementation (e.g., see discussion in McNeill, Pearse and Tate, and Scott, this volume).

(ii) *Water pollution control* should be comprehensive in consideration of the types and sources of polluting materials, the paths by which they reach and flow though the aquatic environment, and opportunities for reducing, reusing, and recycling. Differences in views would include judgements about what should be the minimum level of water quality, how much risk to run of not maintaining this level, how quickly to achieve it and what are the most cost-effective means of implementation. (e.g., see discussion in McNeill, McConnell, Pearse and Tate, and Rankin, this volume).

(iii) *Fisheries management* should be comprehensive in consideration of fisher groups (commercial, sports and Native), fish stocks (resident, migratory and species interactions) and fish habitats (stream, lake, estuarine and ocean ecosystems). Differences in views would include judgements about which groups should be allocated the available harvest, what should be the harvest level, whether and how to restore or enhance stocks, how much risk to run of overfishing, what habitat is required to support a given stock, how much risk to run of maintaining adequate habitat, and what are the most cost-effective means of implementation (see discussion in Dale, Henderson, Kew and Griggs, and Thompson, this volume).

(iv) *Floodplain management* should be comprehensive in its consideration of causes of flooding (snow melt, rainfall and wind elevated water levels), land and water uses (causes of, dependence on and vulnerability to flooding), and means of adapting to floods (structural and non-structural). Differences in views would include judgements about the likelihood of flood flows, the amount of risk to accept, the potential value of damages and the most cost-effective means of implementation (see discussion in Smith and Slaymaker, this volume).

A comparable perspective on the comprehensiveness of and differences in policy views is evident for other natural resource sectors both in terms of their own development and their interactions with water resources management (see discussion by Chapman of energy, by Kimmins and Duffy of forestry, and by Savard of birds, this volume).

The closer the technocentrists are to the ecocentric view, the more their judgement in each of these aspects of water management would be that natural resource systems should be maintained, that they should not be put at risk, and that early restoration is essential. The ecocentrists on the other hand doubt that such substantive policies are adequate; the communalists believe that more emphasis should be given to the design of the decision making processes; and, the deep ecologists believe more fundamental transformations in values are necessary.

Decision Making Perspectives

Underlying differing views on decision making in sustainable development are varied and controversial beliefs about the extent to which it is a matter of science or politics and the possibilities for distinguishing facts and values (Dorcey, 1990). Fundamentally different concepts of the nature of facts and values can greatly confound the debate. At one extreme might be found people who firmly believe that facts can be completely distinguished from values. While at the other extreme are people who equally firmly believe that they never can be distinguished. In between are the vast majority of people who consciously or unconsciously adopt some intermediate view which might favour one extreme more than the other. Depending on the position taken, different opinions are formed about the relationship between knowledge and action, reason and democracy, and science and politics.

The importance of these beliefs in considering alternative approaches to sustainable development is illustrated by the divergent implications of the positions. For those that lean towards the belief that facts and values can be distinguished, sustainable development is more a task for science and require the application of analytical techniques to generate information upon which decisions can be based in the political process. In contrast, those leaning the opposite way see sustainable development as essentially a political task within which science and analytical techniques have secondary roles to the design of decision making processes and the structure of power.

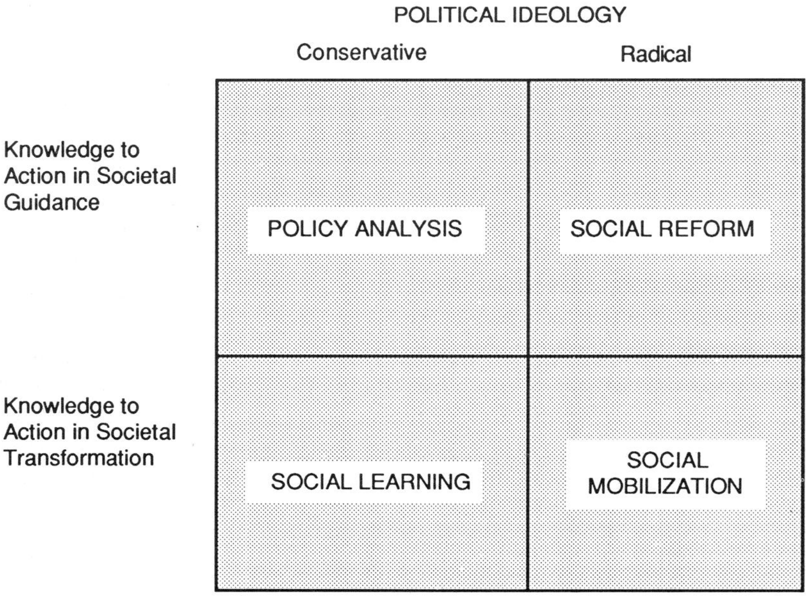

Figure 22.2: The Politics of Knowledge and Action.
(After Friedmann, 1987)

Friedmann (1987) has analysed the richly textured heritage of different decision making models as they have evolved over the last two centuries and grouped them into four major traditions according to their political ideology and how knowledge is related to action (Figure 22.2). The political ideology is classified as being conservative or radical. The relationship between knowledge and action is differentiated in terms of whether the purpose is seen to be societal guidance or social transformation. Friedmann's four major stylised traditions can be summarized as follows:

(i) *Policy Analysis*: Most analysts writing in this tradition are versed in neoclassical economics, statistics and mathematics. They cluster in specialized disciplines such as systems analysis, policy science or operations research. On larger social issues of equity and justice, they are typically conventional in their thinking. They believe that scientific theories and mathematical techniques can, at least in principle, identify and calculate best solutions.

(ii) *Social Reform:* This tradition has roots in sociology, institutional economics and pragmatism and is chiefly concerned with finding ways to make action by the state more effective. Those writing in this tradition see planning as a scientific endeavour and are concerned with ways to institutionalize it while using science to inform and limit politics to what is thought to be its appropriate role.

(iii) *Social Learning*: Theories in this tradition draw on writings from all three of the other traditions but have substantial roots in the organisational development literature. They are distinguished from the preceding traditions in their belief that social learning is derived from experience and is an integral part of action. Further, they do not see social laws as immutable but believe social behaviour can be changed. The scientifically correct way to effect change is through social experimentation, careful observation of the results, and a willingness to admit error and to learn from it.

(iv) *Social Mobilization:* This tradition departs from all the others in asserting the primacy of direct collective action from below. It thus stands in stark contrast to the scientific politics within the established structure of the state as conceived by the social reform and policy analysis traditions. Nevertheless, scientific analysis, particularly in the social learning tradition, plays an important role in the transformative processes which are the primary objectives. There are two kinds of politics in the tradition: for utopians and anarchists, there is the politics of disengagement carried on by alternative communities that demonstrate to others new ways of living; and for Marxists and Neo-Marxists, there is confrontational politics that emphasize political struggle as necessary to transform existing relations of power and create a new order.

This brief summary of Friedmann's four categories can in no way do justice to his detailed analysis of the diverse traditions and their complex cross-currents. In addition, it must be recognised that his analysis is conditioned by a strong belief in the over-riding importance of politics; for a similar analysis by a writer who sees a relatively larger role for science, see Faludi (1987).

Writers on decision making or sustainable development do not necessarily fall neatly into one tradition or another, but it is generally possible to indicate the primary or dominant tradition and how, if at all, others are influential. Clearly, these different views can have major implications for the design of decision making arrangements for sustainable development. The technocentric view is commonly associated with the policy analysis tradition. The challenge to the dominant aquatic cornucopian view by the accommodators and communalists often draws upon the social reform and social learning traditions. In so far as the challenge includes the belief that there must be greater emphasis on bottom-up decision making, it also draws on the social mobilization tradition.

Once again, the contributed papers suggest the differences in perspective but not unambiguously. Several papers, because of their focus, touch upon the relationship between science and politics more explicitly (e.g., Boothroyd, Dale, Fox, Gardner and Rees, this volume). In others, they are only partially or at most implicitly considered. In many instances, a judgement might be made as to what appears to be the dominant tradition. This would likely result in suggestions that all four traditions can variously be found as primary influences among the papers. Such judgement would in most cases be premature based on the inexplicitness with which these issues are addressed in the papers.

Governance Perspectives

There are major differences in views on how governance systems should be re-designed so as to better meet the needs of sustainable development. Even though there might be growing acknowledgement that systems of governance require a superior capability to integrate environmental, economic and social decision-making, different disciplines and associated world views bring distinctive perspectives on how this should be done.

Particular disciplines focus on selected components of the governance system, and consequently tend to emphasize the requirements for reform in their component, while giving less attention to the larger governance system context. Thus political scientists focus on political-legislative mechanisms, lawyers on the judicial-legal, economists on the market-economic, and public administration specialists on the administrative-bureaucratic. The literature is replete with partial analyses of the governance system and is extremely thin on analyses that examine the interdependence of the four major components of the governance system (Figure 22.3). For the most part the background papers examining the governance system reflect this general disciplinary focus, but to a lesser extent than is the norm, particularly in the papers by Boothroyd, Dale, Fox, Gardner, Rankin and Scott in this volume.

Within each of these disciplines can be found analysts who subscribe to different schools of thought and associated world views, each of which see the governance challenge and responses to it in distinctive ways. In the previous chapter, this was illustrated by comparing the mainstream neoclassical and steady state theorists in economics. In political science and public administration, pluralist, elitist, Marxist and corporatist theorists provide differing power perspectives on how governance systems behave and how they should be reformed (e.g., see Ham and Hill, 1984; Pross, 1986; Paehlke and Torgerson, 1990).

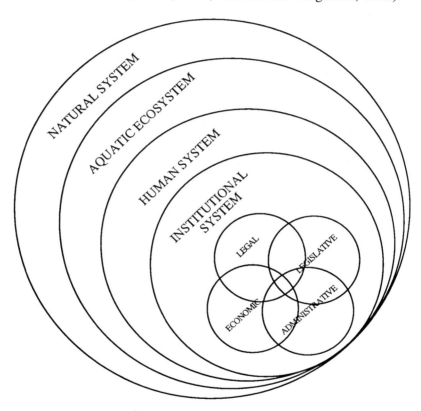

Figure 22.3: The Governance System in the Analysis of Sustainability

The pluralists argue that power in western industrialised societies is widely distributed among different groups. No group is seen to be without power to influence decision making, nor is any group, in particular the state, dominant. The elitists or neo-pluralists challenge this view, asserting that power is concentrated in certain realms, particularly when the diverse sources of power in modern society—including the occupation of formal office, wealth, technical expertise, knowledge etc.—are taken into account. The Marxists variously contend that the elite is specifically drawn from a dominant class. In contrast to the pluralists and neo-pluralists, they see the capitalist state as dominant. The corporatists, on the other hand, argue that there are several predominant sources of power, in particular the state which increasingly shares power with employers and unions.

Explicitly or implicitly, pluralism has pervaded much of the writing and research on politics, government and the state. For these reasons, it is often associated with the dominant technocentric world view, but elitist, Marxist and corporatist theories can also be associated with it. Marxism is perhaps more readily associated with the more radical challenge of the ecocentrists, but again so have been the other three theories. These power theories do not map simply on to the different world views as we have differentiated them. Among the background papers, only Boothroyd explicitly addresses these theories, although others discuss changes in power relationships (e.g., Dale, Fox, Gardner, Kew and Griggs, and Thompson, this volume).

It is in these diverse theoretical contexts that debate rages about how to institutionalize the implementation of sustainable development. Five types of institutional innovation are commonly advanced in both the sustainable development and water resources management literatures in varying forms and degrees, but not always together nor consistently:

(i) *Greater integration of the bureaucracy.* Integrating the consideration of environmental, economic and social systems in decision making is a central theme in both literatures. In the water field, this has long and often focused on the importance of integrating land and water activities within river basins. The traditional sectoral organisation of governments has typically meant that this often did not happen. The reforms that are recommended frequently include various kinds of reorganisation including changes within the existing structures, the addition of new units, the combination of existing ones, and the creation of coordinating arrangements. Such reforms have been typified in recent years by the introduction of environmental and social impact assessment processes, the establishment of environment or natural resources departments with associated planning processes, and the creation of referral mechanisms and special task forces. In the last couple of years, there has been increasing emphasis on greater coordination between organisations concerned with environmental and economic issues primarily through joint committees of cabinet and "round tables".

(ii) *Greater public participation.* Both the sustainable development and water resources management literatures have argued the need for greater public participation in decision making, variously emphasizing democratic principles and practical advantages. Experience over the last two decades has shown that this can have very different meanings for different people. In particular, the distinction has to be made between consultation and making decisions. In very few instances have the innovations in public participation over the last two decades gone beyond some form of consultation to give decision making responsibility to members of the public. Decision making responsibility has been retained by the government, while creating opportunities for consultation to develop new policy and to plan and manage water resources through the increasing use of mechanisms such as opinion surveys, advisory committees, open-houses, hearings, public inquiries and discussion papers.

(iii) *More devolved decision-making.* Again, both the sustainable development and water management literatures advocate more devolved decision making. In the water field, it has long been argued that management should be implemented through regional and watershed institutions. While these arguments always apply to administrative decision-making by regional offices of senior government agencies, they often also involve the use of regional or local institutions. These might take the form of a special purpose organisation (e.g., a water board) or an existing unit of government (e.g., the regional district) and in either case the members might be appointed or elected. While all types of devolution have taken place, the emphasis has been on the regionalisation of government agencies and, to a lesser extent, special purpose organisations, whose members are appointed.

(iv) *Increased use of economic incentives and property rights.* In varying ways, both the sustainable development and water management literatures advocate the increased use of market mechanisms. Water supply pricing, effluent charges and marketable rights for water supply and discharge have long been advocated as means for increasing the economic efficiency of resource use and devolving decision-making. These approaches are slowly becoming more common in practice. Frequently, however, this is not what is meant by some advocates of economic incentives. They are concerned with more payments or subsidies to reduce costs incurred in complying with regulations. The most common form of innovation in recent years has been the increasing use of administered prices and their gradual escalation to better reflect marginal costs and polluter or beneficiary pay principles.

(v) *More effective utilisation of the law and courts.* Enshrining rights and responsibilities more specifically in legislation and making greater use of the courts and quasi-judicial bodies to interpret and enforce them are advocated in both the sustainable development and water resources management literatures. In the water field, attention has been given to the role that the courts might play in improving enforcement of and compliance with environmental regulations, if standing provisions are relaxed and penalties increased. This has increasingly begun to happen in recent years. At the same time, there has been a large expansion in the number of quasi-judicial bodies created to administer review procedures for project development and resource pricing. This expansion, together with the increased regulatory activities of government agencies, has led to recommendations for appeal mechanisms including the appointment of ombudspersons. The adoption of the new Constitution and Bill of Rights has facilitated the increased use of the courts in decision making in all areas of governance including natural resources. An environmental bill of rights has just been introduced in the Yukon (1990)—the first in Canada. In the Canadian context and particularly in the Fraser River Basin, aboriginal claims and associated court cases are having a major influence on aquatic resources management.

Since each of these innovations might be a part of the institutional changes apparently advocated by either technocentrists or ecocentrists, there is the potential for great misunderstanding. The differences in views lie in the particular form and the emphasis given to each innovation and, in particular, their implications for changes in the distribution of power and the structure of values. For example, the accommodators would tend to emphasize reorganisation of the bureaucracy accompanied by more consultation, greater decentralisation of administration, increased use of subsidies and user charges, and more comprehensive legislation with more vigorous enforcement.   The ecocentrists, on the other hand, would perceive this as inadequate, involving little change in the dominant distribution of power and values. They would emphasize the devolution of decision-making giving individuals and local communities greater rights and responsibilities within a restructured federation of governance organisations. These would utilise user charges and subsidies to promote conservation and stronger legislation to facilitate and induce cooperative approaches to management. These two examples could be elaborated in numerous ways with significant differences implied by the words and phrases selected, but they are sufficient to indicate the great difficulty and critical necessity of understanding the subtle and fundamental differences of views about institutional reforms.

In the papers, all five types of innovations are variously advocated among the several that address institutional innovations. Some narrowly focus on one type of change (e.g., McNeill and Pearse and Tate focus on economic incentives, Gardner on the role of ENGO's), while others emphasize the links between changes in two parts of the governance systems (e.g., Rankin examines links between legal and market mechanisms). Several others at least touch upon three or four of the major components of the governance system in the changes they examine (e.g., Boothroyd, Dale, Fox, Rees, and Scott).

Towards Agreement in Acting on Sustainability

Once again, it can be seen that there is considerable scope for agreement on some of the changes required, while at the same time there is immense potential for both misunderstanding and legitimate disagreement. The pervasive necessity of judgement in both science and politics is starkly revealed by the substantive and procedural decisions to be made in acting on sustainability. Yet it appears that there might be considerable agreement about some of the policy and institutional reforms that should be tried. Even though the reforms advocated by the aquatic accommodators might not go far enough to satisfy the transformations sought by those with more ecocentric views, many of them would appear to be moving in the desired direction. Further, it might well be that some of the changes advocated by the aquatic communalists could be found to meet the interests of the accommodators. However, if these possibilities for agreement are to be tested with any chance for success, it will be necessary to address some of the major difficulties that frustrate constructive debate.

Two strategies could be helpful. The first strategy would be to draw on the experience, principles and practices of the emerging field of dispute resolution to guide approaches to decision making wherever decisions are required in acting on sustainability (Dorcey, 1986; 1990; Dorcey and Riek, 1988). Over the last two decades, there has been increasing attention given to the generic problem of reaching agreement in situations where there are disputes about both facts and values. Finding that authoritative techniques often could not respond satisfactorily to such disputes, attention has focused on more consensual approaches. Techniques and procedures have been developed and tested for a wide variety of situations in which conflicts arise and agreements are sought, including unions, corporations, academies, communities, families and governments. General principles for exploiting the advantages of structured conflict and improving the likelihood of agreement have begun to emerge in a number of classic texts including *The Strategy of Conflict* (Schelling, 1960), *Getting To Yes: Negotiating Agreement Without Giving In* (Fisher and Ury, 1981) and *The Art and Science of Negotiation* (Raiffa, 1982). Of major significance is the recognition of the great assistance that can be provided by a third party facilitating or mediating the interactions between the contending parties. Particular attention has been given to third party techniques and principles in resolving environmental and resources disputes (e.g., Bingham, 1985; Cormick and Knaster, 1986; Susskind and Cruikshank, 1987). These techniques and principles could be applied in all of the academic and governance forums where it has been suggested that disputes can be expected in acting on sustainability (see Dale for a discussion of consensus based decision making in the fisheries, and Kew and Griggs in aboriginal societies, this volume).

The second strategy would be to give much greater emphasis to the development and application of the more comprehensive and integrated theories that are emerging from interdisciplinary and transdisciplinary research. Increasingly, these are challenging the dominant disciplinary schools of thought and guiding the design of policy and institutional innovations for sustainable development. In several subject areas, there are groups of theorists and practitioners that are advancing new and more holistic models. They are the progeny of the initial attempts in the sixties and seventies to integrate the biophysical and socioeconomic sciences in environmental and natural resources management and economic development. These new models reflect the belief that both theory and reality, and also principles and practice, must be more closely related. In Friedmann's terms, these writers are strongly influenced by the social learning tradition, but within this they also draw on the social guidance and transformation traditions, with the policy science tradition being selectively applied in the context of the other three traditions. Among such writers are the neo-institutionalists (e.g., Bromley, 1985), progressive planning theorists (e.g., Forester, 1989), community developers (e.g., Daly and Cobb, 1989), and political ecologists (e.g., Dryzek, 1987). While still coming from different perspectives and not agreeing with all the challengers to the dominant view, these writers seem to be coming to remarkably similar conclusions about the nature of the more holistic and integrated institutional innovations that will be necessary for acting on sustainability.

Towards a Model for the Fraser River Basin

It is now necessary to focus on a model of water resources management in sustainable development that can be used in the research program for the Fraser River Basin. The model has to meet several requirements. It must be capable of

(i) *Reflecting evolving principles of sustainable development and water resources management.* It has been argued that these principles have been evolving for many years. In particular, principles of water resources management have evolved greatly over the last two decades. The sustainable development debate stimulated by the Brundtland report points to further and significant innovations. However, while their general nature can be seen, their specifics will only evolve out of future research and experimentation. For these reasons, we need to focus on an evolving model.

(ii) *Exploring differences in views.* It has been argued that the evolution of principles has been the result of the challenges from different world views and schools of thought. The sustainable development debate has greatly expanded the breadth and diversity of views brought to bear on water resources management principles. Even though there now seems to be a remarkable degree of agreement about the general nature of the future model that should be explored, it will be critical to proceed in ways that exploit what can be learnt from differences in views.

(iii) *Being applied within the constraints of the case study.* It has been argued that water resources management must be seen in a much larger context when viewed from the more comprehensive perspective of sustainable development. Indeed, examination of different views on sustainable development principles has led to recognition of much more fundamental questions and associated literatures. There are, however, major constraints on the extent to which this breadth of issues can be addressed within the first phase of our research program. In particular, the severe limitations of existing information together with the small amount of time and resources available to collect and analyse it, make it necessary to define the model in simple enough ways to make it operational.

(iv) *Guiding future research.* It has been argued that there is immense need and potential for progress in future research. Exploring the implications of sustainable development principles for water resources management has been productive in clarifying questions that need to be addressed. However, many of them are not specific to water resources management and should be addressed on a much broader basis than is dictated by our focus on the Fraser

River Basin. Even so, there are many questions within this focus that need to be addressed both in applying and advancing the evolving model.

An Evolving Model of Water Resources Management

At the end of the last chapter, it was suggested that by concentrating on what the challengers to dominant views have in common, there could be widespread agreement that water resource management principles should at least provide for making governance decisions

- based on the consideration of economic, environmental and social values;
- informed by research, project assessment and watershed planning;
- structured for involving stakeholders and elected representatives;
- implemented by combinations of regulatory and market mechanisms; and
- enforced ultimately by the courts.

In this chapter, this simple model has been elaborated by drawing on the background papers, a variety of literatures relating to sustainable development and a diversity of disciplines contributing to the governance of natural resources. This exploration has revealed not only the elements of the evolving model in more detail but also key characteristics in their design that are suggested by emerging principles of sustainable development. *Further, it would appear that despite differences in views, there is a remarkable degree of agreement about the general nature of the innovations required.*

If this is the case, the water resource management model is at a critical stage in its evolution from past to future designs. It is therefore important to recognise the differences between the past and future model. For individual elements, they may only appear to involve small changes in emphasis from ideas that have been in the literature for some time, but cumulatively they imply a fundamental shift in approach. Drawing on the discussion above, the differences can be highlighted and their interrelated and cumulative implications illustrated:

(i) *Greater emphasis on ethics.* Although past approaches to water resources management have increasingly considered a diversity of utilitarian values (i.e., economic, environmental and social), future approaches will be conditioned much more strongly by ethical concerns (i.e., what is morally right). Management decisions in watersheds will be greatly influenced by ethical judgements about not only local, but also global considerations of ecological integrity and compassion for present and future generations (e.g., foregoing water use in order to meet the needs of the disadvantaged or future generations).

(ii) *Greater emphasis on being proactive.* While past approaches to water resources management relied more on reactive strategies (e.g., clean up of pollution), future strategies will rely much more on being proactive (e.g., pollution prevention). Policies will be more comprehensive (e.g., integrating land and water activities) and cautious (e.g., "precautionary", "safe-fail", "no-regrets"). Planning will become much more important and common, often making impact assessment of projects unnecessary or routine (e.g., through zoning and establishment of standards).

(iii)   *Greater emphasis on the integration of science and politics.* In the past, there has been substantial progress in developing both knowledge (e.g., analysis of toxicity) and management processes (e.g., referral, impact assessment and planning processes). In the future, attention will focus on their integration within the broader governance process. It will involve scientists in much more interdisciplinary science, not only within but also between the diversity of natural and social sciences (e.g., integrated research on toxic materials and their impacts on community health or use of indigenous knowledge in fisheries management). It will require elected politicians to provide greater leadership in and be more accountable for policies reflecting the ethics of a more proactive approach (e.g., in establishing environmental standards and decision making processes for their implementation). There will be much greater reliance on all stakeholders, not only scientists, managers and elected politicians, working together to generate the environmental, economic and social information needed for making decisions and implementing adaptive management strategies.

(iv)   *Greater emphasis on consensual decision making.* Past approaches to water resources management have relied heavily on authoritative and adversarial decision-making processes (e.g., formal hearings for impact assessment processes). In the future, there will be growing use of negotiation and more consensual approaches (e.g., mediated negotiations to agree on impacts, mitigation and compensation). Consultation will be replaced by negotiation (e.g., in setting ambient and effluent standards). Management of water resources will involve extensive and diverse co-management arrangements (e.g., co-management of watersheds or fisheries).

(v)   *Greater emphasis on federation.* In the past, water resources management has been largely a top-down process with senior government agencies predominating over the regional and local. In the future, there will be new expectations at each level. Senior resource agencies will be expected to provide the policy framework within which regional and local agencies can be free to make their own decisions (e.g., within minimum environmental standards, decisions would be made locally). Resource management agencies would be much more responsible to regionally and locally elected bodies (e.g., watershed management decisions by regional and municipal governments). While regional and local organisations will be held accountable for more independence, senior government agencies will be expected to be more responsive to the regional and local interests in establishing the policy framework.

(vi)   *Greater emphasis on intersectoral decision making.* Past approaches to water resources management have emphasized the necessity of integrating land and water activities within a watershed. In the future, there will be a broader perspective on the decisions that need to be coordinated. Governance processes will be required that can integrate decisions within and across resource and economic sectors (e.g., the integration of forest, fisheries and recreation developments). While watersheds will be one important focus, it will also be necessary to provide for strong linkages across other boundaries (e.g., integrated resources management across the regions of the province or coordination of resource developments, such as fisheries or pulping, with their international markets). It will also be expected that water and other natural resource developments be integrated with community development in its various social and economic dimensions (e.g., integration of forest development in the watershed with the other resource and non-resource based community activities).

(vii) *Greater emphasis on the integration of regulatory and economic mechanisms.* For a long time, it has been argued that for reasons of economic efficiency there should be greater use of market mechanisms in water resources management (e.g., water supply and effluent discharge pricing or creation of marketable rights). In the future, these arguments will be supplemented by an additional emphasis on their integration with regulatory mechanisms (e.g., effluent standards combined with a discharge fee to induce compliance and a continuing incentive to find more efficient solutions). Regulation will reorient to co-management (co-regulation) and will involve greater use of negotiated contracts that include provisions for performance bonds or automatic financial penalties that escalate with the seriousness of the non-compliance (e.g., exceeding the allowable discharge results in an automatic ticketing that reflects the extent of the violation and previous compliance record). Reflecting the increased emphasis on a proactive approach, user pay principles will be extended to all water uses where administrative and enforcement costs do not outweigh the benefits, and vigorously applied to create revenues for funding maintenance and enhancement of the resource. Much more attention will be given to the principles and decision-making processes for compensation (e.g., compensation of those from whom water rights are taken).

(viii) *Greater emphasis on the design of the total governance system.* In the past, there has been relatively little attention given to the integrated design of the four major components of the formal governance system—legislative-political, judicial-legal, administrative-bureaucratic, and market-economic. In the future, the new emphases in each of the elements listed above will be accompanied by innovations in the organisation of governance. These will be designed to exploit better the components both separately and jointly. There will be greater emphasis on obtaining appropriate and timely decisions from each (e.g., political decisions by the minister or cabinet in order to make it possible for negotiation on standards or a watershed management plan to proceed; a decision by the courts on resource rights in order to allow negotiations to progress further). Overall, there will be a transformation in the governance system. The increasing predominance of the administrative-bureaucratic components in the last half-century will be countered by a revitalization of the traditional importance of the legislative-political components. This will be accompanied by a more selective and effective utilisation of the judicial-legal components. At the same time, the market-economic components will become much more significant as they are expanded and integrated into the administrative-bureaucratic components. The latter will be radically affected by the enhanced roles of the other three governance components and by its own increasing emphasis on consensual decision-making, negotiation and co-management.

In the second volume, these outlines of the past and future models of water resources management can be used to explore progress in the Fraser River Basin towards sustainable development. It will be possible to assess to what extent present approaches to water resource management in the Fraser reflect the principles of either the past or future models. Also, the difference between stated management principles, as reflected in formally established policies and their actual practice can also be examined. In the light of the conclusions, suggestions can be made as to how to move towards the principles of the evolving model of water in sustainable development in both the nearer and longer term.

Advancing Sustainability Research

In concluding, it is important to recognize the broader implications for advancing sustainability research that have been revealed by the background papers and the discussion of them in these last two chapters. The evolution of the water resource management model over the longer term will depend in important ways on progress made on this wider front. There are a number of key questions generated by the sustainability perspective that we have identified but not made too much progress on so far and know that we will not in this first phase of research.

This is particularly evident in the case of the five ethical elements that were suggested to be central to the evolving ideal of sustainable development:

(i)   *Maintaining ecological integrity and diversity.* While this element is widely advanced in the literature and discussed in many of the background papers, present knowledge of aquatic ecology makes it difficult to translate this general norm into specific indicator measures and appropriate strategies.

(ii) *Meeting basic human needs.* There has been relatively little specific discussion of this element and the associated issue of population growth in the background papers (Boothroyd, Rees and Scott being notable exceptions). This is probably because it is extremely difficult to explore what it might imply for a basin in which general living conditions are so much better and population densities so much lower than those in so much of the developing world.

(iii) *Keeping options open for future generations.* Most of the background papers mention this norm and they usually refer to its implications for maintaining the ecological system. There are, however, major uncertainties about what it implies for action, as revealed by the differences in literatures based on fundamentally different views.

(iv) *Reducing injustice.* Several of the papers are premised on a need to reduce injustice, but for the most part discussion of this issue was very general (Boothroyd is a notable exception). There is a very extensive and diverse literature relating to the issue of justice but its specific implications for elaborating the design of policies and institutional arrangements for sustainable development are not clear.

(v) *Increasing self-determination.* A large number of the papers discussed this norm but it had varying meanings. For some it translated into greater use of market mechanisms and for others it meant a greater role in the legislative-political and administrative-bureaucratic components of governance. Once again, the literature reveals fundamental differences in views underlying the advocacy of the various proposals for policy and institutional change.

While we have suggested what might be the elements of an evolving model of water resources management that begins to reflect these norms, its further advancement will depend on these issues being addressed directly and intensively. Based on the analysis in the last two chapters, three priorities are suggested for action on advancing sustainability research on the broader front.

Understanding New World Views

By considering different world views and in particular those that are challenging dominant views, it has been possible to understand better the controversies over the meaning and implications of sustainable development. O'Riordan and Turner's (1983) simple classification of four world views of the environment based on distinctions between a small number of major characteristics has been of powerful assistance in beginning to clarify reasons for differences of opinion on many issues relating to sustainability. But it has little relevance in developing countries. Also, even when restricted to the context of the western industrialized nations, there are limitations to the classification that stem from its simplicity. If issues are examined in more detail from the perspectives of different schools of thought within the academic disciplines, the limitations become evident as was revealed by the consideration of competing theories in both environmental economics and political science. There are also limitations in the O'Riordan and Turner framework that stem from the changes over the last decade in the diversity and intensity of challenges to dominant views in both academic and governance forums.

In some regards, the classification may have become outdated. There would appear to be a new, eclectic and increasingly substantial middle ground emerging between what have been characterised as the technocentric and ecocentric extremes. Some of the old distinctions between views no longer seem to be as relevant. This is starkly evident in governance forums worldwide as the traditional presumptions about capitalist and socialist regimes are contradicted, as well as in a literature which explores new ideologies. For example, Pæhlke (1989) has argued that there is the basis in the Anglo-American democracies for a new environmentally informed progressivism that builds on the classic political ideologies of liberalism, conservatism and socialism, and is emerging as a response to neo-conservatism in the 1990's. Research focused on exploring the definition and implications of different world views and these newly emerging ideological perspectives should be a priority.

Fostering Transdisciplinary Inquiry

From examining illustrative examples of the new schools of thought emerging to challenge traditional disciplinary models, it is clear that they have considerable potential for both refining the understanding of world views and generating disagreement. Much greater emphasis on and capability for transdisciplinary research will be essential for capitalizing on the potential for progress in understanding and avoiding the threats of debilitating disagreement. The transdisciplinary research must involve both the natural and social sciences. Also, it must catalyse and facilitate productive interactions between different schools of thought, such as those examined in environmental economics and political science. More fundamentally, there is a need to re-examine the intellectual traditions linking science and politics that were identified by Friedmann (1987) in the light of the newly emerging schools of thought; his analysis did not include much of the recent environmental or green literature. It seems likely that a revised framework for indicating how different intellectual traditions contribute to various schools of thought could be particularly useful in clarifying the reasons for disagreements.

To foster more radical transdisciplinary learning requires new attitudes, institutional arrangements and funding. It is well recognised that in the past all three have been lacking and difficult to obtain in Canada and elsewhere. It is therefore particularly encouraging that during the last couple of years, there has emerged a marked increase in willingness to become involved in interdisciplinary research, as evidenced by the contributors to this collection of papers. In addition, the University of British Columbia has established this year a Sustainable Development Research Institute involving all disciplines. The Institute will be a think tank on sustainable development and has already become a catalyst for cooperative research across faculties and with other universities and the private sector. This has been encouraged and greatly assisted by the commitment of the Province of British Columbia to provide continuing support for research on sustainability from the revenues generated by new levies on environmentally harmful products (i.e., diapers, lead-acid batteries, tires and waste discharges). At the same time, the Green Plan recently announced by the Federal Government includes proposals for action and research including the Fraser River Basin specifically. There would therefore appear to be greatly improved opportunities for building on the initial steps being taken in the first phase of this research program and addressing the second research priority of fostering more radical transdisciplinary learning.

Facilitating Agreement

While these initiatives in academic and governance forums are encouraging, success in either will depend on the capabilities for reaching agreement. As was indicated at the outset, it would be wrong to interpret this emphasis on reaching agreement to imply that there should not be disagreement. On the contrary, the emphasis should be seen to be on learning from the disagreements that differences in views can generate. This implies the design of strategies for making disagreement productive, while avoiding and rectifying misunderstandings and clarifying reasons for not agreeing. In academic forums, this means much more emphasis on what can be learnt from the insights provided by different schools of thought and transdisciplinary inquiry. In governance forums, it implies a new emphasis on what can be learnt from the different views of the stakeholders and the redesign of institutional arrangements to be more productive and resilient in facilitating disagreement and resolving conflict. From this perspective, both forums are enriched by diversity and eclecticism, but only if they also include the incentives and capability to pursue agreement and cope peacefully with the tensions and turbulence of conflict. The newly emerging field of dispute resolution can assist and its further development is the third priority because of its immense importance to success in both academic and governance forums.

Conclusion

The last two chapters have strongly confirmed the suggestion in the introductory chapter that water management for sustainable development will be a great deal more challenging than it has been in the past. The major reasons for this have been reiterated in numerous ways: the increased number of biophysical and socioeconomic systems to be considered, the associated expansion of spatial boundaries and time scales to be examined, the greater demands that this imposes on science, the growing recognition of pervasive uncertainty, the heightened ethical and moral concerns, and the greater need for consensus. But at the same time, it is evident that there has been substantial progress over the last two decades in developing principles, analytical techniques and decision making processes for the management of water and associated resources that could be used and advanced in assessing and acting on sustainability. The next step in this research program is to test and refine these conclusions through a case study of the Fraser River Basin.

While the case study is a valuable next step, it can be only a small step in moving towards sustainable development of water resources in the Fraser River Basin. Based on the papers and the arguments in this chapter, other steps should include concerted efforts to advance the understanding of different world views and newly emerging schools of thought on sustainability. Although academic institutions have a major role to play in advancing the more radical transdisciplinary learning that this will require, it is essential that this be undertaken in close cooperation with governance institutions. The Fraser River should be only one focus among many for doing this, but it offers immense opportunities for developing both the principles and practice of sustainable development in water resources management.

Acknowledgements

All the contributors of background papers and the members of the Westwater research team have influenced the last two chapters, as indicated in the Acknowledgements. Most useful comments on earlier drafts were also provided by Bruce Mitchell and Mark Roseland.

References

Anderson, M. G., and T. P. Burt (eds.). 1985. *Hydrological Forecasting*. Toronto: John Wiley.

Averous, C. P. 1989. "Reporting on the State of the Environment: A Review of the Experience in OECD Countries." in Dorcey, A. H. J., and H. I. Rueggeberg. Facilitator's Summary Report, *National Workshop on State of the Environment Reporting*, Victoria, B. C. October 24-26, 1989.

Bankes, N., and A. R. Thompson. 1980. *Monitoring for Impact Assessment and Management: An Analysis of the Legal and Administrative Framework*. Vancouver: Westwater Research Centre, The University of British Columbia.

Bingham, G. 1985. *Resolving Environmental Disputes: A Decade of Experience*. Washington, D. C.: Conservation Foundation.

Bird, P. M., and D. J. Rapport. 1986. *State of the Environment Report for Canada*. Ottawa: Environment Canada.

Bromley, D. 1985. "Resources and Economic Development: An Institutionalist Perspective." *Journal of Economic Issues*. 19(3):779-796.

Brown, L. 1981. *Building a Sustainable Society*. New York: W. W. Norton.

Carley, M. 1980. *Rational Techniques for Policy Analysis*. London: Heinemann Educational Books.

Chambers, R. 1986. *Sustainable Livelihoods: An Opportunity for the World Commission on Environment and Development*. Brighton: Institute of Development Studies, University of Sussex.

Clark, W. C., and R. E. Munn. (eds.). 1986. *Sustainable Development of the Biosphere*. Cambridge: Cambridge University Press.

Colborn, T. E., A. Davidson, S. N. Green, R. A. Hodge, C. I. Jackson and R. A. Liroff. 1990. *Great Lakes Great Legacy*? Ottawa: Institute for Research on Public Policy.

Cormick, G. W., and A. Knaster. 1986. "Oil and Fishing Industries Negotiate: Mediation and scientific issues." *Environment*. 28(10):6-15.

Costanza, R. 1989. "What is Ecological Economics?" *Ecological Economics*. 1(1):1-7.

Daly, H. E., and J. B. Cobb. 1989. *For the Common Good: Redirecting the Economy Toward Community, the Environment, and a Sustainable Future*. Boston: Beacon Press.

Dorcey, A. H. J. 1986. *Bargaining in the Governance of Pacific Coastal Resources: Research and Reform*. Vancouver: Westwater Research Centre, The University of British Columbia.

Dorcey, A. H. J. 1987. "Research for Water Resources Management: The Rise and Fall of Great Expectations." in Healey, M. C., and R. R. Wallace (eds.). *Canadian Aquatic Resources*. Canadian Bulletin of Fisheries and Aquatic Sciences. 215:481-511.

Dorcey, A. H. J. 1990. "Negotiation in the Integration of Environmental and Economic Assessment for Sustainable Development." in *Integrating Environmental and Economic Assessment: Analytical and Negotiation Appraoches*. Ottawa: Canadian Environmental Assessment Research Council. [In Press].

Dorcey, A. H. J., and C. L. Riek. 1988. "Negotiation-Based Approaches to the Settlement of Environmental Disputes in Canada." in *The Place of Negotiation in Environmental Assessment*. Ottawa: Canadian Environmental Assessment Research Council.

Dorcey, A. H. J., and H. I. Rueggeberg. 1989. Facilitator's Summary Report, *National Workshop on State of the Environment Reporting*. Victoria, B. C. October 24-26, 1989.

Dryzek, J. S. 1987. *Rational Ecology: Environment and Political Economy*. Oxford: Blackwell.

Faludi, A. 1987. *A Decision-Centred View of Environmental Planning*. Oxford: Pergamon.

Fisher, R., and Ury, W. 1981. *Getting To Yes: Negotiating Agreement Without Giving In*. Boston: Houghton Mifflin.

Fitzsimmons, S. J., and O. A. Salama. 1973. *A Social Report - Man and Water: The Relationship between Social Psychological Systems and Water Resources Development*. Cambridge: Abt Ltd.

Forester, J. 1989. *Planning in the Face of Power*. Berkeley: University of California Press.

Friedmann, J. 1987. *Planning in the Public Domain: From Knowledge to Action*. Princeton: Princeton University Press.

Gardner, J. E., and M. Roseland. 1989a. "Thinking Globally: The Role of Social Equity in Sustainable Development." *Alternatives*. 16(3):26-35.

Gardner, J. E., and M. Roseland. 1989b. "Acting Locally: Community Strategies for Equitable Sustainable Development." *Alternatives*. 16(3):36-48.

Gelinas, R., and J. Slaats. 1989. *Selecting Indicators for State of the Environment Reporting,* (Draft), Report No. 8, SOE Reporting Branch, Environment Canada, Ottawa.

Ham, C. J., and M. J. Hill. 1984. *The Policy Process in the Modern Capitalist State*. Brighton: Wheatsheaf Books.

Holling, C. S. (ed.). 1978. *Adaptive Environmental Assessment and Management*. Chichester: John Wiley.

Liverman, D. M., M. E. Hanson, B. J. Brown and R. W. Merideth. 1988. "Global Sustainability: Toward Measurement." *Environmental Management*. 12(2):133-143.

O'Riordan, T., and R. K. Turner. 1983. *An Annotated Reader in Environmental Planning and Management*. Oxford: Pergammon.

Pæhlke, R. C. 1989. *Environmentalism and the Future of Progressive Politics*. New Haven: Yale University Press.

Pæhlke, R. C., and D. Torgerson. 1990. *Managing Leviathan: Environmental Politics and the Administrative State*. Peterborough: Broadview Press, Ontario.

Pearce, D., A. Markandya and E. B. Barbier. 1989. *Blueprint for a Green Economy*. London: Earthscan Publications.

Potvin, J. R. 1989. *Economic-Environmental Accounts: A Conspectus on Current Developments*. Ottawa: Rawson Academy of Aquatic Science.

Pross, A. P. 1986. *Group Politics and Public Policy*. Toronto: Oxford University Press.

Raiffa, H. 1982. *The Art and Science of Negotiation*. Cambridge: Harvard University Press.

Regier, H. 1989. "The Time is Ripe: Notes on Ecosystem Integrity." in *Towards an Ecosystem Charter for the Great Lakes-St. Lawrence*. Ottawa: Rawson Academy of Aquatic Science.

Repetto, R., W. Magrath, M. Wells, C. Beer and F. Rossini. 1989. *Wasting Assets: Natural Resources in the National Income Accounts*. Washington, D. C.: World Resources Institute.

Sachs, I. 1977. *Environment and Development - A New Rationale for Domestic Policy Formulation and International Cooperation Strategies*. Ottawa: Canadian International Development Agencies

Sale, K. 1985. *Dwellers in the Land: The Bio-regional Vision*. San Francisco: Sierra Club Books.

Schelling, T. 1960. *The Strategy of Conflict*. Cambridge: Harvard University Press.

Schumacher, E. F. 1973. *Small is Beautiful: A Study of Economics As If People Mattered*. New York: Harper and Row.

Sheehy, G. 1989. *Environmental Indicator Research: A Literature Review for State of the Environment Reporting,* (Draft), Report No. 7, SOE Reporting Branch, Environment Canada, Ottawa.

Susskind, L., and J. Cruikshank. 1987. *Breaking the Impasse: Consensual Approaches to Resolving Public Dispute*. New York: Basic Books.

Uno, K. 1988. "Economic Growth and Environmental Change in Japan—Net National Welfare and Beyond." mimeo, Institute of Socio-economic Planning, University of Tsukuba, Japan.

Utton, A. E., W. R. D. Sewell and T. O'Riordan. 1976 *Natural Resources for a Democratic Society: Public Participation in Decision-Making*. Boulder: Westview.

Walters, C. J. 1986. *Adaptive Environmental Assessment and Management*. New York: Macmillan.

World Resources Institute, 1990. *World Resources 1990-91*. New York: Oxford University Press.

Zonneveld, I. S. 1983. "Principles of Bio-indication." *Environmental Monitoring and Assessment*. 3(3-4).

Westwater Publications List

Results of research by Westwater are published in books and a series of reports. Publications presently available are listed below by each of the Centre's four research programs:

I.   Water Resources in the Sustainable Development of River Basins.
II. Management of Human Impacts on Water Quality.
III. Management of Human Activities in Coastal Marine and Estuarine Environments.
IV. International Water Resources Management.

I. Water Resources in the Sustainable Development of River Basins

Books

Bankes, N., and A. R. Thompson. 1981. *Monitoring for Impact Assessment and Management: An Analysis of the Legal and Administrative Framework.* Vancouver: Westwater Research Centre, The University of British Columbia. ($6.00)*

Clarke, S. D. (ed.) 1981. *Environmental Assessment in Australia and Canada.* Vancouver: Westwater Research Centre, The University of British Columbia. ($15.95)

Dorcey, A. H. J. (ed.) 1991. *Perspectives on Water in Sustainable Development: Towards Agreement in the Fraser River Basin.* Vancouver: Westwater Research Centre, The University of British Columbia. ($25.00)

Fox. I. K. (ed.) 1981. *Pipeline Electrification in the Yukon.* Vancouver: Westwater Research Centre, The University of British Columbia. ($4.00)

Fox, I. K., P. J. Eyre and W. Mair. 1983. *Yukon Water Resources Management: Policy and Institutional Issues.* Vancouver: Westwater Research Centre, The University of British Columbia. ($5.00)

Rueggeberg, H. I., and A. R. Thompson. 1984. *Water Law and Policy Issues in Canada.* Vancouver: Westwater Research Centre, The University of British Columbia. ($10.95)

Thompson, A. R. 1981. *Environmental Regulation in Canada: An Assessment of the Regulatory Process.* Vancouver: Westwater Research Centre, The University of British Columbia. ($7.00)*

Thompson, A. R., N. Bankes and J. Souto-Maior. 1981. *Energy Project Approval in British Columbia.* Vancouver: Westwater Research Centre, The University of British Columbia. ($5.00)*

Thompson, J. P. 1981. *Aluminum Smelting in the Yukon: An Assessment of Economic Viability.* Vancouver: Westwater Research Centre, The University of British Columbia. ($6.00)

II. Management of Human Impacts on Water Quality

Books

Barton, B. J., R. T. Franson and A. R. Thompson. 1984. *A Contract Model for Pollution Control.* Vancouver: Westwater Research Centre, The University of British Columbia. ($9.50)

Dorcey, A. H. J. (ed.) 1976. *The Uncertain Future of the Lower Fraser.* Vancouver: Westwater Research Centre, The University of British Columbia. ($6.00)

Sproule-Jones, M. 1980. *The Real World of Pollution Control*. Vancouver: Westwater Research Centre, The University of British Columbia. ($6.00)*
Stephenson, J. B. (ed.) 1977. *The Practical Application of Economic Incentives to the Control of Pollution: The Case of British Columbia*. Vancouver: University of British Columbia Press. (Cloth $23.00, Paper $11.00)

Reports

Bawden, C. A., W. A. Heath and A. B. Norton. 1973. *A Preliminary Baseline Study of Roberts and Sturgeon Banks*. Technical Report No. 1. Vancouver: Westwater Research Centre, The University of British Columbia. ($4.00)*

Benedict, A. H., K. J. Hall and F. A. Koch. 1973. *A Preliminary Water Quality Survey of the Lower Fraser River System*. Technical Report No. 2. Vancouver: Westwater Research Centre, The University of British Columbia. ($3.50)*

Fairbairn, B., and K. Peterson. 1975. *Controlling Sawlog Debris in the Lower Fraser River*. Technical Report No. 5. Vancouver: Westwater Research Centre, The University of British Columbia. ($3.00)*

Hall, K. J., F. A. Koch and I. Yesaki. 1974. *Further Investigations into Water Quality Conditions in the Lower Fraser River System*. Technical Report No. 4. Vancouver: Westwater Research Centre, The University of British Columbia. ($8.00)*

Hall, K. J., I. Yesaki and J. Chan. 1976. *Trace Metals and Chlorinated Hydrocarbons in the Sediments of a Metropolitan Watershed*. Technical Report No. 10. Vancouver: Westwater Research Centre, The University of British Columbia. ($2.50)*

Johnston, N. T., L. J. Albright, T. G. Northcote, P. G. Oloffs and K. Tsumura. 1975. *Chlorinated Hydrocarbon Residues in Fishes from the Lower Fraser River*. Technical Report No. 9. Vancouver: Westwater Research Centre, The University of British Columbia. ($2.50)*

Joy, C. S. 1975. *Water Quality Models of the Lower Fraser River*. Technical Report No. 6. Vancouver: Westwater Research Centre, The University of British Columbia. ($4.00)*

Koch, F. A., and K. J. Hall. 1981. *Survey of Wastewater Quality in the Sewerage Systems of the University of British Columbia*. Technical Report No. 24. Vancouver: Westwater Research Centre, The University of British Columbia. ($4.00)

Koch, F. A., K. J. Hall and I. Yesaki. 1977. *Toxic Substances in the Wastewaters from a Metropolitan Area*. Technical Report No. 12. Vancouver: Westwater Research Centre, The University of British Columbia. ($7.00)*

Northcote, T. G. 1974. *Biology of the Lower Fraser River: A Review*. Technical Report No. 3. Vancouver: Westwater Research Centre, The University of British Columbia. ($2.50)

Northcote, T. G., G. L. Ennis and M. H. Anderson. 1975. *Periphytic and Planktonic Algae of the Lower Fraser River in relation to Water Quality Conditions*. Technical Report No. 8. Vancouver: Westwater Research Centre, The University of British Columbia. ($5.00)*

Northcote, T. G., N. T. Johnston and K. Tsumura. 1975. *Trace Metal Concentrations in Lower Fraser River Fishes*. Technical Report No. 7. Vancouver: Westwater Research Centre, The University of British Columbia. ($2.50)

Northcote, T. G., N. T. Johnston and K. Tsumura. 1976. *Benthic, Epibenthic and Drift Fauna of the Lower Fraser River*. Technical Report No. 11. Vancouver: Westwater Research Centre, The University of British Columbia. ($11.80)*

Northcote, T. G., N. T. Johnston and K. Tsumura. 1978. *A Regional Comparison of Species Distribution, Abundance, Size and Other Characteristics of Lower Fraser River Fishes*. Technical Report No. 14. Vancouver: Westwater Research Centre, The University of British Columbia. ($2.50)

Northcote, T. G., N. T. Johnston and K. Tsumura. 1979. *Feeding Relationships and Food Web Structure of Lower Fraser River Fishes*. Technical Report No. 16. Vancouver: Westwater Research Centre, The University of British Columbia. ($2.50)

Slaymaker, O., and L. M. Lavkulich. 1978. *A Review of Land Use — Water Quality Interrelationships and a Proposed Method for their Study*. Technical Report No. 13. Vancouver: Westwater Research Centre, The University of British Columbia. ($4.50)*

III. Management of Human Activities in Coastal Marine and Estuarine Environments

Books

Dorcey, A. H. J. (ed.) 1979. *Coastal Resources in the Future of British Columbia.* Vancouver: Westwater Research Centre, The University of British Columbia. ($6.70)*

Dorcey, A. H. J. 1986. *Bargaining in the Governance of Pacific Coastal Resources: Research and Reform.* Vancouver: Westwater Research Centre, The University of British Columbia. ($14.95)

Dorcey, A. H. J., and K. J. Hall. 1981. *Setting Ecological Research Priorities for Management: The Art of the Impossible in the Fraser Estuary.* Vancouver: Westwater Research Centre, The University of British Columbia. ($6.95)

Dorcey, A. H. J., K. J. Hall, D. A. Levy and I. Yesaki. 1983. *Estuarine Habitat Management: A Prospectus for Tilbury Slough.* Vancouver: Westwater Research Centre, The University of British Columbia. ($9.95)

Dorcey, A. H. J., M. W. McPhee and S. Sydneysmith. 1980. *Salmon Protection and the B.C. Coastal Forest Industry: Environmental Regulation as a Bargaining Process.* Vancouver: Westwater Research Centre, The University of British Columbia. ($11.95)

Levy, D. A. 1985. *Biology and Management of Surf Smelt in Burrard Inlet, Vancouver, B.C.* Technical Report No. 28. Vancouver: Westwater Research Centre, The University of British Columbia. ($7.50)

Levy, D. A., and K. J. Hall. 1985. *A Review of the Limnology and Sockeye Salmon Ecology of Babine Lake.* Technical Report No. 27. Vancouver: Westwater Research Centre, The University of British Columbia. ($9.50)

Levy, D. A., T. G. Northcote and R. M. Barr. 1982. *Effects of Estuarine Log Storage on Juvenile Salmon.* Technical Report No. 26. Vancouver: Westwater Research Centre, The University of British Columbia. ($7.50)*

McPhee, M. W. 1982. *Offshore Oil and Gas in Canada: West Coast Environmental, Social and Economic Issues.* Vancouver: Westwater Research Centre, The University of British Columbia. ($7.50)

Reports

Boyd, S. 1979. *A Review of Various Tidal Development Techniques.* Information Report No. 1. Vancouver: Westwater Research Centre, The University of British Columbia. ($2.50)*

Dorcey, A. H. J., T. G. Northcote and D. V. Ward. 1978. *Are the Fraser Marshes Essential to Salmon?* Lecture No. 1. Vancouver: Westwater Research Centre, The University of British Columbia. ($2.50)*

Fralick, J. E. 1979. "Economic Analysis of the B.C. Oyster Industry." *The B.C. Oyster Industry: Policy Analysis for Coastal Resource Management.* Volume II. Technical Report No. 20. Vancouver: Westwater Research Centre, The University of British Columbia. ($6.60)*

Fralick, J. E., and D. L. Tillapaugh. 1979. *A Review of Smaller Fishery-Mariculture Industries in B.C.: Mussels, Abalone, Geoducks, Clams, Horse Clams and Marine Plants.* Information Report No. 3. Vancouver: Westwater Research Centre, The University of British Columbia. ($2.50)*

Kistritz, R. U. 1978. *An Ecological Evaluation of Fraser Estuary Tidal Marshes: The Role of Detritus and Cycling of Elements.* Technical Report No. 15. Vancouver: Westwater Research Centre, The University of British Columbia. ($3.50)*

Kistritz, R. U., and I. Yesaki. 1979. *Primary Production, Detritus Flux, and Nutrient Cycling in a Sedge Marsh, Fraser River Estuary.* Technical Report No. 17. Vancouver: Westwater Research Centre, The University of British Columbia. ($3.50)

Levy, D. A., and T. G. Northcote. 1981. *The Distribution and Abundance of Juvenile Salmon in Marsh Habitats of the Fraser River Estuary.* Technical Report No. 25. Vancouver: Westwater Research Centre, The University of British Columbia. ($11.70)*

Levy, D. A., T. G. Northcote and G. J. Birch. 1979. *Juvenile Salmon Utilization of Tidal Channels in the Fraser River Estuary, British Columbia.* Technical Report No. 23. Vancouver: Westwater Research Centre, The University of British Columbia. ($3.50)

McPhee, M. W. 1983. *A Workshop Report on North Coast Native Fisheries — A Review of Major Projects Planned for the North Coast Region of British Columbia*. Information Report No. 4. Vancouver: Westwater Research Centre, The University of British Columbia. ($3.00)

Seale, S., and A. R. Thompson. 1979. "Institutional arrangements for managing the oyster resources." *The B.C. Oyster Industry: Policy Analysis for Coastal Resource Management*. Volume IV. Technical Report No. 22. Vancouver: Westwater Research Centre, The University of British Columbia. ($3.50)

Valiela, D. 1979. "Oyster ecology and culture in British Columbia." *The B.C. Oyster Industry: Policy Analysis for Coastal Resource Management*. Volume I. Technical Report No. 19. Vancouver: Westwater Research Centre, The University of British Columbia. ($3.50)

Valiela, D. 1979. "Policies for the development of the B.C. oyster industry: Analyses based on a computer simulation model." *The B.C. Oyster Industry: Policy Analysis for Coastal Resource Management*. Volume III. Technical Report No. 21. Vancouver: Westwater Research Centre, The University of British Columbia. ($3.50)

Valiela, D., and R. U. Kistritz. 1979. *Dependence of Salmon on Fraser Estuarine Marsh Ecosystems: A Simulation Analysis*. Technical Report No. 18. Vancouver: Westwater Research Centre, The University of British Columbia. ($3.50)

IV. International Water Resources Management

Books

LeMarquand, D. G. 1977. *International Rivers: Politics of Cooperation*. Vancouver: Westwater Research Centre, The University of British Columbia. ($7.00)*

Northcote, T. G., P. Morales S., D. A. Levy and M. S. Greaven (eds.). 1989. *Pollution in Lake Titicaca, Peru: Training, Research and Management*. Vancouver: Westwater Research Centre, The University of British Columbia. ($20.00)

Asterisks (*) mark books and reports that are out of print; reduction photocopies are available at the cost shown.

PLEASE NOTE: *PRICES ARE STATED IN CANADIAN FUNDS AND THEY ARE SUBJECT TO CHANGE WITHOUT NOTICE. PRICES INCLUDE POSTAGE AND HANDLING COSTS. ORDERS SHOULD BE SENT TO:*

WESTWATER RESEARCH CENTRE
THE UNIVERSITY OF BRITISH COLUMBIA
Room 200, 1933 West Mall
Vancouver, British Columbia, Canada
V6T 1Z2